5th Edition

Antique Trader®

Bottles

Identification & Price Guide

Michael Polak

©2006 Michael Polak
Published by

krause publications
An Imprint of F+W Publications

700 East State Street • Iola, WI 54990-0001
715-445-2214 • 888-457-2873
www.krausebooks.com

Our toll-free number to place an order or obtain
a free catalog is (800) 258-0929.

Library of Congress Control Number: 2005922938

ISBN-13: 978-0-89689-243-9
ISBN-10: 0-89689-243-3

Designed by Jamie Griffin
Edited by Dan Brownell

Printed in China

Contents

Dedication 6

Acknowledgments. 7

Photo Credits. 9

Introduction 10

How to Use This Book 12

What's Happening in the
World of Bottle Collecting 13

Bottles: History and Origin 17

The Beginning Collector 33

Bottle Facts 38

Determining Bottle Values 53

Bottle Sources. 57

Digging for Bottles 61

Bottle Handling 75

Old Bottles (Pre-1900) 79
Ale and Gin 81
Barber Bottles 87
Beer Bottles 96
Bitters. 104
Blown Bottles. 118
Cobalt Blue Medicine Bottles 128
Cosmetic Bottles 134
Crocks/Stoneware 142
Figurals 150
Fire Grenades. 158
Flasks. 164
Food and Pickle Bottles. 174
Fruit Jars 181
Hutchinson Bottles 189
Ink Bottles 194
Medicine Bottles 205
Milk Bottles 221
Mineral Water Bottles. 228
Nursing Bottles 243
Patriotic Bottles 246
Pattern-Molded Bottles 258
Perfume and Cologne Bottles 267
Poison Bottles 279
Sarsaparilla Bottles 295
Snuff Bottles 299
Soda Bottles 303
Target Balls 316
Warner Bottles 321
Whiskey Bottles 326

New Bottles (Post-1900) 339
Avon Bottles. 340
Ballantine Bottles 345
Barsottini Bottles 346
Jim Beam Bottles. 346
Bischoff Bottles 363
Borghini Bottles 365
Ezra Brooks Bottles 366
J.W. Dant Bottles 371
Garnier Bottles. 372
Hoffman Bottles. 375
Japanese Bottles 377
Kentucky Gentlemen Bottles 378
Lionstone Bottles. 379
Luxardo Bottle 383
McCormic Bottles 386
Miniature Bottles 390
Old Blue Ribbon Bottles 398
Old Commonwealth Bottles. 399
Old Fitzgerald Bottles 401
Ski-Country Bottles 402
Soda Bottles - Applied Color Label 406
Violin and Banjo Bottles. 412

Trademarks 426

Bottle Clubs 444

Bottle Dealers 472

Auction Companies. 525

Museums and Research Resources . . . 530

Glossary 532

Bibliography. 541

Dedication

This 5th edition is dedicated to the brave men and women of the United States military who have made the ultimate sacrifice, along with their families, in the war against terrorism. Also, to the brave men and women proudly serving in the U.S. military who continue to put themselves in harm's way on a daily basis. Your mission is one of honor and courage.

—THANK YOU!

Acknowledgments

As I completed the 4th edition of Bottles: Identification and Price Guide, I immediately started gathering information for the 5th edition and, as always, I depended on constant additional help from my fellow collectors. Once again, I had plenty of help from those individuals who deserve a big "THANK YOU."

Rodney Baer: Thank you for your contribution of photographs of perfume bottles and for your overall support of the project.

Charles and Julie Blake: Thank you for your contribution of the great photographs and background information and pricing on cobalt blue medicine bottles.

Penny Dolnick: Thank you for writing the great introduction article for the perfume and cologne chapter along with pricing input and background information.

Jim Hagenbuch (Antique Bottle & Glass Collector & Glass Works Auctions): Thank you for the great assortment of photographs, pricing input, and overall support of the project.

Bud Hastin (*Avon Collector's Encyclopedia*): Thanks for the great photographs and for your help with the Avon collectibles pricing.

Norm Heckler (Heckler Auctions): Thank you for your contribution of photographs and for your support of the project.

Fred Holabird: Thanks for your continued help with understanding Nevada bottles and for your great friendship.

David Graci: Thanks for your contribution of photographs and background information on soda and beer bottle closures.

Bob Kay: Thanks for your contribution of pricing input on miniature beer bottles and for your support of the project.

Gary and Vickie Lewis: Thanks for your contribution of photographs of ACL soda bottles and for your overall support of the project.

Randall Monsen: Thank you for your contribution of photographs of perfume bottles and for your overall support of the project.

John Pastor: Thanks for the great photographs of nursing bottles and the input and information on pricing and history.

Jacque Pace Polak: A special thank you to my wife for your continued patience and invaluable moral support.

Steve Ritter (Steve Ritter Auctioneering): Thanks for your help in obtaining the ACL soda bottle photographs and for your help with the pricing input.

David Spaid: Thanks for your help with understanding the world of miniature bottles and for your support of the project.

Rick Sweeney: Thanks for your help and understanding with the pricing input for ACL soda bottles.

John Tutton: Thank you for your contribution of photographs of milk bottles and for your overall support of the project.

Violin Bottle Collectors Association and Members: Thanks for all of your help with the contribution of photographs and an overall understanding of violin bottles and their history. A special thank you specifically to Bob Linden, Frank Bartlett, Samia Koudsi, and Bob Moore for your time and effort in providing the photographs, pricing data, and resource information.

Bruce and Vicki Wassdorp (American Pottery Auction): Thanks for your contribution of photographs and help with the pricing input.

Jeff Wichman (American Bottle Auctions): Thanks for your great assortment of Western bottle photographs and overall support of the project.

Photo Credits

Rodney Baer

Frank Bartlett

Charles and Julie Blake

Jim Hagenbuch (*Antique Bottle & Glass Collector* magazine, Glass Works Auctions)

Bud Hastin (*Avon Collector's Encyclopedia*)

Norman C. Heckler (Norman C. Heckler and Company, Auctions)

The H.J. Heinz Company

Bob Glover

David Graci

Fred Holabird

International Association of Jim Beam Bottle & Specialties Club

Samia Koudsi

Gary and Vickie Lewis

Bob Moore

Randall Monsen

John Pastor

Steve Ritter (Steve Ritter Auctions)

Jan Rutland (National Bottle Museum)

Bob Snyder

David Spaid

Rick Sweeney

Jennifer Tai

John Tutton

Jeff Wichmann (American Bottle Auctions)

Vicki And Bruce Waasdorp (Antique Pottery Auctions)

Willy Young

Introduction

Welcome again to the fun hobby of antique bottle collecting with the 5th edition of Antique Trader® Bottles: Identification and Price Guide. Once again, a special THANK YOU to all my readers for your support in making the 4th edition a huge success. With the publication of every edition, I become re-energized with the continued positive and valuable input and helpful comments from bottle collectors, clubs, and dealers across the United States, Europe, and Asia-Pacific. I have enjoyed writing the 5th edition as much as the first four editions, incorporating all of the positive feedback, and living up to the nickname given the book by collectors and dealers, "The Bottle Bible."

In order to make the 5th edition the most informative reference and pricing guide available, I have continued to provide the beginner and veteran collector with a broader range of detailed information and data. Based on your responses, the 5th edition includes extensive updates and revisions to essentials of the hobby such as the history and origin of glass and bottles, information on how the beginning collector can get started, detailed sections on basic bottle facts, bottle sources, and bottle handling techniques, and one of my favorite chapters, "Digging for Bottles." In response to numerous requests from collectors, I have added two new chapters on the fastest growing segments of bottle collecting—"Patriotic Bottles" and "Perfume and Cologne Bottles."

Another exciting addition to this edition is that the total number of photographs will increase from 300 to 600, and most will be color. The 5th edition also provides complete pricing updates and revisions for both old bottles (pre-1900) and new bottles (post-1900). To help you better understand the details of how to price and evaluate a bottle, the chapter titled "Determining Bottle Values" has also been updated and expanded, along with the reference and research sections on trademarks, bottle clubs and dealers, the bibliography, and the glossary of common bottle terms.

Interest in bottle collecting continues to grow and with new bottle clubs continuing to form throughout the United States and Europe. More collectors

are spending their free time digging through old dumps and foraging through old ghost towns, digging out old out houses (that's right), exploring abandoned mine shafts, and searching out their favorite bottle or antique show, swap meet, flea market, or garage sale. In addition, the Internet has greatly expanded, offering collectors numerous opportunities and resources to buy and sell bottles with many new auction Web sites, without even leaving the house. And, many bottle clubs now have Web sites providing even more information for the collector. A good thing! This new technology continues to help bottle collecting to grow as a hobby and a business, as evidenced by the increasing prices in this 5th edition.

Most collectors, however, still look beyond the type and value of a bottle into its origin and history. In fact, I find that researching the history of bottles has at times been more interesting than finding the bottle itself. I enjoy both pursuits for their close ties to the rich history of the settling of the United States and the early methods of merchandising. My goal has always been to enhance the hobby of bottle collecting for both the beginner and expert collectors and experience the excitement of antique bottle collecting, especially the thrill of making that special find. I hope that the 5th edition continues to bring you an increased understanding and enjoyment of the hobby.

If you would like to provide additional information or input regarding the 5th edition or just talk bottles, I can be contacted at my e-mail address: bottleking@earthlink.net or on my Web site: www.bottlebible.com. Good bottle hunting and have fun with the hobby of bottle collecting.

How to Use This Book

As with previous editions, the 5th edition is formatted to assist all collectors, from the novice to the seasoned veteran. The table of contents clearly indicates chapters such as "The Beginning Collector" that the veteran collector may want to skip. However, other introductory sections, including "Bottles: History & Origin," "Bottle Facts," "Bottle Sources," "Bottle Handling," and the new chapters "Patriotic Bottles" and "Perfume and Cologne Bottles," will contribute information and resource materials to even the expert's store of knowledge about bottles and collecting.

The pricing information has been divided into two sections. The first section begins on page 79 and covers older collectibles, almost exclusively those manufactured before 1900. The section is organized according to categories based on physical type and the bottle's original contents. Where applicable, trade names are listed alphabetically within these sections.

In some categories, such as Flasks, trade names were not embossed on the bottles, so pieces are listed by embossing or other identification that appears on the bottle. Descriptive terms used to identify these pieces are explained in the introductory sections and are also listed in the glossary at the end of the book.

The second pricing section, which begins on page 339, is a guide to pieces produced after the turn of the century, categorized by manufacturer.

Since it is difficult to list prices for every bottle, I've produced a detailed cross section of bottles in various price ranges with the dollar amount for each listing, indicating the value of that particular piece. Similar but not identical bottles could be more or less valuable than those specifically mentioned. This listing will provide a good starting point for pricing pieces in your collection you are considering as additions.

The reference and research sections that include "Trademark Identification" (page 426), "Bottle Clubs" (page 444), "Bottle Dealers" (page 472), "Auction Companies" (page 525), "Museum and Research Resources" (page 530), glossary (page 532), and bibliography (page 541), will provide additional assistance and help to all collectors.

What's Happening in the World of Bottle Collecting

What's been happening? Everything! Antique bottle collecting has gained more popularity and has brought a greater awareness to a wide spectrum of antique collectors, as is evidenced by the many events and discoveries that have occurred between the 4th and 5th editions.

What would you do if you could walk into a grocery store that's been closed for 50 years with everything left on the shelves? The Fifth Avenue Grocery in Roundup, Mont., closed its doors in 1952 with thousands of items still on the shelves, most in mint condition. These items, such as a Coca-Cola display still in the wrapper, a full unopened Kessler Beer bottle, and a full unopened six-pack of Carlin's Beer cans, were auctioned in April 2003. And beneath the store was a small tavern complete with a large assortment of full liquor and beer bottles.

If you think that's a leap back in time, in May 2003 more than 200 artifacts salvaged from the *Titantic* went on display at London's Science Museum. Featured were four miniature scent bottles that belonged to first-class passenger Adolphe Saalfeld, who survived the sinking.

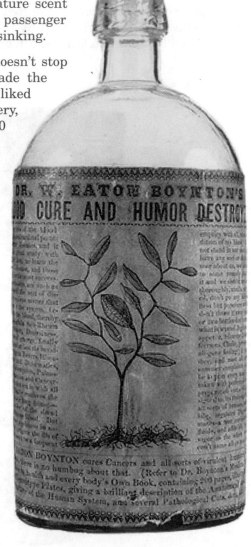

But the trek back into history doesn't stop there. George Washington even made the news. Our first president, who liked cinnamon whiskey, owned a distillery, which at its peak produced 11,000 gallons of liquor. Following Washington's death in 1799, a nephew took over the business, but the building was gone by 1815. Although archeologists uncovered its location in 1932, it wasn't until June 2003 that the Mount Vernon Society for Preservation began to excavate and reached the layers that were in place around 1799. An amber-colored bottle is one of the prized items that was discovered there. The recovered items are being moved to a mound at the site where the reconstruction of the distillery is expected to be completed by 2006.

In July 2003, a team of scientists from Chicago's Field Museum discovered a brewery in the mountains of southern Peru, where members of the Wari Empire made an alcoholic beer-like drink called Chicha more than 1,000 years ago. Based on the brewing room, which contained many pieces of 10- to 15-gallon ceramic preparation vats, it is believed that the facility produced several thousand liters a day.

In August 2003, a Florida salvage company found a paddlewheel steamship, the *S. S. Republic*, which sank almost 140 years ago. The ship's cargo carried $180 million in gold to pay for the reconstruction of the South following the U.S. Civil War. According to the salvage team, the wreck site was littered with bottles and personal items.

Another fascinating discovery took place in Lemoyne, Neb. In the 1940s, a state water project entailed the flooding of Lemoyne, requiring that the town be completely abandoned. Since then, the town has only been seen twice—once recently—because of drought conditions.

The drought has made Lemoyne an antique-treasure paradise, with many adventurers finding old tea cups, medicine bottles (some full), Schlitz Beer cans both full and empty, and other collectibles.

A major event in the beer-collecting world was the announcement that the National Brewery Museum, selected by the American Breweriana Association, will be located in Potosi, Wis., home to the historic Potosi Brewery, which was founded in 1852 and ceased production in 1972. The part of the building that is still standing will house the museum of brewing history and artifacts.

Scheduled to open in three to five years, the museum will have 7,000 square feet of space for permanent and rotating exhibits. A collection of 1,600 beer bottles, all full and with labels intact, and amassed over 50 years, may be displayed as an exhibit, pending a decision by the family that inherited the collection. What a great opportunity to share a collection of this magnitude with collectors from all over the world.

I couldn't give you an update on bottle collecting without a Coca-Cola story. Everyone knows that Georgia is the heart of Coca-Cola country, but did you know that there's one town where the standard flavor isn't king? In Lawrenceville, Ga., at the Las Tarascas Latino Supermarket (only 30 miles from Coca-Cola world headquarters), the preferred drink is Mexican Coke, rather than American Coke.

Each week, the store sells 10 to 15 cases of Mexican Coke, but only five cases of American Coke. The secret is in the cane sugar used in Mexican Coke, which reportedly has a sweeter, cleaner flavor than the high-fructose corn syrup used in the American formula. And the green-tinted, contour glass used in the Mexican Coke bottles has captured the attention of baby boomers because of its retro appeal. This has created major discussions at high levels in the Coca-Cola corporate world, since it seems to be making a financial and marketing difference in other Southwestern states. Stay tuned.

Quite often, bottle collectors collect items associated with glass or bottles called "go-withs," such as glass swizzle sticks from the 1930s and '40s. But, would you believe that someone would collect 2,500 of these antique glass cocktail stirrers and maintain detailed records, sorting the sticks alphabetically, chronologically and geographically?

I've got one very nice swizzle stick from Goldfield, Nev. that I found on a digging trip in Tonopah, Nev., but I can't imagine a collection of 2,500. The collector is Ivan Claman, who six years ago read about the International Swizzle Stick Collectors Association, joined the group and has never quit hunting. He also has a collection of 1,500 casino chips. I think he needs some bottles to go along with those swizzle sticks and casino chips.

As you can see, the discoveries and news events of bottle collecting continue to include all aspects of antique collecting and increase the interest and fun of the hobby of antique bottle collecting.

Bottles:
History and Origin

Glass bottles aren't as recent an invention as some people believe. In fact, the glass bottle has been around for about 3,000 years. During the 2nd century B.C., Roman glass was free-blown with metal blowpipes and shaped with tongs or was formed using molds. The glass was then decorated with enameling or engraving. The Romans even get credit for originating what we think of today as the basic "store bottle" and early merchandising techniques.

In the late 1st century B.C., the Romans began making glass vials that local doctors and pharmacists used to dispense pills, healing powders, and miscellaneous potions. The vials were 3 to 4 inches long and very narrow.

Roman bottles, jars, and glass objects, 1st-3rd century A.D., found in the baths and necropolises of Cimiez Nice, France.

Romans used a small stone rolled in tar as a stopper, while most later bottles were sealed with a cork or glass stopper. The vials contained many impurities like sand particles and bubbles because of the crude manufacturing process. The thickness of the glass and the crude finish, however, made Roman glass very resilient compared to the glass of later times, which accounts for the survival and good preservation of some Roman bottles, which have been dated as old as 2,500 years.

The first attempt to manufacture glass in America is thought to have taken place at the Jamestown settlement in Virginia around 1608. It's interesting to note that the majority of glass produced at the Jamestown settlement was earmarked for shipment to England (because of England's limited resources) and not for the new settlements. As it turned out, the Jamestown glasshouse enterprise was a failure almost as soon as it started. The small quantity and poor quality simply couldn't supply England's needs.

The first successful American glasshouse was opened in New Jersey in 1739 by Caspar Wistar, a brass button manufacturer who immigrated to Philadelphia, Pa., from Germany in 1717. During a trip in Salem County, N.J., Wistar noticed the abundance of white sand, clay, and wood, as well as the proximity of water transportation. He soon bought 2,000 acres of the heavily wooded land and made arrangements for experienced glass workers to come from Europe. The factory was completed in the fall of 1739. Since English law did not permit the colonists to manufacture anything in competition with England, Wistar kept a low profile. In fact, most what was written during the factory's operation implied that that it was less than successful, but Wistar died in 1752 a very wealthy man and left the factory to his son Richard.

Henry Stiegel started the next major glasshouse operation in the Manheim, Pa., area between 1763 and 1774, and eventually established several more. The Pitkin glass works was opened in East Hartford, Conn., around 1783 and was the first American glasshouse to create figured flasks and also the most successful of its time until it closed around 1830 because of the high cost of wood fuel.

To understand the successes and far more numerous failures of early glasshouses, it is essential that the reader get an overview of the challenges that glass workers faced in acquiring raw materials and constructing the glasshouse. The glass factory of the 19th century was usually built near abundant sources of sand and wood or coal near numerous roads, rivers, and other waterways for transportation of raw materials and finished products to the major Eastern markets of Boston, New York, and Philadelphia. Finding a suitable location was usually not a problem, but once production was underway resources quickly diminished. The next major problem was the glasshouse building, which was usually a large wooden structure that housed a primitive furnace about nine feet in diameter and shaped like a beehive.

A major financial drain on the glass companies (and one of the causes of so many of the businesses failing) was the large melting pots inside the furnace that held the molten glass. The melting pot, which cost about $100 and took eight months to build, was formed by hand from a long coil of clay and was the only substance known that would not melt when the glass was heated to 2,700 degrees F. The pots lasted only about eight weeks, as exposure to high temperature caused the clay itself to turn into glass. The cost of regularly replacing melting pots proved to be the downfall of many early glasshouses.

Throughout the 19th century, glasshouses continued to open and close because of changes in demand and technological improvements. Between 1840 and 1890, an enormous demand for glass containers developed to satisfy the whisky, beer, medicine, and food-packing industries. Largely due to this steady demand, glass manufacturing in the United States finally developed into a stable industry. This demand was due in large part to the settling of the Western United States and the great gold and silver strikes between 1850 and 1900.

While the Eastern glasshouses had been in production since 1739, the West didn't begin its entry into glass manufacturing until 1858 when Baker & Cutting started the first glasshouse in San Francisco, Calif. Until that time, the West had to depend on glass bottles from the Eastern glasshouses. The glass manufactured by Baker & Cutting, however, was considered to be poor quality, and production was eventually discontinued.

In 1862, Carlton Newman and Patrick Brennan founded Pacific Glass Works in San Francisco, Calif. In 1876, San Francisco Glass Works bought Pacific Glass Works and renamed the company San Francisco and Pacific Glass Works (SFPGW). Today, these early bottles manufactured in San Francisco are the most desired by Western collectors.

Unlike other industries of the time that saw major changes in manufacturing processes, the process for producing the glass bottles remained the same. It was a process that gave each bottle a special character, producing unique shapes, imperfections, irregularities, and various colors until 1900.

At the turn of the century, Michael J. Owens invented the first fully automated bottle-making machine. Although many fine bottles were manufactured between 1900 and 1930, Owens' invention ended an era of unique bottle design that no machine process could ever duplicate.

Free Blown Bottle-Making Process

In order for a bottle collector, especially a new bottle collector, to better understand the history and origin of antique bottles, it is important to take a look at the development of the manufacturing processes.

Free Blown Bottles: B.C.-1860 (Figure 1)

Around the 1st century B.C., the blowpipe, a long hollow metal rod, was invented. After the tip of the blowpipe was dipped into the molten glass to gather a glob on the end, the glass blower blew into the other end of the pipe. The glassblower then shaped the molten glass into the desired form of bottle, bowl, or other glass container.

Pontil Marks: 1618-1866

Once the bottle was blown, the tip of a 3-foot long metal pontil rod was dipped in molten glass and attached to the bottom of the bottle to hold the bottle after the blowpipe was removed. The blowpipe was then separated from the bottle by touching a tool dipped in cold water to the neck of the bottle, cracking the glass. When the pontil was broken from the base of the bottle, it left a circular scar called a pontil mark.

Figure 1

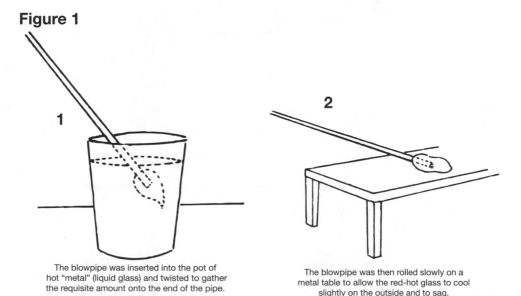

1
The blowpipe was inserted into the pot of hot "metal" (liquid glass) and twisted to gather the requisite amount onto the end of the pipe.

2
The blowpipe was then rolled slowly on a metal table to allow the red-hot glass to cool slightly on the outside and to sag.

3

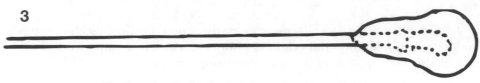

The blower then blew into the pipe to form an internal central bubble.

4

The glass was further expanded and sometimes turned in a wooden block that had been dipped in cold water to prevent charring, or possibly rolled again on the metal table.

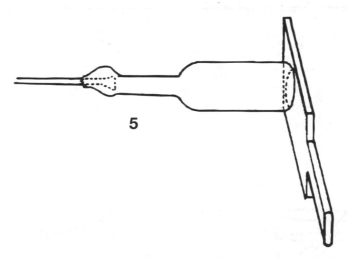

5

The body and neck were then formed by flattening the bottom of the bottle with a wooden paddle called a Battledore, named after the glassblower who developed the techique.

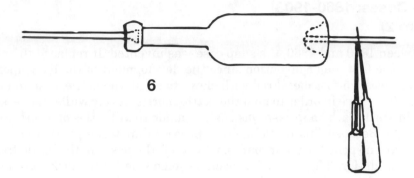

6

One of the irons (called a pontil) was attached to the center bottom of the bottle for
easy handling during the finishing of the bottle neck and lip. A "kick-up" could be
formed in the bottom of the bottle by pushing inward when attaching the iron.

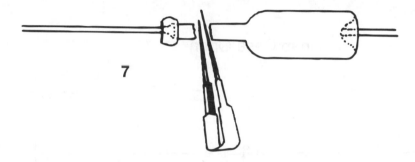

7

The bottle was whetted, or cracked off the blowpipe, by touching the hot
glass at the end of the pipe with a tool dipped in cold water.

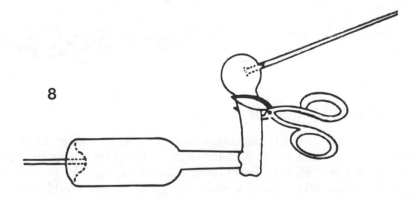

8

With the bottle held on a pontil, the blower reheated the neck to polish the lip and further smoothed
it by tooling. Bottles were created with a variety of applied and tooled ring and collar tops.

Snap Cases: 1860-1903
(Figure 2)

Between 1850 and 1860, the snap case was invented. It replaced the pontil and was the first major invention since the development of the blowpipe. The snap case was a 5-foot metal rod with claws to grasp the bottle. A snap locked the claw into place in order to hold the bottle more securely while the neck was being finished. Each snap case was custom-made to fit bottles of a certain size and shape. Because this bottle-making process didn't use pontil rods, these bottles have no pontil scars or marks, which left the bases of the bottle free for lettering or design. There may, however, be some small grip marks on the side as a result of the claw device. The snap case was used for small-mouth bottle production until the automatic bottle machine came into use in 1903.

Snap Cases: 1860-1903
Figure 2

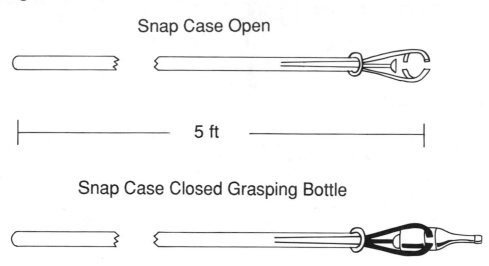

Snap Case Open

|—————————— 5 ft ——————————|

Snap Case Closed Grasping Bottle

Molds: B.C.-1900 (Figure 3)

The use of molds in bottle making, which became prevalent in the early 1800s, actually dates back to the Romans in the 1st century. As detailed earlier in the free-blown process, the glass blower shaped the vessel by blowing and turning it in the air. When using a mold, the glass blower would blow a few puffs while lowering the red-hot shaped mass into the hollow mold. The blower would then continue blowing air into the tube until the glass compressed itself against the sides of the mold to acquire the finished shape.

Molds were made in two or more sections to enable the mold to come apart. The hardened bottle could then easily be removed. Since it was impossible to have the molds fit precisely, the seams show on the surface of the finished article, indicating the method used to produce the bottle. The molds were categorized as "open," in which only the body of the bottle was molded, with the neck and lip being added afterward, and "closed," in which the neck and lip were part of the original mold (Figure 3). Later, two types of molds came into use:

(1) The three-piece mold (1809-1880).

(2) The turn mold or paste mold (1880-1900).

The introduction of the three-piece mold helped the bottle industry become stronger in the 19th century by enabling it to keep up with the increasing demand.

Molds: First Century B.C.-1900

Figure 3

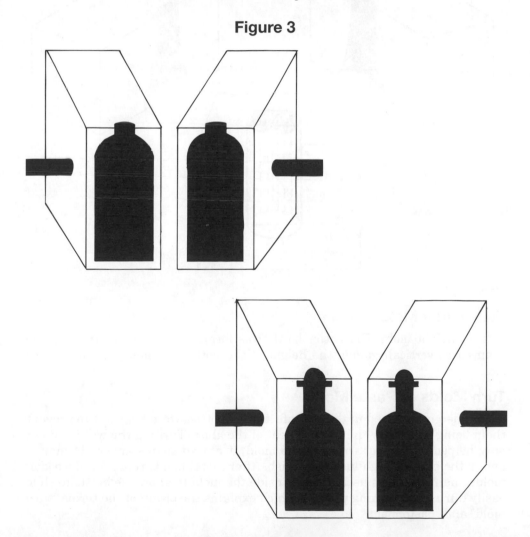

Three-Piece Molds (Figure 4)

Three-piece dip mold: The bottom section of the bottle mold was one piece, and the top, from the shoulder up, was two separate pieces. The mold seams appeared circling the bottle at the shoulder and on each side of the neck.

Three-Piece Mold
Figure 4

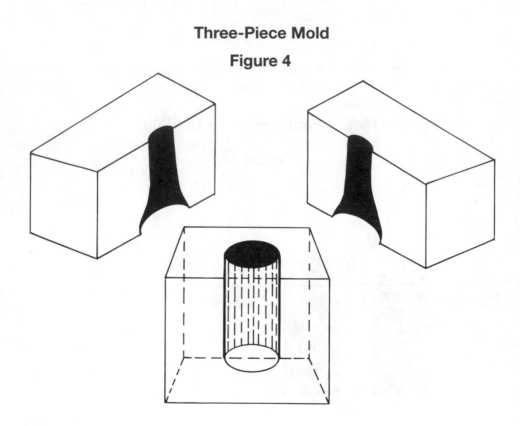

Full-Height Molds

Full height mold: The entire bottle was formed in the mold, and the two seams run vertically along the height of the bottle to below the lip on both sides.

Turn Molds or Paste Molds

Wooden molds used in the manufacture of bottles were kept wet to prevent them being ignited by the intense heat of the glass. Turning the wet mold not only helped prevent charring of the mold, it erased seams and mold marks, giving the bottle a high luster or finish. After metal molds replace the wooden molds, manufacturers used a paste inside the mold to allow the bottle to slide easily during the turning process, which explains the origin of the terms "turn mold" and "paste mold."

Mason Food Jars: 1858

In 1858, Mason invented a wide-mouth jar with a screw top formed in the same mold as the body. The new bottle became famous for its use as a food preservative container. After the jar was blown and broken away from the blowpipe, it was sent to the annealing oven to temper the glass, making it more resistant to breakage. Then the jagged edges of the rims were ground down. Earlier jars can be distinguished from later ones by the rough and sharp edges produced by this grinding down process.

Press and Blow: 1892

A semi-automatic process called "press and blow" was invented in 1892. This process could only be used in the production of wide-mouth containers formed by pressing the molten glass into the mold to form the mouth and lip first. Then, a metal plunger was inserted through the mouth and applied air pressure to form the body of the bottle. This process was used for the production of early fruit jars and milk bottles.

Full height metal mold: front view.

Full height metal mold: side view.

Press and blow milk mold used by Thatcher milk bottles, Lockport Glass Co., Lockport, NY, circa 1927.

Illustration 1

The Original Owens Process

*The basic invention of the Owens Bottle
Machine is fixed on this crude vacuum device.*

The Automatic Bottle Making Machine: 1903

Michael J. Owens, recognized as the inventor of the first automatic bottle-making machine, began as a glass blower in 1874 at 15 years old. Owens proved to be a capable inventor, and in 1888, while working in Toledo, Ohio, for the American Lamp Chimney Company, he invented a semi-automatic

Illustration 2

Machine No. 2

This machine is similar in construction to the original device, except that it is mounted on an upright column, with a wheelbase to move the machine forward to and back from the glass pot.

machine for tumblers and lantern chimneys. Using his engineering talent and his background and experience in glassmaking, he developed his first bottle-making machine in 1899 (Illus. 1). After experimenting with three machines, he perfected the process with his fourth machine in 1903 (Illus. 2, 3, and 4). Owens continued to make additional improvements and introduced Machine No. 5 (Illus. 5) in 1904. This final improvement allowed the continuous movement of the machine and increased both the quantity and quality of bottles.

At first, the Owens machine made only heavy bottles because they were in the greatest demand. In 1909, improvements to the machine made it possible to produce small prescription bottles. Between 1909 and 1917, numerous other

Illustration 3

Machine No. 3

*This was the first rotating machine, and was very novel in
construction. It was for the requirements of this machine
that the revolving glass tank was developed.*

Illustration 4

Machine No. 4

*This machine was the outgrowth of the great encouragement Mr.
Owens received from the the operation of No. 3, and at the time it
was built was considered a marvelous specimen of engineering skill.*

Illustration 5

Machine No. 5

*This machine shows a great improvement over No. 4. It formed
the foundation for the general type in use at the present day.*

automatic bottle-making machines were invented, and soon bottles around the
world were produced by machine.

In 1904, Owens' first machine produced 13,000 bottles a day, but by 1917,
Machine No. 5 was producing 60,000 bottles a day. In 1917, the "Gob Feeder"
was developed, which produced a measured amount of molten glass from which
a bottle could be blown. In this process, a gob of glass was drawn from the tank
and cut off by shears.

Screw-Topped Bottles

One last note about bottle making concerns the process of producing screw-
topped bottles. Early glass blowers produced bottles with inside and outside

threads long before bottle-making machines mechanized the process. Because early methods of production were so complex, screw-topped bottles produced before the 1800s were considered specialty bottles and were expensive to replace. Today, they are considered rare and collectible. In fact, the conventional screw-top bottle didn't become common until after 1924, when the glass industry standardized the threads.

The Beginning Collector

Now that you have learned some things about the history, origin, and the process of producing a bottle, it's time to provide information about how to approach the hobby of bottle collecting, as well as suggestions on books and reference guides, start-up costs, old versus new bottles, and information on bottle clubs and dealers.

So, what approach should you take towards getting started, and what might influence that approach? The first thing to understand about antique bottle collecting is that there aren't set rules. Everyone's finances, spare time, storage space available, and preferences are different, so you will need to tailor your collecting to your own individual circumstances. As a collector, you will need to think about whether to specialize and focus on a specific type of bottle or group of bottles, or become a general or "maverick" collector who acquires everything that becomes available.

The majority of bottle collectors that I've known over the years, myself included, took the maverick approach as new collectors. We grabbed everything in sight, ending up with bottles of every type, shape, and color. Now, after 30 years of collecting, my recommendation to newcomers is to just do a small amount of maverick collecting and focus on a specific or specialized bottle or group of bottles. Taking the more general approach in the early years has given me more breadth of knowledge about bottles and glass, but specializing has the following distinct advantages over the "maverick" approach:

- It reduces the field of collection, which will provide more time for organization, study, and research.

- It allows a collector to become an authority on bottles in a particular or specific field.

- Trading becomes easier with other specialists who may have duplicate or unwanted bottles.

- By becoming more of an authority within a specialty, a collector can negotiate a better deal by spotting bottles that are underpriced.

I need to mention, however, that specialized collectors may be tempted by bottles that don't quite fit into their collections. So, they might cheat a little and give into the maverick urge. This occasional cheating sometimes results in a smaller side collection or, in some cases, turns the collector away from a specialty and back to being a maverick. But, that's OK. Remember, there are no set rules, with the exception of having a lot of fun.

Now, what does it cost to start a collection, and how can you determine the value of a bottle? Aside from digging excursions of which the cost includes travel and daily expenses, starting a collection can be accomplished by spending just a few dollars or maybe just a few cents per bottle. Digging, which is discussed in detail in the chapter "Digging for Bottles" is in this writer's opinion, the ultimate way of adding to your collection and is how I started my addiction to the hobby.

Knowing what and where the best deals are obviously takes time and experience. But, the beginner can do well with just a few pointers. Let's start off with the approach of buying bottles, instead of digging for bottles, since this is a quicker approach with more sources available for the new bottle collector.

Over the years, I've developed a quick-look method of buying bottles by grouping candidates into one of three categories:

- Low-end or common bottles: Bottles in this category reflect noticeable wear and the labels are usually missing or not very visible. In most cases, the labels are completely gone and never have embossing. The bottles will be dirty (although they usually can be cleaned), will have some scrapes, but be free of chips. They are usually clear.

- Average grade/common bottles: Bottles of this type show some wear, and a label may be visible but is usually faded. Some may have minimal embossing, but not likely. They are free of scrapes or chips and are generally clear or aqua.

- High-end and unique bottles: These bottles can be empty, or partially or completely full, with the original stopper

and label or embossing. If it has been stored in a box, the
bottle is most likely in good or excellent condition. Also,
the box must be in very good condition. The bottle will
have no scrapes or chips and will show very little wear.
The bottle can be clear, but is usually green, teal blue,
yellow, or yellow-green.

Pricing ranges will be discussed briefly here since pricing and values are
covered in detail in the "Determining Bottle Values" chapter. Usually the low-
end category can be found for $1 to $5, the average grade will range from $5
to $20, and the high end will range from $20 to $100. Anything above $100
should be looked at closely by someone who has been collecting for a while and
is knowledgeable.

As a general rule, I try not to spend more than $2 per bottle for low-end
and $5 to $7 for average grade. It's easier to stick to this guideline when

you've done your homework, but sometimes you just get lucky. For example, during a number of bottle and antique shows, I have found tables where the seller had shopping bags full of bottles for $2 a bag called "grab bags." I never pass up a bargain like this because of the low price and the lure of the treasures that may be hiding inside. After one show, when I examined my treasures, I discovered a total of nine bottles, some purple, all earlier than 1900, in great shape, with embossing, for a total cost of 22 cents per bottle. Now what could be better than that? Well, what was better was that I found a Tonopah, Nev., medicine bottle valued at $100.

In the high-end category, deals are usually made after some good old horse trading and bartering. But, hey, that's part of the fun. Always let the seller know that you are a new collector with a limited budget. It really helps. I have never run across a bottle seller who wouldn't work with a new collector to try to give the best deal for a limited budget.

A collector should also be aware of the characteristics of old bottle versus new bottles and what the distinctions are among antique bottles, old bottles, and new bottles. Quite often, new collectors assume that any old bottle is an antique and if a bottle isn't old it isn't collectible. In the antique world, an item is defined as an antique if it is 100 years old or more. But quite a number of bottles listed in this book are less than 100 years old, yet are in fact just as valuable—perhaps more so—than those that are more than 100 years old and meet the definition of antique. The history, origin, background, use, and rarity of a bottle can be more important to a bottle collector than how close the bottle comes to the 100-year mark.

The number and variety of old and antique bottles is greater than the new collectible items in today's market. On the other hand, the Jim Beams, Ezra Brooks, Avons, recent Coke bottles, figurals, and miniature soda and liquor bottles manufactured more recently are very desirable and collectible and are, in fact, made for that purpose. If you decide you want to collect new bottles, the best time to buy is when the first issue comes out on the market. When the first issues are gone, the collector market is the only available source, which limits availability and will drive the price up considerably.

The fervor for Coca-Cola collector bottles is a good example of this phenomenon. When Coca-Cola reissued the 8-ounce junior-size Coke bottle in the Los Angeles area to garner attention in a marketplace full of cans, the word spread fast among collectors. This 8-ounce bottle had the same contour as the 6-1/2-ounce bottle that was a Coke standard from the 1920s to the 1950s and has also been issued as a special Christmas issue every year since 1992. The 6-1/2-ounce bottle is available in a few parts of the United States, most noticeably, in Atlanta, Ga., where Coca-Cola has it headquarters. When these reissued 8-ounce bottles were issued, dedicated collectors paid in advance and picked up entire case lots from the bottling operations before they hit the retail market.

For the beginner collector, and even the old-timer, books, references guides, magazines, and other similar literature is readily available at libraries and bookstores. The bibliography in this book lists various types of literature to get you started. Also, joining a bottle club can be of great value, since this will provide numerous new sources of information, as well as an occasional digging expedition. Various bottle clubs and dealers are also listed under separate chapters in this book.

I want to finish with a final note on reproductions and repaired bottles. Always check the bottle, jar, or pottery carefully to make sure that there have been no repairs or special treatments. It's best to hold the item up to the light or take it outside with the dealer to look for cracks, nicks, or dings. Be sure to check for scratches that may have occurred during cleaning. Also, a number of bottles and jars have reproduction closures. The proper closure can make a difference in the value of the bottle, so it's important to make sure the closure fits securely and the metal lid is stamped with the correct patent dates or lettering. If you need help on this, don't hesitate to ask an experienced collector. If you have any doubt, you can ask the dealer for a money-back guarantee, but my approach is to just take a walk or get an experienced collector to help.

Now, get out to the antique and bottle shows, flea markets, swap meets, garage sales, and antique shops. Pick up those bottles, handle that glass, ask plenty of questions, and soon you will be surprised by how much you have learned, not to mention how much fun you'll have.

In order to better understand the hobby, new bottles collectors should learn certain aspects such as age identification, bottle grading, labeling, and glass imperfections and peculiarities.

Bottle Facts

As mentioned in the introduction, usually the first question from a novice is "How do you know how old a bottle is" or "How can you tell if it's really an antique bottle?" Two of the most common methods for determining age involve examining the mold seams and color variations. Also, details on the lip, or top of the bottle, provide further information.

Mold Seams (Figure 1)

Prior to 1900, bottles were either free blown with a blowpipe (to 1860) or made with a mold (to 1900). In both of these processes, the mouth or lip of the bottle was formed last and applied to the bottle after completion. This type of mouth is called an applied lip. An applied lip can be identified by observing the mold seam that runs from the base up to the neck and near the end of the lip. On a machine-made bottle, the lip is formed first and the mold seam runs over the lip. Therefore, the closer to the top of the bottle the seam extends, the newer the bottle.

On the earliest bottles manufactured before 1860, the mold seams end low on the neck or at the shoulder. On bottles made between 1860 and 1880, the mold seam stops right below the mouth and makes it easy to determine that the lip was formed separately. Around 1880, the closed mold was used, wherein the neck and lip were mechanically shaped and the glass was severed from the blowpipe, and the ridge evened off by hand sanding or filing. This mold seam usually ends within 1/4 inch from the top of the bottle. After 1900, the seam extends all the way to the top.

Identifying Bottle Age By Mold Seams

Figure 1

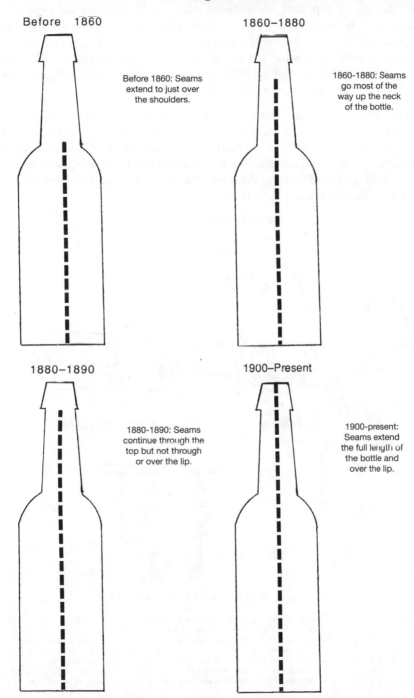

Before   1860

Before 1860: Seams extend to just over the shoulders.

1860–1880

1860-1880: Seams go most of the way up the neck of the bottle.

1880–1890

1880-1890: Seams continue through the top but not through or over the lip.

1900–Present

1900-present: Seams extend the full length of the bottle and over the lip.

Lips and Tops
(Figures 2a and 2b, Figure 3)

Since the lip, or top, was an integral part the bottle-making process, it is important to understand that process. One of the best ways to identify bottles manufactured before 1840 is by the presence of a "sheared lip." This type of lip was formed by cutting or snipping the glass free of the blowpipe with a pair of shears, a process that left the lip with a stovepipe look. Since hot glass can be stretched, some stovepipes have a very distinctive appearance.

Around 1840, bottle manufacturers began to apply a glass ring around the sheared lip, forming a "laid-on-ring" lip. Between 1840 and 1880, numerous variations of lips or tops were produced using a variety of tools. After 1880, manufacturers began to pool their processing information, resulting in a more evenly finished and uniform top. As a general rule, the more uneven and crude the lip or top, the older the bottle is.

Neck-Finishing Tools

Figure 2a

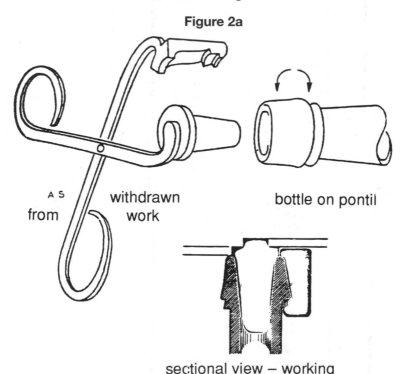

A S
from   withdrawn   bottle on pontil
            work

sectional view – working

A. The line drawings were developed from a description that appeared in the seventh edition (1842) of the *Encyclopedia Britannica*, vol. X, p. 579: "The finisher then warms the bottle at the furnace, and taking out a small quantity of metal on what is termed a ring iron, he turns it once round the mouth forming the ring seen at the mouth of bottles. He then employs the shears to give shape to the neck. One of the blades of the shears has a piece of brass in the center, tapered like a common cork, which forms the inside of the mouth, to the other blade is attached a piece of brass, used to form the ring." This did not appear in the sixth edition (1823), though it is probable the method of forming collars was practiced in some glasshouses at that time.

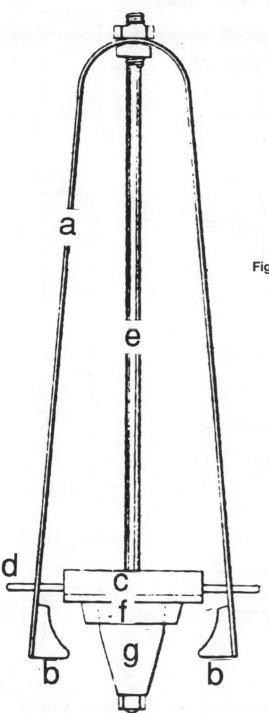

Figure 2b

B. The exact period in which neck finishing tools evolved having metal springs with two jaws instead of one, to form collars, is undetermined. It doubtless was some time before Amosa Stone of Philadelphia patented his "improved tool," which was of simpler construction, as were many later ones. Like Stone's, the interior of the jaws [was] made in such shape as to give the outside of the nozzle of the bottle or neck of the vessel formed the desired shape as it [was] rotated between the jaws in a plastic state..." U.S. Patent Office. From specifications for (A. Stone) patent No. 15,738, September 23, 1856.

Bottle Lips/Tops Identification

Figure 3

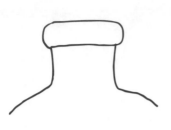

1. Tooled, rounded, rolled-over collar

2. Tooled, flanged, with flat top and squared edges

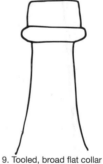

3. Tooled, rounded above 3/4-inch flat band

4. Tooled, flat ring below thickened plain lip

5. Tooled, narrow beveled fillet below thickened plain lip

6. Tooled, broad sloping collar above beveled ring

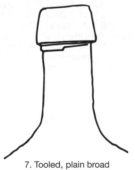

7. Tooled, plain broad sloping collar

8. Tooled, broad sloping collar with beveled edges at top and bottom

9. Tooled, broad flat collar sloping to heavy rounded ring

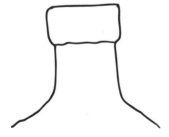

10. Tooled, broad flat vertical collar with uneven lower edge

11. Tooled, double rounded collar, upper deeper than lower; neck slightly pinched at base of collar

12. Tooled, broad round collar with lower level

Closures/Stoppers

As mentioned in the "Bottles: History and Origin" chapter, the Romans used small stones rolled in tar as stoppers, and the following centuries saw little advancement. During most of the 15th and 16th centuries, closures consisted of a sized cloth tied down with heavy thread or string. Beneath the cover was a stopper made of wax or bombase (cotton wadding). Cotton wool dipped in wax was also used as a stopper along with coverings of parchment, paper, or leather. Corks and glass stoppers were still used in great numbers with the cork sometimes tied or wired down for effervescent liquids. When the "closed mold" came into existence, however, the shape of the lip was more accurately controlled, which made it possible to invent and manufacture many different capping devices.

Glass stoppers, 1850-1900

Example of glass stopper with cork as insulator for poison bottles, 1890-1910.

Figure 4
S.A. Whitney Bottle Stopper

No. 31046   Patented Jan. 1, 1861

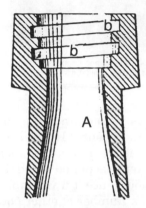
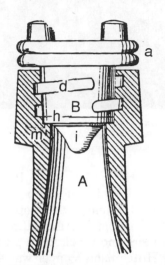

From Samuel A. Whitney's specification for his "Bottle Stopper," Patent No. 31,046, Jan. 1, 1861. The drawing on the left shows grooves in the neck of the bottle. In the drawing on the right, in which "h" is a cork washer, the stopper is in place. "The stopper is formed by pressing or casting the molten...glass in molds of the desired shape...Although...applicable to a variety of bottles and jars, it is especially well adapted to and has been more especiallly designed for use in connection with mineral-water bottles, and such as contain effervescing wines, malt liquors, &c., the corks in this class of bottles, if not lost, being generally so mutilated as to be unfit for second use when the bottles are refilled." (U.S. Patent Office.)

An early closure device was introduced by S.A. Whitney, who owned Whitney Glass Works in Glasborough, N.J. He received Patent No. 31,046 (Figure 4) on Jan. 1, 1861, for the internal screw stopper he created.

A unique closure was developed on July 23, 1872, when British inventor Hiram Codd designed a stopper to contain effervescing liquids. His invention was granted Patent No. 129,652. The bottle was made with a groove inside the neck. A glass marble was first inserted in the bottle, and a ring of cork or rubber was then fitted into the groove. With the glass marble confined inside its neck, the pressure of the gas from the effervescing liquid forced the marble to the top of the neck, sealing the bottle. A second patent, No. 138,230 issued April 29, 1873, contained an interior lug, or ball-holding element. It's interesting to note that many young boys broke the bottle to get the marble.

Hiram Codd interior ball stopper, Patent #129,652, July 23, 1872.

Hiram Codd interior ball stopper, Patent #138,230, April 29, 1873.

From April 8, 1879, when Patent No. 213,992 was issued, until the early 1900s, the Hutchinson stopper was a common bottle closure. Hutchinson's concept used a heavy wire loop to control a rubber gasket that stayed inside the neck of the bottle. After filling the bottle, the gasket was pulled up against the shoulders and was kept in place by the carbonation. Since it was simple to use, the Hutchinson stopper was easily adaptable to a number of other bottle types.

Charles G. Hutchinson stopper, Patent #213,992, April 8, (year uncertain).

The lightning stopper, used from 1880 to the early 1900s, was a porcelain or rubber plug anchored to the outside of the bottle by means of a permanently attached wire. The wire formed a bar that controlled the opening and closing of the bottle. Since the lightning stopper cost more than the Hutchinson stopper, it wasn't used for soft drinks.

In 1892, William Painter invented the "crown cap," which revolutionized the soft drink and beer bottling industry. By 1915, all major bottlers had switched to the crown-type cap. It had been reported that Painter's "crown cork" system had taken three years of constant work to perfect and cost $100,000, a considerable amount of money in 1892. It wasn't until 1960 with the introduction of the screw cap for beer and soda pop bottles that the crown-type cap began to disappear.

William Painter crown cap, Patent #468,226, Feb. 2, 1890.

Dumfries Ale (English) full bottle depicting inside threads.

Dumfries Ale (English) depicting inside threads.

In 1875, some glass manufacturers made an inside screw neck whiskey bottle that used a rubber stopper. This invention wasn't very popular, though, because the alcohol interacted with the rubber, discoloring the rubber and making the whiskey bitter.

The following list reflects a portion of the brands of embossed whiskeys that featured the inside threaded neck and their approximate dates of circulation:

Finally, in 1902, threads were manufactured on the outside of the lip to enable a threaded cap to be screwed onto the mouth of the bottle. This was not a new idea. Early glass blowers produced bottles with inside and outside screw caps long before bottle-making machines came along. Early methods of production were so complex, however, that screw-topped bottles produced before the 1800s were considered specialty bottles. They were expensive to replace and today are considered rare and quite collectible. In fact, the conventional screw-top bottle did not become common until after 1924, when the glass industry standardized the threads.

Glass Color

The next most common method for determining the age of a bottle is examining the color of the glass. The basic ingredients for glass production (sand, soda, and lime) have remained the same for 3,000 years. These ingredients, when mixed together, are collectively called the "batch." When

Whiskey Company	Date of Circulation
Adolph Harris	1907-1912
Chevalier Castle	1907-1910
Crown (squatty)	1905-1912
Crown (pint)	1896-1899
Donnelly Rye	1910-1917
El Monte	1910-1918
H.L. Nye	1900-1905
Hall Luhrs	1880-1918
Hanley	1905-1911
J.C. Donnelly	1907-1915
McDonald/Cohn	1903-1912
Mini Taylor/Williams	1881-1900
Old Gilt Edge	1907-1912
O'Hearns	1907-1916
Posner	1905-1915
Roth (aqua)	1903-1911
Roth (amber sq.)	1898-1909
Roth (amber fluted shoulder)	1903-1911
Roth (amber qt.)	1903-1911
Rusconi-Fisher	1902-1915
Taussig (clear)	1915-1918
Weeks/Potter	1860-1875
Whitney	1860-1875
Wilmerding/Loewe	1907-1917

the batch is heated to a molten state, it is referred to as the "metal." In its soft or plastic stage, the metal can be molded into objects, which when cooled become the solid material we know as glass.

Producing colored and perfectly clear glass were both major challenges for glass manufactures for centuries. In the 13th and 14th centuries, the Venetians produced clear glass using crushed quartz in place of sand. In 1668, the English tried to improve on this process by using ground flint to produce clear glass, and by 1675 an Englishman named George perfected lead glass. Today, this lead glass is referred to as "flint glass." Prior to 1840, intentionally colored or colorless glass was reserved for fancy figured flasks and vessels. The coloration of bottles was essentially considered unimportant until 1880 when food preservation packers began to demand clear glass for food products. Since most glass produced prior to this time was green, glass manufacturers began using manganese to bleach out the green tinge produced by the iron content. Only then did a clear bottle become a common bottle.

Iron slag was used up to 1860 to produce a dark olive-green or olive-amber glass that has become known as "black glass, which was used for wine and beverage bottles that needed protection from light. Colors that are natural to bottle glass are brown, amber, olive-green, and aqua.

The true colors of blue, green, and purple were produced by adding metallic oxides to the glass batch. Cobalt was added for blue glass, sulfur for yellow and green, manganese and nickel for purple, nickel for brown, copper or gold for red, and tin or zinc for milk-colored glass (for apothecary vials, druggist bottles, and pocket bottles). The Hocking Glass Company discovered a process for making a brilliant red-colored glass described as copper-ruby. The color was achieved by adding copper oxide to a glass batch as it was cooling and then immediately reheating the batch before use. Since these bright colors were expensive to produce, they are very rare and sought after by most collectors.

Many bottle collectors consider purple glass the most fascinating and appealing; therefore, it is prized above other glass. As discussed earlier, the iron contained in sand caused glass to take on a color between green and blue. Glass manufacturers used manganese that counteracted the aqua to produce clear glass. Glass with manganese content was most common in bottle production between 1880 and 1914. When exposed to the ultraviolet rays of the sun, the manganese in the glass oxidizes, or combines with oxygen, and turns the glass purple. The longer the glass is exposed to the ultraviolet rays from the sun, the deeper the purple color.

This purple glass has become known as desert glass or sun-colored glass, because the color is activated by exposure to extreme heat. Since Germany was the main source of manganese, the supply ceased with the beginning of World War I. By 1916, the glass-making industry began using selenium as a neutralizing agent. One last note: glass that was produced between 1914 and 1930 is glass that is most likely to change to an amber or straw color.

**The following chart shows how oxides are
used to create various glass colors:**

Color	Oxide Added to the Glass Batch
Yellow	Nickel
Red	Gold, copper, or selenium
Blue	Cobalt
Amber	Impure manganese dioxide, sulphur
Dark Brown	Sulphide of copper and sulphide of sodium
Amethyst (Purple)	Sulphide of nickel
Rose Tinted	Selenium added directly to the batch
Orange-Red	Selenium mixed first with cadmium sulphide
Dark Reddish Brown	Sodium Sulphide
Reddish Yellow	Sulphide of sodium and molybdenite
Green	Iron Oxide
Olive-Green	Iron oxide and black oxide of manganese
Purple	Manganese
Orange	Oxide of iron and manganese

Imperfections

Imperfections and blemishes also provide clues to how old a bottle is and often add to the charm and value to a piece. Blemishes usually show up as bubbles or "seeds" in the glass. During the glass-making process, air bubbles form and rise to the surface where they pop. As the "fining out" process became more advanced around 1920, the bubbles were eliminated.

Another peculiarity of the antique bottle is the uneven thickness of the glass. Often one side of the base has an inch-thick side that slants off to paper thinness on the opposite side. This imperfection was eliminated with the introduction of the Owens bottle-making machine in 1903.

In addition, the various marks of stress and strain, sunken sides, twisted necks, and whittle marks (usually at the neck where the wood mold made impressions in the glass) also give clues to indicate that a bottle was produced before 1900.

Labeling and Embossing

While labeling and embossing were a common practice in the rest of the world for a number of centuries, American bottle manufacturers did not adopt the inscription process until 1869. These inscriptions included information about the contents, manufacturer, distributor, slogans, or other messages advertising the product. Raised lettering on various bottles was produced with a plate mold, sometimes called a "slug plate" that was fitted inside the casting mold. The plate created a sunken area that makes them of special value to collectors. Irregularities such as a misspelled name add to the value of the bottle, as will any name embossed with hand etching or other method of crude grinding. These bottles are very old, collectible, and valuable.

Inscription and embossing ended with the production of machine-made bottles in 1903 and the subsequent introduction of paper labels. In 1933, with the repeal of Prohibition, the distilling of whiskey and other spirits was resumed under new strict government regulations. One of the major regulations was that the following statement was required to be embossed on all bottles containing alcohol: "Federal Law Forbids Sale or Re-Use of this Bottle." This regulation was in effect until 1964 and is an excellent method of dating spirit bottles made from 1933 to 1964.

Determining Bottle Values

Determining an old bottle's value involves a number of variables. The following are most often used by collectors and dealers to determine a bottle's value and are consistent with the methods I have used over the years. All need to be considered when determining value, but rarity, age, condition, and color are considered the most important.

1. **Supply and Demand**
   As with any product, when demand increases and supply decreases, the price rises.

2. **Rarity and Condition**
   See below for a detailed explanation.

3. **Historic Appeal, Significance, and Geographic Location**
   For example, territorial bottles were made in areas that were not yet admitted to the Union.

4. **Embossing, Labeling, and Design**

   - A bottle without embossing is considered common and has little dollar value to many collectors. Exceptions would be early (prior to 1840) hand-blown bottles, which usually did not have embossing.

- Embossing can describe the name of the contents, manufacturer, state, city, dates, trademarks, and other valuable information. Embossed images and trademarks can also enhance and increase the value of a bottle.

- Labeling found intact with specific information also increases the value of the bottle.

5. **Age**

A detailed description of age identification is found in the following chapters: "Bottles: History and Origin;" "Bottle Facts;" and "Digging for Bottles." The following is a brief summary:

- Open Pontil – 1600s-1850s

- Iron Pontil – 1840-1865

- Smooth-Based – 1865-1920

- Machine-Made Threaded Bottles – 1901-Present

6. **Color**

The "Bottle Facts" chapter provides a detailed description of glass color with respect to value and age. The following is a brief summary.

- Low-Price Range: Clear, Aqua, Amber

- Mid-Price Range: Milk Glass, Green, Black, Basic Olive Green

- High-Price Range: Teal Blue, Cobalt Blue, Purple (Amethyst), Yellow, Yellow-Green, Puce

7. **Unique Features**
   These include pontil
   marks, whittle marks, glass
   imperfections (thickness
   and bubbles), slug plates,
   and crudely applied tops
   or lips.

Condition

Mint	An empty or full bottle (preferably full) with a label or embossing. The bottle must be clean and have good color, with no chips, scrapes, or wear. If the bottle comes in a box, the box must be in perfect condition too.
Extra Fine	An empty or full bottle with slight wear on the label or embossing. The bottle must be clean with clear color, and have no chips or scrapes. There is usually no box, or a box not in very good condition.
Very Good	The bottle reflects some wear, and label is usually missing or not very visible. Most likely there is no embossing and no box.
Good	The bottle shows additional wear and label is completely absent. Color is usually faded and bottle is dirty. Usually some scrapes and minor chips. Most likely there is no box.
Fair or Average	Bottle shows a large amount of wear, and the label is missing.

Rarity

Unique   Only one specimen is known to exist. These bottles are the most valuable.

Extremely Rare   Only 5 to 10 specimens are known to exist.

Very Rare   Only 10 to 20 specimens are known to exist.

Rare   Only 20 to 40 specimens are known to exist.

Very Scarce   No more than 50 specimens are known to exist.

Scarce   No more than 100 specimens are known to exist.

Common   Specimens (such as clear 1880-1900 medicine bottles) exist in abundance, are easy to acquire, and usually very inexpensive. These are great bottles for the beginning collector.

Even with the above guidelines, it is important to always have additional resources, especially for rare and unique bottles. The "Bottle Clubs" and "Bottle Dealers" chapters and the bibliography provide references. And remember, never hesitate to ask other collectors and dealers for help and assistance.

Bottle Sources

Antique and collectible bottles can be found in a variety of places and sometimes where you least expect them. Excluding digging for bottles, the following sources are good potential hiding places for that much sought-after bottle.

The Internet

In the 30 years that I have been collecting, I have never seen anything impact the hobby of bottle collecting as much as the Internet. Go to the Internet, type in antique bottle collecting, and check it out. You'll be amazed at all of the data at your fingertips. Numerous Web sites throughout the United States, Canada, Europe, and Asia provide information about clubs, dealers, antique publications, and auction companies. These sites have opened the entire world to the collector and are inexpensive and valuable resources for the collector and dealer.

Flea Markets, Swap Meets, Garage Sales, Thrift Stores, Secondhand Stores, and Salvage Stores

For the beginner collector, these sources will likely be the most fun (next to digging) and yield the most bottles at the best prices. A little homework can result in opportunities to purchase an endless variety of bottles at very low cost. Most bottles from these sources will fall into the "common" or "common but above average" categories.

When searching at flea markets, swap meets, and thrift stores, be sure to focus on places where household goods are sold. It's a good bet they'll have bottles. When targeting garage sales, concentrate on the older areas of town because the goods will be noticeably older and more collectible, perhaps even rare. Salvage stores or salvage yards are good spots to search since these businesses deal with companies that have contracts to demolish old houses, apartments, and businesses and on occasion find treasures. One New York salvage company that was contracted to clean out some old storage buildings discovered an untouched Prohibition-era set-up complete with bottles and unused labels and equipment. What a find!

Local Bottle Clubs and Collectors

By joining a local bottle club or working with other collectors, you'll find yet another source for your growing collection. Members usually have quantities of unwanted or duplicate bottles that they will trade, sell very reasonably, or sometimes even give away, especially to an enthusiastic new collector. In addition, bottle clubs are always a good source for information about digging expeditions.

Bottle Shows

Bottle shows not only expose you to bottles of every type, shape, color, and variety, but also provide the opportunity to talk with many experts in specialized fields. In addition, publications dealing with all aspects of bottle collecting are usually available for sale. Bottle shows can be rewarding learning experiences not only for beginner collectors, but also for veteran collectors. They take place almost every weekend all across the country, and they always offer something new to learn and share and, of course, bottles to buy or trade.

Make sure you look under the tables at these shows because many bargains in the form of duplicates and unwanted items may be lurking where you least expect it. Quite often, diggers find so many bottles that they don't even bother to clean them. Instead, they offer them as is for a very low price. Hey, for a low price I'll clean bottles!

Auction and Estate Sales

Auction houses have become a good source of bottles and glassware over the last few years. Look for an auction company that specializes in antiques and estate buyouts. To promote itself and provide buyers with a better idea of what will be presented for sale, an auction house usually publishes a catalog that provides bottle photographs, descriptions, and conditions. Auctions are fun and can be a very good source of bottles at economical prices. I do recommend, however, that you visit an auction first as a spectator to learn a little about how the whole process works before you decide to participate and buy at one. When buying, be sure of the color and condition of the bottle, and terms of the sale. These guidelines also apply to all Internet auctions.

Since buying and selling at auctions has become very popular, consider the following general information and rules:

Buying Through Auctions

- Purchase the catalog and review all items in the auction. At live auctions, a preview is usually held so customers can see the items before bidding.

- After reviewing the catalog and making your choice, you can usually phone or mail your bid. (Generally, a 10 percent buyer's premium is added to the sale price).

- Callbacks allow you to increase the previous high bid (including yours) on certain items after the close of the auction.

- The winning bidder will receive an invoice in the mail. After the bidder's check clears, the bottle will be shipped.

- The majority of auction houses have a return policy. If the bottle doesn't match the description in the catalog, there is usually a refund policy.

The "Auction Companies" chapter lists a number of quality auction houses that specialize in bottles, pottery, and related glass items.

Selling Through Auctions

- Check your auction source before consigning any merchandise. Make sure the auction venue is legitimate and hasn't had any problems with payment or products.

- Package the item with plenty of bubble wrap, insure it, and mail the package by certified mail, signed receipt requested.

- Allow 30 days to receive the proceeds from the sale. Be aware that most firms charge a 15 percent commission on the sale price.

Estate sales are great sources for bottles if the home is in a very old neighborhood or section of the city that has historical significance. These sales are a lot of fun, especially when the people running the sale let you look over and handle the items for sale to be able to make careful selections. Prices are usually good and are always negotiable.

Knife and Gun Shows

What? Bottles at a knife and gun show? Quite a few knife and gun enthusiasts are also great fans of the West and keep an eye open for related artifacts. Every knife and gun show I have attended, or sold at, has had at least 10 dealers with bottles on their tables (or under the tables) for sale. And the prices were about right since they were more interested in selling their knives and guns than the bottles. Plus, these dealers will often provide information on where they made their finds, which you can put to good use later.

Retail Antique Dealers

This group includes dealers who sell bottles at or near full-market prices. Buying from dealers has advantages as well as disadvantages. They usually have a large selection and will provide helpful information and details about the bottles. It is a safe bet that the bottles for sale are authentic and priced according to the true condition of the bottle. On the other hand, building a collection from these dealers can be very expensive. But these shops are a good place to browse, learn, and to try to add to your collection.

General Antique and Specialty Shops

The difference between a general shop and a retail dealer is the selection (usually more limited in a general shop) and the pricing, which is happily much lower. This is partly because these dealers aren't as knowledgeable about bottles and therefore may incorrectly identify a bottle, overlooking critical areas that determine the value. If a collector is well informed, general antique dealers can provide the opportunity to acquire underpriced quality merchandise.

Digging for Bottles

There are many ways to begin your search for collectible bottles, but few searches are as satisfying and fun as digging up bottles yourself. While the goal is to find a bottle, the adventure of the hunt is as exciting as the actual find. From a beginner's viewpoint, digging is a relatively inexpensive way to start your collection. The efforts of individual and bottle club digging expeditions have turned up numerous important historical finds. These digs surfaced valuable information about the early decades of our country and the history of bottle and glass manufacturing in the United States. The following discussion of how to plan a digging expedition covers the essentials: locating digging sites, equipment and tools, general rules and helpful hints, and a section on privy/outhouse digging for the real adventurer.

Locating the Digging Site

Before any dig, you'll need to learn as much as possible about the area you plan to explore. Don't overlook valuable resources in your own community. You will likely be able to collect important information from your local library, local and state historical societies, various types of maps, and city directories (useful for information about people who once lived on a particular piece of property). The National Office of Cartography in Washington D.C. and the National Archives are excellent resources, as well.

In my experience, old maps are the best guides for locating digging areas with good potential. These maps show what the town looked like in an earlier era and provide clues to where stores, saloons, hotels, red-light districts, and the town dump were located. All are ripe for exploring. The two types of maps that will prove most useful are plat maps and Sanborn Fire Insurance maps.

A plat map, which will show every home and business in the city or area you wish to dig, can be compared to current maps to identify the older structures or determine where they once stood. The Sanborn Insurance maps are the most detailed, accurate, and helpful of all for choosing a digging site. These maps, which have also been published under other names, provide detailed information on each lot, illustrating the location of houses, factories, cisterns, wells, privies, streets, and property lines. These maps were produced for nearly every city and town in the country between 1870 and 1920 and are dated so it's possible to determine the age of the sites you're considering.

Figure 1 depicts an 1890 Sanborn Perris map section of East Los Angeles. This map section was used to locate an outhouse in East Los Angeles that dated between 1885 and 1905. A dig on that site turned up more than 50 bottles. Knowing the appropriate age of the digging site also helps to determine the age and types of bottles or artifacts you find there.

Local chambers of commerce, law enforcement agencies, and residents who have lived in the community for a number of years can be very helpful in your search for information. Other great resources for publications about the area's history are local antique and gift shops, which often carry old books, maps, and other literature about the town, county, and surrounding communities.

Since most early settlers handled garbage themselves, buried bottles can be unearthed almost anywhere, but a little thinking can narrow the search to a location that's likely to hold some treasures. Usually, the garbage was hauled and dumped within a mile of the town limits. Often, settlers or storeowners would dig a hole about 25 yards out from the back of their home or business for garbage and refuse. Many hotels and saloons had a basement or underground storage area where empty bottles were kept.

Ravines, ditches, and washes are also prime digging spots because heavy rains or melting snow often washed debris down from other areas. Bottles can quite often be found beside houses and under porches. Residents stored or threw bottles under their porches when porches were common building features in the late 19th and 20th centuries. Explore wagon trails, old railroad tracks, sewers, and abandoned roads where houses or cabins once stood. Old battlegrounds and military encampments are excellent places to dig if legal

Figure 1

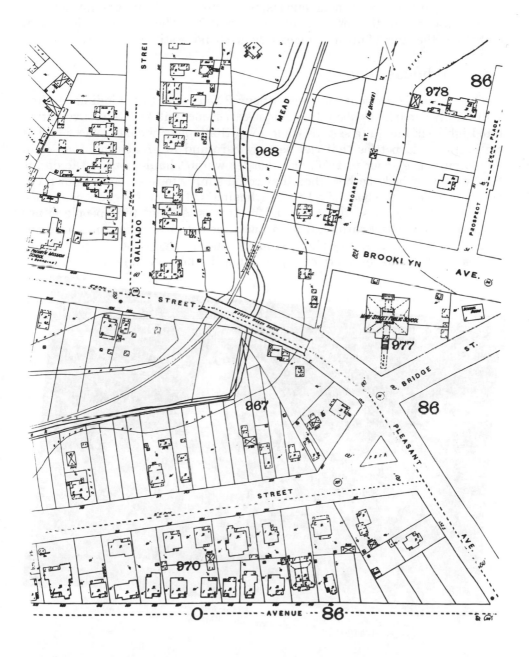

(be sure to check first). Cisterns and wells are other good sources of bottles and period artifacts.

The first love of this bottle hound, and high on the list of most collectors, is an expedition to a ghost town. It's fun and a lesson in history. The best places to search in ghost towns are near saloons, trade stores, and the red-light district, train stations, and the town dump (prior to 1900). The Tonopah, Nev., town dump was the start of my digging experiences and is still a favorite spot.

Privy/Outhouse Digging

"You've dug bottles out of an old outhouse? You've got to be kidding!" Telling your family and friends about this unique experience will kick the conversation into high gear. I'm quite serious when I say that one of the best places to find old bottles—old bottles that can be very rare and in great condition—is in an old outhouse. Prior to 1870, most bottles weren't hauled out to the dump. Why would anybody bother when they could simply toss old bottles down the outhouse hole in the back of a house or business? In fact, very few pontil-age (pre-Civil War) bottles are ever found in dumps. At that time people either dug a pit in their backyard for trash or used the outhouse. These outhouses, or privies, have been know to yield all kinds of other artifacts such as guns, coins, knives, crockery, dishes, marbles, pipes, and other household items.

The Manahans—Ryan (brother), Tim (dad) and Megan (sister)—show off their treasures following a huge dig near their home in Princeton, Ill. Mom (Vickie) took the photographs.

Dad and son display more of their finds from the privy dig. Notice the great condition of some of the pottery finds, especially the white water pitcher.

The Manahan gang, Ryan, Megan, and dad, going down into the privy one more time for a final bottle.

To develop a better sense of where privies can be found, it is important to have an understanding of their construction and uses. The privies of the 19th century (they produce the best results) were deep holes constructed with wood, brick, or sides called "liners." You'll find privies in a variety of shapes—square, round, rectangular, and oval. The chart below summarizes the different types of privies, their locations, and depth.

Types of Privies

Construction	Shape	Location	Depth
Brick	Oval, round, rectangular, square	Big towns and cities, behind brick buildings	not less than 6 feet deep
Stone	Round, square, rectangular	Limestone often used in areas where stone is common	Rectangular, less than 10 feet deep; round, often 20 feet deep or more.
Wood	Square or rectangular	Farms, small towns	May be one privy on lot Not more than 10 to 15 feet deep; often very shallow
Barrel	Round	Cities and towns	8 to 12 feet deep

In general, privies in cities are fairly deep and usually provide more bottles and artifacts. Privies in rural areas are shallower and do not contain as many bottles. Farm privies are very difficult to locate and digs often produce few results.

How long was an outhouse used? The life span of a privy is anywhere from 10 to 20 years. It was possible to extend its useful life by cleaning it out or relining it with new wood, brick, or stone. In fact, nearly all older privies show some evidence of cleaning.

At some point, old privies were filled and abandoned. The fill materials included ashes, bricks, plaster, sand, rocks, building materials, or soil that had been dug out when a new or additional privy was added to the house. Often, bottles or other artifacts were thrown in with the fill. The depth of the privy determined the amount of the fill required. In any case, the result was a privy filled with layers of various materials, the bottom layer being the "use" layer or "trash" layer as shown in Figure 2.

Older Privies

Figure 2

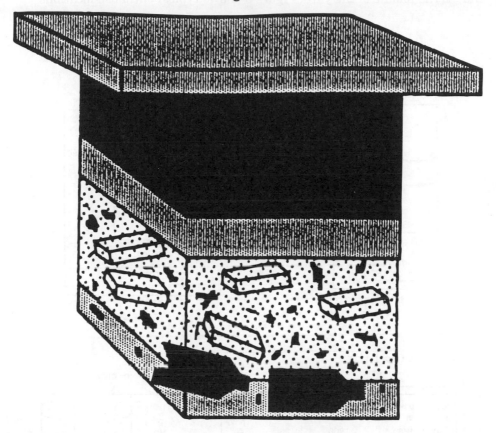

It is possible to locate these old outhouses because of the characteristic differences in density and composition of the undisturbed earth. Because of the manner of construction, it is fairly easy to locate them by probing the area with a metal rod or "probe."

Your own community is a great place to begin the hunt for a privy. A good starting point is to find an old house. Those dating from 1880 to 1920 usually had a least one privy in the backyard. Locate a small lot with few buildings or obstructions to get in the way of your dig. Look for are depressions in the ground, since materials used to fill privies tend to settle; a subtle depression may indicate where a septic tank, well, or privy was once located. In addition, like most household dumps, outhouses were usually located between 15 to 30 yards behind a residence or business. Another good indicator of an old privy site is an unexpected group of vegetation such as bushes or trees that flourishes above the rich fertilized ground. Privies were sometimes located near old trees for shade and privacy.

The most common privy locations were (1) directly outside the back door, (2) along a property line, (3) in one of the back corners or the rear middle of the lot, and (4) the middle of the yard. Figure 3 shows typical outhouse locations.

Typical Privy Configurations

Figure 3

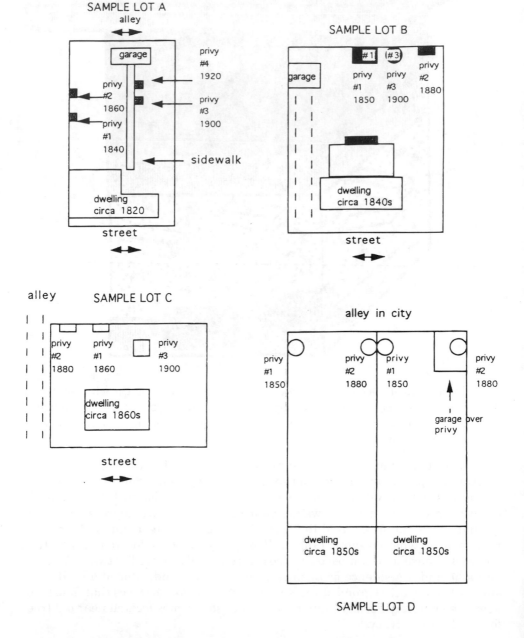

Now that you've located a privy (with luck, it's full of great bottles), it's time to get down and dirty and open up the hole. The approximate dimensions of the hole can usually be determined with your probe. If you know or even think that the hole is deeper than you are tall, it is extremely important to avoid a cave-in by opening up the entire hole. Never attempt to dig half of the hole with hopes of getting to the trash layer quicker. Remember that the fill is looser than the surrounding ground and could come down on you. Also, always dig to the bottom and check the corners carefully. Privies were occasionally cleaned out, but very often bottles and artifacts were missed that were in the corners or on the sides. If you are not sure whether you've hit the bottom, check with the probe. It's easier to determine if you can feel the fill below what you may think is the bottom. In brick and stone-lined holes, if the wall keeps going down, you are not on the bottom.

Quite often it is difficult to date a privy without the use of accurate, detailed maps. But it is possible to determine the age of the privy by the type and age of items found in the hole. The chart lists some types of bottles you might find in a dig and shows how their age relates to the privy's age.

Material	1920+	1900-1919	1880-1900	1860-80	1840-60	Pre-1840
Crown Tops	Yes	Yes	No	No	No	No
Screw Tops	Yes	Yes	No	No	No	No
Aqua Glass	Yes	Some	Yes	Yes	Yes	Yes
Clear Glass	All	Most	Some	Some	Some	Some
Ground Lip Fruit Jar	No	Rare	Yes	Yes	Rare	No
Hinge Mold	No	No	No	Yes	Yes	No
Pontiled	No	No	No	Yes	Yes	Yes
Free Blown	No	No	No	No	No	Yes
Historical Flasks	No	No	No	Yes	Yes	Yes
Stoneware (Crockery)	No	No	Yes	Yes	Yes	Yes

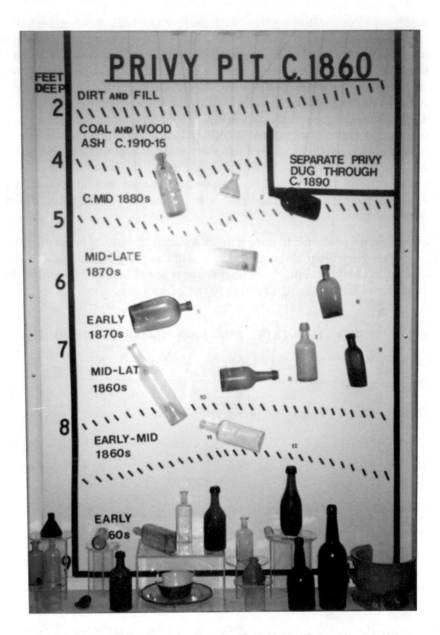

Privy pit display, circa 1860 (actual dug pit), National Bottle Museum, Ballston, Spa, New York.

While finding a prized bottle is great, digging and refilling the hole can be hard work and very tiring. To help make this chore easier, place a tarp on the ground surrounding the hole as you dig, and shovel the dirt on the tarp. Then, shovel the dirt off the tarp and fill five-gallon plastic buckets. The first benefit of this method is the time and energy you'll save filling the hole. The second benefit, and maybe the biggest, is that you'll leave no mess. This becomes important for building a relationship with the property owner. The less mess, the more likely you'll get permission to dig again. Also, your dig will be safer and easier if you use a walk board. Place an 8-foot long, 2-inch x 8-inch plank over the hole for the bucket man to stand on. This will allow him to pull up dirt without hitting the sides. This also reduces the risk of the bucket man falling in or caving in a portion of the hole. Setting up a tripod with a pulley over the hole will help to save time and prevent strain on the back.

The short few paragraphs presented here are really just an outline of privy/ outhouse digging. I recommend two publications that cover the art of privy digging in more detail: *The Secrets of Privy Digging* by John Odell and *Privy Digging 101* by Mark Churchill. Now, let's have some "outhouse" fun.

The Probe

Regardless of whether you're digging in outhouses, old town dumps, or beneath a structure, a probe is an essential tool. The basic probe is actually a very simple device, as depicted in Figure 4.

It is usually 5 to 6 feet long (a taller person may find that a longer probe will work better), with a handle made of hollow or solid pipe, tapered to a point at the end so it is easier to penetrate the ground. Also, welding a ball bearing on the end of the rod will help in collecting soil samples. Examining the soil samples is critical to finding privies. To make your probing easier, add weight to the handle by filling the pipe with lead or welding a solid steel bar directly under the handle. The additional weight will reduce the effort needed to sink the probe. While you can purchase probes in a number of places, you might want to have one custom made to conform to your body height and weight for more comfortable use.

While probing, press down slowly and feel for differences in the consistency of the soil. Unless you are probing into sand, you should reach

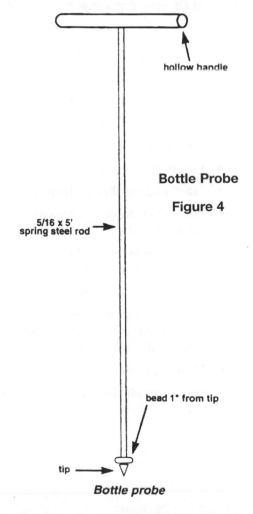

hollow handle

Bottle Probe

Figure 4

5/16 x 5'
spring steel rod

bead 1" from tip

tip

Bottle probe

a point at which it becomes difficult to push, indicating that you've reached a natural bottom. If you find you can probe deeper in an adjacent spot, you may have found an outhouse. When this happens, pull out the probe and plunge it in again, this time at an angle to see if you feel a brick or wood liner. After practice, you'll be able to determine what type of material you are hitting. Glass, brick, crockery, and rocks all have their own distinctive sound and feel.

Digging Equipment and Tools

When I first started digging, I took only a shovel and my luck. I learned I was doing things the hard way, and the result was a few broken bottles. Since then, I've refined my list of tools and equipment. The following list includes items I have found useful and recommended by veteran diggers.

General Digging Equipment

- Probe
- Long-handled shovel
- Short-handled shovel
- Long-handled potato rake
- Small hand rake
- Old table knives
- Old spoons
- Hard and soft bristle brushes
- Gloves/boots/eye protection/ durable clothes
- Insect repellent, snake bite kit, first aid kit
- Extra water and hat
- Dirt sifter (for coins or other items, a 2-foot x 2-foot wooden frame with chicken wire).
- Hunting knife
- Boxes for packing and storing bottles

Privy/Outhouse Digging Equipment

- Long-handled shovel*
- Five-foot probe*
- Slam probe
- Pick*
- Root cutters*
- Short-handled garden scratcher*
- Rope, 1-inch x 15- feet+, with clip
- Tripod with pulley
- Walk board*
- Short-handled shovel
- Ten-foot probes*
- Posthole digger
- Pry bar
- Ax
- Five-gallon buckets
- Heavy tarps
- Hardhat and gloves

*Essential item

General Rules and Helpful Hints

Although I said there were no rules to bottle collecting, when digging there are two major rules you always need to follow.

Rule No. 1:

Always be responsible and ask for permission to dig. As a safety precaution, don't leave any holes open over night. Don't damage shrubs, trees, or flowers unless the owner approves. When the digging is complete, always leave the site looking better than when you started. I can't stress this enough. That means filling in all holes and raking over the area. Take out your trash as well as trash left by previous prospectors or others. Always offer to give the owner some of the bottles. They may not want any, but they will appreciate the gesture. If you adhere to these few rules, the community or owner will thank you, and future bottle diggers will be welcome. The following is a summary of the "Bottle Digger's Code of Ethics" (Compliments of the San Diego Bottle Club).

- Respect property rights and all warning signs.

- Always obtain valid permission to search, probe, or dig on public or private property.

- Do Not park illegally and Do park so that other vehicles can get out.

- Do Not damage or destroy any property improvements on public or private land.

- After digging on a site, try to leave all land and vegetation as it was by taking the necessary time to properly fill all holes and re-root plants when possible.

- Remove or bury existing litter and all unwanted items from your search area, leaving it cleaner than you found it.

- As a representative of all bottle collectors and diggers, be thoughtful, considerate, and courteous at all times.

Rule No. 2:

Do not, under any circumstances, go digging alone. Ignoring this rule is extremely dangerous. When digging up an outhouse, my recommendation is to go with no less than three people, and be sure to tell someone exactly where you're going and how long you expect to be gone.

Two tragic instances—one that occurred in 2002 and one in 2003—show what can happen if this rule isn't followed. On September 23, 2002, in Honolulu, Hawaii, a 55-year-old bottle collector was digging in a trench at the Waipahu Sugar Mill, which is a prized area because of the numerous plantations that were in the area. Without warning, the trench collapsed and he was buried under 6 feet of dirt and suffocated. The other tragedy happened in March 2003 in Ramona, California, when an avid bottle collector, digging in a ravine soaked by several days of heavy rain, was crushed by concrete, stone, dirt, and a large boulder when the unstable ground collapsed. DON'T DIG ALONE!!

When you start to dig, don't be discouraged if you don't find any bottles. If you unearth other objects such as coins, broken dishes, or bottle tops, continue to dig deeper and in a wider circle. If you don't find any bottles, move to another spot. Always work from the edge to the center of the hole. Don't get discouraged! Even the very best have come home with empty bags and boxes but never without the memory of a good time. When you do find a bottle, stop digging and remove the surrounding dirt a little at a time with a small tool, brush, or spoon. Handle the bottle very carefully since old bottles are very fragile.

Now, that you know how to do it, what are you waiting for? Grab those tools, get those maps, and get started making the discoveries of a lifetime.

Bottle Handling

While selling bottles and listening to buyers at various shows, I am inevitably asked questions about cleaning, handling, and storing old bottles. Some collectors believe that cleaning a bottle diminishes its collectible value and desirability.

Leaving a bottle in its natural state, as it was found, can be special. Others prefer to remove as much dirt and residue as possible. The choice rests with the owner. The following information will provide some help with how to clean, store, and take care of those special finds.

Cleaning

Never attempt to clean a find in the field. In the excitement of the moment, it's easy to break the bottle or otherwise damage the embossing. With the exception of soda and ale bottles, glass bottles manufactured prior to 1875 usually have very thin walls. But even bottles with thicker walls should be handled very carefully.

First, remove as much loose dirt, sand, or other particles as possible with a small hand brush or a soft bristled toothbrush, followed by a quick warm water rinse. Then, using a warm water solution and bleach (stir the mixture first), soak the bottles for a number of days (depending upon the amount of caked-on dirt). This should remove most of the excess grime. Adding a little

vinegar to the warm water will give an extra sparkle to the glass.

Other experienced collectors use cleaning mixtures such as straight ammonia, kerosene, Lime-A-Way, Mr. Clean, and chlorine borax bleach. Don't use mixtures that aren't recommended for cleaning glass, never mix cleaners, and don't clean with acids of any type. Mixing cleaners has been known to release toxic gasses.

After soaking, the bottles may then be cleaned with a bottle brush, steel wool, an old toothbrush, any semi-stiff brush, Q-tips, or used dental picks.

At this point, you may want to soak the bottles again in lukewarm water to remove any traces of cleaning materials. Either let the bottles air dry, or dry them with a soft towel. If the bottle has a paper label, the work will be more painstaking, since soaking is not a cleaning option. I've used a Q-tip to clean and dry the residue around a paper label.

Don't clean bottles in a dishwasher. While the hot water and detergent may produce a very clean bottle, older bottles were not designed to withstand the heat of a dishwasher. As a result, the heat combined with the shaking could crack or even shatter the fragile old bottles. Bottles with painted labels may also be severely damaged.

A better option is to take a rare bottle to a specialist, who will clean it with special tumbling or cleaning machines. The machines work on the same principle as a rock tumbler, with two horizontal bars acting as a cradle for the cleaning canisters. The machine cleaning process uses polishing and cutting oxides. The polishing oxides include aluminum, cerium, and tin, which remove stains and give the glass a crystal clean appearance, but do not damage the embossing. The cutting oxides, such as silicon carbide, remove etching and scratching. Many people clean bottles professionally, or you can purchase the machines to use yourself.

Display

Now that you have clean, beautiful bottles, display them to their best advantage. My advice is to arrange your bottles in a cabinet rather than on wall shelving or randomly around the house. While the last two options are more decorative, they also leave the bottles more susceptible to damage. When choosing a cabinet, look for one with glass sides, which will provide more light and better viewing. As an added touch, use a light fixture to set off your collection.

If you still desire a wall-shelving arrangement, make sure the shelf is approximately 12-inches wide, with a front lip for added protection. The lip can be made from quarter-round molding. After the bottle is placed in its spot, draw an outline around the base of the bottle and drill four 1/4-inch holes just outside that outline for pegs. The pegs will provide further stability for the bottle. If you have picked up any other goodies from your digging, like coins or gambling chips, scatter them around the bottles for a little Western flavor.

Protection

Because of earthquake activity, especially in northern and southern California, bottle collectors across the country have taken added steps to protect their valuable pieces.

Since most of us have our collections in some type of display cabinet, it's important to know how to best secure it. First, fasten the cabinet to the wall studs with brackets and bolts. If you're working with drywall and it's not possible to secure the cabinet to a stud, butterfly bolts will provide a tight hold. Always secure the cabinet at both the top and bottom for extra protection.

Next, lock or latch the cabinet doors. This will prevent the doors from flying open. If your cabinet has glass shelves, be sure not to overload them. In an earthquake, the glass shelving can break under the stress of excess weight.

Finally, it's important to secure the bottles to the shelves. A number of materials can be used, such as microcrystalline wax, beeswax, silicone adhesive, double-sided foam tape, and adhesive-backed Velcro spots or strips. These materials are available at local home improvement centers and hardware stores. One of the newest and most commonly used adhesives is called Quake Hold. This substance, available in wax, putty, and gel, is similar to the wax product now used extensively by numerous museums to secure their art work, sculptures, and various glass pieces and is readily available to the general public at many home improvement stores and antique shops.

Storage

For the bottles you've chosen not to display, the best method for storing them is to place them in empty liquor boxes with cardboard dividers (to prevent bottles from bumping each other). As added protection, wrap the individual bottles in paper before packing them in the boxes.

Record Keeping

Last but not least, it's a good idea to keep a record of your collection. Use index cards detailing where the bottle was found or purchased, including the dealer's name and price you paid. Also, assign a catalog number to each bottle, record it on the card, and then make an index. Many collectors keep records with the help of a photocopier. If the bottle has embossing or a label, place the bottle on the machine and make a copy of it. Another method is to make a pencil sketch by placing white paper over the bottle and rubbing the embossing with a No. 2 pencil. Then, type all the pertinent information on the back of the image and file it in a binder. When it comes to trading and selling, excellent record keeping will prove to be invaluable.

Old Bottles (Pre-1900)

The bottles listed in this section have been categorized by physical type and/or by the original contents of the bottle. For most categories, the trade names can be found in alphabetical order if they exist. Note that in the case of certain early bottles, such as flasks, a trade name doesn't appear on the bottle. These bottles have been listed by subject according to the embossing or other identification.

Since it is impossible to list every bottle available, I've tried to provide a good cross section of bottles in various price ranges and categories rather than listing only the rarest or most collectible pieces.

The pricing shown reflects the value of the particular bottle listed. Similar bottles could have higher or lower values than the bottles identified here, but the listing provides a good starting point for determining a price range.

Ale and Gin

Because ale and gin bottles are almost identical in style, it's difficult to determine what a bottle originally contained unless information is provided on the bottle itself. Also, ale bottles can be confused with beer bottles, a common mistake because of the similarity in shape.

Ale was a more popular beverage at a time when available wines were not as palatable. It quickly became a favorite alternative and, with even with the very best ale, was not expensive to make or buy. The bottles used by colonial ale makers were made of pottery and imported from England. When searching for these bottles, keep in mind that the oldest ones had matte or unglazed surfaces.

Unlike ale, gin doesn't have an ancient origin, but it certainly does have a unique one. In the 17th century, a Dutch physician named Francesco De La Bor prepared gin as a medical compound for the treatment of kidney disease. While its effectiveness to purify the blood was questionable, gin drinking became very popular. In fact, it became so popular that many chemists decided to go into the gin brewing business full time to meet the growing demand. During the 19th century, gin consumption in America increased at a steady rate.

The design of the gin bottle, which has a squat body, facilitated the case packing and prevented shifting and possible damage in shipping. The first case bottles were octagonal with short necks and were manufactured with

Albert Von Harten – Savannah, GA, 1870-1885, 7-1/8", $250-350.

straight sides that allowed four to twelve bottles to fit tightly into a wooden packing case. Designs that were introduced later featured longer necks. Bottles with tapered collars are dated to the 19th century. The case bottle sizes vary in size from half-pints to multiple gallons. The early bottles were crudely made and have distinct pontil scars.

A.M. – Bininger & Co – No 19 Broad St N.Y. – Old London Dock – Gin
Medium yellow olive green, 8", smooth base, applied sloping collar mouth.......................................$100-150
American 1860-1870

A.M. – Bininger & Co – No 338 Broadway – Old London Dock – Gin
Medium yellow olive green, 9-3/4", smooth base, applied mouth $50-75
American 1840-1875

A.M. Bininger & Co – No 375 Broadway N.Y.
Pinkish topaz puce, 9", smooth base, applied sloping collar mouth...$500-700
American 1855-1870

Anderson & Co. – Home Brewed Ale – Albany N.Y.
Deep red amber, 1/2 pint, cylindrical soda water bottle form, smooth base, applied sloping collar mouth with ring $1,000-2,000
American 1860-1870

Avan Hoboken & Co. Rotterdam
Medium amber, 11-3/4", smooth base, applied top $50-75
Dutch 1870-1890

Back Bar Bottle – Gin (copper wheel cut on front)
Cobalt blue, 10-1/2", smooth base, tooled lip...$250-350
American

Back Bar Bottle – Gin (on shoulder) – Sterling (on overlay on tooled mouth)
Deep cobalt blue with silver overlay on chain around shoulder, 10-3/4", smooth base, tooled mouth $200-300
American 1890-1920

Booth & Sedgwick's – London – Cordial Gin
Medium blue green, 8", iron pontil, applied sloping collar mouth...$300-400
American 1855-1865

Case Gin – Dip Mold
Yellowish olive green, 9-3/8", smooth base, applied mouth $120-140
Dutch 1770-1800

Case Gin
Deep sapphire blue mouth, neck, and shoulders turning to teal blue toward the base, tapered body, 10", smooth base, tooled mouth $200-400
American 1870-1890

Case Gin
Deep cobalt blue, tapered body, 10-1/8", smooth base, tooled mouth $800-1,000
American 1880-1895

Case Gin – Large Dip Mold
Yellow olive, tapered body, 13-3/4", tubular pontil scar, applied and inverted sloping collar $500-1,000
Dutch 1770-1800

Case Gin – Large Dip Mold
Deep amber with olive tone, 13-3/8", smooth base, applied mouth $350-450
Dutch 1770-1800 (rare in this large size)

Charle's – London – Cordial Gin
Medium olive green, 7-3/4", pontil-scarred base, applied sloping collar mouth $150-250
American 1865-1875

Charle's – London – Cordial Gin
Medium to deep yellow olive, 9-3/4", smooth base, applied sloping collar mouth with ring $150-300
American 1860-1875

Daniel Visser & Zonen Schiedam (on seal) – Case Gin
Clear with blue seal, 11", smooth base, applied top $100-120
American 1860-1875

F. Seitz – Brown – S – Stout
Blue green, 6-3/4", open pontil-scarred base, applied sloping double collar mouth.....................$1,500-2,000
American 1840-1860

Freeblown Gin Bottle
Bright green, 9-3/4", tapered case gin form, pontil scar, sheared mouth $75-150
American 1830-1860

Freeblown Gin Bottle
Yellow olive, 14-7/8", tapered case gin form, smooth base, applied mouth....................................$500-1,000
American 1830-1860

Freeblown Gin Bottle
Dark olive amber, 17-1/2", paddled square form, pontil scar, applied sloping collar mouth $1,000-2,000
American 1780-1820

Freeblown Gin Bottle
Yellow olive, 17-3/4", tapered case gin form, pontil scar, applied mouth $500-1,000
Dutch 1770-1800

Geo. Bibbey & Co – English Ale – Glens Falls – N.Y. – G (inside shield)
Deep emerald green, 10", smooth base, applied sloping double collar mouth...........................$250-350
American 1870-1880

Globular Dutch Gin
Medium olive green, 10", pontil base, applied mouth $150-250
Dutch 1770-1800

H. Ingermann's - XXX - Ale - Cambridge City
- Ind, 1880-1890, quart, $100-150.

H. Ingermann's – XXX Ale – Cambridge City – Ind
Medium amber, 9-1/4", smooth base, "G & Co. Lim" on
bottom, applied sloping collar mouth $150-200
American 1880-1900

Herman Jansen Schiedam (on side) HJ (on seal)
Olive amber, 4-3/8", smooth base,
applied top $350-450
Dutch 1860-1875

Imperial Gin H.H.S. & Co. – Case Gin
Medium amber, 9-3/4", smooth base, applied blob
mouth $75-125
Dutch 1770-1820

J.H. Henkes – Schiedam – Aromatic – Schnapps
Olive green, 9-1/4", smooth base applied sloping collar
mouth $100-150
Dutch 1870-1890

**John Ryan – 1866 – Savannah – Ga.
– Philadelphia – XXX – Ale**
Medium cobalt blue, 6-3/4", smooth base,
applied blob mouth $250-350
American 1860-1875

John Ryan – Philada XX Porter & Ale – 1866
Emerald green, 6-3/4", smooth base, applied double
collar mouth..$150-200
American 1866-1870 (scarce in this green)

**John Ryan – 1852 – Augusta – & Savannah
– Ga – Philada/XX – Porter & Ale**
Cobalt blue, 6-7/8", smooth base,
applied mouth $150-200
American 1860-1870 (scarce double city description)

Juniper - Leaf - Gin - This Bottle is the
Property of Theodore Netter, 10-3/4"; Wolfe's
Schnapps, 1865-1900, 8-1/4", $100-150 (each).

**Juniper – Leaf Gin – Warning – This Bottle
Is The Property Of Theodore Netter**
Medium amber, 10-5/8", case gin form, smooth base,
tooled mouth $75-100
American 1890-1910

John Ryan - 1866 - Savannah, GA - Philadelphia - XXX - Ale, 1860-1870, 6-3/4", $275-375 (front and back).

John Ryan - Philada XX Porter & Ale - 1866, 1866-1870, 6-3/4", $150-200.

John Ryan - Phila. XX Porter & Ale, 1840-1860, 6-7/8", $140-180.

**Jurgen Peters – Trade Mark – JP
(inside motif of Sun and Shield)**
Medium yellow olive, 8-3/4", smooth base, applied
sloping collar mouth...$85-120
German 1090-1910

London - Royal - Imperial Gin , 1870-
1880, 9-3/4", $375-475.

**London (reversed Ns) – Jockey – Club
House – Gin (motif of jockey on horse)**
Deep yellow green, 9-3/4", smooth base, applied
sloping double collar mouth............................$500-700
American 1865-1875

**London – Jockey – Clubhouse – Gin
(motif of jockey on horse)**
Deep yellow green, 10", smooth base, applied sloping
double collar mouth $400-600
American 1865-1875

Meijer & Co. Schiedam (lion in crest) – Case Gin
Medium amber, 9-1/4", smooth base,
applied top $75-125
Dutch 1820-1850

**Newburgh (backwards N) Glass Co – Pat
Feb 27 1866 (base embossed ale bottle)**
Dense amber black, 8-1/4", cylindrical, smooth base,
applied double collar mouth......................$1,000-2,000
American 1865-1875 (rare) Newburgh
Glass Company, Newburgh, N.Y.

P Loopuyt & Co Distillers – Schiedam
Dark amber, 8-1/2", smooth base, applied top...$40-60
Dutch 1860-1880

Philadelphia – XXX – Porter & Ale
Deep teal blue, 6-5/8", iron pontil,
applied mouth $50-75
American 1840-1875

Royal – Imperial Gin – London
Medium cobalt blue, 9-7/8", smooth base, applied
sloping collar mouth.......................................$500-700
American 1870-1880

S.A. Wolf's – Aromatic – Schnapps
Deep olive green, 9-1/2", smooth base,
applied top $50-75
American 1870-1880

Starling Brand Schiedam (bird on seal) Case Gin
Medium blue green, 12", smooth base,
applied top $175-250
Dutch 1865-1880

THC & Co – Hollands T. Harrison & Co.
Amber, 10-1/2", smooth base, applied sloping collar
mouth $175-250
Dutch 1865-1880

Udolpho Wolfe's – Schiedam – Aromatic – Schnapps
Light greenish aqua, 8", iron pontil, applied sloping
double collar mouth $75-125
American 1850-1860

Udolpho Wolfe's – Schiedam – Aromatic – Schnapps
Apricot puce, 8-3/8", smooth base, applied sloping
collar mouth...$300-40
American 1860-1870

Udolpho Wolfe's – Schiedam – Aromatic – Schnapps
Medium copper puce, 9-1/2", smooth base, applied
sloping collar mouth.......................................$350-450
American 1855-1875

**Vanderveer's – Medicated Gin – Or
Real – Schiedam – Schnapps**
Olive green, 9-1/8", case-gin form, smooth base,
applied sloping collar mouth $250-350
American 1870-1880

Volvner's – Aromatic – Schnapps – Schiedam
Yellow olive green, 10", smooth base,
applied mouth $150-250
American 1865-1875

Von Hofen's – Aromatic – Scheidam – Schnapps
Medium emerald green, 8-1/8", iron pontil, applied
mouth $250-350
American 1850-1865

Warners Imported English Gin
Amber, 9", smooth base, applied top................$75-100
American 1860-1880

W.S.C. – Club House Gin (Case Gin)
Medium olive green, 9-1/2", smooth base, applied
mouth $300-400
American 1855-1870 (scarce)

Various gin bottles, 1830-1890, $30-65 (each).

Barber Bottles

Starting in the mid-1860s and continuing to 1920, barbers in America used colorful decorated bottles filled with various tonics and colognes. The colorful designs of these unique pieces originated when the newly created Pure Food and Drug Act of 1906 restricted the use of alcohol-based ingredients in unlabeled or refillable containers.

Very early examples have rough pontil scars with numerous types of ornamentation such as fancy pressed designs, paintings, and labels under glass. The bottles were usually fit with a cork, metal, or porcelain-type closure. Because the value of barber bottles is very dependent on painted or enameled lettering or decoration, it is important to note that when determining the value of a barber bottle, any type of wear, such as faded decoration or color, faded lettering, or chipping, will lower its price.

Barber bottle, cherubs with dove, 1885-1925, 8", $200-300.

Bay Rum
Milk glass with black and gold gilt decoration, 8-5/8", pontil-scarred base, rolled lip..........................**$150-200**
American 1890-1925

Barber Bottle
Cobalt blue with white enamel floral decorations, 8", smooth base, tooled mouth **$75-100**
American 1885-1930 (scarce)

Barber Bottle
Emerald with red and white enamel decorations, 7-3/4", pontil-scarred base, tooled lip **$75-100**
American 1885-1930

Barber Bottle
Yellow green with red and white enamel decorations, 7-3/4", pontil-scarred base, tooled lip **$75-100**
American 1885-1930

Barber Bottle
Deep purple amethyst with white and orange enamel floral decorations, 8", smooth base, ABM lip...**$85-125**
American 1885-1930

Barber bottle,
cherubs
with grapes,
1885-1925, 8",
$200-300.

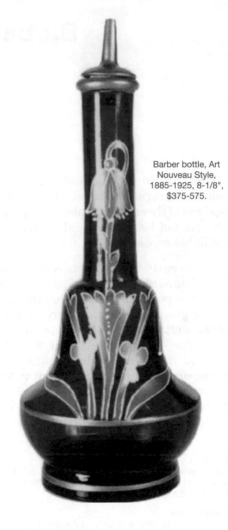

Barber bottle, Art
Nouveau Style,
1885-1925, 8-1/8",
$375-575.

Barber Bottle
Clear glass with Ice blue flashing, white enamel floral
decoration, 8", smooth base, ABM lip $80-140
American 1910-1930

Barber Bottle With Hobnail Pattern
Turquoise blue, 6-3/4", polished pontil,
rolled lip...$60-80
American 1885-1930

Barber Bottle With Hobnail Pattern
Fiery opalescent clear glass, 8-1/2", pontil-scarred,
rolled lip...$100-150
American 1895-1930

Barber Bottle With Hobnail Pattern
Purple amethyst, 7-5/8", smooth base,
rolled lip...$100-150
American 1900-1925

Barber Bottle With Rib Pattern
Frosted lime green, multicolored enamel
rose decoration, 8-1/2'", pontil-scarred base,
tooled lip...$250-350
American 1885-1930

Barber Bottle With Rib Pattern
Deep emerald green with yellow, orange, and white
enamel decoration, 7-1/8", pontil-scarred base, tooled
mouth $100-150
American 1885-1925

Barber Bottle With Rib Pattern
Deep cobalt blue with silver and yellow enamel floral
decoration, 8-1/4", pontil-scarred base,
tooled lip...$80-120
American 1885-1930

Barber bottle, Art
Nouveau style,
1885-1925, 8-1/8",
$300-400.

Barber bottle, hobnail
pattern, 1885-1925,
6-7/8", $150-200.

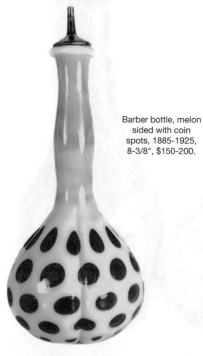

Barber bottle, melon
sided with coin
spots, 1885-1925,
8-3/8", $150-200.

Barber bottle, floral
decoration, 1885-1925,
7-7/8", $150-200.

Barber bottles (lot of 2), 1885-1925, 6-3/4" and 6-7/8", $150-200 (pair).

Barber bottles (lot of 2), 1885-1925, both 7-3/4", $80-120 (pair).

Barber Bottle – Mary Gregory Style Tennis Player
Deep cobalt blue with white enamel decoration, 8-1/8",
pontil-scarred base, rolled lip..........................**$200-300**
American 1885-1930

**Barber Bottle – Mary Gregory
Cameo – Coinspot Pattern**
Light lime green, 8", pontil-scarred base,
rolled lip..**$275-375**
American 1885-1926

**Barber Bottle – Mary Gregory – Girl
With Butterfly Net Decoration**
Medium grass green with white enamel, 8-1/8",
pontil-scarred base, tooled mouth.................**$150-275**
American 1885-1925

Barber Bottle – Art Nouveau Decoration
Dark amethyst with yellow and gold, 8-1/4", pontil-
scarred base, rolled lip **$350-450**
American 1890-1925

Barber Bottle – Art Nouveau Decoration
Frosted lime green, rib pattern with multicolored style
floral decorations, 8-1/4", pontil-scarred base,
rolled lip **$275-375**
American 1890-1925

Barber Bottle – Rib Pattern
Deep purple amethyst, bell pattern form with white,
orange, and gold enamel, 6-7/8", pontil-scarred base,
tooled lip...**$500-700**
American 18901-1910 (rare)

Colyptoline Auxilliator For The Hair
Opalescent milk glass with black, orange,
and blue lettering, 7-3/8", pontil-scarred base,
rolled lip **$600-800**
American 1890-1925 (rare)

Hair Oil – Koken St. Louis (on base)
Milk glass with multicolored enamel rose decoration,
9", smooth base, tooled mouth......................**$375-475**
American 1890-1925

Barber bottle, Lutz art glass, 1885-1925, 7-1/2", $350-450.   Barber bottle, beehive shape, 1885-1925, 6-3/8", $80-140.

Barber bottle,
1885-1925, 8-1/8",
$150-200.

Barber bottle,
1885-1925, 9",
$170-275.

Hair Tonic
Mint green milk glass with multicolored enamel
floral decoration, 9-1/4", pontil-scarred base,
rolled lip...**$700-1,200**
American 1890-1925 (rare in this color)

Hair Tonic – Flying Swallow (on label)
Milk glass with multicolored enamel decoration, 9",
smooth base, rolled lip.....................................**$300-400**
American 1890-1925

Jack Schieles Violet
Milk glass with multicolored enamel floral and clover
decorations, 8", smooth base, tooled lip **$60-80**
American 1885-1930

KDX – Koken Companies – St. Louis, Mo.
Black glass, 8-1/8", smooth base, tooled lip, crown
pour stopper..**$120-140**
American 1895-1930

**Koken Barbers – Supply Co – St. Louis – K
– U.S.A (on base) Toilet Water (on front)**
Milk glass with multicolored floral decoration, 7-7/8",
smooth base, tooled mouth **$175-250**
American 1885-1925

**Labeled Barber Bottle – Arista Antiseptic Face
Tonic Arista M'f'g' Co – Limited Detroit, Mich**
Clear glass with red, black, and white pyro label,
7-1/4", smooth base, tooled mouth **$175-275**
American 1890-1925

**Labeled Barber Bottle – Levigated Barber
Soap, Central Soap Co – Canton, O
– Patented May 25th 1875 (on base)**
Clear glass with black, pink, and gold label, 5-1/2",
smooth base, ground lip **$400-600**
American 1875-1910 (rare)

**Labeled Barber Bottle – Retona A Tonique For
The Hair – F.E. Baker & Co. – Lewiston, Me**
Clear glass with white, blue, yellow, and gold label,
8-1/4", smooth base, tooled lip.......................**$250-350**
American 1890-1925

Mini – Barber Bottle
Opaque milk glass with multicolored enamel
decorations, 5", smooth base, rolled lip **$125-175**
American 1995-1925

N. Wapler – N.Y.
Cobalt blue, 7-1/4", smooth base, rolled lip **$50-75**
American 1885-1930

**PDQ (monogram) – Quinine Tonic
– N. Wapler (on base)**
Milk glass with red transfer, 7-1/2", smooth base,
tooled mouth **$150-200**
American 1890-1925

**Personalized Barber Bottle – Geo. Eissler
Tonic (peafowl sitting on a half moon)**
Milk glass with multicolored enamel decoration,
8", smooth base, group lip, pewter screw
stopper **$400-700**
American 1890-1925 (rare)

Barber bottle, 1885-1925, 8-1/8", $150-200.   Barber bottle, 1885-1925, 8-1/8", $150-200.

Mini-barber bottles, floral decoration, 1885-1925, 5", $250-350 (pair).

Barber bottle (possibly cologne), 1870-1895, 11-1/8", $150-200.

Brillantine barber bottle, 1885-1925, 4-1/4", $140-180.

Personalized Barber Bottle – R.R. Hean – Tonic
Milk glass with floral decoration, 8-7/8", smooth
base, ground lip, original screw of dispensing
cap...**$350-450**
American 1885-1925

Sea Foam
Mint green milk glass with multicolored enamel floral
decorations, 9-1/4", pontil-scarred base,
rolled lip..**$700-1,200**
American 1890-1925 (rare in this color)

Shampoo (on front panel)
Milk glass with photograph of pretty woman, 10-1/4",
smooth base, rolled lip...................................**$500-700**
American 1885-1915

T. Noonan & Co – Barber Supplies – Boston, Mass
Cobalt blue, 7-5/8", smooth base,
tooled mouth **$50-75**
American 1885-1930

T. Noonan & Co – Barber Supplies – Boston, Mass
Frosted green, 7-5/8", smooth base,
tooled mouth **$50-75**
American 1885-1930

Three Cherubs And Dog Head (on label)
Milk glass with labeled decoration, 7-1/2",
pontil-scarred base, tooled lip **$150-200**
American 1885-1925

Vegederma
Deep purple amethyst with white enamel girl
decoration, 8-1/8", pontil-scarred base, rolled
lip..**$500-700**
American 1885-1925

Witch Hazel
Milk glass with multicolored enamel poppy
floral decoration, 9", pontil-scarred base,
applied mouth **$250-350**
American 1890-1925

Brillantine barber
bottle, 1885-1925,
3-1/8", $150-200.

Beer Bottles

Attempting to find an American beer bottle made before the mid-19th century is a difficult task. Until then, most bottles used for beer and spirits were imported. The majority of these imported bottles were black-glass pontiled bottles made in three-piece molds and rarely embossed. There are four types of early beer bottles:

1. Porter, the most common (1820 to 1920)

2. Ale (1845 to 1850)

3. Early lager, rare (1847 to 1850)

4. Late lager (1850 to 1860)

In spite of the large amount of beer consumed in America before 1860, beer bottles were very rare and all have pontiled bases. Most beer manufactured during this time was distributed and dispensed from wooden barrels, or kegs, and sold to local taverns and private bottlers. Collectors often ask why the various breweries didn't bottle the beer they manufactured. The answer is that during the Civil War, the federal government placed a special tax on all brewed beverages that was levied by the barrel. This taxing system prevented the brewery from making and bottling the beer in the same building. Selling the beer to taverns and private bottlers was much simpler than erecting another building just for bottling. This entire process changed after 1890 when the federal government revised the law to allow breweries to bottle the beer straight from the beer lines.

The chart below reflects the age and rarity of beer bottles.

YEAR	RARE	SCARCE	SEMI-COMMON	COMMON
1860-1870	X			
1870-1880		X		
1880-1890			X	
1890-1930				X

Embossed bottles marked "Ale" or "Porter" were first manufactured between 1850 and 1860. In the late 1860s, the breweries began to emboss their bottles with names and promotional messages. This practice continued into the 20th century. It is interesting to note that Pennsylvania breweries made most of the beer bottles from the second half of the 19th century. By 1890, beer was readily available in bottles around most of the country.

The first bottles used for beer in the United States were made of pottery, not glass. Glass did not become widely used until after the Civil War (1865). A wholesaler for Adolphus Busch named C. Conrad sold the original Budweiser beer from 1877 to 1890. The Budweiser name was a trademark of C. Conrad, but in 1891 it was sold to the Anheuser-Busch Brewing Association.

Before the 1870s, beer bottles were sealed with cork stoppers. Late in the 19th century, the lightning stopper was invented. It proved a convenient way of sealing and resealing blob top bottles. In 1891, corks were replaced with the "crown cork closure" invented by William Painter. This made use of a thin slice of cork within a tight-fitting metal cap. Once these were removed, they couldn't be used again.

Bibbey & Ferguson - 101 & 103 - Maple St. - Glens Falls, N.Y. - This Bottle - Not To - Be Sold, Made By - Dean Foster & Co. - Boston (on base), 1880-1895, 9", $140-180.

J.C. Coulter -Cor. 9th & Market - McKeesport, PA - A.G. W. - This Bottle - Not To Be Sold, 1885-1900, 9-5/8", $60-80.

City Brewery (motif of hop) CB - Titusville, PA, 1885-1900, 9-5/8", $60-80.

Until the 1930s, beer came in green glass bottles. After Prohibition, brown glass came into use since it was thought to filter damaging rays of the sun and preserve freshness.

A. Palmtag & Co – Eureka Cal
Medium amber, quart, smooth base,
tooled top..$30-60
American 1885-1900

**Alabama Brewing Co – San
Francisco (with monogram)**
Golden amber, 7-3/4", smooth base, tooled
top...$35-50
American 1880-1890

B. & J. Oakland
Medium light amber, 7-3/8", smooth base,
tooled top..$35-50
American 1880-1890

Breckenfelder & Jochem – Oakland, Cal (with label)
Medium amber, 9-1/4", smooth base, tooled top with
wire bale...$40-50
American 1890-1910

**Buffalo Brewing & Co. – S.F.
Agency (with monogram)**
Medium amber, 7-1/2", smooth base,
crown top..$30-40
American 1900-1910

**C.C. Haley – & Co. – Celebrated – California
– Pop Beer – Trade Mark – Patented – Oct.
29th 1872 – This Bottle – Is Never Sold**
Amber olive, 11-1/2", smooth base,
applied mouth...$50-70
American 1885-1895

Cal. Bottling Co. – Export Beer
Light amber, 6-7/8", smooth base, applied top ..$30-50
American 1880-1890

Cascade Lager – S.F. Cal. (UB & MCo) Monogram
Amber, quart, smooth base, crown top with porcelain
and wire stopper...$15-25
American 1907-1908

City – Bottling Works – McKeesport Pa – H & W
Golden yellow amber, 11-1/2", smooth base, applied
blob gravitating stopper type mouth...............$140-180
American 1875-1885

City Brewery (motif of hop) CB – Titusville, Pa
Golden yellow amber, 9-5/8", smooth base, tooled
mouth for gravitating stopper.............................$60-80
American 1885-1900

**Continental Brewing Co – Philadelphia
(embossed with Revolutionary soldier)**
Aqua blue, pint, smooth base, applied top.........$30-60
American 1870-1880

Dallas Brewery – Malt Wein – Dallas, Texas
Medium amber, 8-1/4", smooth base,
tooled mouth...$80-140
American 1890-1900

Dr. Cronk – R. McC
Deep cobalt blue, 12-sided, 9-3/4", iron pontil, applied
sloping collar mouth.................................$2,500-3,500
American 1850-1865

E. Tousley - Cronk's Beer, 12-sided, 1855-1870, 10", $1,500-2,500 (rare).

E. Tousley – Cronk's Beer
Cobalt blue, 12-sided, 10", smooth base, applied
sloping collar mouth..$400-700
American 1850-1865

Eagle – Bottling Works – Cincinnati, O
Yellow olive, 11-1/2", smooth base,
applied mouth...$50-70
American 1885-1895

Enterprise Brewing Co – S.F. Cal.
Medium amber, quart, smooth base, tooled
top...$30-50
American 1880-1900

Etna Brewery – Etna Mills
Amber, 7-5/8", smooth base, tooled top.............**$30-40**
American 1880-1890

Findlay Bottling Works – E. Bacher – Findlay, O
Aqua, 11", smooth base, tooled mouth **$60-90**
American 1880-1910

Foundersmith's – Beer
Deep amber, 12-sided, 9-7/8", smooth base, applied
sloping collar mouth..**$600-800**
American 1855-1860 (very rare beer from the
Foundersmith's Company of Cincinnati, Ohio)

Foundersmith's – Beer
Deep amber, 12-sided, 10", red iron pontil, applied
sloping collar mouth..**$700-900**
American 1850-1860 (extremely rare beer from the
Foundersmith's Company of Cincinnati, Ohio)

**Fredricksburg Lager Beer – S.F. Bottling
Company (with shield and monogram)**
Light amber, 7-1/2", smooth base, tooled top **$30-50**
American 1880-1890

**Fredricksburg Lager Beer – San Francisco
Cal – Adolph B. Lang (embossed eagle)**
Medium amber, 11-5/8", smooth base,
applied top **$45-55**
Amber 1890-1910

G. Andrae – Port Huron – Mich
Cobalt blue, 11-7/8", smooth base, applied sloping
collar mouth...**$800-1,200**
American 1875-1885

G. H. Hausburg – Blue Island – Ill
Yellow olive green, 8-3/8", smooth base,
tooled mouth **$80-120**
American 1885-1900

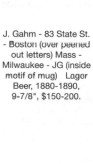

J. Gahm - 83 State St. - Boston (over peened out letters) Mass - Milwaukee - JG (inside motif of mug) Lagor Beer, 1880-1890, 9-7/8", $150-200.

John Stanton Brewing Co - Trade - JSBCO (monogram) Mark - Troy, N.Y., 1885-1900, 9-1/2", $100-150.

Ganbrinus Stock Co. (motif of Gambrinus) - Bottled Beer
- Cincinnati, O, 1875-1885, 10-3/4", $800-1,000; G. Andrae
- Port Huron - Mich., 1875-1885, 11-7/8", $800-1,200.

**Gambrinus Stock Co (motif of Gambrinus)
– Bottled Beer – Cincinnati, O**
Olive amber glass, 10-3/4", smooth base, applied
mouth **$800-1,000**
American 1875-1885 (rare)

**Gowdy's (star) – Medicated Beer – Manufactured
– 10 Ormond Place – This Bottle – Not To Be Sold
– Trade Mark – L & S – Registered July 24th 1890**
Deep bluish aqua, 10-1/2", smooth base,
tooled mouth **$50-75**
American 1885-1895

**Grace Bros. Brewing Co. Gbec (monogram)
– Santa Rosa, Ca – This Bottle Not Be Sold**
Amber, 7-3/4", smooth base, tooled top.............**$35-50**
American 1890-1910

H. Bro's – X.O.
Medium amber, 9", smooth base, applied sloping collar
mouth **$75-125**
American 1875-1885

H. Floto's – Lager Beer – Reading, Pa
Aqua, 7-1/2", smooth base, applied mouth **$70-100**
American 1875-1885

H & K – Dayton, O
Deep red amber, 9-1/2", smooth base, applied sloping
collar mouth..**$75-125**
American 1875-1885

**Haley's – California – Pop Beer – Pat. Oct.
29th 1872 – Manufactured By – McKee & Blehl
– Philadelphia – This Bottle – Not To Be Sold**
Deep yellow amber, 10-3/4", smooth base, applied
mouth **$350-450**
American 1875-1885

Joseph Schlitz's - Milwaukee - Lager Beer
- Registered - J. Gahm - Trade (J.G. inside
motif of mug) - Boston Mass, 1885-1895,
9-3/8", $140-180; John Stanton Brewing
Co - Trade (monogram) Mark -Troy.
N.Y., 1885-1895, 9-1/2", $150-200; City
- Bottling Works - McKeesport PA - H
& W, 1875-1885, 11-1/2", $140-180.

J. Voelker & Bro.
- Cleveland O-V Bro,
1875-1885, 10", $400-600.

P. Stumpf & Co - 1817
Main St - Richmond VA
- This Bottle - Is Never
- Sold 1875-1885,
8-1/4", $250-350.

**Hansen & Kahler – Oakland, Cal. H & K
(monogram) – This Bottle Not Be Sold**
Light amber, quart, smooth base, tooled top......**$30-40**
American 1890-1900

**J.C. Coulter – Cor. 9th & Market – McKeesport,
Pa – A.G.W. – This Bottle – Not To Be Sold**
Golden yellow amber, 9-5/8", smooth base, tooled
mouth for gravitating stopper.............................**$60-80**
American 1885-1900

**J. Gahm – 83 State St. – Boston – Mass – Milwaukee
– Jg (inside motif of mug) – Lager Beer**
Yellow olive, 9-7/8", smooth base, applied sloping
blob top **$150-200**
American 1880-1890

John Rapp & Son – S.F. Cal.
Light amethyst, 7-3/4", smooth base,
crown top **$25-35**
American 1910-1920

**J. Schleenbaker – Bryan – Ohio – This
– Bottle – Not To Be Sold**
Amber olive, 11-1/2", smooth base,
applied mouth **$50-70**
American 1885-1895

**John Stanton Brewing Co – Trade – JSBCO
(monogram) – Mark – Troy, N.Y.**
Bright yellow green, 9-1/2", smooth base,
tooled mouth **$100-150**
American 1885-1900

Phillip Best Brewing Co., Old
Milwaukee Lager Beer, Bottled
by A.P. Fulmer, Lancaster, Pa,
1880-1900, 9-3/4", $50-70.

Robert Portner - Brewing CO - Tivoli (inside diamond)
- Alexandria VA - This Bottle - Not To - Be Sold, 1890-
1910, 9", $75-100; WM Pfeifer - Trade WP (monogram)
Mark - Chicago, 1890-1910, 9-1/2", $75-100.

Schroeder's - B.W.B. Co. - St. Louis Mo, 1890-
1910, 9-1/2", $70-90; Wittemann Rost Brewing
- Co - St. Louis, 1890-1910, 9-1/2", $70-90.

**John Stanton Brewing Co – Trade
– (monogram) – Mark – Troy, N.Y.**
Medium lime green, 9-1/2", smooth base, tooled
mouth, porcelain stopper marked "John Stanton
Brewing Co. Troy, N.Y." $100-150
American 1885-1900

**Joseph Beltz – Weiss Beer – Cor – Slater Ave
– Outwait Ave – Cleveland Ohio – Weiss Beer**
Bluish aqua, 7-5/8", smooth base,
applied mouth $100-150
American 1840-1875

**Joseph Schlitz's – Milwaukee – Lager
Beer – Registered – J. Gahm – Trade (J.G.
inside motif of mug) – Boston Mass**
Medium golden amber, 9-3/8", smooth base, tooled
mouth $140-180
American 1885-1895

Mirrasoul Bros – S.F.
Light amber, 7-5/8", smooth base, tooled top with wire
bale...$30-50
American 1890-1910

**Moerlein's Jug Lager Krug Bier
(Stoneware Ginger Beer)**
Tan pottery with dark brown glaze on neck with black
transfer, 8-3/4", smooth base, tooled mouth $50-80
American 1880-1900

N. Cervelli – 615 Francisco St – S.F.
Medium amber, quart, smooth base,
tooled top $40-80
American 1898-1906

**National Lager Beer – H. Rohrbacher
Agt. – Stockton, Cal**
Golden amber, 7-7/8", smooth base, tooled top with
wire bale $30-50
American 1880-1910

North Star Bottling Works – San Franciso, Cal.
Medium amber, 7-7/8", smooth base,
tooled top $30-60
American 1890-1900

P. Stumpf & Co – 1817 Main St – Richmond
Va – This Bottle – Is Never – Sold
Golden yellow amber, 8-1/4", smooth base, applied
mouth $250-350
American 1875-1885 (Peter Stumpf was
the original distributor in Richmond, Va. for
the Budweiser Brewing Company).

Phillip Best Brewing Co – Old Milwaukee Lager
Beer – Bottled By A.P. Fulmer, Lancaster, Pa
Oliver amber, 9-3/4", smooth base,
tooled mouth $50-70
American 1880-1900

Ruhstaller's Gild Edge Lager Beer
Medium amber, 11-1/2", smooth base,
tooled top $30-50
American 1890-1910 (This beer was produced
by Kenison & Co. in Auburn, Calif.)

Salinas Valley Bottling Co. – Salinas, Cal
Medium amber, 7-5/8", smooth base,
tooled top $35-50
American 1880-1890

San Jose Bottling Com – San Jose Cal.
Medium amber, 7-1/2", smooth base,
tooled top $30-50
American 1880-1890

St. Louis Bottling Co. – MCC. & B – Vallejo, Cal
Amber, quart, smooth base, crown top..............$35-45
American 1900-1920 (rare)

Sunset Bottling Co – San Francisco
(with monogram)
Light amber, 7-1/2", smooth base, tooled top $30-50
American 1880-1890

Take & Veile – Lager Beer – Easton
Pa (in a slug plate)
Medium blue green, 7-1/4", smooth base, applied
sloping double collar mouth...........................$400-600
American 1850-1865

Theodore Lutge & Co – This Bottle
Not To Be Sold – San Jose Cal
Sea foam green, quart, smooth base,
applied top $50-100
American 1875-1890

Thos. Downing Haford, Cal – Not To Be Sold
Medium amber, 7-3/4", smooth base,
crown top $30-40
American 1900-1910

T.L. Neff's Sons – 105 Maujer St
– Brooklyn, N.Y. – Trade (motif of case of
bottles) Mark – Registered – 1895
Deep bluish aqua, 10-1/2", smooth base,
tooled mouth $50-75
American 1885-1895

Ticoulet & Beshorman – Sac. Ca
Medium amber, quart, smooth base,
tooled top $30-40
American 190-1910

Wallabout Pottery Co (stoneware beer)
Reddish brown pottery, 6", smooth base,
tooled top $100-150
American 1870-1890 (rare)

Wunder Bottling – Works – E. Greenwald
– Stockton Cal – Pacific Club Beer, Brewed By
Wunder Brewing Co. – San Francisco, Cal.
Medium amber, 9-1/4", smooth base, tooled mouth,
porcelain stopper marked "D.W. McCarthy Stockton,
Cal"..$70-90
American 1895-1910

Stoneware Ginger Beer,
"Moerlein's Jug Lager
Krug Bier," 1880-1900,
8-3/4", $50-80.

Bitters

Bitter bottles have long been one of the favorite bottles to collect. Because of their uniqueness, they were saved in great numbers, giving the collector of today some great opportunities to build a special and varied collection.

Bitters, which originated in England, were originally a type of medicine made from bitter tasting roots or herbs, giving the concoction its name. During the 18th century, bitters were added to water, ale, or spirits with the intent to cure all types of ailments. Because of the pretense that those mixtures had some medicinal value, bitters became very popular in America since colonists could import them from England without paying the liquor tax. While most bitters had low alcohol content, some brands were as much as 120 proof—higher than most hard liquor available at the time. As physicians became convinced bitters did have some type of healing value, the drink became socially acceptable, promoting use among people who normally weren't liquor drinkers.

The best known among the physicians who made their own bitters for patients was Dr. Jacob Hostetter. After his retirement in 1853, he gave permission to his son

Augauer Bitters
- Augauer Bitter Co -
Chicago - 1890-1910,
8-1/8", $200-300.

David to manufacture it commercially. Hostetter Bitters was known for its colorful, dramatic, and extreme advertising. While Hostetters said it wouldn't cure everything, the list of ailments it claimed to alleviate with regular use covered almost everything: indigestion, diarrhea, dysentery, chills and fever, liver ailments, and pains and weakness that came with old age (at that time, a euphemism for impotence). Despite these claims, David Hostetter died in 1888 from a kidney failure that, ironically, should have been cured by his own bitters formula, had its claims been true.

One of the most sought after bitters bottles, and perhaps the most unique, is the Drakes Plantation Bitters that first appeared in 1860 and recorded a patent in 1862. The Drakes Bitters bottle resembles the shape of a log cabin and can be found in a four-log and a six-log variant, with colors in various shades of amber, yellow, citron, puce, green, and black. Another interesting characteristic of the Drake bitters are the miscellaneous dots and marks, including the "X" on the base of the bottles, which are thought to be identification marks of the various glass houses that manufactured the bottles.

Baker's Orange Grove Bitters - 1865-1875, 9", $75-125.

Most of the bitters bottles—over 1,000 types—were manufactured between 1860 and 1905. The more unique shapes called "figurals" were in the likeness of cannons, drums, pigs, fish, and ears of corn. In addition to these shapes, others were round, square, rectangular, barreled-shaped, gin-bottle shaped, flask-shaped, and 12-sided. The embossed varieties are the oldest, most collectible, and most valuable.

The most common color was amber (pale golden yellow to dark amber brown), then aqua (light blue), and sometimes green or clear glass was used. The rarest and most collectible colors are dark blue, amethyst, milk glass, and puce (a purplish brown).

Big Bill - Best
- Stomach Bitters
- 1890-1905, 12",
$300-450.

Amazon – Bitters – Peter McQuade – New York
Medium amber, 9-3/8", smooth base, applied sloping
collar mouth..**$275-375**
American 1875-1885 (rare)

**Applied Seal Bitters Bottle – HK (above
motif of fish inside star on applied seal)**
Deep olive green, 7-3/8", smooth base, applied mouth
and seal..**$100-150**
German 1880-1895

**Applied Seal Bitters Bottle – IWL
(inside motif of star above fish)**
Medium yellow olive amber, 6-7/8", smooth base,
applied mouth and seal...................................**$140-170**
German 1870-1900

Big – Bill – Best – Bitters
Medium amber, 12-1/8", smooth base,
tooled mouth **$80-120**
American 1900-1910

Bourbon Whiskey – Bitters
Copper puce, 9-1/4", barrel, smooth base, applied
mouth **$200-275**
American 1855-1870

Brown's Catalina – Patd Sept 17th 72
Medium golden amber, 10-5/8", smooth base, applied
mouth **$500-700**
American 1865-1875 (extremely rare)

**Brown's – Celebrated – Indian Herb
Bitters – Patented – Feb. 11 – 1868**
Medium amber, 12-1/8", Indian queen, smooth base,
group lip **$500-700**
American 1863-1870

Bryant's – Stomach – Bitters
Olive green, 12-1/2", 8-sided lady's leg,
pontil-scarred base, applied sloping double
collar mouth...**$3,500-4,500**
American 1865-1875

Brown's Celebrated Indian
Herb Bitters - 1867-1875,
12-1/4", $600-900.

Castillian Bitters - 1865-
1880, 10", $300-400.

B.T. 1865 S.C. – Smiths – Druid Bitters
Medium yellow amber, 9-1/2", barrel, smooth base,
applied mouth **$1,000-1,500**
American 1855-1870

Buhrer's – Gentian Bitters – S. Buhrer – Proprietor
Yellow amber, 9", smooth base, applied sloping collar
mouth **$60-80**
American 1870-1880

**California Fig & Herb – Bitters – California
Fig Products Co – San Francisco, Cal**
Medium amber, 9-7/8", smooth base,
tooled mouth **$80-120**
American 1890-1900

**Carl Mampe – Berlin (motif of elephant
inside oval) – Carlampe**
Golden amber, 8", smooth base,
tooled mouth **$140-180**
German 1890-1915 (scarce variant)

**Carl Mampe Berlin (motif of elephant
inside oval) – S.W. Halleschestrasse 17**
Olive green, 10", smooth base, applied sloping collar
mouth **$120-160**
German 1880-1895

Castilian Bitters
Medium golden amber, 10", smooth base, applied
mouth **$800-1,200**
American 1865-1875 (scarce figural cannon bitters)

**Celebrated – Crown Bitters – F.
Chevalier & Co – Sole Agents**
Medium amber, 8-7/8", smooth base, applied sloping
collar mouth..**$300-400**
American 1885-1895 (scarce California bitters)

**Celebrated Nectar – Stomach Bitters – And Nerve
Tonic – The – Nectar Bitter Co – Toledo, O**
Medium yellow green, 9-3/8", smooth base, tooled
mouth **$700-900**
American 1890-1900 (rare)

Dandelion & Wild Cherry
Bitters - 1850-1870,
8-7/8", $275-375.

Dr. Geo. Pierce's -
Indian Restorative Bitters
- Lowell Mass - 1840-
1860, 7-1/2", $150-200.

Group of six bottles: Dr. Harter's - Wild
Cherry Bitters -1890-1910, 3-7/8", 8-1/8",
$250-350 (entire lot of six bottles).

C.H. Swains – Bourbon – Bitters
Amber, 9-1/4", smooth base, applied
mouth $275-375
American 1865-1875

**Clarke's – Vegetable – Sherry Wine
– Bitters – Sharon Mass**
Bluish aqua, 14", smooth base, applied sloping collar
mouth $500-700
American 1850-1865

**Dingen's – Napolean Cocktail Bitters
– Dingen Brothers – Buffalo N.Y.**
Medium olive green, 10-1/4", lady's leg drum, iron
pontil, applied sloping collar mouth $15,000-20,000
American 1865-1875 (rare color and form)

Dr. C.W. Roback's – Stomach Bitters – Cincinnati, O
Medium amber, 9-3/8", barrel, smooth base, applied
sloping collar mouth..$250-300
American 1860-1870

Dr. Green's Polish Bitters
Yellow amber, 10-7/8", iron pontil,
applied mouth $400-600
American 1845-1860 (rare)

Dr. J. Hostetter's – Stomach Bitters
Deep olive green, 9-1/2", smooth base, applied sloping
collar mouth...$275-375
American 1865-1875

Dr. J. Hostetter's – Stomach Bitters
Medium golden amber, 8-3/4", smooth base, applied
sloping collar mouth..$275-375
American 1875-1885

Dr. MacKenzie's – Wild Cherry – Bitters – Chicago
Clear glass, 8-3/8", smooth base,
tooled mouth $175-275
American 1890-1900

**Dr. Shoule's – Hop – Bitters – 1872
(motif of hop berries and leaves)**
Yellow olive, 10", semi-cabin, smooth base, applied
sloping double collar mouth............................$200-300
American 1872-1880

**Dr. Shoule's – Hop – Bitters – 1872
(motif of hop berries and leaves)**
Yellow olive green, 9-5/8", semi-cabin, smooth base,
applied sloping double collar mouth.........$1,400-1,800
American 1872-1880 (rare)

**Dr. Sperry's – Female – Strengthening
– Bitters – Waterbury Ct**
Deep bluish aqua, 9-1/8", smooth base,
applied mouth $200-300
American 1880-1890

Dr. Wood's – Sarsaparilla – & – Wild Cherry – Bitters
Aqua, 8-3/4", open pontil, applied mouth.......$250-350
American 1845-1855

**Edw Wilder's – Stomach Bitters (motif
of five story building) – Edw Wilder & Co
– Wholesale Druggists – Louisville, Ky.**
Clear glass, semi-cabin, 10-3/4", smooth base, applied
sloping double collar mouth............................$375-475
American 1880-1890 (rare variant)

Dr. Loews Celebrated
- Stomach Bitters &
Nerve Tonic - 1890-1910,
3-1/2", $375-475.

Dr. J. Hostetter's Stomach Bitters - 1910-
1915, 8-7/8", $75-150 (front and side).

E.S. Royer's – Excelsior Bitters
Yellow amber, 9-1/2", smooth base,
applied mouth $175-275
American 1870-1880

Faith – Whitcomb's – Bitters – Faith
Whitcomb's Agency – Boston Mass, U.S.A.
Aqua, 9-1/2", smooth base, applied double collar
mouth $175-275
American 1880-1890

Fulton M. McRae – Yazoo Valley Bitters
Medium amber, 8-3/4", smooth base, applied sloping
collar mouth..$200-300
American 1875-1885

German Balsam Bitters – W.M. Watson
& Co – Sole Agents For U.S.
Milk glass, 9", smooth base, applied sloping collar
mouth $500-800
American 1879-1880

Greeley's – Bourbon Whiskey – Bitters – Greeley's
Bluish aqua, 9-3/8", barrel, smooth base, applied
mouth $3,000-4,000
American 1855-1870

Greeley's Bourbon – Bitters
Smoky olive topaz, 9-3/8", barrel, smooth base,
applied mouth $1,400-1,800
American 1855-1870

Hall's Bitters – E.E. Hall New
Haven – Established 1842
Medium amber, 9-1/4", barrel, smooth base, applied
mouth $300-400
American 1860-1870

Hesperidina – Bagles – Un Barril
Medium yellow amber, 9-5/8", barrel, smooth base,
"Rio De La Plaata – Brazil," smooth base, applied
mouth $120-140
Brazil 1875-1895

H.P. Herb – Wild – Cherry – Bitters – Reading
– Pa – Wild Cherry (motif of cherry tree)
– Bitters – Bitters (on four roof panels)
Amber, 10-1/8", cabin, smooth base,
tooled mouth $300-400
American 1885-1895

Hunki Dori – Bitters – H.B. Matthews – Chicago
Medium amber, 8-7/8", smooth base, applied sloping
collar mouth..$175-275
American 1875-1885 (scarce)

1834 – John Roots Bitters – 1834 – Buffalo, N.Y.
Medium blue green, 10-1/8", semi-cabin, smooth base,
applied sloping collar mouth $1,200-1,800
American 1865-1875

E. Dexter Loveridge
- Yahoo Bitters - 1870-
1880, 10", $700-900.

Figural Pineapple
Bitters - 1870-1880,
9", $175-250.

J.W. Hutchinson's – Tonic Bitters – Mobile Ala
Deep olive green, 9", smooth base, applied sloping
collar mouth..$2,500-3,500
American 1865-1875 (one of only two known examples)

J.W. Hutchinson's – Tonic Bitters – Mobile Ala
Medium golden amber, 8-7/8", smooth base, applied
sloping collar mouth..............................$3,500-4,500
American 1865-1875 (one of only two known examples)

John Moffat – Phoenix – Bitters
– New York – Price 1 Dollar
Medium amber, 5-1/2", open pontil,
rolled lip...$1,000-1,500
American 1835-1845

John Root's Bitters – Buffalo, N.Y. – 1834 – 1834
Medium blue green, 10-1/4", semi-cabin, smooth base,
applied mouth $2,500-3,000
American 1865-1875

**John Steele's – Niagara (star) Bitters – John
Steele's Niagara Star Bitters – 1864 (on roof).**
Deep amber, semi-cabin, 9-7/8", smooth base, applied
mouth $375-475
American 1865-1875

**Karlsbader Sprudel Bitter – G (motif of
fountain) – G – Karlsbader Sprudel Likor
– Ges Gesch – Edmund – Weiss – Karlsbad**
Milk glass, 8-1/8", smooth base,
tooled mouth...$140-100
German 1880-1895

Hertrich's
Gesundheits Bitter
- Hans Hertirich Hof
- Erffinderu
Allein - Destillateur
- Gesetzlich
Geschutzt, 1900-
1915, 11-7/8",
$800-1,200 (rare).

**Kelly's – Old Cabin – Bitters – Patented – 1863
– Kelly's – Old Cabin – Bitters – Patented – 1863**
Amber, 9-1/4", log cabin, smooth base, applied sloping
collar mouth.......................................$1,500-2,000
American 1865-1875

Kimball's – Jaundice – Bitters – Troy N.H.
Medium yellow amber, 7", iron pontil, applied sloping
collar mouth..$1,000-1,500
American 1840-1860

**Leopold Sahl's – Aromatic – Stomach
Bitters – Pittsburgh, Pa**
Medium amber, 10-1/4", smooth base, applied sloping
collar mouth..$2,500-3,500
American 1855-1870

**McConnon's – Stomach Bitters – McConnon
& Company – Winona, Minn**
Medium reddish amber, 9-1/8", smooth base, tooled
mouth $350-550
American 1880-1900

McKeever's Army Bitters (cannon balls on drums)
Medium amber, 10-5/8", smooth base, applied sloping
collar mouth...$1,500-2,500
American 1865-1875

**Mishler's Herb Bitters – Tablespoon
Graduation – Dr. S.B. Hartman & Co**
Yellow with copper tone, 8-3/4", smooth base,
"Stoeckel's Grad Pat Feb 6 66," applied sloping collar
mouth $300-400
American 1866-1875

National – Bitters
Medium amber, 12-3/8", smooth base, applied collar
mouth $375-475
American 1867-1875

Holtzermann's
Patent Stomach
Bitters, 1865-
1875, 9-1/2",
$1,800-2,800
(front and side).

Miniature Bitters - A. Gilka-Schutzen STR No. 9 - J.A. Gilka/Berlin - 1890-1910, 3-1/8", $100-150.

Mack's Orange Tonic Bitters, 1885-1895, 9", $150-250 (front and back).

National Bitters, 1867-1875, 12-1/8", $600-900.

Morning (star) Bitters - Inceptum 5869, 1870-1880, 12-1/2", $150-200.

Normandy - Herb & Root - Stomach Bitters - Normandy - Medicine M'F'G. Co - Louisville, KY (lot of 2), 1890-1910, 4" and 7-3/4", $150-200 (pair).

Philadelphia Hop Bitters, 1840-1860, 9", and Pepsin Calisaya Bitters, 1840-1860, 8-1/8", $150-200 (for both).

Patented – A863 – OK – Plantation – 1840
Medium amber, 11", triangular shape, smooth base, applied mouth $2,500-3,500
American 1863-1870 (rare)

Old – Homestead – Wild Cherry – Bitters – Patent
Medium amber, 9-3/4", cabin, smooth base, applied sloping collar mouth.......................................$140-180
American 1865-1875

Old – Homestead – Wild Cherry – Bitters – Patent
Golden yellow amber, 9-5/8", cabin, smooth base, applied sloping collar mouth $350-450
American 1865-1875

Old Sachem – Bitters – And – Wigwam Tonic
Deep strawberry puce, 9-3/8", barrel, smooth base, applied mouth $500-800
American 1855-1870

Old Sachem – Bitters – And – Wigwam Tonic
Bright yellow amber, 9-1/4", barrel, smooth base, applied mouth $150-200
American 1855-1870

Orient Bitters – Wm. M. Leslie – N.Y.
Clear glass, 9-1/2", smooth base, tooled lip...$175-275
American 1880-1895 (rare)

Poor Man's - Family Bitters, 1870-1875, 6-3/8", $200-275 (front and back).

Prickly Ash – Bitters Co.
Medium amber, 9-7/8", smooth base, applied sloping collar mouth..$150-250
American 1880-1890

Red Jacket – Bitters – Bennett Peters & Co.
Root beer amber, 9-3/4", smooth base, applied sloping
collar mouth..$200-300
American 1870-1880

Reed's – Bitters – Reed's Bitters
Medium golden yellow amber, 12-1/2", lady's leg,
smooth base, applied mouth $300-400
American 1875-1885

Rising Sun – Bitters – John C. Hurst – Philada
Yellow with light amber and olive, 9-1/4", smooth base,
applied mouth $300-400
American 1870-1880

Rocky Mountain – Tonic Bitters – 1840 Try Me 1870
Medium yellow amber, 9-3/4", smooth base, applied
mouth $350-450
American 1870-1880 (rare)

**Royal – Italian Bitters – Registered (motif
of crown, shield and crossed flags) – Trade
Mark – A.M.F. Gianelli – Genova**
Medium pink amethyst, 13-3/4", smooth base, applied
mouth $600-900
Canadian 1875-1885

Rush's – Bitters – A.H. Flanders, Md. – New York
Yellow with light amber, 9-1/4", smooth base, applied
mouth $100-175
American 1875-1885

**Sanitarium – Bitters – Hi Hi Bitters
Co. – Rock Island, Ill**
Bright lime green, 9-1/2", smooth base,
tooled lip..$250-350
American 1880-1890

Shurtleff's – Bitters – Shurtleff's – Bitters
Amber, 12-1/2", lady's leg, smooth base, applied
mouth $500-700
American 1870-1880 (one of the rarest
bitters bottles in the lady leg form)

S.O. Richardson – Bitters – South – Reading – Mass
Aqua, 6-1/2", open pontil, flared out
tooled lip..$100-175
American 1845-1855

**Solomons' – Strengthening & – Invigoration
Bitters – Savannah – Georgia**
Deep cobalt blue, 9-7/8", smooth base, applied sloping
collar mouth...$1,000-1,500
American 1870-1880

**St – Drakes – 1860 – Plantation – X
– Bitters – Patented – 1862**
Deep purple amethyst, 10", smooth base, applied
sloping collar mouth..................................$1,400-1,800
American 1862-1875

**St – Drakes – 1860 – Plantation – X
– Bitters – Patented – 1862**
Dark cherry puce, 10", 6-log cabin, smooth base,
applied sloping collar mouth $1,400-1,800
American 1862-1875

**St. – Nicholas – Stomach – Bitters
– Imported – By – Gentry – & Otis – N.Y.**
Amber, 7-5/8", pontil-scarred base, wedge form,
applied collar mouth..$400-700
American 1865-1875

Suffolk Bitters – Philbrook & Tucker – Boston
Golden amber, 10", smooth base, applied double collar
mouth $600-800
American 1865-1875

The – Fish Bitters – W.H. Ware – Patented 1866
Amber, 11-3/4", fish form, smooth base, "W.H. Ware
– Patent 1866," applied mouth........................$250-350
American 1866-1875

Tyree's – Chamomile – Bitters
Yellow amber, 6-5/8", smooth base,
tooled lip..$175-275
American 1880-1890

**Von Humboldt's – German Bitters
– Dyspepsia & C. – Liver Complaint**
Bluish aqua, 7", pontil-scarred base,
applied mouth $500-700
American 1845-1855

**Warner's – Safe – Bitters (motif
of safe) – Rochester N.Y.**
Yellow amber, 7-1/2", smooth base,
applied mouth $600-800
American 1880-1895

The - Fish Bitters - W.H. Ware
- Patented 1866, 1866-
1875, 11-3/4", $250-350.

Wheeler's – Genuine – Bitters
Aqua, 9-1/4", pontil-scarred base,
applied mouth **$400-600**
American 1845-1855 (rare with pontil)

Winter's – Stomach Bitters
Reddish amber, 9-5/8", smooth base,
tooled lip..**$175-275**
American 1880-1895

W.R. Tyree's – Chamomile – Bitters – 1880
Amber, 8-5/8", semi-cabin, smooth base,
tooled mouth **$800-1,200**
American 1880-1890 (rare)

Sample Bitters Bottles

As discussed earlier, bitters bottles were made in the early 1800s, but sample bitters and other types of samples weren't introduced until the 1890s. What makes these sample bottles so interesting is that, except for their smaller size, they were identical to the standard-sized bitters bottles. The sample bitters bottles shown are from the collection of Omer and Helen Sherwood, who began collecting sample bitters in the mid-1960s. Another interesting aspect of the Sherwoods' collection is that along with each sample bitters, they also collected a matching full-size bottle.

Augauer Bitters – Augauer Bitters Co – Chicago
Medium emerald green, 4-1/4", smooth base, tooled
mouth **$275**
American 1890-1910

**California – Fig & Herb – Bitters – California
Fig Products Co – San Francisco, Cal.**
Yellow amber, 4-1/2", smooth base, tooled lip **$700**
American 1885-1900

Carl – Mampe (motif of elephant) – Berlin
Medium amber, 2-1/4", smooth base, tooled mouth,
99% label **$50**
German 1900-1915

**Carmeliter – Stomach Bitters Co. – New
York – SJ (monogram) Registered**
Medium amber, 4-7/8", smooth base, tooled mouth,
original labels, foil neck seal, and contents **$850**
American 1890-1910

Deimel Bros & Co – New York – U.S.A.
Milk glass, 4-1/8", case gin, smooth base, tooled
mouth **$150**
American 1890-1900

Digestine – Bitters
Yellowish amber, 3-1/2", smooth base, tooled lip**$1,300**
American 1890-1900

**Dr. Loew's Celebrated – Stomach Bitters – Nerve
Tonic – The – Loew & Sons Co. – Cleveland, O**
Pale aqua, 3-7/8", smooth base, tooled mouth **$160**
American 1890-1910

Eagle Angostura Bark Bitters
Medium amber, 3-7/8", smooth base,
tooled mouth **$425**
American 1895-1910

Sample Bitters - Carl Mampe - Berlin - 1900-1915, 2-1/4", $80-120 (front and back).

Sample Bitters - Holtzermann's Stomach Bitters, Piqua,
O - 1885-1900, 4-1/8", $300-400 (front and back).

**Ferro Quina – Bitters – D.P. Rossi
– Dogliani – Italia – S.F. Cal**
Yellow amber, 3-3/4", smooth base, tooled lip **$120**
American 1890-1910

**Geo. Benz – & – Sons – Appetine
– Bitters – St. Paul, Minn**
Amber, 3-1/2", smooth base, "Pat – Nov. 23 – 1897,"
tooled lip **$425**
American 1897-1910

**Golden – Bitters – Geo. C. Hubbel
& Co – Geo. C. Hubbel & Co.**
Pale aqua, 3-5/8", semi-cabin, smooth base, inward
rolled lip **$275**
American 1875-1885

**H. Kantorowicz – Co – Hamburg
– Berlin – Posen – New York**
Milk glass, 4-1/8", case gin, smooth base, tooled
mouth **$120**
American 1880-1890

Holtzermann's Stomach Bitters – Piqua O
Medium amber, 4-1/8", log cabin, smooth base, tooled
mouth, original label, foil neck seal and contents .. **$850**
American 1885-1900

**Hops – & – Malt – Bitters (on four roof panels)
– Hops & Malt – Trade (sheaf of grain) Mark – Bitters**
Yellow amber, 3-5/8", semi-cabin, smooth base, tooled
mouth **$1,500**
American 1885-1895

**Kennedys – East India – Bitters
– Iler & Co – Omaha, Neb**
Clear glass, 4-1/8", smooth base, tooled mouth ... **$100**
American 1885-1895

**Morning (star) – Bitters – Inceptum
5869 – Patented – 5869**
Yellow amber, 5-1/8", smooth base,
tooled mouth **$1,400**
American 1880-1890 (only two known examples)

**Pepsin Bitters – R.W. Davis Drug
Co. – Chicago. U.S.A.**
Apple green, 4-1/2", smooth base, tooled top **$250**
American 1890-1910

Sarasina – Stomach Bitters
Amber, 4", smooth base, tooled lip **$325**
American 1890-1910

Schroeder's – Bitters – Louisville, Ky
Medium amber, 5-1/4", lady leg, smooth base,
tooled lip **$275**
American 1880-1890

Sample Bitters - Old
Hickory Celebrated
Stomach
Bitters - J. Grossman
- New Orleans, La , 1890-
1900, 4-5/8", $140-180.

S.O. Richardson's
Bitters - South
Reading, Mass
- 1840-1860,
6-1/4", $100-150.

The Loew & Sons Co. -
Cleveland, Ohio - 1863-
1870, 10", $300-400.

W.C. Bitters -
Brobst & Rentschler -
Reading, Pa, 1885-1895,
10-3/4", $600-800.

Williams Allens
- Congress Bitters -
20th Century,
7-3/4", $500-700.

Blown Bottles

Free-blown bottles, also called blown bottles, were made without molds and were shaped by the glassblower. It is difficult to determine age and the origin of these bottles, since many were produced in Europe and America long before records were kept.

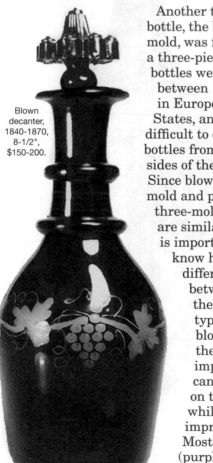

Blown decanter, 1840-1870, 8-1/2", $150-200.

Another type of blown bottle, the blown three-mold, was formed from a three-piece mold. These bottles were manufactured between 1820 and 1840 in Europe and the United States, and it is quite difficult to distinguish bottles from different sides of the Atlantic. Since blown three-mold and pressed three-mold bottles are similar, it is important to know how to differentiate between the two types. With blown glass, the mold impression can be felt on the inside, while pressed-glass impressions can only be felt on the outside. Most blown three-mold bottles came in amethyst (purple), sapphire blue, and a variety of greens.

Blown copper - wheel-cut decanter, 1820-1835, 8-1/4", $275-375.

Black Glass Seal Bottle (motif of crown above shield with hounds on either side)
Olive amber, 9-3/4", smooth base, applied mouth and seal, blown in a three-part mold......................**$375-475**
English 1850 1870

Black Glass Seal Bottle – I.L.M. Smith – Wine Mercht. – Baltimore (on applied seal)
Olive amber, 10-1/4", pontil-scarred pointed kick-up, applied double collar mouth, blown in a dip mold...**$800-1,400**
American 1810-1825

Black Glass Seal Bottle – J.W.C. (on applied seal) Patent (on shoulder)
Deep olive green, 11", pontil-scarred base, "H. Rickett's & Co Glass Works Bristol," applied sloping double collar mouth and seal, blown in a three-part mold **$600-800**
English 1825-1840

Blown Decanter
Clear glass with ruby red overlay, copper wheel cut grape and vine decoration, 8-1/2", ground glass stopper, pontil-scarred base, applied neck rings, tooled out flared lip..**$150-200**
American 1840-1870

Blown Decanter
Clear glass with ruby red overlay, copper wheel cut diamond pattern, 10-1/2", ground glass stopper, pontil-scarred base, applied neck rings, tooled out flared lip..**$150-200**
American 1840-1870

Blown Globular Bottle
Yellow amber, 9-3/4", pontil-scarred base, applied sloping collar mouth.......................................**$400-600**
American 1810-1830

Blown Spirits Flask
Clear glass, 7-1/2", pontil-scarred base, applied pewter neck band with screw threads **$100-150**
German 1780-1820

Blown spirits flask (German), 1780-1820, 7-1/2", $100-150.

Blown decanter, 1830-1860, 10", $700-1000.

Blown Three–Mold Decanter
Deep olive green, 8-3/8", pontil-scarred base, applied double collar mouth $2,500-3,500
American 1820-1835 (rare with medicine top)

Blown Three-Mold Decanter
Yellow olive, quart, pontil-scarred base, sheared mouth $150-300
American 1820-1840 (Keene Marlboro Street Glassworks, Keene, N.H.)

Blown Wine Decanter
Clear glass with etched scenes of sailboats, grape clusters, and windmills, 12", pontil-scarred base, tooled top $250-350
European 1830-1850

Blown decanter, 1840-1860, Sandwich Glassworks, 10-1/2", $1,000-1,500 (extremely rare).

Blown Three-Mold Flask
Moonstone, 5", half pint, pontil-scarred base, tooled mouth $1,500-3,000
American 1820-1840 (rare, Boston and Sandwich Glass Works, Sandwich, Mass.)

Blown Three-Mold Castor Bottle
Honey amber, 4", smooth base, ground mouth with screw threads, metal shaker cap $250-500
American 1860-1880 (rare in any color)

Blown Three-Mold Toilet Water Bottle
Deep cobalt blue with purple tone, pontil-scarred base, tooled flared mouth with stopper....................$200-400
American 1820-1840 (Boston and Sandwich Glass Works, Sandwich, Mass.)

Blown Two-Mold Decanter
Medium amethyst, 6-3/4", ground pontil-scarred base, tooled flared mouth $2,000-4,000
American 1820-1840

Chestnut Flask
Pink amethyst, 18 vertical rib pattern, 6-1/4", pontil-scarred base, sheared lip $150-250
European 1830-1860

Freeblown Bottle (teardrop form)
Medium cobalt blue, 4-1/8", tubular pontil-scarred base, inward rolled mouth..............................$300-600
American 1750-1800

Freeblown Back Bar Bottle
Medium amethyst with gold and black painted "Brandy," 10-7/8", pontil-scarred base, tooled mouth with applied string lip $150-250
American 1830-1860

Freeblown Chestnut Bottle
Yellow green, 5-1/8", pontil-scarred base, rolled collar mouth $250-450
American 1780-1830

Freeblown Chestnut Bottle
Medium yellow green, 6-3/4", pontil-scarred base, applied collar mouth..$225-450
American 1783-1830

Freeblown Chestnut Bottle
Yellow olive, 7-1/2", pontil-scarred base, applied collar mouth $250-500
American 1780-1830

Freeblown Chestnut Bottle
Yellow green, 8-1/4", pontil-scarred base, applied collar mouth...$250-500
American 1780-1830

Freeblown Miniature Globular Bottle
Greenish aquamarine, 2-7/8", small globular form with long neck, tubular pontil-scarred base, outward rolled mouth $500-1,000
American 1780-1830

Freeblown Globular Bottle
Deep aquamarine, 3-1/8", pontil-scarred base, rolled collar mouth...$150-300
American 1815-1830

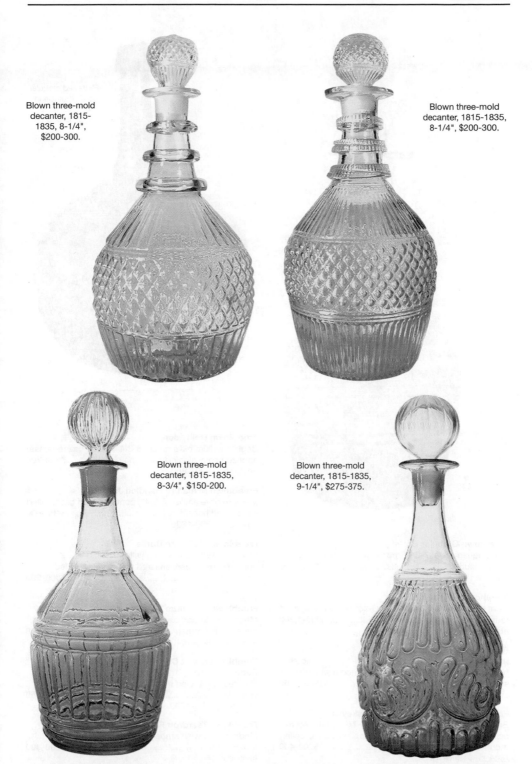

Blown three-mold decanter, 1815-1835, 8-1/4", $200-300.

Blown three-mold decanter, 1815-1835, 8-1/4", $200-300.

Blown three-mold decanter, 1815-1835, 8-3/4", $150-200.

Blown three-mold decanter, 1815-1835, 9-1/4", $275-375.

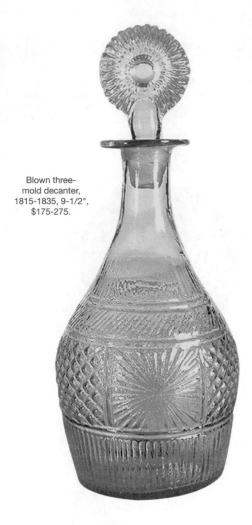

Blown three-mold decanter, 1815-1835, 9-1/2", $175-275.

Flattened globular bottle (European), 1850-1870, 12", $250-350.

Freeblown Globular Bottle
Deep aquamarine, 7-3/4", pontil-scarred base, applied collar mouth...$150-300
American 1815-1830

Freeblown Globular Bottle
Light yellow olive, 11-1/4", pontil-scarred base, applied round collar mouth $600-1,200
American 1780-1830

Freeblown Globular Bottle
Medium reddish amber, 11-7/8" h., 5-1/2" b., smooth base with pointed kick-up, sheared mouth with applied string lip...$250-350
European 1840-1870

Freeblown Handled Globular Whiskey Jug
Brilliant medium strawberry puce, 5-7/8", pontil-scarred base, applied solid glass handle, applied sloping collar mouth $200-400
American 1840-1870

Freeblown Utility Jar
Bright medium olive green, 6-3/4", pontil-scarred base, applied heavy sloping collar mouth................$350-700
American 1820-1860

Freeblown Miniature Handled Jug
Medium olive amber, 2-3/4", pontil-scarred base, rolled lip, applied handle $400-600
American 1800-1830

Freeblown Miniature Bottle
Medium olive green with a yellow tone, 3-1/2", pontil-scarred base, sheared mouth with applied string rim $300-600
American 1780-1800

Freeblown Miniature Decanter
Medium yellowish olive green, 3-3/8", pontil-scarred base, tooled mouth $500-1,000
American 1800-1840

Freeblown Squat Chestnut Flask
Reddish amber, 6-1/2", pontil scar on deep kick-up, sheared and tooled mouth with applied string lip...$250-350
European 1770-1790

Freeblown Teardrop Flask
Medium yellowish amber, 7", pontil-scarred base, tooled mouth $200-300
American 1825-1850

Freeblown back bar
bottle, "Brandy," 1830-
1860, 10-7/8", $150-250.

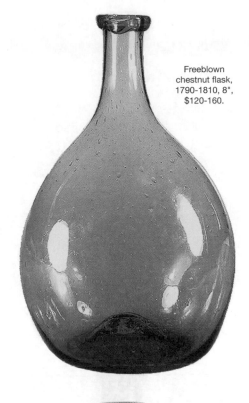

Freeblown
chestnut flask,
1790-1810, 8",
$120-160.

Freeblown Teardrop Flask
Yellow green with dense olive amber tones above
shoulder and in the base, 5-5/8", tubular pontil-scarred
base, sheared mouth......................................**$200-400**
American 1815-1830 (Keene Marlboro
Street Glassworks, Keene, N.H.)

Freeblown Utility Medicine Bottle
Medium olive green, 2-1/2", pontil-scarred base, tooled
flared mouth **$400-800**
American 1780-1830

Freeblown Utility Bottle
Medium yellow olive, 8-1/8", square form,
pontil-scarred base, applied double collar
mouth **$300-600**
American 1800-1840

Midwestern Club Bottle
Blue aqua, 8", 24 rib-pattern swirled to right, open
pontil, applied mouth **$175-275**
American 1820-1835

Freeblown globular bottle, 1815-1825, 8-1/2", $150-200.

Freeblown globular bottle, 1800-
1820, 7-1/2", $250-300.

Nailsea Flask
Medium yellow amber with white looping, 4-7/8",
pontil-scarred base, tooled mouth.................**$400-600**
European 1830-1860

Nailsea Flask
Clear glass with cobalt blue looping, 6-3/4", pontil-
scarred base, tooled mouth **$120-160**
English 1880-1910

Nailsea Flask
Light turquoise blue with opalescent looping, 7-3/8",
pontil-scarred base, tooled mouth.................**$275-375**
English 1880-1910

Pinch Waist Chestnut Flask
Smoky clear glass, 8", polished pontil base, applied
mouth, neck rings..**$400-600**
European 1820-1850

Pinch Waist Chestnut Flask
Clear glass, 8-1/4", polished pontil base, applied
mouth, neck rings...**$375-475**
European 1820-1850

Freeblown globular bottle, 1815-
1825, 8-1/8", $250-350.

Freeblown Ludlow bottle, 1780-
1810, 9-1/4", $200-300.

Nailsea flask, 1870-1890,
7-1/4", $200-300.

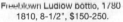

Freeblown Ludlow bottle, 1780
1810, 8-1/2", $150-250.

Pitkin Flask
Medium green, 4-1/2", 20 broken-rib-pattern swirled to
right, pontil-scarred base, tooled lip **$500-700**
American 1815-1830

Pitkin Flask
Greenish aqua, 6-1/2", 32 broken-rib-pattern swirled to
right, pontil-scarred base, tooled lip **$375-475**
American 1810-1820

Pitkin Flask
Medium olive green, 36 broken-rib-pattern swirled to
right, 6-5/8", pontil-scarred base,
sheared lip...**$400-600**
American 1780-1810

Pocket Flask
Deep emerald green, 4-1/4", pontil-scarred base,
tooled lip, applied double handles **$150-200**
Middle Eastern 1800-1840

Sandwich Type Decanter
Deep pinkish amethyst, 11-1/2", cut fluted
panels on shoulder and base, polished pontil,
tooled mouth **$200-300**
American 1840-1870

Sandwich Type Decanter
Deep emerald green, 11-1/2", 10-sided corset
waist form, polished pontil, tooled mouth, applied
mouth with original shot glass lid, applied
neck ring..**$2,000-3,000**
American 1840-1870 (extremely rare)

Sandwich Type Decanter
Deep teal green, 10-1/4", 8-sided polished pontil,
applied mouth pewter stopper.................**$2,500-3,500**
American 1830-1860 (extremely rare color)

Wide Mouth Food Jar
Deep ruby red, 9-3/4", polished pontil, tooled flared
out lip, thick heavy glass................................**$375-475**
European 1900-1925

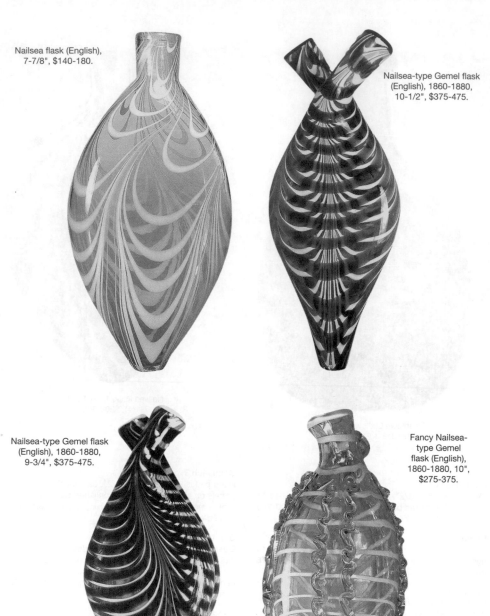

Nailsea flask (English), 7-7/8", $140-180.

Nailsea-type Gemel flask (English), 1860-1880, 10-1/2", $375-475.

Nailsea-type Gemel flask (English), 1860-1880, 9-3/4", $375-475.

Fancy Nailsea-type Gemel flask (English), 1860-1880, 10", $275-375.

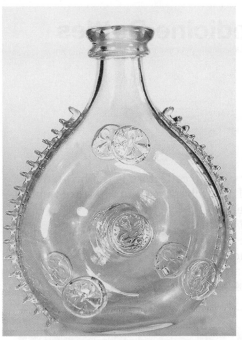

Pinch waist chestnut flask (European),
1820-1850, 8-1/4", $375-475.

Pinch-waist chestnut flask (European),
1820-1850, 8", $400-600.

Sandwich-type decanter,
1830-1860, 10-1/4",
$2,500-3,500 (rare color).

Sandwich-type
decanter, 1840-1870,
11-1/2", $2,000-3,000
(extremely rare).

Cobalt Blue Medicine Bottles

One of the most sought after colors by bottle collectors is the brilliant cobalt blue. As discussed in the "Bottle Facts" chapter, colors natural to bottle glass production are brown, amber, olive-green, and aqua. The true blue, green, and purple colors were produced by metallic oxides added to the glass batch. The blue was specifically produced by adding cobalt oxide to the basic glass batch. Since blue and other bright colors were expensive to produce and were usually manufactured for specialty items, bottles with these colors are very rare and highly sought after by most collectors. Cobalt blue bottles stood out among all other colors, so many chemist, druggist, and pharmacist bottles were made with cobalt along with elaborate monograms, pictures, and unique designs.

This chapter presents a cross-section of many cobalt blue medicine bottles manufactured across the United States before 1920. For a complete and detailed collection of these brilliant bottles, add the following book to your references: *Cobalt Medicine Bottles* by Charles E. Blake (e-mail: dig632@aol.com)

Eau De Rabel
(French), 1880-1910,
6-3/4", $150-250.

**Acker's English Remedy – W.H. Hooker &
Co. – Sole Agent – North & South America
– For All Throat & Lung Diseases**
Cobalt blue, 7", smooth base, tooled mouth ..**$120-160**
American 1885-1900

Ackerman – & – Stewart – Palakta, Fla
Cobalt blue, 3", smooth base, tooled mouth ..**$100-150**
American 1880-1890

Apothecaries' Hall – San Francisco – AH (mongram)
Light cobalt, 5-1/4", smooth base,
tooled mouth **$200-400**
American 1890-1910

Ayer's – Hair Vigor
Cobalt blue, 7-1/4", smooth base, ABM lip, original
matching color stopper **$125-150**
American 1890-1910

**B. Ward – Druggist (O. Festina Lente and BW
monogram inside a wreath) Mobile, Ala**
Cobalt blue, 5-1/4", smooth base,
tooled mouth **$350-450**
American 1880-1900

Boynton's Pharm. – Biddeford, Me
Dark cobalt blue, 5-1/8", smooth base, "Pat. Jan.
24,'88 A. W. T. Co. U.S.A.," tooled top............**$200-250**
American 1880-1890

Boswell & Warner's – Colorific
Deep cobalt blue, 5-5/8", smooth base,
tooled mouth **$150-200**
American 1880-1890

**Buck & Rayner – Chicago – I, C, 9, B, W
(design in fragmented diamond shape)**
Light cobalt blue, 6-3/4", smooth base,
tooled top **$100-150**
American 1885-1900

**Buffum's Sarsasparilla & Lemon
Mineral Water – Pittsburgh**
Medium cobalt blue, 7-5/8", iron pontil, applied collar
top **$700-900**
American 1850-1860

C. Heimstreet & Co – Troy N.Y.
Medium cobalt blue, 7", 8-sided, pontil-scarred base,
applied double collar mouth...........................**$375-475**
American 1840-1860

**Chelfs Comp. – Celery – Caffein – Trade C.C.C.C.
Mark – Chelf Chemical Co. – Richmond, Va U.S.A.**
Dark cobalt blue, 4-3/4", smooth bottom,
tooled top **$20-30**
American 1890-1900

Citrate – Of Magnesia
Deep cobalt blue, 7-1/4", smooth base, applied double
collar mouth...**$250-350**
American 1875-1880

Daniel J. Mahler – Providence, R.I.
Cobalt blue, 5-3/4", smooth base,
tooled top **$250-350**
American 1885-1900 (rare)

Dr. Chasussier's – Empress (labeled)
Cobalt blue, 7-3/8", smooth base, applied
collar mouth...**$150-300**
American 1860-1880 (rare with label)

Dr. Eliel's – Silver Regulator – South Bend, Ind
Cobalt blue, 5-5/8", smooth base,
tooled top **$500-600**
American 1880-1900

Dr. J.B. Henion's – Sure Cure – For – Malaria
Cobalt blue, 6-3/8", smooth base, large applied disc-
type mouth ....,**$5,000-7,000**
American 1880-1890

Dr. J. J. Hogan – Next To Post Office – Vallejo, Cal
Cobalt blue, 7-1/4", smooth base, "WT & Co. U.S.A.,"
tooled mouth **$125-225**
American 1880-1890

Edwin J. Kuhns – Druggist & Chemist – Lansdale, Pa
Cobalt blue, cylinder shape, 6-1/4", smooth base, "WT
& Co. U.S.A.," tooled mouth **$275-375**
American 1890-1910

**Farrand Williams & Co. – FW & Co
(monogram) – Detroit, Mich.**
Dark cobalt blue, 8", smooth base,
tooled top **$200-250**
American 1880-1900

Frank Morgan & Sons – Philadelphia
Deep cobalt blue, 10-5/8", smooth base,
tooled mouth **$150-200**
American 1890-1910

Fraser & Co. – 28 Washington St., Chicago
Cobalt blue, 5-5/8", smooth base "WT & Co. 2 U.S.A.,",
tooled top **$200-250**
American 1890-1900

**From – Frough's (in script) Odel
Drug Store – Watsonville, Cal**
Cobalt blue, 4-3/4", smooth base, "WT & Co. U.S.A.
– Pat. Dec 11. 1894," tooled mouth **$300-400**
American 1894-1900 (rare)

Geller's – Hair Producer – Boston – Mass
Cobalt blue, 7-3/4", smooth base, tooled
collar mouth...**$100-200**
American 1870-1890

Geo. W. Laird & Co. – Oleo – Chyle
Medium cobalt blue, 10", smooth base,
tooled mouth **$200-300**
American 1880-1895

Gooch's – Extract Of – Sarsaparilla – Cincinnati, O
Light cobalt blue, 9-3/8", smooth base,
tooled mouth **$250-350**
American 1880-1890

Hall's – Hair Renewer
Electric cobalt blue, 6-1/2", smooth base, ABM lip,
original glass stopper **$140-180**
American 1910-1915

Elixir Visc: Hoffm: (French), 1880-1910, 6-3/4", $150-250.

Ether Acetiq (French), 1880-1910, 6-3/4", $150-250.

Imperial Embrocation – For Veterinary Use – The Acme Medical Supply Co. – Denver Colo.
Cobalt blue, 7", smooth base, tooled mouth ..**$400-600**
American 1875-1890 (very rare)

Indian – Hair Restorer – A.A. Snyder – Paterson N.J.
Deep cobalt blue, 8-3/4", smooth base, applied square collar mouth...**$1,500-2,500**
American 1870-1880 (extremely rare)

Iron Tonic – Talbot Bro's – Lawrence, Mass
Medium cobalt blue, 7-1/4", smooth base,
tooled top **$150-200**
American 1875-1885

J. & G. Maguire – Chemists And – Druggists – St. Louis, Mo
Medium cobalt blue, 9", smooth base,
applied mouth **$150-250**
American 1865-1875

J. Personeni – Sole Agent – & – Importer – New York
Cobalt blue, 9-1/4", smooth base,
tooled mouth **$140-180**
American 1890-1910 (very rare)

J. R. Nichols & Co – Chemists – Boston
Deep cobalt blue, 9-1/2", smooth base,
tooled mouth **$150-250**
American 1890-1910

Kickapoo – Sage – Hair Tonic
Cobalt blue, 4-5/8", smooth base,
tooled mouth **$300-400**
American 1880-1895

**Lucien Pratte – Le – Renovateur – De
La – Femme – Waterbury Conn**
Cobalt blue, 9-1/4", rectangular with beveled corners
and three indented embossed panels, smooth base,
applied square collar mouth...........................**$250-500**
American 1860-1880 (rare)

Melvin & Badger – Apothecaries – Boston, Mass
Cobalt blue, 6-3/8", smooth base, "C.L.G. & Co.
– Patent Appl'd For," tooled lip **$150-250**
American 1890-1915

Mortons – Citrate – Of – Magnesia – Milwaukee
Medium cobalt blue, 7-3/8", smooth base, applied
double collar mouth **$350-450**
American 1885-1895

Mrs. Dr. Secor – Boston, Mass
Cobalt blue, 9-1/2", smooth base, tooled lip ..**$300-400**
American 1880-1895

**O'Rourke + Hurley – Druggists + Pharmacists
– 501 Main Street – Little Falls, N.Y.**
Cobalt blue, 4-1/4", smooth base,
tooled mouth **$45-55**

**R.A. Robinson & Co. – Importers &
Wholesale Druggists – Louisville, Ky**
Medium cobalt blue, 6", smooth base,
tooled top **$100-175**
American 1895-1900

R.C. & A. – New York
Deep cobalt blue, 9-3/8", smooth base,
tooled mouth **$100-150**
American 1880-1895

R.P. Hall's – Improved – Preparation – For The Hair
Medium cobalt blue, 7-1/2", smooth base, applied
double collar mouth **$140-180**
American 1879-1880 (rare)

**Sanford's – Extract Of – Hamamelis
– Or Witch Hazel**
Medium cobalt blue, 9-1/4", smooth base, applied
mouth **$275-375**
American 1870-1880

**Solomon's Co. Branch Drug Stores
– Bull St. – Savannah, Ga (in script)**
Cobalt blue, 7", smooth base, "WT & Co. U.S.A.,"
tooled mouth **$35-45**
American 1885-1895

Melvin & Badger - Apothecaries - Boston,
Mass, 1890-1915, 6-3/8", $150-250.

Mrs. Dr. Secor - Boston,
Mass, 1880-1895,
9-1/2", $300-400.

**Strong Cobb & Co – Wholesale
– Druggist – Cleveland**
Deep cobalt blue, 8-1/4", smooth base, applied square
collar mouth..**$350-450**
American 1870-1880

**Sutter – Ludman Drug Co. – Two Stores
– Burlington, Ia (in circular slug plate horizontally
embossed above) Solution – Citrate Of Magnesia
– Dose For Adults – One Half To One Full
Bottle – Children – In Proportion To Age**
Dark cobalt blue, 7-1/2", smooth base, applied double
collar mouth..**$500-700**
American 1890-1900

Swift's – Syphilitic Specific
Deep cobalt blue, 9", smooth base,
applied mouth **$800-1,200**
American 1870-1880

**The Adam's Sanatorium – Cure For
The Tobacco Habit – Mexico, Mo**
Medium cobalt blue, 5-1/4", smooth base,
tooled top **$275-375**
American 1890-1900

U.S.A. Hosp. Dept
Cobalt blue, 2-1/2", smooth base,
tooled lip...**$350-450**
American 1860-1875

U.S.A. Hosp. Dept
Cobalt blue, 4-7/8", smooth base,
tooled lip...**$300-400**
American 1860-1875

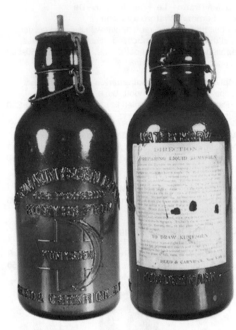

Siphon Kumysgen Bottle - For Preparing - Kumyss
From - Kumysgen - Reed & Carnrick, N.Y. - Water
Mark - Powder Mark, 1890-1900, 9-1/8", $150-250.

Not To Be Taken
- Poisonous,
1890-1910,
7-3/8", $120-140.

Prof. I. Huberts
- Malvina Lotion
- Toledo, Ohio,
1880-1895, 5",
$100-150.

U.S.A. Hosp. Dept
Cobalt blue, 9-1/8", smooth base,
tooled lip...**$375-475**
American 1860-1875

Weaver & Wentz – Pharmacists – Gilroy, Cal
Cobalt blue, 5-1/2", smooth base, "WT & Co. U.S.A.,"
tooled mouth **$500-700**
American 1880-1890

Super - Pittsburgh, 1862-1863, 3-3/8", $150-250 (possibly a poison bottle due to the rib pattern).

U.S.A. Hosp. Dept, 1860-1875, 4-7/8", $300-400.

Turlock Drug Co, Prescription Druggists Turlock, Turlock, CAL, 1880-1890, $450-550 (rare).

Pair of U.S.A. Hosp. Dept, 1860-1875, 2-1/2", $175-225 (each).

U.S.A. Hosp. Dept, 1860-1870, 9-1/8", $375-475.

Cosmetic Bottles

This category includes bottles that originally contained products to improve personal appearance, including treatments for skin, teeth, and the scalp (hair and restoring agents). The more popular of these are the hair treatment bottles.

Hair bottles are popular as collector items because of distinctive colors like amethyst and various shades of blues. The main producer of American-made perfume bottles in the 18th century was Casper Wistar, whose clients included Martha Washington. Another major manufacturer of the 18th century was Henry William Stiegel. While most of Wistar's bottles were plain, Stiegel's were decorative and are more appealing to collectors.

In the 1840s, Solon Palmer began to manufacture and sell perfumes. By 1879, his products were being sold in drugstores around the country. Today, Palmer bottles are sought for their brilliant emerald-green color.

Acme Hair Vigor – Phil. Eisemann
(label under glass bottle)
Clear glass with white, red, blue, and gold label, 8-1/4", smooth base, tooled mouth **$250-350**
American 1890-1925

A.J. Green – Highgate Vt – Professor Motts – Magic – Hair Invigorator – Price Fifty Cents
Greenish aquamarine, 7-3/4", pontil-scarred base, applied double collar mouth...........................**$175-350**
American 1840-1860

Ames – Caucasian – Hair Tonic – Springfield Mass
Aquamarine, 5-3/4", pontil-scarred base, applied collar mouth **$100-200**
American 1840-1860

Arista Antiseptic Face Tonic – Arista M'f'g' Co. Limited Detroit, Mich.
Clear glass with red, black, and white pyro label, 7-1/4", smooth base, tooled mouth **$175-275**
American 1890-1925

Boswell & Warner's Colorific, 1880-1890, 5-5/8", $150-200.

Bowens Genuine Crude Oil Products - Bowen's Genuine Crude Oil Hair Grower - Liquid Velvet (figural oil derrick bottle), 1880-1900, 6-1/2", $250-300 (front and side).

Bunker Hill Monument
cologne bottle -
cologne water, 1865-1880,
6-5/8", $150-200.

Church's Circassian Hair
Restorer, 1870-1880,
7-5/8", $140-200.

Ayer's – Hair Vigor
Peacock, 7-1/4", smooth base, tooled top, original
stopper..**$125-150**
American 1890-1910

Ayer's – Hair Vigor
Cobalt blue, 7-1/4", smooth base, ABM lip, original
stopper..**$125-150**
American 1890-1910

Bogle's – Hyperion Fluid – For The Hair
Aquamarine, 7-1/2", pontil-scarred base, applied collar
mouth **$70-100**
American 1840-1860

Brown's – Liquid – Hair Dye – No 1
Light blue green, 2-7/8", pontil-scarred base, tooled
top **$70-100**
American 1840-1860

Burger's – Hair – Restorative – New York
Opalescent milk glass, 7-1/8", pontil-scarred base,
tooled mouth **$1,500-2,000**
American 1840-1860 (rare)

**Cabiria – Hair Color – Restorer
– Cabiria Co. – New York**
Bright yellow green, 7-1/2", smooth base,
tooled mouth **$150-250**
American 1890-1910

**C.F. Collins – Kallocrine – For The Skin
– & Hair – Middletown Conn**
Light blue green, 6-3/8", pontil-scarred base,
tooled top **$70-100**
American 1840-1860

Circassian – Hair – Restorative – Cincinnati
Yellow amber, 7-3/8", smooth base,
applied mouth **$150-200**
American 1870-1880

Chadwick's – Hair Renewer
Bluish aqua, 7-7/8", smooth base, applied double
collar mouth..**$140-180**
American 1855-1865 (rare)

Church's – Circassian – Hair – Restorer
Medium amber, 7-5/8", smooth base,
applied mouth **$150-200**
American 1870-1880 (rare)

C.S. Emerson's American Hair
Restorative, 1840-1860, 6-3/8",
$350-450. (front and back)

Chas. C. Dissel
Tonic (personalized
bottle), 1885-1925,
11-1/4", $200-300.

Cologne
Water for
Toilet, 1870-
1880, 5-5/8",
$140-180.

Dodge Brothers
- Melanine -Hair
Tonic, 1865-1875,
7-1/2", $600-800.

"Cremex" – Shampooing – Vase – Registered Design
Cobalt blue, 8", smooth base,
tooled mouth $175-275
American 1890-1935 (long crooked
neck with finger grooves)

**C.S. Emerson's – American Hair – Restorative
– Cleveland – Ohio – Price 15c**
Clear glass, 6-3/8", pontil-scarred base,
tooled mouth $350-450
American 1840-1850

**Daniel's – Daniverian – So. Adams
Mass – For The – Hair And Skin**
Aquamarine, 6-1/8", pontil-scarred base,
tooled mouth $100-200
American 1840-1860

Dimick's – Capillary Balm – For The Hair
Aquamarine, 5-7/8", smooth base,
tooled top $70-125
American 1860-1870

Dodge Brothers – Melanine – Hair Tonic
Deep pink amethyst, 7-1/2", smooth base, applied
double collar mouth $600-800
American 1865-1875

Dr. Tebbetts Physiological
Hair Regenerator, 1870-
1880, 7-5/8" $600-900.

Dr. Leons' Electric Hair
Renewer - Ziegler &
Smith, 1870-1880,
7-3/8" $500-
700 (scarce).

Hall's - Hair Renewer, 1890-
1910, 7-1/4", $150-200.

Dr. Leons – Electirc – Hair Renewer
– Ziegler & Smith – Philada
Pink amethyst, 7-3/8", smooth base,
tooled mouth **$500-700**
American 1770-1800 (scarce)

Dr. Tebbetts – Physiological – Hair – Regenerator
Deep strawberry puce, 7-3/8", smooth base, applied
double collar mouth **$200-300**
American 1856-1875

Harris And Morse – Hair Dye – No 1
– Made By – J.B. Harris & Co.
Light blue green, 3-3/8", pontil-scarred base, tooled
top **$70-100**
American 1840-1860

Indian – Hair Restorer – A.A.
Snyder – Paterson – N.J.
Deep cobalt blue, 8-3/4", smooth base, applied square
collar mouth...**$1,500-2,500**
American 1870-1880 (rare)

Ess-Tee-Dee Stops The Dandruff
– S.T. Fustin, Mfr. 2120 W. Van Buren St.
Chicago (label under glass bottle)
Clear glass with red, white, green, and gold label,
8-1/4", smooth base, tooled mouth................**$300-400**
American 1900-1925

Hall's Hair Renewer
Teal blue, 7-1/4" (including stopper), smooth base,
"R.P.H. & Co.," tooled lip.................................**$150-250**
American 1890-1910

Kennedy's Dandruff Cure – Hair
Restorer (label under glass bottle)
Clear glass with white, black, and red label, 7", smooth
base, tooled mouth **$300-400**
American 1895-1930

Kickapoo – Sage – Hair Tonic
Cobalt blue, 4-5/8", smooth base,
tooled mouth...**$300-400**
American 1880-1895

Koken's Heather Bloom (label under glass bottle)
Clear glass with black, white, gold, and red label,
8-3/8", smooth base, "Koken – St. Louis,"
tooled mouth **$250-350**
American 1890-1910 (rare)

Koken's Tonique De Luxe – The Liquid Head Rest
– Design Pat. Applied For (label under glass bottle)
Clear glass with gold, yellow, and red label, 7-3/4",
smooth base, "Koken – St. Louis U.S.A.,"
ABM lip..**$250-350**
American 1920-1930

LeVarn's Golden
Wash Shampoo
- Manufactured by
the Mettowee Toilet
Specialty Co., Granville,
New York, 1890-1920,
7-3/4", $80-120.

Mahdeen For Dandruff
- For Extreme Use Only
-The Mahdeen Company,
Nacogdoches, Texas, 1925-
1935, 8-1/4", $140-180.

Levarn's Antiseptic – Manufactured By The Mettowee Toilet Specialty Co. – Granville, New York (label under glass bottle)
Clear glass with white, gold, and black label, 7-3/4", smooth base, tooled mouth **$60-90**
American 1890-1930

Levarn's Golden Wash Shampoo – Manufactured By The Mettowee Toilet Specialty Co. – Granville, New York (label under glass bottle)
Clear glass with white, gold, and black label, 7-3/4", smooth base, tooled mouth **$80-120**
American 1890-1920

Levarn's Rose Hair Tonic And Dandruff Cure – Manufactured By The Mettowee Toilet Specialty Co. – Granville, New York (label under glass bottle)
Clear glass with white, gold, and black label, 7-3/4", smooth base, tooled mouth **$60-90**
American 1890-1920

Levigated Barber Soap (label under glass bottle)
Clear glass with black, pink, and gold label, 5-1/2", smooth base, "Central Soap Co.-Canton, O – Patented May 25th 1875," ground lip **$400-600**
American 1875-1910 (extremely rare)

Mahdeen For Dandruff – For External Use Only – The Mahdeen Company – Nacogdoches, Texas
Clear glass with white and blue enamel, smooth base, ABM lip **$150-200**
American 1925-1935

Minehaha – Hiawatha – Hair Restorative – Mudjekee Wis
Aquamarine, 6-3/4", smooth base, tooled top..**$70-125**
American 1860-1870

Mrs. S.A. Allen's – Worlds Hair – Restorer – New York
Medium pink amethyst, 7-3/8", smooth base, applied double collar mouth **$250-350**
American 1865-1875

Newbro's Herpicide For The Hair And Scalp (label under glass bottle) [reverse embossed] This Bottle – Is Owned By – The Herpicide Co. – Detroit, Mich – U.S.A.
Clear glass, 8-1/8", smooth base, tooled mouth
....**$375-475**
American 1910-1930

Oldridge's – Balm Of Columbia – For Restoring – Hair – Philadelphia
Aqua, 6-3/8", pontil-scarred base, flared lip ...**$375-500**
American 1830-1850

Osage Rub – Manufactured Only By The Bonheur Company Inc., Syracuse, New York (label under glass bottle)
Clear glass with black, white, and gold label, 8-1/4", smooth base, tooled mouth **$250-350**
American 1900-1920

Mrs. S.A. Allen's Worlds Hair Restorer - New York, 1865-1875, 7-1/4", $200-350.

Oldridge's - Balm Of Columbia - For Restoring - Hair - Philadelphia, 1830-1850, 6-3/8", $375-550 (front and back).

R. R. Hean Tonic
(personalized
bottle), 1885-1925,
8-7/8", $350-450.

**Professor Wood's – Hair Restorative – Depo
– St. Louis, Missouri – And New York**
Aquamarine, 9-1/8", iron pontil base, applied sloping
collar mouth..**$200-400**
American 1845-1860 (rare in this size)

**Property – Of – Lucky Tiger – Dandruff Co.
– K.C. Mo (label under glass bottle)**
Clear glass with yellow, red, black, and white celluloid
label, 7-3/4", smooth base, tooled mouth **$250-350**
American 1900-1925 (rare)

**Property – Of – Lucky – Tiger – Remedy – Co.
– Kansas – City – Mo (painted label bottle, label
reads: Lucky Tiger, For Dandruff and Eczema,
Luck Tiger Remedy Co. Kansas City, Mo)**
Clear glass, 8-5/8", smooth base, tooled mouth with
dispensing top..**$150-250**
American 1890-1930

**Quinine Hair Tonic – Buckeye Barber's Supply
Co. – Dayton, Ohio (label under glass bottle)**
Clear glass with white enamel label with black and gold
decoration, 7-1/8", smooth base, tooled mouth
....**$250-300**
American 1890-1910

W.C. Montgomery's Hair
Restorer, 1865-1875,
7-1/2", $375-475.

Tone 3 Scalp Tonic
- A Pinol Product, 1910-
1925, 9", $150-200.

Over The Top Hair Tonic – Malchior Supply Company, Chicago (label under glass bottle)
Clear glass with black, yellow, red, and white label, 7-7/8", smooth base, tooled mouth $300-400
American 1900-1920

Race's Hair Tonic (label)
Amber, 8-1/8", smooth base, tooled mouth........$40-80
American 1900-1930

Retona A Tonique For The Hair – F.E. Baker & Co. – Lewiston, Me (label under glass bottle)
Clear glass with white, blue, yellow, and gold label, 8-1/4", smooth base, tooled mouth $250-350
American 1890-1925

The Chief – Indian Root And Herb Hair Tonic For Exzema, Dandruff, Falling Hair – Wavenlock Perfume & Supply Co. – Detroit, Mich (label under glass bottle)
Clear glass with multicolored label with an Indian in headdress, 8-1/4", smooth base,
tooled mouth $400-600
American 1900-1920

Tone 3 Scalp Tonic – A Pinol Product
Clear glass, 9", horizontal rib pattern with original painted label, smooth base, ABM lip $140-180
American 1910-1925

Watkins Dandruff Remover – And – Scalp Tonic – J.R. Watkins Company – Winona, Minn U.S.A.
Amber, 7-1/8", smooth base, tooled top.........$300-400
American 1880-1910

W.C. Montgomery's – Hair – Restorer – Philada
Medium copper puce, 7-1/2 ", smooth base, applied double collar mouth $350-450
American 1865-1875

W.C. Montgomery's – Hair – Restorer – Philada
Deep pink amethyst, 7-3/4", smooth base, applied double collar mouth $350-450
American 1865-1875

Wavenlock For The Hair And Scalp (label under glass bottle)
Clear glass with black, white, gold, and yellow, 8-3/8", smooth base, tooled mouth $150-170
American 1880-1920

Crocks/Stoneware

Although crocks are made of pottery rather than glass, many bottle collectors also have crock collections, since they have been found wherever bottles are buried. Crock containers were manufactured in America as early as 1641 and were used extensively in the sale of retail products during the 19th and early 20th centuries. Miniature stoneware jugs were often used for advertising, as were some stoneware canning jars. Storeowners favored crocks because they kept beverages cooler and extended the shelf life of certain products. Crocks appeal to collectors because of their interesting shapes, painted and stenciled decorations, lustrous finishes, and folk art value. In addition, molded stoneware shouldn't be considered mass-produced, as a great deal of detailed design and handwork had to be accomplished on each crock before it was complete.

In the late 1800s, the discovery of microbes in disease-causing bacteria prompted many medicine makers to seize a profitable if not unethical opportunity. An undocumented number of fraudulent cures were foisted on gullible customers. The most infamous of these so-called cures were produced and sold in pottery containers made by William Radam. He was given a patent for his "Microbe Killer" in 1886 and stayed in business until 1907 when the Pure Food and Drug Act ended his scheme. His "cure" was nothing but watered-down wine (wine comprised only one percent of the total contents.)

With the invention of the automatic bottle machine in 1903, glass bottles became cheaper to make and, hence, more common. This contributed to the steady decline of production and the use of pottery crocks and containers.

Advertising Saltglaze Jug (one-half gallon) – Gus Curry 15 & 17 Broad St. Utica NY
Tan, 9-1/2"..**$90-110**
American 1870-1880

Advertising Saltglaze Jug (one-half gallon) – This Jug Not To Be Sold Registered – Hollander Bros – 1-3-5 – Main St. – Paterson – N.J.
Tan, 9", handle..**$100-125**
American 1880-1890

Advertising Pottery Mug – Compliments Of Louis Rupprecht, Scranton, Pa
Cream, black and brown transfer, 4-3/8" **$70-90**
American 1910-1920

Advertising Stoneware Jug – Registered John Dudor Perth Amboy, N.J.
Light cream, blue transfer, 9-1/4", handled.....**$100-150**
American 1890-1910

George Kepnwein - Washington, D.C., 1855-1875, 7-5/8", $100-150.

L.L. Smith - Atlanta, Ga (on shoulder), 1880-1890, 13", $180-250.

One gallon stoneware crock, 1870-1885, 9", $150-250.

One gallon stoneware jug - I.D. McClasky - Wine Merchant - No. 92 Fulton St. Brooklyn, 1869-1875, 10-1/2", $150-200.

Advertising Saltglaze Jug (one-half gallon) – Thos. E. McLaughlin – Wholesale Liquors – Little Falls, NY
Brown and white, 8-1/2" **$20-30**
American 1900-1910

Bellarmine Jug
Orange brown, impressed grotesque face above serpent cartouche, 8-3/4", handle **$300-400**
German 1600-1700

Five-Gallon Saltglaze Stoneware Crock – Evan R. Jones Pittston, Pa
Tan, cobalt slip bird on flower decoration, 13", handled **$2,000-2,500**
American 1870-1880

Four-Gallon Stoneware Crock – Brown Brothers, Huntington L.A. 4'
Grayish tan, cobalt slip floral decoration, 11-1/2", closed double handles **$140-180**
American 1880-1900

Four-Gallon Stoneware Jug – E & L.P. Norton Bennington Vt 4'
Gray, cobalt slip flower decoration, 11-1/2", closed handles **$250-350**
American 1875-1881(rare)

Four-Gallon Stoneware Jug – 4 Satterlee & Mory Ft. Edward, N.Y.
Cream, cobalt slip bird on flower decoration, 17-3/8", handled...**$400-600**
American 1880-1900

Ovoid saltglaze stoneware jug, 1815-1825, 13-1/2", $1,000-1,500.

Four-Gallon Stoneware Water Cooler – Ice Water 4'
Gray, cobalt slip glaze, 17-1/2" $300-400
American 1890-1910

Mini Ovoid Saltglaze Stoneware Oil Jug
Tan, 4-1/8", handle...$140-180
European 1760-1790

**One-Gallon Saltglaze Stoneware Handled
Jug – A.P. Donagho – Parkersburg, W. Va.**
Gray, dark cobalt blue stencil, 11" $70-90
American 1880-1900

**One-Gallon Stoneware Jug – I.D. McClasky
Wine Merchant, No 92 Fulton St. Brooklyn**
Tan, 10-1/2", handled.....................................$150-200
American 1860-1875

**One-Gallon Saltglaze Stoneware Jug
– Nichols & Co. Burlington Vt**
Light gray, dark cobalt slip flower decoration, 11-3/8",
handle...$275-375
American 1854-1860

**One-Gallon Stoneware Jug – Pichel &
Schwab 174 Beckford Ave. Brooklyn**
Cream, cobalt slip lettering, 11",
open handle..$150-200
American 1880-1900

Saltglaze stoneware water cooler, 1875-
1895, 12-1/2", $600-800.

Saltglaze stoneware crock,
J.M. Pruden Manufacturer
Elizabeth, N.J., 1880-
1895, 7-1/2", $200-300.

**One-Gallon Saltglaze Stoneware
Crock – Whites Utica**
Grayish tan, cobalt slip flower decoration, 9-1/4",
closed handles $175-275
American 1856-1860

**One & A Half Gallon Saltglaze Stoneware Crock
– T. Schneider & Sons Union Hill, N.J. 1 1/2'**
Light gray, cobalt slip decoration, 11",
closed handle $350-450
American 1880-1895

**One & A Half Gallon Preserve Jar – W.A. MacQuoid
& Co. Potter Works Little West 12th St. N.Y.**
Tan, 10-1/2", lion's face design $1,200-1,500
American 1870-1880

Ovoid Bellarmine Jug
Brown glaze, 17-1/2", handle.......................$700-1,000
European 1500-1600

Ovoid Stoneware Jug – D. Goodale
Gray, 10-5/8", handle $100-150
American 1818-1822

Ovoid Redware Handled Jug
Redware glaze, 6-3/4", handled......................$150-200
American 1820-1860

Ovoid Redware Handled Jug
Black alkaline glaze, 8-1/4", handled..............$140-160
American 1830-1860

Six gallon saltglaze stoneware crock, O.L. & A.K. Ballard
- Bennington, Vt - 6', 1880-1900, 13-3/4", $400-600.

Saltglaze stoneware water cooler,
1830-1850, 18", $400-500.

Fancy Stoneware Urn - Chas. Graham Patd
April 7th 1885, 1885, 7-5/8", $200-300.

Saltglaze Stoneware Open-Handled Crock – 3 Boston
Dark brown, 14-1/2"......................................$700-900
American 1804-1812

Saltglaze Stoneware Batter Jug – Cowden & Wilcox Harrisburg Pa
Gray, cobalt slip 'Spitting Tulip' floral decoration, 8-5/8", closed handle...............................$1,500-2,500
American 1865-1880

'2' Jas. Benjamin - Stoneware - Depot - Cincinnati, O, 1880-1900, 14", $160-200.

Stoneware ointment pot - T.P. Wreaks Glossop (English), 1860-1880, 2-1/8", $100-145.

Stoneware batter jug - Lewis Jones Pittston, PA 4', 1880-1900, 9", $300-400 (front and side).

Two gallon saltglaze stoneware crock, H.C. Ward - Stoneware - Depot - Zanesville, O, 1880-1900, 9-1/2", $275-375.

Two gallon saltglaze stoneware crock, A.O. Whittemore - Havana, N.Y. - 2', 1880-1900, 11", $1,400-1,800.

Saltglaze Stoneware Barrel
Dark gray, cobalt slip on raised barrel
staves, 22"...**$675-875**
American 1865-1880

Saltglaze Stoneware Crock – Appleby & Helme – 133 Water St. S.E. Cor. Pine
Gray, cobalt slip over lettering, 8-1/4" **$140-180**
American 1855-1865

Saltglaze Stoneware Crock – C. Hart & Son, Sherburne
Gray, cobalt slip over decoration (bird in flight),
7-1/2" **$800-900**
American 1870-1885

Saltglaze Stoneware Crock
Tan, cobalt blue decoration, 4-1/2"....................**$40-60**
American 1870-1890

Saltglaze Stoneware Crock
Tan, cobalt blue decoration, 7" **$40-60**
American 1870-1890

Saltglaze Stoneware Pitcher
Gray, cobalt blue floral decoration, 12-1/2",
handle...**$1,000-1,500**
American 1855-1875

Saltglaze Stoneware Stein – 4 M.C.S. 1824
Light gray, dark cobalt slip on an incised decoration of
a jumping stag, 8-3/4", handle........................**$500-800**
German 1824

Six Gallon Stoneware Water Cooler – Monmouth Filter, Western Stoneware Co.
White, raised floral band around top with raised leaf
decoration around base, cobalt stenciling, 15-3/4"
....**$250-350**
American 1920-1935

Two gallon stoneware jug - '2' - J.J. Duffy - 38 River Street - Troy, N.Y. 1880-1900, 14-1/8", $300-400.

Three gallon saltglaze stoneware crock,
1885-1900, 10-1/4", $250-350.

Three gallon stoneware crock - F.B. Norton & Co.
Worcester, Mass. 3", 1875-1895, 10-1/2", $80-140.

Three gallon saltglaze stoneware crock, Ottman Bro's &
Co - Fort Edward, N.Y. - 3', 1880-1900, 10-1/4", $70-100.

Three gallon ovoid stoneware jug - 3 -
1842, 1840-1850, 14", $375-475.

Small-Size Open-Ear Saltglaze Stoneware Crock
Gray, cobalt slip decoration, 4", open
 handles **$100-150**
German 1830-1860

**Stoneware Handled Jug – Lewis
Fischer & Bro., Jersey City, N.J.**
Cream, black lettering, 14-1/4" **$150-250**
American 1880-1900

Stoneware Batter Jug – Lewis Jones Pittston, Pa 4'
Cream, cobalt slip floral decoration, 9", closed handles
and pour spout..**$300-400**
American 1880-1900

Stoneware Ointment Pot – T.P. Wreaks Glossop
Grayish tan, 2-1/8" **$100-150**
English 1860-1880

**Stoneware Souvenir Mug – World's
Fair Chicago 1893**
Gray, cobalt slip over decoration, 5", handle ..**$100-150**
American 1893

**Two-Gallon Saltglaze Stoneware Crock
– Brady & Ryan Ellenville, N.Y. 2'**
Grayish tan, cobalt slip bird decoration, 9", closed
handles...$375-475
American 1880-1890

**Two-Gallon Saltglaze Stoneware Crock
– G.W. Fulper & Bros., Flemington. N.J.**
Gray, cobalt slip flower decoration, 9-1/4", closed
handles...$300-400
American 1870-1890

**Two-Gallon Saltglaze Stoneware Jug – J.A.
& C.W. Underwood Fort Edward, N.Y. 2'**
Tan, cobalt slip flower decoration, 14-1/4",
handle...$275-400
American 1870-1890

**Two-Gallon Stoneware Jug – 2 J.J.
Duffy, 38 River Steet, Troy, N.Y.**
Cream, cobalt slip stenciling, 14-1/8",
handled...$300-400
American 1880-1900

**Three-Gallon Saltglaze Stoneware Crock
– Adam Caire Poughkeepsie NY 3'**
Cream, cobalt slip flower decoration, 10-1/4", closed
handles...$125-150
American 1875-1890

**Three-Gallon Saltglaze Stoneware Crock
– 3 Cowden & Wilcox – Harrisburg Pa**
Tan, cobalt blue decoration, 10", closed
handle...$200-300
American 1880-1900

**Three Gallon Stoneware Crock – F.B.
Norton & Co. Worcester, Mass. 3'**
Grayish tan, cobalt slip floral decoration, 10-1/2",
closed handles $80-140
American 1875-1895

**Three-Gallon Saltglaze Stoneware Crock – Fort
Edward Stoneware Co, Fort Edward N.Y. 3'**
Gray, cobalt slip flower decoration, 10-1/2", closed
handles...$140-180
American 1870-1890

**Three-Gallon Saltglaze Stoneware
Jug – John Burger Rochester**
Grayish tan, cobalt slip flower decoration, 16-1/8"
handle...$250-350
American 1850-1870

**Three-Fourth Gallon Saltglaze Stoneware Crock
– Feeling Brothers & Co Druggist 142 Water St N.Y.**
Grayish brown, cobalt slip over name,
9-1/8" $600-800
American 1840-1860

Figural Bottles

Figural bottles were produced in large numbers in the late 19th century and early 20th century. The whimsical bottles took on the shapes of animals, people, boots, and books, among other objects. They came in a wide variety of colors and sizes and were quite popular among wealthy aristocrats of that time.

Figural Applied Face
Bear bottle, 1885-1910,
10-7/8", $400-600.

Figural Artillery Shell
bottle (French), 1885-
1900, 9-3/4", $150-200.

Apple Bottle
Frosted green glass, apple form, 5-1/8", smooth base,
ground lip, applied handle..............................**$150-200**
European 1890-1920

Banjo Bottle – Pan-American (motif of bison) – Exposition
Clear glass, 7", smooth base, ground lip, metal screw
cap..**$140-180**
American 1901 (rare Pan-American Expo item)

Barrel Dispensing Bottle – 10
Deep cobalt blue, 14-7/8", smooth base, ground lip,
applied ring of glass around dispensing hole..**$500-700**
French 1880-1910

Beehive Bottle
Clear glass, beehive shape, 6-1/2", smooth base,
tooled mouth **$80-140**
American 1890-1915

Bon-Bon Jar
Clear glass, 12", embossed with wreaths on front,
smooth base, sheared and ground lip.............**$200-300**
French 1890-1910

Cannon Bottle (miniature)
Medium yellow amber with olive tone, 9-3/4",
smooth base, tooled mouth, blown-in four-part
mold **$175-275**
American 1890-1910

Cannon Bottle – R & G.A. Wright – Philada (Label: The Great Gun Lau De Cologne, Gold Medal Perfumery, Manufactured By R. & G.A. Wright Philadelphia)
Smoky copper with puce tone, 12-1/4", smooth base,
tooled mouth **$500-700**
American 1865-1875

Car (miniature) – Mirabel (across hood)
Deep blue aqua, 2-7/8" long, tooled mouth........**$70-90**
European 1900-1920

Castle Bottle
Clear glass castle with Eiffel Tower embossed
on one side and a castle on the other side, 10" h.,
pontil-scarred base, tooled mouth..................**$150-200**
French 1890-1910

Figural Cannon bottle - Phalon & Son, 1890-1910, 5-5/8", $200-300.

Figural Cannon bottle, 1890-1910, 9-3/4", $175-275.

Figural Ear of Corn bottle (European), 1890-1920, 8-3/4", $350-400.

Christmas Tree – Kyselak (on side at base)
Olive green, 9-1/2", smooth base, tooled
mouth **$150-180**
American 1900-1920

Cockatoo Bottle
Black amethyst, 13-1/2", smooth base,
ground lip **$300-400**
American 1890-1910

Double Cherub Bottle – Aottaoio – Aspasia
Mint green milk glass, 9-3/4", smooth base, "Salve" on
bottom, applied sloping collar mouth **$400-600**
European 1890-1920

Dutchman Bottle
Clear glass, 4", smooth base, sheared
tooled lip **$80-120**
European 1900-1920

**Falcon Bottles (2) – Distilerias El Lorito
Benetuser Valencia (around base)**
Milk glass, 8" and 10" h., smooth bases,
ABM lips **$140-180**
European 1920-1930

Fish
Clear glass, 11-7/8", smooth base,
tooled mouth **$275-375**
American 1880-1900

Goose Egg Whiskey Nip
Milk glass with multicolored floral decoration with the
words "Jed Clayton Rye," 4-3/8", smooth base, ground
lip, metal screw-on cap **$250-350**
American 1890-1910

Grants Tomb
Milk glass monument with pewter bust of Grant,
smooth base, ground lip **$800-1,200**
American 1893-1895 (rare)

Hand (ceramic) Bottle
Yellow ware pottery, 10-7/8", bottle narrows to the
wrist and becomes the bust of Admiral Dewey at the
mouth **$350-450**
American 1880-1900

Lemon – Paul Mangiet – Will Hand – You One
Pale aqua, 4-1/4" long, sheared and ground lip
....**$80-140**
American 1890-1915

Lighthouse Bottle
Frosted clear glass, 6-sided, 9-1/4" h., smooth base,
tooled mouth **$200-300**
French 1880-1910

Locomotive
Clear glass, 4-3/4" h., smooth base, ground
lip...**$150-250**
French 1890-1915

Maiden Bottle
Medium blue green, 13", pontil-scarred base, tooled
mouth **$600-800**
French 1890-1910

Man Smoking A Long-Stemmed Pipe Bottle
Medium amber, 11-3/4", smooth base, tooled
mouth **$275-375**
American 1890-1910

**Monkey Sitting On A Barrel Pulling
Hat Down Over Ears**
Milk glass, 9-3/8", smooth base, "Glschutt" on bottom,
tooled lip..**$500-700**
European 1890-1915 (rare)

Moon Mullins Bottle
Brown glazed pottery, 7", smooth base..........**$500-700**
American 1923-1930

Figural Fountain bottle
(French), 1890-1920,
11", $200-300.

Figural Grandfather's
Clock bottle,
1885-1910, 7-7/8",
$140-180.

Figural Guard House bottle (French), 1890-1915, 13-1/8", $350-450.

Figural Hand Holding a Bottle (French), 1890-1920, 7-1/8", $150-200.

Figural Ladies Lower Leg with Victorian Period Shoe bottle, 1885- 1910, 14-3/4", $200-275.

Figural Liberty Bell, 1876 (Proclaim Liberty Throughout The Land, 1776 Centennial Exposition 1876), $150-250.

Figural Man Sitting on a Barrel bottle,
1895-1910, 9-1/2", $200-275.

Rabbit candy container,
1925-1935, 5-1/2", $250-300.

Negro Waiter
Frosted clear glass with black glass head, 14-3/8",
smooth base, sheared and ground lip,
original stopper $300-400
American 1890-1910

Oyster Bottle
Aqua, 6" h, smooth base, ground lip, screw-on
cap...$80-140
American 1890-1910

Pistol (freeblown)
Medium amethyst (barrel and handle), clear glass (hand
grips), 13-1/8" h., sheared and ground lip (end
of barrel) $275-475
European 1900-1910

Pocket Watch Bottle
Clear glass, 5-1/4", "Time To Drink" on back, smooth
base, ground lip, screw-on cap.......................$150-200
American 1885-1910

Policeman Bottle
Deep green aqua, 8-3/4", pontil scar base,
sheared lip $70-100
German 1890-1920

**Political Coin Bottle – E. Pluribus Unum – Bust Of
Miss Liberty With Word "Liberty" In Head Band,
"1885" (on front) – (on reverse) United States Of
America One Dollar – In God We Trust – Eagle**
Clear glass, 4-1/2", smooth base, ground lip, screw-on
cap...$250-350
American 1885-1900

**Revolver – Standard Perf Wk's
– Patented Nov 6th 1883**
Deep amber, 10" long, tooled mouth $150-200
American 1883-1900

Roasted Turkey Bottle
Clear glass, 4-3/4" l., smooth base, ground lip, screw-
on cap $80-120
American 1885-1910

Ship Bottle
Frosted clear glass, 6-1/2" h., 9-1/4" l., smooth base,
ground lip $250-350
French 1890-1915 (scarce)

Shirt Bottle
Milk glass, 4-5/8", smooth base, ground lip, metal
screw cap $70-100
American 1890-1910

Figural Santa Claus bottle - Super Fine Liquor, Crème De Menthe, Artificially Colored, Extra Quality, 1885-1910, 12-1/4", $400-500.

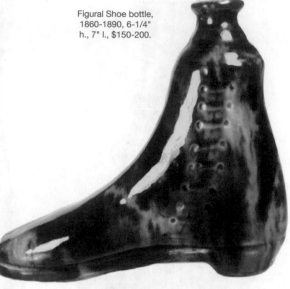

Figural Shoe bottle, 1860-1890, 6-1/4" h., 7" l., $150-200.

Sitting Bear With Paw In Air Bottle
Blue and white bisque, 7-1/4", "Teddy's Bear" embossed on back...**$400-600**
European 1900-1920

Sitting Oriental Man Bottle
Clear glass, 5-7/8", smooth base, ground lip...**$180-275**
American 1885-1910

Shoe With Protruding Toe Bottle
Black glass, 5-1/2" l., smooth base, ground lip, screw-on cap **$140-180**
American 1885-1910

Shore Bird
Milk glass, pontil-scarred base, tooled mouth **$600-900**
American 1890-1910 (scarce)

Standing Portly Man Bottle
Bluish aqua, 11-3/4", "M. Husted" between legs, smooth base, tooled mouth **$600-900**
American 1885-1910

Steamer Trunk Whiskey Nip Bottle (Label: A Merry Christmas And A Happy New Year, J. Christman)
Clear glass, 5", smooth base, tooled lip **$150-200**
American 1885-1910

Three Cherubs Holding A Ball Over Their Heads Bottle
Bluish aqua, 8-1/2", pontil-scarred base, tooled lip..**$200-300**
French 1885-1910

Truffle Bottle
Dark smoky puce, 3-7/8" h., pontil-scarred base, tooled mouth **$100-150**
European 1890-1920

Turk Sitting On A Drum Bottle
Red amber, 11-3/4", smooth base, applied mouth **$800-1,200**
European 1875-1885 (rare)

Turtle Bottle – Good Luck And Horseshoe Embossed On Underside
Clear glass, 5-1/4" l., smooth base, ground lip, original screw-on cap..**$150-200**
American 1885-1910

U.S. Mail Box Whiskey Bottle – U.S. (motif of flying eagle) Mail (on both panels) (Label: U.S. Mail Box Rye Special Delivery, Rheinstrom Bros, Sole Proprietors, Cincinnati, U.S.A.)
Clear glass, 8-3/4", smooth base, "Patented – Dec. 15 1891," tooled lip **$300-500**
American 1891-1910 (rare with label)

Violin Bottle
Yellow amber, 6-1/2", rough sheared lip **$350-450**
American 1885-1910

Violin Bottle
Yellow amber, 18", smooth base, tooled lip **$350-450**
American 1885-1910 (rare in this size)

Windmill Decanter
Turquoise blue with multicolored enamel decoration
of a tree, two windows and a door, smooth base,
ground lip **$250-350**
American 1890-1920

Young Girl Sitting On A Basket Bottle
Clear glass with frosted girl, 8-1/2", pontil-scarred
base, tooled lip **$200-300**
European 1890-1920

Figural Wall Clock bottle,
early Clevenger Brothers
piece (20th century),
11-3/8", $80-120.

Fire Grenades

Fire grenades are highly prized items among bottle collectors and represent one of the first modern improvements in fire fighting. A fire grenade is a water-filled bottle about the size of a baseball. It was designed to be thrown into a fire, where it would break and (hopefully) extinguish the flames. They worked best when the fire was noticed immediately.

The first American patent on a fire grenade was issued in 1863 to Alanson Crane of Fortress Monroe, Va. The best known manufacturer of these highly specialized bottles was the Halden Fire Extinguisher Co., Chicago, Ill., which was awarded a patent in August 1871.

Fire grenade, horizontal rib pattern, 1880-1895, 6-1/4", $250-350.

The grenades were manufactured in large numbers by companies with names as unique as the bottles themselves: Dash-Out, Diamond, Harkness Fire Destroyer, Hazelton's High Pressure Chemical Firekeg, Magic Fire, and Y-Burn. The fire grenade became obsolete with the invention of the fire extinguisher in 1905. Many of these grenades can still be found with the original closures, contents, and labels.

Grenade, ETS.
Hofer Sapfeu
Caluire (Rhone)
Extinctrice, Label:
Grenade, Ets.
Hofer, Sapfeu,
Caluire (Rhone),
Extinctrice
(European), 1890-
1910, 8-1/2",
$400-600.

**Babcock – Hand Grenade – Non-Freezing
– Manf'd By Fire Extinguisher M'f'g Co
– 325 – 331 S. Des Plaines St. Chicago**
Medium cobalt blue, 7-1/2", smooth base, sheared and
ground lip **$3,000-4,000**
American 1875-1895 (rare)

**Babcock – Hand Grenade – Non-Freezing
– Manufactured By American-La France
Fire Engine Co – Elmira, N.Y.**
Medium amber, 7-1/2", smooth base,
ground lip **$2,000-3,000**
American 1875-1895 (Note: rare Babcock from Elmira
N.Y. These grenades were made only for a short time by
the American-La France Fire Engine Co. of Elmira. Today,
American-La France is one of the major manufacturers of
firefighting equipment).

Harden Grenade
Sprinkler (English),
1880-1900,
17-1/4", $700-800.

Grenade - Unic
- Extingrice
(embossed on
three circular
shoulder panels)
(French), 1880-
1900, 5-3/4",
$375-475.

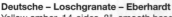

Harden's Hand Fire Extinguisher Grenade - Patented
No.1 - Aug. 8, 1871 Aug.14, 1883, 6-1/4", $60-80.

Harden's Hand Grenade Fire
Extinguisher, 1880-1895, 6-3/4", $80-120.

Deutsche – Loschgranate – Eberhardt
Yellow amber, 14-sides, 8", smooth base, "Gesetzlich-
Geschutzt," sheared and ground lip................**$400-600**
German 1910-1930 (very rare)

Fire Grenade – Vertical Rib-Pattern
Medium green, 5-1/2", smooth base, ABM
mouth **$275-375**
English 1910-1920 (rare)

Fire Grenade – Vertical Rib-Pattern
Cobalt blue, 6-1/4", smooth base, tooled
mouth **$350-400**
American 1880-1895

Fire Grenade
Medium amber, 6-1/2", smooth base, tooled lip, back
panel is flat with center groove **$375-500**
American 1880-1900 (rare, had a metal holder allowing it
to be hung on a wall)

**Fire Grenade – C & NW RY (Chicago
& Northwestern Railroad)**
Clear glass, 17-3/4", smooth base, sheared
lip..**$175-275**
American 1880-1900

**Grenade – Extincteur – Systeme
– Labbe – L'Incombustibilite Paris**
Yellow amber, 5", smooth base, ground lip, original
contents..**$300-400**
French 1880-1890

Grenade – L'urbaine
Cobalt blue, rib-pattern, 6-1/2", smooth base, ground
lip..**$400-600**
French 1880-1900 (scarce)

**Harden's Improved Grenade Fire
Extinguisher Patd. Oct. 7th 1884**
Two piece grenade wired together, half is cobalt
blue and other half is clear, 4-3/4", smooth base,
ground lip **$375-475**
American 1885-1895 (rare)

**Harden's Hand – Grenade – Fire – Extinguisher
– Patented – No. 7 – Aug. 8 1871 – Aug 14 1883**
Smoky light green, 6-1/4", smooth footed base, tooled
mouth **$400-600**
American 1875-1895 (rare color)

**Harden's Hand – Grenade – Fire – Extinguisher
– Patented – No. 2 – Aug. 8 1871 – Aug 14 1883**
Turquoise blue, 5-1/8", smooth footed base, rough
sheared and ground lip **$175-250**
American 1875-1895

**Harden's Hand – Grenade – Fire
– Extinguisher – Patented**
Lavender blue, 4-7/8", smooth footed base, rough
sheared lip **$250-350**
American 1875-1895

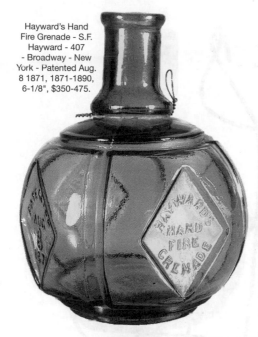

Hayward's Hand
Fire Grenade - S.F.
Hayward - 407
- Broadway - New
York - Patented Aug.
8 1871, 1871-1890,
6-1/8", $350-475.

Hayward's Hand
Fire Grenade - S.F.
Hayward - 407 -
Broadway - New
York - Patented Aug.
8 1871, 1875-1895,
6-1/8", $200-300.

Hazelton's - High Pressure - Chemical - Fire
Keg, 1880-1900, 11", $250-300.

Harden's Hand – Grenade – Fire – Extinguisher – Patented – No. 2 – Aug. 8 1871 – Aug 14 1883
Light sapphiro blue, 5-1/4", smooth footed base, rough sheared and ground lip **$175-250**
American 1875-1895

Harkness – Fire – Destroyer
Medium sapphire blue, 6-1/4", smooth base, ground lip, original contents **$500-700**
American 1880-1900

Harkness – Fire Extinguisher
Medium cobalt blue, horizontal rib-pattern, 6-1/8", smooth base, ground lip **$600-800**
American 1880-1900

Harkness – Fire Extinguisher
Medium blue, horizontal rib-pattern, 6-1/8", smooth base, ground lip...**$500-700**
American 1880-1900 (scarce)

Harkness – Fire – Destroyer (Label: Patented Sept. 19th 1874 And February 1878, Improved 1881)
Cobalt blue, horizontal-rib pattern, 6-1/4", smooth base, ground lip...**$250-300**
American 1871-1895

Hayward Hand Grenade Fire Extinguisher – New York
Pale aqua, pint, 6", smooth base, "Design Patd,," tooled lip, original contents............................**$275-375**
American 1875-1885

The Imperial Grenade - Fire - Extinguisher (with original metal carrier) (English), 1880-1900, 6-5/8", $600-800.

Imperial Grenade Fire Extinguisher (English), 1880-1895, 6-1/2", $375-475.

Star (inside star) Harden Star Hand Grenade - Fire Extinguisher, Label: How To Use, Throw the Grenade Into the Hottest Part of the Fire (English), 1880-1900, 7", $250-350.

Hayward Hand Grenade Fire Extinguisher – New York (pleated panel grenade)
Cobalt blue, pint, 6", smooth base, "Design Patd.," tooled lip, original contents **$300-400**
American 1875-1885 (pleated panels are more scarce than diamond panels)

Hayward Hand Grenade Fire Extinguisher – New York
Medium grass green, 6", smooth base, "Design Patd.," embossed neck foil has "Trade Mark" and "Hayward Hand Fire Grenade," tooled lip, original contents **$600-800**
American 1875-1885

Hayward – Hand Fire – Grenade – Patented – Aug-8-1871 – S.F. Hayward – 407 – Broadway – New York
Turquoise blue, 6-1/4", smooth base, tooled lip **$350-450**
American 1871-1895

HSN (Harvey S. Nutting – monogram on two diamond panels)
Yellow with amber tone, 7", grooved smooth base, rough sheared lip **$180-200**
American 1880-1890

Imperial Grenade – Fire – Extinguisher
Medium emerald green, 6-1/2", smooth base, ground lip **$375-475**
English 1880-1900

Magic – Fire – Extinguisher Co.
Yellow with amber tone, 6-1/4", smooth base, rough sheared lip **$600-800**
American 1875-1895

PSH (monogram on two diamond panels)
Yellow amber, 7", grooved smooth base, tooled lip **$250-350**
American 1880-1890

Rockford – Kalamazoo – Automatic And – Hand Fire Extinguisher – Patent Applied For
Deep cobalt blue, 10-3/4", smooth base, tooled mouth, original contents...**$400-600**
American 1875-1895

Soda – Acid Fire Extinguisher Bottle – Acid Line – Manufactured By – Badger Fire – Extinguisher Co. – Boston, Mass. – U.S.A.
Clear, 6", smooth base, tooled mouth.............**$100-125**
American 1890-1900

Star (inside star on flat panel) – Harden Star Hand Grenade – Fire Extinguisher
Deep cobalt blue, pint, 6-1/2", smooth base, "Regd – No – 10490," ground lip, original contents ...**$250-350**
English 1884-1895

Star (inside star on flat panel) – Harden Star Hand Grenade – Fire Extinguisher
Brilliant green, quart, 7-7/8", smooth base, "M 7 84," ground lip, original contents............................**$200-250**
American 1884-1895

Star (inside star on flat panel) – Harden Star Hand Grenade – Fire Extinguisher
Deep blue, pint, 6-5/8", smooth base ground lip, original contents..**$200-250**
American 1884-1895

Star (inside a star) – Harden Grenade – Sprinkler
Deep cobalt blue, 17-1/4", smooth base, "RD No 60064," tooled lip **$700-900**
English 1880-1900 (scarce)

Systeme – Labbe (motif of anchor) Grenade – Extincteur (diamond pattern inside four circular panels) L'incombustibilite – Paris
Golden yellow amber, 5-7/8", smooth base, ground lip **$275-375**
French 1880-1900

The Kalamazoo – Automatic And – Hand Fire Extinguisher – Patent Applied For
Cobalt blue, 10-7/8", smooth base, tooled mouth **$300-400**
American 1875-1895

W.D. Allen Manufacturing Company – Chicago, Illinois (crescent moon)
Medium yellowish green, 8-1/4", smooth base, ground lip...**$500-700**
American 1875-1895 (rare in this color)

Systeme - Labbe (motif of anchor) Grenade - Extincteur (diamond pattern inside four circular panels) L'incombustibilite - Paris (French), 1880-1900, 5-7/8", $275-375.

Flasks

Flasks have become a most popular and prized item among collectors due to the variety of decorative, historical, and pictorial depictions on many pieces. The outstanding colors have had a major effect on their value, more so than on most other collectible bottles.

American flasks were first manufactured by the Pitkin Glasshouse in Connecticut around 1815 and quickly spread to other glasshouses around the country. Early flasks were free-blown and represent some of the better craftsmanship, displaying more intricate designs. By 1850, approximately 400 designs had been used. Black graphite pontil marks were left on the bottles because the pontils were coated with powdered iron to allow the flask's bottom to break away without damaging the glass. The flasks made between 1850 and 1870, however, had no such markings because of the widespread use of the newly invented snap case.

Since flasks were intended to be refilled with whiskey or other spirits, more time and effort was expended on manufacturing them than on most other types of bottles. Flasks soon became a popular item for use with all types of causes and promotions. Mottos were frequently were embossed on flasks and included a number of patriotic sayings and slogans. George Washington's face commonly appeared on flasks, as did Andrew Jackson's and John Quincy Adams', the candidates for the presidential elections of 1824 and 1828. Events of the time were also portrayed on flasks.

One of the more controversial specimens was the Masonic flask, which bore the order's emblem on one side and the American eagle on the other. At first, the design drew strong opposition from the public, but the controversy soon passed, and Masonic flasks are now a specialty item for collectors.

Another highly collectible flask was the Pitkin-type flask, named for the Pitkin Glassworks where it was exclusively manufactured. While Pitkin-type flasks and ink bottles are common, Pitkin bottles, jugs, and jars are very rare. German Pitkin flasks are heavier and straight-ribbed, while the American patterns are swirled and broken-ribbed with unusual colors such as dark blue.

Because flasks were widely used for promoting various political and special interest agendas, they represent a major historical record of the people and events of those times.

Baltimore Glass Works
- Resurgam, 1865-1875,
8", $800-1,000.

Clasped Hands
- Eagle, 1865-1870,
6-1/4", $150-200.

Bennington flask
(English), 1875-
1895, 7-5/8",
$140-180.

Corn For The World
- Ear Of Corn -
Monument - Baltimore,
1870-1875, 8-1/2",
$6,000-8,000.

**Adams & Jefferson July 4 A.D. 1776
– General Washington – Bust Of Washington
– Kensington Glass Works Philadelphia
– E. Pluribus Unum – Eagle – T.W.D.**
Medium blue green, pint, pontil-scarred base, sheared
lip...**$4,500-6,500**
American 1825-1835 (Note: commemorates the death of
Presidents Thomas Jefferson and John Adams)

**A – Merry – Christmas (girl on a barrel)
– And A – Happy New Year – (cock on
barrel staves) Pictorial Flask**
Light yellow amber, pint, smooth base, tooled double
collar top **$500-1,000**
American 1880-1900 (extremely rare)

**American System – Paddle Wheeler – Use Me
But Do Not Abuse Me – Sheaf Of Wheat**
Greenish aqua, pint, pontil-scarred base, rough
sheared lip...**$15,000-20,000**
American 1824-1828 (Note: a sought-after historic flask
that was blown in the Page & Bakewell Glasshouse in
Pittsburgh to commemorate the passing of the Protective
Tariff Act of 1824)

**Andy Balich – 170 Pacific Ave. – Santa
Cruz, Cal. – Net Contents 6 Oz.**
Aqua, half-pint, smooth base, tooled mouth.......**$75-95**
American 1908-1918

**Arnett G. Smith – 14 – Fulton – St – New
York (strapside flask – partial label reading
Irish Whiskey – Arnett G. Smith)**
Amber, quart, smooth base, tooled double
collar mouth...**$80-100**
American 1885-1910

Baltimore – Anchor – Glassworks – Sheaf Of Grain
Orange amber, quart, pontil-scarred base, sheared and
tooled lip...**$600-800**
American 1865-1875

**Bininger's – Clock Face – Regulator
– 19 Broad St – New York**
Deep amber, pint, pontil-scarred base, applied double
collar mouth...**$350-450**
American 350-450

Booth & Co. – Sacramento (embossed anchor)
Clear, pint, smooth base, tooled mouth **$100-125**
American 1890-1903 (rare)

**Bridgeton New Jersey – Bust Of Washington
– Bridgeton New Jersey – Bust Of Taylor**
Bluish aqua, quart, pontil-scarred base,
tooled mouth **$125-175**
American 1820-1835

C.C. Goodale – Full 1/2 Pt – Rochester N.Y.
Golden yellow amber, half-pint, smooth base,
tooled mouth **$140-180**
American 1880-1890 (scarce)

Corset waist
"J.R. & Son"
scroll flask,
1840-1850,
7-1/2",
$700-1,000.

Eagle with Banner,
calabash, 1855-
1860, $300-400.

Eagle - Eagle,
1835-1845, 6-3/4",
$180-275.

Eagle - Pittsburgh
- Pa - Eagle,
1865-1875, 8-3/4",
$400-700.

Eagle - Pittsburgh - Pa
- Eagle, 1865-1875,
9-1/4", $140-180.

C.C. Goodale – Full Pt – Rochester N.Y.
Medium apple green, pint, smooth base,
tooled mouth $400-600
American 1885-189 (rare in this color)

**Civil War Period Whiskey Flask – E.
Wattis Jr – Philada (on base)**
Clear glass, pint, upper half wrapped in leather, smooth
base, ground lip...$175-275
American 1860-1870

Cluster Of Grapes – Coat Of Arms
Lime green, half-pint, pontil-scarred base,
tooled lip..$75-125
European 1850-1890

Coffin Flask (unembossed)
Deep opalescent milk glass, pint, smooth base,
tooled mouth $150-200
American 1880-1900

Concentric Ring Eagle – Eagle Flask
Medium yellow green, quart, pontil-scarred base,
tooled lip..$6,000-9,000
American 1825-1835 (rare)

Corn For The World – Ear-Of-Corn – Monument
Clear glass with amethyst tint, quart, pontil-scarred
base, sheared lip **$600-800**
American 1825-1835

Cornucopia – Urn
Golden yellow amber, half-pint, pontil-scarred base,
tooled lip...**$140-180**
American 1825-1835

Cornucopia – Urn
Bluish aqua, pint, pontil-scarred base, tooled
mouth **$250-350**
American 1840-1850

Cornucopia – Urn
Deep blue green, pint, open pontil,
tooled lip..**$475-600**
American 1835-1845 (scarce color)

**Cunninghams & Ihmsen
– Glassmakers Pittsburgh, Pa**
Bluish aqua, strapside pint, smooth base, applied
mouth **$100-150**
American 1880-1890

D. Kirkpatrick & Co – Eagle – Chattanooga – Tenn
Greenish aqua, quart, smooth base,
applied mouth **$2,500-3,500**
American 1865-1880 (extremely rare Tennessee flask)

Horse Pulling
Cart - Eagle,
1825-1835, 8-1/2",
quart, $275-375.

Eagle - Louisville - KY - Glassworks,
1840-1850, half-pint, $150-200.

Easley's (motif of hand) Saloon - Huntsville - Rough &
(man walking with bottle in hand) Ready H. Easley's, 1860-
1870, 6-3/8", $5,500-7,000. (front and back)

Dancer – Chapman – Soldier – Balt. Md
Olive green, pint, smooth base, applied
ring mouth **$1,800-2,800**
American 1865-1875 (desirable color)

Dancer – Chapman – Soldier – Balt. Md
Teal blue, pint, smooth base, applied
mouth **$250-350**
American 1865-1875

Eagle – Coffin & Hay – Standing Deer – Hammonton
Aqua, pint, pontil-scarred base, sheared and
tooled lip..**$375-475**
American 1825-1835 (scarce, South Jersey Glasshouse)

**Eagle – Continental – Indian Shooting Bire
– Cunninghams & Co – Pittsburgh, Pa**
Deep yellow green, quart, smooth base, applied square
collar mouth..**$2,500-3,500**
American 1865-1875

**Eagle – Continental – Indian Shooting Bire
– Cunninghams & Co – Pittsburgh, Pa**
Deep aqua, quart, smooth base, applied collar
mouth **$200-300**
American 1860-1875

Label-under-glass pocket flask - Compliments of Reiff
& Adams Bridgeport, Conn, 1880-1900, 6", $500-700.

Eagle – Geo. A. Berry & Co. – Eagle
Bluish aqua, pint, smooth base, applied
ringed lip...**$120-180**
American 1860-1870

Eagle – Eagle
Yellow amber, half-pint, pontil-scarred base, sheared
and tooled lip..**$120-140**
American 1855-1870

Eagle – Farley & Taylor – Richmond, Ky
Greenish aqua, gallon, open pontil, tooled
mouth **$5,000-7,000**
American 1830-1840

**Easley's (motif of hand) – Saloon
– Huntsville – Rough & (man walking with
bottle in hand) Ready – H. Easley's**
Aqua, half-pint, 6-3/8", smooth base, applied ringed
mouth **$5,500-7,000**
American 1860-1870

Flower – Heart
Blue green, quart, pontil-scarred base,
sheared lip...**$2,500-3,500**
American 1845-1860 (rare)

For Pike's Peak – Prospector – Eagle – Pittsburgh Pa
Deep bluish aqua, pint, smooth base, applied
mouth **$100-175**
American 1965-1875

**French Brandy – From – F.L. Allan – 33 State Street
New London, Conn (labeled whiskey flask)**
Reddish amber, pint, smooth base, applied double
collar mouth..**$250-500**
American 1860-1866 (New London Glassworks, New
London, Conn.)

**Frigate – Franklin – Free Trade And Sailors
Rights – Masonic Arch – Kensington
Glass Works Philadelphia**
Pale greenish aqua, pint, pontil-scarred base,
tooled lip..**$200-275**
American 1825-1835

Granite – Glass – Co. – Stoddard – N.H.
Olive amber, pint, pontil-scarred base, sheared and
tooled lip..**$350-450**
American 1850-1865

**Hendricks (bust of Hendricks)
– Cleveland (bust of Cleveland)**
Clear glass, pint pumpkinseed flask, smooth base "J.R.
Hartigans – Patent, Pitts," tooled mouth.........**$700-900**
American 1884 (Note: rare political flask made for 1884
Presidential campaign between Grover Cleveland and
James Blaine

Hourglass Masonic Flask
Light yellow olive, swirl of amber at base, half-pint,
pontil-scarred, sheared mouth................**$6,000-12,000**
American 1814-1830 (Coventry Glass Works, Coventry,
Conn.)

Horse Pulling Cart – Eagle
Yellow olive, pint, pontil-scarred base, sheared and
tooled lip..**$200-250**
American 1825-1835

Hunter – Hound (handled)
Medium amber, pint, pontil-scarred base, tooled lip and
pour spout **$7,000-8,000**
American 1855-1870 (rare, only a few known to exist)

Iron Front (motif of steer's head)
Neff & Duff – Austin Texas
Clear glass with amethystine tint, pint, cobweb pattern,
6-5/8", smooth base, tooled mouth **$6,000-8,000**
American 1879-1881 (most desirable Texas flask)

Isabella – Anchor – Glassworks – Glass Factory
Aqua green, quart, 9-3/8" open pontil, applied collar
mouth **$275-375**
American 1865-1875

Jno. F. Horne – Knoxville, Tenn (strapside flask)
Amber, quart, smooth base, applied mouth **$80-100**
American 1885-1910

Liberty – Eagle – Willington – Glass
– Co – West Willington – Conn
Medium blue green, half-pint, smooth base, applied
double collar mouth **$500-700**
American 1856-1875

L.N. Kreinbrook's – Bitters – Mt.
Pleasant – Pa (flask bitters bottle)
Bright yellow amber, pint, coffin-shaped form, smooth
base, tooled sloping collar mouth with
ring **$750-1,500**
American 1860-1890

Log Cabin – Hard Cider (below
flag, barrel, and plow)
Deep blue aqua, pint, pontil-scarred base,
sheared lip **$6,000-8,000**
American 1840-1845 (made for William Henry Harrison
Presidential campaign of 1840)

Louis Kossuth – Bust Of Kossuth – Frigate – U.S.
Steam Frigate – Mississippi – S. Huffsey
Medium blue green, calabash, pontil-scarred base,
"Dolphin Mould Maker – Nth 5T ST 84," applied sloping
collar mouth...**$1,200-1,800**
American 1850-1860

Masonic Arch – Eagle
Medium blue green, pint, pontil-scarred base, tooled
mouth **$3,500-4,500**
American 1815-1825 (rare)

Masonic Arch – Zanesville – Eagle – Ohio
(inside oval) J. Shepard & Co.
Bright yellow olive, pint, pontil-scarred base, tooled
mouth **$3,000-4,000**
American 1825-1835

M'Carty & Torreyson – Manufacturers
– Wellsburg, Va (sunburst)
Light blue apple green, quart, iron pontil,
sheared lip **$1,800-2,800**
American 1845-1855 (very rare)

Mohns & Kaltenbach – M & K – 29
Market Street – San Francisco
Clear, pint, smooth base, tooled mouth **$125-150**
American 1890-1910 (rare)

Monument – A – Little – More – Grape – Capt Bragg
Medium yellow olive, half-pint, pontil-scarred base,
sheared and tooled lip.............................**$2,500-3,500**
American 1825-1835 (rare color)

Nailsea Flask
Clear glass with white loopings, 8-3/8", pontil-scarred
base, tooled mouth **$350-450**
English 1840-1860

Newmark Gruenberg & Co. – Old Judge Pony S.F.
Clear, pint, smooth base, tooled mouth **$100-150**
American 1900-1910 (rare)

Octopus Draped Over Silver Dollar Flask
Milk glass, 4-1/2", smooth base, ground lip, metal
screw-on cap..**$500-900**
American 1901 (1901 is embossed near the base)

Our Choice – Bust Of Cleveland Facing Bust
Of Stevenson – Cleve & Steve – November
8th 92 – March 4th 93 – Rooster
Aqua, half-pint, smooth base, tooled mouth...**$250-350**
American 1892 (made for the 1892 Presidential
campaign)

Patrick Smith
- 1313 - Sec.
Ave. - NW
Corner 69th
St. - New York
- One - Half Pint
- Full Measure,
1890-1910, half-
pint, $80-150.

Success To The Railroad - Locomotive (reverse
same), 1825-1835, pint, $1,800-2,000.

Success To The
Railroad - Horse
Pulling Cart (reverse
same), 1825-1835,
pint, $150-200.

Sunburst flask,
1850-1850, 5-5/8",
$300-400.

**Pocket Spirits Flask (walking bear on one
side and trees and the date 1851)**
Clear glass with copper wheel cut decoration, pontil-
scarred base, wide outward rolled lip **$250-350**
German 1851

**Republican Gratitude – General La Fayette
– Bust Of La Fayette – Kensington Glass Works
Philadelphia – E. Pluribus Unum – Eagle – T.W.D**
Aqua, pint, 6-5/8", open pontil, tooled and
sheared lip **$300-400**
American 1825-1830 (scarce, Kensington Glassworks)

S (motif of palm tree) C – Dispensary
Clear glass, 6-3/4", smooth base, tooled
mouth **$45-60**
American 1893-1900

SCD (monogram) – S.C. – Dispensary
Clear glass, 6-3/4", smooth base, tooled
mouth **$45-60**
American 1893-1900

SCD (monogram) – S.C. – Dispensary
Clear glass, 7-7/8", smooth base, "C.F.F.C.CO.," tooled
mouth **$45-60**
American 1893-1900

U.S. (Battleship Maine) Battleship Maine, 1898-1905, 5-3/4", $250-350.

The Hero Of Manila (bust of Admiral Dewey), 1898-1910, 5-3/4", $250-350.

Schwan – Palerson – N.J. (strapside flask)
Amber, quart, smooth base, tooled double
collar mouth..**$80-100**
American 1885-1910

Scroll Flask (corset waist)
Medium blue green, pint, pontil-scarred base,
sheared lip..**$250-300**
American 1840-1850

Scroll Flask
Medium yellow apple green, quart, red iron pontil,
sheared lip..**$600-800**
American 1840-1850 (scarce color)

Scroll Flask
Ice blue, pint, iron pontil, applied mouth.........**$150-200**
American 1840-1850

Scroll Flask
Deep amber, pint, pontil-scarred base, sheared and
tooled mouth **$500-700**
American 1840-1850

Scroll Flask – JR. & S. – Anchor
Yellow green, half-pint, pontil-scarred base, tooled
mouth **$4,000-6,000**
American 1845-1860 (extremely rare color)

Scroll Flask – Louisville – Glass Works
Medium yellow amber, pint, red iron pontil,
ground lip **$400-600**
American 1845-1860

Sheaf Of Grain – Star
Light to medium teal blue, calabash, iron pontil, applied
double collar mouth **$375-475**
American 1850-1860

Sheets & Duffy – Kensington
Bluish aqua, strapside quart, 8-1/2", smooth base,
applied ringed lip..**$250-350**
American 1870-1880

Sitting Dog – Stag's Head With Horn And Rifle
Cobalt blue, quart, pontil-scarred base,
tooled lip..**$75-125**
European 1850-1860

Spring Garden – Anchor – Glass Works – Log Cabin
Yellow olive, pint, 7-3/4", open pontil,
sheared lip...**$1,000-2,000**
American 1865-1875

Standing Soldier – Sunflower
Deep bluish aqua, calabash, iron pontil,
applied mouth $375-550
American 1855-1865 (scarce)

Strapside Flask
Yellow olive, quart, smooth base, "A. & D. H. C.,"
applied ring collar mouth................................$140-180
American 1875-1885 (rare color)

Strapside Flask
Dark amber, pint, smooth base, ground lip,
metal screw cap $80-120
American 1875-1900

Success To The Railroad – Locomotive
Medium cobalt blue, pint, pontil-scarred base,
sheared lip...$5,000-7,000
American 1830-1840

Sunburst Flask
Greenish aqua, pint, pontil-scarred base,
sheared lip..$275-375
American 1825-1835

Sunburst Flask
Blue green, half-pint, pontil-scarred base,
tooled lip...$300-400
American 1820-1835

Sunburst Flask
Aqua, half-pint, 5-5/8", open pontil, sheared
lip...$300-400
American 1840-1850

Sunburst Flask (wide mouth) – Keene – P&W
Yellow olive amber, half-pint, pontil-scarred base,
tooled expanded mouth $5,000-7,000
American 1815-1835 (rare)

**Sunburst Flask – M'Carty & Torreyson
– Manufacturers – Weburg, Va**
Deep bluish aqua, pint, red iron pontil,
sheared lip...$1,000-1,500
American 1845-1860

Sunburst Flask – Schooner
Aqua, half-pint, pontil-scarred base,
sheared lip...$140-160
American 1820-1835

**Token Flask (pocket plask with a United States
quarter attached to an indented panel)**
Deep teal green, 5-3/4", smooth base, tooled mouth,
original metal and cork stopper with time screw shot-
glass cover $100-150
American 1890-1910

**Traveler's – Companion – Star (Label:
Bourbon Whisky, F. French & Son, Wholesale
Druggists, Union Block, Hillsdale, Mich)**
Medium amber in lower half shading to a pure yellow
in the upper half, half-pint, iron pontil, sheared and
tooled lip...$600-800
American 1860-1870

Tree – Tree
Bluish aqua, half-pint, smooth base, applied double
collar mouth...$150-200
American 1860-1870

**Union – Clasped Hands And
Masons Compass – Eagle**
Bluish aqua, half-pint, smooth base, applied
mouth $80-120
American 1865-1875

**Union – (pair of flags and three embossed
bottles) Bottle – Reverse Plain Flask**
Clear glass, pint, smooth base, applied sloping collar
mouth with ring...$200-400
American 1880-1900

**W. Ihmsen's   Eagle – Glass – Agriculture
– Sheaf Of Grain And Tools**
Light green, pint, open pontil, sheared and
tooled lip..$1,400-1,800
American 1835-1845

Waterford – Clasped Hands – Eagle
Aqua, quart, 8-7/8", smooth base, applied double
collar mouth...$175-275
American 1865-1875

**Westford Glass Co – Westford
– Conn – Sheaf Of Wheat**
Olive green, pint, smooth base, applied double
collar mouth...$120-160
American 1865-1875

Woman On Bicycle – Eagle – A – DHC (inside oval)
Bright yellow olive, pint, smooth base, applied square
collar mouth..$1,000-1,500
American 1865-1875

Zanesville – City – Glass Works
Aqua, strapside pint, smooth base, applied
mouth $100-175
American 1875-1895

Food and Pickle Bottles

Food bottles are one of the largest and most diverse categories of collectible bottles. They were made for the commercial sale of a wide variety of food products (including milk, but excluding other beverages). Food bottles are an ideal specialty for the beginning collector, since as a group they are so readily available. Many collectors are attracted to food bottles for their historical value. Nineteenth and early twentieth century magazines and newspapers contained so many illustrated advertisements for food products that many collectors keep scrapbooks of ads to help date and price the bottles.

Before bottling, food could not to be transported long

A. Stone & Co. - Philada, 1855-1865, 5-7/8", $500-700.

distances or kept long because of spoilage. Bottling revolutionized the food industry and began a new chapter in American business merchandising and distribution. With the glass bottle, producers were able to use portion packaging, save labor, and sell from long distances.

Suddenly local producers faced competition from great distances, so many interesting bottles were created specifically to distinguish them from others. Green and clear peppersauce bottles, for instance, were made in the shape of Gothic cathedrals with arches and windows; mustard jars and chili sauce bottles were designed with unique embossing; cooking oil bottles were made tall and narrow, and pickle bottles were manufactured with large mouths.

The pickle bottle is one of the largest of the food bottles, with a wide mouth and a square or cylindrical shape. While the pickle bottle was often unique in shape and design, its color was almost exclusively aqua, although occasionally you may find a multicolored piece. Since there are many variations of Gothic-looking pickle jars with many different colors, it's difficult to identify the bottle manufacturers and contents. While the oldest bottles may have used foil labels for identification, paper labels and embossing provide additional identification. When looking through ghost-town dumps and digging behind older pioneer homes, you are sure to find many food and pickle bottles in large numbers, since pickles were a popular food, especially in mining communities.

Two of the more common food bottles are the Worcestershire sauce bottles distributed by Lea & Perrins, and the Heinz sauce bottles. The Worcestershire sauce in the green bottle was in high demand during the 19th century and is quite common.

Henry J. Heinz introduced his sauces in 1869 with the bottling of horseradish but didn't begin bottling ketchup until 1889.

A.N. Thompson – & Co – New York
Deep blue aqua, 8-5/8", pontil-scarred base, applied double collar mouth...**$120-160**
American 1850-1865

Cathedral pickle jar, 1850-1860, 6-1/2", $140-180.

Cathedral pickle jar, 1860-1870, 7-1/8", $1,000-1,500.

Cathedral pickle jar, 1860-1870, 11-5/8", $350-450.

Cathedral pickle jar, six-sided, 1865-1875, 13-7/8", $400-500 (rare).

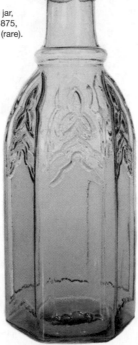

Belfast – Cigars – United Cut Plug (tobacco jar)
Yellow amber, 6-3/4", smooth base, "Factory No 1054 -50-3rd District N.Y.," original metal screw lid **$140-180**
American 1885-1910

Blueberry Preserve Jar
Yellow olive, 11-1/8", smooth base, applied double collar mouth..**$1,200-2,400**
American 1860-1872 (Willington Glass Works, West Willington, Conn.)

C.D. Brooks – Boston
Yellow amber, 6-1/2", smooth base, applied mouth **$40-60**
American 1880-1900

Cala Bonzest (relish jar) ·
Blue aqua, 6-1/2", smooth base, applied lip...**$300-350**
American 1870-1880 (Wm F. Swasey Company)

Cathedral Peppersauce Bottle
Cornflower blue, 8-3/8", smooth base, applied double collar mouth...**$350-700**
American 1860-1870

Cathedral Peppersauce – Peppersauce – W.K. Lewis & Bros.
Pale greenish aqua, 10-1/8", smooth base, applied. double collar mouth $175-275
American 1855-1865

Cathedral Pickle – E.H.V.B. – N.Y. (Elias H. Van Benschoten Company)
Deep blue green, 6-sided, 9", iron pontil base, rolled lip..$1,000-1,500
American 1850-1865 (scarce jar with rare color)

Cathedral Pickle – E.H.V.B. – N.Y. (Elias H. Van Benschoten Company)
Bluish aqua, 6-sided, 14-1/4", smooth base, applied mouth $400-600
American 1850-1865 (rare)

Cathedral Pickle – R & F. Atmore
Bluish aquamarine, 11-3/8", smooth base, outward rolled mouth $200-400
American 1860-1880

Cathedral Pickle – Wellington
Deep bluish aqua, 13-1/4", square form, pontil-scarred base, outward folded lip.................................$600-800
American 1850-1860

Cloverleaf Pickle Jar
Light yellow green, 7-3/4", pontil-scarred, outward rolled mouth $1,000-2,000
American 1840-1860 (Stoddard Glasshouse, Stoddard, N.H.)

Cloverleaf Pickle Jar
Reddish amber, 8-1/8", smooth base, outward rolled mouth $600-1,200
American 1840-1860 (Stoddard Glasshouse, Stoddard, N.H.)

Crown Celery Salt – Horton Cato & Co Detroit
Medium amber, 8-1/8", smooth base, ground lip, original yellow and black label and metal shaker screw top...$200-300
American 1885-1890

G. P. Sanborn & Son - Union - Boston Pickles, 1870-1885, 7-5/8", $75-110 (pair).

**Diamond Packing (diamond) Bridgeton
– N.J. – Design Pat. Feb. 1st. 1870
(around shoulder) (sauce bottle)**
Aqua, 8-1/4", smooth base, applied mouth........**$50-75**
American 1870-1880

**Dodson Braun Mfg. Co – St. Louis. U.S.A.
– 1904 (countertop display food jar)**
Clear glass with amethyst tint, 11", smooth base,
ground lip, original glass lid............................**$140-180**
American 1904-1915

E.T. Cowdrey – Boston
Medium amber, 7-3/4", smooth base,
applied mouth **$40-60**
American 1880-1900

Food Jar (unembossed)
Medium apple green, 5-1/4", pontil-scarred base,
rolled lip..**$40-70**
European 1850-1870

Food Jar (unembossed)
Deep emerald green, 8", pontil-scarred base,
rolled lip..**$40-70**
European 1850-1870

**Glass Syrup Dispenser Bottle – Fowlers
5c – Cherry Smash (label under glass)**
Clear glass, 12", smooth base, tooled lip with original
metal cover...**$150-200**
American 1910-1920

**Glass Syrup Dispenser Bottle – Trade Mark
Registered (cluster of grapes) – Grape
Smash (label under glass)**
Clear glass, 11-7/8", smooth base, tooled lip with
original metal cover **$200-300**
American 1910-1920

**Glass Syrup Dispenser Bottle – The Best What Gives
– John Graf Co. – Lemon Life – Milwaukee Wis.**
Clear glass, 12-1/4", smooth base, ABM lip with
original metal cover **$200-300**
American 1910-1920

**Globe – Tobacco Company – Detroit &
Windsor – Pat. Oct. 10, 1882 (tobacco jar)**
Medium yellow amber, 6-7/8", smooth base, ground lip
with original screw-on lid **$80-120**
American 1882 –1900

Heinz's Keystone Ketchup, (produced in Heinz Glass
factory - Sharpsburg, PA), 1889-1913, $35-45.

Peppersauce bottle,
1860-1870,
8-3/8", $400-600.

G.P. Sanborn & Son – Union – Boston Pickles
Yellow green, 7-5/8", smooth base,
tooled mouth **$40-50**
American 1870-1885

**G.W. Gable – Manufacturer – Factory 706
– 9th District – Of Pa – 25 (tobacco jar)**
Straw yellow, 6-7/8", barrel shape, smooth base,
ground lip, original metal screw lid.................**$150-200**
American 1890-1910

**Golden Tree – Pure – Cane Syrup – New
England – Maple Syrup – Company – Boston**
Clear glass, pint, smooth base, ABM lip **$70-90**
American 1910-1930

**Hale & Parshall Lyons N.Y. (Labeled Extract) Label:
Hale & Parshall Growers And Manufacturers
Of First Premium Peppermint Oil, Lyons,
Wayne Co. New York State U. S. America)**
Medium sapphire blue, 10", smooth base, applied
sloping double collar mouth...........................**$140-180**
American 1860-1870

**Hiawatha Tobacco Works – Detroit,
Mich (on base) (tobacco jar)**
Medium yellow amber, 6-3/4", smooth base, ground lip
with original metal screw-on lid......................**$200-300**
American 1885-1900 (rare)

Joseph Campbell – JP (monogram) – Camden, N.J.
Aqua quart, 9-1/4", smooth base, applied
mouth **$150-250**
American 1880-1895 (early jar of the Campbell Soup
Company)

Lime Juice (below an arrow on shoulder)
Deep olive amber, 10-1/4", smooth base, applied
mouth, blown-in three-part mold **$250-350**
American 1865-1885

**Loren J. Wicks (diamond) Bridgeton – N.J. – Design
Pat. Feb. 1st. 1870 (around shoulder) (sauce bottle)**
Aqua, 6-7/8", smooth base, applied mouth........**$50-75**
American 1870-1880

**Mecantile (air-tight) Havana – Cigar – St.
Louis, Mo – Patented – Nov. 13-94 – Jan. 15-95
– Patented Dec. 11-94 – June 24-02 (tobacco jar)**
Amber, 5-1/4", smooth base, "Factory No. 305, 1st
Dist. – Of Mo. – 50 Cigars," ground lip with original
metal screw-on lid **$80-140**
American 1894-1902

**Mi Lola Cigar Co. (motif of bust of
woman) Cigar (tobacco jar)**
Amethyst, 5-3/8", smooth base, "Mi Lola Cigar Co
–Milwaukee – 50-Factory No 207 – 1st Dist. Wis,"
original glass lid, ABM lip **$70-90**
American 1910-1920

Skilton Foote & CO's - Trade
(monument) Mark - Bunker Hill
Pickle, 1870-1885, 5",
$75-110 (pair).

Mustard Jar (embossed eagle)
Straw yellow, smooth base, ground lip, glass insert and
metal screw band **$90-140**
American 1890-1910

Mustard Jar (embossed eagle)
Blue milk glass, smooth base, ground lip, glass insert
and metal screw band **$90-140**
American 1890-1910 (scarce)

**Mustard Jar – Moutard A Maille Disd
Vinalgrier Boulevard Des Italienes A Paris,
Manufactured For Richd Willamson Grocer
And Wine Merchant 19 Maiden Lane, N. York**
White pottery with black transfer on both sides, 4-3/4",
smooth base..**$400-600**
American 1810-1820 (extremely rare)

**New England Tomato Relish – Skilton, Foote & Co.,
Boston, Mass. U.S.A. (labeled stoneware jug)**
Cream pottery with dark brown glaze,
handled..**$80-120**
American 1890-1900

**Newlin's Coffee – Newlin Tea Co – City
Of New York – Borough Of Brooklyn**
Brilliant yellow, 6-1/4", smooth base, ground mouth, tin
lid...**$400-800**
American 1880-1900 (extremely rare)

**Shaker Pepper Relish, E.D.
Pettengill Co., Portland, Me**
Aqua, 5-3/8", smooth base, ground lip **$100-150**
American 1880-1895

**Shaker Pepper Relish, E.D.
Pettengill Co., Portland, Me**
Aqua, 7-5/8", smooth base, ground lip **$100-150**
American 1880-1895

Sheehan Bros (handled metal creamer)
Soldered metal construction, 5-3/4", soldered handle,
wooden stopper **$100-150**
American 1860-1880

**Siphon Jumysgen Bottle – For Preparing
– Kumyss From – Jumysgen – Reed &
Carnrick, N.Y. – Water Mark – Powder Mark**
Cobalt blue, 9-1/8", smooth base, tooled lip, original
metal closure **$170-250**
American 1890-1900

**Skilton Foote & Cos – Bunker Hill Brand
– Trade (motif of Bunker Hill Monument)
Mark – Bunker Hill – Brand**
Bright yellow amber with olive tone, 6-3/4", smooth
base, applied mouth..**$140-180**
American 1880-1890

**Skilton Foote & Co – Trade (motif of Bunker Hill
Monument) Mark – Bunker Hill Pickle's (Label:
Gherkins, Skilton, Foote & Co. Manufacturers
Of Bunker Hill Pickles, Boston, Mass. U.S.A.)**
Yellow olive, 7-3/4", smooth base, tooled
mouth **$150-200**
American 1875-1890

**The Aristocratic – Cigar – a 10c – Manufactured
By – Factory No. 3492 – 9th District of Pa – 25**
Yellow amber, 5-1/4", smooth base, ground lip, original
screw-on metal lid..**$80-140**
American 1885-1900

**The Ribbon – Havana Cigars – Geo. Fehl.
B.R.C. Co. – St. Louis, Mo (tobacco jar)**
Amethyst, 5-1/2", smooth base, "Factory No. 731. 1st
District – State Of Missouri – 50 Cigars" original tin
screw lid, ABM lip..**$70-90**
American 1910-1920

**This Trade Mark Registered – Maple
Sap And Boiled Cider – Vinegar – The
C.I. Co. Lt'd – East Rindge, N.H.**
Cobalt blue, 11-3/8", smooth base,
tooled mouth **$800-1,200**
American 1880-1895

W.D. – N.Y. (W. D. Smith Company) – Pickle Jar
Bluish aqua, fluted shoulder with raised beads
around shoulder and base, 11-7/8", iron pontil,
rolled lip **$500-700**
American 1850-1870 (very rare)

Wells – Miller – & Provost
Medium cobalt blue, 8-1/8", 8-round panels, open
pontil, applied mouth **$600-800**
American 1850-1860 (less than eight known examples in
this color)

**Wendell & Espy – Mince Meat
– 152 So Front – Philada**
Aqua, 8-1/2", pontil-scarred base, rolled lip ...**$500-700**
American 1850-1860 (rare)

W. H. Clay's – Richmond – Sauce Bottle
Aquamarine, 10", smooth base, applied sloping
collar mouth..**$250-500**
American 1860-1870 (extremely rare)

Wm. S. Kimball & Co – Rochester N.Y. (tobacco jar)
Golden green amber, 7", smooth base, ground lip,
original metal screw lid......................................**$70-90**
American 1890-1910

Wm. Underwood & Co Boston – 32 Oz (on shoulder)
Medium blue green, 8-1/4", open pontil,
rolled lip **$275-375**
American 1845-1860

Wm. Underwood & Co Boston
Deep blue aqua, 10-7/8", iron pontil, applied sloping
collar mouth..**$250-350**
American 1845-1860

Yeoman's – Fruit Bottle
Aqua, quart, smooth base, applied mouth......**$100-150**
American 1890-1910

Yeoman's – Fruit Bottle
Aqua, half-gallon, smooth base, applied
mouth **$100-150**
American 1890-1910

Fruit Jars

Unlike food bottles, fruit jars were sold empty for home preservation of many different types of food. They were predominant in the 1800s when prepackaged foods weren't available and home canning was the only option. Although fruit jars carry no advertising, they aren't necessarily common or plain, since the bottle manufacturer's name is usually embossed in large letters along with the patent date. The manufacturer whose advertising campaign gave fruit jars their name was Thomas W. Dyott, who was in the market early, selling fruit jars by 1829.

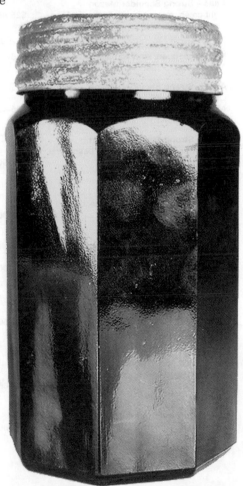

For the first 50 years, the most common closure was a cork sealed with wax. In 1855, an inverted saucer-like lid was invented that could be inserted into the jar to provide an airtight seal. The Hero Glassworks invented the glass lid in 1856 and improved on it in 1858 with a zinc lid invented by John Landis Mason, who also produced fruit jars. Because the medical profession warned that zinc could be harmful, Hero Glassworks developed a glass lid for the Mason jar in 1868. Mason eventually transferred his patent rights to the Consolidated Fruit Jar Company, which let the patent expire.

In 1880, the Ball Brothers began distributing Mason jars, and in 1898 the use of a semi-automatic bottle machine increased the output of the Mason jar until the automatic machine was invented in 1903.

D. H. McAlpin & Co - New York (on base),
1880-1895 6-1/2", $60-80.

Fruit jars were made in a wide range of sizes and colors, but the most common are aqua and clear. The rarer jars were made in various shades of blue, amber, black, milk glass, green, and purple.

A.G. Smalley & Co – Patented – April 7th 1896 – Boston & New York (on base)
Amber, quart, smooth base, ground lip...............$40-70
American 1895-1910

A.Stone & Co. – Philad'a
Bluish aqua, half-pint, 5-7/8", smooth base, applied mouth, "A.Stone & Co.-Philad'a" (on closure)..$500-700
American 1855-1865

Atherhold, Fisher & Co. – Philada
Aquamarine, quart, smooth base, applied collar mouth with blown glass "Kline" stopper $200-400
American 1920-1940

Atlas – Strong Shoulder Mason
Light green, quart, smooth base, ABM lips.........$25-45
American 1925-1940

Atlas – Strong Shoulder Mason
Light olive, quart, smooth base, ABM lips $25-45
American 1925-1940

Atlas – Strong Shoulder Mason
Light olive yellow, quart, smooth base, ABM lips $25-45
American 1925-1940

Atlas – Strong Shoulder Mason
Cornflower blue, quart, smooth base, ABM lip $70-100
American 1925-1940

Bee
Aquamarine, quart, smooth base, ground mouth $500-1,000
American 1869-1880

Chef – Trade Mark (Chef) – The Berdan Co.
Clear, half-pint, smooth base, ground mouth, glass lid $75-100
American 1910-1920

Chef – Trade Mark (Chef) – The Berdan Co.
Clear, half-gallon, smooth base, ground mouth, glass lid $35-50
American 1910-1920

Cohansey – Glass Mfg Co – Pat Mar 20 77
Aqua, quart barrel, smooth base, applied groove ring wax seal, glass lid embossed, "Cohansey Glass Mfg Co – Philada, Pa" $140-160
American 1877-1885

Columbia (monogram)
Aqua, quart, smooth base, ground lip.................$60-80
American 1884-1900

Dexter (encircled by fruit and vegetables)
Aqua, quart, 7-1/4", smooth base, "D," ground lip, original glass lid embossed "Patd Aug. 8th 1865" $200-250
American 1865-1870

Doane's Great Air Tight – Preserving Jar
Aqua, bulbous body, quart, smooth base, applied mouth $3,500-4,500
American 1865-1870

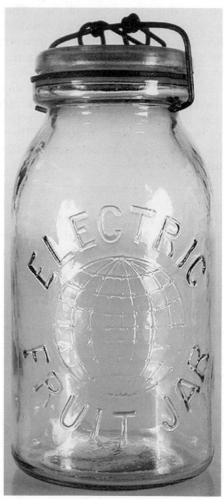

Electric - Fruit Jar (around globe),
1885-1895, quart, $150-250.

Eagle
Aquamarine, quart, smooth base, ground
mouth **$150-300**
American 1860-1870

Electric – Fruit Jar (around globe)
Bluish aqua, pint, smooth base, "Pat Apd For,"
ground lip **$140-180**
American 1885-1895

Electric – Fruit Jar (around globe)
Bluish aqua, quart, smooth base, "Pat Apd For,"
ground lip **$150-225**
American 1885-1895

Eureka – A7 – Patd Dec 27th – 1864
Bluish aqua with light olive green in shoulder and neck,
half-gallon, smooth base, ground lip..................**$70-90**
American 1865-1875

Figural Own Fruit Jar
Milk glass owl, smooth base, rough sheared lip, original
glass insert with embossed eagle **$100-150**
American 1890 -1910

Flaccus Bros – Steer's (steers head) Head – Fruit Jar
Clear, pint, 6-1/8", smooth base, ground lip, original
screw-on lid..**$250-350**
American 1890-1910

Flaccus Bros – Steer's (steer's head) Head – Fruit Jar
Milk glass, pint, 6-1/8", smooth base, ground lip,
original screw-on lid **$250-350**
American 1890-1910

Hartell's Glass Air Tight Cover - Patented   Oct
19 1858, 1860-1870, pint, $300-400.

Figural Owl fruit jar, 1890-
1910, $100-150.

Flaccus Bros - Steer's (steer's head) Head - Fruit
Jar, 1890-1910, 6-1/8", $500-700 (pair).

Gilberds (star) Jar
Aqua, pint, 5-1/4", smooth base, ground lip, original clear glass lid embossed "Jas Gilberds – Patd-Jan 30, 1883 – Jamestown, N.Y." **$1,000-1,500**
American 1883-1885

Globe
Reddish amber, quart, smooth base, "62," ground lip, original glass lid embossed "Patented May 25th 1886" **$150-200**
American 1886-1895

Globe
Yellow amber, quart, smooth base, ground lip, original glass lid embossed "Patented May 25th 1886" **$75-125**
American 1886-1895

Globe
Orange amber, quart, smooth base, ground lip, original glass lid embossed "Patented May 25th 1886" **$75-125**
American 1886-1895

Haines's – Improved – March 1st – 1870
Bluish aqua, quart, smooth base, applied mouth **$90-125**
American 1870-1880

H & S (in script)
Aqua, quart, smooth base, applied mouth, original attached metal yoke and lid is embossed "William Haller Patd. Aug 7 1860" **$2,500-3,500**
American 1860-1865 (very rare)

H.W. Pettit – Westville, N.J. (on base)
Aqua, pint, smooth base, applied lip..................**$40-50**
American 1870-1900

Huyett & Fredley – Carisle, Pa – Ladies Choice
Aquamarine, quart, smooth base, ground mouth **$500-1,000**
American 1860-1870 (rare)

Mason's - C.F. J. Co (monogram) Patent - Nov 30th 1858, 1875-1895, quart, $100-150.

Mason's - CFJ Co (monogram) Patent - Nov 30th - 1858, 1875-1895, quart, $140-180.

John F. Henry – N.Y.
Golden yellow amber, 4-3/8", smooth base, tooled
mouth **$140-180**
American 1855-1875 (rare)

Keystone
Bluish aqua, half-gallon, red iron pontil, applied
mouth **$200-300**
American 1860-1870

LaFayette (bust of LaFayette)
Aqua, quart, smooth base, applied mouth, original
3-piece metal and glass stopper marked "Patented
– Sept 21, 1994-Aug, 1885".......................**$1,500-2,000**
American 1885-1895

LaFayette (in script)
Smoky clear glass, half-gallon, smooth base, tooled
mouth, original three-piece metal and glass stopper
marked "Patented – Sept 21, 1994-Aug,
1885"...**$1,500-2,000**
American 1885-1895

Ludlow's Patent – June 28th 1859
Aqua, pint, 6-1/8", smooth base, ground lip...**$400-600**
American 1859-1865

**Magic – Fruit Jar – Wm. McCully & Co
– Pittsburgh Pa – Sole Proprietors – No. 6
– Patented – By – R.M. Dalbey – June 6th 1866**
Aquamarine, half-gallon, smooth base, ground
mouth **$500-1,000**
American 1865-1870 (rare)

**Manufactured For – Rice & Burnett
– Cleveland. O – L & W**
Aquamarine, quart, smooth base, applied mouth with
"Kline" stopper **$250-500**
American 1860-1880 (rare)

M.G. Co (on base), 1870-1875, quart; Haine's - Improved
- March 1st - 1870, 1870-1875, quart, $175-250 (both).

Mason's - Patent - Nov 30th - 1858,
1875-1895, half-gallon, $100-200.

Mason's - SG CO (monogram) Patent - Nov. 30th - 1858 (lot of
two), 1875-1897, half-gallon and quart, $140-180 (both).

Mason's – C.F.J. Co. (monogram)
Improved – Butter Jar
Aqua, half-gallon, smooth base, rough sheared and ground lip **$200-275**
American 1880-1895

Mason's – Patent – Nov. 30th – 58 (on front)
And "The Ball – Jar" (on reverse)
Aqua, pint, smooth base, ground lip **$150-200**
American 1875-1890

Mason's – Patent – Nov 30th – 1858
Greenish aqua with olive amber striations, 8-3/4", smooth base, ABM lip **$180-250**
American 1920-1930

Mastodon (wax sealer jar)
Bluish aqua, quart, smooth base "T.A. Evans & Co Pittsburgh Pa," applied groove ring wax sealer, original tin lid...**$200-300**
American 1870-1885

M.G.Co. (on base)
Yellow green, quart, smooth base, applied groove wax sealer...**$90-125**
American 1870-1880

M G M Co (monogram)
Pale amethyst, midget-pint, smooth base, ground mouth **$250-500**
American 1880-1900

Millville – Atmospheric – Fruit Jar
– Whitall's Patent – June 18th 1861
Bluish aqua, pInt, smooth base, applied mouth, embossed glass lid "Whitall's Patent –June 18th 1861"..**$60-80**
American 1861-1870

Millville – Atmospheric – Fruit Jar
– Whitall's Patent – June 18th 1861
Bluish aqua, quart, smooth base, applied mouth, embossed glass lid "Whitall's Patent –June 18th 1861"..**$70-90**
American 1861-1870

Patented - Oct 19 1858 (on lid), 1860-1870, quart, $140-180.

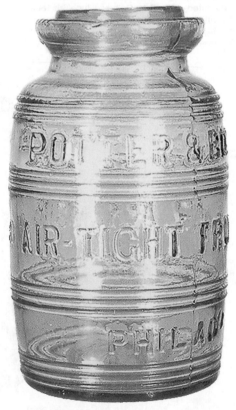

Potter & Bodine's - Air-Tight Fruit Jar - Philada - Patented - April 13th 1858, 1855-1865, quart, $475-575.

**Millville – Atmospheric – Fruit Jar
– Whitall's Patent – June 18th 1861**
Bluish aqua, half-gallon, smooth base, applied mouth,
embossed glass lid "Whitall's Patent – June 18th
1861" **$90-100**
American 1861-1870

**Millville – Atmospheric – Fruit Jar
– Whitall's Patent – June 18th 1861**
Bluish aqua, 72 oz., smooth base, applied mouth,
embossed glass lid "Whitall's Patent – June 18th"
1861" **$90-100**
American 1861-1870

Millville – Whitall's Patent
Bluish aqua, half-pint, smooth base "W.T.&CO.
– U.S.A.," applied mouth, embossed glass lid "Whitall's
Patent – June 18th 1861" **$90-100**
American 1861-1870

Michigan Mason
Aqua, smooth base, ground lip **$25-30**
American 1910-1920

Moore's – Patent – Dec 3d 1861
Bluish aqua, half-gallon, smooth base, applied
mouth **$150-200**
American 1861-1870

**Ne Plus Ultra Air-Tight Fruit Jar (row of squares)
– Made By Bodine & Bors Wmstown, N.J. (row of
circles) For Their Patent Glass Lid – (row of squares)**
Deep bluish aqua, half-gallon, smooth base, applied
mouth, original glass lid embossed, "Patented – Aug
3rd 1858" **$2,000-3,000**
American 1858-1865 (rare)

Patented – Oct 19 1958
Apple green, quart, smooth base, ground lip, original
glass screw lid...**$140-180**
American 1860-1870

Patented Imperial
Clear glass, quart, smooth base, "The G.H.
Hammond Co. – Hammond, Ind – Imperial Pat –
April 20th 1886," ground lid embossed "The G.H.
Hammond Co. – Hammond, Ind – Imperial Pat – April
20th 1886" **$200-300**
American 1886-1890 (very rare)

Petal Jar
Emerald green, 10 panels around shoulder, 8-3/4", red
iron pontil, applied mount **$1,800-2,500**
American 1850-1860

Petal Jar
Deep bluish aqua, 10-3/8", iron pontil, applied
mouth **$375-475**
American 1855-1865

Porcelain – BBGM Co (monogram) Lined
Aquamarine, midget-pint, smooth base, ground
mouth **$500-1,000**
American 1880-1900 (rare)

**Potter & Bodine's – Air-Tight – Fruit Jar
– Philada – Patented – April 13th – 1858**
Bluish aqua, half-gallon barrel, pontil-scarred base,
applied groove wax ring sealer **$250-300**
American 1855-1865

Protector
Aqua, quart, smooth base, tinned iron lid, "Cohansey
Mfg Co." **$100-125**
American 1867-1880

Safety
Medium yellow amber, quart, smooth base, ground lip,
original glass lid embossed "Patent Applied
For"...**$175-250**
American 1880-1890

Safety
Yellow amber, half-gallon, smooth base, ground lip,
original glass lid embossed "Patent Applied
For"...**$200-300**
American 1880-1890

**Safety Valve – HC (superimposed
over triangle) Patd May 21 1895**
Grass green, pint, smooth base, ground lip, original
lid **$150-200**
American 1895-1910

The - Mason's - Improved -Label: Little Rhody
Cut Plug, George R. Young & Bros., Providence,
R.I., 1890-1900, half-gallon, $150-250.

San Francisco – Glass Works (wax sealer jar)
Bluish aqua, quart, smooth base, applied groove ring
wax sealer, original tin lld $90-150
American 1870-1885

**Stevens – Tin Top – Patd July 27 1875 – Lewis
& Neblett – Cincinnati. O (wax sealer jar)**
Bluish aqua, quart, smooth base, applied groove ring
wax sealer, original tin lid $90-150
American 1870-1885

The Ball – Pat. Apld. For
Aquamarine, quart, smooth base, ground
mouth $250-500
American 1890-1900

The Canton – Domestic – Fruit Jar
Clear, pint, smooth base, ground mouth, glass
lid...$150-300
American 1889-1900

The Darling
Aqua, quart, smooth base, ground lip.................$60-80
American 1884-1900

The Howe – Jar – Scranton – Pa
Aqua, quart, smooth base, ground lip.................$40-60
American 1888-1910

The Howe – Jar – Scranton – Pa
Clear, pint, smooth base, ground mouth, glass
lid...$75-100
American 1888-1910

The – King – Pat. Nov. 2, 1869
Bluish aqua, quart, 7-1/2", smooth base, "3", ground
lip, original glass lid...$275-375
American 1869-1875

**The Ladies Favorite (fullbodied Victorian woman
holding a jar) – Wm. L. Haller – Carlisle – Pa**
Aquamarine, quart, smooth base, ground
mouth $3,000-6,000
American 1860-1870

The Leader
Medium amber to yellow amber, pint, 6", smooth base,
"3," ground lip, original amber domed lid embossed
"Patd June 28 1892" $300-400
American 1892-1895 (scarce in pint)

The Leader
Yellow amber, quart, 8", smooth base, "23," ground lip,
original amber domed lid embossed "Patd June 28,
1892" $300-450
American 1892-1895

The – Paragon – Valve Jar – Patd. April 19th 1870
Bluish aqua, quart, 7-3/4", smooth base, "MCE & CO
– 2," ground lip...$400-600
American 1870-1875 (rare)

The – Reservoir
Bluish aqua, half-gallon, smooth base "C.& I," applied
mouth, glass screw-in stopper, "Mrs. G.E. Haller
– Patd. Feb 25. 73"...$400-500
American 1873-1880

The Rose
Clear, midget-pint, smooth base, machined mouth,
glass lid $200-400
American 1880-1900

The – Smalley – Jar
Aquamarine, quart, smooth base, ground
mouth $200-400
American 1890-1900

The – Van Vliet – Jar – Of 1881
Aqua, quart, 7-1/4", smooth base, "7,"
ground lip, original glass lid embossed "Pat
May 3d 1881"...$600-800
American 1881-1885

Thrift – Thrift Jar Co. – Baltimore, Md
Clear, pint, smooth base, metal lid.....................$25-35
American 1913-1920

Trade Mark – Lightning
Golden yellow olive, half-gallon, smooth base,
"Putnam," ground lip, lid is embossed, "Patd Jan 5. 75
Reisd. June 5. 77. Patd Aprl. 25. 82" $200-300
American 1885-1895

**Trademark – Masons – CFJ Co
(monogram) – Improved**
Aqua, half-pint, smooth base, ABM lip $40-50
American 1870-1900

Trade Mark – The Dandy
Medium amber, half-gallon, smooth base. "Gilberds,"
ground lip, glass lid embossed, "Pat. Oct. 13th
1885" $150-200
American 1885-1895

U.S. Patented – May 12 1863 (wax sealer jar)
Bluish aqua, half-gallon, smooth base, applied groove
ring wax sealer, original tin lid $150-200
American 1863-1870

Union – No 4
Aquamarine, quart, smooth base, ground
mouth $300-600
American 1860-1880

**Victory – 1 – Patd Feby 9th 1864
– Reisd June 22d 1867**
Aqua, quart, smooth base, rough sheared and ground
lip..$70-90
American 1870-1895

Wm. Frank & Sons Pitts
Ice blue, quart, smooth base, groove wax ring
sealer...$50-70
American 1910-1920

Woodbury Improved – WGW (monogram)
Aqua, half-gallon, smooth base, "Woodbury Glass
Work – 20 - Woodbury, N.J.," ground lip...........$90-125
American 1861-1885

**Yeoman's – Fruit Bottle – Patent
– Applied For (on shoulder)**
Aqua, half-gallon, smooth base, ground
mouth $60-90
American 1870-1900

Hutchinson Bottles

Charles A. Hutchinson developed the Hutchinson bottle in the late 1870s. Interestingly, the stopper, not the bottle itself, differentiated the design from others. The stopper, which Hutchinson patented in 1879, was intended as an improvement over cork stoppers, which eventually shrank and allowed the air to seep into the bottle.

The new stopper consisted of a rubber disc held between two metal plates attached to a spring stem. The stem was shaped like a figure eight, with the upper loop larger than the lower to prevent the stem from falling into the bottle. The lower loop could pass through the bottle's neck and push down the disc to permit the filling or pouring of it contents. A refilled bottle was sealed by pulling the disc up to the bottle's shoulder, where it made a tight fit. When opened, the spring made a popping sound. Thus, from the Hutchinson bottle came the term "pop bottle," which is how soda came to be known as "pop."

Hutchinson stopped producing bottles in 1912, when warnings about metal poisoning were issued. As collectibles, Hutchinson bottles rank high on the curiosity and price scales, but pricing varies quite sharply by geographical location, compared to the relatively stable prices of most other bottles.

Hutchinson bottles carry abbreviations, of which the following three are the most common:

TBNTBS—This bottle not to be sold

TBMBR—This bottle must be returned

TBINS—This bottle is not sold

Daniel Ritter - Allentown - Pa, 1890-1910, 6-3/8", $600-800.

D.W. Powell - Soda
Water - Evergreen,
Ala, 1890-1910,
7-1/8", $375-475.

H.W. Elson's - Bottling
- Works - Ishpeming,
Mich, 1889-1910,
9", $80-120.

Arcata Soda Works – B.P.
Aqua, 6-3/4", smooth base, tooled top...............$50-80
American 1875-1890

Artic – Soda Works – Berkeley – Cal
Aqua, 7", smooth base, tooled top $100-300
American 1893-1903 (extremely rare)

Black Diamond – A1 – Soda Works
Green hue, 7", smooth base, tooled top.........$100-200
American 1902-1910 (scarce)

C. Valer & Co – Electric Bottlers – Charlotte, N.C.
Aqua, 6-3/4", smooth base, tooled top...............$50-65
American 1875-1895

California – S.C.&Co. – Soda Works
Aqua, 6-1/2", smooth base, tooled top...........$100-200
American 1884 (rare)

Cape Argo – Soda Works – Marshfield, Ore
Aqua, 6-7/8", smooth base, tooled top...............$45-65
American 1880-1890

Crystal Bottling Co. – Charleston – W. Va
Aqua, 6-3/4", mug based, tooled top $35-45
American 1880-1890

Daniel Ritter – Allentown – Pa
Medium amber, 6-3/8", smooth base, tooled
top $600-800
American 1890-1910

**D.W. Bostelmann – Trade Mark (anchor)
Registered – Chicago Ill.**
Deep aqua, 6-7/8", smooth base, tooled top $45-55
American 1880-1900

D.W. Powell – Soda Water – Evergreen, Ala.
Light pink amethyst, 7-1/8", smooth base, tooled
top $375-475
American 1890-1910 (rare in this color)

E.L. Billings – Sacramento Cal
Green aqua, 7-1/8", smooth base, applied top...$45-60
American 1880-1890

Empire Soda Works – Weiss & Company
Aqua, 6-1/2", smooth base, applied top......**$500-1,000**
American 1883-1887 (extremely rare)

Eureka California (eagle) Soda Water Co. – S.F.
Aqua, 6-1/2", smooth base, tooled top...........**$100-150**
American 1889-1907

Eureka Soda Works – 723 Turk St – S.F.
Aqua, 6-1/2", smooth base, applied top.............**$50-75**
American 1884-1898 (scarce)

F. Schmidt – Leadville – Colorado
Clear, 6-1/2", smooth base **(S)**, tooled top **$100-300**
American (Colorado Territory) 1870-1880

F. Schmidt – Leadville – Colorado
Clear, 6-1/4", smooth base, tooled top...........**$100-300**
American (Colorado Territory) 1870-1880

H & M Eureka – Cal
Aqua, 7", smooth base, tooled top **$50-75**
American 1875-1890

H. Rummel – Charleston – W. Va
Pale green, 7", smooth base, tooled top.............**$25-35**
American 1880-1900

Haywards – S.J. Simons – Soda Works
Light green aqua, 6", smooth base, tooled
top **$80-150**
American 1890-1902

Jas. F. Taylor – New Berne – N.C.
Clear, 6-1/2", smooth base, "T 36," tooled top...**$50-60**
American 1880-1890

Leadville
Clear, 6-3/4", smooth base, tooled top...........**$100-300**
American (Colorado Territory) 1870-1880

Leonard – Sonora – Cal.
Aqua, 6-7/8", smooth base, tooled top.............**$75-100**
American 1880-1907

Mason & Co – Sausalito
Aqua, 6-1/2", smooth base (four "M"s embossed on
base), tooled top **$500-1,000**
American 1900-1910 (extremely rare)

Mendocino – Bottling Works – A.L. Reynolds
Light blue aqua, 7", smooth base, tooled
top **$100-200**
American 1905-1910

Home Soda Works
- Chas. Peverley - Prop. -
Douglas, A. I., 1890-1910,
7-1/4", $200-300 (scarce
Arizona Territory soda).

Registered -
Biedenharn - Candy
Co - Vicksburg
- Miss, 1890-1900,
7-1/4", $275-375.

S.C. Palmer -
Washington - D.C.
- This Bottle - Is - Never
Sold, 1890-1900,
7-1/8", $350-450.

Simon James - 27 -
Brunswick St. - Jersey City,
NJ - Registered, 1890-
1910, 7-3/8", $250-350.

Monroe Cider & Vinegar Co. – Ferndale Cal.
Aqua, 6-1/8", smooth base, tooled top.............**$75-150**
American 1895-1905 (rare)

Monroe Bottling – Works – Fortuna, Cal.
Light green, 7", smooth base, tooled top........**$100-250**
American 1898-1899 (scarce)

Montgomery – Carbonating Co.
– Montgomery, W. Va.
Ice blue, 6-1/2", smooth base, tooled top **$65-85**
American 1880-1890

Morgan & Co – Selma, Cal.
Pale aqua, 7", smooth base, tooled top, four-piece
mold **$300-600**
American 1905-1920 (rare)

**Nevada – Soda Water – Grass Valley – Nevada Co
– Cal. (on one side) W.E. Deamer (on other side)**
Medium aqua, 6-1/2", smooth base (embossed with
gravitating stopper made by John Matthews Pat
October 11 1864 NY), tooled top **$60-100**
American 1880-1890 (scarce)

New River – Bottling Co. – Sewell, W. Va
Green tinted, 7", smooth base, "The Liquid," tooled
top **$35-45**
American 1880-1890

Nome – Brewing – And – Bottling Co.
Aqua, 7-13/16", smooth base (no embossing on base),
four-piece mold, tooled top......................**$1,000-2,000**
American (Alaska Territory) 1895-1905 (very rare)

**Otto Brandt – 287 Washington – St
– Newark – N.J. (front) – Trade Mark – O.B.
– This Bottle – Not To Be Sold (back)**
Aqua, 6-7/8", smooth base, "Pat 8," tooled
top **$20-30**
American 1890-1910

P.J. Fitzpatrick – Newburgh – N.Y. – PJG (monogram)
Bluish aqua, smooth base, "Gravitating Stopper
– Made By – John Matthews – Pat – Oct 11 – 1864
– New York," tooled mouth **$45-60**
American 1864-1870

**Palmyra Bottling Work – Palmyra Pa – Registered
(embossed with "P" in oval slug plate)**
Ice blue, 6-3/4", smooth base, tooled top $20-30
American 1880-1890

Paul Jeenicke – San Jose
Amber, 6-3/4", smooth base, applied
top $2,000-4,000
American 1880-1890 (rare)

**Pioneer – Trade (motif of anchor)
Mark – Soda Works – P.O.**
Blue aqua, 6-1/8", smooth base, tooled top.......$40-60
American 1880-1895

Property Of – Monterey Soda Works – Cal.
Aqua, 7", smooth base, tooled top $75-125
American 1890-1910

Quinnimont – Bottling Co. – Quinnimont, W. Va.
Green tint, 7", smooth base "This Bottle Is Never Sold-
M.G. & G. Co.," tooled top $55-75
American 1870-1880

Ramona – Bottling – Works – Los Angeles, Cal.
Dark aqua, 6-1/2", smooth base, tooled top ..$100-200
American 1905-1909 (rare)

**Registered – Biedenharn – Candy
Co – Vicksburg – Miss.**
Aqua, 7-1/4", smooth base, "B.C.C.," tooled
top $275-375
American 1890-1900 (bottle that started The Coca-Cola
Company)

**Registered – Lynch & Livingston
– Point Pleasant – N.J.**
Aqua, 6-5/8", mug-based, tooled top $40-50
American 1870-1890

Richmond Soda Works – R.S.W. – Point Richmond
Light aqua, 7", smooth base, tooled top.........$100-300
American 1902-1914 (rare)

**The Standard Bottling Works & Mfg.
Co – Cripple Creek – Colo.**
Aqua green, 6-5/8", smooth base, tooled top.....$40-55
American 1880-1890

San Diego – Trade (star) Mark – Soda Works
Light purple, 6-3/4", smooth base, tooled
top $150-300
American 1888-1889

**Santa Rosa Bottling Co. – SRBCO
(intertwined in center) – Santa Rosa, Cal.**
Aqua, 7", smooth base, tooled top $60-80
American 1887-1910

**S.C. Palmer – Washington – D.C.
– This Bottle – Is Never Sold**
Deep amber, 7-1/8", smooth base, tooled
top $350-450
American 1890-1900

**Simon James – 27 – Brunswick St.
– Jersey City, NJ – Registered**
Lime green, 7-3/8", smooth base, tooled
top $250-350
American 1890-1910 (rare in this color)

Solano Soda Work – Vacaville – California
Aqua, 6-1/2", smooth base, tooled top...............$40-75
American 1903-1910

Standard – Bottling Works – Minneapolis – Minn.
Medium amber, 6-7/8", smooth base (H.R.),
tooled top $55-65
American 1880-1890

The C.C. Co. – Charleston, W. Va
Ice blue, 7", smooth base, tooled top $40-65
American 1880-1890

**Tri-State – Bottling Co. – Huntington, W. Va. (front)
– This Bottle Never Sold – M.B. & G. Co. (back)**
Green tint, 6-1/2", smooth base, tooled top $50-60
American 1880-1910

Ukiah Soda Works – Ukiah – Cal.
Purple tint, 7", smooth base, tooled top $100-150
American 1808-1910

West Va. – Carbonating Co. – Hinton, W. Va
Aqua, 6-1/2", smooth base, tooled top...............$35-50
American 1880-1900

Winslow Junction Bottling Co. (W & R) – N.J.
Aqua, 8", 10 vertical panels around base,
tooled top $45-55
American 1880-1890

**Wm. A. Kearney – Shamokin – Pa
– This Bottle – Never Sold**
Deep amber, 8-7/8", smooth base, tooled
collar mouth..$300-600
American 1880-1900

Ink Bottles

Ink bottles are unique because of their centuries-old history, which provides collectors today with a wider variety of designs and shapes than any other group of bottles. People often ask why a product as cheap to produce as ink was sold in such decorative bottles. While other bottles were disposed of or returned after use, ink bottles were usually displayed on desks in dens, libraries, and studies. It's safe to assume that even into the late 1880s people who bought ink bottles considered the design of the bottle as well as the quality of its contents.

Prior to the 18th century, most ink was sold in brass or copper containers. The wealthy would then refill their gold and silver inkwells from these storage containers. Ink that was sold in glass and pottery bottles in England in the 1700s had no brand name identification and, at best, would have a label identifying the ink and/or the manufacturer.

In 1792, the first patent for the commercial production of ink was issued in England, 24 years before the first American patent, which was issued in 1816.

Bank of England, 1880-1890, 3-1/2", $250-300.

Molded ink bottles began to appear in America around 1815 to 1816, and the blown three-mold variety came into use during the late 1840s. The most common ink bottle shape, the umbrella, is a multisided conical that can be found with both pontiled and smooth bases. One of the more collectible ink bottles is the teakettle, identified by the neck, which extends upward at an angle from the base.

As the fountain pen grew in popularity between 1885 and 1890, ink bottles gradually became less decorative and soon became just another plain bottle.

Bauman's Ink - Pittsburgh, 1880-1890, 2-3/4", $150-250.

Assortment of ink bottles, 1875-1900, 1-7/8" - 7-1/2", $200-300 (all).

Alling's – Pat'd Apl 25 1871 (Label: Jet Black High School Ink, Manufactured Solely By Fred D. Alling, Rochester, N.Y.)
Pale blue green, 1-7/8", smooth base, tooled mouth
....**$100-150**
American 1871-1875

Bank – Of – England – Cottage Ink
Aqua, 3-1/2", smooth base, tooled mouth......**$250-350**
American 1880-1890

Bauman's – Ink – Pittsburgh
Clear, 2-3/4", smooth base, ground lip **$150-250**
American 1880-1890 (rare)

Blown three-mold geometric ink, 1810-1835,
1-5/8" h. x 2-1/4" dia., $150-250.

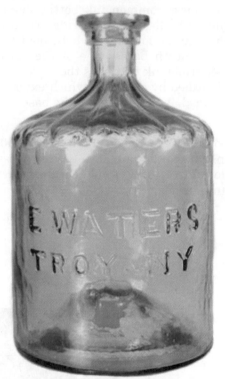

E. Waters - Troy, NY, 1840-1860, open
pontil, 6-7/8", $275-375.

Elgin Ink, 1885-1895, 2", $75-100; Higgins American India Ink, Brooklyn, 1885-1895, 1-7/8", $75-100.

Bertinguiot
Medium yellow olive, 2", pontil-scarred base, tooled
mouth **$400-500**
American 1845-1860

Blake – N.Y. Umbrella Ink
Pale aqua, 3", 8-sided, open pontil, rolled lip
....**$500-700**
American 1845-1860

Blake & – Herring – N.Y. – Umbrella Ink
Emerald green 3", 8-sided, open pontil, rolled lip
....**$3,000-4,000**
American 1845-1860 (rare color, size, and embossing)

**Blackwood & Co. (monogram in
diamond) London – Igloo Ink**
Pale greenish aqua, 2", smooth base,
sheared lip **$50-100**
English 1875-1895

Blackwood & Co. – 18 Bread St. Hill – London
Cobalt blue, 2-1/8", 8-sided, smooth base,
flared lip **$80-120**
English 1890-1910

**Blue Black Ledger, United Manufacturing
Stationers, William Eden & Co. Importing
Stationers' – 430 Broadway, New York**
White pottery, smooth base, 98% original label .**$60-90**
American 1890-1920

Buller Ink – Cincinnati – Sided Ink
Bluish aqua, 2-1/4", 12-sided, pontil-scarred base,
rolled lip **$150-250**
American 1840-1860

Carter's (on base) – Clover Ink
Cobalt blue, 3", 6-sided, smooth base,
ABM lip **$140-180**
American 1920-1930

Carter's – Ink (around shoulder) – Master Ink
Medium yellow green, 9-3/4", smooth base,
applied sloping double collar mouth with tooled
pour spout **$100-150**
American 1870-1885

Commercial (monogram) Ink London
Deep teal blue, barrel shape, 5-5/8", pontil-scarred
base, tooled lip with double pour spout..........**$150-250**
English 1845-1865

Davids & Black – New York
Medium blue green, 5-1/4", open pontil, applied
sloping collar mouth..**$275-375**
American 1845-1860

Harrison's Columbian Ink, 1840-1860,
open pontil, 2", $250-350.

Harrison's Columbian Ink, 1840-1860, open
pontil, 4" each, $300-400 (pair).

Harrison's Columbian Ink, 1840-1860, open
pontil, 4-5/8", each, $300-400 (pair).

Davids & Black – New York
Deep blue green, 10-1/8", open pontil, three-piece
mold, applied sloping collar mouth with tooled pour
spout **$500-700**
American 1845-1860 (rare size)

Davis & – D M – Miller – Umbrella Ink
Bluish aqua, 2-1/2", rib pattern with two embossed
panels, open pontil, rolled lip **$400-700**
American 1845-1860

Derby – All British
Deep cobalt blue, 2-3/8", triangular shape, smooth
base, rough sheared mouth **$80-140**
English 1880-1890

E. Waters – Troy – NY
Light blue green, 5-1/4", iron pontil,
applied mouth **$600-900**
American 1845-1890

Elgin – Ink
Clear, 2", smooth base, tooled lip **$75-100**
American 1885-1895

Harrison's
Columbian Ink,
1840-1860, 5-5/8",
$200-300.

Harrison's Columbian
Ink - Patent, 1840-1860,
5-3/4", $140-180.

Harrison's Columbian Ink, 1840-1860,
open pontil, 5-5/8" $200-300.

Estes – N.Y. Ink – Umbrella Ink
Aqua, 4-1/8", 8-sided, open pontil,
rolled lip..$175-275
American 1840-1860

Farley – Sided Ink
Medium amber, 1-5/8", 8-sided, pontil-scarred base,
rolled lip..$300-400
American 1845-1860

**Fine – Black Ink – Made & Sold – By
– J.L. Thompson – Troy NY**
Yellow olive with amber tone, 5-7/8", pontil-scarred
base, flared lip..$700-900
American 1840-1860

Gaylord's – Superior – Record – Ink – Boston
Deep olive green, 5-7/8", pontil-scarred base,
flared lip..$2,500-3,500
American 1835-1860

G & Rs – American Writing Fluid
Bluish aqua, 2", pontil-scarred base,
rolled lip..$400-600
American 1845-1860

Government – W.B. Todd's – Writing Ink
Medium teal blue, 3-1/8", smooth base, "
tooled mouth $100-150
American 1885-1895

**Granite State Ink – L.P. Farley
Marlow, N.H. – Igloo Ink**
Bluish aqua, 1-7/8", smooth base,
ground lip...$100-150
American 1875-1890

Harrison's – Indelible – Preparation
Clear, 2-3/8", 8-sided, pontil-scarred base,
rolled lip..$350-450
American 1845-1860

Harrison's – Columbian – Ink
Bluish aqua, 10-3/4" (gallon), 12-sided, pontil-scarred
base, applied mouth................................$1,200-1,800
American 1845-1860

Harrison – Tippecanoe – Cabin Ink
Clear, 4-1/8", rectangular form, pontil-scarred base,
rolled lip...$15,000-25,000
American 1840 (very rare, made for William Henry
Harrison's 1840 presidential campaign)

Harrison's
Columbian
Ink – Patent,
1840-1860, open
pontil, 3-7/8",
$150-200.

Harrison's
Columbian Ink,
1840-1860,
pontil-scarred
base, 11",
$3,500-5,500.

J. K. Palmer
- Chemist - Boston,
1840-1860,
$700-900.

Master Ink, 1865-
1880, 9-3/4",
$375-550.

**Hohenthal – Brothers & Co
– Indelible – Writing Ink – N.Y.**
Deep olive amber, 9-1/8", pontil-scarred base, applied
sloping collar **$800-1,200**
American 1845-1865

Hover – Phila – Umbrella Ink
Bluish aqua, 2-3/8", 8-sided, open pontil,
rolled lip **$300-400**
American 1845-1860

Hyde – London
Deep cobalt blue, 5-3/4", smooth base, tooled lip with
pour spout **$100-200**
English 1880-1895

III – IV Rd 12 6 (inside diamond) – Isaac & C L – Pool
Deep purple amethyst, 5", smooth base, tooled
pour spout **$80-120**
English 1880-1895

J.E. – Peterman – Ink – Philada
Greenish aqua, 3-3/4", 12-sided, open pontil,
flared lip **$375-475**
American 1840-1860

J/J. Butler – Cin
Bluish aqua, 2-7/8", pontil-scarred base,
rolled lip **$100-150**
American 1845-1855

J.W. – Seaton – Louisville – Ky
Medium blue green, 2-1/8", 10-sided, open pontil,
rolled lip..**$1,000-1,500**
American 1840-1860 (rare with color and embossing)

James S – Mason & Co – Umbrella Ink
Aqua, 2-1/2", 8-sided, pontil-scarred base,
rolled lip...**$275-375**
American 1845-1860

Jones – Empire – Ink – N.Y.
Deep olive green, 7-1/8", 12-sided, open pontil,
applied mouth **$3,500-4,500**
American 1840-1860

T & M - T & M,
1840-1860, 2-5/8",
$100-170.

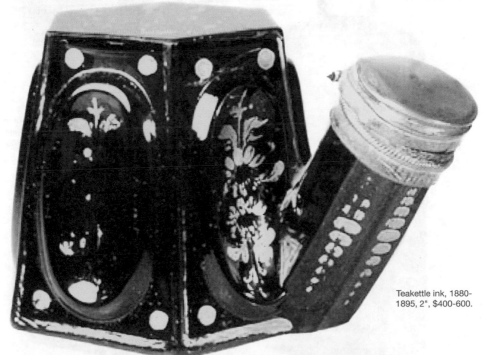

Teakettle ink, 1880-
1895, 2", $400-600.

**Josiah – Johnson – Japan – Writing – Fluid
– London – Stoneware Teakettle Ink**
Light brown pottery, 2-1/2", 6-sided, smooth
base...**$150-200**
English 1875-1900

Kirtland's – Ink – W & H – Igloo Ink
Yellow with amber tone, 1-7/8", smooth base, sheared
lip..**$800-1,200**
American 1875-1895

L.C. – Vertu Bordeaux – Engre De La Grange
Deep amber, 2", pontil-scarred base,
tooled lip..**$250-350**
French 1845-1860

Levison's – Inks – St. Louis
Aqua, 2-1/2", smooth base, tooled mouth......**$300-500**
American 1880-1895

M & P – New York – Umbrella Ink
Light blue green, 2-3/4", 6-sided, pontil-scarred base,
rolled lip...**$1,000-1,500**
American 1845-1860 (rare in aqua, extremely rare in other
colors)

Pattern Molded Handled Inkwell
Light yellow green, 2-1/4", 19-rib pattern, pontil-
scarred base, flared rim, applied handle...**$1,800-2,800**
American 1825-1840

Perkins – Superior – Indelible – Ink
Clear, 2-5/8", open pontil, flared lip................**$200-300**
American 1845-1860 (rare embossed ink)

**Pomeroys Inks – Keystone Potter Co.
– Rochester, Pa – Pottery Master Ink**
Cream, 7-3/4", smooth base, pour spout.......**$100-150**
American 1880-1900

Umbrella Ink,
1840-1860,
pontil-scarred
base, 2-5/8",
$700-1,000 (rare).

T.K. Hibbert -
Pittsburgh, 1840-1860,
open pontil, 5-5/8",
$2,500-3,500.

Umbrella ink, 1840-
1860, open pontil,
2-5/8", $200-300.

R.B. – Snow – St. – Louis – Umbrella Ink
Yellow olive, 2-1/8", 12-sided, smooth base, rough
sheared and unfinished lip **$1,500-2,500**
American 1855-1865

Runge – Tinte (motif of horse) – Mf & R – Master Ink
Black amethyst, 8-1/8", smooth base, tooled mouth
and pour spout **$140-180**
German 1880-1910

**Saltglaze Stoneware Bulk Ink Jug, (embossed),
"Harrison's Patent Columbian Ink"**
Gray pottery, 11", applied handle....................**$700-900**
American 1840-1860

S. Fine – Blk. Ink
Medium amber, 3-1/4", open pontil,
rolled lip **$175-275**
American 1845-1860 (extremely rare color for this ink)

S.I. – Comp
Milk glass, 2-3/8", barrel shape,smooth base,
tooled mouth **$400-600**
American 1870-1890

**S.O. Dunbar – Taunton – Mass (Label:
Dunbar's Black Ink, Superior To Any Other
Ink In Use, S.O. Dunbar, Taunton, Mass)**
Aqua, 3-7/8", 8-sided, open pontil,
flared lip **$300-400**
American 1850-1860

Umbrella ink,
1840-1860,
open pontil,
2-3/8",
$80-150.

Umbrella ink,
1840-1860,
open pontil,
2-1/2",
$200-300.

Umbrella ink,
1840-1860,
pontil-scarred
base, 2-1/4",
$2,000-3,000.

Umbrella ink, 1840-
1860, open pontil,
2-5/8", $150-200.

Stafford's Carmine Non-Copying – Master Ink
Clear, smooth base, 98% label **$60-90**
American 18901920

Stafford's – Ink – Made In U.S.A – Master Ink
Amber, 9-1/8", smooth base, tooled mouth........**$35-45**
American 1890-1910

Superior Black Ink Preparte By Stretch, Bennett & Co. Philadelphia – Labeled Umbrella Ink
Medium sapphire blue, 2-3/4", 8-sided, smooth base, tooled mouth **$275-375**
American 1875-1895

Teakettle Ink – China
White bisque china with red, gold, and black Japanese flower, bird, and tree decoration, 3", applied frond on top and applied bird on original stopper **$400-600**
European 1875-1890

Teakettle Ink – Double Font
Milk glass, 2-1/4", 8-sided, smooth base, ground lips, applied mother of pearl panels........................**$700-900**
American 1875-1895

Teakettle Ink – Miniature
Medium green, 1-1/8", 8-sided, polished pontil, polished lip **$400-600**
American 1875-1890

T. Davids & Co (along the edge of an English registry stamp) – Pottery Master Ink
Cream, 8-1/4", smooth base, pour spout **$40-60**
English 1880-1900

T. Davids & Co (along the edge of an English registry stamp) – Pottery Master Ink
Cream, 7-1/2", smooth base, pour spout **$40-60**
English 1880-1900

T.K. Hibbert – Pittsburgh
Cobalt blue, 5-5/8", open pontil, applied mouth **$2,500-3,500**
American 1840-1860

Thacker – London – Domed Ink
Blue green with amber streaks, 1-5/8", smooth base, tooled top **$35-45**
English 1885-1895

Unoco Fast Black Writing Ink – Umbrella Ink
Yellow olive green, 2-3/4", 8-sided, smooth base, tooled mouth, 97% label **$250-350**
American 1870-1885

Ward's Ink
Emerald green, 4-3/4", smooth base, applied mouth with tooled pour spout **$150-200**
American 1860-1870

Warrens – Congress – Ink – Sided Ink
Medium olive green, 2-7/8", 8-sided, pontil-scarred base, rolled lip **$800-1,200**
American 1845-1860

W.E. Bonney – Barrel Ink
Light blue green, 2-1/2", pontil-scarred base, rolled lip...**$400-700**
American 1845-1860 (rare in this color)

Wood's – Black Ink – Portland
Deep olive amber, 2-3/8", pontil-scarred base, tooled lip...**$1,000-1,500**
American 1845-1860

Writing – Fluid – Petroleum – P.B. & Co. – Barrel Ink
Aqua, 2-1/2", smooth base, applied mouth....**$300-400**
American 1875-1895

Figural Inks

Ink – Adrien Maurin – Depose – Locomotive
Bluish aqua, 2-1/8", smooth base, ground lip
....**$800-1,200**
American 1875-1890

Ink – Building (1776-1876)
Clear glass, 3-1/2", "Patented – April," smooth base, "Patented – April 11 1876," ground lip............**$400-600**
American 1876

Ink – BF– House
Milk glass, 4-7/8", smooth base, tooled mouth **$600-800**
American 1875-1890

Ink – Liberty Bell – 1776-1926
Clear, 2-5/8", smooth base, tooled mouth......**$175-275**
American 1926 (made for the 150th anniversary of the signing of the Declaration of Independence)

Inkwell – Luzia – Depose Made In France
Frosted aqua, 1-7/8", coiled snake form, smooth base, polished lip, domed lid **$150-250**

Inkwell – Ma & Pa Carter Inkwells – Carter's Inx
Bisque pottery with multicolored paint, both 3-3/4", smooth base, "Pat'd Jan 6 1914, Germany"...**$200-300**
American 1914-1920

Teakettle Ink – Benjamin Franklin
Cobalt blue, 2-3/4", smooth base, ground lip **$700-1,000**
American 1875-1895

Teakettle Ink – Figural Cat
Clear glass, 2-1/8", smooth base, ground lip **$400-600**
American 1875-1890

Teakettle Ink – Figural Foot Wearing A Sandal
Clear glass, 1-1/2", smooth base, rough sheared and ground lip **$275-375**
French 1875-1900

Teakettle Ink – Snail
Clear glass, 1-5/8", smooth base, ground lip **$300-400**
English 1875-1900

Inkwell – E. Mauring (on back of shoe)
Deep cobalt blue, 2-1/8", smooth base, sheared and ground lip **$1,000-1,800**
French 1880-1900

Medicine Bottles

The medicine bottle group includes all pieces specifically made to hold patented medicines. Bitter and cure bottles, however, are excluded from this category because the healing powers of these mixtures were very questionable.

A patent medicine was one whose formula was registered with the U.S. Patent office, which opened in 1790. Not all medicines were patented, since the procedure required the manufacturer to reveal the medicine's contents. Following the passage of the Pure Food and Drug Act of 1907, most patent medicine companies went out of business after consumers learned that most medicines consisted of liquor diluted with water and an occasional pinch of opiates, strychnine, and arsenic. I have spent many enjoyable hours reading the labels on these bottles and wondering how anyone survived the recommended doses.

One of the oldest and most collectible medicine bottles—the embossed Turlington "Balsam of Life" bottle—was manufactured in England from 1723 to 1900. The first embossed U.S. medicine bottle dates from around 1810. When searching for these bottles, always look for embossing and original boxes. Embossed "Shaker" or "Indian" medicine bottles are very collectible and valuable. Most embossed medicines made before 1840 are clear and aqua, with the embossed greens, amber, and various shades of blues, specifically the darker cobalt blues, being much more collectible and valuable.

Aikins - Tonic - Syrup, 1830-1845, 4-1/4", $250-350 (extremely rare).

**A.L. Scovill – Dr. A. Rogers – Liverwort
Tar – & Canchalagua – Cincinnati**
Deep bluish aqua, 7-1/2", open pontil, applied
mouth $150-200
American 1840-1860

**Althrop's – Constitutional Tonic
– Chicago – & – New York**
Aqua, 9-7/8", smooth base, "D.S.G.CO," applied
mouth $100-150
American 1870-1880

American – Eagle – Liniment
Bluish aqua, 5-1/8", 6-sided, smooth base,
flared lip...$140-180
American 1850-1860

American Quinine – Elixir – Chicago – Ills
Medium amber, 9-3/8", smooth base, tooled
mouth $150-200
American 1880-1890

Anderson's – Dermador
Pale aqua, 4-1/8", open pontil, rolled lip.............$40-70
American 1880-1890

Atkins – Tonic – Syrup
Light green, 4-1/4", 8-sided, open pontil, inward
rolled lip..$500-700
American 1830-1845 (extremely rare)

**Atwood's Vegetable Dysentery Drops, Manufactured
By Moses Atwood, Georgetown, Mass**
Olive amber, 6-1/4", pontil-scarred base, applied
sloping collar mouth..$250-350
American 1835-1850

Ayers – Ague – Cure – Lowell – Mass
Aqua, 7", pontil-scarred base, applied
mouth $150-200
American 1840-1855 (scarce)

Bach's – American – Compound – Auburn, N.Y.
Aqua, 5-3/8", pontil-scarred bases, applied sloping
collar mouth...$30-40
American 1840-1865

**Baker's Vegetable – Blood & Liver – Cure – Lookout
– Mountain – Medicine Co. – Manufacturers
– & – Proprietors – Greenville – Tenn**
Medium amber, 9-3/4", smooth base, tooled
mouth $250-350

**Balm – Of – X Thousand – Flowers
– Merchant – New York**
Aqua, 5-1/8", pontil-scarred base, applied
mouth $150-200
American 1845-1855 (rare)

**Barnes Magnolia Water – Nueva
York – Ph.H. Drake Y.Cia.**
Milk glass, 7-1/2", smooth base, tooled lip.....$100-150
American 1880-1900

**Brant's Indian – Purifying Extract
– M.T. Wallace – Proprietor**
Bluish aqua, 6-3/4", open pontil, applied sloping collar
mouth $140-180
American 1840-1860

Bringhurst's – King's – Mixture – Wilmington
Aqua, 6-1/8", open pontil, applied mouth.......$350-450
American 1840-1860

Brown's – Blood Cure – Philadelphia
Medium green, 6-3/8", smooth base, "M.B.W. –U.S.A.,"
tooled mouth $150-200
American 1890-1910

**B.W. Fetters – Druggist – Philadelphia
– Patented August 1, 1876**
Medium blue green, 8-5/8", smooth base,
tooled mouth $200-300
American 1880-1890 (rare)

**C. Brinckerhoffs – Health Restorative
– Price 1.00 – New York**
Yellow olive green, 7-1/4", pontil-scarred base,
applied mouth $1,000-1,500
American 1840-1860

Brants Indian
- Purifying Extract
- M.T. Wallace
-Proprietor,
1840-1860 6-3/8",
$140-180.

**Christian Xander's – Melliston – Wild
Cherry Cordial – Washington, D. C.**
Clear, 9-3/8", smooth base, tooled mouth **$80-100**
American 1890-1910

**Cibil's Fluid Extract Of Beef, Cibils
Co Importers, New York**
Emerald green, 4", smooth base, tooled
mouth **$40-60**
American 1890-1925

**Citrate Of Magnesia – Sanford-
Frazier – Drug Co. – Enid, Okla**
Bright green, 7-3/4", smooth base, tooled mouth,
original porcelain stopper..............................**$150-200**
American 1890-1910

**Clemens Indian (motif of Indian) Tonic
– Prepared By – Geo. W. House**
Aqua, 5-5/8", open pontil, folded lip **$800-1,200**
American 1840-1860

**Connell S. Brahminical – Moonplant
– East Indian – Remedies (motif of feet
surrounded by stars) Trade Mark**
Medium amber, 8-1/2", smooth base, applied double
collar mouth..**$175-225**
American 1880-1890

**Damascus (motif of an Arab, city, and
camel) San Francisco – Cor. Geary & Mason
Sts. – Trade Mark – Stoddart Bros**
Yellow amber, 4-1/2", smooth base, "W.T. & CO.,"
tooled lip..**$150-200**
American 1890-1900

**Dandelion & Tomato – Panacea – Ransom
& Steven – Druggists Boston**
Aqua, 9", open pontil, applied sloping collar
mouth **$500-700**
American 1840-1855

Davison & Son – Fleet Street
Yellow olive green, 6", pontil-scarred base, applied
string lip...**$200-300**
English 1770-1790

Ditchett's – Remedy For – The Piles N.Y.
Olive green, 9", smooth base, applied sloping double
collar mouth..**$3,000-4,000**
American 1855-1865 (extremely rare)

Doct. – Harrison's – Tonic – Chalybeate
Medium emerald green, 9", smooth base, applied
mouth **$275-550**
American 1865-1875 (rare)

C. Heimstreet & Co.
- Troy, N.Y., 1840-1855,
7-1/8", $250-375.

Carter's - Spanish
- Mixture, 1840-1860,
8-3/8", $700-900.

Doctor – Warren's (backward "S") – Cough – Mixture
Clear, 4", pontil-scarred base, flared lip $150-200
American 1840-1855 (rare)

**Dr. Bell's – British Liniment – S.M.
Shaw & Co – Alfred Me U.S.A.**
Bluish aqua, 6-1/8", open pontil, rolled lip $350-450
American 1845-1855 (extremely rare)

Dr. Birminghan's – Antibillious – Blood Purifier
Medium teal blue, 8-5/8", smooth base, applied square
collar mouth.. $400-600
American 1865-1875

**Dr. C.W. Roback's – Scandinavian – Blood Purifier
– Purely Vegetable – Dyspepsia – Liver Complaint**
Deep aqua, 8-1/2", iron pontil, applied double collar
mouth $350-450
American 1840-1860 (scarce)

Dr. Davis's – Departure – Phila
Medium blue green, 9-1/2", iron pontil, applied sloping
collar mouth... $1,500-2,000
American 1840-1860

Dr. E. Blecker's – Tonic Mixture – For – Chills & Fever
Deep bluish aqua, 6-7/8", pontil-scarred base, applied
sloping collar mouth.. $600-800
American 1840-1855 (rare)

**Dr. Edward's – Tar Wild Cherry – &
Naptha – Cough Syrup**
Aqua, 5-1/8", open pontil, rolled lip $200-300
American 1840-1860

Dr. F. Houck's – Panacea – New York
Bluish aqua, 8-1/2', smooth base, applied sloping
double collar mouth $150-200
American 1855-1865

Dr. Fenner's – Kidney & Backache – Cure
Medium amber, 10-1/4", smooth base, tooled
mouth $50-75
American 1880-1895

Dr. Friend's – Cough Balsam – Morristown N.J.
Bluish aqua, 6-3/8", open pontil, applied sloping collar
mouth $375-475
American 1840-1860 (very rare)

Clemens Indian (motif of
Indian) Tonic - Prepared
By - Geo. W. House
1840-1860, 5-5/8", $800-
1,200. (front and back)

Dr. Geo. W. Fisher's – Catarrh Cure – Baltimore, Md
Golden yellow amber, 5-7/8", smooth base,
tooled lip..**$140-180**
American 1890-1910 (rare colored cure bottle)

Dr. H. Van Vleck's – Family Medicine – Pittsburgh Pa
Cornflower blue, 8-1/8", pontil-scarred base, applied
sloping collar mouth..................................**$2,200-3,200**
American 1845-1855

Dr. H.W. Bergner's – Stomach – Reading, Pa
Aqua, 4-3/4", open pontil, rolled lip **$150-200**
American 1840-1860

**Dr. H.W. Swartz – Cancer Specialist
– New Oxford, Pa**
Clear, 6-1/2", smooth base, tooled mouth......**$100-150**
American 1885-1900 (very rare)

**Dr. H. James – N0, 19 Grand St. – Jersey City
– N.J. – Also No 14 Decil St – Strand – London**
Bluish aqua, 8-1/8", open pontil, applied
mouth **$180-275**
American 1840-1860

Dr. J.A. Goodale – Newton & Dover – N.J.
Bluish aqua, 3-7/8", open pontil, rolled lip **$150-200**
American 1840-1860

Dr. Jackson's – Pile – Embrocation – Phila
Pale green aqua, 3-7/8", pontil-scarred base, wide
flared out lip..**$200-300**
American 1845-1855

**Dr. Jacob Webber's – Invigorating Cordial
– T. Jones Agent & Proprietor – New York**
Aqua, 9-3/4", smooth base, applied double collar
mouth **$150-175**
American 1855-1865

Dr. Cavanuagh's - Pile Salve - St. Louis, Mo,
1840-1860, 2-3/8", $350-450 (rare).

Dr. Jayne's – Alterative – Philada
Aqua, 5-3/4", pontil-scarred base, applied sloping
collar mouth..**$30-40**
American 1840-1865

**Dr. Jones – Red (motif of 3-leaf clover)
– Clover – Tonic – E. Y. Griggs – Ottawa, Ills**
Medium amber, 9", smooth base, tooled
mouth **$70-90**
American 1880-1890

**Dr. Kilmer & Co – Catarrh – Dr. Kilmer's
– Cough Cure – Consumption Oil
– Specific – Binghamton, N.Y.**
Aqua, 8-5/8", smooth base, tooled mouth......**$500-700**
American 1880-1895

Dr. King's – Croup – & – Cough – Syrup
Pale aqua, 5", open pontil, applied double collar
mouth **$120-160**
American 1840-1860 (scarce)

**Dr. Mann's – Celebrated – Ague
Balsam – Galion, Ohio**
Deep aqua, 7", iron pontil, applied double collar
mouth **$350-460**
American 1840-1860

Dr. Markley's – Family – Medicine – Lancaster, Pa
Aqua, 6-1/2", open pontil, applied double collar
mouth **$275-375**
American 1854-1860

**Dr. Ordway's Celebrated Pain Destroyer (Label:
Dr. Ordway's Celebrated Pain Destroyer, Ordway
& Wadleigh Sole Proprietors, Lawrence, Mass)**
Clear, 5-1/8", 12-sided, open pontil, flared
out lip...**$70-100**
American 1835-1850

Dr. S.A. Weaver's – Cerate
Aqua, 2-3/4", open pontil, rolled lip **$250-350**
American 1840-1860

**Dr. S.F. Stowe's – Ambrosial Nectar
(motif of stemmed glass inside vine
frame) – Patented May 22, 1866**
Light yellow green (citron), 8", smooth base, applied
mouth **$150-200**
American 1885-1895 (scarce)

Dr. D.P. Brown - Buffalo - N.Y. - 12-sided, 1850-
1860, 1-3/16" h., 2-3/8" base dia., $400-700.

Dr. S. Hart – New York – Vegetable – Extract
Aqua, 7-1/4", open pontil, applied tapered
mouth $300-400
American 1840-1860 (rare)

**Dr. Sage's – Catarrh – Remedy – Buffalo
– Dr. Pierce's – Buffalo – N.Y.**
Emerald green, 2-1/8", smooth base, tooled
mouth $80-100
American 1880-1890

Dr. Swayne's – Panacea – Philada
Clear with amethyst tint, 8", smooth base,
tooled lip...$140-180
American 1880-1890

**Dr. Taylor's Chronothermal – Balsam Of – Liverwort
– For Consumption – Asthma & C.G.J.L.**
Bluish aqua, 8-1/8", pontil-scarred base, applied
sloping collar mouth.......................................$275-375
American 1840-1855 (rare)

**Dr. W. Eaton Boynton's Blood Cure And
Humor Destroyer (labeled medicine bottle)**
Bluish aqua, 7-1/2", pontil-scarred base, applied
sloping collar mouth..$140-180
American 1830-1850

**Drink – Wm Radam's – Microbe
– Killer (around shoulder)**
Medium amber, 10-3/8", smooth base, tooled
mouth $250-350
American 1895-1905 (one of the rarest of the Radam
bottles)

Duffy's Formula
Amber, 9-7/8", smooth base, applied
mouth $100-150
American 1875-1890

Extract – Valaria – Shaker – Fluid
Bluish aqua, 3-3/4", open pontil, flared lip......$125-150
American 1845-1855

Dr. H. James - No.
19 Grand St. - Jersey
City - N.J.- Also No.
14 Cecil St - Strand
- London, 1840-1860,
8-1/8", $180-275
(extremely rare).

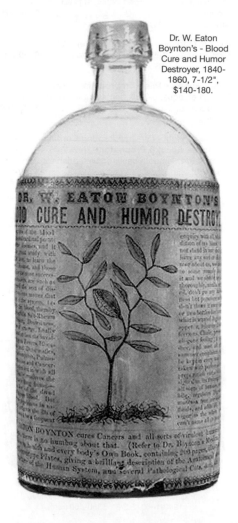

Dr. W. Eaton
Boynton's - Blood
Cure and Humor
Destroyer, 1840-
1860, 7-1/2",
$140-180.

Fairchild's – Sure – Remedy
Bluish aqua, 7-7/8", pontil-scarred base, applied
sloping collar mouth **$800-1,200**
American 1840-1860 (extremely rare)

**Fisher's – Seaweed – Extract – Manx Shrub
(motif of shrub) – Registered – Company
– Ulverston – Quarrie's Patent**
Yellow green, 5-1/4", triangular form with bulged neck,
smooth base, tooled lip **$250-350**
American 1890-1910

Forestine Kidney Cure
Medium amber, 9-3/8", smooth base, tooled
mouth **$50-75**
American 1880-1895

From – Dr. H.C. Porter – & – Son's – Drug Store
Clear, 7-5/8", smooth base, tooled mouth **$175-275**
American 1885-1900

Gell's – Dalby's Carminative
Pale blue green, 3-7/8", open pontil, flared
out lip..**$200-300**
American 1825-1835

**Germ Bacteria Or – Fungus Destroyer – Wm Radams
– Microbe (man beating a skeleton) Registered
Trade Mark Dec. 13, 1887 – Cures – All – Diseases**
Amber, 10-1/4", smooth base, tooled lip **$200-300**
American 1887-1895

**Gun Wa's – Chinese – Herb – &
– Vegetable – Remedies**
Amber, 6-3/4", smooth base (**H**), tooled lip.....**$300-400**
American 1890-1900

Gell's - Dalby's
- Carminative,
1825-1835, 3-7/8",
$200-300.

Germ Bacteria Or
- Fungus Destroyer
- Wm Radams
- Microbe Killer
(man beating a
skeleton) Registered
Trade Mark Dec. 13
1887 - Cures - All -
Diseases, 1887-1895,
10-1/4", $200-300.

**Guinn's Pioneer – Blood Renewer
– Macon Medicine Co. – Macon Ga**
Reddish amber, 11-1/8", smooth base, applied double
collar mouth...**$350-450**
American 1875-1885

G.W. Merchant – Lockport – N.Y.
Blue green, 5-1/8", open pontil-scarred base, applied
sloping collar mouth..**$250-350**
American 1840-1860

H. Lake – Indian – Specific
Aqua, 8-1/4", open pontil, applied mouth....**$800-1,400**
American 1840-1860

Hermanu's – Germany's Infallible – Dyspepsia Cure
Yellow amber, 2-7/8", smooth base,
tooled lip...**$80-100**
American 1880-1890

**Hoffman's Mixture – For – Gonorrhea Gleet
& C. – Solomons & Co. – Savannah, Geo**
Aqua, 5-7/8", smooth base, tooled lip **$80-120**
American 1880-1890 (rare)

Holdens – Dysentery – & – Diarrhoea – Cordial
Aqua, 5-1/4", open pontil, applied mouth.......**$350-450**
American 1840-1860 (rare)

Holme & Kidd
Deep bluish aqua, 6-1/2", pontil-scarred base,
rolled lip **$200-300**
American 1840-1860

Hop – Tonic (on 4 roof panels) Hop Tonic
Medium amber, 9-7/8", smooth base, tooled
mouth **$175-250**
American 1880-1890

Gun Wa's -
Chinese - Herb
& Vegetable
- Remedies,
1890-1900,
6-3/4",
$300-400.

G.W. Merchant
- Lockport
- N.Y., 1840-
1860, 5-1/8",
$250-350.

Hurd's Cough – Balsam
Bluish aqua, 4-5/8", open pontil, rolled lip..........**$40-70**
American 1840-1860

Improved – Distilled – Microbe Killer
Clear, 9-3/4", smooth base, "I.G.CO,"
tooled lip...**$150-200**
American 1890-1910

**Indian – Specific – For Coughs
– Prepared By – Dr. C. Freeman**
Bluish aqua, 5", pontil-scarred base,
flared lip...**$375-500**
American 1835-1850

James L. Bispham – No. 710 – So 2d St – Philada
Teal green, 8-1/4", smooth base, applied
mouth **$140-160**
American 1865-1875

Jas. Tarrant – Druggist – New York
Aqua, 5-1/2", pontil-scarred base, applied sloping
collar mouth...**$30-40**
American 1840-1865

J.B. Hicks – Reading, Pa
Aqua, 4-1/8", open pontil, flared out lip............**$80-100**
American 1840-1860

**Jelly Of – Pomegranate – Preparate
– By – Dr. Gordak – Only**
Aqua, 6-3/4", pontil-scarred base, flared lip ...**$300-400**
American 1840-1860 (scarce)

J.W. Bull's – Recto – Mistura – Baltimore
Aqua, 5-7/8", open pontil, applied mouth.......**$400-600**
American (extremely rare)

Hermanu's -
Germany's Infallible
- Dyspepsia
Cure, 1880-1890,
2-7/8", $80-120.

Improved - Distilled
- Microbe Killer,
1890-1910, 9-3/4",
$150-250.

Jn Sullivan – Pharmacist (JS monogram) – Boston
Milk glass, 5", smooth base, tooled lip **$100-150**
American 1880-1900

John C. Baker Co – Cod Liver Oil – Philadelphia
Clear, 9", smooth base, tooled mouth.............**$120-140**
American 1900-1910

John A. Jones – Baltimore – No 1
Pale aqua, 3-3/8", open pontil, flared lip...........**$70-100**
American 1845-1855

**Jos. Fleming – Druggist – Cor. Market
& Diamond – Pittsbg Pa**
Ice blue, 7-5/8", iron pontil, applied double collar
mouth **$175-275**
American 1845-1855 (extremely rare)

**Lipman Wolfe & Co. / Portland, Oregon (Label:
Extract Of Witch Hazel Bottled By Drug Dept.
Lipman Wolfe & Co. Portland, Oregon)**
Bright green, 7-1/4", smooth base, tooled
mouth **$150-200**
American 1890-1910

Log Cabin – Hops And Buchu – Remedy
Amber, 10-1/8", smooth base, "**Pat. Sept. 6/87,**"
applied blob type mouth **$100-125**
American 1887-1895

Longley's – Panacea
Olive green, 6-3/4", pontil-scarred base, applied double
collar mouth..**$3,500-4,500**
American 1840-1860

John C. Baker - Cod Liver Oil
- Philadelphia, 1900-1910, 9",
$120-140. (front and back)

Lyon's – Power – B & P – N. Y.
Medium blue green, 4-1/4", smooth base,
tooled lip..**$140-180**
American 1860-1880

Lyon's – Power – B & P – N. Y.
Deep reddish puce, 4-1/8", open pontil, inward
rolled lip...**$150-250**
American 1860-1880

**L.Q.C. Wishart's Pine Tree – Tar Cordial
– Phila – Trade (motif of tree) Mark**
Blue green, 10-1/4", smooth base, tooled
mouth...**$150-200**
American 1885-1895

Mad. M.J. Goodman's – Excelsior – Pearl – Drops
Milk glass, 4-5/8", smooth base, rolled lip......**$150-200**
American 1880-1895

Magnes – Carbonic
Amber with white and blue enameled background,
black lettering, 9", smooth base, tooled lip, original
glass stopper...**$140-180**
American 1890-1910

Magnetic – Aether By – Halsted & Co
Aqua, 4-3/8", 9-sided, open pontil, flared
out lip..**$400-600**
American 1840-1860 (extremely rare)

M.B. Riberts's – Vegetable – Embrocation
Light emerald green, 5", pontil-scarred base, applied
sloping collar mouth.......................................**$200-300**
American 1840-1860

**McDonald's – Annihilator – Bronchitis
– Coughs & Colds**
Medium amber, 7-3/4", smooth base, tooled
mouth...**$100-150**
American 1880-1890

Jones - Drops - For
Humors - Or - Anti-
Impetigines, 1840-1860,
4-7/8", $200-275.

Longley's
- Panacea,
pontil-scarred
base, 1840-
1860, 6-3/4",
$3,500-4,500.

M.K. Paine Druggist – & Apothecary – Windsor, Vt
Milk glass, 6-1/2", smooth base, applied
mouth **$150-200**
American 1880-1895

Morley's – Liver And Kidney – Cordial
Medium amber 9", smooth base, tooled
mouth **$70-90**
American 1880-1890

Mother's – Worm Syrup (building with windows and doors) – Edward Wilder & Co – Wholesale Druggists
Clear, 4-5/8", smooth base, tooled mouth **$140-180**
American 1885-1900

Mrs. E. Kidder – Dysentery – Cordial – Boston
Aqua, 7-7/8", open pontil, applied mouth.......**$180-225**
American 1840-1860

Murray & Lanman – Chemists & Druggists – No 69 Water St – New York
Medium apple green, 10-1/2", open pontil, applied
sloping double collar mouth.....................**$1,500-2,500**
American 1845-1855

Myers – Rock Rose – New Haven
Aqua, 8-7/8", iron pontil, applied mouth.........**$400-600**
American 1840-1860

N.W. Seat (letter "S" is backwards on bottle) MD – Negative – Electric Fluid – New York
Aqua 3-1/4", open pontil, rolled lip **$150-200**
American 1840-1860

Normal Liquid – Ipecac – Parke, Davis & Co – Detroit Michigan, U.S.A
Amber, 4-1/2", smooth base, tooled mouth........,**$40-60**
American 1890-1925

L.Q.C. Wishart's - Patent (motif of tree) 1859 - Pine Tree - Tar Cordial - Phila, 1860-1875, 7-7/8", $200-275.

N.W. Seat, MD - Negative - Electric Fluid - New York, 1840-1860, 3-1/4", $150-200.

Owl Drug Co. (owl on mortar) San Francisco
Deep yellow green, 9-3/4", smooth base, tooled
mouth **$200-300**
American 1900-1915

**Paul G. Schuh – Rattle Snake Oil
(inside a coiled snake) Cairo, Ill**
Clear, 5-1/2", smooth base, tooled mouth **$200-300**
American 1885-1895

**Prairie Weed – Balsam – Austin Bros &
Steere – Boston (sheaf of weeds)**
Aqua, 7", smooth base, tooled mouth **$70-90**
American 1885-1900

**Primley's – Iron & Wahoo – Tonic – Jones
& Primley Co. – Elkhart, Ind**
Yellow olive amber, 9-1/2", smooth base (F.C. MFG.
CO), applied mouth **$250-350**
American 1870-1880

Purcell – Ladd & Co – Druggist – Richmond, Va
Aqua, 3-7/8", open pontil, rolled lip **$300-400**
American 1840-1860

Querus – Cod Liver Oil – Jelly
Bluish aqua, 5-3/8", wide mouth jar, pontil-scarred
base, folded rim...**$200-300**
American 1845-1855 (scarce)

R.A. Boyd – Belvedere. N.J.
Aqua, 6-1/4", open pontil, applied double collar
mouth **$175-275**
American 1840-1860 (very rare)

R.E. Sellers – Druggist – Pittsburgh
Clear, 4-3/4", pontil-scarred base, rolled lip **$50-75**
American 1840-1860

Owl Drug Co (owl on mortar)
San Francisco, 1900-
1915, 9-3/4", $200-300.

Rheumatic - Trade
(motif of tree) Mark
- Syrup - 1887
- R.S. Co - Rochester,
N.Y., 1887-1890,
9-3/4", $150-250.

Rhode's – Antidote – To – Malaria
– Fever & Ague Cure
Deep bluish aqua, 8-1/4", pontil-scarred base, applied
sloping collar mouth......................................**$375-475**
American 1845-1855 (rare pontiled cure bottle)

Richards & Perkins – Druggists – Bangor Me
Deep bluish aqua, 7-1/4", pontil-scarred base, applied
sloping collar mouth......................................**$150-200**
American 1840-1860 (very rare)

Robbins – Anod. Drops, – Balto
Aqua, 4-1/4", open pontil, applied mouth.......**$225-300**
American 1840-1860

Rogers – Vegetable – Work Syrup – Cincinnati
Deep aqua, 4-7/8", open pontil, applied mouth
....**$200-300**
American 1840-1860 (very rare)

Rohrer's - Expectoral
- Wild - Cherry
- Tonic - Lancaster
PA, 1870-1880,
10-3/4", $800-1200.

Rohrer's – Expectoral – Wild – Cherry
– Tonic – Lancaster, Pa
Medium golden amber, 10-3/4", smooth base, applied
mouth **$200-300**
American 1865-1870

Rothe – Boston – No 1
Aqua, 3-5/8", open pontil-scarred base,
rolled lip...**$75-125**
American 1840-1860

R.W. Davis Drug Co – Chicago, U.S.A.
Milk glass, 11-1/8", smooth base, tooled
mouth **$100-150**
American 1890-1910

Samuel Simes – Pharmacien – Chestnut St. Phil
Aqua, 8-7/8", open pontil, applied mouth.........**$70-100**
American 1845-1855

Scarpa's – Oil For – Deafness
Aqua, 2-1/2", 6-sided, open pontil, flared
out lip..**$450-550**
American 1840-1860 (very rare)

Selden's – Wigwam – Liniment – N.Y
Aqua, 7-7/8", open pontil, applied mouth.......**$300-400**
American 1840-1860 (rare)

Schwartz & Haslett – C.F. Galton's
– Dyspepsia Remedy – Pittsburgh, Pa
Amber, 7-3/4", smooth base, applied mouth ..**$120-150**
American 1870-1880

Shaker – Anodyne – Nth Enfield – N.H.
Bluish aqua, 4", smooth base, tooled mouth....**$80-120**
American 1875-1885

Shaker Cherry – Pectoral Syrup
– Canterbury – N.H. No 1
Aqua, 5-3/8", open pontil, applied mouth.......**$150-200**
American 1840-1860

S.S. Ryckman – Sole Mfg Hamilton – Ont (Label:
Ryckman's Srs Kootenay Cure, S.S. Ryckman
Medicine Co, Hamilton, Canada)
Medium amber, 10-1/8", smooth base, tooled
mouth **$100-125**
Canadian 1880-1890

Swaim's – Panacea – Philada
Medium olive green, 7-3/4", smooth base, applied
mouth **$150-200**
American 1855-1865

Sweet Spirits, Nitre, Put Up By N. Wood
& Son, 428 & 430, Fore Street, Portland,
Me (labeled medicine bottle)
Yellow olive, 5", open pontil, flared out lip **$150-175**
American 1835-1855

T. Morris Perot & Co – Druggists – Philada
Aqua, 4-7/8", open pontil, rolled lip **$250-300**
American 1850-1880

T. Morris Perot & Co – Druggists – Philada
Sapphire blue, 4-7/8", open pontil, rolled lip ..**$250-300**
American 1850-1880

Scarpa's - Oil For - Deafness, 1840-1860, 2-1/2", $450-550 (very rare).

Swaim's - Panacea - Philada, 1840-1855, 8", $200-300.

Tarpant – Druggist – New York
Bluish aqua, 5", pontil-scarred base, rolled lip ...**$50-75**
American 1840-1860

Telsier-Prevost – A Paris
Medium blue green, 7-3/4", pontil-scarred base,
applied sloping collar mouth **$250-400**
American 1840-1860

**The Great European Cough Remedy,
Prepared By Rev. Walker Clark, Minot,
Maine (labeled medicine bottle)**
Olive amber, 4-5/8", pontil-scarred base, applied
mouth **$150-200**
American 1835-1855

**The Great – Shoshonees – Remedy
Of – Dr. Josephus**
Deep bluish aqua, 9-1/4", smooth base, applied
sloping collar mouth.....................................**$80-100**
American 1870-1880

**The River Swamp – Chill And (motif of
alligator) Fever Cure – Augusta, Ga**
Yellow amber, 6-1/4", smooth base,
tooled lip..**$500-700**
American 1880-1890

**Thompsonian – Appetizer – Trade Mark
(motif of portly man) – Prepared By
– J.J. Vogt & Co – Cleveland O**
Medium yellow amber, 9-1/8", smooth base, "**B.F.C.
CO,**" applied sloping collar mouth **$150-200**
American 1875-1885 (rare)

Thron's – Compound – Syrup Of – Cod Liver – Oil
Deep aqua, 7-3/8", 8-sided, open pontil, applied
mouth **$400-600**
American 1840-1860 (extremely rare)

**Trade Mark – Est 1842 – (motif of
castle) Duffy's Tower Mint**
Amber, 9", tower with windows and doors, smooth
base, applied mouth......................................**$500-700**
American 1875-1885

Trade Mark – Sparks – Perfect Health (upper torso of a man) For – Kidney & Liver – Diseases – Camden
Deep amber, 9-1/2", smooth base,
tooled lip..**$250-350**
American 1885-1895

U.S.A – Hosp. Dept
Yellow amber with olive tone, 9-1/2", smooth base,
applied double collar mouth............................**$500-800**
American 1860-1870 (used during the Civil War by the Union Army Medical Corp.)

**Vaughn's – Vegetable – Lithotriptic
– Mixture – Buffalo**
Deep bluish aqua, 8-1/8", smooth base, applied
sloping collar **$140-180**
American 1855-1870

Western – Moxie – Nerve Food Co. – Chicago
Aqua, 9-7/8", smooth base, tooled blob top ..**$150-160**
American 1890-1910

**White & Hill – Dr. Warren's
– Expectorant – Nashua, N.H.**
Aqua, 6-3/8", open pontil, applied double collar
mouth **$200-250**
American 1840-1860

**Whitwell's – Patent – Volatile
– Aromatic & – Headache – Snuff**
Clear, 3-5/8", pontil-scarred base, inward
rolled lip... **$250-350**
American 1830-1850

Sweet Spirits - Nitre - Put Up By - N.Wood & Son - 428 & 430 - Fore Street - Portland, ME, 1835-1855, 5", $150-200.

The Great - European Cough Remedy - Prepared By - Rev. Walter Clark - Minot, Maine, 1835-1855, 4-5/8", $150-200.

Wild Cherry Tonic – Wm. F. Zoeller – Pittsburgh, Pa
Amber, 10-3/4", smooth base, applied
mouth $300-400
American 1870-1880 (very rare)

**Winans Bros (motif of Indian) Indian
– Cure – For The – Blood – Price $1.00
– Winams Brothers – Indian Cure**
Bluish aqua, 9-1/4", smooth base, tooled
mouth $150-250
American 1880-1890

Milk Bottles

The first patent for a milk bottle was issued to the "Jefferson Co. Milk Assn." in January 1875. The bottle featured a tin top with a spring clamping device. The first known standard-shaped milk bottle (pre-1930) was patented in March 1880 and was manufactured by the Warren Glass Works of Cumberland, Md.

In 1884, A.V. Whiteman patented a jar with a dome-type tin cap to be used with the patented Thatcher and Barnhart fastening device for a glass lid. No trace exists of a patent for the bottle itself, however. Among collectors today, the Thatcher milk bottle is one of the most prized. There are several variations on the original. Very early bottles were embossed with a picture of a Quaker farmer milking his cow while seated on a stool. "Absolutely Pure Milk" is stamped into the glass on the bottle's shoulder.

An important development in the design of the milk bottle was the patent issued to

Gallon, Bolin Dairy Farm, Bradford, Pa., $50.

H.P. and S.L. Barnhart on Sept. 17, 1889, for their method of capping and sealing. Their invention involved the design of a bottle mouth that received and retained a wafer disc or cap. It was eventually termed the milk bottle cap and revolutionized the milk bottling industry.

Between 1900 and 1920, not many new bottles were designed or patents issued. With the introduction of the Owens semi-automatic and automatic bottle machines, milk bottles became mass produced. Between 1921 and 1945, the greatest number of milk bottles were manufactured and used. After 1945, square milk bottles and paper cartons became common.

In recent years, there has been a renewed interest in collecting milk bottles. Two types of milk bottles are especially collectible. The first is the "baby top" bottle, which featured an embossed baby's face on the upper part of the bottle's neck. The second is the "cop-the-cream" bottle, which displayed a policeman's head and cap embossed into the neck. The "baby top" design was created in 1936 by Mike Pecora Sr. of Pecora's Dairy in Drums, Pa. Pecora's Dairy used quart, pint, and half pint round bottles with pyro printing. Fifteen years after the original baby face was introduced, a twin face baby top was made, with two faces, back to back, on opposite sides of the bottle. Both the baby top and cop-the-cream bottles, as well as their tin tops, are very rare and valuable.

The color mentioned in the following bottle descriptions is the color of the lettering on the bottle.

Baby Tops

Dressel Dairy Co – Granite City, Il
Red $100

Edgewood Dairy – Beloit, Wi
Orange and black (semi-rare) $100

Embassy Dairy – Washington, D.C.
Red $50

Fox Dairy – Fostoria, O – Home Owned
Red $75

Frozen Gold – Safe Milk – Sheboygan, Wi
Black (rare) $75

J.J. Brown Dairy – Troy, N.Y.
Orange $75

Lemke's Deluxe – Wausau, Wi
Camel tan $75

North Jersey – Irvington, N.J.
Orange $50

Page's – Pittsburgh, Pa
Orange $50

Pecora's – Hazleton, Pa
Red $50

Rando Milk Co – Quality Milk For The Baby – Endicott, N.Y.
Orange (semi-rare) $75

Springfield Plantation Dairy – Savannah, Ga
Orange $100

Baby top, Dressel Dairy, Granite City, Il., $100 (semi-rare).

Baby top, North Jersey, Irvington, N.J., $50.

Baby top, Rando Milk Co., Endicott, N.Y., $75.

Baby top, Upton's Farm, Bridgewater, Mass., $50.

Cop the cream, Crombie Dairy, Joliet, Ill., $150.

Cop the cream, Hy-Point Dairy, Wilmington, Del., $150.

Cop the cream, Leighty Dairy, Connelleville, Pa., $75.

Cop the cream, Pitstick Dairy, Ottawa, Ill., $150.

Cream top, Arctic Dairy, $20.

Cream top, Belleview Farms, Ilimrod, N.Y., $30.

Cream top, Central Special, $20.

Cream top, Greenville Dairy, Greenville, Pa., $50.

Cream top, Hoak's Dairy, Harrisburg, Pa., $20.

Cream top, Maple Tree Dairy, Fall River, Mass., $50.

Swayer Farms – Gilford, N.H. – For Health
Orange and black (semi-rare).................................. $150

Sunnyhurst Dairy – Reading, Ma
Orange (semi-rare)... $150

United Farm – Albany, N.Y.
Red $100

Upton's Farm – Bridgewater, Ma
Black... $50

Cop The Cream

Crombie Guernsey Dairy – Joliet, Ill
Red (semi-rare).. $150

Fountain Head Dairy – Hagerstown, Md
Tan (semi-rare).. $150

Furman Bros – Ithaca N.Y.
Orange.. $150

Hillside Dairy Milk – Whately, Ma
Black (semi-rare) $150

Hy-Point Dairy – Wilmington, De
Orange (rare)... $150

Leighty Pure Milk Co – Connelleville, Pa
Red $75

Morningcrest Farms – Eau Claire, Wi
Orange (semi-rare)... $150

Pitstick Farm – Dairy – Ottawa, Ill
Red (semi-rare).. $150

Royal Farms Dairy – Baltimore, Md
Orange (semi-rare)... $150

Silver Hill Dairy – Portland,Or
Red (semi-rare).. $150

West Side Dairy – Albans, Vt
Red (semi-rare).. $150

Cream Tops

Burg's – Model Dairy – Clintonville, Wi
Orange.. $50

Consumers Dairy Co. – Westerly, R.I.
Black... $50

Greenville Dairy Banquet Products – Greenville, Pa
Green.. $50

Green Meadow Farm – Rye, N.Y.
Green (semi-rare)... $75

LaRose Dairy – So. Hadley Falls, Ma
Red $50

McAdams Dairy Products – Chelsea, Ma
Orange.. $50

Queen City Dairy – Cumberland, Md
Orange.. $20

Shamrock Dairy – Tucson, Az
Black... $50

Tru-Li-Pure – Nashville, Tn
Red $30

Week's Dairy – Laconia, N.H.
Red $30

Quarter Pints

Almida County – Oakland, Ca
Orange.. $30

Bay City Creamery – San Leanadro, Ca
Red $30

El Camino Creamery – San Bruno, Ca
Black... $30

Elkhorn Farm – Watsonville, Ca
Orange.. $20

Hygienic Dairy Co. – Watertown, N.Y.
Orange.. $10

Pratt's Dairy – Visalia, Cal.
Black... $30

Rivera Dairy – Santa Barbara, Ca
Green.. $30

Virginia Dairy – The Home Of Better Milk – Richmond, Va
Red (semi-rare).. $50

Wildwood Dairy – Santa Rosa, Ca
Green.. $30

Zenda Farms – Clayton, N.Y.
Orange.. $20

Gallons

Bolin Dairy Farm – Bradford, Pa
Red $50

Cream top, Puritan Super Cream, $30.

Gallon, Bolin Dairy Farm, Bradford, Pa., $50.

Gallon, DuBois Dairy, DuBois, Pa., $50.

Gallon, Ka-Vee Milk, Belleville, Pa., $50.

Gallon, Silvis Farms, Greensburg, Pa., $50.

Square quart, Burch Dairy, Jamestown, N.Y, $50.

Square quart, Guard Your Health with Guernsey Milk, $10.

Square quart, J.D. Poole & Sons, Minford, Ohio, $10.

Square quart, Northland, $50.

Carron Country Creamery – Rawlins, Wy
Yellow **$50**

Guernsey Milk – Champaign, Il
Orange... **$50**

**Harmony Dairy – Country Style
– Buttermilk – Pittsburgh, Pa**
Red **$50**

Ka-Vee – Best By Test – Milk
Belleville, PA **$50**

Lewis Dairies Inc – Grove City, Pa
Green... **$50**

Marburger Farm Dairy – Evans City, Pa
Black.. **$50**

Otto's Milk – Pittsburgh, Pa
Red **$50**

Purity Milk Co. – Phillipsburg, Pa
Red **$50**

Sanitary Milk Co – Rantoul, Il
Orange... **$50**

Square Quarts

Armstrong Dairy Inc – Locust Valley, N.J.
Orange (semi-rare).. **$30**

Big Boy Milk – Rochester, N.Y.
Amber **$10**

Blue Spruce Dairy – Freehold, N.J.
Blue **$20**

Broadway Farms Dairy – New York City, N.Y.
Red **$20**

Fitchett Bros – Lake View Dairy – Poughkeepsie, N.Y.
Orange... $20

Harrisburg Milk – Harrisburg, Pa
Green and orange... $50

Hy Vita Milk Co – Ship Bottom, N.J.
Orange (semi-rare)... $50

J.D. Poole & Sons – Minford, Ohio
Red.. $20

J & J Dairy Products Inc. – Jersey City, N.J.
Red.. $10

Little Dairy – Let Us Serve You – Namog, Id
Green... $30

Model Dairy – Huron, S.D.
Red (semi-rare).. $30

Momence Dairy – Momence, Il
Purple $10

Rutland Hills Co-Op Inc – Watertown, N.Y.
Orange... $20

Seegert's Milk – Forestville, N.Y.
Orange... $20

University Of New York – Delhi, N.Y.
Green... $30

Coffee Creamers

Carrigan's – Niagara Falls, N.Y.
Green... $30

Coffee creamer, Blanding Dairy (front), $50.

Coffee creamer, Blanding Dairy (reverse) St. Johns, Mich.

Coffee creamer, Dart's Dairy, Manchester, Conn., $30.

Coffee creamer, Idlenot Farm Dairy, $30.

Coffee creamer, Lincoln Trail Motel and Restaurant, Highway 66, Tell City, Indiana, $50.

Coffee creamer, Links, Randolph, N.Y., $40.

Dart's Dairy – Manchester, Ct
Orange... $30

Girton Dairy Equipment – Girton Mfg. – Millville, Pa
Orange (semi-rare)... $70

Johnson's Dairy – Cooperstown, N.Y.
Black (semi-rare) $75

Kyles Dairy – Mackeyville, Pa
Orange... $30

**Lincoln Trail – Motel And Restaurant
– Highway 66 – Tell City, Indiana**
Red $50

Neidig's Dairy – Sunbury, Pa
Orange... $20

N. Mex Milk Prods. Inc – Belen, N.M.
Orange (rare).. $100

Picket's Pasteurized Products – Sheridan, In
Orange... $40

Ramon's – Hickory – Foods – Florence, Al
Green... $50

Richard Dairy – Neward, Ne
Orange (semi-rare)... $60

Sharpes Dairy – Jackson, Mich
Green... $50

Strickler's – It's Better – Cream – Huntingdon, Pa
Orange... $20

Twin Cedar Dairy – McClure, Pa
Red $30

Waynesburg Sanitary Dairy Co – Waynesburg, Pa
Orange... $30

Miscellaneous

A.G.S. & Co. – Patented – April 5, 1898
Clear, quart, smooth base, tooled mouth..........$75-100
American 1890-1900

**Arborvitae – Lodge Farm – Succasunna – N.J.
– This Bottle – To Be Washed – And Returned**
Clear, 6-7/8", smooth base, tooled mouth......$100-150
American 1910-1920

Country Store Countertop Milk Jar
Deep bluish aqua, 17-1/2" H, 12" dia., smooth base,
ABM lip..$700-800
American 1920-1935 (made by Owens Illinois Glass Co.)

Ferme – Des – Vauzillons (On Lid)
Milk glass encased in clear quart, pontil-scarred base,
tooled mouth $150-250
French 1910-1920

Greenfield – Dairy Co – Jersey City
Clear, 1/4 pint, smooth base, ABM lip.............$100-150
American 1915-1925

**One Quart – Liquid – E.F. Mayer – Phone
– Glen'd 3887R-289 Hollenbeck St.**
Amber, quart, smooth base (M)......................$120-160
American 1920-1935

**This Bottle – The Property Of And Filled
By – The Page Dairy Oo. – Toledo – Ohio
– Sealed – One Quart – No. 5**
Deep amber, quart, smooth base, ABM lip $100-150
American 1920-1935

**Trade Mark – Union Milk Company (cow's
head) Milk & Cream – Registered – The Public
Cautioned – Not To Use This Bottle**
Clear, quart, smooth base, tooled lip $80-120
American 1915-1925

Coffee creamer,
Ramon's Foods,
Florence, Ala., $50.

Coffee creamer,
Valley Farm
Dairy, $20.

Mineral Water Bottles

Drinking water from mineral springs was very popular for a full century, with the peak between 1860 and 1900. Consequently, most collectible bottles were produced during these years. Although the shapes and sizes of mineral bottles are not very creative, the lettering and design, both embossed and paper, are bold and interesting. Mineral bottles can range from 7 inches to 14 inches high. Most were cork-stopped, manufactured in a variety of colors, and embossed with an eagle and the name of the glasshouse manufacturer.

Akesion Spring - Owned By - Sweet Springs Co - Saline Co - Mo, 1875-1885, pint, $200-300.

Adirondack Spring – Whitehall – N.Y.
Deep blue green, pint, smooth base, applied sloping double collar mouth **$275-375**
American 1865-1875

Artesian Water – Louisville – Ky. – Dupont
Deep amber, 7-3/4", iron pontil, applied collar mouth **$500-700**
American 1850-1860

Bedford – Springs Co
Aqua, quart, smooth base, "MC.C," tooled mouth **$140-180**
American 1870-1880

Beverwyck – N.Y.
Aqua, 9-1/4", smooth base, tooled top...............**$25-35**
American 1880-1910

Blount Springs – Natural – Sulphur Water – Trade (monogram) Mark
Medium cobalt blue, 7-1/2" smooth base, applied mouth **$120-160**
American 1870-1880

Boyd & Beard – Mineral Water – B – Patent
Medium emerald green, 6-3/4", iron pontil, applied sloping collar mouth..**$140-180**
American 1835-1845

Bowden – Lithia Water (spring house) – Lithia Springs, Ca – Trade Mark – Registered
Aqua, half-gallon, smooth base, tooled mouth **$70-90**
American 1885-1910

Buffalo – Lithia Water (motif of seated woman) – Natures – Materia – Medica – Trade Mark
Medium blue green, 9-3/4", open pontil, applied mouth **$125-175**
American 1850-1860

Bridgeton Glass Works – N.Y.
Medium blue green, 7-3/8", smooth base, applied mouth, original metal band closure stamped "John Allender, Patent July 24 1866" **$150-250**
American 1855-1865 (scarce)

C. A. Dubois & Bros – Philada – D & B
Medium blue green, 6-3/4", smooth base, applied mouth **$50-75**
American 1860-1875

Caledonia – Spring – Wheelock Vt
Golden yellow, quart, smooth base, applied sloping collar mouth..**$400-800**
American 1860-1880

Congress & Empire Spring Co – E – Saratoga N.Y. – Empire Water
Deep blue green, quart, 9-1/2", smooth base, applied sloping double collar **$60-80**
American 1865-1875

D.A. Knowlton – Saratoga N.Y.
Red amber, quart, 9-1/8", smooth base, applied double collar mouth..**$1,400-1,800**
American 1860-1870

Alburgh - A - Springs VT, 1865-1880, 9-3/4", $1,500-2,000.

Artesian Spring Co (monogram) Ballston - N.Y. - Ballston Spa - Lithia - Mineral - Water, 1865-1875, 7-5/8", $80-140.

Artesian Water - Louisville - Ky. - Dupont, 1855-1865, mug base, pint, $500-700.

Avon - Spring Water, 1865-1875, quart, $80-120.

Darien – Mineral Springs – Tifft & Perry – Darien Centre – N.Y.
Bluish aqua, pint, smooth base, applied sloping double collar mouth.....................................**$500-700**
American 1870-1880

Deep Rock Spring – Trade – Deep Rock – Mark Oswego N.Y. – S
Aqua, pint, smooth base, applied sloping double collar mouth **$200-300**
American 1870-1880

E. Mcintire – Mineral Water – Patent
Medium emerald green, 6-1/2", open pontil, applied tapered collar mouth **$1,000-1,500**
American 1830-1840

F.H. Suppe – Franklin Springs – Franklin – Iron Works, N.Y. – This Bottle Not To Be Sold
Amber, quart, 11-3/8", smooth base, "Clyde Glass Works – Clyde – N.Y.," tooled blob top **$150-200**
American 1885-1895

Fonticello – Trade Mark – Mineral Water – Spring – Chesterfield Co, Va – Monticello Mineral Spring Co – Richmond, Va
Bluish aqua, 10-3/8", smooth base, tooled mouth **$80-120**
American 1880-1900

G.a. Kohl – Lambertville – N.J. – K
Deep blue green, 7-1/4", iron pontil, applied sloping double collar mouth **$200-300**
American 1845-1855

**G. Snider – Cold Spring – N.Y. – This
Bottle – Not To Be – Sold**
Golden amber, 8", smooth base, applied
mouth **$80-150**
American 1870-1880

G. Upp Jr. – Your Pa
Medium emerald green, 7-1/4", iron pontil, applied blob
type mouth **$375-475**
American 1845-1855 (scarce)

G.W. Weston & Co – Saratoga N.Y.
Deep green, pint, pontl scarred base, sloping collar
mouth with ring...**$200-400**
American 1840-1860

Gardner & Landon – Sharon – Sulphur Water
Medium yellow green, quart, pontil-scarred base,
applied sloping double collar mouth........**$1,200-1,800**
American 1860-1870

**Guilford Mineral (monogram)
– Spring Water – Guilford – Vt**
Deep blue green, quart, smooth base, applied sloping
double collar mouth **$150-200**
American 1870-1880

**Hamilton (in a slug plate) – & Church
– Excelsior – Mineral Water – Brooklyn**
Medium teal blue, 8-sided, 7-1/4", iron pontil, applied
blob type mouth **$600-800**
American 1840-1860

Bedford - Springs
Co, 1880-
1900, 10-5/8",
$200 300.

Bolen Waach & Co
New York - Mineral
Spring Water,
1870-1880 6-7/8",
$250-350.

Hanbury Smith's – Kissingen Water
Blue green, 7-7/8", oval form, iron pontil, applied blob
type mouth $200-300
American 1845-1860 (rare pontil in this color)

Hanbury Smith – Mineral Water
Yellow olive green, pint, smooth base, applied sloping
collar mouth..$100-150
American 1870-1885

Heffernan – N.Y.
Aqua, 9-1/4", smooth base, tooled top...............$25-35
American 1880-1910

Hubbell – Philad "A" (inside a scrolled circle)
Olive yellow, pint, 7-5/8", smooth base, applied
mouth $200-300
American 1865-1875

Hulschizer & Co (in a slug plate)
– Premium – Mineral – Waters
Medium blue green, 8-sided, 7-1/2", red iron pontil,
applied blob type mouth $1,400-1,800
American 1845-1855

I.D. Buttles – Rome – N.Y. – Mineral – Water
Ice blue, quart, smooth base, applied sloping collar
mouth $200-300
American 1870-1880 (rare)

J. Donnell's – Premium – Mineral – Waters
Medium emerald green, 8-sided, 7-3/8", iron pontil,
applied sloping collar mouth $400-600
American 1845-1855 (rare)

Caledonia - Spring
- Wheelock VT,
1865-1880, quart,
$500-700.

Chalybeate
Water - Of The
- American
- Spring - Water,
1870-1880 7-1/2",
$500-700.

J. Harvey & Co – Providence, R.i. – H
Olive amber, 7", pontil-scarred base, applied blob
mouth **$500-600**
American 1840-1855

**J. Wise – Allentown – Pa – This Bottle
– Belongs To James Wise**
Deep cobalt blue, 7-1/4", smooth base, applied blob
type mouth **$150-250**
American 1855-1870

John B. Welscher – Philada
Deep blue green, 7-3/8", smooth base, applied sloping
double collar mouth **$150-250**
American 1855-1865

**J. Cosgrove – & – Son – Charleston
– Trade – JC (monogram) – Mark**
Electric cobalt blue, 7-1/2", smooth base, applied blob
type mouth **$275-375**
American 1865-1875

Kohl & Beans – Mineral Water – Easton – Pa
Medium blue green, 7-1/2", iron pontil, applied
mouth **$120-180**
American 1840-1860

Ledlie – Trenton – N.J. – Elliott & – Trenton
Medium green, 6-7/8", smooth base, applied sloping
double collar mouth **$60-90**
American 1870-1885

Clarke & Co - New
York, 1850-1860,
pint, $100-150.

Clarke & White - New
York, 1855-1865,
7-1/2", $200-300.

McKinna & Connolly – 1861 – New York – McK & C
Medium teal blue, 7-1/4:, smooth base, applied
mouth **$50-75**
American 1860-1875

Meyer & Rottman – New York
Medium blue green, 7-1/4", iron pontil, applied blob
type mouth **$100-150**
American 1845-1855

Middletown – Healing – Springs
– Grays & Clark – Middletown Vt
Golden yellow amber, quart, smooth base, applied
sloping double collar mouth..............................**$80-120**

N. Richardson – Trenton – N.J.
– This Bottle – N – Never Sold
Deep emerald green, 7", iron pontil, applied sloping
double collar mouth **$60-80**
American 1845-1855

Oak Orchard – Acid Spring – Address
– G.W. Merchant – Lockport. N.Y.
Medium blue green, quart, smooth base, applied
sloping double collar mouth...........................**$100-200**
American 1865-1875

Pavilion United States Spring Co – P
– Saratoga – N.Y. Pavilion – Water
Medium yellow green, pint, smooth base, applied
sloping double collar mouth...........................**$175-275**

Congress &
Empire Spring Co
- Hotchkiss' Sons
- C - New York -
Saratoga N.Y., 1865-
1875, pint, $70-90.

Cooper's Well Water
- Miss, 1870-1885,
pint, $80-120.

R.C. & T. – New York
Deep cobalt blue, 7-1/2", iron pontil, applied blob
mouth **$275-375**
American 1845-1855

Robert Weller – N.Y.
Aqua, 9-1/4", smooth base, tooled mouth..........**$25-35**
American 1880-1910

Sheldon – A – Spring – Sheldon, Vt
Deep amber, quart, smooth base, applied sloping
double collar mouth **$300-400**
American 1865-1875 (scarce)

St. Leon Spring Water – J (in diamond)
Trademark – Earl W. Johnson Boston
Teal green, quart, applied sloping collar mouth
....**$400-800**
American 1860-1880

Congress Spring Co SS NY (on base);
label only bottle (lot of 2) Label:
Natural - Saratoga Vichy - Water
- Fine Table Water, The Only Alkaline
Spring at Saratoga, N.Y., 1880-
1890, both 9-3/8", $70-140 (pair).

Crystal Spring - Sunderlin & Snook, 1870-1880, pint, $400-600.

D. A. Knowlton - Saratoga - N.Y., 1855-1865, 9", $150-200.

St. Regis – Water – Massena Springs
Teal blue , pint, smooth base, applied sloping double collar mouth..**$375-475**
American 1870-1880

Stirling – Magnetic Mineral – Spring – Eaton Rapids – Mich
Medium amber , 9-7/8", smooth base, "L & W," applied sloping double collar mouth...........................**$375-475**
American 1875-1885

The – Excelsior – Water
Medium teal blue, 8-sided, 7-1/4", iron pontil, applied blob type mouth **$150-200**
American 1840-1860

Tiffany & Allen – Trade (monogram) – Mark – Paterson N.J. – Do Not Steal – This Bottle
Medium amber, pint, smooth base, tooled mouth **$250-350**
American 1870-1880

Triton Spouting Spring – T – Saratoga N.Y. – Triton Water
Deep blue aqua, pint, 7-3/8", smooth base, applied sloping collar mouth......................................**$500-800**
American 1865-1875

Vermont Spring – Saxe & Co. – Sheldon, Vt
Olive green, quart, smooth base, applied mouth **$50-90**
American 1864-1880

W. Eagle – New York – Superior – Mineral Water
Medium cobalt blue, 7-1/4", iron pontil, applied blob
type mouth **$300-400**
American 1845-1855 (scarce)

W. Riddle – Philada
Medium blue green, 7-1/2", iron pontil, applied sloping
collar mouth...**$140-180**
American 1845-1855

Yuengling – N.Y.
Aqua, 9-1/4", smooth base, tooled top...............**$25-35**
American 1880-1910

Eureka Spring Co
- Saratoga N.Y. (and
stand), 1870-1875,
9", $400-700.

G.W. Weston &
Co - Saratoga
- N.Y., 1850-1860,
9-5/8", $250-275.

Haskins' Spring Co
- H - Shutesbury - Mass
- H.S. Co, 1865-1875,
8-1/2", $400-600.

Hathorn Spring
- Saratoga N.Y.,
1865-1875,
9-3/8", $100-150.

Hopkins - Chalybeate
- Baltimore, 1855-1865,
7-3/8", $200-300.

Hubbell - Philada (inside
a scrolled circle), 1865-
1875, 7-5/8" $200-300.

Kissingen Water -
Hanbury Smith (lot of
2), 1870-1880, 6-3/4"
(both), $160-220 (pair).

Lynch & Clarke
- New York, 1845-
1855, pint, $250-350.

Magnetic Spring
- Hennikr NH, 1870-
1880, quart, $500-700.

Minnequa Water
- Bradford Ct - PA, 1870-
1880, 7-5/8", $200-300.

Minnequa Water - Bedford
Co - PA, 1870-1880,
9-5/8", $200-300.

Saratoga - A - Spring
Co. - N.Y., 1865-1875,
pint; Congress & Empire
Spring Co - E - Saratoga,
N.Y., 1865-1875, pint,
$100-150 (pair).

Saratoga (star)
Spring, 1865-1875,
quart, $250-350.

Saratoga - Red
- Spring, 1865-
1875, pint,
$140-200.

Saratoga - Vichy - Water
- Saratoga, N.Y. - V,
1870-1880, $100-150.

Syracuse Springs
- Excelsior, 1865-1875,
7-7/8", $200-300.

Vichy Water
- Hanbury Smith,
1870-1880,
pint, $120-160
(scarce color).

Weller Saratoga Springs Blob
Tops (lot of 4), 1880-1910,
7-1/2" to 9-1/4", $80-120 (all).

Nursing Bottles

Nursing bottles and associated items such as sterilizers, bottle warmers, trading cards, advertisements, have long been a favorite of many bottle collectors. In fact, in 1973, The American Collectors of Infant Feeders (ACIF) was founded by a group of devoted collectors to promote the hobby of collecting nursing bottles and related items. Today, that membership now extends throughout the United States and to Canada, Australia, Germany, and other numerous countries.

Nursing bottles have a colorful history dating back to the early 1600s. Nursing bottles were better known then as "sucking bottles" and were usually made of leather or wood, the nipples fashioned from rags, skins, or sponges. Toward the end of the 1600s and into the 1700s, the pewter sucking bottle was introduced. By the late 1790s and early 1800s, tubular-shaped pottery nursing bottles were used in England and eventually were manufactured in American glasshouses.

In the 1800s, a competition arose between the American and English glass manufacturers. Dr. T.W. Dyott began advertising his free-blown glass decanter and tubular nursing bottles in America in the1820s, and shortly after, in 1832, Solomon Maw began producing glass nursing bottles in England. By 1832, many New York drug companies were advertising nursing bottles and nursing flasks. In 1841, Charles Windship of Massachusetts registered the first nursing bottle with the U.S. Patent Office, and in 1845, Dr. Elijah Pratt of New York registered the first rubber nipple. This was a welcome event for the babies of the world who up to that point, had to make do with hard nipples of pewter, silver, wood, or ivory.

The latter part of the 1800s brought a virtual explosion of various designs and methods for nursing bottles and feeding devices. Following are highlights of these milestones:

1851 - The first nursing bottle using a long sucking tube was introduced at the Great Exposition in England.

1854 - Paneled glass nursing bottles fitted with an internal tube, stopper, and hard nipples were advertised by Bullock & Crenshaw.

1864 - The turtle-shaped nursing bottle was patented in England and brought to the United States.

1869 - The first nursing bottle with graduated markings was patented by Drs. H and A.M. Knapp of Providence, R.I.

1872 - The corset-shaped nursing bottle was patented by Milo S. Burr.

1873 - The two-hole (vented) nursing bottle was patented by William Hobson.

1894 - The wide-mouthed Hygeia nursing bottle was patented by Dr. William Decker.

1896 - The double-ended Allenbury nursing bottle was patented in England.

With the invention of the Owens automatic bottle machine in 1903, blown-in-mold (BIM) bottles were phased out, and the early 1900s saw a new 8-ounce tapered wide-mouth nursing bottle manufactured by companies such as Pyrex, Hygeia, Vita-Flo, Curity, and Armstrong. One of the most popular brands, Evenflo, was introduced in 1947. In 1905, the flask-shaped nursing bottle, the first style produced by the automatic bottle machine, was phased out. Although today's nursing bottles have replaced glass with plastic, we can still enjoy these rare and unique collectibles of the past.

Baby (picture of seated bunny – bunting)
Clear glass, wide mouth cylinder, ABM, embossed within 2" shield, "Baby Bunting" in script, 8 oz. scale on reverse, smooth base....................................**$25-30**
American 1930-1940

Baby's – Pet
Clear glass, oval shape, 8 oz., smooth base, ABM...**$10-15**
American 1910-1940

Betsy Brown – Safety – Nursing Bottle
Clear glass, flask shape, BIM, sheared lip with screw threads on neck..**$10-15**
American 1890-1910

Cat And Two Kittens (embossed picture)
Clear glass, oval shape, ABM, 8 oz. scale on reverse, "2" on smooth base **$15-20**
American 1930-1944

Comfy (embossed Felix cartoon character)
Clear glass, oval shape, ABM, 8 oz. scale embossed on reverse, "C" within triangle and "2" on base...**$40-50**
Canada 1925

Cow & Gate (embossed picture of baby's shoulders and head with crown)
Feeding Bottle (with original box)
Clear glass, round shape, ABM, 8 oz. and 16 tablespoon scales on reverse, smooth base.....**$75-100**
England 1950-1960

Dog (embossed picture)
Clear, oval shape, ABM, 8 oz. scale on reverse, "2" embossed on base...**$10-13**
American 1930-1944

Dominion Glass Nursery Rhyme: "Ding Dong Bell – Pussy's In The – Well" (embossed picture of well, child, and cat in well)
Clear glass, oval shape, ABM, 8 oz. scale on reverse, "D" within diamond and numbers "3", "1", and "6" on base..**$30-40**

Elephant (embossed picture of elephant on front)
Clear glass, wide mouth......................................**$20-25**
American 1900-1912

Fireking – Heatproof (embossed vertically on alternate panels)
Pale blue, rounded hexagon, ABM, smooth base, "Fireking – guaranteed – two years"...........................**$20-25**
American 1935-1950

Flask-type Nurser
Clear glass, 6 oz. scale on front and reverse, smooth base, BIM, tooled lips...**$10-30**
American 1890-1910

Glaxo (with original box)
Clear glass, double ended, BIM, "Glaxo" in double lined script letter, smooth base, 4 oz. and 8 tablespoon scales on opposite sides, tooled lip....................**$50-60**
English 1910-1925

Handy – Wt (monogram) – Nurser
Clear glass, flask shape, BIM, tooled lip.............**$10-15**
American 1900-1910

Home Nursing – W.T. & Co. (within diamond) – Bottle
Clear glass, turtle shape, BIM, tooled lip............**$15-20**
American 1930-1945

Phone Hyd. 1545
Clear glass, red pyroglazing, oval shape, horizontal ribbing on sides, ABM, smooth base ("K" within keystone –Knox Glass C. Knox, PA)...................**$20-25**
American 1930-1945

Kesso (with underline extending from base of "K")
Clear glass, oval, ABM, vertical ribs encircle the bottle, smooth base...**$10-12**
American 1930-1940

Mellin's Trade (motif of bird) Mark – Food – For One Meal At (graduation) Months – Rd Nos – 434 884-7008 – Glass Made In France (on base) Table – Spoon
Clear glass, 7-1/2", tooled mouths at both ends, smooth base...**$140-180**
English 1890-1910

N. Wood & Son's – Nursing – Bottle
Clear glass, turtle shape, BIM, tooled lip............**$30-35**
American 1890-1910

Phoenix – Ovale Nurser
Clear glass, oval shape, 8 oz., ABM, smooth base..**$20-25**
American 1910-1940

Teddy's Pet Peaceful Nights - For Your Baby, 1904, $210; Comfy, 1925, $170; The Little Papoose - Patd, 1865-1885, $325; Sweet Babee Nurser - Patd May 3-10,1910-1920, $85; Medallion Nursing bottle - Trade - M.S. Burr and Co., 1878-1895, $60.

Rabbit (embossed picture)
Clear glass, oval shape, ABM, 8 oz. scale on reverse, four graduated lines are embossed on the side, "1" on smooth base..**$15-20**
American 1930-1940

Savory & Moore's – Valveless
– Feeder (with original Box)
Clear glass, elongated turtle shape, BIM, embossed within 2-1/4" seal on front: "Made In England", tooled lip..**$95-110**
English 1880-1900

Stork – Nursing – Bottle – Easily Cleaned
– And Hygienic (with original box)
Clear glass, wide mouth cylinder, ABM, "Stork" in script...**$30-35**
American 1930-1940

Submarine-Shaped Nurser
White ceramic with medium-blue transfer pattern of a landscape, 7" length **$175-200**
English 1830-1850 (Staffordshire region)

Submarine-Shaped Nurser
Clear, 7-1/8" length, freeblown, polished pontil-scarred base, small tooled lip with flange....................**$140-160**
English 1840-1880

Submarine-Shaped Nurser
Clear, 8" length, freeblown, polished pontil-scarred base, small tooled lip with flange......................**$95-110**
English 1840-1880

Submarine-Shaped Nurser
Clear, 9-1/2" length, freeblown, polished pontil-scarred base, small tooled lip with flange.......................**$35-50**
English 1840-1880

Temp-guard – Baby Bottle – Eisele & Co
Clear glass, oval shape, ABM, smooth base, red pyroglazing..**$10-15**
American 1930-1945

The 'Ovale' Nurser – Non-Rolling
– Whitall Tatum Company
Clear glass, oval shape, 8 oz., smooth base, ABM..**$20-25**
American 1910-1940

Tuffy – Heat Proof – Tuffy – Cold Proof
(embossed vertically on side panels)
Pale blue, rounded hexagon, ABM, smooth base, "Brockway (in script) - made In USA" **$20-25**
American 1935-1950\

Walker-gordon – Modified – Milk – Laboratory
Clear glass, 4 oz., round shape, BIM, tooled lip, smooth base..**$25-30**
American 1900-1910

Patriotic Bottles

    At the beginning of World War II, the bottling industry, specifically milk bottle manufacturers, began a patriotic campaign that had never been experienced before in American history. World War II resulted in some of the most unique and collectible bottles, with war slogans depicting tanks, soldiers, fighter planes, "V" signs, and saying and slogans about Pearl Harbor. While some bottles, especially milk bottles, were colorful and had detailed graphics, many displayed simple slogans such as "Buy Bonds and Stamps" or "Buy War Savings Bonds-Keep it Up" on the wings of bombers and fighter planes.

The Applied Color Label (ACL) soda pop bottle was conceived in the 1930s when Prohibition forced brewing companies to sell soda pop. During World War II, soda pop bottlers throughout the United States created labels that will forever preserve unique patriotic moments and figures in American history such as American flags, the Statue of Liberty, the "V" symbol, soldiers, pilots and fighter planes. Bottles with images of Uncle Sam and the American flag are the most popular.

Other groups of bottles such as historical flasks, figurals, and Jim Beam bottles have depicted patriotic figures, embossed images, and paintings of important patriotic milestones in the history of America. In fact, 25 types of flasks depict the American flag as a symbol of patriotism, a rallying cry for battle, and the celebration of the re-establishment of the Union following the Civil War.

Milk Bottles

Quarts 1942-1945

Anderson Erickson Dairy, Des Moines, IA
Picture of Abraham Lincoln "That Freedom Shall Not Perish From The Earth!" Buy War Bonds **$100-125**

Clarksburg Dairy, Clarksburg, WV
Conserve "V" For Victory-Buy War Bonds And Stamps **$85-100**

Cloverleaf Dairy, MD
Red stars around bottle, bomber with "Buy War Savings Bonds" on wings-Keep It Up **$75-100**

Compston Bros. Dairy, Corning, CA
Black lettering, Milk For Victory with "V" symbol...**$75-100**

Crane Dairy, Utica, NY
Red lettering, Buy War Bonds And Stamps For Victory **$45-55**

Dykes Dairy, Warren, PA
The United States Is A Good Investment (picture of Statue of Liberty) Buy War Bonds And Stamps ..**$75-85**

Buy Bonds, $100.

Buy War Bonds, $150.

Wilson Dairy, For Victory, Ferndale, Wis., $150.

V for Victory, $250.

V, Bancroft Dairy, $150.

My War Stamps
Are Adding Up,
Renovo, Pa., $150.

We're All Pulling for
Uncle Sam, $75.

Our Country Needs
Your Cooperation, $50.

Selection of various milk labels, Owens - Illinois Glass Company, Toledo, Ohio (1942), $125.

Return! Save!,
Indianapolis, Ind., $50.

V for Victory, $50.

M.G. Nevius
(front) $250.

M.G. Nevious (reverse),
Even a fish wouldn't
get into trouble if he
kept his mouth shut.

Milk, the First Line of
Health Defense, Titusville,
Dairy, Titusville, Pa., $50.

For Victory Buy United
States Savings Bonds,
Frear, Dover, Del., $70.

The Navy Our
Protection, $250.

Hasten the Day,
Laramie, Wyo., $75

The U.S. Needs Us Strong, $35.

For Energy Drink Milk, $50.

Elmwood Dairy, Oxbridge, MA
We Need Your Help (Uncle Sam pointing) It's Your Right -It's Your Responsibility-Buy More Bonds $60-70

Ferry Hills Farms, Prairie View, IL
It's Patriotic To Save (fighter plane) Buy War Bonds And Stamps $75-85

Geneva Dairy, Geneva, NY
"V" For Victory – sailor standing by battleship..$75-100

Golden Crest, Bordens
Buy War Bonds $75-100

Hansen Dairy, Deer Lodge, MT
Black lettering, Bonds Buy Bombs $75-100

Haskels Dairy, Augusta, CA
Back Their Attack – Buy More War Bonds – Drink Milk For Health...............$50-60

Haskels Dairy, Augusta, CA
Milk Helps To – Keep 'Em Flying – Do Your Part-Buy War Bonds And Stamps (picture of pilot)............$75-85

Heisler's Cloverleaf Dairy, Tamaqua, PA
Armaments And Good Health – For Victory – Drink More Milk...............$100-125

HyGrade Dairy, Buffalo, NY
Give A Pint Of Blood And Help Save A Life (rare) $175-200

Illinois Valley, Strator, Ottawa IL
Orange lettering, Revenge Pearl Harbor $75-100

Kentucky Acres Dairy, Crestwood, KY
Buy War Bonds, Everybody-Every Payday (on arrow pointing to target) $50-60

Lavine's Dairy, Potsdam, NY
Victory (picture of soldier in middle of "V")........$75-100

Melrose Dairy, Dyersburg, TN
Red lettering, fighter plane "Keep 'Em Flying, Buy War Bonds Today" $100-125

Perry Creamery, Tuscaloosa, AL
National Defense Starts – Buy Defense Bonds – With Health Defense...............$60-75

Shamrock Dairy, Tucson, AZ
America Has A Job To Do! "V" symbol with picture of pilot...............$75-100

Shums Dairy, Jeanette, PA
(Picture of eagle) National-Defense Starts With Good Health-Build America's Future-Drink More Milk..$35-45

Sunshine Dairy, St. Johns, Newfoundland, Canada
Black and orange lettering, Victory sign with Churchill, tanks, and ships $200-250

Thatchers Manufacturing Glass Co. – Series of eight slogans ....$100-150 each
- Victory–Comes A Little Closer Every Time You Buy a–War Bond (fighter plane)
- We Need Your Help–It's Your Fight–It's Your Responsibility–Buy War Bonds (Uncle Sam pointing)

Anderson Erickson Dairy, Des Moines, IA
- "That Freedom Shall Not Perish From the Earth!"–Buy War Bonds (Abraham Lincoln)
- Think–Act–Work (picture of eagle)–Victory
- You Can Keep 'Em Flying By Buying (fighter plane) U.S. War Bonds-Stamps
- Action Speaks Louder Than Words–What Are You Doing To Help Uncle Sam?

Royale Dairy, Elmira, NY
- Keep Them Rolling (tank) Buy Bonds and Stamps
- You Owe It To Your Country–Buy War Bonds–You Owe It To Your Health–Drink Milk

Common Quarts

A Healthy Nation Is A Strong Nation – Uncle Sam holding a glass of milk $35-45

America Is A Great Place To Be – Lets Keep It That Way $35-40

Buy Defense Bonds And Stamps For Victory – "V" Symbol...............$45-55

Food Fights Too – (picture of Uncle Sam) Conserve What You Buy – Plan All Meals For Victory $45-50

For Our Defense – Battleship – 1,200 Men $50-55

God Bless America – Pearl Harbor Remembered – made for collectors market – 1992 ....$15-20

Help Save The Life Of A Soldier Or Sailor (picture of Red Cross) Donate To The Blood Plasma Program Of The Red Cross (rare) $200-250

It's Great To Be An American, picture of Uncle Sam and eagle $35-45

Invest In Victory (picture of bombers) War Savings – Bonds – Stamps $75-100

Remember Pearl Harbor – Safe Guard Your Country – By Doing Your Bit Now – Be Prepared – "V" Symbol $125-150

Uncle Sam pointing to the signs: Your Country First, Your Family Second, Yourself Last $45-55

U.S. Savings Bonds And Freedom Shares $20-25

We Cherish Liberty – Health – Let's Protect Them –1943 .... $35-45

50th Anniversary Of Pearl Harbor – made for collectors market –1992 .... $15-20

Cream Tops

Shamrock Dairy, Tucson, AZ
America Has A Job To Do, "V" symbol with fighter pilot $75-100

Common Bottle
Food For Victory – Careful Wartime Meal Planning Will Help Us Win $75-100

Common Bottle
Uncle Sam Prescribes Milk For The Army (rare) $150-200

Common Bottle
V For Victory – Guernsey Milk For Health $75-85

Common Bottle
Making It Together (picture of Uncle Sam and milk man) An American Tradition $35-45

Gateway Dairy
My WAR STAMPS Are Adding Up $85-95

Walnut Grove Dairy, Alton, IL
Buy War Bonds and Stamps For Victory $75-95

Half-Pints

Alden's Dairy
Speed Victory $25-30

Common Bottle
Do Your Part Too! Buy War Bonds & Stamps $35-40

Common Bottle
You Can Keep Them Flying By Buying U.S. War Bonds And Stamps $30-35

Common Bottle
War Bonds For Victory $20-25

Dairylea Dairy
Buy Bonds For Victory $35-45

Live Oak Riviera Farms, Santa Barbara, CA
USA food emblem, red and blue, flying eagle surrounded by stars $35-40
Buy Bonds For Victory $35-45

War Slogans

Action Speaks Louder Than Words, Help Uncle Sam
Round red quart $75

Air – Land – Sea (in circle with large V in background) Sanida Dairy, Erie PA
Round red gallon $75

Buy War Bonds & Stamps
Round red quart $50

Conserve For Victory
Round red quart $100

Do Your Part Too! Buy war Bonds & Stamps
Round half pint $35

For Freedom Buy War Bonds, Wrightwood Dairy, Chicago, IL
Round red quart $50

For Our Defense, Pete Miller's Dairy, Sauquoit, NY
Round red quart $100

Make America Strong, Mountain Gold Dairy, Walsenberg, CO
Round red quart $35

My War Stamps Are Adding Up, Gateway Dairy
Round green and red cream top quart $85

Pledge of Allegiance
Square red two quart $35

Prepared and Ready For Order, Are You?
Round green quart $75

Remember Pearl Harbor, Be Prepared, High Grade Dairy, Harrington, DE
Round red quart $100

Soldier, Sailor, Marine, They Guard Your Home (photos of soldiers)
Round cream top quart $45

Speed Victory, Alden's Dairy
Round red half pint $25

Turner & Wescott V For Victory, Morse Code for V
Round black quart $75

U.S. Savings Bonds And Freedom Shares
Round orange quart $20

War Bonds For Victory (Uncle Sam in center)
Green Round quart $35

We Cherish Liberty, Let's Protect Them (pyro)
Round maroon quart $35

We Need Your Help, It's Your Fight, It's
Your Responsibility, Buy More Bonds,
Elmwood Dairy, Oxbridge, MA
Round green quart $60

Your Country First, Your Family Second,
Yourself Last (picture of Uncle Sam)
Round red quart $45

Beer Bottles

"Buy U.S. War Bonds"
9-1/2", Metz Brewing Co. $25-35

Pioneer "Victory" Beer
9-1/2" $25-35

**Uncle Sam Beer – Glencoe Brewing
Company, Glencoe, Minnesota –1918**
Amber, 9-1/4", two paper labels with picture depicting
Uncle Sam holding a bottle of beer next to the brewery,
14 oz. **$125-150**

Figurals

**Canteen – 25th Annual Encampment – GAR
– Department of Ohio – 1891 – Steubenville (bust
of man on one side and Filson on reverse side)**
White pottery with maroon transfer and gold trim, 3-
1/4", smooth base, original mouth ring **$150-250**
American 1891

**Canteen – Souvenir – Twenty Sixth Grand
Annual – Encampment – Washington , DC
Sept. 20th to 23rd 1892, Reverse side: GAR
1861 to 1865 1892 – Patented April 16, 1885**
Stamped metal canteen with stamped copper
embossing, 5", original cork stopper on chain **$150-200**
American 1892

**Independence Hall Bank – "Bank Of Independence
Hall 1776-1876 – Patent Pending**
Pressed clear glass, 7-1/4", tin base sliding
closure **$375-475**
American 1876 (rare souvenir candy container from the
Philadelphia Centennial Exposition of 1876)

Figural Liberty
Dollar Coin flask:
United States Of
America - In God
We Trust (American
Eagle) - One Dollar
(on one side), E.
Pluribus Unum
(bust of Columbia)
1885 (on reverse
side), 1885-1895,
4-1/2", $250-350.

Liberty Bell Candy Container – "Proclaim Liberty Throughout The Land – 1776/ Centennial Exposition/1876
Clear, 3-1/2", smooth base, sheared and ground lip **$175-275**
American 1875-1876

Liberty Dollar Coin Flask – on one side "United States Of America/In God We Trust" (American eagle)/One Dollar, on other side "E. Pluribus Unum"/ (bust Of Columbia)
Clear, 4-1/2", smooth base, ground lip **$250-350**
American 1885-1895

Military Hat Candy Container
Clear, cap reading "U.S. Military Hat, Pla-Toy Company, Greensburg, PA **$80-140**
American 1930-1940

Statue of Liberty Jars (two)
Both clear glass, 12-1/2", smooth base, ground rims..**$275-375**
American 1886-1890 (Brought from France in 1885 and unveiled on October 28, 1886. President Cleveland received this gift from France for the American people.)

Statue of Liberty
Milk glass base with cast metal Statue of Liberty,15-1/2" (including statue), smooth base, sheared and ground lip **$400-500**
American 1890-1900

Uncle Sam Candy Container
Clear glass with 50 percent of original red, white, and blue paint - Uncle Sam standing next to container...**$300-400**
American 1915-1925

Uncle Sam
Clear, 9-1/2", smooth base, tooled top, 'Tall Hat' screw-on cap...**$80-120**
American 1890-1910

Flasks And Bottles

Ceramic G.A.R. Presidents Flask
White with multicolored transfers of G.A.R. Medal on one side depicting Lincoln April 14th 1865; Garfield July 2nd 1884 and McKinley Sept 6th 1901 on reverse, 5-3/4" **$350-450**
(rare flask showing the three Presidents who were assassinated while in office)

Eagle With Banner
Medium yellow olive green quart, smooth base, applied top **$500-800**
American 1855-1860

Eagle – Eagle
Greenish aqua pint, pontil-scarred base, sheared lip..**$150-200**
American 1835-1845

Selection of flasks: Eagle (reverse plain), 1830-1845, 2-1/2 quart, $4,000-6,000 (extremely rare size);
Eagle - Eagle, 1835-1845, quart, $175-250; Eagle - Eagle, 1835-1845, pint, $150-200.

Eagle – Furled Flag – "For Our Country"
Medium yellow green pint, pontil-scarred base, tooled
lip...$1,500-2,500
American 1825-1835 (rare)

Eagle – "Liberty" Tree
Light green half-pint, pontil-scarred base,
tooled top $700-900
American 1820-1835

**Franklin D. Roosevelt Flask, bust of Roosevelt
on one side above an American eagle.
Reverse side has image of hydroelectric
dam and hand grasping a lightning bolt with
TVA 1936, Tennessee Valley Authority.**
Aqua, 10", smooth base, tooled top $100-200
American 1936

Eagle – Morning Glory – Stoneware Flask
Tan pottery with dark brown Bennington-type
glaze, pint, pontil-scarred base, applied double
collar mouth..$700-1,000
American 1840-1845

**"Liberty"/Eagle – Willington Glass
Co. – West Willington – Conn**
Deep olive green pint, smooth base, applied sloping
collar top $200-300
American 1865-1875

**Teddy Roosevelt and Cabinet Whiskey Bottle
– "Cabinet (Three – Eagle Picture – Star)
Whiskey – A Blend Bottled By – Robert & Lindley
– Salt Lake City, Utah (labeled bottle)**
Medium amber, 9", smooth base, tooled
top $300-400
American 1905 (label depicts President Theodore
Roosevelt and Vice President Charles Fairbanks
presiding with full Cabinet)

**U.S. Patented Applied For – E. Pluribus
Unum – C. Packman Jr. & Co. Baltimore,
Md – Label Under Glass Flask**
Clear glass with multicolored label depicting an
eagle with crossed flags, shield, and cannons,
smooth base, ground lip, original metal cap and
strap rings $375-475
American 1885-1900

Eagle - Cornucopia, 1825-1835, 7", $150-200.

Eagle - Eagle, 1855-1865, Ohio Glasshouse,
pint, $3,000-4,500 (rare).

Jim Beam Bottles

American Bald Eagle – 1966
White head, golden beak, and rich brown plumage,
yellow claws grip branch of tree.........................**$25-35**

AMVETS – 1970
Commemorates the 25th anniversary of the Veterans
of American Wars (World War II, Korea, and Vietnam).
Gold metal eagle designed for stopper above the red,
white, blue, and yellow bottle. Embossed war scene is
on the reverse, 11-3/4".......................................**$20-30**

Bald Eagle – 1985
Bald eagle with spread wings **$25-30**

Boots and Helmet – 1984
Army helmet atop combat boots........................**$25-35**
(very collectible among military personnel and collectors)

Crispus Attucks – 1976
Picture of Crispus Attucks, American Revolutionary war
hero with American flag in background.................**$5-10**

Franklin Mint – 1970
Liberty Bell on one side, and blue and white shield with
Liberty on other side **$5-10**

Pearl Harbor – 1072
Dec 7 1941 – Pearl Harbor – Pearl Harbor Survivors
Association, Bald eagle sitting on top of bottle ..**$25-35**

Statue of Liberty – 1975
"Give Me Your Tired" on back **$20-25**

Statue of Liberty – 1985
"Give me your tired"on back **$20-30**

U.S. Open – Pebble Beach, Cal – June 12-18 1972
Red, white, and blue Uncle Sam hat doubling as a gold
bag **$25-30**

Washington State Bicentennial – 1976
Revolutionary War drummer on red and white base with
a gold Liberty Bell reading "1776-1976" and round blue
sign with stars reading "200 Years" **$15-20**

Shot Glasses and Stir Sticks
Blown glass Uncle Sam top hat with blown glass
stir sticks (set of six). Hat 2" x 2-1/4", stir sticks each
5-1/4" .... **$125-150 (set)**

Soda Bottles

**Dunn's Beverages – Statue of Liberty
in front of clouds –1954**
Clear glass, 10 oz., Sedalia, Mo.........................**$15-20**

Liberty Bottling Co. – Statue of Liberty – 1950
Green glass, 12 oz., Memphis, Tenn. **$65-85**

**My Pic – 1949 – Statue of Liberty
with stars erupting from torch**
Clear glass, 10 oz., Alexandria, La. **$30-35**

**Uncle Sam's Beverage (picture of
Uncle Sam on yellow label) –1947**
Clear glass, 7 oz., Houston, Texas...................**$90-100**

Victory Beverage – 1944
Dark glass, 9-1/2" **$25-30**

Victory Root Beer (picture of Stars & Stripes) – 1947
Dark glass, 10 oz..**$50-65**

Whiskey Bottles

Royal Doulton Dewars White Label Bottle
High-glazed porcelain with a dark brown base and
dark brown top fading to a light brownish gold center,
picture of Uncle Sam smoking a pipe, 7-1/4" x 6-1/2" x
2-3/4" **$300-400**
Royal Doulton, England 1907

Whiskey nipper - Uncle
Sam - Your Health
- 1930s, $45-55.

Miscellaneous

Opalescent milk glass with Uncle Sam seated between the smokestacks of the ship U.S.S. Olympia
The bottom of the boat has an eagle on the bow with portholes and guns on the sides, 6-1/2" x 3" x 4-5/8" **$125-150**
American 1898

Franklin D. Roosevelt Glass Goblet – Top of glass: "1933 – Franklin D. Roosevelt – 32nd President of the United States of America. Inaugurated March 4, 1933"; Front of glass: (bust of Roosevelt) – Reverse side of glass: (image depicting birds on a grape vine) – Repeal of the 18th Amendment Dec 7th 1933; Base of glass: "Asst. Sec. Of Navy 1915-20, Gov. of New York State 1929-1933"
Frosted glass, 6-1/4", smooth base...............**$200-300**
American 1933

Gilbert Stuart Portrait of George Washington on Liverpool Pitcher
White pottery, 7-1/2", smooth base, "Herculaneum" imprint **$900-1,200**
English 1790-1905. Extremely rare, Gilbert Stuart (1755-1828) painted all the notable American figures of the Federal period and was considered "Father of American Portraiture." This image of George Washington is on the most famous The "Herculaneum" imprinted on the base of the pitcher identifies it as a product of one of the more renowned pottery manufacturers of the period for the Liverpool region of England.

Gravy Boat
Union Porcelain Works (Green Point) Brooklyn, NY- Fine Porcelain Gravy Boat with Uncle Sam and John Bull reclining on top of boat, 7-1/2" x 3-1/2" x 5-1/8" **$1,200-1,500**
American 1868

McKinley – Bryan Campaign Bottles (two) – Bottle 1: "In Bryan We Trust" – Free Silver 16-1 (bust of Williams Jennings Bryan); Bottle 2: "In McKinley We Trust" – Gold Standard (bust of William McKinley)
Clear glass, 6-1/2", smooth base, tooled tops **$500-700**
American 1896 (extremely rare)

McKinley – Roosevelt Campaign Flask – "Our Candidates" (bust of William McKinley and Teddy Roosevelt)
Clear glass, 5", smooth base, screw-on metal cap, blue and white support rope for hanging purposes **$500-700**
American 1900

Occupational Shaving Mug Made For "Adolph Market"
Picture on mug depicting a flexed arm holding a hammer in front of the American flag, maroon wrap with a gold gilt edge **$300-400**
American 1880-1920

For Pike's Peak - Traveler - Eagle, 1870-1875, 6-1/8", $80-120.

Label-under-glass flask, U.S. - Patented Applied For - E. Pluribus Unum - C. Packman Jr. & Co. Baltimore, MD, 1885-1900, 5", $375-475.

Barber bottle, red stars & stripes pattern, 1885-1925, 7", $250-350.

Barber bottle, blue stars & stripes pattern, 1885-1925, 7", $250-350.

Patriotic shaving mug, made for Jacob Bauer, 1885-1925, 3-3/8", $100-150.

Patriotic shaving mug, made for William Parilla, 1885-1925, 3-7/8", $140-180.

St. Louis World's Fair – Ceramic Mug
Ceramic mug, 4-1/2", logo depicting Washington, Jefferson, Lafayette, Napoleon, and St. Louis, 1904. Crossed American flags, shield, and eagle, smooth base, "Sinclair Art. Co, Decorators of China, East Liverpool" **$125-150**
American 1904

Woodrow Wilson Royal Staffordshire Caricature Toby Jug
Red, white, and blue, 11", smooth base **$400-500**
English 1918. In 1918, an English political cartoonist designed a set of Toby jug caricatures to honor the leaders of World War I, manufactured by Royal Staffordshire Pottery, Staffordshire, England. President Woodrow Wilson is depicted astride a biplane in a flying position wearing a Colonial hat.

Pattern-Molded Bottles

A pattern-molded bottle is one that is blown into a ribbed or patterned mold. This group includes globular and chestnut flasks. One of these, the Stiegel bottle, produced during the late 18th century, is considered very rare and valuable. The two types of Stiegel bottles manufactured at the Stiegel Glass Factory are the diamond daisy and hexagon designs. Since pattern-molded bottles are among the more rare and valuable pieces, collectors should become familiar with their types, sizes, colors, and manufacturers.

Chestnut flask, 20-rib pattern, swirled to right, 1815-1835, 3-5/8", $400-600.

Blown Decanter
Medium lavender, 6", 15-vertical rib pattern, applied
ring mouth **$400-700**
American 1840-1860

Blown Three-Mold Toilet Water Bottle
Cobalt blue, 5-1/4", pontil-scarred base, flared out
mouth with inward folded rim..........................**$200-300**
American 1815-1835

Blown Three-Mold Toilet Water Bottle
Cobalt blue, 6-1/8", pontil-scarred base, inward
rolled lip **$200-300**
American 1815-1835

Chestnut Flask
Medium amber, 4-3/4", 24-vertical rib pattern, pontil-
scarred base, tooled mouth **$250-350**
American 1820-1835

Chestnut Flask
Golden yellow amber, 5-1/2", 16-vertical rib pattern,
pontil-scarred base, sheared lip......................**$100-150**
American 1820-1835

Chestnut Flask
Medium cobalt blue, 5-1/8", 22-broken rib
'Popcorn' pattern swirled to right, pontil-scarred
base, tooled mouth **$700-900**
American 1815-1835

Club Bottle
Blue aqua, 8-1/4", 16-rib pattern swirled to left, open
pontil, applied collar mouth............................**$100-150**
American 1815-1825

Elongated Flask
Pale green aqua, 7-1/4", 16-diamond over rib pattern,
open pontil, sheared lip...................................**$250-350**
American 1815-1825

Club bottle, 24-rib pattern, swirled to
right, 1810-1825, 7-7/8", $150-200.

Club Bottle
Blue aqua, 8-1/4", 16-rib pattern swirled to left, open
pontil, applied collar mouth............................**$100-150**
American 1815-1825

Club Bottle
Blue aqua, 8-1/2", 23-broken rib pattern to right, open
pontil, applied collar mouth............................**$170-2 50**
American 1815-1825

Freeblown Chestnut Flask
Aqua, 7", pontil-scarred base, sheared and tooled
lip...**$100-150**
American 1815-1835

Freeblown Globular Bottle
Greenish aqua, 8", open pontil, applied string
lip...**$200-275**
American 1780-1800

Freeblown Globular Bottle
Medium green, 8-7/8", open pontil, applied string
lip...**$150-200**
American 1770-1800

Freeblown Globular Bottle
Medium yellow olive green, 8-1/4", open pontil,
outward lip...**$300-400**
American 1770-1800

Freeblown Flattened Globular Bottle
Bluish aqua, 9-1/2", pontil-scarred base, applied
sloping collar mouth...**$75-125**
American 1780-1810

Freeblown Flattened Globular Bottle
Bluish aqua, 10-1/4", pontil-scarred base, applied
sloping collar mouth...**$75-125**
American 1780-1810

Freeblown Teardrop Flask
Medium sapphire blue, 4-1/2", pontil-scarred base,
tooled lip..**$100-150**
European 178-1920

Globular Bottle
Medium amber, 7-3/4", 24-rib pattern swirled to left,
pontil-scarred base, rolled lip..........................**$500-700**
American 1815-1835

Globular Bottle
Yellow amber with olive tone, 7-3/4",
24-vertical rib pattern, pontil-scarred base,
outward rolled lip.......................................**$1,200-1,600**
American 1815-1835

Globular Bottle
Medium golden amber, 8-1/8", 24-rib pattern
swirled to right, pontil-scarred base, outward
rolled lip...**$250-350**
American 1815-1835

14-diamond
pattern flask,
1815-1835,
6-1/8",
$250-350.

Midwestern chestnut flask, 24-vertical rib
pattern, 1820-1835, 4-1/2", $275-375.

Midwestern chestnut flask, 24-vertical rib
pattern, 1815-1835, 4-1/2", $400-600.

Midwestern chestnut flask, 24-vertical rib pattern
swirled to left, 1815-1835, 4-1/2", $375-500.

Midwestern chestnut flask, 24-rib pattern, swirled
to right, 1815-1835, 5-1/4", $300-400.

Midwestern chestnut flask, 24-vertical rib
pattern, 1815-1835, 5-1/4", $375-550.

Midwestern Chestnut Flask
Yellow amber, 24-verical rib pattern, 4-1/2", pontil-scarred base, sheared and tooled lip..............**$275-375**
American 1915-1835 (Zanesville Glassworks)

Midwestern Chestnut Flask
Medium golden amber, 24-rib pattern swirled to right, 5-1/4", pontil-scarred base, sheared and too led lip..**$300-400**
American 1915-1835

Midwestern Club Bottle
Deep bluish aqua, 8-1/8", 23-rib pattern swirled to right, pontil-scarred base, applied mouth.......**$175-275**
American 1815-1835

Midwestern Cruet
Light green, 5-7/8", 18-rib pattern swirled to right, open pontil, tooled mouth.......................................**$250-350**
American 1820-1835

Midwestern Elongated Chestnut Flask
Light emerald green, 24-vertical rib-pattern, 5-3/4", pontil-scarred base, sheared lip......................**$200-300**
American 1815-1835

Midwestern Flattened Globular Bottle
Deep blue aqua, 25-swirl rib pattern to right, 9", applied mouth **$120-140**
American 1815-1845

Midwestern club bottle, 24-broken rib pattern, swirled to right, 1815-1835, 8-1/4", $200-300.

Midwestern club bottle, 31-vertical rib pattern, 1810-1820, 7-1/2", $150-200.

Midwestern club bottle, 25-vertical rib pattern, 1815-1835, 8-1/2", $200-300.

Midwestern globular bottle, 24-vertical rib pattern, 1815-1835, 7-1/8", $250-300.

Midwestern globular bottle, 24-rib pattern, swirled to left, 1815-1835, 7-5/8", $200-275.

Midwestern globular bottle, 24-rib pattern, swirled to right, 1815-1835, 7-7/8", $150-200.

Midwestern globular bottle, 24-rib pattern, swirled to right, 1815-1835, 7-1/2", $500-700.

Midwestern Globular Bottle
Deep bluish aqua, 24-swirl rib pattern to right, 7-3/8",
pontil-scarred base, outward rolled lip............**$250-300**
American 1815-1835

Midwestern Globular Bottle
Medium amber, 8-1/8", pontil-scarred base,
applied lip...**$375-475**
American 1815-1835

Midwestern Globular Swirl Bottle
Golden yellow amber, 8-3/8", 24-rib pattern swirled to
right, pontil-scarred base, rolled lip.................**$500-800**

Midwestern Handled Globular Bottle
Medium amber, 6-5/8", 24-broken rib pattern
swirled to right, pontil-scarred base, applied
mouth and handle **$25,000-30,000**
American 1820-1835 (one of the rarest and most
desirable Midwestern glass items)

Midwestern Handled Jug
Deep amber, 4-3/4", pontil-scarred base, tooled mouth,
applied handle..**$375-475**
American 1820-1835 (rare, Zanesville Glassworks)
American 1812-1835

Midwestern Melon – Ribbed Flask
Medium blue green, 5-7/8", 16-vertical rib pattern,
pontil-scarred base, tooled lip **$200-300**
American 1820-1835

Nailsea Flask
Clear glass with white opalescent loops, 8-1/8", vertical
bands of applied rigaree on each side, pontil-scarred
base, tooled lip...**$80-140**
English 1850-1880

Nailsea Flask
Yellow amber with white looping, 5-3/8", pontil-scarred
base, tooled mouth **$175-300**
English 1820-1850

Nailsea Flask
Clear glass with white and blue alternating looping,
7-1/4", pontil-scarred base, tooled mouth......**$375-475**
American 1850-1870

Nailsea Flask – Rib Pattern
Red and yellow over milk glass, 7", 12-rib
pattern swirled to right, pontil-scarred base,
tooled mouth **$140-180**
English 1860-1880

Pattern-Molded Bottle
Light olive green, 4-1/4", 16-rib pattern swirled to right,
pontil-scarred base, tooled lip **$250-350**
American 1820-1835

Pattern-Molded Oil Bottle
Greenish aqua, 16-swirl rib pattern to left, 12-1/4",
smooth base, deep kick-up, applied mouth ...**$125-150**
European 1850-1865

Midwestern globular
bottle, 24-rib pattern
swirled to right,
1815-1835, 8-1/4",
$2,500-3,500.

Pattern-molded
pocket flask,
1940s, made by
Clevenger Brothers
Glassworks,
5-3/8", $250-350.

Pitkin flask,
36-broken rib
pattern, 1780-
1820, 5-3/8",
$600-800.

Pattern-Molded Chestnut
Yellow amber with olive tone, 6-5/8",15-broken rib
pattern, pontil-scarred base, applied mouth...**$600-800**
American 1820-1835

Pattern-Molded Flask
Medium green, 7-3/4", 20-ogival pattern, open pontil,
sheared lip..**$500-700**
American 1820-1835

Pinch-Sided Spirits Bottle
Clear glass, 7-3/8", pontil-scarred base with applied
foot, tooled top...**$200-300**
European 1780-1830

Pitkin Flask
Yellow olive, 5-3/8", 36-broken rib pattern swirled to
right, open pontil, sheared and tooled lip **$600-800**
American 1780-1820

Pitkin Flask
Deep emerald green, 6-3/8", 30-broken rib
pattern swirled to left, pontil-scarred base,
tooled mouth **$180-275**
American 1780-1810

Pitkin Flask
Medium yellow green, 6-1/4", 32-broken rib
pattern swirled to right, pontil-scarred base,
tooled mouth **$650-750**
American 1780-1810

Pitkin flask,
32-broken rib
pattern, swirled to
right, 1780-1810,
6-1/4", $600-800.

Pitkin flask,
30-broken rib
pattern, swirled to
right, 1780-1810,
6-3/8", $180-275.

Pocket Flask
Clear glass, 4-3/4", vertical rib pattern, pontil-scarred
base, tooled lip **$150-250**
German 1780-1830

Pocket Flask
Clear glass, 5", overall diamond pattern, pontil-scarred
base, outward rolled lip **$150-250**
German 1780-1830

Rib-Pattern Cruciform Type Bottle/Decanter
Clear glass with amethyst tine, 8-5/8", rib pattern
swirled to right, pontil-scarred base, applied
string lip..**$350-450**
American 1750-1780

Rib-Pattern Flask
Medium purple amethyst, 3-1/2", 18-vertical rib
pattern, pontil-scarred base, tooled mouth **$275-450**
European 1815-1835

Rib-Pattern Pocket Flask
Medium green, 20-vertical rib pattern, pontil-scarred
base, applied mouth......................................**$300-400**
European 1800-1830 (possibly German)

Rib-Pattern Chestnut Spirits Flask
Medium cobalt blue, 7-1/2", 24-vertical rib pattern,
pontil-scarred base, tooled mouth..................**$250-450**
German 1780-1820

Rib-Pattern Flask
Medium cobalt blue, half-pint, 5-1/2",
16-vertical rib pattern on both sides,
pontil-scarred base, tooled lip **$1,000-1,500**
American 1840-1850 (rare in this color)

Teardrop flask,
European, 22-vertical
rib pattern, 1830-1850,
7-1/8", $140-180.

Pocket flasks, German,
1780-1830, 4-3/4" and
5", $170-250 (both).

Perfume and Cologne Bottles

With each revised edition of this book, I receive valuable feedback from bottle and glass collectors from across the United States and Europe on how to make each new edition better than the last. One question I am constantly asked is, "When are you going to add a chapter about perfume bottles?" OK, I have listened, and here's the chapter. But it didn't happen without a lot of help from Penny Dolnick, who provided the background and pricing information, and from Randy Monsen and Rodney Baer, who provided the great photographs.

Penny's credentials speak for themselves, as she is a past president of the International Perfume Bottle Association (IPBA), and the author of the *Penny Bank Commercial Perfume Bottle Price Guide*, 7th Edition, the *Penny Bank Miniature Perfume Bottle Price Guide*, 2nd Edition, and the *Penny Bank Solid Perfume Bottle Price Guide*, 3rd Edition. Penny is willing to help fellow collectors

Benoit Nuit de Paques (Easter Evening), 1925, 4.4", $3,500-4,500. (Extremely rare in flask form, with only five known to exist of this model. The back is molded H. Benoit Paris).

identify and date bottles, but not conduct appraisals. She can be contacted at alpen@gate.net.

The International Perfume Bottle Association is an organization of 1,500 perfume bottle collectors in several countries. Its main objective is to foster education and comradeship for collectors through its quarterly full-color magazine, its regional chapters, and its annual convention. If interested in obtaining further information or becoming a member, visit the association's Web site at www.perfumebottles.org.

In addition, each year, the IPBA convention hosts the Monsen and Baer Perfume Bottle Auction, featuring approximately 400 perfume bottles and related items. A full-color, 128-page hardbound catalogue entitled "The World of Perfume" is available by contacting Randall Monsen and Rodney Baer at monsenbaer@errols.com.

Collectors look for two types of perfume bottles—decorative and commercial. Decorative bottles are those sold empty and meant to be filled with your choice of scent. Commercial bottles are sold filled with scent and usually have the label of a perfume company. Because there are thousands of different perfume bottles, most collectors specialize in a subcategory.

Among decorative perfume bottle collectors, popular specialties include ancient Roman or Egyptian bottles; cut glass bottles with or without gold or sterling silver trim or overlay; bottles by famous glassmakers like Moser, Steuben, Webb, Lalique, Galle, Daum, Baccarat, and Saint Louis; figural porcelain bottles from the 18th and 19th centuries or from Germany between 1920 and 1930; perfume lamps (with wells to fill with scent); perfume burners; laydown and double-ended scent bottles; atomizer bottles; pressed or molded early American glass bottles; matched dresser sets of bottles; and hand-cut Czechoslovakian bottles from the early 20th century.

Commercial perfume collectors often collect by categories such as color of glass; bottles by a single parfumer (Guerlain, Caron, or Prince Matchiabelli); bottles by famous fashion designers (Worth, Paul Poiret, Chanel, Dior, Schiaparelli, or Jean Patou); bottles by a

Clear glass bottle, sterling silver top, Birmingham, England, 1897, 8", $450-650.

particular glassmaker or designer (Lalique, Baccarat, Viard, or Depinoix); giant factice bottles (store display bottles not filled with genuine fragrance); small compacts (often figural) holding solid (cream) perfume; tester bottles (small bottles with long glass daubers); figural; novelty; or miniature perfumes (usually replicas of regular bottles given as free samples at perfume counters).

Novice perfume bottle collectors may be surprised to learn that the record price for a perfume bottle at auction was more than $80,000, and the little sample bottles that were given free at perfume counters in the '60s can now bring as much as $300 to $400! They may also be surprised that European collectors prefer miniature bottles to their full-size counterparts, and bottles by American perfume companies are more desirable to European collectors than to Americans, and vice-versa. Also, most collectors of commercial perfume bottles will buy empty examples, but those still sealed with the original perfume carry a premium, and the original packaging can raise the price by as much as 300 percent! The rubber bulbs on atomizer bottles dry out over time, but the lack of one or the presence of a modern replacement does not really affect the price.

Collecting perfume bottles is one of those hobbies that can begin with little or no investment. Just ask your friend who wears Shalimar to save her next empty bottle for you. But beware! Investment-quality perfume bottles can be pricey! The factors determining value are the same as for any other kind of glass—rarity, condition, age, and quality.

Some special considerations should be taken into account for perfume bottles:

> 1. A commercial bottle isn't investment quality (one that will appreciate in value over time) unless it has its original stopper and label. (This rule only applies to commercially made perfume bottles).

> 2. An investment quality bottle must have high quality glass (must not be a lower-end eau de cologne or eau de toilette bottle) and must not have any corrosion on any metal part.

> 3. In 1963, small plastic liners were added to the dowel end of the stopper on commercial bottles. Before then, each stopper had to be ground to match the neck of its bottle. Bottles without liners (pre-1963) are preferred to those that have them (post-1963).

Special Note: All dates given are for the introduction of the scent (if applicable), not for the issue of the particular bottle.

Decorative Perfume Bottles

German ceramic crown top of Dutch boy holding flowers, 4.2", c1920 .... $150

German ceramic crown top of seated kewpie doll, 2.9", c1930s $125

Baccarat signed atomizer for Marcel Franck, 3.75", c1930s $90

Ruby cut glass w/sterling neck and elaborate stopper, French, 3.8", c1855 .... $575

English ruby glass, double-ended scent w/sterling mounts, signed, 4.5", 1905 .... $350

R. Lalique "Myosotis #3," green stain, nude stopper, signed, 9.0", c1928 .... $4,000

R. Lalique "Sirenes" perfume burner, blue stain, nude figures, signed, 7.0", c1920 .... $2,200

Webb red glass w/sterling stopper and white cameo overlay, unsigned, 4.4", c1910 .... $1,250

Limoges enameled w/lady, enameled overcap, inner stopper, 2.5", c19th C. $800

Volupte atomizer enameled w/Art Deco motifs, unsigned, 9.3", c1930s $1,150

DeVilbiss black glass w/gold mica "lady leg" atomizer, label, 6.8", c1930s $275

Devilbiss perfume lamp enameled w/dancing girls, metal cap and base, 7.5", c1930s $460

Austrian square metal filigree over glass w/glass jewels, 2.1", c1920s $115

Czech pale blue cut glass w/matching keyhole stopper, 5", c1920s $175

Birmingham engraved sterling laydown w/glass liner, hinged cover, 4.5", 1885 .... $475

Ingrid Czech lapis lazuli glass atomizer cut w/roses, label, 5", c1920s $350

Moser amber w/gold frieze of female warriors, signed, 6", c1920s $250

Cologne bottle,
1860-1880,
5-3/4", $175-275.

Cologne bottle,
1860-1880,
9-3/4", $275-375.

Cologne bottle,
1845-1865, 12",
$200-300.

Hoffman clear w/amber lady and cherub stopper, many jewels, signed, 6.8", c1920s $1,600

Czech clear w/pale blue nude figure dauber, blue jewels, unsigned, 5.7", c1920s $6,300

Shuco mohair monkey figure w/perfume tube inside 5", c1930s $265

American molded paperweight bottle w/bird stopper, unsigned, 5.3", c1940s $25

American clear bottle w/elaborate silver overlay, ball stopper, 5.1", c1930s $100

Kosta faceted bottle and stopper, signed V Lindstand, 3.5", c1950 .... $40

Gallé atomizer, yellow w/maroon berry and leaf overlay, cameo signed, 7.36", c1910 .... $2,200

Daum, Nancy peach w/amber leaf and flower overlay, cameo signed, 6.5", c1915 .... $1,000

Baccarat two dolphins bottle, ball stopper, signed, 6", c1925 .... $300

Fenton blue opalescent coin dot atomizer for DeVilbiss, 4", c1940s $75

Steuben blue aurene atomizer, acorn finial, for DeVilbiss, 9.5", c1930 .... $1,050

Cambridge pink foot urn, stopper w/long dauber, label, 4.75", c1940s.. $75

L.C. Tiffany blue favrile footed urn, signed, 6", c1930s... $700

Commercial Perfume Bottles

Elizabeth Arden It's You, MIB, Baccarat white figural hand in dome, 6.5", c1938 .... $4,300

Babs Creations Forever Yours Heart, in composition hands w/dome, 3.5", c1940 .... $233

Fancy cologne bottle, 1850-1870, 9-7/8", $800-1,200.

Guerlain Le Mouchoir de Monsieur (A Gentleman's Handkerchief), clear glass and stopper, 1902, 5", $300-400. The bottle, the Escargot (or "Snail") by Pochet et du Courval dates from 1902.

Guerlain Rose du Moulin,
1907, 1.7", $125-175.

Bourjois Evening in Paris, cobalt w/fan stopper, banner label, 4.5", c1928.....................................$265

Bourjois Evening in Paris, cobalt bullet shape laydown, good label, tassel, 3.5", c1928 ....$22

Hattie Carnegie, clear head and shoulders bottle, label, 3.25", c1944...$123

Caron Nuit de Noel, MIB, black glass, gold label, faux shagreen box w/tassel, 4.36", c1922............$98

Chanel Chanel #5, glass giant factice, 10.5", c1921 ....$595

Mary Chess Souvenir d'un Soir, MIB, replica of Plaza Hotel fountain, 3.62", c1956 ....$2,875

Colgate Cha Ming glass stopper, flower label, box, 3", c1917...$46

Corday Toujours Moi, MIB, clear bottle w/gold trim, glass stopper, 2.5", c1924.......................................$81

Corday Tzigane R Lalique, tiered bottle and stopper, label, 5.5", c1940s...$291

Houbigant La Belle Salson
(The Beautiful Season), 1926,
3.9", $4,000-6,000 (signed
in the mold R. Lalique).

Label-under-glass cologne bottle, Eau De Cologne, J. Quinlan - New York (on base), 1880-1910, 6-7/8", $400-500.

Coty Ambre Antique R Lalique w/gray stained maidens, 6", c1913 ....$1,380

Coty L'Origan, MIB, Baccarat, flat rectangle, sepia stained moth stopper, 3.25", c1903 ....$205

D'Albert Ecusson Urn w/gold label, box, 3.87", c1952 ....$52

Jean Desprez Votre Main Sevres, porcelain hand w/applied flowers, 3.2", c1939 ....$1,900

Dior Diorissimo, MIB, clear amphora, glass stopper, 3.87", c1956 ....$148

Dior Diorissimo Urn w/gilt bronze flowers stopper, box, 9", c1956 ....$1,850

Luxor Lybis, clear glass and blue glass stopper, 1924, 5.4", $500-750.

D'Orsay Toujours Fidele Baccarat, pillow shape w/bulldog stopper, box, 3.5", c1912 ....$520

Duchess of Paris Queenly Moments Queen Victoria bottle on wood base, 3.5", c1938.........................$33

Faberge Woodhue, oversize upright logo stopper, 3.5", c1940..$75

Forvil Relief R Lalique, round bottle w/swirl pattern, no label, 6.87", c1920 ....$475

Dorothy Gray Savoir Faire Bottle w/enameled mask, gold stopper, 4", c1947 ....$460

Jacques Griffe Griffonage square bottle, flat top glass stopper, box, 2.25", c1949 ....$23

Guerlain Shalimar Baccarat signed classic winged bottle, blue stopper, 5.5", c1921...........................$155

Guerlain Shalimar, MIB, donut-shape cologne, pointed glass stopper, 11", c1921 ....$36

Houbigant Parfum Ideal Baccarat, faceted stopper, gold label, box, 4.2", c1900....................................$80

Isabey Bleu de Chine Viard, gray stain w/enameled flowers, 5.75", c1926 ....$1,325

Andrew Jergens Ben Hur, rounded bottle, frosted stopper, black label, 5.25", c1904 ....$50

Lander Gardenia, dime store bottle w/orange plastic tiara stopper, 4.75", c1947.........................$19

Lanvin Arpege, MIB, black boule w/gold logo, gold raspberry stopper, 3.5", c1927 ....$255

Lucien Lelong Indiscret, draped bottle, glass bow stopper, label, 4.75", c1935...................................$50

Prince Matchabelli Added Attraction, MIB, red crown, velvet case, 2.12", c1956.........................$394

Prince Matchabelli Crown Jewel, MIB, clear crown, cross stopper, chain, 2", c1945 ....$51

Molinard Xmas Bells, MIB, black glass figural bell, gold lettering, 4.25", c1926 ....$460

Solon Palmer Gardenglo Simple bottle, glass ball stopper, label, 4.75", c.1913...................................$20

Raphael Replique, MIB, R logo stopper, red seal, 3.25", c1944..$50

Nina Ricci L'Air du Temps, MIB, Lalique, double dove stopper, 4.5", c1948....................................$250

Elsa Schiaparelli Shocking Torso w/flowers, tape measure, dome, 4", c1936 ....$185

Tre Jur Suivez Moi Lady, figure bottle w/long dauber, 2.5", c1925..$215

Opaque glass scent bottle with décor of leaves, 5.2"; Glass stopper and silver cap with hallmarks for London 1903; Opaque white glass bottle and stopper, 3.2"; Porcelain handpainted bottle, no stopper, 2.4"; Porcelain honeycomb bottle with a green bee on both sides 4.1", $400-600.

Vigny Golliwogg, MIB, black face stopper w/seal fur hair, 3.5", c1919..$347

Worth Dans la Nuit R Lalique, matt blue boule, name on stopper, 5.75", c1920.......................................$865

Ybry Femme de Paris Baccarat, green opaque w/enameled overcap, 2.25", c1925.....................$500

Miniature Perfume Bottles

Elizabeth Arden, blue glass blown bottle w/blue horse figure inside, box, 2.2", c1934...................$870

Bourjois Evening in Paris, cobalt mini in green bakelite shell, 2", c1928 ....$280

Bourjois On The Wind, peach label and cap, 1.5", c1930, ...$26

Hattie Carnegie A Go Go, square mini in hat box, 1.36", c1969..$55

Caron Nuit de Noel Tester, black cap and label, full, 1.75", c1922..$31

Ciro Chevalier de la Nuit, frosted figural knight, black head, 2.36", c1923 ....$250

Colgate Caprice, worn label, twisted screw cap, 2", c1893 ....$18

Corday Toujours Moi, shield-shape label, pink plastic cap, 1.75", c1923.......................................$25

Coty A'Suma Boule with embossed flowers, no label, 1.5", c1934...$87

Jean Desprez Sheherazade, MIB, tall spire stopper, 3", c1960s..$155

Dior Diorama, round laydown "pebble," black label, 1", c1950...$71

Dior Miss Dior, round laydown "pebble," white label, 1", c1953...$33

D'Orsay Intoxication, draped bottle, gold label, gold pouch, 1.62", c1942..$29

Evyan Great Lady, laydown heart bottle, full, 2.25", c1958 ....$8

Guerlain Chamade, green plastic pagoda cap, 1.25", c1969 ....$275

Guerlain L'Heure Bleu Tester, black cap w/dauber, horse label, 2.25", c1912.....................................$160

Guerlain Mitsouko, replica mini, glass stopper, full, 1.5", c1919...$22

Richard Hudnut Le Debut Bleu, MIB, blue w/gold raspberry stopper, 1.25", c1927 ....$255

Richard Hudnut Le Debut Noir, MIB, black w/gold raspberry stopper, 1.25", c1927 ....$778

Karoff Buckarettes, set of two, cowboy and cowgirl w/wooden heads, 1.87", c1940 ....$91

Lanvin Arpege, tiny black boule w/logo, 1.2", c1927 ....$545

Le Galion Sortilege, tiny mini w/ship cap and gold label, 1.25", c1937..$29

Sandwich cologne, 1970-1890, 4-7/8", $275-375.

Sandwich cologne, 1850-1870, 3-3/8", $140-180.

Lucien Lelong Passionment, tiny mini w/pearl cap, label, 1.12", c1940..$14

Germain Monteil Laughter, blown bottle, blue threaded stopper, full, 1.5", c1941 ....$52

Raphael Replique, MIB, Lalique, acorn in plastic case, 2", c1944...$145

Revillon Detchma, MIB, urn shape, metal cap, 2.25", c1955 ....$14

Nina Ricci, set of three sunburst, leaf and heart minis in box, 1.25"-1.5", c1952............................$663

Rochas Femme, round laydown "pebble," gold label, 1.5", c1945...$48

Elsa Schiaparelli Shocking, set of three torsos in jack-in-box w/flowers, 1.36", c1936 ....$1,100

Rose Valois Canotier, figural mini wearing hat in plastic case, 2.3", c1950 ....$256

Weil Cobra, MIB, ball stopper, worn box, 1.5", c1941 ....$34

Weil Secret of Venus (antelope), waisted bottle, blue cap, full, 1.36", c1942 ....$32

Miscellaneous Perfume/ Cologne/Scent Bottles

Blown Cologne Bottle
Opalescent sapphire blue, 6-1/8", swirl line throughout bottle, pontil-scarred base, rolled lip...............**$250-350**
American 1855-1865

Bunker Hill Monument Cologne (Label: Cologne Water For The Toilet)
Deep purple amethyst, 6-1/2", smooth base, rolled lip **$700-900**
American 1875 (rare color for this bottle)

Cologne Bottle
Purple amethyst, 4-5/8", 8-sided, corset waist shape, smooth base, rolled lip **$600-800**
American 1865-1875

Cologne Bottle (Label: Eau de Cologne Paris)
Aqua, 6-3/8", plume and vine design on three panels, open pontil, thin flared out lip............................**$70-100**
American 1840-1860

Scent bottle, 1850-1880, 2-1/2", $150-250.

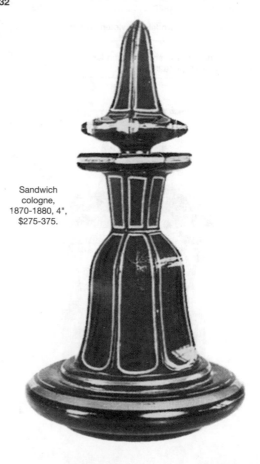

Sandwich cologne, 1870-1880, 4", $275-375.

Cologne Bottle (Label: Eau De Cologne) – Label Under Glass
Clear glass, 6-7/8", copper wheel cut decoration reading 'Sarah', label under glass is red, blue, gold with black and white photo of a woman, smooth base, "J. Quinlan - New York," tooled mouth.................**$400-500**
American 1880-1910

Cologne Bottle (Label: Cologne Water For Toilet)
Clear glass, 5-5/8", obelisk with herringbone corners and stars on two side panels, smooth base, tooled lip..**$140-180**
American 1870-1880

Cologne Bottle (Label: Double Extract D'eau De Cologne)
Deep cobalt blue, 4-1/4", 12-sided with sloped shoulder, smooth base, rolled lip **$300-400**
American 1865-1885

Cologne Bottle (Label: Double Extract D'eau De Cologne Perfectionee)
Medium cobalt blue, 6-3/8", 12-sided, pontil-scarred base, rolled lip **$300-400**
American 1860-1880

Seahorse scent bottle, 1820-1835, 2-3/4", $100-150.

Sterling silver covered perfume bottle with inner stopper, 2.8"; Bottle with ornate sterling silver top, hallmarked Birmingham, 1892; Sterling silver covered bottle, 3.6", hallmarked London 1907, $200-300 (all).

Victorian bottles: green glass bottle, 3.3"; Clear glass bottle, 3.2"; Red glass bottle, 4"; Clear glass bottle with sterling top marked Birmingham, 1924; Clear glass bottle, 3.7"; circa 1920s, $200-300 (all).

Sterling silver perfume bottle and stopper, 3.1", the front carved with flowers, the reverse with the initials HS, the back marked Sterling and with various hallmarks, circa 1900-1920, $69.

Vaseine glass bottle and stopper, 7.5", the bottle created with eight ridges, conforming stopper, possibly of Bohemian manufacture, circa 1900-1920, $104.

White porcelain oval bottle with brass cap, 2.3", handpainted on both sides with blue flowers, circa 1900-1924, $58.

Cologne Bottle – Perfume – Aimee – Richard Hudnut – New York
Porcelain with light blue glazing and blue lettering, 10", smooth base, "This Bottle Is The Property Of R. Hudnut's Pharmacy New York," tooled top.....**$200-300**
American 1890-1920

Fancy Cologne Bottle
Milk glass, 5", embossed Indians on two panels, pontil-scarred base, tooled mouth **$1,800-2,800**
American 1845-1865 (rare color)

Fancy Cologne Bottle
Medium sapphire blue, 5-7/8", pontil-scarred base, flared lip...**$2,000-3,000**
American 1825-1845

Pattern-Molded Cologne Bottle
Medium purple amethyst, 4-1/2", 12-vertical rib-pattern swirled to left, pontil-scarred base, flared lip ..**$400-600**
American 1820-1835

Scent Bottle
Deep cobalt blue, 3-1/4", swirl pattern, pontil-scarred base, tooled mouth **$100-150**
American 1840-1860

Sunburst Scent Bottle
Medium cobalt blue, 2-7/8", pontil-scarred base, rolled lip...**$400-600**
American 1820-1835

Teardrop Cologne Bottle
Clear glass with alternating blue, white, and pink vertical strips, 4-3/4", pontil-scarred base, tooled mouth **$175-275**
American 1840-1870

Poison Bottles

By the very nature of their contents, poison bottles form a unique category for collecting. While most people assume that poison bottles are plain, most are very decorative, making them easy to identify their toxic contents. In 1853, the American Pharmaceutical Association recommended that laws be passed requiring identification of all poison bottles. In 1872, the American Medical Association recommended that poison bottles be identified with a rough surface on one side and the word *poison* on the other. But as so often happened during that era, passing of these laws was very difficult and the manufacturers were left to do whatever they wanted. Because a standard wasn't established, a varied group of bottle shapes, sizes, and patterns was manufactured, including skull and crossbones, or skulls, leg bones, and coffins.

Brecklein, 1890-1915, 7-1/2", $2,000-3,000 (very rare).

The bottles were manufactured with quilted or ribbed surfaces and diamond/lattice-type patterns for identification by touch. Colorless bottles are very rare since most poison bottles were produced in dark shades of blues and browns, another identification aid. When collecting these bottles, caution must be exercised because it is not unusual to find a poison bottle with its original contents. If the bottle has the original glass stopper, the value and demand for the bottle will greatly increase.

Brecklein
Cobalt blue, 7-1/2", irregular hexagon form,
smooth base, "C.L.G.CO. Patent Appl'd For,"
tooled lip..$2,000-3,000
American 1890-1915 (rare)

**Champion – Embalming Fluid – The Champion
– Chemical Co. – Springfield – Ohio – Poison**
Clear glass, 8-1/2", smooth base, tooled mouth
....$150-200
American 1890-1915

**Motif of skull and crossed bones inside triangle)
De – Dro – Giftflasche – Des – Deutschen
– Drogisten – Verbandes – DDV (monogram)
– (motif of skull and crossed bones inside
triangle) De – Dro – Giftflasche – Des – Deutschen
– Drogisten – Verbandes – DDV (monogram)**
Medium green, 9-5/8", triangular form, smooth base.
"750," ABM lip...$275-375
German 1910-1930 (scarce)

**Doctor Oreste – Sinanide's – Medicinal
– Preparations – Orestorin – Prolong Or Restore –
Youthfulness – A Youthful Appearance – Is A Social
Necessity – Not A Luxury – Sole Representative
– Adele Morel – 24 East 61 Street – New York**
Milk glass, 4-5/8", coffin form, smooth base, tooled
mouth, original ground stopper.......................$150-200
American 1890-1910

**Durfee – Embalming – Fluid Co.
– Grand Rapids – Mich – Poison**
Medium amber, 8-1/2", smooth base, tooled
mouth $150-200
American 1890-1915

**(Motif of skull and crossed bones
on 6 panels) Federation Francaise
Droguistes Merchands De Couleurs**
Light yellow green, 10-3/4", 6-sided, smooth base,
"1 Litre Depose Model," ABM lip $300-400
French 1910-1930 (rare)

Columbian Pharmacy,
Inc. - 461 State St. Perth
Amboy, N.J., 1890-1915,
5", $1,200-1,800 (only one
of two known examples).

F. & E. Bailey
& Co. -
Lowell, Mass,
1890-1915,
5", $300-400.

Gift (skull and crossbones) – Gift
Medium amber, 5-1/2", smooth base, "200,"
tooled lip...$300-400
German 1900-1920

Gray & Pearse – Druggist – Poison
– Take Care – Cheyenne – Wyo
Cobalt blue, 3-5/8", smooth base, "W.T. & CO,"
tooled lip..$800-1,200
American 1890-1915 (extremely rare Western poison)

Hydrarg Salicyl Poison
Amber, 4-1/8", smooth base, "Pat. Apr. 2, 1889
–W.T.CO," tooled lip $70-90
American 1880-1910

Jacob Hulle – Not To Be Taken – Strychnine
Deep cobalt blue, 3-5/8", smooth base, tooled
mouth $35-45
American 1890-1915

(Skull and crossed bones) Poison
– Jacobs – Bichloride – Tablets
Yellow amber, 2-1/4", 8-sided, smooth base, tooled
mouth $800-1,200
American 1890-1910

Lattice And Diamond Pattern – Poison
Deep cobalt blue, 7", smooth base, tooled lip, original
glass "Poison" stopper...................................$275-375
American 1890-1910

Lattice And Diamond Pattern – Poison
Medium cobalt blue, 9-3/8", smooth base, tooled lip,
original glass "Poison" stopper, "Poison" embossed on
label panel $1,200-1,800
American 1890-1910

Melvin & Badger – Apothecaries – Boston, Mass
Cobalt blue, 3-3/8", smooth base, "C.L.G. CO. – Patent
Applied For," tooled mouth $125-150
American 1890-1920 (scarce in this size)

Corrosive Sublimate - Poison, 1890-1910, 2-7/8"; Antiseptic Tablets - Poison, 1890-1910, 3-1/4", $100-150 (both).

Nicoticide
Cobalt blue, 4", smooth base, tooled mouth $40-55
English 1890-1915

Phenol Poison
Amber, 6-5/8", smooth base, tooled lip, original ground
glass stopper...$70-90
American 1880-1910

**Poison (motif of star above and below
skull and crossed bones) Poison**
Yellow amber, 4-3/4", smooth base, tooled
mouth $500-700
American 1890-1910 (scarce)

Poison Poison (Label: Poison Caution)
Medium golden amber, 2-3/4", smooth base, tooled
mouth $150-200
American 1890-1910 (scarce)

Poison (on shoulder)
Deep cobalt blue, 3-1/2", smooth base (PATENT –T & L
CO), tooled mouth..$150-250
American 1890-1910 (scarce)

Poison (embossed on two sides)
Medium amber, jar, smooth base, ABM lip $275-375
Australian 1920-1930 (scarce)

Poison – Bowker's Pyrox (on base)
Clear glass, 5", smooth base, ABM lip................$15-20
American 1895-1900

**Poison – Davis & Geck (monogram)
Brooklyn, N.Y. – Germicidal Tablets**
Cobalt blue, 3-1/8", smooth base, tooled
lip...$600-800
American 1890-1915

**Poison (on neck) – Electric Balm – G.M.
Rhoades – Grand Rapids – Mich**
Clear glass, 6-5/8", smooth base, tooled
mouth $150-200
American 1885-1895

**Poison – H.K. Mulford Co – Chemist
– Philadelphia – Poison**
Cobalt blue, 1-7/8", smooth base, tooled
mouth $15-20
American 1890-1900

**Poison – (Label: Coffinoids, Manufactured
By Crystal Chen Co., New York City)**
Deep cobalt blue, 3-1/4", coffin shape, smooth base,
tooled top $400-600
American 1890-1910

Poison – F.A. – Thompson – & Co – Detroit – Poison
Medium amber, 3-1/8", coffin form, smooth base,
tooled mouth $600-900
American 1890-1910

Posion – (figural grim reaper)
Bisque with brown and tan glaze, 7", smooth base,
original stoppers...$35-45
American 1900-1920

Poison – Nit. Strychnia, Chas. Pfizer & Co. New York
Cobalt blue, 2-3/8", smooth base, tooled top $15-20
American 1895-1910

Poison – Pat Appl'd For (figural skull poison)
Cobalt blue, 4-1/8", smooth base, tooled
mouth $700-900
American 1890-1910

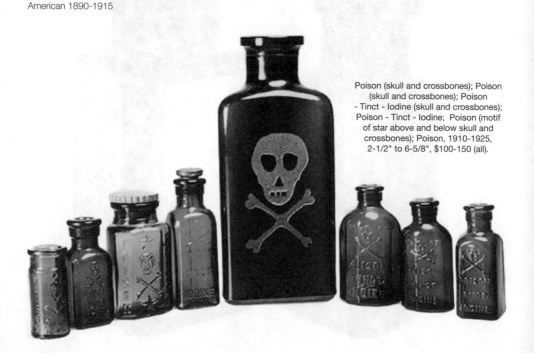

Poison (skull and crossbones); Poison
(skull and crossbones); Poison
- Tinct - Iodine (skull and crossbones);
Poison - Tinct - Iodine; Poison (motif
of star above and below skull and
crossbones); Poison, 1910-1925,
2-1/2" to 6-5/8", $100-150 (all).

Poison – Poison Phosp. Strchnia
Clear glass, 3-1/4", smooth base, tooled top **$15-20**
American 1890-1910

Poison Flask
Ice blue with overall hobnail pattern, 4-5/8", pontil-scarred base, tooled mouth **$150-200**
German 1890-1915

Poison Flask
Medium olive green, 5-5/8", overall hobnail pattern, pontil-scarred base, sheared lip......................**$150-200**
American 1820-1835

Poison – (submarine-shaped poison)
Deep cobalt blue, 2-1/2", smooth base, "Registered No 336907," tooled lip **$400-600**
English 1890 1915

Poison – The Owl Drug Co (motif of double winged owl on mortar and pestle)
Medium cobalt blue, 5", triangular form, smooth base, ABM lip **$140-180**
American 1915-1925

Poison – The Owl Drug Co (motif of double winged owl on mortar and pestle)
Medium cobalt blue, 8-1/2", triangular form, smooth base, tooled mouth **$300-400**
American 1915-1925

Poison – The Owl Drug Co (motif of owl on mortar and pestle) – Aqua Ammonia, Poison
Deep cobalt blue, 9-5/8", triangular form, smooth base, tooled mouth **$700-900**
American 1890-1910 (scarce)

Figural Skull Poison - Poison - Pat. Appl'd For, 1880-1910, 2-7/8", $2,500-3,500 (rare).

For - External - Use Only - Prescriptions - Reese Chem. Co - 1000 - External - Use 4 Times Daily - Mfg. By - Reese Chem. Co - Cleveland - O, 1915-1925, 5-1/2", $80-120.

Poison – Use With Caution – 16 Oz
Cobalt blue, 8-3/4", smooth base, tooled
mouth $200-300
Canadian 1890-1910

**Poison – O.K. Is Absolutely Sure – Special
– Is King Of All (embalming fluid bottle)**
Clear glass, 11", smooth base, tooled
mouth $40-60
American 1880-1920

**Poison – Poison (Label: Poison – Diamond
– Antiseptics – For External Use Only – Lilly
– Eli Lilly And Company, Indianapolis, U.S.A.)**
Medium amber, 10-1/2", smooth base, tooled
mouth $200-300
American 1890-1910

**Poison – Poison (Label: Coffin Shape
– Corrosive – Mercuric Chloride – The Norwich
Pharmacal Co, Norwich, New York)**
Medium cobalt blue, 7-1/2", smooth base, (Norwich
-16A), tooled mouth $1,000-15,000
American 1890-1910

Rat – Poison
Clear glass, 2-3/8", smooth base, tooled
mouth $40-80
American 1890-1920

**Rough On Rats – Poison Made By E.W.
Wells, Chemist, Jersey City, N.J. – U.S.A.**
Wooden cylindrical box, 2-1/2", original label and
contents...$80-160

**Ser C Sol – Elliott – Poison – Poison
– Not To Be Taken – Ser C Sol – Elliotts
– Poison – Not To Be Taken**
Medium amber, 5-1/8", triangular form, smooth base,
"L," tooled mouth $80-120
French 1890-1920

Strychnia – Poison
Clear glass, 2-1/2", oval form, smooth base, tooled
mouth $100-150
American 1890-1910

**Strychn – Pulv (above an orange enameled
skull and crossbones) – Apothecary Jar**
Medium amber with gold, red, white, and black enamel
label, 5", smooth base, tooled mouth, original glass
hollow blown stopper.....................................$200-300
European 1900-1925

**The – Egyptian – Chemical – Company
Poison – Boston – Mass (embalming fluid)**
Clear glass, 8-5/8", smooth base, tooled
mouth $40-60
American 1890-1910

**The – Oriental – Embalming – Fluid – Poison – The
– Egyptian – Chemical Co. – Boston – Mass**
Clear glass, 11-1/2", smooth base, tooled
mouth $40-60
American 1890-1920

**Contents – 16 Fl. Oz – The – JMF Hartz Co.
– Limited – Toronto (inside embossed heart)**
Deep cobalt blue, 7-3/4", smooth base, tooled
mouth $700-1,000
Canadian 1890-1925

Usage Externe
Medium golden amber, 9", 6-sided, smooth base (500),
tooled mouth $150-250
German 1890-1920

Zewnetrznie
Aqua, 8-1/2", 6-sided, smooth base (500),
tooled top $200-300
German 1890-1920

Figural Grim Reaper Poison bottles, 7"; Four skull shot
glasses,1-7/8", 1900-1920, $200-250 (all).

Gift (skull and crossbones) - Giftglasche - Gift, 1910-1930, 7-3/4", $150-200.

Gray & Pearse - Druggist - Poison - Take Care - Cheyenne – Wyo, 1890-1915, 3-5/8", $800-1,200.

Giftflasche (skull and crossbones) and (skull and crossbones); Giftflasche (skull and crossbones) (both German), 1890-1930, 6-1/4" and 5-1/4", $120-160 (both).

Poison (skull and crossbones)
Caution, 1890-1910,
2-3/4", $150-200.

Jacob Hulle - Not To Be Taken
- Strychnine; Poisonous - Not To Be
Taken; Not To Be Taken; Owbridge's
Embrocation - For Outward -
Application - Only; Usage Externe - Not
To Be Taken - Use With Caution; Oval
Poison; Poision - Not To Be Taken;
Not To Be Taken; Triangular Poison;
Not To Be Taken (Foreign), 1895-1920,
3-1/2" to 7-3/4", $100-150 (all).

Poison (motif of star above and below skull and crossbones) Poison, 1890-1910, 4-3/4", $500-700.

Label-under-glass jar, Hydrarg. Ammon. Poison, 1890-1910, 3-5/8", $150-250.

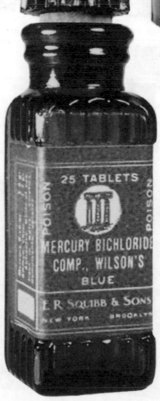

Mercury Bichloride Comp. Wilson's - Blue - E.R. Squib & Sons Brooklyn New York, 1890-1910, 3-1/8", $50-75.

Lattice and diamond
pattern poison, 1890-
1920, 7", 3-3/4", 3-1/2",
$250-450 (all three).

16 (Arrow) N OZ;
Nicoticide; 1 (Arrow) N
Oz (English), 1890-1915,
6-5/8", 3-3/4", 2-3/4",
$120-150 (all three).

Poison - Jacobs - Bichhoride - Tablets (skull and crossbones) Poison, 1890-1915, 2-1/4", $1,400-1,800.

Poison flask (German), 1890-1915, 4-5/8", $150-200.

Poison - 100 - Germicidal Tablets - Davis & Geck - Brooklyn, N.Y. 1890-1915, 3-1/8", $600-800.

Poison, 1890-1910, 3", $250-350.

Poison (poison jar - European), 1925-1935, 3-1/2", $80-150.

Poison, 1890-1910, 4-7/8", $150-200.

Poison bottle, 1890-1910, 2-3/4", $80-140.

Poison - Poison, 1890-1910, 5-1/8";
Melvin & Badger - Apothecaries - Boston,
Mass, 1890-1910, 5-3/8", $200-300 (both).

Poison - Poison (lot of eight), 1890-
1910, 2" to 8-1/4", $100-200 (all).

Poison - Poison - Eli Lilly and
Company, Indianapolis, U.S.A.,
1890-1910, 10-1/2", $200-300.

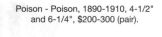

Poison - Poison, 1890-1910, 4-1/2"
and 6-1/4", $200-300 (pair).

Poison - Poison, The Norwich Pharmacal Co, Norwich, New York, 1890-1910, 7-1/2", $1,000-1,500.

Poison - Poison, The Norwich Pharmacal Co, Norwich, New York, 1890-1910, 3-1/2", $275-375.

Rat - Poison, 1890-1920, 2-3/8"; Rough on Rats Poison made by E.S. Well, chemist, Jersey City, N.J. U.S.A, 1890-1920, wooden cylindrical box (lot of two), $80-160 (both).

Poison; Poison - Poison, 1890-1915, 2-1/2" and 2-3/4", $100-150 (pair).

Strychn. Pulv. (skull and crossbones) (European), 1900-1925, 5", $200-300.

Sarsaparilla Bottles

Sarsaparilla was advertised as a "cure-all" elixir, which actually makes these bottles a subset of the "cures" or "bitters" category. In the 17th century, sarsaparilla was touted as a blood purifier and later as a cure for the dreaded disease syphilis. The drink became popular in the United States in the 1820s as a cure-all for a number of different ailments but soon was recognized as nothing more than "snake oil" sold at the medicine shows. As you can see from the "The Red Root of Jamaica" label, the bottle labels were very ornate. One of the most popular brands among collectors is Doctor Townsend, which was advertised as "The most extraordinary medicine in the world." The bottles are usually aqua or green, with blues or dark colors much rarer.

Dr. Guysott's - Yellow Dock & - Sarsaparilla - John D. Park - Cincinnati, O, 1880-1890, 9-3/4", $150-275.

Allen Sarsaparilla Co.
Aqua, 9-1/2", smooth base, applied mouth........**$50-75**
American 1860-1870

Bell's Sarsaparilla – AM Robinson
Aqua, 9-1/4", smooth base, tooled mouth........**$85-100**
American 1880-1900

Bristol's Extract Of Sarsaparilla
Blue aqua, 5-1/2", open pontil, applied
mouth **$75-100**
American 1885-1900

Corwitz Sarsaparilla
Aqua, 9-1/2", smooth base, tooled top..............**$55-75**
American 1880-1900

Dalton's Sarsaparilla & Nerve Tonic
Blue aqua, 9-1/2", smooth base, tooled top.......**$35-45**
American 1885-1900

Dr. Blackwell's Sarsaparilla
Aqua, 9-3/4", iron pontil, applied collar
mouth **$150-200**
American 1860-1870

Dr. Cumming – Compound – Extract Of Sarsaparilla
Aqua, 7-1/2", smooth base, tooled mouth........**$75-100**
American 1885-1900

Dr. Guysott's – Compound Extract
– Of Yellow Dock – Sarsaparilla
Blue aqua, 9-1/2", smooth base, applied double collar
mouth **$150-250**
American 1850-1860

Dr. James – Sarsaparilla – J.W.
James & Co – Pittsburgh, Pa
Aqua, 9-1/4", smooth base, tooled mouth........**$80-140**
American 1885-1900 (scarce)

Dr. Frederick's Sarsaparillas, Prepared Only By Nichols & Marr Medicine Co. Belle Plaine, Iowa, 1880-1895, 9", $100-150.

Dr. Guysott's - Compound Extract - Of Yellow Dock & Sarsaparilla, 1855-1870, 9-5/8", $275-375.

Dr. – Keeler's – (full figure of Indian warrior) – Sole Proprietor – Sarsaparilla – Philada (reversed and backwards)
Aquamarine, 9-5/8", tall oval form, pontil-scarred base, applied sloping collar mouth **$2,000-4,000**
American 1840-1860

Dr. Long's – Sarsaparilla – Jacobs' Pharmacy – Atlanta, Ga
Clear glass, 9", smooth base, tooled mouth...**$100-150**
American 1885-1900 (rare)

Dr. Morley's Sarsaparilla & 100 Potash
Aqua, 9-1/2", smooth base, tooled top.............**$85-125**
American 1880-1900

Dr. Myers Vegetable – Extract – Sarsaparilla – Wild Cherry – Dandelion
Deep blue aqua, 8-3/8", iron pontil-scarred base, applied mouth **$100-125**
American 1840-1860 (rare)

Dr. Stocker's Sarsaparilla
Pale greenish aqua, 9-1/2", open pontil, applied mouth **$350-450**
American 1850-1860

Dr. Townsend's – Aromatic – Hollands – Tonic
Golden amber, 9", smooth base, applied sloping collar mouth **$250-350**
American 1860-1880 (rare)

Dr. Myers Vegetable - Extract - Sarsaparilla - Wild Cherry Dandelion, 1840-1860, 0-1/0", $600 800.

Dr. Townsend's - Sarsaparilla - Albany - N.Y., 1840-1860, 9-3/4", $250-350.

Kenifick & Skrine
- Comp. Fluid Extract Of
- Sarsaparilla - Queen's
Delight & C - Charleston,
SC, 1850-1865, 9-1/4",
$175-275 (extremely rare).

Old Dr. - Townsend's
- Sarsaparilla - New
York, 1840-1860,
9-1/2", $170-200.

Dr. Townsend's – Comp. Extract – Sarsaparilla
Aquamarine, 9-1/2", iron pontil mark, applied sloping
collar mouth..$2,000-4,000
American 1845-1860 (rare embossing)

Dr. Wood's – Sarsaparilla – & – Will Cherry – Bitters
Aqua, 8-3/4", open pontil, applied mouth.......$250-350
American 1845-1855

Emerson's – 50 Cts. Sarsaparilla
Blue aqua, 9", smooth base, tooled mouth $80-150
American 1885-1900

**Gilbert's – Sarsaparilla – Bitters – N.A.
Gilbert & Co-enosburgh Falls Vt**
Golden amber, 8-5/8", octagonal form, smooth base,
applied square collar mouth...........................$350-700
American 1860-1880

Gold Metal Sarsaparilla – Albany N.Y.
Amber, 9", smooth base, tooled top $90-125
American 1880-1900

**Kenifick & Skrine – Comp. Fluid Extract Of –
Sarsaparilla – Queen's Delight & C – Charleston, SC**
Green aqua, 9-1/4", smooth base, applied double
collar mouth..$175-275
American 1850-1865 (extremely rare)

J.J. Mack & Co – Indian Sarsaparilla
Blue aqua, 9-1/4", smooth base, tooled
mouth $350-450
American 1880-1900

Kelley & Co Sarsaparilla
Aqua, 7-3/4", open pontil, applied mouth.......$100-150
American 1860-1870

Kennedy's Sarsaparilla
Aqua, 9-1/2", smooth base, applied double
collar mouth..$100-150
American 1880-1900

Leon's Sarsaparilla
Aqua, 9", smooth base, tooled top **$75-100**
American 1881-1900

McLean's Sarsaparilla
Light green, 9-1/4", smooth base, tooled
mouth **$85-100**
American 1875-1895

**Old Dr. – Townsend's – United States
– Sarsaparilla – New York**
Light emerald green, 8-1/2", pontil-scarred base,
applied sloping double collar mouth **$1,000-1,500**
American 1840-1855 (rare)

Sand's Genuine Sarsaparilla – New York
Aqua, 10", rectangular shape, smooth base,
tooled top **$100-125**
American 1880-1900

Wetherell's Sarsaparilla
Aqua, 9-3/8", smooth base, tooled top...........**$100-125**
American 1875-1890

Yager's Sarsaparilla
Medium amber, 8-3/4", smooth base,
tooled top **$75-100**
American 1880-1900

Snuff Bottles

Snuff was a powdered form of tobacco mixed with salt, various scents, and flavors such as cinnamon and nutmeg. Inhaling snuff was considered much more fashionable than smoking or chewing tobacco. It was yet another substance touted as a cure-all for ailments like sinus problems, headaches, and numerous other problems.

Most snuff bottles from the 18th and early 19th centuries were embossed, dark brown or black, and straight sided. They were either square or rectangular, with beveled edges and narrow bodies and wide mouths. In the latter part of the 19th century, the bottles were colorless or aqua and rectangular or cylindrical, with occasional embossing or labels.

Snuff bottle,
1825-1840,
4-3/8", $375-475.

Snuff bottle,
1820-1835,
4-1/2",
$175-275.

Snuff bottle
(English), 1780-
1810, 5-1/2",
$200-275.

**Appleby & Helme's – Rail Road – Mills
Snuff – 133 Water St – New York**
Medium amber, square form, 4", smooth base, tooled
mouth $150-180
American 1880-1890

Black Glass Snuff Bottle
Medium olive green, 4-3/4", cylindrical, open pontil,
rolled lip $275-375
American 1800-1820

Black Glass Snuff Bottle
Medium olive green, 5-5/8", cylindrical, pontil-scarred
base, applied string lip, blown in a dip mold...$275-375
English 1780-1810

Black Glass Snuff Bottle
Light olive green, 8-1/4", pontil-scarred base, tooled
mouth $175-275
European 1770-1810

E. Roome – Troy – New York
Medium yellow olive amber, 4-1/2", rectangular with
beveled corner panels, pontil-scarred base, tooled
mouth $300-400
American 1835-1855

Freeblown And Paddled Snuff Jar
Yellow olive, 4-3/4", square form, pontil-scarred base,
sheared flared mouth $400-800
American 1815-1840

Freeblown Snuff Bottle
Yellow amber, 4-3/8", open pontil, tooled flared
out lip..$150-200
American 1790-1820

Freeblown Snuff Bottle
Yellow amber with olive tone, 4-1/2", tubular pontil
scar, tooled mouth...$150-300
American 1830-1860

Freeblown Snuff Bottle
Golden amber, 6-1/2", rectangular with beveled
corners, smooth base, tooled mouth..............$200-400
American 1850-1870

**Freeblown Snuff Jar (Label: Wholesale
Medicines Retail Dealer Paint, Oils,
And Groceries – Norwich, N.Y.)**
Medium yellow olive, 5-5/8", pontil-scarred base,
heavy applied mouth $250-500
American 1800-1840

Octagonal Snuff Bottle
Medium olive green, 8-sided, 3-1/4", pontil-scarred
base, tooled lip..$300-400
American 1800-1820

Octagonal Snuff Bottle
Deep emerald green, 8-sided, 4-1/2", pontil-scarred
base, tooled lip..$275-375
American 1800-1820

Sided Snuff Bottle
Yellow amber with olive tone, 12-sided, 4-7/8", open
pontil, rolled lip **$375-475**
American 1820-1840

Snuff Bottle
Blue green, 4-1/2", square form, open pontil, tooled
and slightly flared out lip **$175-275**
American 1820-1835

Snuff Bottle
Deep green aqua, 7-3/4", square form,
pontil-scarred base, original pewter neck
band and screw-on lid.....................................**$400-500**
European 1780-1820

Snuff Jar
Medium amber, 4", square form, open pontil, tooled
mouth **$150-200**
American 1850-1860

Snuff Jar
Medium yellow green, 4-1/8", square form, open pontil,
tool flared lip...**$140-200**
American 1800-1830

Snuff Jar
Deep yellow amber, 4-3/8", open pontil, tool
flared lip...**$100-150**
American 1800-1830

Snuff Jar
Medium yellow green, 7", rectangular with beveled
corners, pontil-scarred base, tooled flared
mouth **$250-500**
American 1780-1840

Snuff bottle
(European), 1820-
1835, 9-5/8",
$200-300.

Snuff bottle (European), 1780-1810, 5-3/4", $300-400.

Snuff Jar
Medium blue green, 11" h, 4-1/8" base diameter,
tubular pontil-scarred base, sheared mouth with
applied metal threaded neck ring (no cap)......**$400-600**
German 1770-1800

Sunburst Snuff Jar
Dark green, 7" h, 3-7/8" w, 3-5/16" d, rectangular form,
pontil-scarred base, sheared mouth **$2,500-5,000**
American 1815-1830 (extremely rare, Keene Marlboro
Street Glassworks, Keene, N.H.)

Snuff bottle
(German),
1770-1800, 11",
$400-600.

Soda Bottles

After years of selling, buying, and trading, I have come to believe that soda bottles support one of the largest collector groups in the United States. Even collectors who don't normally seek out soda bottles always seem to have a few on their tables for sale (or under the table).

Albert Vonharaten Savannah, GA - Ginger Ale, 1870-1885, 7-1/8", $250-350.

Soda is basically artificially flavored or unflavored carbonated water. In 1772, an Englishman named Joseph Priestley succeeded in defining the process of carbonation. Small quantities of unflavored soda were sold by Professor Benjamin Silliman in 1806. By 1810, New York druggists were selling homemade seltzer as cure-all for stomach problems, with flavors being added to the solution in the mid-1830s. By 1881, flavoring was a standard additive in these seltzers.

Because of pressure caused by carbonation, bottle manufacturers had to use a much stronger type of bottle, which eventually led to the heavy-walled blob-type soda bottle. Manufacturers also had to develop more effective closures because corks tended to blow out. Some of the more common closures were the Hutchinson-type wire stoppers, lightning stoppers, and Codd stoppers.

Soda bottles generally aren't unique in design, since manufacturers had to produce them as cheaply as possible to keep up with demand. The only way to distinguish among bottles is by the lettering, logos, embossing, or by labels, which weren't very common.

**A.Schroth – Sch.Ll Haven – Superior
– Mineral Water – Union Glass Works**
Cobalt blue, 7-1/4", mug base, iron pontil, applied blob
top **$1,200-1,600**
American 1840-1855 (rare)

Albert Fischer – Atlantic City, N.J.
Deep amber, 7", smooth base, tooled mouth .**$150-200**
American 1865-1876

B. Carter – West Chester (in slug plate)
Medium blue green, 7", iron pontil, applied
mouth **$300-400**
American 1840-1860 (scarce)

Bridgeton Glass Works – N.J
Medium blue green, 7-3/8", smooth base, applied
mouth, original metal band closure stamped "John
Allender, Patent July 24 1855" **$150-200**
American 1855-1865 (scarce)

**Buffums – Sarsaparilla & Lemon
– Mineral Water – Pittsburgh**
Bluish aqua, 10-sided, 8", iron pontil, applied tapered
collar mouth..**$500-700**
American 1840-1855

C. Mack's – Phillipson – Reading, Pa – M & P
Light green, 7-1/2", smooth base, applied
mouth **$70-100**
American 1875-1885

C. Mack
- Reading (in
slug plate),
1840-1860, 7",
$200-300.

Carpenter - & Cobb
- Knickerbocker - Soda
Water - Saratoga
Springs, 1840-1860,
9-1/2", $400-700.

CHS. A. H. Umbach & Co - Savannah - Geo (eagle and shield), 1860-1870, 7-5/8", $200-300.

Edward Moyle - Savannah - GA, 1880-1890, 7-1/2", $375-450.

**Carl H. Schultz – C – P M – S – Pat.
May – 1868 – New York**
Medium green, 6-3/4", smooth base, applied
blob top **$70-90**
American 1880-1890

**Carpenter – & Cobb – Knickerbocker
– Soda Water – Saratoga – Springs**
Blue green, 7-3/8", 10-sided, iron pontil, applied blob
top **$500-700**
American 1840-1855 (rare)

City Bottling Works – Toledo. Ohio
Medium sapphire blue, 6-3/8", smooth base, large
applied mouth **$275-375**
American 1875-1885

Clarke & Co – New York
Medium amber with olive tone, pint, pontil-scarred
base, applied sloping collar mouth **$120-150**
American 1855-1865

**Crystal Palace – Premium – Soda Water
– W. Eagle – New York (motif of crystal
palace) – Union Glass Works**
Deep teal blue green, 7-3/8", iron pontil, applied
blob top **$500-700**
American 1845-1860

**Crump & Fox – Bernardston – Mass
– Superior – Soda Water**
Deep blue green, 7-1/4", iron pontil, applied blob
top **$800-1,200**
American 1840-1855

Dean & Paxton – Newark – N.J.
Deep cobalt blue, 7-1/8", iron pontil, applied
blob top **$250-350**
American 1840-1855 (very rare)

Empire Bottling
Works - Reading,
PA, 1875-1885,
6-5/8"; Roland
& UPP-Reading,
PA, 1875-1885,
6-5/8" (lot of two),
$120-160 (pair).

Deer Park – L. I.
Cobalt blue, 8-sided, 7-1/4", iron pontil, applied blob
top **$1,000-1,500**
American 1840-1855 (rare)

Dr. Brown N.Y. – B
Medium blue green, 6-3/4", iron pontil, applied sloping
collar mouth...**$375-475**
American 1840-1860

Dyottville Glass Works – Philada
Medium cobalt blue, 7-1/2", smooth base, applied
blob top **$80-120**
American 1850-1860

Early Sided Soda Bottle (unembossed)
Dark amber, 8-3/8", 8-sided, smooth base, applied
mouth **$200-300**
American 1855-1865

**E. Roussel – Philada – Cyottville Glass Works
– R – Philada – This Bottle – Is Never Sold**
Medium cobalt blue, 7-1/2", iron pontil, applied sloping
collar mouth...**$100-150**
American 1840-1860

E. Smith – Elmira – N.Y.
Deep cobalt blue, 7-1/8", smooth base, applied
blob top **$500-700**
American 1855-1865

**E. S. Hart – Canton – Ct – Superior
– Soda Water – Union Glass Works**
Bluish aqua, 7-5/8", pontil-scarred base, applied
blob top **$80-120**
American 1845-1855

F. Oerling & Bror
- Reading - PA
- Union Glass
Works - Phila,
1840-1860,
7-1/4", $150-250.

F.H. Suppe - Franklin
Springs - Franklin
- Iron Works, N.Y.
- This Bottle - Not To
Be Sold, Clyde Glass
Works - Clyde - N.Y.
(on base), 1885-1895,
11-3/8", $150-200.

Empire Bottling Works – Reading Pa
Aqua, 6-5/8", smooth base, applied mouth........**$60-80**
American 1875-1885

**Excelsior – Ginger Ale – 1852
– John Ryan – Savannah. Ga**
Medium amber, 7-1/4", smooth base, applied
blob top **$250-350**
American 1875-1890

Francis Dusch – This Bottle Is Never Sold
Deep cobalt blue, 7-1/2", smooth base, applied
blob top **$200-250**
American 1865-1885

G.A. Sammis – Hemstead – L.I.
Medium aquamarine blue green, 7-3/8", iron pontil,
applied sloping collar mouth **$250-350**
American 1845-1855 (scarce)

G. Gent – New York
Greenish aqua, 7-1/8", iron pontil, applied
blob top **$200-300**
American 1845-1855 (scarce)

G.H. Hausburg – Blue Island – III – I.G. Co. 3-1 1/2
Deep yellow green, 8-1/2", smooth base, tooled
mouth **$100-150**
American 1890-1910

G. Lauter – Reading – Pa – Walater – L – Reading, Pa
Aqua, 7", smooth base, applied mouth.............**$70-100**
American 1875-1885

Ghirardelli's – Branch – Oakland
Cobalt blue, 7-1/2", smooth base, applied
mouth **$100-150**
American 1855-1870

Geo. Gemenden
 - Savannah
 - Geo (eagle
  and shield),
  1845-1860,
 6-3/4, $80-120.

Henry Lubs - & Co - 1885
- Savannah - GA, 1855-
1870, 7-1/4", $80-140.

Gleason – & Cole – Pittsbg – Mineral Water
Cobalt blue, 7-3/4", 10-sided, iron pontil, applied
sloping collar mouth...................................**$700-1,000**
American 1840-1855 (rare_

Hamilton Glass Works – N.Y.
Aquamarine, 7", iron pontil, applied mouth.....**$100-150**
American 1840-1860

Hathorn Spring – Saratoga. N.Y.
Deep yellow olive, pint, smooth base, applied sloping
double collar mouth **$45-60**
American 1865-1875

Hoxsie Jeffers & Co – Albany
Blue green, 7", smooth base, applied
mouth **$140-180**
American 1855-1870

**Hutchinson & Co – Celebrated
– Mineral – Water – Chicago**
Medium cobalt blue, 7-1/4", iron pontil, applied
blob top **$600-800**
American 1840-1855

J.A. Dearborn – New York (in slug plate)
Medium teal blue, 6-3/4", iron pontil, applied sloping
collar mouth..**$200-300**
American 1840-1855

**J. B. Bryant – Wilmington (in slug
plate) – Porter – Ale Cider**
Medium emerald green, 7", iron pontil, applied sloping
double collar mouth **$700-900**
American 1840-1855

Heller & Co - Savannah
- Geo, 1860-1870,
6-7/8", $300-400.

John Fehr - Reading
- PA (in slug plate)
Bodine & Son,
1840-1860, 7-1/8",
$275-375.

J. Boardman – New York
Medium yellow olive green, 7-1/4", iron pontil, applied
sloping collar mouth..**$200-300**
American 1845-1855

**J. D. Ludwick – Pottstown, Pa – This Bottle
– Not To – Be Sold – Registered 1889**
Deep green, 7-1/4", smooth base, tooled lip **$70-100**
American 1890-1910

J. H. Magee (in slug plate) – Vine St – Philada
Medium cobalt blue, 7-3/8", iron pontil, applied sloping
double collar mouth **$150-200**
American 1840-1860

**J. Johnston – Superior – Soda Water – New
York – Union Glass Works – Phila**
Teal blue, 7-1/4", iron pontil, applied mouth ...**$140-180**
American 1845-1855 (scarce)

James Wise - Allentown - PA
- This Bottle - Belongs To - James
Wise, 1855- 1870, 7"; Vincent
- Hathaway - & Co - Boston
- Ginger - Ale, 1855-1870, 9-5/8"
(lot of two), $150-200 (pair).

**J. Lampin – Utica – Mineral Waters
– L – This Bottle – Is Never Sold**
Cobalt blue, 7-5/8", iron pontil, applied sloping collar
mouth **$600-800**
American 1840-1855 (scarce)

**J. Schweinhart – Pittsburgh – Pa – 10th
Ward – Bottling Works – A.&D.H.C.**
Cobalt blue, 7", smooth base, "J.S.," applied
blob top **$125-150**
American 1870-1885

**J. T. Brown – Chemist – Boston
– Double – Soda – Water**
Medium blue green, 8-3/4", torpedo shape, smooth
base, applied blob top **$375-475**
American 1850-1860

J. Voelker & Bro. – Cleveland. O – V & Bro
Medium cobalt blue, 10", smooth base, applied
mouth **$400-600**
American 1875-1885

J.W. Harris – Soda – New Haven – Conn
Cobalt blue, 8-sided, 7-5/8", iron pontil, applied
blob top **$250-350**
American 1845-1855

**J & W. Coles – Superior – Soda &
– Mineral Water – Staten Island**
Blue green, 7-1/2", iron pontil, applied sloping collar
mouth **$375-475**
American 1840-1855 (rare)

Knauss &
Lichtenwallner
- Allentown - PA
- K&L, 1855-1876,
6-7/8", $275-375.

Maick's - Porter
- Reading, 1840-
1860. 7-1/8",
$170-250.

**James Wise – Allentown – Pa – This
Bottle – Belongs To – James Wise**
Cobalt blue, 7", smooth base, applied mouth ..**$75-100**
American 1855-1870

John Clarke – New York
Medium yellow olive amber, pint, pontil-scarred base,
applied sloping collar mouth **$150-200**
American 1845-1860

L. Gahre – Bridgeton – N.J. – G
Blue green, 7", smooth base, applied sloping
collar mouth..**$120-160**
American 1855-1870

Lancaster – Glass Works – N.Y.
Cobalt blue, 7-1/8", iron pontil, applied sloping
collar mouth..**$150-200**
American 1840-1860

M. Monju & Co – Mobile
Aqua, 7-3/8", pontil-scarred base, applied
blob top **$125-175**
American 1840-1860

M. Monju & Co – Mobile
Teal blue, 7-3/8", pontil-scarred base, applied
blob top **$125-175**
American 1840-1860

Neptune – Glass Works
Pale green, 7-3/8", pontil-scarred base, applied sloping
blob top **$350-450**
American 1840-1860 (rare)

Owen Case – Eagle Soda – Works – Sac City
Cobalt blue, 7-1/2", smooth base, applied
blob top **$150-200**
American 1870-1880

M. Monju & Co - Mobile
(lot of two), 1840-
1860, 7" and 7-1/2",
$250-350 (pair).

P. Conway – Bottler – Philada – No 8 Hunter St – & 108 Filbert St – Mineral Waters
Cobalt blue, 7-1/4", iron pontil, applied blob top $100-175
American 1840-1860

P. Divine – Bottler – Philada.
Light green, 7-1/2", smooth base, applied mouth $50-80
American 1855-1870

Quinan & Studer – 1888 – Savannah – Ga
Deep cobalt blue, 7-7/8", smooth base, tooled top $150-175
American 1880-1890

Robert Portner – Brewing Co – Tivoli (inside diamond) Alexandria Va – This Bottle – Not To – Be Sold
Olive green, 9", smooth base, applied mouth.....$70-90
American 1885-1900

Roland & Upp – Reading, Pa
Aqua, 6-5/8", smooth base, applied mouth $60-80
American 1875-1885

Soda Water
Emerald green, 7-3/4", torpedo shape, smooth base, applied mouth $500-700
American 1850-1860

Walter & Brother - Reading, PA - W&B, 1860-1870, 6-3/4", $120-160

N. A. Felix (in slug plate)-Dyottville Glassworks - Philada, 1840-1860, 6-7/8", $250-350.

S. Keys – Burlington – N.Y. – Union Glass Works Philad. – Superior – Mineral Water
Cobalt blue, 7-3/8", mug base, iron pontil, applied tapered collar mouth **$800-1,200**
American 1840-1855 (extremely rare)

S. Smith – Auburn – 1857
Medium cobalt blue, 10-sided, 7-3/4", iron pontil, applied blob top **$600-800**
American 1840-1855

S.S. – Knicker – Bocker – Soda – Water
Deep cobalt blue, 8-sided, 8", iron pontil, applied blob top **$400-600**
American 1840-1855

Seitz Bros. – Easton. Pa – S
Medium teal blue, 6-3/4", smooth base, applied blob top **$40-70**
American 1865-1875

Sloper & Frost
Medium cobalt blue, 7-1/2", iron pontil, applied mouth **$300-400**
American 1845-1860

Smith & – Fotheringham – Soda Water – St. Louis – This Bottle – Is Never Sold
Deep cobalt blue, 7-1/2", 10-sided, iron pontil, applied sloping collar mouth......................................**$200-300**
American 1845-1855 (scarce)

Smith's – Mineral – Soda Water – New York – Premium – S
Pale blue green, 7-1/2", iron pontil, applied sloping collar mouth...**$45-60**
American 1855-1875

Schick & Fett - Reading - PA - S&F, 1870-1880, 7-1/4"; Herman Floto - Reading, PA - F, 1870-1880, 7" (lot of two), $120-180 (pair).

Soda Water – Von – Dr. Struve
Olive green, 7-3/4", smooth base, applied
mouth $120-150
German 1850-1870

**Steinke & – Kornahrens (in slug plate) – Soda
Water – Return This Bottle – Charleston S.C.**
Deep cobalt blue, 8-1/4", 8-sided, iron pontil, applied
sloping collar mouth..$500-700
American 1845-1855

**Suydam & Dubois – N.Y. – Union Glass
Works – Superior – Mineral Water**
Cobalt blue, 7-1/2", mug base, iron pontil, applied
tapered collar mouth $1,500-2,500
American 1840-1855 (rare)

**T.S. Waterman – 11 St Paul St
– N.O. – W. Mineral Water**
Deep aqua, 7-1/4", iron pontil, applied
mouth $150-200
American 1840-1860

Torpedo Soda – Unembossed
Medium blue green, 8-1/2", smooth base, applied
sloping collar mouth $140-180
American 1850-1865

Twitchell – T – Philada (reverse same)
Light green, 7", smooth base, applied mouth $50-80
American 1855-1870

W. Dean – Newark – N.J.
Deep blue aqua, 6-3/4", iron pontil, applied
blob top $150-200
American 1840-1855

**Waring – Webster – & Co – 192
West St. N.Y. – Soda Water**
Deep cobalt blue, 8-sided, 7-3/8", iron pontil, applied
blob type mouth $150-200
American 1840-1855

W.H.H. – Chicago
Medium cobalt blue, 7-1/2", iron pontil, applied blob
top $150-200
American 1845-1855

W. Morton – Trenton – N.J. – W
Medium emerald green, 7-1/8", iron pontil, applied
mouth $140-180
American 1845-1855 (scarce)

Willis & Ripley – Portsmouth – W & R
Deep sapphire blue, 7-3/8", iron pontil, applied sloping
collar mouth..$400-600
American 1840-1855

**Wm. Heiss Jr – Manufacturer Of – Superior
Mineral – And Soda Waters – No 213 North 2d
St – Philada   This Bottle – To Be Returned**
Medium cobalt blue, 7-3/8", 8-sided, iron pontil,
applied sloping collar mouth $250-350
American 1840-1860

Twitchell - T - Philada (2) 1855-1870, 7"; Youngblood (large letters around entire bottle), 1855-
1870, 7-1/2"; P. Divine - Bottler - Philada, 1855-1870, 7-1/2", $150-250 (all).

**W.P. – Knicker – Bocker – Soda
Water – 164 18th St. N.Y. 1848**
Deep cobalt blue, 7-1/4", 10-sided, iron pontil, applied
blob top **$400-600**
American 1840-1855

**Wm. W. Lappeus – Premium – Soda
Or – Mineral – Waters – Albany**
Deep cobalt blue, 7-1/8", 10-sided, iron pontil, applied
blob type **$500-700**
American 1840-1855 (scarce)

Youngblood (large letters around bottle)
Light green, 7-1/2", smooth base, applied
mouth **$50-80**
American 1855-1870

Target Balls

Target balls, which are small rounded bottles, were filled with confetti, ribbon, and other items. They were used for target practice from the 1850s to early 1900s. They gained considerable popularity during the 1860s and 1870s with the Buffalo Bill Cody and Annie Oakley Wild West Shows. Around 1900, clay pigeons started to be used in lieu of target balls. Because they were made to be broken, they are unfortunately extremely difficult to find, and have become very rare, collectible, and valuable.

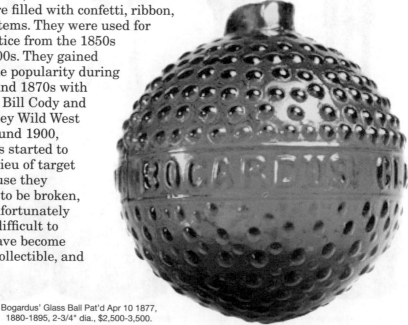

Bogardus' Glass Ball Pat'd Apr 10 1877,
1880-1895, 2-3/4" dia., $2,500-3,500.

Dr. A. Frank Glasshutten – Charlottenburg
(German), 1890-1910, 2-5/8" dia., $275-375.

For Hockey Patent Trap (English), 1880-
1900, 2-1/2" dia., $500-700.

Ira Paine's Filled Ball Pat Apl'd For, 1880-1895,
2-5/8" dia.., $100-1,500 (front and reverse).

A.J. Legorone (range target ball)
Light cobalt blue, 2-1/4" dia., rough sheared
mouth **$300-400**
English 1880-1900 (rare)

**Bo't. Of – Jas. Bown & Sons – 136 Wood St. – Pittsg.
Pa – Manufacturers – And – Dealers In – Fire Arms**
Medium amber, 2-3/4" dia., rough sheared
mouth **$3,000-4,000**
American 1880-1900 (rare)

E. Jones Gunmaker Blackburn Lanc (target ball)
Medium cobalt blue, 2-3/4" dia., diamond pattern,
rough sheared mouth **$250-350**
English 1880-1900

Freeblown Target Ball
Medium pink amethyst, 2-1/2" dia., sheared mouth
....**$120-160**
American 1880-1900

**Grafl – Zu – Solms – Glasfab
– Andreashutte (target ball)**
Medium amber, 2-5/8" dia., diamond pattern, sheared
mouth on unusually long neck **$1,400-1,800**
German 1880-1900 (extremely rare, made by German
Glasshouse Andreashutte founded in1858 in Schlesien,
Germany, now part of Poland)

N.B. Glassworks Perth – N.B. Glassworks Perth
(English), 1880-1900, 2-5/8" dia., $150-200.

**Grafl – Zu – Solms – Glasfab
– Andreashutte (target ball)**
Clear glass, 2-5/8" dia., diamond pattern, sheared
mouth on unusually long neck **$1,400-1,800**
German 1880-1900 (extremely rare, made by German
Glasshouse Andreashutte founded in1858 in Schlesien,
Germany, now part of Poland)

Greene – London (range target ball)
Medium sapphire blue, 2-1/4" dia., rough sheared
mouth **$275-375**
English 1880-1900

Gurd & Son – 185 Dundas Street – London Ont
Medium yellow amber, 2-3/4" dia., square pattern,
rough sheared mouth **$1,000-1,600**
Canadian 1880-1900 (rare variant with embossed
squares above and below center band)

**From J. Palmer O'Neil – & Co
– Pittsburgh (target ball)**
Medium amber, 2-3/4" dia., rough sheared
mouth **$4,500-6,500**
American 1880-1900 (extremely rare, one of only two
known to exist. J. Palmer O'Neil was president of
Pittsburgh Firearms Company from 1878 to 1886 and
bought the Pittsburgh Pirates in 1891.)

Made By Rutherford & Co Hamilton Ont
Golden yellow amber, 2-5/8" dia, diamond pattern,
rough sheared mouth **$2,500-3,500**
Canadian 1880-1900 (rare)

N.B. Glass Works Perth – N.B. Glass Works Perth
Cobalt blue, 2-5/8" dia, diamond pattern, rough
sheared mouth **$150-200**
English 1880-1900 (variant with backward "S")

Range balls (English), 1880-1900, 1-1/4" dia., $140-180 (pair).

Range Target Ball
Dark emerald green, 1-1/4" dia., rough sheared
lip..**$100-150**
English 1880-1915

Range Target Ball
Deep emerald green, 1-1/2" dia., rough sheared
lip..**$70-100**
American 1880-1910

Range Target Ball
Medium emerald green, 1-1/2" dia., rough sheared
mouth **$40-70**
American 1880-1910

Range Target Ball
Clear glass, 2" dia., sheared mouth **$70-100**
American 1880-1910

Range Target Ball – BMP – London
Deep cobalt blue, 2-1/4" dia., long neck to fit over a
wooden peg, sheared mouth **$200-300**
English 1880-1900

Target ball, 1880-1900, 2-3/4" dia., $150-200.

Target ball (French), 1880-1900, 2-5/8" dia., $300-400.

Target ball (German), 1880-1910, 2-5/8" dia., $200-300.

Target ball (German), 1890-1910, 2-5/8" dia., $150-200.

Sophienhutte In Ilmeenau (Thur)
Bluish aqua, 2-5/8" dia., diamond pattern, rough
sheared mouth $700-900
German 1880-1900 (extremely rare)

Sophienhutte In Ilmeenau (Thur)
Reddish amber, 2-5/8" dia., diamond pattern, rough
sheared mouth $500-700
German 1880-1900 (rare)

Target ball (Czechoslovakia), 1890-
1910, 2-1/2" dia., $150-200.

Stacey & Co – London
Medium cobalt blue, 2-5/8" dia., square pattern, rough
sheared mouth $400-600
English 1880-1900 (extremely rare)

Target Ball
Bright yellow green, 2-1/2" dia,, overall diamond
pattern, sheared lip $150-200
Czechoslovakia 1890-1910

Target Ball
Persian blue, 2-1/2" dia., overall fern, star, and
pinwheel pattern, sheared mouth..............$2,500-3,500
English 1880-1900 (scarred and unique)

**Target Ball – F.B.H. (at base) – Two
Unembossed Circular Panels**
Medium cobalt blue, 2-5/8" dia., diamond pattern,
rough sheared mouth $500-700
Australian 1880-1900 (made by Fredric Bolton Hughes,
owner of South Australian Glass Bottle Company from
1896-1913)

Target Ball
Black amethyst, 2-5/8" dia., overall diamond pattern,
sheared and ground lip $150-200
German 1890-1910

Target Ball
Deep cobalt blue, 2-5/8" dia., overall square pattern,
rough sheared lip...$1,400-1,800
Australian 1880-1900 (only a few type of target balls
were made in Australia)

Target Ball
Cobalt blue, 2-5/8" dia., square pattern above and
below a plain center band, rough sheared and outward
flared lip...$150-200
French 1880-1900

Target ball (Czechoslovakia), 1890-
1910, 2-1/2" dia., $150-200.

Target ball (Australian), 1880-1900,
2-5/8" dia., $1,400-1,800.

Target Ball
Yellow amber, 2-5/8" dia., horizontal ribs down both mold seams, overall pimple design, rough sheared mouth **$1,500-2,000**
American 1880-1900 (extremely rare)

Target Ball
Light cobalt blue, 2-5/8" dia., blown in three-part mold, rough sheared mouth **$140-180**
American 1880-1900

Target Ball
Yellow amber, 2-3/4"dia., 6 raised beads on shoulder near the lip, rough sheared lip, blown in three-part mold **$150-200**
American 1880-1900

Target Ball
Medium yellow amber, 2-3/4" dia., three sizes of embossed circles around entire ball, rough sheared mouth **$1,500-2,000**
American 1880-1900 (extremely rare, referred to as the "nickel, dime, quarter ball")

Target Ball (motif of man shooting)
Medium purple amethyst, 2-5/8" dia., diamond pattern, rough sheared mouth **$140-180**
American 1880-1900

Target Ball (motif of man shooting)
Deep purple amethyst, 2-3/4" dia., diamond pattern, rough sheared mouth **$500-700**
English 1880-1900

Target Ball (motif of man shooting)
Medium green, 2-5/8" dia., diamond pattern, rough sheared mouth **$350-450**
English 1880-1900

Target Ball (composite)
Pale aqua, 2-3/4" dia., impressed on bottom, "Patented Sept 3, 1879, March 3, 1880, Lockport, N.Y.," hollow with roughly formed mouth **$400-600**
American 1880-1910 (very rare)

Van Cutsem – A St. Quentin
Deep cobalt blue, 2-5/8" dia., diamond pattern, sheared flared out mouth **$100-150**
French 1880-1900

WW Greener St Marys Works Birmm & 68 Haymarket London
Medium yellow amber, 2-5/8" dia., diamond pattern, rough sheared mouth **$1,400-1,800**
English 1880-1900

Warner Bottles

The Warner bottle was named for H.H. Warner, who sold a number of remedies developed by a Doctor Craig. Warner developed his bottle for those and other cures and began producing great volumes and varieties (more than 20) in 1879 in Rochester, N.Y. In addition, Warner bottles were marketed and sold in major European cities such as London, Melbourne, Frankfurt, and Prague. The bottles can frequently be found with their original labels and boxes, giving additional value to these already expensive and rare pieces.

Warner bottles can be categorized according to the following varieties:

- Warner's Safe Kidney & Liver Remedy
- Warner's Safe Diabetes Remedy
- Warner's Safe Cure
- Warner's Safe Bitters
- Warner's Safe Rheumatic Cure
- Warner's Safe Cure (around shoulders – rare)
- Log Cabin Cough & Consumption Remedy

- Log Cabin Hop & Buchu Remedy
- Log Cabin Sarsaparilla
- Log Cabin Scalpine (hair tonic)
- Log Cabin Scalpine
- Log Cabin Extract, Rochester, N.Y.
- Log Cabin Rose Cream (extremely rare)

Warner's - Log Cabin - Extract - Rochester. N.Y., 1887-1895, 6-1/2", $200-275. (front and back)

H.H. Warner's Co (motif of safe)
Deep yellow amber, 9", smooth base, "Pat. Nov. 20, 83
–Rochester, N.Y.," applied flared mouth..........**$140-180**
American 1850-1860

H.H. Warner's Co (motif of safe)
Medium amber, 8-7/8", smooth base "Pat. Nov. 20, 83
–Rochester, N.Y.," applied flared mouth..........**$200-250**
American 1850-1860

Tippecanoe – H.H. Warner & Co.
Amber, 9", figural log, smooth base "Pat.
Nov. 20, 83 –Rochester, N.Y.," smooth base,
applied mouth **$80-140**
American 1883-1895

Tippecanoe – H.H. Warner & Co.
Golden yellow amber, 9", figural log, smooth
base, "Rochester – N.Y.," smooth base, applied
mouth **$150-200**
American 1883-1895

Warner's Log Cabin – Extract – Rochester, N.Y.
Medium yellow amber, 8-1/4", smooth base, "Patd
Sept 6 -1887," tooled mouth..........................**$150-200**
American 1887-1895

Warner's – Safe – Bitters (motif of safe)
Rochester, N.Y. (in a slug plate)
Amber, 7-1/2", smooth base, "A. & D.H.C.," applied
mouth **$500-800**
American 1880-1885 (scarce slug plate variant)

Warner's - Safe
Cure (motif of safe)
Frankfurt (German),
1890-1910, 9-1/8",
$250-500

Warner's - Safe
Cure (motif of safe)
Frankfurt (German),
1890-1910, 9-1/2",
$250-375

Warner's – Safe – Bitters (motif of safe)
Rochester, N.Y. (in a slug plate)
Amber, 7-3/8", smooth base, "A. & D.H.C.," applied
mouth **$500-700**
American 1880-1885 (scarce slug plate variant)

Warner's Safe Cure – Concentrated
Medium amber, 5-3/4", smooth base, tooled
mouth **$60-80**
Australian 1885-1895

Warner's – Safe Cure (motif of safe) Frankfurt – A/M
Deep olive green, 9", smooth base, tooled
top **$375-475**
German 1890-1900

Warner's – Safe Cure (motif of safe) Frankfurt – A/M
Deep red amber, 9-1/2", smooth base, applied blob
mouth **$250-375**
German 1890-1910 (scarce in this color)

Warner's – Safe Cure (motif of safe) Pressburg
Reddish amber, 9-3/8", smooth base, applied
mouth **$350-450**
Austria 1890-1900

Warner's – Safe Cure (motif of safe) Pressburg
Red amber, 9-1/2", smooth base, applied
mouth **$300-400**
German 1885-1900

Warner's – Safe Cure (around shoulder)
Medium amber, 9-5/8", smooth base, applied double
collar mouth...**$150-250**
American 1880-1895

Warner's – Safe – Diabetes – Cure
(motif of safe) Rochester, N.Y.
Amber, 9-5/8", smooth base, "A. & D.H.C.," applied
double collar mouth **$200-300**
American 1885-1895 (scarce slug plate variant)

Warner's - Safe - Remedies Co. - (motif of safe) - Rochester, N.Y. U.S.A, Label: Warner's Acute Rheumatic Compound, 1910-1915, 9-1/8", $150-200. (front and back)

**Warner's – Safe – Diabetes – Cure
(motif of safe) London**
Yellow amber, 9-1/2", smooth base, applied
mouth **$250-350**
English 1885-1900

**Warner's – Safe – Diabetes Cure (motif
of safe) – Melbourne Aus – London Eng
– Toronto Can – Rochester, N.Y. U.S.A.**
Medium amber, 9-1/2", smooth base, tooled
mouth **$375-475**
Australian 1885-1900

**Warner's – Safe – Diabetes Cure (motif
of safe) – Melbourne Aus – London Eng
– Toronto Can – Rochester, N.Y. U.S.A.**
Yellow with amber tone , 9-5/8", smooth base, applied
blob mouth **$275-375**
Australian 1885-1895

**Warner's – Safe – Kidney & Liver – Remedy
(motif of safe) Rochester, N.Y.**
Clear glass, 9-3/4", smooth base, tooled
mouth **$150-200**
American 1885-1895 (scarce in colorless glass)

**Warner's – Safe – Kidney & Liver – Remedy
(motif of safe) Rochester, N.Y.**
Medium amber, 9-3/8", smooth base, applied
mouth **$150-200**
American 1880-1890 (rare variant with two series of eight
circular impressions behind the words "Safe Kidney &
Liver Cure")

**Warner's – Safe – Medicines
(motif of safe) Melbourne**
Reddish amber, 9-1/2", smooth base, tooled
mouth **$60-80**
Australian 1885-1895

**Warner's – Safe – Nervine (motif
of safe) – Rochester N.Y.**
Medium amber, 7-1/2", smooth base, applied
mouth **$140-180**
American 1880-1895 (scarce slug plate variant made in
Pittsburgh District Glasshouse)

**Warner's – Safe – Nervine (motif
of safe) – Rochester N.Y.**
Medium golden amber, 9-5/8", smooth base, tooled
mouth **$120-150**
American 1885-1895

**Warner's – Safe – Remedies Co. – (motif of
safe) Rochester, N.Y. U.S.A (Label: Warner's
Acute Rheumatic Compound – Also
For Muscular Pains And Gout)**
Medium amber, 9-1/8", smooth base,
ABM lip..**$150-200**
American 1910-1915

**Warner's – Safe – Rheumatic – Cure
(motif of safe) Rochester N.Y. U.S.A.**
Medium amber, 9-1/2", smooth base, applied
mouth **$150-250**
American 1880-1895

**Warner's – Safe Tonic – (motif
of safe) Rochester, N.Y.**
Amber, 9-3/4", smooth base, applied double collar
mouth **$375-475**
American 1880-1895 (scarce slug plate variant)

Whiskey Bottles

Whiskeys, sometimes referred to as spirits, come in an array of sizes, designs, shapes, and colors. The whiskey bottle dates back to the 19th century and provides the avid collector with numerous examples of rare and valuable pieces.

In 1860, E.G. Booz manufactured a whiskey bottle in a cabin design embossed with year 1840 and the words "Old Cabin Whiskey." One theory suggests that the word "booze" was derived from his name and came to mean any hard liquor. This bottle has been credited as being the first to have a name embossed on a whiskey bottle.

After the repeal of Prohibition in 1933, the only inscription that could be found on any liquor bottles was "Federal Law Forbids Sale or Re-use of This Bottle," which was continued through 1964.

Ambrosial - B.M. & E.A.W. & Co. (sealed chestnut), 1855-1870, 8-7/8", $200-300.

A.P. Hotaling & Co's – Old Bourbon Whisky (motif of kangaroo inside a shield) Barron, Moxhah & Co – Sydney – Sole Agents For – Australia
Medium orange amber, 11-3/4", smooth base, applied sloping double collar mouth......................**$7,000 0,000**
American 1885-1895 (rare)

Albro & Bro's – 156 – Bowery – N.Y. – Strapside
Medium olive amber, quart, smooth base, applied mouth, ...**$150-175**
American 1880-1890

Casper's Whiskey - Made By Honest - North - Carolina People, 1885-1895, 12-1/4", $400-500.

A.M. Bininger & Co. - No 19 Broad St. New York, 1865-1875, 8-5/8", $90-150.

Chicken Cock
(standing rooster)
Bourbon (rare back
bar bottle) 1890-1915,
7", $1,400-2,000.

Ambrosial – B.M. & F. AW Co (on applied seal)
Deep amber, 9", pontil-scarred base, applied mouth
and handle..**$200-300**
American 1860-1870

**Belle – Of – Anderson – Old – Fashion
– Hand Made – Sour – Mash**
Milk glass, 8-1/4", smooth base, tooled
mouth **$80-100**
American 1885-1895

Bennett & Carrol – 120 Wood St – Pittsburgh
Medium golden amber, 9-1/2", barrel shape, smooth
base, applied mouth....................................**$800-1,200**
American 1865-1975 (rare whiskey barrel)

Bininger's Nightcap – No 19 – Broad St. N.Y.
Golden amber, 8-1/4", smooth base, applied collar
mouth with internal screw threads **$150-300**
American 1860-1880

**Bottle For – Truet Jones – & – Arrington
– Eichelberger – Dewdrop (Label:
Superior – Old Rye—Whiskey)**
Deep reddish amber, 10", smooth base, applied square
collar mouth...**$1,000-2,000**
American 1860-1870 (rare, Stoddard Glasshouse,
Stoddard, N.H.)

B.M. & E.A. Whitlock & Co – New York
Bluish aqua, 8-1/8", barrel shape, open pontil, applied
mouth **$500-700**
American 1855-1865 (scarce)

C. A. Richards & Co – 99 Washington St. – Boston
Medium amber, 9-1/2", smooth base, applied sloping
collar mouth..**$150-200**
American 1865-1875

**Casper's Whiskey – Made By Honest
– North – Carolina People**
Medium cobalt blue, 12", smooth base, tooled
mouth **$400-600**
American 1880-1900

**Chestnut Grove – Whiskey – G.W.
(on seal) – Handled Whiskey**
Orange amber, 8-7/8", open pontil, applied seal,
handle, and mouth **$250-350**
American 1860-1875

E. G. Booz's - Old Cabin - Whiskey - (1840) - 120
Walnut St - Philadelphia E.G. Booz's - Old Cabin
- Whiskey, 1865-1875, 7-3/4", $2,500-3,500.

Flora Temple (motif of horse) Harness Trot
2:19, 1859-1860, 8", $140-180.

Distilled In 1848 – Old Kentucky – 1849 – Reserve – Bourbon – A.M. Bininger & Co 19 Broad St. N.Y.
Amber, 8-1/8", barrel shape, pontil-scarred base, applied double collar mouth...........................**$400-600**
American 1855-1865

Golden Eagle - Distilleries Co (picture of eagle) San Francisco, Cal., 1905-1910, 11", $350-450.

Durham (standing steer) Whiskey
Orange amber, 11-1/2", smooth base, applied mouth, blown in four-piece mold................................**$600-900**
American 1880-1890

E.G. Booz's – Old Cabin – Whiskey – 120 Walnut St – Philadelphia – (1840)
E.G. Booz's – Old Cabin – Whiskey
Deep amber, 7-3/4", cabin shape, smooth base, applied sloping collar mouth **$3,500-4,500**
American 1860-1875 (earlier and rarer of the E.G. Booz cabin bottles)

Evans & Ragland – Old – Ingledew – Whiskey – LaGrange Ga
Medium amber, 10-1/4", smooth base, tooled mouth **$200-300**
American 1870-1880

Ewyssons – Denver – Colo. – U.S.A.
Medium amber, 10-5/8", smooth base, ground lip, original screw-on cap......................................**$80-120**
American 1890-1910

Hunter - Fisherman, 1850-1860, 9-1/8", $350-450.

Forest – Lawn – J.V.H.
Medium olive amber, 7-1/4", pontil-scarred base,
applied sloping collar mouth **$400-600**
American 1855-1875

**G.O. Blake's – Ky – Whiskey – Gob
And G.O. Blake's – Bourbon Co – Ky
– Whiskey (inside barrels) Adams, Taylor & Co
– Proprietors – Boston & Louisville**
Deep sun-colored amethyst, 12-1/2", smooth base,
tooled mouth **$50-75**
American 1880-1890

**Golden Eagle Distilleries Co (picture
of eagle) San Francisco, Cal**
Amber, 11", smooth base, tooled top **$250-350**
American 1904-1910

**Greeting – Theodore Netter – 1232
Market St. – Philadelphia**
Deep cobalt blue, 6", barrel shape, smooth base,
tooled mouth **$350-550**
American 1890-1910

**Griffith Hyatt & Co – Baltimore
– Handled Whiskey Jug**
Amber, 7-1/2", globular with flattened label panels
and applied handle, tubular pontil scar, applied square
collar mouth...**$400-800**
American 1840-1860

**H. Rickett's & Co Glassworks Bristol
(on base) And Patent (on shoulder)**
Medium green, 10-1/4", pontil-scarred base, applied
sloping double collar mouth, three-piece mold
....**$100-150**
American 1835-1855

H.A. Graef's Son Canteen – N.Y.
Deep yellow olive, 6-1/2", canteen shape,
smooth base, applied square collar mouth,
applied handle...**$200-400**
American 1860-1880

**Hilbert Bros – Wine – And – Liquor – Merchants
– 101 Powell St – San Francisco, Cal**
Amber, 12", smooth base, blob top **$2,000-3,000**
American 1892-1901

**Imperial – Levee – J. Noyes Hollywood,
Miss (cluster of grapes on stump)**
Medium golden yellow amber, 9-3/8", red iron pontil,
applied mouth **$2,500-4,500**
American 1865-1875 (considered by many collectors to
the State of Mississippi's No. 1 bottle)

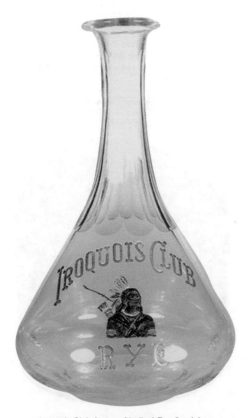

Iroquois Club (torso of Indian) Rye (back bar
bottle), 1890-1915, 8-7/8", $1,200-2,000.

J. T. Bickford & Bartlett - Boston (sealed whiskey),
1865-1875, 8-3/4", $375-475 (extremely rare).

Imperial – Measure (around shoulder) – J.W. Watts – Wine – Merchant – Coleford (on applied seal)
Greenish aqua, 9", smooth base, applied mouth and seal, three-piece mold.....................................**$175-275**
English 1870-1880

J.N. Kline & Co – Aromatic – Digestive Cordial
Medium amber, pumpkinseed flask, 5-1/2", smooth base, applied mouth..**$400-600**
American 1860-1870

J.T. Bickford & Bartlett – Boston – Handled Whiskey
Medium amber, 8-3/4", open pontil, applied seal, handle and mouth **$375-475**
American 1865-1875 (rare)

Joseph Fetz – Importer – 3rd & – Mission Sts – S.F.
Clear, 12", smooth base, tooled top **$75-100**
American 1885-1890

L.L. Lyons – Pure Ohio – Catawba Brandy – Cini
Golden amber, 13-3/4", smooth base, applied mouth with ring...**$200-400**
American 1860-1880 (rare)

Lindley & Co – (monogram) – Sacramento, Cal
Clear, 11-7/8", smooth base, tooled top.............**$35-50**
American 1895-1905

Mansion House – 478 – 4th Ave. N.Y. – Wm. Brandes & Co Props – Strapside Flask
Medium amber, half –pint, smooth base, applied mouth **$40-60**
American 1880-1900

(American eagle) M.G. Landsberg – Chicago – 1771-1876
Medium amber, 11", smooth base, applied mouth **$1,500-2,500**
American 1876 (bottled for the 1876 Centennial)

Mist Of The Morning – SM – Barnett & Company
Dark amber, 10", barrel shape, smooth base, applied sloping double collar mouth...........................**$150-200**
American 1865-1875

Mohawk Whiskey – Pure – Rye – Patented – Feb 11 1868 (Indian queen)
Medium golden amber, 12-1/2", smooth base, inward rolled lip..**$2,500-3,500**
American 1868-1875 (rare)

Myers & Company Dist's – Pure – Fulton – Whiskey – Patap. – Covington, Ky. U.S.A.
Aqua, 9-1/8", smooth base, tooled mouth......**$100-150**
American 1885-1895

N. Van Bergen & Co – Gold Dust Kentucky Bourbon – N. Van Bergen & Co. – Sole Propts
Clear, 11-3/4", smooth base, applied top **$800-1,000**
American 1880-1882

Mitchell's - MB
- Ltd - Heather Dew
- Scotch Whiskey
- Glasgow 1890-1920,
23-1/2", $500-700.

Myers & Company Dist's-Pure - Fulton - Whiskey - Patap
- Covington, KY. U.S.A., 1885-1895, 9-1/8", $100-150.

Nathan Bros – Philad
Medium golden amber, 7-1/2", smooth base, applied
water seal above crescent-shaped label panel, applied
mouth $300-400
American 1855-1870 (rare)

**Net Contents 25 Oz – McLeod – Hatje Co – Wine
& Liquor – M Co L – Merchants – San Francisco**
Orange amber, 11-3/4", smooth base,
tooled lip..$50-80
American 1900-1905

**Old Bourbon – Whiskey – For Medicinal – Purposes
– Wilson Fairbank & Co – Sole Agents**
Bluish aqua, 10", smooth base, applied
mouth $250-350
American 1865-1875

**Old Continental – Whiskey (standing
Continental soldier) 1776**
Medium yellow amber, 9-1/2", smooth base, applied
mouth $2,500-3,500
American 1865-1875

**Patrick Smith – 1313 – Sec. Ave – NW Corner 69th
St – New York – One Half – Pint – Full Measure**
Amber, half-pint, smooth base, "L & Mc –A82 Fulton St
–N.Y." tooled mouth $80-150
American 1890-1910

**Perrine's – Apple – Ginger – Phila
– Perrine's (motif of apple) Ginger**
Amber, 10", smooth base, tooled mouth $200-275
American 1880-1890

**Phoenix – Old (picture of bird) Bourbon
– Naber, Alfs & Brune – S.F. – Sole Agts.**
Amber, 11-3/4", smooth base,
applied top $1,000-2,000
American 1880-1895

Pure Malt Whiskey – Bourbon Co. Kentucky
Amber, 8-3/4", open pontil, applied handle and
mouth $400-600
American 1860-1875 (scarce)

O.K. - Old Bourbon
- Castle - Whiskey
- F. Chevalier - Sole
Agents, 1880-1895,
12", $150-200.

Old Bourbon - Whiskey
- For Medicinal
- Purposes - Wilson
Fairbank & Co. - Sole
Agents, 1865-1875,
10", $250-375.

R.B. Cutter – Pure – Bourbon
Deep cherry puce, 8-1/2", pontil-scarred base, applied
mouth and handle $800-1,200
American 1855-1870

Reed's Old Lexington Club
Medium golden amber, 11", smooth base, applied
sloping collar mouth.....................................$140-180
American 1870-1880

Robinson & Lord – 88 & 90 – Lombard St – Baltimore
Deep amber, barrel shape, 10-1/8", iron pontil, applied
mouth $800-1,200
American 1860-1870 (rare)

Roehling & Schutz, Inc. – Chicago
Amber, 9-5/8", cabin shape, smooth base,
tooled lip...$275-375
American 1880-1890

Salem – Thd (monogram) – Mass – Strapside Flasks
Aqua, half-pint, smooth base, tooled mouth.......$40-60
American 1880-1900

Silas F. Miller & Co – Galt House – Louisville
Medium amber, 6-1/4", flask, smooth base, applied
double collar mouth $350-450
American 1875-1885 (very rare)

**Simmond's – Nabob – Trade (picture of nabob)
Mark – Pure – Ky Bourbon – Whiskey**
Red amber, 10-3/4", smooth base, blob
top $1,000-2,000
American 1878-1890

**Smokine – Imported And Bottled – By – Alfred
Andersen & Co – The Western Importers
– Minneapolis Minn – And – Winnipeg, Man**
Reddish amber, 5-1/4", cabin shape, smooth base,
tooled lip...$275-375
American 1880-1895

**Spruance Stanley & Co – Wholesale
– Liquor Dealers – San Francisco
– Cal – 1869 (inside horseshoe)**
Medium amber, 11-5/8", smooth base, applied sloping
glob top $175-275
American 1885-1900

**Star Whiskey – New York – W.B.
Crowell Jr – Handled Whiskey**
Medium yellow amber, 8-1/8", pontil-scarred base,
applied handle, double collar mouth, tooled mouth
spout $500-700
American 1855-1870

S.S. Smith Jr. & Co – Cincinnati, O
Medium cobalt blue, 9-3/4", smooth base, applied
sloping collar mouth.................................$1,500-2,500
American 1865-1875 (very rare)

**Stoneware Canteen – Pat. Aug 11 1891 – The
Old Dexter Jug Whiskey (reverse) Old Dexter
Distilling Co, Butler Kentucky Distillers**
Gray pottery, 7-1/4", smooth base, handled.....$80-120
American 1891-1900

Poole & Anderson's
Whiskies - Poole &
Anderson's - Tartan Blend
- & - Zephyr Liqueur - Old
Scotch Whiskies (English)
(stoneware pub jug) 1880-
1900, 6-3/8", $150-250
(Doulton - Lambeth -
England stamped on base).

The Campus – Gossler Bros. Prop's – N.W. Cor. 104 Ste. & Columbus Av. – N.Y. – Handled Whiskey
Reddish amber, 9-5/8", smooth base, "The Campus – Gossler – Bros. Prop's – N.W. Cor. 104 Ste. & Columbus Av. – N.Y," applied handle and mouth **$150-200**
American 1885-1895

Thos M Jacobs & Co (on seal)
Teal blue, 11-3/4", half-gallon, iron pontil, applied seal and mouth **$150-250**
American 1850-1860

Thos Taylor & Co – Importers – Virginia, NV
Medium amber, 11-3/4", smooth base, blob top **$3,000-4,000**
American 1870-1880

Udolpho Wolf's – Schiedam – Aromatic – Schnapps (sample size)
Light green, 3-5/8", smooth base, applied mouth **$150-250**
American 1870-1880

United We Stand – Old Bourbon – Whiskey – Wilmerding & Co – Sole Agent's – S.F. Ca. – W. & Co
Yellow amber, 12", smooth base, applied sloping double collar mouth **$3,000-4,000**
American 1878-1883

Van Dunck's – Genever – Trade Mark – Ware & Schmitz
Deep amber, 8-3/4", smooth base, applied mouth **$150-200**
American 1880-1890

Walther's – Peptonized Port – Pittsburgh, Pa – Miniature
Medium amber, 4-3/8", smooth base, tooled mouth **$80-120**
American 1890-1900

Weeks & Gilson So. Stoddard N.H.
Medium golden amber, 11-1/2", three-piece mold, smooth base, applied sloping double collar mouth...**$400-600**
American 1855-1870

Wharton's – Whiskey – 1850 – Chestnut Grove
Medium cobalt blue, pumpkinseed flask, 5-1/4", smooth base, applied mouth **$400-600**
American 1860-1870

Wm. H. Spears & Co – Pioneer Whiskey – (picture of a walking bear) – Fenkhausen & – Braunschweiger – Sole Agents , S.F.
Light amber, 11-3/4", smooth base, applied top **$2,500-5,000**
American 1878-1882

Willmington Glass Works (on base)
Deep amber, 11-5/8", smooth base, blown in three-part mold applied sloping double collar mouth......**$100-150**
American 1855-1875

Whiskey Flask – Plain And Unembossed
Light to medium pink, pint, smooth base, applied double collar mouth **$400-800**
American 1860-1880 (rare due to unique color)

Stoneware canteen, Pat. Aug. 11 1891, The Old Dexter Jug Whiskey (reverse) Old Dexter Distilling Co, Butler Kentucky Distillers, 1891-1900, 7-1/4", $80-120.

Wormser Bros – San Francisco
Golden yellow amber, 9-1/2", barrel shape, smooth
base, applied sloping collar mouth **$1,500-2,000**
American 1870-1872

Back Bar Bottles and Decanters

Angelo Myers Philadelphia Rye Whiskey
Clear, 11-1/8", polished pontil, tooled
mouth **$250-300**
American 1885-1910

Brandy (label under glass bottle)
Clear, 10-7/8", multicolored label showing a pretty
woman, smooth base, tooled mouth, original metal and
cork stopper on chain **$500-700**
American 1890-1910

Chicken Cock (standing rooster) Bourbon
Clear with amethyst tint, 7", smooth base,
tooled lip..**$1,400-2,000**
American 1890-1915 (rare)

**Established In 1844 – Robert Johnston Distiller
Of Copper Double Distilled – Rye – Wheat
And Malt – Whiskies – Warranted Without
The Use Of Steam – The Only Whiskey
Fit For Medicinal Use & C. – Greencastle,
Franklin Co. Pa (label under glass bottle)**
Clear, 11-3/8", smooth base, tooled mouth **$500-700**
American 1880-1910

Hawthorne
Clear, 11-1/4", rib-pattern swirled to right and white
enameled lettering, smooth base, tooled mouth,
original 30 cent pour stopper **$180-250**
American 1880-1910

Iroquois Club (torso of an Indian) Rye
Clear, 8-7/8", polished pontil, tooled lip....**$1,200-1,600**
American 1890-1915

Kellerstrass Belle Of Missouri Rye
Clear, 9-1/8", multicolored enamel floral decoration,
smooth base, tooled mouth, original ground glass
stopper **$600-800**
American 1880-1910

Maryland Club
Clear, 8-1/4", white enamel and green shamrock
decoration, polished pontil, tooled mouth, ground glass
stopper **$300-400**
American 1885-1910

Thos Jacobs & Co
(on seal), 1850-
1860, 11-3/4",
$150-250 (large
iron pontil).

Union Clasped Hands
- Eagle, 1860-1865,
8-7/8", $350-450.

Old Rosebud Whiskey
Clear, 9", multicolored enamel decoration showing a jockey on a horse, smooth base, tooled mouth, mother-of-pearl "Whiskey" stopper **$600-800**
American 1885-1910

Old Underwood Baltimore Pure Rye
Clear, 11-1/4", white enamel lettering, smooth base, tooled mouth **$140-180**
American 1890-1915

Phoenix Club (bird coming out of the fire)
Clear, 8-1/2", vertical rib pattern, polished pontil...**$250-350**
American 1890-1910

Prentice, Hand Made Sour Mash J.T.S. Brown & Sons, Spring 1871 (label under glass bottle)
Clear, 9-3/4", smooth base, tooled liop with original ground glass stopper **$375-500**
American 1875-1910 (rare)

Rye And Scotch – Set Of Two
Medium amber, 8-1/2", applied metal cages and stoppers, smooth base, tooled mouth............**$100-150**
American 1880-1890

Scotch Decanter
Straw yellow, 11", rib-pattern with silver overlay lettering, smooth base, polished lip, original sterling collar and shot glass lid..................................**$250-350**
American 1880-1910

Sunny Brook Whiskey
Clear, 10-7/8", multicolored enamel decoration showing an inspector, "The Inspector is Back of Every Bottle" holding a bottle of Sunny Brook Whiskey, smooth base, tooled mouth, ground glass stopper...............**$500-700**
American 1890-1910

West Point
Medium amber, 11-1/8", white enamel lettering on shoulder, smooth base, tooled mouth, copper stopper **$200-300**
American 1890-1910

Yellowstone 100 Proof Kentucky Straight Bourbon Whiskey, Yellowstone, Inc. Louisville, Ky
Clear, 11-3/4", multicolored enamel decoration showing waterfall scene, smooth base, tooled mouth and rim, metal cage stopper **$1,500-2,500**
American 1890-1910 (very rare)

Pottery Whiskey Jugs

Auld Lang Syne – Pure Old Barley Malt Whiskey – The Weideman Company Proprietors – Cleveland, O
Cream with brown glaze, 7-3/4", smooth base, applied handlo...**$100-150**
American 1890-1915

WM. H. Spears & Co - Pioneer Whiskey (picture of walking bear) A. Fenkhausen & CO -Sole Agents, S. F., 1875-1893, 11-1/2", $500-700.

Back bar decanter, Scotch, 1880-1910, 11", $250-350; Cartan, McCarthy & Co (monogram) San Francisco, 1880-1894, 11-7/8", $75-100.

Chapin & Gore's Bourbon – 1867 – Sour Mash Whiskey – Chapin & Gore Chicago
Tan with brown glaze, 8-5/8", smooth base......**$80-120**
American 1890-1915

Gilmour Thomson's Royal Stag Whisky, Gilmour Thomson & Co. Ltd Glasgow
White with brown glaze, 8-1/4", smooth base, "Kennedy Bakersfield Potteries Glasgow," applied handle............**$80-120**
Scottish 1890-1915

Grannie – Taylor's – Liqueur Whisky – Taylor Brothers Co. Glasgow & London
Cream with brown glaze, 8-1/4", smooth base, "Govancroft Co. Glasgow," applied handle **$80-120**
English 1890-1915

Happy Day – Famous – Old Rye Whiskey
Cream with brown glaze, 7-3/4", smooth base, applied handle............**$80-140**
American 1890-1915

Kentucky Belle – Eight Year Old Hand Made Sour Mash – Bourbon – Bottled At The Distillery – Anderson Co. Ky
Cream with brown glaze, 8-3/8", smooth base, applied handle............**$250-350**
American 1890-1915 (rare)

O'Donnel's Old Irish Whisky Belfast
Cream with brown glaze, 7-5/8", smooth base, applied handle............**$100-150**
Irish 1890-1915

Pennsylvania Club Pure Rye Whiskey
White china with dark green transfer, 7-5/8", smooth base............**$275-375**
American 189-1915

Pointer – The Gottschalk Co – Baltimore, Md – Maryland Rye
Cream with brown glaze, black transfer, 7-3/8" smooth base............**$175-275**
American 1890-1910

Roche Brand – Irish Whiskey – Type – Compounded With Pure Grain Distillates
Cream with brown glaze, 7-3/8", smooth base
............**$200-300**
American 1890-1915 (rare)

The Cream Of Irish Whiskey Shamrock
Cream with brown glaze, 8-3/4", smooth base, applied handle............**$100-150**
Irish 1890-1915

The Cream Of Old Scotch Whiskey Bonnie Castle
Tan with brown glaze, 9", smooth base **$100-150**
Scottish 1890-1915

Watson's Dundee Whisky
Cream with dark brown glaze, 8-5/8", smooth base, "Port-Dundas Pottery Co. Glasgow," applied handle............**$140-180**
Scottish 1890-1915

Back bar decanters (set of two) Rye and Scotch, 1880-1900, 8-1/2", $100-150 (for set).

New Bottles (Post 1900)

The bottles listed in this section have been classified according to individual categories and/or type, since the contents hold little interest for the collector. New bottles covered in this section are valued for their decorative—and sometimes unique—designs.

The goal of most new-bottle collectors is to collect a complete set of items designed and produced by a favorite manufacturer. As with the reproduction of old bottles such as Coca-Cola, or new items such as Avon, the right time to purchase is when the first issue comes out on the retail market (or before retail release, if possible). As with the old bottles, I have provided a broad cross section of new bottles in various price ranges and categories rather than listing only the rarest or most collectible pieces.

The pricing shown reflects the value of particular items listed. Newer bottles are usually manufactured in limited quantities without any reissues. Because retail prices are affected by factors such as source, type of bottle, desirability, condition, and the possibility the bottle was produced exclusively as a collector's item, the pricing can fluctuate radically at any given time.

Avon Bottles

The cosmetic empire known today as Avon began as the California Perfume Company. It was the creation of D.H. McConnell, a door-to-door book salesman who gave away perfume samples to stop doors from being slammed in his face. Eventually, McConnell gave up selling books and concentrated on selling perfumes instead. Although based in New York, the name "Avon" was used in 1929 along with the name California Perfume Company or C.P.C. After 1939, the name Avon was used exclusively. Bottles embossed with C.P.C. are very rare and collectible due to the small quantities issued and the even smaller quantity that have been well preserved.

Today, Avon offers collectors a wide range of products in bottles shaped as cars, people, chess pieces, trains, animals, sporting items (footballs, baseballs, etc.), and numerous other objects. The scarcest and most sought-after pieces are pre-World War II figurals, since very few were well preserved.

To those who collect Avon items, anything Avon-related is also considered collectible. That includes boxes, brochures, magazine ads, or anything else labeled with the Avon name. Since many people who sell Avon items are unaware of their value, collectors can find great prices at swap meets, flea markets, and garage sales.

While this book offers an good cross-section of Avon collectibles, I recommend that serious collectors obtain Bud Hastings new 16th edition of *Avon Products & California Perfume Co. (CPC) Collector's Encyclopedia,* which offers photos and pricing of thousands of Avon & California Perfume Co. (C.P.C.) products from 1886 to the present.

A Man's World, Globe On Stand, 1969 .... **$7-10**

A Winner, Boxing Gloves, 1960 .... **$20-25**

Abraham Lincoln, Wild Country After Shave, 1970-1972.................. **$3-5**

After Shave On Tap, Wild Country **$3-5**

Aladdin's Lamp, 1971 .... **$7-10**

Alaskan Moose, 1974 .... **$5-8**

Alpine Flask, 1966-1967 .... **$35-45**

American Belle, Sonnet Cologne, 1976-1978 ...... **$5-7**

American Buffalo, 1975 .... **$6-8**

American Eagle Pipe, 1974-1975........................ **$6-8**

American Eagle, Windjammer After Shave, 1971-1972 .... **$3-4**

American Ideal Perfume, California Perfume Comp., 1911 .... **$125-140**

American Schooner, Oland After Shave, 1972-1973 .... **$4-5**

Andy Capp Figural (England), 1970 .... **$95-105**

Angler, Windjammer After Shave, 1970................. **$5-7**

1971-73 Aladdin's Lamp, 6 oz., green
glass bottle with gold cap, $11-13.

1966-67 Alpine Flask, 8
oz., brown glass, gold cap
and neck chain, $28-33.

Apple Blossom Toilet Water, 1941-1942 .... **$50-60**

Apothecary, Lemon Velvet Moist Lotion, 1973-1976
.... **$4-6**

Apothecary, Spicy After Shave, 1973-1974 .... **$4-5**

Aristocat Kittens Soap, (Walt Disney) **$5-7**

Armoire Decanter, Charisma Bath Oil, 1973-1974 **$4-5**

Armoire Decanter, Elusive Bath Oil, 1972-1975 ... **$4-5**

Auto Lantern, 1973 .... **$6-8**

Auto, Big Mack Truck, Windjammer After Shave, 1973-
1975 .... **$5-6**

Auto, Cord, 1937 Model, Wild Country After Shave,
1974-1978 .... **$7-8**

Auto, Country Vendor, Wild Country After Shave, 1973
.... **$7-8**

Auto, Duesenberg, Silver, Wild Country After Shave,
1970-1972 .... **$8-9**

Auto, Dune Buggy, Sports Rally Bracing Lotion, 1971-
1973 .... **$4-5**

Auto, Electric Charger, Avon Leather Cologne, 1970-
1972 .... **$6-7**

Auto, Hayes Apperson, 1902 Model, Avon Blend 7 After
Shave, 1973-1974 .... **$5-7**

Auto, Maxwell 23, Deep Woods After Shave, 1972-1974
.... **$5-6**

Auto, MG, 1936, Wild Country After Shave, 1974-1975
.... **$4-5**

Auto, Model A, Wild Country After Shave, 1972-1974
.... **$4-5**

Auto, Red Depot Wagon, Oland After Shave, 1972-1973
.... **$6-7**

Auto, Rolls Royce, Deep Woods After Shave, 1972-
1975 .... **$6-8**

Auto, Stanley Steamer, Windjammer After Shave, 1971-
1972 .... **$6-7**

Auto, Station Wagon, Tai Winds After Shave, 1971-
1973 .... **$7-8**

Auto, Sterling Six, Spicy After Shave, 1968-1970 . **$6-7**

Auto, Sterling Six II, Wild Country After Shave, 1973-
1974 .... **$4-5**

Auto, Stutz Bearcat, 1914 Model, Avon Blend 7 After
Shave, 1974-1977 .... **$5-6**

Auto, Touring T, Tribute After Shave, 1969-1970 ... **$6-7**

Auto, Volkswagen, Red, Oland After Shave, 1972 **$5-6**

Avon Calling, Phone, Wild Country After Shave, 1969-
1970 .... **$15-20**

Avon Dueling Pistol II, Black Glass, 1972 .... **$10-15**

Avonshire Blue Cologne, 1971-1974 .... **$4-5**

Baby Grand Piano, Perfume Glace, 1971-1972 . **$8-10**

Baby Hippo, 1977-1980 .... **$4-5**

Ballad Perfume, 3 Drams, 3/8 Ounce, 1939. **$100-125**

Bath Urn, Lemon Velvet Bath Oil, 1971-1973 .... **$4-5**

Beauty Bound Black Purse, 1964 .... **$45-55**

Bell Jar Cologne, 1973 .... **$5-10**

Benjamin Franklin, Wild Country After Shave, 1974-
1976 .... **$4-5**

Big Game Rhino, Tai Winds After Shave, 1972-1973
.... **$7-8**

Big Whistle, 1972 .... **$4-5**

Bird House Power Bubble Bath, 1969 .... **$7-8**

1972-74 Maxwell '23 Decanter, 6 oz., green glass with beige plastic top and trunk over cap, $12-14.

1969-70 Avon Calling for Men, 6 oz., gold paint over clear glass, gold cap, black mouthpiece, black plastic earpiece, $16-18.

Bird Of Paradise Cologne Decanter, 1972-1974
.... $4-5

Blacksmith's Anvil, Deep Woods After Shave, 1972-1973 .... $4-5

Bloodhound Pipe, Deep Woods After Shave, 1976 $5-6

Blue Blazer After Shave Lotion, 1964 .... $25-30

Blue Blazer Deluxe, 1965 .... $55-65

Blue Moo Soap On A Rope, 1972 .... $5-6

Blunderbuss Pistol, 1976 .... $7-10

Bon Bon Black, Field & Flowers Cologne, 1973 ... $5-6

Bon Bon White, Occur Cologne, 1972-1973 .... $5-6

Bon Bon White, Topaz Cologne, 1972-1973......... $5-6

Boot Gold Top, Avon Leather After Shave, 1966-1971
.... $3-4

Boot Western, 1973 .... $4-5

Boots & Saddle, 1968 .... $20-22

Brocade Deluxe, 1967 .... $30-35

Buffalo Nickel, Liquid Hair Lotion, 1971-1972...... $4-5

Bulldog Pipe, Oland After Shave, 1972-1973 .... $4-5

Bunny Puff & Talc, 1969-1972 .... $3-4

Bureau Organizer, 1966-1967 .... $35-55

Butter Candlestick, Sonnet Cologne, 1974.......... $7-8

Butterfly Fantasy Egg, First Issue, 1974 .... $20-30

Butterfly, Unforgettable Cologne, 1972-1973 .... $4-5

Butterfly, Unforgettable Cologne, 1974-1976 .... $1-2

Cable Car After Shave, 1974-1975 .... $8-10

Camper, Deep Woods After Shave, 1972-1974 .... $6-7

Canada Goose, Deep Woods Cologne, 1973-1974
.... $4-5

Candlestick Cologne, Elusive, 1970-1971 .... $5-6

Car, Army Jeep, 1974-1975 .... $4-5

Casey's Lantern, Island Lime After Shave, 1966-1967
.... $30-40

Catch A Fish, Field Flowers Cologne, 1976-1978 $6-7

Centennial Express 1876, Locomotive, 1978... $11-12

Chevy '55, 1974-1975.. $6-8

Christmas Ornament, Green Or Red, 1970-1971
.... $1-2

Christmas Ornament, Orange, Bubble Bath, 1970-1971 .... $2-3

Christmas Tree Bubble Bath, 1968...................... $5-7

Classic Lion, Deep Wood After Shave, 1973-1975
.... $4-5

Club Bottle, 1906 Avon Lady, 1977.................. $25-30

Club Bottle, 1st Annual, 1972 .... $150-200

Club Bottle, 2nd Annual, 1973 .... $45-60

Club Bottle, 5th Annual, 1976 .... $25-30

Club Bottle, Bud Hastin, 1974 .... $70-95

Club Bottle, CPC Factory, 1974 .... $30-40

Collector's Pipe, Windjammer After Shave, 1973-1974
.... $3-4

Colt Revolver 1851, 1975-1976 .... $10-12

Corncob Pipe After Shave, 1974-1975............... $4-6

Corvette Stingray '65, 1975................................ $5-7

Covered Wagon, Wild Country After Shave, 1970-1971
.... $4-5

Daylight Shaving Time, 1968-1970 .... $5-7

Defender Cannon, 1966 .... $20-24

Dollar's 'N' Scents, 1966-1967 .... $20-24

Dutch Girl Figurine, Somewhere, 1973-1974 ..... $8-10

Duck After Shave, 1971 .... $4-6

Dueling Pistol 1760, 1973-1974 .... $9-12

Dueling Pistol II, 1975 .... $9-12

Eight Ball Decanter, Spicy After Shave, 1973 ...... $3-4

Electric Guitar, Wild Country After Shave, 1974-1975
.... $4-5

Enchanted Frog Cream Sachet, Sonnet, 1973-1976
.... $3-4

Fashion Boot, Moonwind Cologne, 1972-1976 .... $5-7

Fashion Boot, Sonnet Cologne, 1972-1976 .... $5-7

Fielder's Choice, 1971-1972 .... $4-6

Fire Alarm Box, 1975-1976 .... $4-6

First Class Male, Wild Country After Shave, 1970-1971
.... $3-4

First Down, Soap On A Rope, 1970-1971 .... $7-8

First Down, Wild Country After Shave $3-4

First Volunteer, Tai Winds Cologne, 1971-1972 .... $6-7

Fox Hunt, 1966 .... $25-30

French Telephone, Moonwind Foaming Bath Oil, 1971
.... $20-24

Garnet Bud Vase, To A Wild Rose Cologne, 1973-1976
.... $3-5

Gavel, Island Lime After Shave, 1967-1968 .... $4-5

George Washington, Spicy After Shave, 1970-1972
.... $2-3

George Washington, Tribute After Shave, 1970-1972
.... $2-3

Gold Cadillac, 1969-1973 .... $7-10

Gone Fishing, 1973-1974 .... $5-7

Grade Avon Hostess Soap, 1971-1972 .... $6-8

Hearth Lamp, Roses, Roses, 1973-1976 .... $6-8

Hobnail Decanter, Moonwind Bath Oil, 1972-1974 $5-6

Hunter's Stein, 1972 .... $10-14

Indian Chieftain, Protein Hair Lotion, 1972-1975
.... $2-3

Indian Head Penny, Bravo After Shave, 1970-1972
.... $4-5

Inkwell, Windjammer After Shave, 1969-1970 ...... $6-7

Iron Horse Shaving Mug, Avon Blend 7 After Shave,
1974-1976 .... $3-4

Jack-In-The-Box, Baby Cream, 1974 .... $4-6

Jaguar Car, 1073 1076 .... $6-8

Jolly Santa, 1978 .... $6-7

Joyous Bell, 1978 .... $5-6

King Pin, 1060 1070 .... $4-6

Kodiak Bear, 1977 .... $5-10

Koffee Klatch, Honeysuckle Foam Bath Oil, 1971-
1974 .... $5-6

Liberty Bell, Tribute After Shave, 1971-1972 .... $4-6

Liberty Dollar, After Shave, 1970-1972 .... $4-6

Lincoln Bottle, 1971-1972 .... $3-5

Lip Pop Colas, Cherry, 1973-1974 .... $1-2

Lip Pop Colas, Cola, 1973-1974 .... $1-2

1968-72 Charlie Brown, 4 oz., red, white, and black plastic, $3-5.

1975-76 Chess Piece Decanter, 3 oz., sprayed silver over glass with amber plastic tops, $7-9.

1967 Christmas Ornament, 4 oz., bubble bath, silver cap, $9-14.

1968-70 Christmas Tree, 4 oz., bubble bath, red paint over silver glass, $8-12.

1976 Liberty Bell, 5 oz., sprayed bronze with bronze cap, $10-12.

1974-75 Mallard Duck, 5 oz., amber glass with green plastic head, $11-13.

Lip Pop Colas, Strawberry, 1973-1974 .... **$1-2**

Longhorn Steer, 1975-1976 .... **$7-9**

Looking Glass, Regence Cologne, 1970-1972 ..... **$7-8**

Mallard Duck, 1967-1968 .... **$8-10**

Mickey Mouse, Bubble Bath, 1969 .... **$10-12**

Mighty Mitt Soap On A Rope, 1969-1972 .... **$7-8**

Ming Cat, Bird Of Paradise Cologne, 1971 .... **$5-7**

Mini Bike, Sure Winner Bracing Lotion, 1972-1973 **$3-5**

Nile Blue Bath Urn, Skin So Soft, 1972-1974 .... **$3-4**

Nile Blue Bath Urn, Skin So Soft, 1972-1974 .... **$4-6**

No Parking, 1975-1976 .... **$5-7**

Old Faithful, Wild Country After Shave, 1972-1973 **$4-6**

One Good Turn, Screwdriver, 1976 .... **$5-6**

Opening Play, Dull Golden, Spicy After Shave, 1968-1969 .... **$8-10**

Opening Play, Shiny Golden, Spicy After Shave, 1968-1969 .... **$14-17**

Owl Fancy, Roses, Roses, 1974-1976 .... **$3-4**

Owl Soap Dish And Soaps, 1970-1971 .... **$8-10**

Packard Roadster, 1970-1972 .... **$4-7**

Pass Play Decanter, 1973-1975 .... **$6-8**

Peanuts Gang Soaps, 1970-1972 .... **$8-9**

Pepperbox Pistol, 1976 .... **$5-10**

Perfect Drive Decanter, 1975-1976 .... **$7-9**

Pheasant, 1972-1974 .... **$7-9**

Piano Decanter, Tai Winds After Shave, 1972 ...... **$3-4**

Pipe, Full, Decanter, Brown, Spicy After Shave, 1971-1972 .... **$3-4**

Pony Express, Avon Leather After Shave, 1971-1972 .... **$3-4**

Pony Post "Tall," 1966-1967 .... **$7-9**

Pot Belly Stove, 1970-1971 .... **$5-7**

President Lincoln, Tai Winds After Shave, 1973 ... **$6-8**

President Washington, Deep Woods After Shave, 1974-1976 .... **$4-5**

Quail, 1973-1974 .... **$7-9**

Rainbow Trout, Deep Woods After Shave, 1973-1974 .... **$3-4**

Road Runner, Motorcycle **$4-5**

Rook, Spicy After Shave, 1973-1974 .... **$4-5**

Royal Coach, Bird Of Paradise Bath Oil, 1972-1973 .... **$4-6**

Scent With Love, Elusive Perfume, 1971-1972 .. **$9-10**

Scent With Love, Field Flowers Perfume, 1971-1972 .... **$9-10**

Scent With Love, Moonwind Perfume, 1971-1972 .... **$9-10**

Side-Wheeler, Tribute After Shave, 1970-1971 ..... **$4-5**

Side-Wheeler, Wild Country After Shave, 1971-1972 .... **$3-4**

Small World Perfume Glace, Small World, 1971-1972 .... **$3-4**

Snoopy Soap Dish Refills, 1968-1976 .... **$3-4**

Snoopy's Bubble Tub, 1971-1972 .... **$3-4**

Spark Plug Decanter, 1975-1976 .... **$2-5**

Spirit Of St. Louis, Excalibur After Shave, 1970-1972 .... **$3-5**

Stage Coach, Wild Country After Shave, 1970-1977 .... **$5-6**

Tee Off, Electric Pre-Shave, 1973-1975 .... **$2-3**

Ten Point Buck, Wild Country After Shave, 1969-1974
.... **$5-7**

Twenty-Dollar Gold Piece, Windjammer After Shave,
1971-1972 .... **$4-6**

Uncle Sam Pipe, Deep Woods After Shave, 1975-1976
.... **$4-5**

Viking Horn, 1966.. **$12-16**

Western Boot, Wild Country After Shave, 1973-1975
.... **$2-3**

Western Saddle, 1971-1972 .... **$7-9**

Wild Turkey, 1974-1976 .... **$6-8**

World's Greatest Dad Decanter, 1971................. **$4-6**

Ballantine Bottles

Ballantine bottles, brightly colored and ceramic, contain imported Scotch whiskey and usually read "Blended Scotch Whiskey, 14 Years Old." Most depict sporting or outdoor themes, such as ducks or fishermen, whose heads form the cap on the bottle. The more collectible items, however, are the older bottles (1930 and earlier), which are non-figural and very decorative.

Charioteer	**$8-12**
Discus Thrower	**$8-12**
Duck	**$8-12**
Fisherman	**$20-25**
Gladiator	**$8-12**
Golf Bag	**$15-20**
Knight	**$15-20**
Mallard Duck	**$10-15**
Mercury	**$7-10**
Old Crow Chessman	**$9-10**
Scottish Knight	**$10-12**
Seated Fisherman	**$10-12**
Silver Knight	**$12-15**
Zebra	**$12-15**

Ballantine's Liqueur Blended Scotch Whisky, Product of Scotland, 1950-1955, $50-$75.

Barsottini Bottles

Barsottini bottles, manufactured in Italy, don't use any American or geographic themes for the U.S. marketplace. The bottles are ceramic and colored gray and white to represent the brickwork of buildings. They usually portray European subjects such as the Eiffel Tower or the Florentine Steeple.

Alpine Pipe, 10"	$10-12	**Florentine Steeple,** Gray And White	$10-12
Antique Automobile, Ceramic, Coupe	$7-10	**Monastery Cask,** Ceramic, 12"	$15-20
Antique Automobile, Open Car	$7-10	**Paris Arc De Triomphe,** 7-1/2"	$10-12
Clock, With Cherub	$30-40	**Pisa's Leaning Tower,** Gray And White	$10-12
Clowns, Ceramic, 12" Each	$10-12	**Roman Coliseum,** Ceramic	$10-12
Eiffel Tower, Gray And White, 15"	$10-12	**Trivoli Clock,** Ceramic, 15"	$12-15
Florentine Cannon, L, 15"	$14-20		

Jim Beam Bottles

The James B. Beam distilling company was founded in Kentucky in 1778 by Jacob Beam and now bears the name of Col. James B. Beam, Jacob Beam's grandson. Beam whiskey was very popular in the South during the 19th and 20th century but was not produced on a large scale. Because of low production, the early Beam bottles are very rare, collectible, and valuable.

Angelo's Delivery Truck
- 1984, $180-200

In 1953, the Beam company packaged bourbon in a special Christmas/ New Year ceramic decanter—a rarity for any distiller. Because the decanters sold well, Beam decided to redevelop its packaging, leading to production of a number of series in the 1950s. The first was the Ceramics Series in 1953. In 1955, the Executive Series was issued to commemorate the 160th anniversary of the corporation. In 1955, Beam introduced the Regal China Series, issued to honor significant people, places, and events, with an emphasis on America and contemporary situations. In 1956, political figures were introduced, with the elephant and the donkey, as well as special productions for customer specialties made on commission. In 1957, the Trophy Series honored various achievements within the liquor industry. The State Series was introduced in 1958 to commemorate the admission of Alaska and Hawaii into the Union. The practice has continued, with Beam still producing decanters to commemorate all 50 states.

In total, over 500 types of Beam bottles have been issued since 1953. For further information, contact the International Association of Jim Beam Bottle and Specialties Clubs, PO Box 486, Kewanee, IL 61443, 309-853-3370, www. beam-wade.org.

AC Spark Plug, 1977
Replica of a spark plug in white, green, and gold
....**$22-26**

AHEPA 50th Anniversary, 1972
Regal China bottle designed in honor of AHEPA'S (American Hellenic Education Progressive Association) 50th Anniversary..**$4-6**

Aida, 1978
Figurine of character from the opera *Aida* **$140-160**

Akron Rubber Capital, 1973
Regal China bottle honoring Akron, Ohio............**$15-20**

Alaska, 1958
Regal China, 9-1/2", star-shaped bottle **$55-60**

Alaska, 1964-1965
Reissue of the 1958 bottle **$40-50**

Alaska Purchase, 1966
Regal China, 10", blue and gold bottle **$4-6**

American Samoa, 1973
Regal China, with the seal of Samoa **$5-7**

American Veterans **$4-7**

Antique Clock **$35-45**

Antioch, 1967
Regal China, 10", commemorates Diamond Jubilee of Regal **$5-7**

Antique Coffee Grinder, 1979
Replica of a box coffee mill used in mid-19th century...**$10-12**

Antique Globe, 1980
Represents the Martin Behaim globe of 1492.......**$7-11**

Antique Telephone (1897), 1978
Replica of an 1897 desk phone, second in a series **$50-60**

Antique Trader, 1968
Regal China, 10-1/2", represents *Antique Trader*
newspaper..$4-6

Appaloosa, 1974
Regal China, 10", represents favorite horse of the Old
West..$12-15

Arizona, 1968
Regal China, 12", represents the State of Arizona..$4-6

Armadillo $8-12

Armanetti Award Winner, 1969
Honors Armanetti, Inc. of Chicago as "Liquor Retailer of
the Year"...$6-8

Armanetti Shopper, 1971
Reflects the slogan, "It's fun to Shop Armanetti Self-
Service Liquor Store," 11-3/4" $6-8

Armanetti Vase, 1968
Yellow-toned decanter embossed with flowers $5-7

Bacchus, 1970
Issued by Armanetti Liquor Stores of Chicago, Illinois,
11-3/4" $6-9

Barney's Slot Machine, 1978
Replica of the world's largest slot machine.........$14-16

Barry Berish, 1985
Executive series $110-140

Barry Berish, 1986
Executive series, bowl....................................$110-140

Bartender's Guild, 1973
Commemorative honoring the International Bartenders
Assn..$4-7

Baseball, 1969
Issued to commemorate the 100th anniversary of
baseball $18-20

Beam Pot, 1980
Shaped like a New England bean pot, club bottle
for the New England Beam Bottle and Specialties
Club $12-15

Beaver Valley Club, 1977
A club bottle to honor the Beaver Valley Jim Beam Club
of Rochester...$8-12

Bell Scotch, 1970
Regal China, 10-1/2", in honor of Arthur Bell &
Sons $4-7

Beverage Association, NLBA................................$4-7

The Big Apple, 1979
Apple-shaped bottle with "The Big Apple" over
the top $8-12

Bing's 31st Clam Bake Bottle, 1972
Commemorates 31st Bing Crosby National Pro-Am
Golf Tournament in January 1972 ....$25-30

Bing Crosby National Pro-Am, 1970 ....$4-7

Bing Crosby National Pro-Am, 1971 ....$4-7

Bing Crosby National Pro-Am, 1972 ....$15-25

Bing Crosby National Pro-Am, 1973 ....$18-23

Bing Crosby National Pro-Am, 1974 ....$15-25

Bing Crosby National Pro-Am, 1975 ....$45-65

Bing Crosby 36th, 1976 ....$15-25

Bing Crosby National Pro-Am, 1977 ....$12-18

Bing Crosby National Pro-Am, 1978 ....$12-18

Black Katz, 1968
Regal China, 14-1/2"..$7-12

Blue Cherub Executive, 1960
Regal China, 12-1/2".......................................$70-90

Blue Daisy, 1967
Also known as Zimmerman Blue Daisy...............$10-12

Blue Gill, Fish $12-16

Blue Goose Order $4-7

Blue Jay, 1969 ....$4-7

Blue Goose, 1979
Replica of blue goose, authenticated by Dr. Lester
Fisher, Director of Lincoln Park Zoological Gardens in
Chicago $7-9

Blue Hen Club $12-15

Blue Slot Machine, 1967 ....$10-12

Bobby Unser Olsonite Eagle, 1975
Replica of the racing car used by Bobby Unser .$40-50

Bob Devaney...$8-12

Bob Hope Desert Classic, 1973
First genuine Regal China bottle created in honor of the
Bob Hope Desert Classic $8-9

Bob Hope Desert Classic, 1974.......................$8-12

Bohemian Girl, 1974
Issued for the Bohemian Cafe in Omaha, Nebraska,
to honor Czech and Slovak immigrants in the United
States, 14-1/4" $10-15

Bonded Gold $4-7

Bonded Mystic, 1979
Urn-shaped bottle, burgundy-colored $4-7

Bonded Silver...$4-7

Boris Godinov, With Base, 1978
Second in Opera series...................................$350-450

Bourbon Barrel $18-24

Bowling Proprietors $4-7

Boys Town Of Italy, 1973
Created in honor of the Boys Town of Italy $7-10

Bowl, 1986
Executive series $20-30

Broadmoor Hotel, 1968
To celebrate the 50th anniversary of this famous hotel in Colorado Springs, Colorado, "1918-The Broadmoor-1968"..$4-7

Buffalo Bill, 1971
Regal China, 10-1/2", commemorates Buffalo Bill .$4-7

Bull Dog, 1979
Honors the 204th anniversary of the United States Marine Corps..$15-18

Cable Car, 1968
Regal China, 4-1/2"...$4-6

Caboose, 1980 ....$50-60

California Mission, 1970
This bottle was issued for the Jim Beam Bottle Club of Southern California in honor of the 120th anniversary of California Missions, 14"..$10-15

California Retail Liquor Dealers Association, 1973
Designed to commemorate the 20th anniversary of the California Retail Liquor Dealers Association $6-9

Cal-Neva, 1969
Regal China, 9-1/2"...$5-7

Camellia City Club, 1979
Replica of the cupola of the California state capitol building in Sacramento $18-23

Cameo Blue, 1965
Also known as the Shepherd Bottle........................$4-6

Cannon, 1970
Bottle issued to commemorate the 175th anniversary of the Jim Beam Co. Some of these bottles have a small chain shown on the cannon and some do not. Those without the chain are harder to find and more valuable, 8"
With chain...$2-4
Without chain $9-13

Canteen, 1979
Replica of the exact canteen used by the armed forces...$8-12

Captain And Mate, 1980....................................$10-12

Cardinal (Kentucky Cardinal), 1968.................$40-50

Carmen, 1978
Third in the Opera series $140-180

Carolier Bull, 1984
Executive series $18-23

Catfish $16-24

Cathedral Radio, 1979
Replica of one of the earlier dome-shaped radios...$12-15

Cats, 1967
Trio of cats: Siamese, Burmese, and Tabby............$6-9

Cedars Of Lebanon, 1971
Issued in honor of the Jerry Lewis Muscular Dystrophy Telethon in 1971 ....$5-7

Charisma, 1970
Executive series $4-7

Charlie McCarthy, 1976
Replica of Edgar Bergen's puppet from the 1930s
....$20-30

Cherry Hills Country Club, 1973
Commemorating 50th anniversary of Cherry Hills Country Club $4-7

Cheyenne, Wyoming, 1977 ....$4-6

Chicago Cubs, Sports Series $30-40

Chicago Show Bottle, 1977
Commemorates 6th Annual Chicago Jim Beam Bottle Show $10-14

Christmas Tree...$150-200

Churchill Downs, Pink Roses, 1969
Regal China, 10-1/4" $5-7

Churchill Downs, Red Roses, 1969
Regal China, 10-1/4" $9-12

Circus Wagon, 1970
Replica of a circus wagon from the late 19th century $24-26

Civil War North, 1961
Regal China, 10-1/4" $10-15

Civil War South, 1961
Regal China, 10-1/4" $25-35

Clear Crystal Bourbon, 1967
Clear glass, 11-1/2"...$5-7

Clear Crystal Scotch, 1966 ....$9-12

Clear Crystal Vodka, 1967....................................$5-8

Cleopatra Rust, 1962
Glass, 13-1/4" $3-5

Cleopatra Yellow, 1962
Glass, 13-1/4", rarer than Cleopatra rust..............$8-12

Clint Eastwood, 1973
Commemorating Clint Eastwood Invitational Celebrity Tennis Tournament in Pebble Beach...................$14-17

Cocktail Shaker, 1953
Glass, fancy dis. bottle, 9-1/4"...............................$2-5

Coffee Grinder $8-12

Coffee Warmers, 1954
Four types are known: red, black, gold, and white
....$7-12

Coffee Warmers, 1956
Two types with metal necks and handles................$2-5

Coho Salmon, 1976
Offical seal of the National Fresh Water Fishing Hall of Fame is on the back...$10-13

Colin Mead $180-210

Convention Series Number 18: Buck Beaver 1988, $30-40; Bottle & Rose (red), $30-40; Bottle & Rose (yellow), $30-40.

Cobalt, 1981
Executive Series..**$18-23**

Collector's Edition, 1966
Set of six glass famous paintings: The Blue Boy, On the Terrace, Mardi Gras, Austide Bruant, The Artist Before His Easel, and Laughing Cavalier...................**$2-5 each**

Collector's Edition Volume II, 1967
A set of six flask-type bottles with famous pictures: George Gisze, Soldier and Girl, Night Watch, The Jester, Nurse and Child, and Man on Horse ..**$2-5 each**

Collector's Edition Volume III, 1968
A set of eight bottles with famous paintings: On the Trail, Indian Maiden, Buffalo, Whistler's Mother, American Gothic, The Kentuckian, The Scout, and Hauling in the Gill Net.....................................**$2-5 each**

Collector's Edition Volume IV, 1969
A set of eight bottles with famous paintings: Balcony, The Judge, Fruit Basket, Boy with Cherries, Emile Zola, The Guitarist Zouave, and Sunflowers ....**$2-5 each**

Collector's Edition Volume V, 1970
A set of six bottles with famous paintings: Au Cafe, Old Peasant, Boaring Party, Gare Saint Lazare, The Jewish Bride, and Titus at Writing Desk.....................**$2-5 each**

Collector's Edition Volume VI, 1971
A set of three bottles with famous pieces: Charles I, The Merry Lute Player, and Boy Holding Flute...**$2-5 each**

Collector's Edition Volume VII, 1972
A set of three bottles with famous paintings: The Bag Piper, Prince Baltasor, and Maidservant Pouring Milk ....**$2-5 each**

Collector's Edition Volume VIII, 1973
A set of three bottles with famous portraits: Ludwig Van Beethoven, Wolfgang Mozart, and Frederic Francis Chopin...**$2-5 each**

Collector's Edition Volume 1X, 1974
A set of three bottles with famous paintings: Cardinal, Ring-Neck Pheasant, and Woodcock ....**$3-6 each**

Collector's Edition Volume X, 1975
A set of three bottles with famous pictures: Sailfish, Rainbow Trout, and Largemouth Bass ....**$3-6 each**

Collector's Edition Volume XI, 1976
A set of three bottles with famous paintings: Chipmunk, Bighorn Sheep, and Pronghorn Antelope ......**$3-6 each**

Collector's Edition Volume XII, 1977
A set of four bottles, each with a different reproduction of James Lockhart on the front ....**$3-6 each**

Collector's Edition Volume XIV, 1978
A set of four bottles with James Lockhart paintings: Raccoon, Mule Deer, Red Fox, and Cottontail Rabbit ....**$3-6 each**

Collector's Edition Volume XV, 1979
A set of three flasks with Frederic Remington's paintings: The Cowboy 1902, The Indian Trapper 1902, and Lieutenant S.C. Robertson 1890.............**$2-5 each**

Collector's Edition Volume XVI, 1980
A set of three flasks depicting duck scenes: Mallard, Redhead, and Canvasback ....**$3-6 each**

Collector's Edition Volume XVII, 1981
A set of three flasks bottles with Jim Lockhart paintings: Great Elk, Pintail Duck, and Horned Owl ....**$3-6 each**

Colorado, 1959
Regal China, 10-3/4" **$20-25**

Colorado Centennial, 1976
Replica of Pike's Peak...**$8-12**

Colorado Springs...**$4-7**

Computer, Democrat, 1984...............................**$12-18**

Computer, Republican, 1984 ....**$12-18**

Convention Bottle, 1971
Commemorates the first national convention of the National Association of Jim Beam Bottle and Specialty Clubs hosted by the Rocky Mountain Club, Denver, Colorado...**$5-7**

Convention Number 2, 1972
Honors the second annual convention of the National
Association of Jim Beam Bottle and Specialty Clubs in
Anaheim, Calif. **$20-30**

Convention Number 3 – Detroit, 1973
Commemorates the third annual convention of Beam
Bottle Collectors in Detroit, Mich. **$10-12**

Convention Number 4 – Pennsylvania, 1974
Commemorates the annual convention of the Jim
Beam Bottle Club in Lancaster, Pa. **$80-100**

Convention Number 5 – Sacramento, 1975
Commemorates the annual convention of the Camellia
City Jim Beam Bottle Club in Sacramento, Calif. ...**$5-7**

Convention Number 6 – Hartford, 1976
Commemorates the annual convention of the Jim
Beam Bottle Club in Hartford, Conn. **$5-7**

Convention Number 7 – Louisville, 1978
Commemorates the annual convention of the Jim
Beam Bottle Club in Louisville, Ky............................**$5-7**

Convention Number 8 – Chicago, 1978
Commemorates the annual convention of the Jim
Beam Bottle Club in Chicago, Ill. **$8-12**

Convention Number 9 – Houston, 1979
Commemorates the annual convention of the Jim
Beam Bottle Club in Houston, Texas **$20-30**
Cowboy, beige..**$35-45**
Cowboy, in color...**$35-45**

Convention Number 10 – Norfolk, 1980
Commemorates the annual convention of the Jim
Beam Bottle Club at the Norfolk Naval Base **$18-22**
Waterman, pewter **$35-45**
Waterman, yellow **$35-45**

Convention Number 11 – Las Vegas, 1981
Commemorates the annual convention of the Jim
Beam Bottle Club in Las Vegas, Nev..................**$20-22**
Showgirl, blonde **$45-55**
Showgirl, brunette **$45-55**

Convention Number 12 – New Orleans, 1982
Commemorates the annual convention of the Jim
Beam Bottle Club in New Orleans, La................**$30-35**
Buccaneer, gold **$35-45**
Buccaneer, in color...**$35-45**

Convention Number 13 – St. Louis, 1983 (Stein)
Commemorates the annual convention of the Jim
Beam Bottle Club in St. Louis, Mo. **$55-70**
Gibson girl, blue **$65-80**
Gibson girl, yellow **$65-80**

Convention Number 14 – Florida, King Neptune, 1984
Commemorates the annual convention of the Jim
Beam Bottle Club in Florida **$15-20**
Mermaid, blonde **$35-45**
Mermaid, brunette...**$35-45**

Convention Number 15 – Las Vegas, 1985
Commemorates the annual convention of the Jim
Beam Bottle Club in Las Vegas, Nev...................**$40-50**

Convention Number 16 – Boston, Pilgrim Woman,
1986
Commemorates the annual convention of the Jim
Beam Bottle Club in Boston, Mass. **$35-45**
Minuteman, color **$85-105**
Minuteman, pewter **$85-105**

Convention Number 17 – Louisville, 1987
Commemorates the annual convention of the Jim
Beam Bottle Club in Louisville, Ky.......................**$55-75**
Kentucky Colonel, blue **$85-105**
Kentucky Colonel, gray **$85-105**

Convention Number 18 – Bucky Beaver, 1988
....**$30-40**
Portland rose, red...**$30-40**
Portland rose, yellow..**$30-40**

Convention Number 19 – Kansas City, 1989
Commemorates the annual convention of the Jim
Beam Bottle Club in Kansas City, Mo. **$40-50**

Cowboy, 1979
Awarded to collectors who attended the 1979
convention for the International Association of Beam
Clubs **$35-50**

Duck Stamp Series: Pin Tails, 1983-1984, $30-40; Canvasbacks, 1982-1983, $30-40; Ruddy Ducks, 1981-1982, $30-40.

CPO Open $4-7

Crappie, 1979
Commemorates the National Fresh Water Fishing Hall of Fame $10-14

Dark Eyes Brown Jug, 1978.................................$4-6

D-Day...$12-18

Delaware Blue Hen Bottle, 1972
Commemorates the State of Delaware $4-7

Delco Freedom Battery, 1978
Replica of a Delco battery $18-22

Delft Blue, 1963...$3-5

Delft Rose, 1963...$4-6

Del Webb Mint, 1970
Metal stopper $10-12
China stopper...$50-60

Devil Dog $15-25

Dial Telephone, 1980
Fourth in a series of Beam telephone designs....$40-50

Dodge City, 1972
Issued to honor the centennial of Dodge City.........$5-6

Doe, 1963
Regal China, 13-1/2" $10-12

Doe – Re-Issued, 1967 ....$10-12

Dog, 1959
Regal China, 15-1/4" $20-25

Don Giovanni, 1980
The fifth in the Opera series $140-180

Donkey And Elephant Ashtrays, 1956
Regal China, 12" (pair).......................................$12-16

Donkey And Elephant Boxers, 1964 (pair) $14-18

Donkey And Elephant Clowns, 1968
Regal China, 12" (pair)..$4-7

Donkey And Elephant Football Election Bottles, 1972
Regal China, 9-1/2" (pair).......................................$6-9

Donkey New York City, 1976
Commemorates the National Democratic Convention in New York City...$10-12

Duck, 1957
Regal China, 14-1/4"..$15-20

Ducks And Geese, 1955 ....$5-8

Ducks Unlimited Mallard, 1974 ....$40-50

Ducks Unlimited Wood Duck, 1975 ....$45-50

Ducks Unlimited 40th Mallard Hen, 1977 ....$40-50

Ducks Unlimited Canvasback Drake, 1979.....$30-40

Ducks Unlimited Blue-Winged Teal, 1980
The sixth in a series, 9-1/2"...............................$40-45

Ducks Unlimited Green-Winged Teal, 1981.....$35-45

Ducks Unlimited Wood Ducks, 1982................$35-45

Ducks Unlimited American Widg Pr, 1983.......$35-45

Ducks Unlimited Mallard, 1984 ....$55-75

Ducks Unlimited Pintail Pr, 1985 ....$30-40

Ducks Unlimited Redhead, 1986......................$15-25

Ducks Unlimited Blue Bill, 1987 ....$40-60

Ducks Unlimited Black Duck, 1989.................$50-60

Eagle, 1966
Regal China, 12-1/2" $10-13

Eldorado, 1978 ....$7-9

Election, Democrat, 1988...................................$30-40

Election, Republican, 1988 ....$30-40

Elephant And Donkey Supermen, 1980
Set of two $10-14

Elks $4-7

Elks National Foundation...................................$8-12

Emerald Crystal Bourbon, 1968
Green glass, 11-1/2" $3-5

Emmett Kelly, 1973
Likeness of Emmett Kelly as sad-faced Willie the Clown $18-22

Emmett Kelly, Native Son $50-60

Ernie's Flower Cart, 1976
In honor of Ernie's Wines and Liquors of Northern Calif $24-28

Evergreen, Club Bottle......................................$7-10

Expo, 1974
Issued in honor of the World's Fair held at Spokane, Wash...$5-7

Falstaff, 1979
Second in Australian Opera series, limited edition of 1,000 bottles..$150-160

Fantasia Bottle, 1971..$5-6

Father's Day Card...$15-25

Female Cardinal, 1973..$8-12

Fiesta Bowl, Glass..$8-12

Fiesta Bowl, 1973
The second bottle created to honor the Fiesta Bowl $9-11

Figaro, 1977
Character Figaro from the opera *Barber of Seville* $140-170

Fighting Bull $12-18

Fiji Islands $4-6

First National Bank Of Chicago, 1964
Commemorates the 100th anniversary of the First
National Bank of Chicago. Approximately 130 were
issued, with 117 being given as mementos to the bank
directors with none for public distribution. This is the
most valuable Beam bottle known. Also, beware of
reproductions **$1,900-2,400**

Fish, 1957
Regal China, 14" $15-18

Fish Hall Of Fame $25-35

Five Seasons, 1980
Club bottle for the Five Seasons Club of Cedar Rapids
honors the State of Iowa $10-12

Fleet Reserve Association, 1974
Issued by the Fleet Reserve Association to honor the
Career Sea Service on its 50th anniversary $5-7

Florida Shell, 1968
Regal China, 9" $4-6

Floro De Oro, 1976..$10-12

Flower Basket, 1962
Regal China, 12-1/4" $30-35

Football Hall Of Fame, 1972
Reproduction of the new Professional Football Hall of
Fame Building $14-18

Foremost – Black And Gold, 1956
First Beam bottle issued for a liquor retailer, Foremost
Liquor Store of Chicago $225-250

Foremost – Speckled Beauty, 1956
The most valuable of the Foremost bottles.....**$500-600**

Fox, 1967, Blue Coat $65-80

Fox, 1971, Gold Coat..$35-50

Fox, Green Coat..$12-18

Fox, White Coat $20-30

Fox, On A Dolphin..$12-15

Fox, Uncle Sam..$5-6

Fox, Kansas City, Blue, Miniature $20-30

Fox, Red Distillery $1,100-1,300

Franklin Mint...$4-7

French Cradle Telephone, 1979
Third in the Telephone Pioneers of America
series $20-22

Galah Bird, 1979...$14-16

Gem City Club Bottle...$35-45

George Washington Commemorative Plate, 1976
Commemorates the U.S. Bicentennial, 9-1/2" $12-15

German Bottle – Weisbaden, 1973......................$4-6

German Stein $20-30

Germany, 1970
Issued to honor the American Armed Forces in
Germany...$4-6

Glen Campbell 51st, 1976
Honors the 51st Los Angeles Open at the Riviera
Country Club in February 1976 ....$7-10

Golden Chalice, 1961 ....$40-50

Golden Jubilee, 1977
Executive Series...$48-12

Golden Nugget, 1969
Regal China, 12-1/2"...$35-45

Golden Rose, 1978 ....$15-20

Grand Canyon, 1969
Honors the Grand Canyon National Park 50th
Anniversary...$7-9

Grant Locomotive, 1979.................................. $55-65

Harley-Davidson Stein, $175-200; Harley-Davidson Decanter, $180-220; Seoul Korea 1988 Olympic, $60-75.

Gray Cherub, 1958
Regal China, 12" **$240-260**

Great Chicago Fire Bottle, 1971
Commemorates the great Chicago fire of 1871
and salutes Mercy Hospital, which helped the fire
victims **$18-22**

Great Dane, 1976 ....**$7-9**

Green China Jug, 1965
Regal glass, 12-1/2" **$4-6**

Hank Williams, Jr. **$40-50**

Hannah Dustin, 1973
Regal China, 14-1/2" **$10-12**

Hansel And Gretel Bottle, 1971 ....**$44-50**

Harley Davidson 85th Anniversary Decanter
....**$175-200**

Harley Davidson 85th Anniversary Stein **$180-220**

Harolds Club – Man-In-A-Barrel, 1957
First in a series made for Harolds Club in Reno,
Nev. **$380-410**

Harolds Club – Silver Opal, 1957
Commemorates the 25th anniversary of Harolds
Club **$20-22**

Harolds Club – Man-In-A-Barrel, 1958.........**$140-160**

Harolds Club – Nevada (Gray), 1963
Created for the Nevada Centennial 1864-1964 as a
state bottle. This is a rare and valuable bottle ..**$90-110**

Harolds Club – Nevada (Silver), 1964.............**$90-110**

Harolds Club – Pinwheel, 1965.........................**$40-45**

Harolds Club – Blue Slot Machine, 1967 ....**$10-14**

Harolds Club – VIP Executive, 1967
Limited quantity issued **$50-60**

Harolds Club – VIP Executive, 1968 ....**$55-65**

Harolds Club – Gray Slot Machine, 1968 ....**$4-6**

Harolds Club – VIP Executive, 1969
This bottle was given as a Christmas gift to the casino's
executives **$260-285**

Harolds Club – Covered Wagon, 1969-1970.......**$4-6**

Harolds Club, 1970 ....**$40-60**

Harolds Club, 1971 ....**$40-60**

Harolds Club, 1972 ....**$18-25**

Harolds Club, 1973 ....**$18-24**

Harolds Club, 1974 ....**$12-16**

Harolds Club, 1975 ....**$12-18**

Harolds Club VIP, 1976.....................................**$18-22**

Harolds Club, 1977 ....**$20-30**

Hollywood, Florida, Glass Convention Bottles - 1984: Bourbon, $25-30; Canadian Whiskey, $25-30.

Harolds Club, 1978 ....**$20-30**

Harolds Club, 1979 ....**$20-30**

Harolds Club, 1980 ....**$25-35**

Harolds Club, 1982 ....**$110-145**

Harp Seal...**$12-18**

Harrah's Club Nevada – Gray, 1963
This is the same bottle used for the Nevada Centennial
and for Harolds Club **$500-550**

Harry Hoffman **$4-7**

Harvey's Resort Hotel At Lake Tahoe **$6-10**

Hatfield, 1973
The character of Hatfield from the story of the Hatfield
and McCoy feud..**$15-20**

Hawaii, 1959
Tribute to the 50th state **$35-40**

Hawaii – Re-Issued, 1967................................**$40-45**

Hawaii, 1971 ....**$6-8**

Hawaii Aloha, 1971 ....**$6-10**

Hawaiian Open Bottle, 1972
Honors the 1972 Hawaiian Open Golf
Tournament **$6-8**

Hawaiian Open, 1973
Second bottle created in honor of the United Hawaiian
Open Golf Classic **$7-9**

Hawaiian Open, 1974
Commemorates the 1974 Hawaiian Open Golf
Classic...**$5-8**

Hawaiian Open Outrigger, 1975 ....**$9-11**

Hawaiian Paradise, 1978
Commemorates the 200th anniversary of the landing of Captain Cook **$15-17**

Hemisfair, 1968
Commemorates the "Hemisfair 68-San Antonio" **$8-10**

Herre Brothers **$22-35**

Hobo, Australia **$10-14**

Hoffman, 1969...**$4-7**

Holiday-Carolers...**$40-50**

Holiday-Nutcracker **$40-50**

Home Builders, 1978
Commemorates the 1979 convention of the Home Builders **$25-30**

Hone Heke..**$200-250**

Honga Hika, 1980
First in a series of Maori warrior bottles. Honga Hika was a war-chief of the Ngapuke tribe **$220-240**

Horse (Appaloosa) **$8-12**

Horse (Black) **$18-22**

Horse (Black) Re-Issued, 1967 ....**$10-12**

Horse (Brown) **$18-22**

Horse (Brown) Re-Issued, 1967........................**$10-12**

Horse (Mare And Foal) **$35-45**

Horse (Oh Kentucky) **$70-85**

Horse (Pewter) **$12-17**

Horse (White) **$18-20**

Horse (White) Re-Issued, 1967 ....**$12-17**

Horseshoe Club, 1969 ....**$4-6**

Hula Bowl, 1975 ....**$8-10**

Hyatt House – Chicago **$7-10**

Hyatt House – New Orleans.............................**$8-11**

Idaho, 1963...**$30-40**

Illinois, 1968
Honors Illinois' Sesquicentennial (1818-1968) **$4-6**

Indianapolis Sesquicentennial **$4-6**

Indianapolis 500...**$9-12**

Indian Chief, 1979 ....**$9-12**

International Chili Society, 1976.........................**$9-12**

Italian Marble Urn, 1985
Executive series **$12-17**

Ivory Ashtray, 1955 ....**$8-10**

Jackalope, 1971
Honors the Wyoming jackalope **$5-8**

Jaguar..**$18-23**

Jewel T Man – 50th Anniversary **$35-45**

John Henry, 1972
Commemorates the legendary Steel Drivin' Man**$18-22**

Joliet Legion Band, 1978
Commemorates the 26th national championships **$15-20**

Kaiser International Open Bottle, 1971
Commemorates the 5th Annual Kaiser International Open Golf Tournament **$5-6**

Kangaroo, 1977.. **$10-14**

Kansas, 1960
Commemorates the "Kansas 1861-1961 Centennial"..**$35-45**

Kentucky Black Head – Brown Head, 1967
Black Head..**$12-18**
Brown Head..**$20-28**
White Head..**$18-23**

Kentucky Derby 95th, Pink, Red Roses, 1969.....**$4-7**

Kentucky Derby 96th, Double Rose, 1970.......**$15-25**

Kentucky Derby 97th, 1971....................................**$4-7**

Kentucky Derby 98th, 1972....................................**$4-6**

Kentucky Derby 100th, 1974...............................**$7-10**

Key West, 1972
Honors the 150th anniversary of Key West, Fla. **$5-7**

King Kamehameha, 1972
Commemorates the 100th anniversary of King Kamehameha Day **$8-11**

King Kong, 1976
Commemorates Paramount's movie release in December 1976...**$8-10**

Kiwi, 1974 ....**$5-8**

Koala Bear, 1973 ....**$12-14**

Laramie, 1968
Commemorates the Centennial Jubilee, Laramie Wyo. 1868-1968 ....**$4-6**

Largemouth Bass Trophy Bottle, 1973
Honors the National Fresh Water Fishing Hall of Fame..**$10-14**

Las Vegas, 1969
Bottle used for Customer Specials, Casino series..**$4-6**

Light Bulb, 1979
Honors Thomas Edison.......................................**$14-16**

Lombard, 1969
Commemorates "Village of Lombard, Illinois-1869 Centennial," 1969...**$4-6**

London Bridge $4-7

Louisville Downs Racing Derby, 1978.................$4-6

Louisiana Superdome $8-11

LVNH Owl $20-30

Madame Butterfly, 1977
Figurine of Madame Butterfly, music box plays "One
Fine Day" from the opera $340-370

The Magpies, 1977
Honors an Australian football team....................$18-20

Maine, 1970 ....$4-6

Majestic, 1966 ....$20-24

Male Cardinal...$18-24

Marbled Fantasy, 1965 ....$38-42

Marina City, 1962
Commemorates modern apartment complex in
Chicago $10-15

Marine Corps $25-35

Mark Antony, 1962...$18-20

Martha Washington, 1976 ....$5-6

McCoy, 1973
Character of McCoy from the story of the Hatfield and
McCoy feud..$14-17

McShane – Mother-Of-Pearl, 1979
Executive series $85-105

McShane – Titans, 1980 ....$85-105

McShane – Cobalt, 1981
Executive series $115-135

McShane – Green Pitcher, 1982
Executive series $80-105

McShane – Green Bell, 1983
Executive series $80-110

Mephistopheles, 1979
Figurine depicts Mephistopheles from the opera *Faust*,
music box plays "Soldier's Chorus" $160-190

Michigan Bottle, 1972...$7-9

Milwaukee Stein $30-40

Minnesota Vikings, 1973 ....$9-12

Mint 400, 1970 ....$80-105

Mint 400, 1970 ....$5-6

Mint 400, 1971 ....$5-6

Mint 400, 1972
Commemorates the 5th annual Del Webb Mint 400$5-7

Mint 400, 1973
Commemorates the 6th annual Del Webb Mint
400...$6-8

Mint 400, 1974..$4-7

Mint 400 7th Annual, 1976................................$9-12

Mississippi Fire Engine, 1978 ....$120-130

Model A Ford, (1903) 1978 ....$38-42

Model A Ford, (1928) 1980 ....$65-75

Montana, 1963
Tribute to "Montana, 1864 Golden Years Centennial
1964"...$50-60

Monterey Bay Club, 1977
Honors the Monterey Bay Beam Bottle and Specialty
Club...$9-12

Mortimer Snerd, 1976.......................................$24-28

Mother-Of-Pearl, 1979......................................$10-12

Mount St. Helens, 1980
Depicts the eruption of Mount St. Helens...........$20-22

Mr. Goodwrench, 1978 ....$24-28

Musicians On A Wine Cask, 1964 ....$4-6

Muskie, 1971
Honors the National Fresh Water Fishing Hall of Fame
....$14-18

National Tobacco Festival, 1973
Commemorates the 25th anniversary of the National
Tobacco Festival..$7-8

Nebraska, 1967 ....$7-9

Nebraska Football, 1972
Commemorates the University of Nebraska's national
championship football team of 1970-1971 ....$5-8

Nevada, 1963...$34-38

New Hampshire, 1967 ....$4-8

New Hampshire Eagle Bottle, 1971 ....$18-23

New Jersey, 1963...$40-5o

New Jersey Yellow, 1963...................................$40-50

New Mexico Bicentennial, 1976 ....$8-12

New Mexico Statehood, 1972
Commemorates New Mexico's 60 years of
statehood $7-9

New York World's Fair, 1964 ....$5-6

North Dakota, 1965...$45-55

Northern Pike, 1977
The sixth in a series designed for the National Fresh
Water Fishing Hall of Fame $14-18

Nutcracker Toy Soldier, 1978........................$90-120

Ohio, 1966 ....$5-6

Ohio State Fair, 1973
In honor of the 120th Ohio State Fair.....................$5-6

Olympian, 1960 ....$2-4

One Hundred First Airborne Division, 1977
Honors the division known as the Screaming Eagles
....$8-10

Opaline Crystal, 1969 ....$4-6

Oregon, 1959
Honors the centennial of the state $20-25

Oregon Liquor Commission $25-35

Osco Drugs $12-17

Panda, 1980..$20-22

Paul Bunyan $4-7

Pearl Harbor Memorial, 1972
Honoring the Pearl Harbor Survivors
Association..$14-18

Pearl Harbor Survivors Association, 1976...........$5-7

Pennsylvania, 1967 ....$4-6

Pennsylvania Dutch, Club Bottle.......................$8-12

Permian Basin Oil Show, 1972
Commemorates the Permian Basin Oil Show in
Odessa, Texas..$4-6

Petroleum Man $4-7

Pheasant, 1960 ....$14-18

Pheasant, 1961 Re-Issued; Also '63, '66, '67, '68
....$8-11

Phi Sigma Kappa (Centennial Series), 1973
Commemorates the 100th anniversary of this
fraternity $3-4

Phoenician, 1973 ....$6-9

Pied Piper Of Hamlin, 1974..................$3-6

Ponderosa, 1969
A replica of the Cartwrights of "Bonanza" TV fame $4-6

Ponderosa Ranch Tourist, 1972
Commemorates the one millionth tourist to the
Ponderosa Ranch...............................$14-16

Pony Express, 1968 ....$9-12

Poodle – Gray And White, 1970 ....$5-6

Portland Rose Festival, 1972
Commemorates the 64th Portland, Ore., Rose
Festival $5-8

Portola Trek, 1969
Issued to celebrate the 200th anniversary of
San Diego..$3-6

Poulan Chain Saw, 1979..................$24-28

Powell Expedition, 1969
Depicts John Wesley Powell's survey of the Colorado
River $3-5

Preakness, 1970
Issued to honor the 100th anniversary of the running of
the Preakness..$5-6

Preakness Pimlico, 1975...................$4-7

Presidential, 1968
Executive series $4-7

Prestige, 1967
Executive series $4-7

Pretty Perch, 1980
Eighth in a series, this fish is used as the official seal of
the National Fresh Water Fishing Hall of Fame ...$13-16

Prima-Donna, 1969...........................$4-6

Professional Golf Association $4-7

Queensland, 1978.............................$20-22

Rabbit $4-7

Rainbow Trout, 1975
Produced for the National Fresh Water Fishing Hall of
Fame..$12-15

Ralph Centennial, 1973
Commemorates the 100th anniversary of the Ralph
Grocery Co. $10-14

Ralph's Market..$8-12

Ram, 1958..$40-55

Ramada Inn, 1976...........................$10-12

Red Mile Racetrack...........................$8-12

Redwood, 1967 ....$6-8

Reflections, 1975
Executive series $8-12

Regency, 1972..$7-9

Reidsville, 1973
Issued to honor Reidsville, N.C. on its centennial...$5-6

Rennie The Fox, 1974
Represents the companion for the International
Association of Jim Beam Bottle and Specialities Club's
mascot..$7-9

Rennie The Runner, 1974 ....$9-12

Rennie The Surfer, 1975 ....$9-12

Reno, 1968
Commemorates "100 Years - Reno".......................$4-6

Republic Of Texas, 1980...................$12-20

Republican Convention, 1972.....................$500-700

Republican Football, 1972 ....$350-450

Richard Hadlee $110-135

Richards – New Mexico, 1967
Created for Richards Distributing Co. of Alburquerque,
N.M...$8-10

Robin, 1969 ....$5-6

Rocky Marciano, 1973......................................$14-16

Rocky Mountain, Club Bottle $10-15

Royal Crystal, 1959...$3-6

Royal Di Monte, 1957 ....$45-55

Royal Emperor, 1958 ....$3-6

Royal Gold Diamond, 1964 ....$30-35

Royal Gold Round, 1956...................................$80-90

Royal Opal, 1957 ....$5-7

Royal Porcelain, 1955...................................$380-420

Royal Rose, 1963 ....$30-35

Ruby Crystal, 1967..$6-9

Ruidoso Downs, 1968
Pointed ears $24-26
Flat ears...$4-6

Sahara Invitational Bottle, 1971
Introduced in honor of the Del Webb 1971 Sahara
Invitational Pro-Am Golf Tournament $6-8

San Bear – Donkey, 1973
Political series $1,500-2,000

Samoa...$4-7

San Diego, 1968
Issued by the Beam Co. for the 200th anniversary of its
founding in 1769...$4-6

San Diego – Elephant, 1972 ....$15-25

Santa Fe, 1960 ....$120-140

SCCA, Etched $15-25

SCCA, Smoothed...$12-18

Screech Owl, 1979...$18-22

Seafair Trophy Race, 1972
Commemorates the Seattle Seafair Trophy Race ... $5-6

Seattle World's Fair, 1962.................................$10-12

Seoul – Korea, 1988..$60-75

Sheraton Inn...$4-6

Short Dancing Scot, 1963 ....$50-65

Short-Timer, 1975 ....$15-20

Shriners, 1975 ....$10-12

Shriners – Indiana...$4-7

Shriners Pyramid, 1975
Issued by the El Kahir Temple of Cedar Rapids,
Iowa..$10-12

Shriners Rajah, 1977 ....$24-28

Shriners Temple, 1972.......................................$20-25

Shriners Western Association..........................$15-25

Sierra Eagle..$15-22

Sigma Nu Fraternity, 1977...................................$9-12

Sigma Nu Fraternity – Kentucky $8-12

Sigma Nu Fraternity – Michigan......................$18-23

Smith's North Shore Club, 1972
Commemorating Smith's North Shore Club, at Crystal
Bay, Lake Tahoe $10-12

Smoked Crystal, 1964 .... $6-9

Snow Goose, 1979.. $8-10

Snowman $125-175

South Carolina, 1970
In honor of celebrating its tricentennial 1670-1970.$4-6

South Dakota – Mouth Rushmore, 1969............. $4-6

South Florida – Fox On Dolphin, 1980
Bottled sponsored by the South Florida Beam Bottle
and Specialties Club $14-16

Sovereign, 1969
Executive series $4-7

Spenger's Fish Grotto, 1977 ....$18-22

Sports Car Club Of America................................$5-7

Statue Of Liberty, 1975......................................$8-12

Statue Of Liberty, 1985.....................................$18-20

Trophy Series: Duck Decoy $40-50; Organization Series: Ducks
Unlimited $40-50; Regal China Series: Fathers Day Card, $15-25.

St. Bernard, 1979 ....$30-35

St. Louis, Club Bottle $10-15

St. Louis Arch, 1964..$10-12

St. Louis Arch – Re-Issue, 1967.......................$16-18

St. Louis Statue, 1972 ....$8-10

Sturgeon, 1980
Exclusive issue for a group that advocates the
preservation of sturgeons...................................$14-17

Stutz Bearcat (1914), 1977 ....$45-55

Submarine – Diamond Jubilee $35-45

Submarine Redfin, 1970
Issued for Manitowoc Submarine Memorial
Association...$5-7

Superdome, 1975
Replica of the Louisiana Superdome $5-8

Swagman, 1979
Replica of an Australian hobo called a swagman
who roamed that country looking for work during the
Depression $10-12

Sydney Opera House, 1977...............................$9-12

Tall Dancing Scot, 1964......................................$9-12

Tavern Scene, 1959 ....$45-55

Telephone No. 1, 1975
Replica of a 1907 phone of the magneto wall type
....$25-30

Telephone No. 2, 1976
Replica of an 1897 desk set...............................$30-40

Telephone No. 3, 1977
Replica of a 1920 cradle phone $15-20

Telephone No. 4, 1978
Replica of a 1919 dial phone..............................$40-50

Telephone No. 5, 1979
Replica of a pay phone $25-35

Telephone No. 6, 1980
Replica of a battery phone $20-30

Telephone No. 7, 1981
Replica of a digital dial phone............................$35-45

Ten-Pin, 1980..$8-11

Texas Hemisfair $7-11

Texas Rose, 1978
Executive series $14-18

Thailand, 1969..$4-6

Thomas Flyer (1907), 1976 ....$60-70

Tiffiny Poodle, 1973
Created in honor of Tiffiny, the poodle mascot of the
National Association of the Jim Beam Bottle and
Specialties Clubs...$20-22

Tiger – Australian...$14-18

The Tigers, 1977
Issued in honor of an Australian football team....$20-24

Titian, 1980..$9-12

Tobacco Festival $8-12

Tombstone $4-7

Travelodge Bear...$4-7

Treasure Chest, 1979..$8-12

Trout Unlimited, 1977
To honor the Trout Unlimited Conservation
Organization $14-18

Truth Or Consequences Fiesta, 1974
Issued in honor of Ralph Edwards' radio and televison
show..$14-18

Turquoise China Jug, 1966 ....$4-6

Twin Bridges Bottle, 1971
Commemorates the largest twin bridge between
Delaware and New Jersey...................................$40-42

Twin Cherubs, 1974
Executive series $8-12

Twin Doves, 1987
Executive series $18-23

US Open, 1972
Honors the US Open Golf Tourney at Pebble Beach,
Calif. $9-12

Vendome Drummers Wagon, 1975
Honored the Vendomes of Beverly Hills, Calif. ...$60-70

VFW Bottle, 1971
Commemorates the 50th anniversary of the
Department of Indana VFW.....................................$5-6

Viking, 1973 ....$9-12

Volkswagen Commemorative Bottle – Two Colors,
1977
Commemorates the Volkswagen Beetle $40-50

Vons Market..$28-35

Walleye Pike, 1977
Designed for the National Fresh Water Fishing Hall of
Fame..$12-15

Walleye Pike, 1987...$17-23

Washington, 1975
A state series bottle to commemorate the Evergreen
State $5-6

Washington – The Evergreen State, 1974
The club bottle for the Evergreen State Beam Bottle
and Specialties Club $10-12

Washington State Bicentennial, 1976..............$10-12

Waterman, 1980..$100-130

Western Shrine Association, 1980
Commemorates the Shriners convention in Phoenix,
Ariz. **$20-22**

West Virginia, 1963 ....**$130-140**

White Fox, 1969
Issued for the second anniversary of the Jim Beam
Bottle and Specialties Club in Berkley, Calif. **$25-35**

Wisconsin Muskie Bottle, 1971 ....**$15-17**

Woodpecker, 1969 ....**$6-8**

Wyoming, 1965...**$40-50**

Yellow Katz, 1967
Commemorates the 50th anniversary of the Katz
Department Stores **$15-17**

Yellow Rose, 1978
Executive series **$7-10**

Yellowstone Park Centennial **$4-7**

Yosemite, 1967...**$4-6**

Yuma Rifle Club **$18-23**

Zimmerman – Art Institute...................................**$5-8**

Zimmerman Bell, 1976
Designed for Zimmerman Liquor Store of Chicago **$6-7**

Zimmerman Bell, 1976 ....**$6-7**

Zimmerman – Blue Beauty, 1969......................**$9-12**

Zimmerman – Blue Daisy **$4-6**

Zimmerman Cherubs, 1968 ....**$4-6**

Zimmerman – Chicago...**$4-6**

Zimmerman – Eldorado **$4-7**

Zimmerman – Glass, 1969 ....**$7-9**

Zimmerman Oatmeal Jug...............................**$40-50**

Zimmerman – The Peddler Bottle, 1971 ....**$4-6**

Zimmerman Two-Handled Jug, 1965..............**$45-60**

Zimmerman Vase, Brown...................................**$6-9**

Zimmerman Vase, Green **$6-9**

Zimmerman – 50th Anniversary **$35-45**

Automobile and Transportation Series

Chevrolet

1957 Convertible, Black, New **$85-95**

1957 Convertible, Red, New **$75-85**

1957, Black...**$70-80**

1957, Dark Blue, Pa. **$70-80**

1957, Red..**$80-90**

1957, Sierra Gold **$140-160**

1957, Turquoise...**$50-70**

1957, Yellow Hot Rod **$65-75**

Camaro, 1969, Blue **$55-65**

Camaro, 1969, Burgundy **$120-140**

Camaro, 1969, Green....................................**$100-120**

Camaro, 1969, Orange **$55-65**

Camaro, 1969, Pace Car **$60-70**

Camaro, 1969, Silver **$120-140**

Camaro, 1969, Yellow, Pa................................**$55-65**

Corvette, 1986, Pace Car, Yellow, New...........**$60-85**

Corvette (red) 1984, $55-65; Corvette 1984, $55-65; Democratic
Convention 1988, $30-40; Republican Convention 1988, $30-40.

Train Series: Caboose (Grey), $45-55; Flat Car, $20-30; Wood Tender $40-45.

Corvette, 1984, Black $70-80

Corvette, 1984, Bronze............................... $100-200

Corvette, 1984, Gold.................................... $100-120

Corvette, 1984, Red... $55-65

Corvette, 1984, White...................................... $55-65

Corvette, 1978, Black $140-170

Corvette, 1978, Pace Car $135-160

Corvette, 1978, Red... $50-60

Corvette, 1978, White...................................... $40-50

Corvette, 1978, Yellow.................................... $40-50

Corvette, 1963, Black, Pa............................... $75-85

Corvette, 1963, Blue, N.Y. $90-100

Corvette, 1963, Red... $60-70

Corvette, 1963, Silver $50-60

Corvette, 1955, Black, New $110-140

Corvette, 1955, Copper, New........................ $90-100

Corvette, 1955, Red, New $110-140

Corvette, 1954, Blue, New $90-100

Corvette, 1953, White, New $100-120

Duesenburg

Convertible, Cream $130-140

Convertible, Dark Blue................................. $120-130

Convertible, Light Blue $80-100

Convertible Coupe, Gray $160-180

Ford

International Delivery Wagon, Black $80-90

International Delivery Wagon, Green.............. $80-90

Fire Chief, 1928 .... $120-130

Fire Chief, 1934 .... $60-70

Fire Pumper Truck, 1935 .... $45-60

Model A, Angelos Liquor $180-200

Model A, Parkwood Supply $140-170

Model A, 1903, Black.................................... $35-45

Model A, 1903, Red...................................... $35-45

Model A, 1928 .... $60-80

Model A Fire Truck, 1930 .... $130-170

Model T, 1913, Black $30-40

Model T, 1913, Green...................................... $30-40

Train Series: Combination Car, $55-65; Holiday Series: Carolers, $40-50; Presidential Series: Carolers 1988, $40-50.

Mustang, 1964, Black $100-125

Mustang, 1964, Red $35-45

Mustang, 1964, White $25-35

Paddy Wagon, 1930 .... $100-120

Phaeton, 1929 .... $40-50

Pickup Truck, 1935 .... $20-30

Police Car, 1929, Blue $75-85

Police Car, 1929, Yellow $350-450

Police Patrol Car, 1934 .... $60-70

Police Tow Truck, 1935 .... $20-30

Roadster, 1934, Cream, Pa., New $80-90

Thunderbird, 1956, Black $60-70

Thunderbird, 1956, Blue, Pa. $70-80

Thunderbird, 1956, Gray $50-60

Thunderbird, 1956, Green $60-70

Thunderbird, 1956, Yellow $50-60

Woodie Wagon, 1929 .... $50-60

Mercedes

1974, Blue $30-40

1974, Gold $60-80

1974, Green $30-40

1974, Mocha $30-40

1974, Red $30-40

1974, Sand Beige, Pa. $30-40

1974, Silver, Australia $140-160

1974, White $35-45

Trains

Baggage Car $40-60

Box Car, Brown $50-60

Box Car, Yellow $40-50

Bumper $5-8

Caboose, Gray $45-55

Caboose, Red $50-60

Casey Jones With Tender $65-80

Casey Jones Caboose $40-55

Casey Jones Accessory Set $50-60

Coal Tender, No Bottle $20-30

Combination Car $55-65

Dining Car $75-90

Flat Car $20-30

General Locomotive $60-70

Grant Locomotive $50-65

Log Car $40-55

Lumber Car $12-18

Observation Car $15-23

Passenger Car $45-53

Tank Car $15-20

Track $4-6

Turner Locomotive $80-100

Watertower $20-30

Wood Tender $40-45

Wood Tender, No Bottle $20-25

Other

Ambulance $18-22

Army Jeep $18-20

Bass Boat $12-18

Cable Car $25-35

Circus Wagon $20-30

Ernie's Flower Cart $20-30

Golf Cart $20-30

HC Covered Wagon, 1929 .... $10-20

Jewel Tea $70-80

Mack Fire Truck, 1917 .... $120-135

Mississippi Pumper Firetruck, 1867 .... $115-140

Oldsmobile, 1903 .... $25-35

Olsonite Eagle Racer $40-35

Police Patrol Car, 1934, Yellow $110-140

Space Shuttle $20-30

Stutz, 1914, Gray $40-50

Stutz, 1914, Yellow $40-50

Thomas Flyer, 1909, Blue $60-70

Thomas Flyer, 1909, Ivory $60-70

Vendome Wagon 40-50

Volkswagen, Blue $40-50

Volkswagen, Red $40-50

Bischoff Bottles

Bischoffs, which was founded in Trieste, Italy, in 1777, issued decorative figurals in the 18th century long before any other company. The early bottles are rare because of the limited production and the attrition of the bottles over the years.

Modern Bischoffs were imported into the United States beginning in 1949. Collectors haven't shown intense interest in modern imports, and since sales have not been made often enough for a reliable value to be established, prices for modern pieces are not included in this book.

Three other types of Bischoffs will be covered: Kord Bohemian decanters, Venetian glass figurals, and ceramic decanters and figurals.

Kord Bohemian Decanters

Kord Bohemian decanters were hand blown and hand painted glass bottles created in Czechoslovakia by the Kord Company with a tradition of Bohemian cut, engraved, etched, and flashed glass. Stoppers and labels with the bottles are considered very rare and valuable today. The cut glass and ruby-etched decanters were imported to the U.S. in the early 1950s, with the ruby-etched being considered rare only if complete with the stopper.

Most of these decanters were made with a matching set of glasses. The value will be even greater if the entire set is intact.

Amber Flowers, 1952
A two-toned glass decanter, 15-1/2", dark amber stopper **$30-40**

Amber Leaves, 1952
Multi-toned bottle with long neck, 13-1/2" **$30-40**

Anisette, 1948-1951
Clear glass bottle with ground glass stopper, 11" **$20-30**

Bohemian Ruby-Etched, 1949-1951
Round decanter, tapered neck, etched stopper, 15-1/2" **$30-40**

Coronet Crystal, 1952
Tall round bottle, multi-toned with a broad band of flowers, leaves, and scrolls, 14" **$30-40**

Cut Glass Decanter (Blackberry), 1951
Geometric design, handcut overall, ground stopper, 10-1/2" **$32-42**

Czech Hunter, 1958
Round thick clear glass, heavy round glass base, 8-1/2" **$18-26**

Czech Hunter's Lady, 1958
"Mae West" shaped decanter of cracked clear glass, 10" **$18-26**

Dancing – Country Scene, 1950
Clear glass handblown decanter with peasant boy and girl doing a country dance beside a tree, 12-1/4" **$25-35**

Dancing – Peasant Scene, 1950
Pale and amber glass decanter, peasants in costume dancing to music of bagpipes, 12" **$25-35**

Double – Dolphin, 1949-1969
Fish-shaped twin bottles joined at the bellies, handblown clear glass..**$20-30**

Flying Geese Pitcher, 1952
Green glass handle and stopper, glass base, 9-1/2" **$15-25**

Flying Geese Pitcher, 1957
Clear crystal handled pitcher, gold stopper,
9-1/2" **$15-25**

Horse Head, 1947-1969
Pale amber-colored bottle in the shape of a horse's
head, round pouring spout on top, 8" **$15-25**

Jungle Parrot – Amber Glass, 1952
Hand etched jungle scenes with a yellow amber color,
15-1/2" **$25-35**

Jungle Parrot – Ruby Glass, 1952
Hand etched jungle scenes with a ruby colored body,
15-1/2" **$20-30**

Old Coach Bottle, 1948
Pale amber color, round glass stopper, 10" **$25-35**

Old Sleigh Bottle, 1949
Glass decanter, handpainted, signed, 10" **$22-32**

Wild Geese – Amber Glass, 1952
Tall round decanter with tapering etched neck, flashed
with a yellow amber color, 15-1/2" **$25-35**

Wild Geese – Ruby Glass, 1952
Tall round decanter with tapering etched neck, flashed
with ruby red color, 15-1/2" **$25-35**

Venetian Glass Figurals

These figurals are produced in limited editions by the Serguso Glass Company in Morano, Italy, and are unique in design and color with birds, fish, cats, and dogs.

Black Cat, 1969
Glass black cat with curled tail, 12" l. **$18-25**

Dog – Alabaster, 1966
Seated alabaster glass dog, 13" **$33-45**

Dog – Dachschund, 1966
Alabaster long dog with brown tones, 19" l. **$40-50**

Duck, 1964
Alabaster glass tinted pink and green, long neck,
upraised wings, 11" l. **$42-52**

Fish – Multicolor, 1964
Round fat fish, alabaster glass, green, rose,
yellow **$18-25**

Fish – Ruby, 1969
Long, flat, ruby glass fish, 12" l. **$25-35**

Ceramic Decanters and Figurals

These are some of the most interesting, attractive, and valuable of the Bischoff collection and are made of ceramic, stoneware, and pottery. Decanters complete with handles, spouts, and stoppers conmand the highest value.

African Head, 1962	**$15-18**
Alpine Pitcher, 1969	**$25-30**
Amber Flower, 1952	**$30-35**
Amber Leaf, 1952	**$30-35**
Amphora, Two Handles, 1950	**$20-25**
Ashtray, Green Striped, 1958	**$10-15**
Bell House, 1960	**$30-40**
Bell Tower, 1960	**$15-30**
Boy (Chinese) Figural, 1962	**$30-40**
Boy (Spanish) Figural, 1961	**$25-35**
Candlestick, Antique, 1958	**$20-25**
Candlestick, Clown, 1963	**$8-10**
Canteen, Floral, 1969	**$15-20**
Canteen, Fruit, 1969	**$18-20**
Cat, Black, 1969	**$20-25**
Clown With Black Hair, 1963	**$30-40**
Clown With Red Hair, 1963	**$15-25**
Chariot Urn, 1966 (two sections)	**$20-25**
Christmas Tree, 1957	**$50-55**
Dachshund Figural	**$35-45**
Deer Figural, 1969	**$20-25**
Duck Figural	**$35-45**
Egyptian Dancing Figural, 1961	**$12-17**
Egyptian Pitcher, Two Musicians, 1969	**$15-24**
Egyptian Pitcher, Three Musicians, 1959	**$20-28**
Girl In Chinese Costume, 1962	**$30-40**
Girl In Spanish Costume, 1961	**$30-40**
Greek Vase Decanter, 1969	**$13-19**
Mask, Gray Face, 1963	**$16-26**
Porcelain Cameo, 1962	**$15-20**
Oil And Vinegar Cruets, Black And White, 1959	**$18-25**
Vase, Black And Gold, 1959	**$19-22**
Watchtower, 1960	**$12-16**

Borghini Bottles

Borghini bottles are ceramics of modernistic style with historical themes manufactured in Pisa, Italy. They vary greatly in price depending on location. The lowest values are in areas closest to the point of distribution or near heavy retail sales. Recent bottles are stamped "Borghini Collection Made In Italy."

Cats
Black with red ties, 6" $11-15

Cats
Black with red ties, 12" $10-15

Female Head
Ceramic, 9-1/2" $11-15

Penguin
Black and white, 6" $8-11

Penguin, 1969
Black and white, 12" $12-16

Fruit Bowl, 1970, $15-20; Penguin, 1969, $10-12; Cardinal, 1969, $10-12; Black Cat, 1969, $10-15.

Ezra Brooks Bottles

The Ezra Brooks Distilling Company began issuing figurals in 1964, 10 years after the Jim Beam company, and quickly became a strong rival because of their effective distribution, promotion techniques, unique design, and choice of subjects.

While many of the Brooks bottles depict the same themes as those of Jim Beam (Sports and Transportation series, for example), they also produced bottles based on original subjects. One is the Maine lobster, which looks good enough to put on anyone's dinner table. The most popular series depict antiques such as an Edison phonograph and a Spanish cannon. Yearly new editions highlight American historical events and anniversaries. One of my favorites is the Bucket of Blood (1970), a bucket-shaped bottle from the Virginia City, Nev., saloon by the same name. While Ezra Brooks bottles are still purchased for their contents, most of the figurals are bought by collectors.

Alabama Bicentennial, 1976 ....$12-14

American Legion, 1971
Distinguished embossed star emblem from
WWI $20-30

American Legion, 1972
Salutes Illinois American Legion 54th National
Convention $45-55

American Legion, 1973
Salutes Hawaii, which hosted the American Legion's
54th National Convention....................................$10-12

American Legion, Denver, 1977......................$19-22

American Legion, Miami Beach, 1973 ....$8-12

AMVETS, Dolphin, 1974 ....$8-10

AMVETS, Polish Legion, 1973 .... $14-18

Antique Cannon, 1969..$6-9

Antique Phonograph, 1970 ....$8-12

Arizona, 1969
Man with burro in search of Lost Dutchman Mine ..$4-8

Auburn 1932 Classic Car, 1978........................$18-20

Badger No. 1 Boxer, 1973 ....$9-11

Badger No. 2 Football, 1974 ....$10-14

Badger No. 3 Hockey, 1974 ....$9-12

Baltimore Oriole Wildlife, 1979........................$20-30

Bare Knuckle Fighter, 1971..................................$5-7

Baseball Hall Of Fame, 1973............................$20-22

Baseball Player, 1974 ....$14-16

Bear, 1968...$5-9

Beaver, 1973..$10-15

Bengal Tiger Wildlife, 1979 ....$20-30

Betsy Ross, 1975 ....$8-12

Bicycle, Penny-Farthington, 1973 ....$10-15

Big Bertha
Nugget Casino's very own elephant with a raised
trunk $10-13

Big Daddy Lounge, 1969
Salute to South Florida's state liquor chain and Big
Daddy Lounges $4-6

Bighorn Ram, 1973...$14-18

Bird Dog, 1971 ....$12-14

Bordertown
Salutes Borderline Club on border of California and
Nevada $5-10

Bowler, 1973 ....$4-6

Bowling Tenpins, 1973 ....$9-12

Brahma Bull, 1972...$10-12

Bucket Of Blood, 1970
Salutes the famous Virginia City, Nev., saloon. Bucket-
shaped bottle $5-7

Bucking Bronco, Rough Rider, 1973...................$7-9

Bucky Badger, Football...................................$20-25

Bucky Badger, Hockey, 1975 ....$18-24

Bucky Badger, No. 1 Boxer, 1973 ....$9-12

Buffalo Hunter, 1971 ....$5-7

Bulldog, 1972
Mighty canine mascot and football symbol $10-14

Bull Moose, 1973 ....$12-15

Busy Beaver $4-7

Cabin Still $20-35

Cable Car, 1968..$5-6

California Quail, 1970 ....$8-10

Canadian Honker, 1975 ....$9-12

Canadian Loon Wildlife, 1979 ....$25-35

Cardinal, 1972 ....$20-25

Casey At Bat, 1973 ....$6-10

Ceremonial Indian, 1970 ....$15-18

CB Convoy Radio, 1976 ....$5-9

Charolais Beef, 1973 ....$10-14

Cheyenne Shoot-Out, 1970
Honoring the Wild West and its Cheyenne Frontier
Days $6-10

Chicago Fire, 1974...$20-30

Chicago Water Tower, 1969 ....$8-12

Christmas Decanter, 1966....................................$5-8

Christmas Tree, 1979...$13-17

Churchill, 1970
Commemorating "Iron Curtain" speech at Westminster
College by Churchill $5-9

Cigar Store Indian, 1968.......................................$4-6

Classic Firearms, 1969
Embossed gun set consisting of Derringer, Colt 45,
Peacemaker, Over and Under Flintlock, and Pepper
Box $15-19

Clowns, Imperial Shrine, 1978...........................$9-11

Clown Bust No. I, Smiley, 1979.......................$22-28

Clown Bust No. 2, Cowboy, 1979 ....$20-25

Clown Bust No. 3, Pagliacci, 1979 ....$15-22

Clown Bust No. 4, Keystone Cop....................$30-40

Clown Bust No. 5, Cuddles.............................$20-30

Clown Bust No. 6, Tramp $20-30

Clown With Accordion, 1971 ....$15-18

Clown With Balloon, 1973...............................$20-32

Club Bottle, Birthday Cake $9-12

Club Bottle, Distillery $9-12

Club Bottle, 1973
The third commemorative Ezra Brooks Collectors Club
in the shape of America.......................................$14-18

Clydesdale Horse, 1973 ....$8-12

Colt Peacemaker Flask, 1969.............................$4-8

Conquistadors
Tribute to the great Drum and Bugle Corps $6-9

Conquistadors Drum And Bugle, 1972 ....$12-15

Corvette Indy Pace Car, 1978 ....$45-55

Corvette 1957 Classic, 1976 ....$110-140

Court Jester $5-7

Dakota Cowboy, 1975 ....$34-44

Dakota Cowgirl, 1976.......................................$20-26

Dakota Grain Elevator, 1978 ....$20-30

Dakota Shotgun Express, 1977 ....$18-22

Dead Wagon, 1970
Made to carry gunfight loser to Boot Hill $5-7

Delta Belle, 1969...$6-7

Democratic Convention, 1976.........................$10-16

Derringer Flask, 1969 ....$5-8

Distillery, 1970
Reproduction of the Ezra Brooks Distillery in Kentucky
....$9-11

Duesenberg..$24-33

Elephant, 1973 ....$7-9

Elk
Salutes those organizations who practice benevolence
and charity...$20-28

English Setter, Bird Dog, 1971 ....$14-17

Equestrienne, 1974..$7-10

Esquire, Ceremonial Dancer............................$10-16

Farthington Bike, 1972 ....$6-8

Fire Engine, 1971 ....$14-18

Fireman, 1975...$18-23

Fisherman, 1974 ....$8-12

Flintlock, (Two Versions; Japanese And Heritage), 1969
Japanese...$7-9
Heritage...$12-16

Florida "Gators," 1973
Tribute to the University of Florida Gators Football
Team...$9-11

Foe Eagle, 1978...$15-20

Foe Flying Eagle, 1979 ....$20-25

Foe Eagle, 1980..$25-40

Foe Eagle, 1981..$18-28

Football Player, 1974 ....$10-14

Ford Mustang Pace Car, 1979 ....$25-35

Ford Thunderbird 1956, 1976.........................$70-80

Foremost Astronaut, 1970
Tribute to major liquor supermart, Foremost Liquor
Store..$5-7

Fresno Decanter $5-12

Fresno Grape With Gold $48-60

Fresno Grape, 1970 ....$6-11

Gamecock, 1970..$9-13

Go Big Red No. 1, No. 2, And No. 3 – Football Shaped Bottle
No. 1 with football, 1972 ....$20-28
No. 2 with hat, 1971 ....$18-22
No. 3 with rooster, 1972 ....$10-14

Golden Antique Cannon, 1969
Symbol of Spanish power $5-7

Golden Eagle, 1971..$18-22

Golden Grizzly Bear, 1970 ....$4-6

Golden Horseshoe, 1970
Salute to Reno's Horseshoe Club $7-9

Golden Rooster No. 1
Replica of solid gold rooster on display at Nugget
Casino in Reno, Nev. $35-50

Gold Prospector, 1969...$5-9

Gold Seal, 1972 ....$12-14

Gold Turkey $35-45

Go Tiger Go, 1973..$10-14

Grandfather Clock, 1970 ....$5-7

Grandfather Clock, 1970...................................$12-20

Greater Greensboro Open, 1972 ....$16-19

Greater Greensboro Open, 1972 ....$15-20

Greater Greensboro Open Golfer, 1973 ....$17-24

Greater Greensboro Open Map, 1974..............$29-36

Greater Greensboro Open Cup, 1975 ....$25-30

Greater Greensboro Open Club And Ball, 1977
....$20-25

Great Stone Face, Old Man Of The Mountain, 1970
....$10-14

Great White Shark, 1977 ....$8-14

Hambletonian, 1971..$13-16

Happy Goose, 1975 ....$12-15

Harolds Club Red Dice, 1968...............................$8-12

Hereford, 1971 ....$12-15

Hereford, 1972 ....$12-15

Historical Flask Eagle, 1970 ....$3-5

Historical Flask Flagship, 1970 ....$3-5

Historical Flask Liberty, 1970 ....$3-5

Historical Flask Old Ironsides, 1970 ....$3-5

Historical Flask, 1970..$3-5

Hollywood Cops, 1972 ....$12-18

Hopi Indian, 1970
Kachina Doll $15-20

Hopi Kachina, 1973..$50-75

Horseshoe Casino Gold $8-10

Idaho, Ski The Potato, 1973
Salutes the State of Idaho......................................$8-10

Indianapolis 500...$30-35

Indy Pace Car, 1978..$50-60

Indian Ceremonial, 1970 ....$13-18

Indian Hunter, 1970..$12-15

Iowa Farmer, 1977 ....$55-65

Iowa Grain Elevator, 1978 ....$25-34

Iron Horse Locomotive $8-14

Jack O'Diamonds, 1969 ....$4-6

Jay Hawk, 1969..$6-8

Jester, 1971 ....$6-8

Jug, Old Time 1.75 Liter $9-13

Kachina Doll No. 1, 1971 ....$80-100

Kachina Doll No. 2, 1973 ....$10-60

Kachina Doll No. 3, 1974 ....$50-60

Kachina Doll No. 4, 1975 ....$20-25

Kachina Doll No. 5, 1976 ....$30-40

Kachina Doll No. 6, 1977 ....$25-35

Kachina Doll No. 7, 1978 ....$35-45

Kachina Doll No. 8, 1979 ....$50-60

Kansas Jayhawk, 1969 ....$4-7

Katz Cats, 1969
Siamese cats are symbolic of Katz Drug Co. of Kansas
City, Kan. $8-12

Katz Cats Philharmonic, 1970
Commemorating its 27th annual Star Night $6-10

Keystone Cop, 1980 ....$32-40

Keystone Cops, 1971 ....$25-35

Killer Whale, 1972 ....$15-20

King Of Clubs, 1969 ....$4-6

King Salmon, 1971 ....$18-24

Liberty Bell, 1970 ....$5-6

Lincoln Continental Mark I, 1941 ....$20-25

Lion On The Rock, 1971 ....$5-7

Liquor Square, 1972 ....$5-7

Little Giant, 1971
Replica of the first horse-drawn steam engine to arrive
at the Chicago fire in 1871 ....$11-16

Maine Lighthouse, 1971 ....$18-24

Maine Lobster, 1970 ....$15-18

Mako Shark, 1962 and 1979 ....$15-20

Man-O-War, 1969 ....$10-16

M & M Brown Jug, 1975b $15-20

Map, Usa Club Bottle, 1972 ....$7-9

Masonic Fez, 1976 ....$12-15

Max, The Hat, Zimmerman, 1976 ....$20-25

Military Tank, 1971 ....$15-22

Minnesota Hockey Player, 1975 ....$18-22

Minuteman, 1975 ....$10-15

Missouri Mule, Brown, 1972 ....$7-9

Moose, 1973 ....$20-28

Motorcycle $10-14

Mountaineer, 1971
One of the most valuable Ezra Brooks figural
bottles $40-55

Mr. Foremost, 1969 ....$7-10

Mr. Maine Potato, 1973 ....$6-10

Mr. Merchant, 1970 ....$6-10

Mule $8-12

Mustang Indy Pace Car, 1979 ....$20-30

Nebraska – Go Big Red! $12-15

New Hampshire State House, 1970 ....$9-13

North Carolina Bicentennial, 1975 ....$8-12

Nugget Classic
Replica of golf pin presented to golf tournament
participants $7-12

Oil Gusher $6-8

Old Capital, 1971 ....$30-40

Old EZ No. 1 Barn Owl, 1977 ....$25-35

Old EZ No. 2 Eagle Own, 1978 ....$40-55

Old EZ No. 3 Show Owl, 1979 ....$20-35

Old Man Of The Mountain, 1970 ....$10-14

Old Water Tower, 1969
Famous landmark, survived the Chicago fire of
1071 ....$12-16

Oliver Hardy Bust $12-18

Ontario 500, 1970 ....$18-22

Overland Express, 1969 ....$17-20

Over-Under Flintlock Flask, 1969 ....$6-9

Panda – Giant, 1972 ....$12-17

Penguin, 1972 ....$8-10

Penny Farthington High-Wheeler, 1973 ....$9-12

Pepperbox Flask, 1969 ....$4-6

Phoenix Bird, 1971 ....$20-26

Phoenix Jaycees, 1973 ....$10-14

Phonograph $15-20

Piano, 1970 ....$12-13

Pirate, 1971 ....$6-10

Polish Legion American Vets, 1978 ....$18-26

Portland Head Lighthouse, 1971
Honors the lighthouse that has guided ships safely into
Maine Harbor since 1791 ....$18-24

Pot-Bellied Stove, 1968 ....$5-6

Queen Of Hearts, 1969
Playing card symbol with royal flush in hearts on front
of the bottle $4-6

Raccoon Wildlife, 1978 ....$30-40

Ram, 1973 ....$13-18

Razorback Hog, 1969 ....$12-18

Razorback Hog, 1979 ....$20-30

Red Fox, 1979 ....$30-40

Reno Arch, 1968
Honoring the Biggest Little City in the World, Reno,
Nev. $4-8

Sailfish, 1971 ....$7-11

Salmon, Washington King, 1971 ....$20-26

San Francisco Cable Car, 1968 ....$4-8

Sea Captain, 1971..$10-14

Sea Lion, Gold, 1972..$11-14

Senators Of The US, 1972
Honors the Senators of the United States of
America $10-13

Setter, 1974 ....$10-15

Shrine King Tut Guard, 1979............................$16-24

1804 Silver Dollar, 1970 ....$8-10

Silver Saddle, 1973 ....$22-25

Silver Spur Boot, 1971
Cowboy-boot-shaped bottle with silver spur buckled
on "Silver Spur-Carson City Nevada" embossed on
side of boot $7-11

Simba, 1971..$9-12

Ski Boot, 1972 ....$5-7

Slot Machine, 1971
A replica of the original nickel Liberty Bell slot machine
invented by Charles Fey in 1895 ....$18-24

Snowmobiles, 1972 ....$8-11

South Dakota Air National Guard, 1976...........$18-22

Spirit Of '76, 1974 ....$5-7

Spirit Of St. Louis, 50th Anniversary, 1977 ....$6-11

Sprint Car Racer...$30-40

Stagecoach, 1969 ....$10-12

Stan Laurel Bust, 1976 ....$10-16

Stock Market Ticker, 1970
A unique replica of a ticker-tape machine.............$8-11

Stonewall Jackson, 1974 ....$22-28

Strongman, 1974..$8-12

Sturgeon, 1975..$20-28

John L. Sullivan, 1970..$15-20

Syracuse, New York, 1973 ....$11-16

Tank, Patton, 1972
Reproduction of a U.S. Army tank $16-20

Tecumseh, 1969
Figurehead of the U.S.S. Delaware, this decanter is an
embossed replica of the statue at the United States
Naval Academy $5-6

Telephone, 1971
Replica of the old-time upright handset
telephone..$16-19

Tennis Player, 1972 ....$8-12

Terrapin, Maryland, 1974...................................$14-16

Texas Longhorn, 1971 ....$18-22

Ticker Tape, 1970...$8-12

Tiger On Stadium, 1973
Commemorates college teams who have chosen the
tiger as their mascot..$12-17

Tom Turkey..$18-24

Tonopah, 1972 ....$12-15

Totem Pole, 1972 ....$10-14

Tractor, 1971
A model of the 1917 Fordson made by Henry
Ford $9-11

Trail-Bike Rider, 1972 ....$10-12

Trojan Horse, 1974...$15-18

Trojans, USC Football, 1973 ....$10-14

Trout & Fly, 1970..$7-11

Truckin' & Vannin', 1977 ....$7-12

Vermont Skier, 1972...$10-12

VFW, Veterans Of Foreign Wars, 1973 ....$6-10

Virginia, Red Cardinal, 1973 ....$15-20

Walgreen Drugs, 1974 ....$16-24

Weirton Steel, 1973..$15-18

Western Rodeos, 1973 ....$17-23

West Virginia, Mountaineer, 1971.....................$65-75

West Virginia, Mountain Lady, 1972.................$14-20

Whale, 1972..$14-20

Wheat Shocker, 1971
The mascot of the Kansas football team in a fighting
pose..$5-7

Whiskey Flasks, 1970
Reproduction of collectible American patriotic whiskey
flasks of the 1800s: Old Ironsides, Miss Liberty,
American Eagle, Civil War Commemorative........$12-14

Whitetail Deer, 1974...$18-24

White Turkey, 1971...$20-25

Wichita...$4-8

Wichita Centennial, 1970 ....$4-6

Winston Churchill, 1969 ....$6-10

Zimmerman's Hat, 1968
A salute to "Zimmerman's-World's Largest Liquor
Store" $5-6

J.W. Dant Bottles

The J.W. Dant Distilling Company produces bottles similar to the Brooks and Beam bottles, which gives them strong collector appeal. They usually portray American themes such as patriotic events and folklore in addition to various types of animals.

Because Dant has such an affinity for American history and its traditions, most bottles are decorated in full color. Some bottles carry an embossed American eagle and shield with stars. The bottles are limited editions and the molds are not reused.

Alamo, 1969	$4-6	Fort Sill Centennial, 1969	$7-11
American Legion, 1969	$3-7	Patrick Henry, 1969	$4-7
Atlantic City, 1969	$4-6	Indianapolis 500, 1969	$7-11
Bobwhite, 1969	$6-8	Mountain Quail, 1969	$7-9
Boeing 747	$5-8	Mt. Rushmore, 1969	$5-9
Boston Tea Party, eagle to left	$4-6	Prairie Chicken	$5-7
Boston Tea Party, eagle to right	$9-12	Reverse Eagle	$5-8
Bourbon	$3-5	Ring-Necked Pheasant	$7-9
Paul Bunyan, 1969	$5-7	Ruffed Grouse, 1969	$4-7
California Quail, 1969	$7-9	San Diego Harbor, 1969	$4-6
Chukar Partridge	$7-9	Speedway 500	$6-9
Clear Tip Pinch	$7-9	Stove, Pot Belly, 1966	$9-11
Constitution And Guerriere	$5-7	Washington Crossing Delaware	$5-7
Duel Between Burr And Hamilton	$8-106	Woodcock, 1969	$6-9
Eagle	$6-9	Wrong-Way Charlie	$15-20

Garnier Bottles

Garnet Et Cie, a French firm founded in 1858, has long been given credit as the pioneer of the modern collectible liquor bottle because it introduced Garnier figural bottles in 1899. During Prohibition and World War II, production temporarily halted, but resumed in the 1950s.

Bottles manufactured before World War II are the rarest and most valuable but are not listed in this book due to the difficulty in establishing accurate prices. Among these are the Cat (1930), Clown (1910), Country Jug (1937), Greyhound (1930), Penguin (1930), and the Marquise (1931).

Aladdin's Lamp, 1963 ....$40-50

Alfa Romeo 1913, 1970....................................$20-30

Alfa Romeo 1929, 1969....................................$20-30

Alfa Romeo Racer, 1969...................................$20-30

Antique Coach, 1970 ....$25-30

Apollo, 1969
Apollo Spaceship, 13-1/2" $17-22

Aztec Vase, 1965...$15-20

Baby Foot, Soccer Shoe, 1963
Black with white trim 3-3/4" x 8-1/2" $10-20
1962 soccer shoe, large $7-11

Baby Trio, 1963 .... $7-10

Baccus Figural, 1967 .... $20-25

Bahamas
Black policeman, white jacket and hat, black pants, red stripe, gold details...$15-24

Baltimore Oriole, 1970..................................... $10-16

Bandit Figural, 1958.. $10-14

Cardinal; Robin; Goldfinch; Mockingbird; Road Runner, all 1971, $10-15 (all).

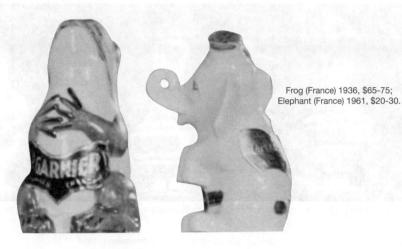

Frog (France) 1936, $65-75;
Elephant (France) 1961, $20-30.

Bedroom Candlestick, 1967 ...... $20-25	Clown Holding Tuba, 1955 ...... $15-25
Bellows, 1969 ...... $14-21	Coffee Mill, 1966 ...... $20-30
Bird Ashtray, 1958 ...... $3-4	Coffee Pot, 1962 ...... $30-35
Bluebird, 1970 ...... $12-18	Columbine Figural, 1968
Bouquet, 1966 ...... $15-25	Female partner $20-30
	Harlequin $30-40
Bull (And Matador) Animal Figural, 1963 ...... $17-23	Diamond Bottle, 1969 ...... $10-15
Burmese Man Vase, 1965 ...... $15-25	Drunkard, Drunk On Lamppost $15-20
Canada $11-14	Duckling Figural, 1956 ...... $18-26
Candlestick, 1955 ...... $25-35	Duo, 1954
Candlestick Glass, 1965 ...... $15-25	Two clear glass bottles stacked, two pouring
Cannon, 1964 ...... $50-60	spouts $12-18
Cardinal State Bird, Illinois, 1969 ...... $12-15	Egg Figural, 1956 ...... $70-80
Cat, Black, 1962 ...... $15-25	Eiffel Tower, 1951
Cat, Gray, 1962 ...... $15-25	13-1/2" $15-25
	12-1/2" $14-20
Chalet, 1955 ...... $40-50	Elephant Figural, 1961 ...... $20-30
Chimney, 1956 ...... $55-65	Empire Vase, 1962 ...... $10-18
Chinese Dog, 1965 ...... $15-25	Fiat 500 1913, 1970
Chinese Statuette, Man, 1970 ...... $15-25	Yellow Body $20-30
Chinese Statuette, Woman, 1970 ...... $15-25	Fiat Neuvo 1913, 1970
Christmas Tree, 1956 ...... $60-70	Blue body $20-30
Citroen 1922, 1970 ...... $20-30	Flask Garnier, 1958 ...... $9-12
Classic Ashtray, 1958 ...... $20-30	Flying Horse Pegasus, 1958 ...... $50-60
Clock, 1958 ...... $20-30	Football Player, 1970 ...... $13-17
	Ford 1913, 1970 ...... $20-30
Clown's Head, 1931 ...... $65-75	Fountain, 1964 ...... $25-35

Nice Pitcher; Centaur Pitcher; Biarritz Pitcher; Pegasus Pitcher; Deauville Pitcher, all 1971, $20-25 Ea (all).

Giraffe, 1961 ....$20-35

Goldfinch, 1970..$12-16

Goose, 1955 ....$14-24

Grenadier, 1949..$55-65

Guitar And Mandolin $20-25

Harlequin Standing, 1968................................$13-19

Harlequin With Mandolin, 1958 ....$30-40

Hockey Player, 1970 ....$15-20

Horse Pistol, 1964..$15-25

Hula Hoop, 1959 ....$25-30

Hunting Vase, 1964..$25-35

Hussar, 1949
French Cavalry soldier of 1800s...........................$25-35

India $10-15

Indian, 1958 ....$15-20

Indy 500, No. 1, 1970 ....$35-40

Jockey, 1961 ....$25-35

Lancer, 1949 ....$15-22

Locomotive, 1969 ....$15-25

Log, Round, 1958..$20-30

London, Bobby...$12-18

Loon, 1970...$10-18

Maharajah, 1958 ....$70-80

Mallard Duck...$15-20

M.G. (1933), 1970 ....$15-25

Mockingbird, 1970..$8-14

Montmartre Jug, 1960......................................$12-18

Monuments, 1966
A cluster of Parisian monuments $15-25

Napoleon On Horseback, 1969 ....$20-30

Nature Girl, 1959 ....$10-15

New York Policeman $9-13

Packard (1930), 1970..$20-30

Painting, 1961 ....$25-35

Paris, French Policeman................................$10-15

Paris Taxis, 1960 ....$20-30

Partridge, 1961..$25-35

Pheasant, 1969 ....$25-35

Pigeon, Clear Glass, 1958..............................$10-15

Pony, 1961 ....$25-35

Poodle, 1954..$12-15

Rainbow Trout...$20-25

Renault (1911), 1969 ....$20-30

Road Runner, 1969 ....$10-15

Robin, 1970 ....$10-15

Rocket, 1958 ....$10-15

Rolls Royce (1908), 1970..................................$20-30

Rooster, 1952 ....$15-25

Saint Tropez Jug, 1961b..................................$20-30

Scarecrow, 1960 ....$25-35

Sheriff, 1958 ....$15-25

Snail, 1950 ....$58-68

Soccer Shoe, 1962...$30-40

Soldier With Drum And Rifle...........................$15-20

S.S. France, Large, 1962 .... $80-130	**Valley Quail,** 1969 .... $8-12
S.S. France, Small, 1962 .... $50-60	**Violin,** 1966 .... $30-36
S.S. Queen Mary, 1970 .... $25-35	**Watch, Antique,** 1966 .... $20-30
Stanley Steamer (1907), 1970 .... $20-30	**Water Pitcher,** 1965 .... $12-18
Teapot, 1961 .... $15-25	**Woman With Jug** $20-25
Teapot, 1935 .... $20-30	**Young Deer Vase,** 1964 .... $25-35
Trout, 1967 .... $17-22	

Hoffman Bottles

Hoffman bottles are considered limited editions, since each issue is restricted in quantity produced. Once the predetermined number is reached, the molds are destroyed, which quickly establishes the designs as rare, collectible, and valuable.

While these bottles often depict European figures in various occupations, they have also focused on American subjects, such as the 1976 Centennial bottle and the 1976 Hippie bottle.

Bears and Cubs, 1977, $10-20; Duck Decoy, 1976, $15-20; Leprechaun "Mr." Carpenter, 1979, $20-25.

Bicentennial Series
4/5 Qt. Size

Betsy Ross With Music Box
"Star Spangled Banner" $30-40

Generation Gap
Depicts "100 Years of Progress," 2 oz. size $30-38

Majestic Eagle With Music Box
"America the Beautiful" $60-80

Cheerleader Series

Dallas, 1979 .... $30-35

Houston, 1980 .... $25-30

Rams, 1980 .... $25-30

St. Louis, 1980 .... $25-30

Washington, 1980 .... $25-30

Children Of The World Series

France With Music Box, 1979 .... $30-35

Jamaica With Music Box, 1979 .... $30-35

Mexico With Music Box, 1979 .... $30-35

Panama With Music Box, 1979 .... $30-35

Spain With Music Box, 1979 .... $30-35

Yugoslavia With Music Box, 1979 .... $30-35

Occupation Series

Mr. Bartender With Music Box
"He's a Jolly Good Fellow" $25-30

Mr. Charmer With Music Box
"Glow Little Glow Worm" $10-15

Mr. Dancer With Music Box
"The Irish Washerwoman" $18-22

Mr. Doctor With Music Box
"As Long as He Needs Me" $20-25

Mr. Fiddler With Music Box
"Hearts and Flowers" $20-22

Mr. Guitarist With Music Box
"Johnny Guitar" $20-22

Mr. Harpist With Music Box
"Do-Re-Mi" $10-15

Mr. Lucky With Music Box
"When Irish Eyes Are Smiling" $15-20

Mrs. Lucky With Music Box
"The Kerry Dancer" $12-15

Mr. Policeman With Music Box
"Don't Blame Me" $30-35

Mr. Sandman With Music Box
"Mr. Sandman" $10-20

Mr. Saxophonist With Music Box
"Tiger Rag" $15-20

Mr. Shoe Cobbler With Music Box
"Danny Boy" $15-20

C.M. Russell Series
4/5 Qt. Size

Buffalo Man, 1976 .... $20-25

Cowboy, 1978 .... $30-35

Flathead Squaw, 1976 .... $15-20

Half-Breed Trader, 1978 .... $40-45

I Rode Him, 1978 .... $35-40

Indian Buffalo Hunter, 1978 .... $40-45

Last Of Five Thousand, 1975 .... $14-18

Northern Cree, 1978 .... $35-40

Prospector, 1976 .... $25-30

Red River Breed, 1976 .... $23-30

The Scout, 1978 .... $30-40

The Stage Coach Driver, 1976 .... $20-30

The Stage Robber, 1978 .... $45-50

Trapper, 1976 .... $20-30

Pistol Series With Stand

Civil War Colt, 1975 .... $25-35

Dodge City Frontier, 1975 .... $25-35

.45 Automatic, 1975 .... $25-35

German Luger, 1975 .... $20-30

Kentucky Flintlock, 1975 .... $30-35

The Lawman, 1978 .... $35-40

The Outlaw, 1978 .... $35-40

Pistol Framed Series

Civil War Colt, 1978 .... $30-35

Derringer, Gold, 1978 .... $25-30

Derringer, Silver, 1978 .... $25-30

Dodge City Frontier, 1978 .... $30-35

.45 Automatic, 1978 .... $30-35	**Lawman,** 1978 .... $15-20
German Luger, 1978 .... $30-35	**Outlaw,** 1978 .... $15-20
Kentucky Flintlock, 1978 .... $15-20	

Japanese Bottles

While bottle making in Japan has always been an ancient art, the collectible bottles now produced are mainly for export. Even though these bottles are available in higher numbers in the American market, prices have remained reasonable.

Daughter, 1970 .... $15-20

Faithful Retainer, 1970 .... $25-35

"Kiku" Geisha, Blue 13-1/4", 1970 .... $20-30

Maiden, 1970 .... $20-25

Noh Mask, 1961 .... $40-45

Okame Mask, 1961 .... $40-45

Playboy, 1970 .... $20-25

Princess, 1970 .... $20-25

Sake God, Colorful Robe, Porcelain 10",
1969 .... $20-30

Sake God, White, Bone China 10", 1969 .... $12-15

"Yuri" Geisha, Pink, Red Sash 13-1/4", 1969 ... $35-45

House Of Koshu

Angel, With Book 7 Oz. $5-10

Child, Sitting On A Barrel 17 Oz. $5-10

Beethoven Bust 7 Oz. $5-10

Centurian Bust 7 Oz. $5-10

House of Koshu - "Boy"
- 1969, $20-25.

Children 7 Oz. $7-10

Declaration Of Independence $4-6

Geisha, Blue, 1969 .... $40-45

Geisha, Cherry Blossom, 1969 .... $30-35

Geisha, Lily, 1969 .... $25-35

Geisha, Violet, 1969 .... $30-40

Geisha, Wisteria, 1969 .... $30-40

Geisha, Lavender With Fan, 1969 .... $45-50

Geisha, Reclining, 1969 .... $60-70

Geisha, Sitting, 1969 .... $45-50

Lantern, Doro, 1961 .... $55-65

Lionman, Red, 1967 .... $25-35

Lionman, White, 1969 .... $35-40

Pagoda, Green, 1969 .... $25-30

Pagoda, White, 1961 .... $20-25

Pagoda, Gold, 1970 .... $15-20

Sailor With A Pipe, 1969 .... $6-10

Kamotsuru Bottles

Daokoru, God Of Wealth, 1965 .... $15-20

Ebisu, God Of Fishermen, 1965 .... $15-20

Fukurokujin, God Of Wisdom, 1965 .... $15-20

Goddess Of Art, 1965 .... $15-20

Golden House, 1969 .... $15-20

Hotei, God Of Wealth, 1965 .... $15-20

Jurojin, God Of Longevity, 1965 .... $15-20

Sedan Chair, 1966 .... $15-20

Treasure Tower, 1966 .... $20-25

Kentucky Gentlemen Bottles

These bottles are similar in design to the Beam and Brooks bottles but are released less frequently. Generally they depict costumes of various periods of American history, most notably around the Civil War.

Confederate Infantry
In gray uniform with sword, 13-1/2" $10-15

Frontiersman (1969)
Coonskin cap, fringed buckskin, powder horn, long rifle, 14" $12-15

Pink Lady (1969)
Long bustle skirt, feathered hat, pink parasol, 13-1/4" $20-32

Kentucky Gentleman (1969)
Figural bottle, frock coat, top hat and cane, "Old Colonel," gray ceramic, 14" $12-15

Revolutionary War Officer
In dress uniform and boots, holding sword, 14" $12-16

Union Army Sergeant
In dress uniform with sword, 14" $9-13

Lionstone Bottles

Lionstone bottles, manufactured by Lionstone Distillery, reflect a great deal of detail and realism in their designs. As an example, their bottle "Shoot-Out at O.K. Corral" consists of three bottles with nine figures and two horses.

The Lionstone bottles are issued in series, such as the Sport, Circus, and Bicentennial series. The most popular among collectors is the Western series. Since the prices of these bottles have continued to stay firm, collectors should watch for old uncirculated stock.

Bar Scene No. 1, 1970	$125-140	Cherry Valley Club, Gold, 1971	$25-35
Bartender, 1969	$35-40	Cherry Valley Club, Silver, 1971	$35-45
Belly Robber, 1969	$15-20	Chinese Laundryman, 1969	$15-20
Blacksmith, 1973	$25-30	Annie Christmas, 1969	$20-25
Molly Brown, 1973	$30-35	Annie Oakley, 1969	$25-35
Buffalo Hunter, 1973	$25-35	Circuit Judge, 1969	$15-20
Calamity Jane, 1973	$35-40	Corvette, 1.75 Liters	$60-75
Camp Cook, 1969	$25-30	Country Doctor, 1969	$12-18
Camp Follower, 1969	$25-30	Cowboy, 1969	$15-20
Canadian Goose, 1980	$75-100	Frontiersman, 1969	$14-16
Casual Indian, 1969	$8-12	Gambels Quail, 1969	$15-20
Cavalry Scout, 1969	$8-12	Gentleman Gambler, 1969	$25-35

Old Time Steam Engine, 1976, $20-25; Insignia of "I.A.F.F.", 1976, $20-25; Old Time Fire Engine, 1976, $20-30.

Top Row: Proud Indian, 1969, $10-15; Cowboy, 1969, $15-20; Gambler, 1969, $25-35.

Bottom Row: Casual Indian, 1969, $8-12; Cavalry Scout, 1969, $8-12; Sheriff, 1969, $10-12.

God Of Love, 1969 .... $17-22	Mint Bar With Nude And Frame $1,000-1,250
God Of War, 1978 .... $35-40	Mountain Man, 1969 .... $15-20
Goddess Of War, 1978 .... $35-40	Pintail Duck, 1969 .... $40-55
Gold Panner, 1969 .... $15-20	Proud Indian, 1969 .... $10-15
Highway Robber, 1969 .... $15-20	Railroad Engineer, 1969 .... $15-18
Jesse James, 1969 .... $18-23	Renegade Trader, 1969 .... $15-18
Johnny Lightining #1, Gold, 1972 .... $50-65	Riverboat Captain, 1969 .... $10-15
Judge Roy Bean, 1973 .... $20-30	Roadrunner, 1969 .... $28-36
Lonely Luke, 1974 .... $35-45	Saturday Night Bath, 1976 .... $60-70
Lucky Buck, 1974 .... $35-40	Sheepherder, 1969 .... $50-60
Mallard Duck, 1972 .... $35-45	Sheriff, 1969 .... $10-12
Miniatures, Western (Six) $85-110	Sod Buster, 1969 .... $13-16
Mint Bar With Frame, 1970 .... $700-900	Squawman, 1969 .... $20-30

Stagecoach Driver, 1969 .... $45-60

STP Turbocar, Red, 1972 .... $25-35

STP Turbocar With Gold And Platinum (Pair), 1972 .... $150-185

Telegrapher, 1969 .... $15-20

Tinker, 1974 .... $25-35

Tribal Chief, 1973 .... $25-35

Al Unser No. 1 .... $15-20

Wells Fargo Man, 1969 .... $8-12

Woodhawk, 1969 .... $35-40

Bicentennial Series

Firefigher No. 1, 1972 .... $110-120

Firefighter No. 3, 1975 .... $55-65

Mail Carrier, 1975 .... $25-30

Molly Pitcher, 1975 .... $25-30

Paul Revere, 1975 .... $25-30

Betsy Ross, 1975 .... $25-30

Sons Of Freedom, 1975 .... $25-35

George Washington, 1975 .... $25-30

Winter At Valley Forge, 1975 .... $30-35

Bicentennial Westerns

Barber, 1976 .... $30-40

Indian Weaver, 1976 .... $30-35

Photographer, 1976 .... $35-40

Rainmaker, 1976 .... $22-28

Trapper, 1976 .... $30-35

Capistrano Swallow, 1974, $15-20.

Bird Series, 1972-1974

Bluebird, Eastern $18-24

Bluebird, Wisconsin $20-30

Bluejay $20-25

Peregrine Falcon $15-18

Meadowlark $15-20

Mourning Doves $50-70

Swallow $15-18

Circus Series (Miniatures), 1973

The Baker $10-15

Burmese Lady $10-15

Fat Lady $10-15

Fire-Eater $10-15

Giant With Midget $10-15

Giraffe-Necked Lady $10-14

Snake Charmer $10-15

Strong Man $10-15

Sword Swallower $10-15

Tattooed Lady $10-15

Dog Series (Miniatures), 1975-1977

Boxer $10-15

Cocker Spaniel $9-12

Collie $10-15

Pointer $10-15

Poodle $10-15

European Worker Series, 1974

The Cobbler $20-35

The Horseshoer $20-35

The Potter $20-35

The Silversmith $25-35

The Watchmaker $20-35

The Woodworker $20-35

Oriental Worker Series, 1974

Basket Weaver $25-35

Egg Merchant $25-35

Gardner $25-35

Sculptor $25-35

Tea Vendor $25-35

Timekeeper $25-35

Sports Series, 1974-1980

Baseball $22-30

Basketball $22-30

Boxing $22-30

Football $22-30

Hockey $22-30

Tropical Bird Series (Miniatures), 1974

Blue-Crowned Chlorophonia $12-16

Emerald Toucanet $12-16

Northern Royal Flycatcher $12-16

Painted Bunting $12-16

Scarlet Macaw $12-16

Yellow-Headed Amazon $12-16

Miscellaneous Lionstone Bottles, 1971-1974

Buccaneer $25-35

Cowgirl $45-55

Dancehall Girl $50-55

Falcon $15-25

Firefighter No. 2 .... $80-100

Firefighter No. 3 .... $25-35

Firefighter No. 5, 60th Anniversary $22-27

Firefighter No. 6, Fire Hydrant $40-45

Firefighter No. 6, In Gold Or Silver $250-350

Firefighter No. 7, Helmet $60-90

Firefighter No. 8, Fire Alarm Box $45-60

Firefighter No. 8, In Gold Or Silver $90-120

Firefighter No. 9, Extinguisher $55-60

Firefighter No. 10, Trumpet $55-60

Firefighter No. 10, Gold $200-260

Firefighter No. 10, Silver $125-175

Indian Mother And Papoose $50-65

The Perfesser $40-45

Roses On Parade $60-80

Screech Owls $50-65

Unser-Olsonite Eagle $35-45

Miscellaneous Miniatures, 1978

Bartender $12-15

Cliff Swallow Miniature $9-12

Dancehall Girl Miniature $15-22

Firefighter Emblem $24-31

Firefighter Engine No. 8 .... $24-31

Firefighter Engine No. 10 .... $24-31

Horseshoe Miniature $14-20

Kentucky Derby Race Horse, Cannonade $35-45

Lucky Buck $10-12

Rainmaker $10-15

Sahara Invitational No. 1 .... $35-45

Sahara Invitational No. 2 .... $35-45

Sheepherder $12-15

Shootout At OK Corral, Set Of Three $250-300

Woodpecker $10-15

Luxardo Bottles

The Girolamo Luxardo bottle is made in Torreglia, Italy, and was first imported into the United States in 1930. The Luxardo bottle usually contained liquors or wine.

Luxardo bottles are well designed and meticulously colored, adding to the desirability of this line. Most are figural and consist of historical subjects and classical themes. The most popular bottle, the Cellini, was introduced in the early 1950s and is still used. The names and dates of many of the earlier bottles are not known due to owners removing the tags. Bottles in mint conditions with the original label, whether with or without contents, are very rare, collectible, and valuable. One of the rarer and more valuable of these bottles is the Zara, which was made before World War II.

African Head **$20-25**

Alabaster Fish Figural, 1960-1968....................**$30-40**

Alabaster Goose Figural, 1960-1968
Green and white, wings.......................................**$25-35**

Ampulla Flask, 1958-1959 ....**$20-30**

Apothecary Jar, 1960
Handpainted multicolor, green and black **$20-30**

Assyrian Ashtray Decanter, 1961
Gray, tan, and black **$15-25**

Autumn Leaves Decanter, 1952
Handpainted, two handles **$35-45**

Autumn Wine Pitcher, 1958
Handpainted country scene, handled pitcher **$30-40**

Babylon Decanter, 1960
Dark green and gold..**$16-23**

Bizantina, 1959
Gold embossed design, wide body **$28-38**

Blue And Gold Amphora, 1968
Blue and gold with pastoral scene in white
oval..**$20-30**

Blue Fimmetta Or Vermillian, 1957
Decanter..**$20-27**

Baroque gold ruby pitcher, 1958, $15-20; Baroque green and gold amphora, 1958, $20-30; White topaz majolica pitcher, 1958, $20-30.

Apple, 1960-1961, $25-30; Pear, 1960-61, $25-30; Queen chess piece $75-85;
Orange, 1960-1961, $25-30; Banana, 1960-1961, $25-30.

Brocca Pitcher, 1958
White background pitcher with handle, multicolor
flowers, green leaves...**$28-37**

Buddha Goddess Figural, 1961
Goddess head in green-gray stone....................**$14-19**
Miniature...**$11-16**

Burma Ashtray Speicalty, 1960
Embossed white dancing figure, dark green
background **$20-25**

Burma Pitcher Specialty, 1960
Green and gold, white embossed dancing
figure...**$14-19**

Calypso Girl Figural, 1962
Black West Indian girl, flower headdress in bright color
$20-25

Candlestick Alabaster, 1961 ....**$30-35**

Cannon
Brass wheels **$25-30**

Cellini Vase, 1958-1968
Glass and silver decanter, fancy **$14-19**

Cellini Vase, 1957
Glass and silver handled decanter with serpent
handle..**$14-19**

Ceramic Barrel, 1968
Barrel shaped with painted flowers.....................**$14-19**

Cherry Basket Figural, 1960
White basket, red cherries...................................**$14-19**

Classical Fragment Specialty, 1961
Roman female figure and vase............................**$25-33**

Cocktail Shaker, 1957
Glass and silver decanter, silver painted top **$14-19**

Coffee Carafe Specialty, 1962
Old-time coffee pot, white with blue flowers.......**$14-19**

Curva Vaso Vase, 1961
Green, green and white, ruby red.......................**$22-29**

Deruta Amphora, 1956
Colorful floral design on white............................**$11-16**

Deruta Cameo Amphora, 1959
Colorful floral scrolls and cameo head on eggshell
white...**$25-35**

Deruta Pitcher, 1953
Multicolor flowers on base perugia **$11-16**

Diana Decanter, 1956
White figure of Diana with deer on black **$11-16**

Dogal Silver And Green Decanter, 1952-1956
Handpainted gondola..**$14-19**

Dogal Silver Ruby, 1952-1956
Handpainted gondola..**$14-18**

Dogal Siver Ruby Decanter, 1956
Handpainted Venetian scene and flowers...........**$17-22**

Dogal Silver Smoke Decanter, 1952-1955
Handpainted gondola..**$14-19**

Dogal Silver Smoke Decanter, 1953-1954
Handpainted gondola..**$11-16**

Dogal Silver Smoke Decanter, 1956
Handpainted silver clouds and gondola..............**$11-16**

Dogal Silver Smoke Decanter, 1956
Handpainted gondola, buildings, flowers............**$14-18**

Dolphin Figural, 1959
Yellow, green, blue..**$42-57**

"Doughnut" Bottle, 1960 ....**$15-20**

Dragon Amphora, 1953
Two-handled white decanter with colorful dragon and
flowers **$10-15**

Dragon Amphora, 1958
One handle, white pitcher, color dragon **$14-18**

Duck - Green Glass Figural, 1960
Green and amber duck, clear glass base............**$35-45**

Eagle, 1970 ....**$45-55**

Egyptian Specialty, 1960
Two-handled amphora, Egyptian design on tan and
gold **$14-19**

Etruscan Decanter, 1959
Single-handled black Greek design on tan background
$14-19

Euganean Bronze, 1952-1955..........................**$14-19**

Euganean Coppered, 1952-1955 ....**$13-18**

Faenza Decanter, 1952-1956
Colorful country scene on white single-handled
decanter **$21-28**

Fighting Cocks, 1962
Combination decanter and ashtray.....................**$14-19**

Fish - Green And Gold Glass Figural, 1960
Green, silver, and gold, clear glass base.............**$30-40**

Fish - Ruby Murano Glass Figural, 1961
Ruby-red tone of glass......................................**$30-40**

Florentine Majolica, 1956
Round-handled decanter, painted pitcher **$20-30**

Fruit, 1960..**$10-15**

Gambia, 1961
Black princess, kneeling holding tray...................**$8-12**

Golden Fakir, Seated Snake Charmer
With Flute And Snakes
1961 gold **$26-37**
1960 black and gray..**$26-37**

Gondola, 1959
Highly glazed abstract gondola and gondolier in
black...**$21-27**

Gondola, 1960 ....**$14-19**

Grapes, Pear Figural **$25-40**

Mayan, (1960
Mayan temple god head mask...........................**$15-25**

**Mosaic Combination
Decanter Ashtray,** 1959
Black, yellow, green 11-1/2" **$15-25**
Black, green; miniature 6" **$10-14**

Nubian
Kneeling black figure...**$14-19**

Opal Majolica, 1957
Two gold handles, translucent top **$14-19**

Penguin Murano Glass Figural, 1968
Black and white penguin **$25-30**

Pheasant Murano Glass Figural, 1960
Red and clear glass on a crystal base **$35-45**

Pheasant Red And Gold Figural, 1960
Red and gold glass bird **$40-60**

Primavera Amphora, 1958
Two-handled vase shape **$14-19**

Puppy Cucciolo Glass Figural, 1961
Amber and green glass **$26-37**

Puppy Murano Glass Figural, 1960
Amber glass **$26-37**

Silver Blue Decanter, 1952-1955
Handpainted silver flowers and leaves...............**$22-28**

Silver Brown Decanter, 1952-1955
Handpainted silver flowers and leaves...............**$26-37**

Sir Lancelot, 1962
Figure of English knight in full armor **$14-19**

Springbox Amphora, 1952
Leaping African deer **$14-19**

Squirrel Glass Figural, 1968
Amethyst-colored squirrel on crystal base..........**$40-50**

Sudan, 1960
African motif in browns, blue, yellow and gray ...**$14-19**

Torre Rosa, 1962
Rose tinted tower of fruit....................................**$16-24**

Torre Tinta, 1962
Multicolor tower of fruit **$18-22**

Tower Of Flowers, 1968....................................**$15-20**

Tower Of Fruit, 1968
Various fruit in natural colors..............................**$16-24**

Tower Of Fruit Majolicas Torre Bianca, 1962
White and gray tower of fruit..............................**$16-24**

Venus, 1969 ....**$15-20**

McCormic Bottles

McCormic bottles are similar in design to the Beam and Brooks bottles but are released in limited numbers. The McCormic Distilling Company was eventually bought by Midwest Grain Products in 1950, and the company discontinued making the decanters in 1987.

The McCormic bottles, which contain McCormic Irish Whiskey, were manufactured in four series: Cars, Famous Americans, Frontiermen Decanters, and Gunfighters. The Famous Americans series has been the most produced and represents celebrities from colonial times to the 20th century.

Barrel Series

Barrel, With Stand And Shot Glasses, 1958 ... $25-30

Barrel, With Stand And Plain Hoops, 1968 ..... $15-20

Barrel, With Stand And Gold Hoops, 1968 ..... $20-25

Bicentennial Series

Benjamin Franklin, 1975 .... $25-30

Betsy Ross, 1975 .... $35-40

Ben Franklin, 1976 .... $15-20

George Washington, 1975 .... $40-45

John Hancock, 1975 .... $25-30

John Paul Jones, 1975 .... $25-30

Patrick Henry, 1975 .... $20-25

Paul Revere, 1975 .... $40-50

Thomas Jefferson, 1975 .... $25-30

Bicentennial Set (all of the above figurals), 1976 .... $250-300

Spirit Of '76, 1976 .... $90-100

George Washington, 1976, $20-30; Betsy Ross, 1976, $20-25;

John Hancock, 1976, $15-20; Paul Revere, 1976, $20-25.

Bird Series

Blue Jay, 1971 .... $20-25

Canadian Goose, Miniature $18-25

Gambel's Quail, 1982 .... $45-55

Ring Neck Pheasant, 1982 .... $45-55

Wood Duck, 1980 .... $30-35

Car Series

Packard, 1937 .... $25-35

The Pony Express $20-25

The Sand Buggy Commemorative
Decanter $35-50

Confederate Series

Jeb Stuart $25-35

Jefferson Davis $25-30

Robert E. Lee $25-35

Stonewall Jackson $25-35

Country and Western Series

Hank Williams Sr., 1980 .... $50-55

Hank Williams Jr., 1980 .... $70-80

Tom T. Hall, 1980 .... $32-42

Elvis Presley Series

Elvis '55, 1979 .... $40-50

Elvis '55 Mini $25-35

Elvis '55 Mini, 1980 .... $20-30

Elvis '68, 1980 .... $40-50

Elvis '68 Mini, 1980 .... $25-35

Elvis '77, 1978 .... $65-80

Elvis '77 Mini, 1979 .... $32-40

Elvis Bust, 1978 .... $24-35

Elvis Designer I
Music box plays "Are You Lonesome
Tonight?" $85-100

Elvis Designer II
Music box plays "It's Now or Never" $140-160

Elvis Gold, 1979 .... $180-220

Elvis Karate $100-130

Elvis Sergeant $190-210

Elvis Silver, 1980 .... $120-135

Famous American Portrait Series

Abe Lincoln With Law Book In Hand $35-45

Alexander Graham Bell With Apron $10-15

Captain John Smith $12-20

Charles Lindbergh $24-28

Eleanor Roosevelt $12-20

George Washington Carver $28-40

Henry Ford $20-25

Lewis Meriwether $16-20

Pocahontas $30-42

Robert E. Perry $25-35

Thomas Edison $35-45

Ulysses S. Grant With Coffee Pot And Cup $15-25

William Clark $15-20

Patrick Henry, 1976, $15-20; John Paul Jones, 1976, $15-20; Thomas Jefferson, 1976, $15-20.

Football Mascots

Alabama Bamas.. $26-34

Arizona Sun Devils $39-48

Arizona Wildcats... $21-27

Arkansas Hogs, 1972 .... $42-48

Auburn War Eagles... $16-24

Baylor Bears, 1972.. $24-30

California Bears... $20-25

Drake Bulldogs, Blue Helmet And Jersey,
1974... $15-20

Georgia Bulldogs, Black Helmet And Red
Jersey.. $12-19

Georgia Tech Yellowjackets $15-25

Houston Cougars, 1972 .... $20-30

Indiana Hoosiers, 1974.................................... $15-25

Iowa Cyclones, 1974 .... $45-55

Iowa Hawkeyes, 1974...................................... $60-70

Iowa Purple Panthers...................................... $32-42

Louisiana State Tigers, 1974 .... $15-20

Michigan State Spartans $15-20

Michigan Wolverines, 1974 .... $15-25

Minnesota Gophers, 1974................................ $8-12

Mississippi Rebels, 1974.................................. $8-12

Mississippi State Bulldogs, Red Helmet
And Jersey, 1974... $12-18

Nebraska Cornhuskers, 1974.......................... $12-18

Nebraska Football Player $35-45

Nebraska, Johnny Rogers, No. 1................ $230-260

New Mexico Lobo.. $32-40

Oklahoma Sooners Wagon, 1974.................... $20-28

Oklahoma Southern Cowboy, 1974 .... $14-18

Oregon Beavers, 1974..................................... $10-18

Oregon Ducks, 1974.. $12-18

Purdue Boilermakers, 1974 .... $15-25

Rice Owls, 1972 .... $20-30

Smu Mustangs, 1972....................................... $17-24

Tcu Horned Frogs, 1972 .... $25-30

Tennessee Volunteers, 1974 .... $8-12

Texas A & M Aggies, 1972............................... $22-30

Texas Tech Raiders, 1972 .... $20-26

Texas Horns, 1972 .... $23-33

Washington Cougars, 1974.............................. $20-25

Washington Huskies, 1974............................... $15-25

Wisconsin Badgers, 1974 .... $15-25

Frontiersmen Commemorative Decanters, 1972

Daniel Boone.. $15-22

Davy Crockett $17-25

Jim Bowie... $12-15

Kit Carson $14-18

General

A & P Wagon $50-55

Airplane, Spirit Of St. Louis, 1969 .... $60-80

American Bald Eagle, 1982 .... $30-40

American Legion Cincinnati, 1986 .... $25-35

Buffalo Bill, 1979 .... $70-80

Cable Car $25-30

Car, Packard, 1980 .... $30-40

Chair, Queen Anne $20-30

Ciao Baby, 1978 .... $20-25

Clock, Cuckoo, 1971 .... $25-35

De Witt Clinton Engine, 1970 .... $40-50

French Telephone, 1969 .... $20-28

Globe, Angelica, 1971 .... $25-32

Henry Ford, 1977 .... $20-24

Hutchinson Kansas Centennial, 1972 .... $15-25

Jester, 1972 .... $20-28

Jimmy Durante, 1981
With music box, plays "Inka Dinka Do" $31-40

Joplin Miner, 1972 .... $15-25

JR Ewing, 1980
With music box, plays theme song from
"Dallas" $22-27

JR Ewing, Gold-Colored $50-55

Julia Bulette, 1974 .... $140-160

Lamp, Hurricane $13-18

Largemouth Bass, 1982 .... $20-28

Lobsterman, 1979 .... $20-30

Louis Armstrong $60-70

Mark Twain, 1977 .... $18-22

Mark Twain, Mini $13-18

McCormick Centennial, 1956 .... $80-120

Mikado, 1980 .... $60-80

Missouri Sesquicentennial China, 1970 .... $5-7

Missouri Sesquicentennial Glass, 1971 .... $3-7

Ozark Ike, 1979 .... $22-27

Paul Bunyan, 1979 .... $25-30

Pioneer Theatre, 1972 .... $8-12

Pony Express, 1972 .... $20-25

Renault Racer, 1969 .... $40-50

San Houston, 1977 .... $22-28

Stephen F. Austin, 1977 .... $14-18

Telephone Operator $45-55

Thelma Lu, 1982 .... $25-35

US Marshal, 1979 .... $25-35

Will Rogers, 1977 .... $18-22

Yacht Americana, 1971 .... $30-38

Gunfighter Series

Bat Masterson $20-30

Billy The Kid $25-30

Black Bart $26-35

Calamity Jane $25-30

Doc Holiday $25-35

Jesse James $20-30

Wild Bill Hickok $21-30

Wyatt Earp $21-30

Jug Series

Bourbon Jug $62-70

Gin Jug $6-10

Old Holiday Bourbon, 1956 .... $6-18

Platte Valley, 1953 .... $3-6

Platte Valley, 1/2 Pt $3-4

Vodka Jug $6-10

King Arthur Series

King Arthur On Throne $30-40

Merlin The Wizard With His Wise Old Magical Robe,
1979 .... $25-35

Queen Guinevere, The Gem Of The Royal
Court $12-18

Sir Lancelot Of The Lake In Armor, A Knight Of The
Roundtable $12-18

The Literary Series

Huck Finn, 1980 .... $20-25

Tom Sawyer, 1980 .... $22-26

Miniatures

Charles Lindbergh Miniature, 1978 .... $10-14

Confederates Miniature Set (Four), 1978 .... $40-50

Henry Ford Miniature, 1978 .... $10-14

Mark Twain Miniature, 1978............................. $12-18

Miniature Gunfighters (Eight), 1977 .... $110-140

Miniature Noble, 1978 .... $14-20

Miniature Spirit Of '76, 1977 .... $15-25

Patriot Miniature Set (Eight), 1976 .... $250-350

Pony Express Miniature, 1980 .... $15-18

Will Rogers Miniature, 1978............................ $12-16

Pirate Series

Pirate No. 1, 1972.. $10-12

Pirate No. 2, 1972.. $10-12

Pirate No. 3, 1972.. $8-12

Pirate No. 4, 1972.. $8-12

Pirate No. 5, 1972.. $8-12

Pirate No. 6, 1972.. $8-12

Pirate No. 7, 1972.. $8-12

Pirate No. 8, 1972.. $8-12

Pirate No. 9, 1972.. $8-12

Pirate No.10, 1972... $20-28

Pirate No.11, 1972... $20-28

Pirate No.12, 1972... $20-28

Rural Americana Series

Woman Feeding Chickens, 1980..................... $25-35

Woman Washing Clothes, 1980....................... $30-40

Shrine Series

Circus $20-35

Dune Buggy, 1976... $25-35

Imperial Council.. $20-25

Jester (Mirth King), 1972................................ $30-40

The Noble, 1976.. $25-32

Sports Series

Air Race Propeller, 1971.................................. $15-20

Air Race Pylon, 1970 .... $10-15

Johnny Rodgers No. 1, 1972 .... $160-195

Johnny Rodgers No. 2, 1973 .... $70-85

KC Chiefs, 1969 .... $18-25

KC Royals, 1971.. $10-15

Mohammad Ali, 1980....................................... $20-30

Nebraska Football Player, 1972....................... $33-45

Skibob, 1971.. $10-11

Train Series

Jupiter Engine, 1969.. $20-25

Mail Car, 1970... $25-28

Passenger Car, 1970.. $35-45

Wood Tender, 1969 .... $14-18

Miniature Bottles

When a discussion on bottle collecting begins, most collectors focus their attention on physically large containers such as beer, whiskey, or maybe bitter bottles. But a distinct group of collectors set their sights on the small. Their quest for a special find leads them into the world of miniatures. Until I started bottle collecting, the only miniatures I knew of were the ones passengers bought on airline trips. Today, there is tremendous enthusiasm for miniature bottle collecting. Not only are there specialty clubs and dealers across the United States but throughout the world in the Middle East, Japan, England, Scotland, Australia, and Italy to name just a few countries. The new collector will soon discover that miniatures are fascinating in their own way. Because of the low average cost per bottle ($1-$5) and the relatively small amount of space required for storing them, it's easy to start a collection. There are some rare and expensive miniatures, however.

A number of miniatures were manufactured in the 1800s, but most were made from the late 1920s to the 1950s, with peak production in the 1930s. While miniatures are still produced today, some of the most interesting and sought after are those produced before 1950. Louisiana legalized the sale of miniatures in 1934, Nevada in 1935, and Florida in 1935.

If you're looking for a 19th century miniature, miniature beer bottles are ideal. They are a good example of a bottle that was produced for uses other than containing beer. Most of the major breweries produced them as advertisements, novelties, and promotional items. In fact, the majority of the miniatures didn't even contain beer. A number were made with perforated caps so they could be used as salt and pepper shakers. The Pabst Blue Ribbon Beer Company was the first brewery to manufacture a beer bottle miniature commemorating the Milwaukee Convention of Spanish American War Veterans in 1898. Pabst's last miniature was manufactured around 1942. Most of the miniature beers you'll find today date from before World War II. In 1899, there were as many as 1,507 breweries, all of which all produced miniatures.

Beyond the whiskey, beer, and soda pop bottles identified in this chapter, don't overlook earlier chapters, including Luxardo, Garnier, Lionstone, and Barsottini, which include other miniatures.

Collecting miniature liquor bottles has become a special interest for other collectors as well. For instance, a number of state liquor stamps from the early 1930s and 1940s have specific series numbers that are valuable to stamp collectors. As a reference guide for pricing purposes, I've used Robert E. Kay's *Miniature Beer Bottles & Go-Withs* price guide and reference manual with corresponding pricing codes (CA-1, California; MN-1, Minnesota; etc.).

Beer Bottles

Pre-Prohibition – Circa 1890 - 1933

Bohemian Beer, Pabst Brewing Co. (WI-5)
Paper label, 5-1/2", Milwaukee, Wis., 1890 ....**$100-150**

George Brehn (Trade Mark) Baltimore County, MD – This Bottle Not To Be Sold (MD-1)
Embossed, 5-1/8", Baltimore, Md., 1895............**$30-50**

Indianapolis Brewing Co. (IN-2)
Paper label, 4-1/2", Indianapolis, Ind., 1900...**$100-150**

L. Hoster Brewing Co. (OH-1)
Paper label, 5-1/2", Columbus, Ohio, 1900 ....**$100-150**

Oakland Bottling Co. (CA-4)
Embossed, 5-1/4", Oakland, Calif., 1905............$30-50

Seipp's (IL-4)
Embossed, 5-1/2", Chicago, Ill., 1900 ....$30-50

Silver Foam, Grand Rapids Brewing Co. (MI-3)
Paper label, 5-1/8", Mercury glass bottle, Grand
Rapids, Mich. $100-150

Post-Prohibition – Circa 1933-Present

Acme Beer, Acme Brewing Co. (CA-8)
Decal paper label, 3", Los Angeles, Calif.,
1940...$100-150

Atlantic Beer, Atlantic Co. (NC-2)
Foiled paper label, 4", Charlotte, N.C., 1950 ....$75-100

Ballantine's Export Beer, P. Ballantine & Sons (NJ-8)
Paper label, 4-1/4", Newark, N.J., 1950................$5-10

Barbarossa Beer, Red Top Brewing Co. (OH-10)
Paper label, 4", Cincinnati, Ohio, 1950 ....$10-20

Blatz Old Heidelberg Beer, Blatz Brewing Co. (WI-6)
Decal paper label, 4-1/4", Milwaukee, Wis.,
1936...$10-20

Coors Beer, Adolph Coors Co. (CO-4)
Paper label, 4", Golden, Colo., 1950...............$100-150

Champagne Velvet Brand Beer (IN-14)
Foiled paper label, 4", Terre Haute, Ind., 1950....$10-20

Country Club Pilsener Beer, M.K.
Goetz Brewing Co. (MO-3)
Decal foiled label, 4-1/4", St. Joseph, Mo.,
1934...$30-50

E & O Pilsener Beer, Pittsburgh Brewing Co. (PA-4)
Decal paper label, 4-1/4", Pittsburgh, Pa.,
1936...$30-50

Eastside Beer, Los Angeles Brewing Co (CA-13)
Foil paper label, 4-1/4", Los Angeles, Calif.,
1950...$100-150

Falls City Beer, Falls City Brewing Co., Inc. (KY-4)
Paper label, 4-1/4", Louisville, Ky., 1950...............$5-10

Felsenbrau Beer, The Clyffside Brewing Co. (OH-6)
Decal paper label, 4-1/4", Cincinnati, Ohio, 1936$10-20

Fisher Beer, Fisher Brewing Co. (UT-1)
Decal paper label, 3-1/4", Salt Lake City, Utah,
1936...$20-30

Anderson Club, 1960; Barclay's Bourbon, 1967; Barclay's Gold Label, 1936;
Barclay's Niagara, 1937; Bass River Skipper's Choice, 1960; $10-55.

Echo Spring, 1950; Echo Spring, 1968; Echo Spring, 1972; Ezra Brooks, 1960; Ezra Brooks, 1960; $10-25.

8-Ball Whiskey, 1940; Family Club, 1940; Fleischmann's Preferred, 1953;
Fleischmann's Preferred, 1960; Fleischmann's Preferred, 1967; $10-30.

E.M. Fleischmann's Reserve, 1940; E.M. Fleischmann's Special, 1940; Fort McHenry, 1939;
Four Decades Brand, 1941; Samuels Four Decades Brand, 1940; $20-40.

Belle Of Anderson,
1927-1930, $25-45.

Stagg's Elkhorn,
1919, $45-55.

Early Times Brand,
1936, $35-50.

Old Sunny Brook, 1933, $50-75.

Belle of Kentucky,
1927, $50-75.

Broad Ripple, 1934, $40-55.

Whiskey nipper, Here's to Both
of You, 1930s, $45-55.

Whiskey nipper, A Wee Scotch - Old Whiskey, 1930s, $40-50.

Whiskey nipper, Old Scotch, 1930s, $50-60.

Frederick's 4 Crown Lager Beer (IL-9)
Decal paper label, 4-1/4", Chicago, IL, 1940..**$100-150**

Gettleman $100 Beer, Gettleman Brewing Co. (WI-34)
Foiled paper label, 4-1/4", Milwaukee, Wis.,
1945-1950 ....**$5-10**

Grain Belt Beer, Minneapolis Brewing Co. (MN-13)
Decal paper label, 4", Minneapolis, Minn.,
1950..**$10-20**

Harry Mitchell's Beer, Harry Mitchell Brewing Co. (TX-1)
Decal paper label, 4-1/4", El Paso, Texas,
1936..**$100-150**

Jax Beer, Jackson Brewing Co. (LA-2)
Foiled paper label, 4-1/4", New Orleans, La.,
1952..**$5-10**

Lang's Bohemian Beer, Gerhard Lang Brewery (NY-25)
Decal paper label, 3", Buffalo, N.Y., 1940 ....**$100-150**

Meister Brau, Peter Hand Brewery Co. (IL-15)
Foil paper label, 4-1/4", Chicago , Ill., 1952..........**$5-10**

Million's Wisconsin Select Beer, Million Brewery, Inc. (WI-97)
Decal paper label, 3", New Lisbon, Wis., 1940...**$50-75**

Old Craft Brew, Menominee-Marinette Brewing Co. (MI-4)
Decal paper label, 4-1/4", Menominee, Mich.,
1936..**$100-150**

Old Export Beer, The Cumberland Brewing Co. (MD-6)
Decal paper label, 4", Cumberland, Md., 1948...**$20-30**

Old Milwaukee Beer, Bottled By G. Ferlita & Sons (FL-3)
Decal paper label, 3", Tampa, Fla., 1940 ....**$100-150**

Old Tap Brand Bohemian Beer, Enterprise Brewing Co. (MA-2)
Decal paper label, 3", Fall River, Mass., 1940.....**$10-20**

Nectar Beer, Ambrosia Brewing Co. (IL-8)
Decal paper label, 4-1/4", Chicago, Ill.,
1941..**$100-150**

Royal Pilsen Beer, Abne Drury Brewery, Inc. (DC-2)
Decal paper label, 4-1/4", Washington, D.C.,
1934..**$100-150**

Senate Beer, Diamond State Brewery, Inc. (DC-3)
Decal paper label, 4", Washington, D.C.,
1950..**$100-150**

Southern Beer, Southern Breweries, Inc. (VA-2)
Decal paper label, 3-1/4", Norfolk, Va., 1936..**$100-150**

Southern Select Beer, Galveston-Houston Breweries, Inc (TX-6)
Decal paper label, 3-1/4", Galveston, Texas,
1936..**$75-100**

Spearman Beer, The Spearman Brewing Co. (FL-2)
Decal paper label,4-1/4", Pensacola, Fla.,
1936..**$100-150**

Stein's Beer, George F. Stein Brewery, Inc. (NY-11)
Decal paper label, 3", Buffalo, N.Y., 1940 ....**$10-20**

Topper Beer (IL-11)
Decal paper label, 3", Chicago, Ill., 1940 ....**$100-150**

Valley Forge Beer, Adam Scheidt Brewing Co. (PA-27)
Decal paper label, 4", Norristown, Pa., 1952 ......**$10-20**

**West Virginia Special Export Beer,
Fesenmeier Brewing Co. (WV-1)**
Decal paper label, 4-1/4", Huntington, W.V.,
1936... $3,040

Foreign Beer Bottles

Guinness Extra Stout, Arthur Guinness (IRL-30)
Foiled paper label, 4-1/4", Dublin, Ireland, 1960... $5-10

O'Keefe Ale, O'keefe Ale Brewery Limited (CAN-1)
Decal paper label, 4-3/4", Toronto, Ottawa, Winnipeg,
Saskatoon, Canada (CA-1).................................. $5-10

**Castle Ale, Type 1, Rhodesian
Breweries Ltd. (RHOD-1)**
Paper label, 4-1/4", Rhodesia, 1960 .... $10-20

Sol (MEX-2)
Enamel label, 4-1/4", Mexico, 1965 .... $10-20

Stjerne Export Beer, Brewery Stjerne (DEN-4)
Foiled paper label, 4", Copenhagen, Denmark,
1955.. $10-20

Whiskey Flasks (Circa 1928-1935)

Boss Of The Road	$175
Clipper's Special	$200
Hello World	$150
Kentucky Prince	$150
Lord Cedrio	$100
Murlee	$175
99	$75
Old Armitage	$75
Old Colonel Dan	$175
Old Forman–Distilled Spring	$150
Old Guide	$175
Old Honesty	$175
Old Kentucky Home	$50
Old Reliable	$175
Old Royalty	$200
Old 73	$200
Pride Of Nelson	$60
R. A. Baker	$100
Special Select	$150
Stone Haven	$75

Scotch Whisky

Ambassador	$130-175
Ancient Memories	$130-175
Auld Glen Ross	$175-255
B. Grant's	$250-350
Bentley Royal	$90-175
Bonnie Charlie	$45-90
Cardhu Highland Malt Whisky (French)	$130-175
Dalmore 8	$250-350
Eddie Cairns	$90-175
Gannochy Brig	$250-350
Glenfiddich	$450-550
John Adair	$45-90
Heather Bell	$250-350
Highland Shepherd	$175-255
House Of Commons	$450-550
Invercauld	$90-175
King Edward	$90-175
MacKinlay's Old Benvorlich	$175-255
O B Saunders	$45-90
Old Bar	$130-175
Old Keg	$130-175
Pageant	$130-175
Queen Elizabeth	$130-175
Real MacKay	$250-350
Royal Highlander	$90-175
Royal Mackenzie	$90-175
Royal Toby	$450-550
Scots Piper	$90-175
Stag's Head	$175-255
Sterlini	$45-90
Talisker	$175-255
Teachers	$250-350
Tiny Tot	$450-550
Trocadero	$175-255
Weston's 8 Years Old	$45-90

Soda Pop Bottles (3" To 5", Circa 1930s To 1950s)

Applied Color Painted Label (ACL)

Braunel $10

Dad's Root Beer...$40

Fanta...$5

Frostie...$15

Hires Root Beer $30

Mission Beverages $15

Orange Crush...$45

Virginia Dare...$20

Paper Labels

A-Treat $8

Canada Dry Ginger Ale $20

Pepsi $50

7-Up $30

Wonder Mix $10

Embossed

Dr. Pepper $45

RC $30

Smile (Pat. July 11, 1922) $15

Squirt $15

Vess..$10

Whistle...$10

Old Blue Ribbon Bottles

These bottles, containing Old Blue Ribbon liquor, are figurals made from 1969 to 1974. They are noted for their realistic depiction of historical themes and railroad cars from the 19th century.

In addition, Blue Ribbon is the only manufacturer to produce a hockey series, with each bottle commemorating a different hockey team.

Air Race Decanter $18-26

Blue Bird...$14-19

Caboose Mkt...$20-30

Eastern Kentucky University $15-21

Jupiter '60 Mail Car $13-17

Jupiter '60 Passenger Car $16-23

Jupiter '60 Wood Tender $13-17

Jupiter '60 Locomotive $15-22

KC Royals...$19-26

Pierce Arrow $13-15

Santa Maria Columbus Ship $15-20

Titanic Ocean Liner $100-125

Transportation Series

Balloon... $9-12

5th Ave Bus $14-21

Prairie Schooner... $10-11

River Queen $10-15

River Queen, Gold $20-25

Hockey Series

Boston Bruins $14-18

Chicago Black Hawks....................................... $14-18

Detroit Red Wings $14-18

Minnesota North Stars..................................... $14-18

New York Rangers.. $14-18

St. Louis Blues... $14-18

Old Commonwealth Bottles

The Old Commonwealth brand, produced by J.P. Van Winkle and Son, is one of the newer companies (1974) to produce whiskey in collectible decanters. The ceramic decanters themselves are manufactured in Asia, while the whiskey and bottling is done at the Hoffman Distilling Co. in Lawrenceburg, Ky.

Today, the majority of the decanters are produced in regular and miniature sizes with the titles of most pieces appearing on the front plaques.

Alabama Crimson Tide, 1981
University of Alabama symbol............................**$23-30**

Bulldogs, 1982
The mascot of the Georgia Bulldogs..................**$20-30**

Chief Illini No. 1, 1979
The mascot for the University of Illinois **$70-85**

Chief Illini No. 2, 1981
The mascot for the University of Illinois **$55-65**

Chief Illini No. 3, 1989
The mascot for the University of Illinois **$65-75**

Coal Miner No. 1, 1975
Standard size..**$80-100**

Mini, 1980 ....**$20-30**

Coal Miner No. 2, 1976
Standard size...**$20-30**
Mini, 1982..**$19-23**

Coal Miner No. 3, 1977
Standard size...**$28-36**
Mini, 1981 ....**$20-25**

Coal Miner – Lunch Time No. 4, 1980
Standard size...**$33-43**
Mini...**$15-20**

Cottontail, 1981..**$25-35**

Elusive Leprechaun, 1980 ....**$24-30**

Fisherman, "A Keeper," 1980............................$20-30

Golden Retriever, 1979......................................$30-40

Kentucky Thoroughbreds, 1976......................$30-40

Kentucky Wildcat...$32-42

LSU Tiger, 1979...$45-55

Lumberjack...$15-25

Missouri Tiger...$35-45

Old Rip Van Winkle No. 1, 1974......................$40-50

Old Rip Van Winkle No. 2, 1975......................$35-45

Old Rip Van Winkle No. 3, 1977......................$30-40

Pointing Setter Decanter, 1965........................$16-23

Quail On The Wing Decanter, 1968....................$7-12

Rebel Yell Rider, 1970......................................$23-32

Rip Van Winkle Figurine, 1970.........................$32-40

Songs Of Ireland, 1972....................................$15-20

Sons Of Erin, 1969..$6-9

South Carolina Tricentennial, 1970.................$12-19

Tennessee Walking Horse, 1977......................$24-35

USC Trojan, 1980
Standard size...$45-55
Mini..$11-16

Weller Masterpiece, 1963................................$26-35

Western Boot Decanter, 1982
Standard size...$20-25
Mini..$8-12

Western Logger, 1980.....................................$25-34

Wildcats, 1982...$40-46

Wings Across The Continent, 1972.................$16-23

Yankee Doodle...$25-32

Modern Firefighters Series

Modern Hero No. 1, 1982
Standard size...$25-35
Mini..$8-12

The Nozzleman No. 2, 1982
Standard size...$30-40
Mini..$17-24

On Call No. 3, 1982
Standard size...$45-55
Mini..$15-24

Fallen Comrade No. 4, 1982
Standard size...$30-40
Mini..$17-25

Fireman #1, 1976
Cumberland Valley...$40-50

Fireman #2, 1978
Volunteer..$35-40

Fireman #3, 1980
Valiant Volunteer..$40-50

Fireman #4, 1981
Heroic Volunteer...$40-50

Fireman #5, 1982
Lifesaver...$45-55

Fireman #6, 1982
Breaking Thru...$55-65

Waterfowler Series

Waterfowler No. 1, 1979...................................$40-50

Here They Come No. 2, 1980.............................$32-42

Good Boy No. 3, 1981.......................................$32-42

Old Fitzgerald Bottles

Old Fitzgerald bottles are manufactured by the Old Fitzgerald Distilling Company to package its whiskey and bourbon. The bottles are often called Old Cabin Still bottles based on one of the brand names under which they were distributed and sold.

The bottles are issued in both decanter and figural designs in various types and colors portraying various Irish and American subjects. The bottles are produced in very limited numbers.

American Sons, 1976 .... $10-15	Hillbilly Bottle, Gal (Very Rare), 1954 .... $60-85
Americas Cup Commemorative, 1970 .... $15-22	Irish Charm, 1977 .... $15-20
Birmingham, 1972 .... $45-50	Irish Luck, 1972 .... $15-20
Blarney Castle, 1970 .... $12-19	Irish Patriots, 1971 .... $10-15
Browsing Deer Decanter, 1967 .... $15-22	Jewel Decanter, 1951-1952 .... $9-15
California Bicentennial, 1970 .... $15-22	Leaping Trout Decanter, 1969 .... $11-16
Cabin Still, Hillbilly, 1854 .... $75-80	Leprechaun Bottle, 1968 .... $25-32
Cabin Still, Hillbilly, 1954 .... $15-20	LSU Alumni Decanter, 1970 .... $25-32
Candelite Decanter, 1955 .... $9-12	Man O' War Decanter, 1969 .... $5-9
Classic, 1972 .... $5-10	Memphis Commemorative, 1969 .... $8-12
Colonial Decanter, 1969 .... $4-7	Nebraska, 1971 .... $27-32
Crown Decanter $5-9	Nebraska, 1972 .... $18-25
Eagle, 1973 .... $5-10	Ohio State Centennial, 1970 .... $12-18
Gold Coast Decanter, 1954 .... $10-15	Old Cabin Still Decanter, 1958 .... $16-23
"Golden Bough" Decanter, 1971 .... $4-9	Old Ironsides, 1970 .... $5-10
Gold Web Decanter, 1953 .... $10-16	Pilgrim Landing Commemorative, 1970 .... $14-24
Hillbilly Pt., 1969 .... $13-18	Rip Van Winkle, Blue, 1971 .... $45-50
Hillbilly Bottle, Pt, 1954 .... $13-18	Sons Of Erin, 1969 .... $15-20
Hillbilly Bottle, Qt, 1954 .... $13-18	Tree Of Life, 1964 .... $5-10

Ski-Country Bottles

Ski-Country bottles are produced by the Foss Company in Golden, Colo. They are issued in limited editions and offer a variety of subjects such as Indians, owls, game birds, Christmas themes, and customer specialties. Since Foss didn't start manufacturing its decanters until 1973, a number of limited editions have high quality detailing. These bottles are rated high on the list of most collectors.

Animals

Badger Family
Standard size.. $35-45
Mini...$16-24

Bobcat Family
Standard size...$45-60
Mini...$16-25

Coyote Family
Standard size.. $37-48
Mini...$17-23

Kangaroo
Standard size...$22-32
Mini...$18-28

Koala... $20-28

Raccoon
Standard size...$36-45
Mini...$25-30

Skunk Family
Standard size...$40-50
Mini...$22-26

Snow Leopard
Standard size...$36-43
Mini...$30-35

Birds

Blackbird
Standard size...$34-40
Mini...$29-30

P.T. Barnun, 1976, $30-40; Circus Lion, 1975, $30-35; Circus Clown, 1974, $45-55.

Landlocked Salmon, 1976, $40-50; Trout, 1975 $30-35; Muskie, 1977, $30-40.

Black Swan
Standard size...$30-35
Mini...$18-24

Blue Jay
Standard size...$50-60
Mini...$42-49

Cardinal
Standard size...$55-70
Mini...$35-45

Condor
Standard size...$45-55
Mini...$25-30

Gamecocks
Standard size...$120-130
Mini...$40-46

Gila Woodpecker
Standard size...$55-65
Mini...$26-32

Peace Dove
Standard size...$50-60
Mini...$20-26

Peacock
Standard size...$80-100
Mini...$45-60

Penguin Family
Standard size...$45-55
Mini...$21-27

Wood Duck
Standard size...$175-200
Mini...$125-150

Sage Grouse, 1974, $40-50; Red Shouldered Hawk, 1973, $60-70; Peacock, 1972, $80-100.

Christmas

Bob Cratchit
Standard size..$40-50
Mini..$25-30

Mrs. Cratchit
Standard size..$40-50
Mini..$25-30

Scrooge
Standard size..$40-50
Mini..$15-20

Circus

Clown
Standard size..$44-52
Mini..$27-33

Elephant On Drum
Standard size..$35-45
Mini..$35-45

Jenny Lind, Blue Dress
Standard size..$55-75
Mini..$48-60

Lion On Drum
Standard size..$31-36
Mini..$23-28

Palomino Horse
Standard size..$40-48
Mini..$30-40

P.T. Barnum
Standard size..$32-40
Mini..$20-25

Ringmaster
Standard size..$20-25
Mini..$15-18

Tiger On Ball
Standard size..$35-44
Mini..$31-37

Tom Thumb
Standard size..$20-25
Mini..$16-21

Customer Specialties

Ahrens-Fox Engine......................$140-180

Bonnie And Clyde (Pair)
Standard size..$60-70
Mini..$55-62

Caveman
Standard size..$16-23
Mini..$18-22

Mill River Country Club....................$38-47

Olympic Skier – Gold......................$85-110

Olympic Skier, Red
Standard size..$22-30
Mini..$30-35

Olympic Skier, Blue
Standard size..$25-32
Mini..$35-40

Political Donkey And Elephant......................$50-60

Domestic Animals

Basset Hound
Standard size..$45-55
Mini..$26-32

Holstein Cow................................$45-60

Eagles, Falcons, And Hawks

Birth Of Freedom
Standard size..$85-95
Mini..$65-75

Eagle On The Water
Standard size..$90-110
Mini..$38-45

Easter Seals Eagle
Standard size..$48-60
Mini..$22-29

Falcon, Gallon............................$350-425

Gyrfalcon
Standard size..$54-60
Mini..$27-34

Happy Eagle
Standard size..$85-105
Mini..$80-95

Mountain Eagle
Standard size..$130-150
Mini..$100-120

Osprey Hawk
Standard size..$140-160
Mini..$100-120

Peregrine Falcon
Standard size..$75-85
Mini..$18-25

Prairie Falcon
Standard size..$65-80
Mini..$35-48

Red Shoulder Hawk
Standard size..$60-70
Mini..$34-40

Redtail Hawk
Standard size..$75-95
Mini..$33-40

White Falcon
Standard size.................................$68-75
Mini...$30-40

Fish

Muskellunge
Standard size.................................$30-37
Mini...$17-21

Rainbow Trout
Standard size.................................$40-50
Mini...$24-30

Salmon
Standard size.................................$30-35
Mini...$18-22

Trout...$27-32

Game Birds

Banded Mallard.................................$50-60

Chukar Partridge
Standard size.................................$33-40
Mini...$16-21

King Eider Duck.................................$50-60

Mallard 1973.................................$50-60

Pheasant, Mini $52-62

Pheasant, Golden
Standard size.................................$40-45
Mini...$24-30

Pheasant In The Corn
Standard size.................................$50-60
Mini...$30-39

Pheasants Fighting
Standard size.................................$70-80
Mini...$35-45

Pheasants Fighting, 1/2 Gal........................$145-165

Pintail...$76-85

Prairie Chicken $55-65

Ruffed Grouse
Standard size.................................$40-50
Mini...$22-28

Turkey
Standard size.................................$80-100
Mini...$100-120

Horned and Antlered Animals

Antelope $45-60

Desert Sheep
Standard size.................................$75-90
Mini...$25-30

Big-Horn Ram
Standard size.................................$65-75
Mini...$25-31

Mountain Goat
Standard size.................................$30-45
Mini...$38-48

Mountain Goat, Gal $525-600

Mountain Sheep
Standard size.................................$50-60
Mini...$24-30

Stone Sheep
Standard size.................................$50-65
Mini...$27-34

White Tail Deer
Standard size.................................$30-95
Mini...$34-40

Indians

Ceremonial Antelope Dancer
Standard size.................................$52-62
Mini...$36-45

Ceremonial Buffalo Dancer
Standard size.................................$150-185
Mini...$32-38

Ceremonial Deer Dancer
Standard size.................................$85-100
Mini...$40-48

Ceremonial Eagle Dancer
Standard size.................................$185-205
Mini...$24-34

Ceremonial Falcon Dancer
Standard size.................................$85-100
Mini...$34-45

Ceremonial Wolf Dancer
Standard size.................................$50-60
Mini...$32-40

Chief No. 1
Standard size.................................$105-125
Mini...$14-20

Chief No. 2
Standard size.................................$105-125
Mini...$14-20

Cigar Store Indian.................................$32-40

Dancers of the Southwest

Dancers Of The Southwest, Set
Standard size.................................$250-300
Mini...$140-175

Arizona Ceremonial Eagle Dancer, 1978
Standard Size.................................$100-125
Mini...$20-30

Acoma, 1975
Standard Size $40-50
Mini $15-20

Drummer, 1975
Standard Size $35-45
Mini $15-20

Eagle Dancer, 1975
Standard Size $35-45
Mini $15-20

Hoop Dancer, 1975
Standard Size $35-40
Mini $15-20

Shield Dancer, 1975
Standard Size $40-50
Mini $15-20

Sun Dancer, 1975
Standard Size $40-50
Mini $15-20

Owls

Barn Owl
Standard size $48-55
Mini $20-24

Great Gray Owl
Standard size $48-55
Mini $20-25

Horned Owl
Standard size $60-70
Mini $70-80
Horned Owl, Gal $700-800

Saw Whet Owl
Standard size $40-45
Mini $20-25

Screech Owl Family
Standard size $80-90
Mini $68-75

Spectacled Owl
Standard size $70-85
Mini $58-68

Rodeo

Barrel Racer
Standard size $58-68
Mini $20-26

Bull Rider
Standard size $42-49
Mini $22-28

Wyoming Bronco
Standard size $48-66
Mini $25-35

Soda Bottles - Applied Color Label

Anyone who has ever had a cold soda on a hot summer day from a bottle with a painted label probably didn't realize that the bottle would someday become rare and collectible. Today, collecting applied color label (ACL) soda bottles has become one of the fastest growing and most affordable areas of bottle collecting. This rapid growth has resulted in the Painted Soda Bottle Collectors Association, which is the nationwide collectors group dedicated to the promotion and preservation of ACL soda bottles.

So, what is an applied color label soda bottle? The best description is this excerpt from an article written by Dr. J.H. Toulouse, a noted expert on bottle collecting and glass manufacturing in the late 1930s:

"One of the developments of the last few years has been that of permanent fused on labels on glass bottles. The glass in a glass furnace is homogenous in character, all of one color and composition. When the bottles are ready for decoration, the color design is printed on them in the process that superficially resembles many printing or engraving processes. The color is applied in the form of a paste-like material, through a screen of silk, in which the design has been formed. The bottle, which contains the impression of that design must then be dried and then fired by conducting it thorough a lehr, which is long, tunnel-like enclosure through which the bottles pass at a carefully controlled rate of speed and in which definite zones of temperature are maintained. The maximum temperature chosen is such that the glass body will not melt, but the softer glass involved in the color will melt and rigidly fuse on the glass beneath it."

The first commercially sold soda was Imperial Inca Cola, whose name was inspired by the Native American Indian. Coca-Cola, the first truly successful cola drink, was developed in 1886 by Dr. John Styth Pemberton of Atlanta, Ga. Carbonated water was added in 1887, and by 1894, bottled Coca-Cola was in full production. Alex Samuelson designed the famous hobbleskirt-shaped bottle in 1915. Numerous inventors attempted to ride on the coattails of Coke's success. The most successful of these inventors was Caleb Bradham, who started Brad's drink in 1890 and in 1896 changed its name to Pep-Kola. In 1898, it was changed to Pipi-Cola and by 1906 to the now-familiar Pepsi-Cola.

The ACL soda bottle was conceived in the 1930s when Prohibition forced numerous brewing companies to sell soda. What started out as a temporary venture saved many brewing companies from bankruptcy, and some never looked back. From the mid-1930s to the early 1960s, with peak production in the 1940s and 1950s, many small, local bottlers throughout the United States created bottle labels that will forever preserve unique moments in American history. The labels featured western scenes, cowboys, Native Americans, bi-planes to jets, clowns, famous figures, birds, bears, boats, Donald Duck, and even Las Vegas (Vegas Vic).

Since Native Americans and cowboys were popular American figures, these bottles are among the most popular and most collectible. In fact, the Big Chief ACL sodas are the most popular bottles—even more than the embossed types. These small bottlers actually produced the majority of the better-looking labels in contrast to the largely uniform bottles by major bottlers like Coca-Cola and Pepsi-Cola. Because these bottles were produced in smaller quantities, they are rarer and more valuable. While rarity affects value, a bottle with a larger label is even more desirable for collectors. The most sought-after bottles are those with a two-color label, each color adding more value to the bottle.

Unless Otherwise Noted, All Soda Bottles Listed Have A Smooth Base And A Crown Top:

Applied Color Label Bottles

A Good, Anderson, In
Orange, 8 oz., 1948 .... $49

Ace High, Albert Lea, Mn
Light green, 7 oz., 1945 .... $24

Artic, Conroe, Tx
Dark green, 10 oz., 1948 .... $15

Bali, Los Angeles, Ca
Amber, 7 oz., 1941 .... $22

Barr's Soda, Hardwick, Vt
Orange, 8 oz., 1967 .... $10

Bells Of Kentucky, Paris, Ky
Dark green, 7 oz., 1946 .... $9

Bingo, Waukesha, Wi
Dark green, 10 oz., 1966 .... $20

Blue Bird, Chicago, Il
Clear, 7 oz., 1947 .... $5

Bubble Up, St. Louis, Mo
Dark green, 7 oz., 1946 .... $5

Cannon, Dodge City, Ks
Orange, 10 oz., 1958 .... $20

Castle Beverages, Ansonia, Ct
Dark green, 7 oz., 1957 .... $8

Circle A, Booneville, Mo
Clear, 10 oz., 1954 .... $5

Clear Water, Pittsburgh, Pa
Dark green, 32 oz., 1961 .... $10

College Club, Windsor, Pa
Dark green, 30 oz., 1969 .... $12

Dart, Emporia, Ks
Clear, 8 oz., 1952 .... $75

Dash, Verona, Pa
Light green, 7 oz., 1945 .... $7

Desert Cooler, Tucson, Az
Dark green, 10 oz., 1954 .... $18

Dixie Dew, Waynesboro, Ga
Medium green, 10 oz., 1952 .... $25

Eight Ball, Altoona, Pa
Green, 16 oz., 1955 .... $46

Elk's Beverages, Leavenworth, Ks
Light brown, 12 oz., 1941 .... $8

Flathead, Kalispell, Mt
Clear, 12 oz., 1953 .... $175

Frostie, Camden, NJ
Clear, 10 oz., 1965 .... $6

Fudgy, Ludlow, Ma
Amber, 6 oz., 1943 .... $395

Fuller's Spring, Jamestown, ND
Amber, 7 oz., 1952 .... $15

Golden Age, Youngstown & Akron, Oh
Clear, 12 oz., 1938 .... $51

Golden Harvest, Freeport, Il
Clear, 10 oz., 1959 .... $15

Golden Slipper, Philadelphia, Pa
Clear, 7 oz., 1951 .... $80

Hall Of Waters, Excelsior Springs, Mo
Clear, 10 oz., 1959 .... $20

Hava Drink, Monett, Mo
Clear, 12 oz., 1948 .... $5

Chey Rock $31; Wyoming $150; Old Faithful $70; Oregon Trail $75; Alamo $300; Santa Fe Trail $130, circa 1925-1960.

Hazel Club, Ellwood City, Pa
Dark green, 32 oz., 1962 .... $7

Herby Cola, Leavenworth, Ks
Clear, 10 oz., 1959.. $5

Hornet Brand, Tulia, Tx
Clear, 10 oz., 1962.. $40

I C Cola, Denver, Co
Clear, 16 oz., 1959.. $21

Idaho, Caldwell & Buhl, Id
Clear, 10 oz., 1950.. $25

Indian Club, Santa, Ana, Ca
Clear, 9 oz., 1950.. $60

Jet, Waco, Tx
Clear, 8 oz., 1958.. $33

Jo-Jo, Milwaukee, Wi
Clear, 7 oz., 1956.. $35

Ju-See, Brookfield, Mo
Clear, 10 oz., 1949.. $5

Kanner's 7-11, Los Angeles, Ca
Green, 7 oz., 1946 .... $5

Kik, Canada
Clear, 12 oz., 1940.. $35

Kist, Chicago, Il
Clear, 10 oz., 1959.. $5

Kleer Kool, Topeka, Ks
Clear, 10 oz., 1954.. $25

Lemmy, Tecumseh, Nb
Clear, 10 oz., 1950.. $35

Log Cabin, Niagra Falls, NY
Clear, 10 oz., 1956.. $105

Coca-Cola - Jackson, Tenn - Coca-Cola - Registered - Coca-Cola Bottling Wks, 1900-1910, $150-200.

Dad's Root Beer $7; Dad's Root Beer $5; Duffy's $8; Duffy's $8; Elwing $5; Elks $12; Elks $11; Elks $15, circa 1950s.

Drink Mor $13; Dr. Enuf $18; Dr. Nut $5; Dr. Pepper 10-2-4 $5; Dr. Pepper $10; Dr. Pepper $5; Dr. Pepper $12; Dr. Swells Root Beer $11, circa 1950s-early 1960s.

Los Banos, Los Banos, Ca
Clear, 7 oz., 1948.. $10

Mason's Root Beer, Chicago, Il
Amber, 10 oz., 1954 .... $5

Mountain Maid, Nevada City, Ca
Clear, 10 oz., 1964.. $20

Mountaineer, Clarskburg, Va
Clear, 9 oz., 1957... $15

Nesbitt's , Los Angeles, Ca
Clear, 7 oz., 1954.. $5

Norton Big Chief, Norton, Ks
Clear, 9 oz., 1956.. $20

Nugget, Providence, RI
Clear, 12 oz., 1956.. $16

Old Time Root Beer, Reading, Pa
Clear, 12 oz., 1950... $40

Old Mill, Brookville, In
Green, 7 oz., 1957 .... $37

Orange Crush, Evanston, Il
Amber, 7 oz., 1966 .... $5

Pep-Up, Wilkes-Barre, Pa
Dark green, 32 oz., 1973 .... $11

Polar Club, Salem, Ma
Clear, 12 oz., 1938.. $10

Polly's Soda, Independence, Mo
Clear, 12 oz., 1961.. $10

Pop Kola, Marceline, Mo
Clear, 10 oz., 1952.. $5

Quality Beverages, Manitowoc, Wi
Green, 7 oz., 1953 .... $8

Rancho, Ontario, Ca
Clear, 10 oz., 1948... $40

Royal Flush, Portland, Or
Clear, 7 oz., 1947.. $30

Sal-U-Taris, St. Clair, Mn
Amber, 7 oz., 1950 .... $12

Legge's Quality $5; Legge's Quality $5; Laynes $5; LC Cola $5; Mountain Dew $21; Mason's Root Beer $5; Mason's Root Beer $5; Mug Root Beer $12, circa 1950s-early 1960s.

Mission $5;
Mission $5;
NuGrape $5;
Nesbitt's $5; NC
$8; Orange Crush
$6; Orange Crush
$5; Orange Crush
$5, circa 1950s.

Spring Grove, Spring Grove, Mn
Clear, 10 oz., 1960... **$15**

Stone Fort, Nacogdoches, Tx
Clear, 9 oz., 1950.. **$100**

Swallow's Root Beer, Lima, Oh
Clear, 10 oz., 1952.. **$35**

Tally Ho, Los Angeles, Ca
Clear, 10 oz., 1947.. **$25**

Terry's, Scottsdale, Ne
Clear, 12 oz., 1949.. **$140**

Twang Root Beer, Chicago, Il
Clear, 12 oz., 1956.. **$75**

Uncle Dan's Root Beer, Detroit, Mi
Clear, 16 oz., 1961.. **$29**

Valley Spring, Phoenix, Az
Clear, 32 oz., 1949.. **$10**

Viking, St. Paul, Mn
Clear, 12 oz., 1972.. **$20**

West Bend, West Bend, Wi
Clear, 7 oz., 1950.. **$5**

Whistle, St. Louis, Mo
Clear, 10 oz., 1950... **$5**

Wolf's, Harrisburg, Il
Clear, 10 oz., 1974... **$5**

X-Tra, Wolcott, Ct
Clear, 12 oz., 1966... **$5**

Yakima Chief, Yakima, Wa
Clear, 10 oz., 1955... **$35**

Yorkshire Ginger Beer, Los Angeles, Ca
Clear, 12 oz., 1941... **$35**

Yucca, Clovis, NM
Clear, 12 oz., 1941... **$15**

Zee Beverages, Erie, Pa
Clear, 7 oz., 1958... **$11**

Zeisler, St. Charles, Mo
Clear, 10 oz., 1951... **$10**

Embossed

Big Chief, Clinton, Mo
Light green, 9 oz., 1948... **$25**

Sun Glo $6; Sunset
$5; Sun-Shine $5;
Sun-Rich $33;
Sun-Rich $25;
SunTex $5; SunTex
$5, circa 1950s.

Crystal, Osceola, Mo
Light green, 7 oz., 1930.. $5

Kramer's, Mt. Carmel, Pa
Clear, 7 oz., 1965... $5

Dr. Pepper, Dennison, Ia
Clear, 6-1/2 oz., 1947 .... $10

Pepsi-Cola, Durham, NC
Light green, 6-1/2 oz., 1929 .... $105

Treasure Isle $4; My Pic $35; Lindy $41; Lift $22, circa 1940s-1950s.

Violin and Banjo Bottles

While roaming the aisles of bottle and antique shows, I have often seen a violin- or banjo-shaped bottle on a table, admired its shape and color, then set it back down and moved on to whiskey bottles and medicine bottles. I didn't fully appreciate them, until I attended the June 1999 National Bottle Museum Antique Bottle Show in Saratoga, N.Y., to participate in a book signing. Before the show, a silent auction was held that included a spectacular display of violin and banjo bottles. At that time, I had the pleasure of meeting several knowledgeable collectors and members of the Violin Bottle Collectors Association and received a short lesson and history of violin bottles. With the help of many dedicated members of the Violin Bottle Collectors Association, we've written a chapter that will assist both the veteran and the novice collector with understanding the fun and collecting of violin and banjo bottles.

While gathering the information for this chapter, it became clear that the majority of bottle and antique collectors and dealers (including this collector) had very little knowledge about violin and banjo bottles and their beginnings. Are they considered antiques? How old are violin bottles? Why and where were they manufactured?

First, most were manufactured in the 20th century, with heavy production not taking place until the 1930s. One interesting aspect about violin and banjo bottles is that they are completely original designs and not copied from any earlier bottle types such as historic flasks or bitters. This makes these bottles antique in that they are the first of their design and style.

Selection Of Bard's Town Violin Bottles: Bard's Town, 1939, 5"; Bard's Town, 1940, 4-7/8"; Bard's Town, 1938, 4-7/8"; Bard's Town Bond, 1940, 4-7/8"; Bourbon Springs, 1938, 4-7/8"; Bourbon Springs, 1939, 4-7/8"; Old Anthem Brand, 1938, 4-7/8"; Old Bard Brand, 1938, 4-7/8"; Old Fiddle, 1950, 4-3/4"; Old Fiddle, 1950, 4-3/4". (All Items $50-75 each)

As with other specialty groups, violin and banjo bottles have specific categories and specific classes and codes with each category. For the serious collector, I recommend *The Classification of Violin Shaped Bottles, 2nd Edition (1999)*, and *3rd Edition (2004)* by Robert A. Linden, and *Violin Bottles, Banjos, Guitars, and Other Novelty Glass, 1st Edition (1995)* by Don and Doris Christensen. Information on the association can be obtained by writing to the Violin Bottle Collector's Association, 1210 Hiller Road, McKinleyville, CA 95519, or by contacting Frank Bartlett, Membership Chairman, at fbviobot@hotmail.com.

Violin Bottles:

Category 1:
American Styles

LV: Large Violin-Shaped Bottles (Figure 1)

- Eight molds have been identified:
  - Molds 1, 4, and 6: Produced at Clevenger Brothers Glass Works.
  - Molds 2, 3, and 7: Produced at Dell Glass Company.
  - Mold 5: Maker unidentified.
  - Mold 8: Produced in Japan.
- Bottles had no contents and were made only for decorative purposes.
- Production began in the 1930s; first identified in the marketplace in the 1940s.
- Height range of 9"–10-1/4"; Body width 4-1/4"– 4-3/8"; 1-1/2" thick near base.
- Colors: various shades of amber, amberina, amethyst, blue, cobalt, green, yellowish, and vaseline.

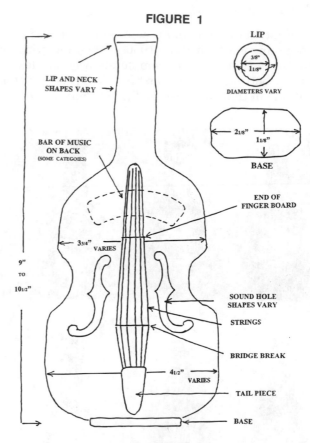

FIGURE 1

SV: Small Violin-Shaped Bottles (Figure 2)

SV: Small Violin-Shaped Bottles

- Three molds have been identified:
  - Mold 1: Produced at Clevenger Brothers Glass Works and Old Jersey Glass Co. (a Dell Glass Company).
  - Mold 2: Produced at Dell Glass Company.
  - Mold 3: Produced at Clevenger Brothers Glass Works.
- Less common than large violin bottles.
- Bottles had no contents and were made only for decorative purposes.
- First identified in the marketplace in the '40s.
- Height range of 7-1/4"; Body width 3"; 1-1/4" thick near base.
- Colors: various shades of cobalt, clear, blue, green, amber, and amethyst.

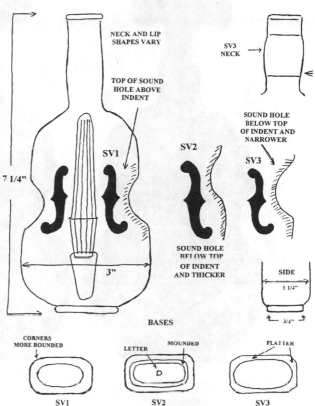

FIGURE 2

NECK AND LIP SHAPES VARY

TOP OF SOUND HOLE ABOVE INDENT

SV1

SV2

SV3 NECK

SOUND HOLE BELOW TOP OF INDENT AND NARROWER

SV3

7 1/4"

3"

SOUND HOLE BELOW TOP OF INDENT AND THICKER

SIDE
1 1/4"

3/4"

BASES

CORNERS MORE ROUNDED

SV1

LETTER   MOUNDED

D

SV2

FLATTER

SV3

EV: Violin-Shaped Bottles With "Ears" Or Tuning Pegs On The Neck (Figure 3)

- Four molds have been identified. Four neck shapes represent four mold patterns. Numerals 1-7 are cavity numbers. (Figure 4).
  - EVA1 to EVA7: Each has an "A" neck shape.
  - EVB1 to EVB7: Each has a "B" neck shape.
  - EVC1 to EVC7: Each has a "C" neck shape.
  - EVD1 to EVD7: Each has a "D" neck shape.
- Produced at Maryland Glass Company.
- ABM product (mold line goes up through neck, ears, and lip).
- Bottles had contents such as cosmetic lotion.
- Labeled as flasks, figurals, vases, and cosmetic bottles.
- Production began in the mid-1930s and lasted through the mid-1950s.
- Height 8"; Body width 4".
- Colors: various shades of blue, amber, and clear.

Violin bottle (EV) with "Ears" or "Tuning Pegs," cobalt blue $10-20.

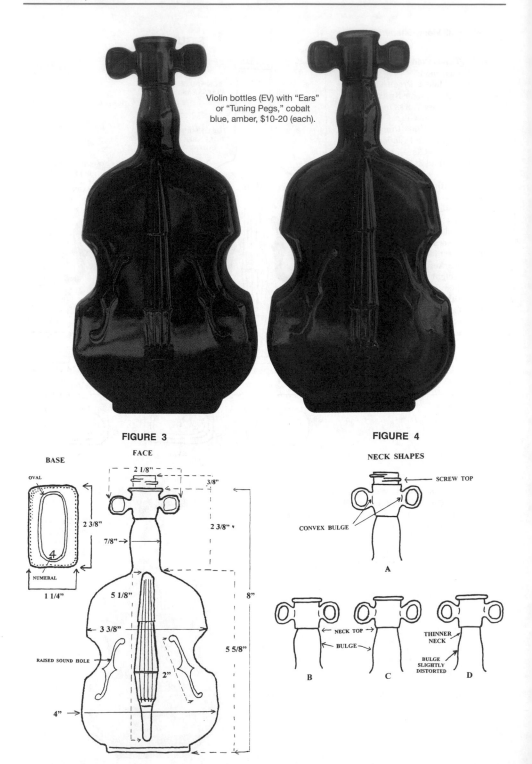

Violin bottles (EV) with "Ears" or "Tuning Pegs," cobalt blue, amber, $10-20 (each).

FIGURE 3

BASE

OVAL

2 3/8"

4

NUMERAL

1 1/4"

FACE

2 1/8"

3/8"

2 3/8" "

7/8"

5 1/8"

3 3/8"

RAISED SOUND HOLE

2"

4"

8"

5 5/8"

FIGURE 4

NECK SHAPES

SCREW TOP

CONVEX BULGE

A

NECK TOP

BULGE

B

C

THINNER NECK

BULGE SLIGHTLY DISTORTED

D

During the late 1930s, bourbon whiskey was distilled in Bardstown, Ky., and distributed throughout the eastern United States and Canada. Bardstown's violin-shaped bottles were made in several sizes and had many attractive labels that became common identifiers until production ceased in 1940. Interestingly, while the violin-bottle molds spanned 16 years, the molds were only used for four years. Because of limited production, Bardstown bottles with full labels are very difficult to find.

BV: Bardstown Violin-Shaped Whiskey Bottle (Figures 5 and 6)

- Two molds have been identified (produced at Owens-Illinois and Anchor-Hocking)
- Mold 1 (Cork Top)
  - BVC1: 11" (quart)
  - BVC2: 11" (4/5 quart)
  - BVC3: 10-1/8" (pint)
  - BVC4: 9-5/8" (pint)
  - BVC5: 8-1/8" (half pint)
- Mold 2 (Screw Top)
  - BVS1: 14" (half gallon)
  - BVS2: 9-1/2" to 10" (pint)
  - BVS3: 7-3/4" to 8-1/8" (half pint)
  - BVS4: 4-3/4" to 4-7/8" (nip)
- Only American violin figural designed and patented specifically with alcoholic content.
- Production began in the 1930s and lasted until 1940, when production ceased.
- Color: amber

FIGURE 5

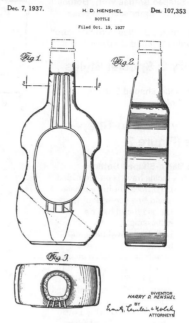

FIGURE 6

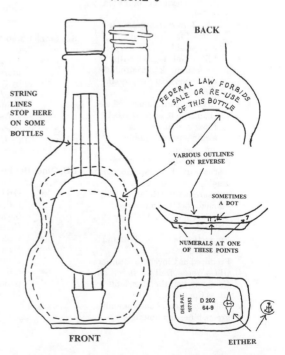

Category 2: European Styles

DV: Definitive Violin-Shaped Bottles

FV: Violin-Shaped Bottles With "Bottles Made In France" Embossed On Base.

CV: Violin Shaped Bottles With "Czecho" And "Slovakia" Etched On Base.

Category 3: Special Styles

OV: Other Violin-Shaped Bottles, Including Miniatures.

Category 4: Banjo-Shaped Bottles (Figure 7)

LB: Large Banjo-Shaped Bottles
- Six molds have been identified
    - LB1: Does not have a base (mold line goes all around the body) and has no embossing.
    - LB2: Plain oval base and no embossing. Possible prototype for future models.
    - LB3: Only type produced to contain alcohol. LB3 bottles have the following embossed legend: "Federal Law Forbids Sale or Reuse of this Bottle," which was required from 1933 (repeal of Prohibition) to 1966.
    - LB4: Minor changes with a "new" face and a clean reverse side.
    - LB5: Same as LB4, with a pontil mark but without the famous base embossing removed.
    - LB6: No pontil marks, since snap case tools were used. Finer and more delicate string and sound hole embossing.
- All large banjos have the same discus body shape, approximate height, width, and neck measurements. (Height 9-1/2"; diameter 5-1/4"; thickness 1-5/8"; oval base 1-1/2" long by 3/4" wide)
- Production began in 1942 and continued until 1975.
- Produced at Clevenger Brothers Glass Works, Dell Glass Company, and the Maryland Glass Company.
- Colors: various shades of amber, green, blue, and amethyst.

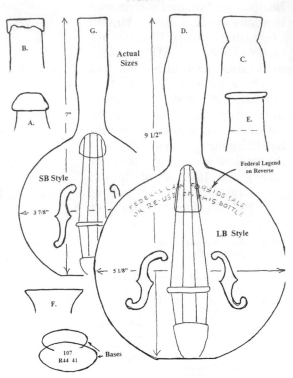

FIGURE 7

Actual Sizes

7"

9 1/2"

SB Style

3 7/8"

5 1/8"

Federal Legend on Reverse

LB Style

FEDERAL LAW FORBIDS SALE OR RE-USE OF THIS BOTTLE

107 R44 41 — Bases

SB: Small Banjo-Shaped Bottles
- Two molds have been identified:
    - SB 1: Smaller version of LB; height 7"; discus diameter 3-7/8"; lady's neck 3-1/8"; oval base 1-1/8" by 3/4".
    - SB 2: Squared sides with height 7-7/8"; discus diameter 4-1/2"; straight neck 3-1/2"; oval base 2" by 1-1/8", with a 1" kick-up in center of bottle (scarce).
- Produced at Clevenger Brothers Glass Works, Dell Glass Company, and the Maryland Glass Company.
- Colors: various shades of amber, green, blue, amethyst.

OB: Other Banjo-Shaped Bottles
- Three molds have been identified:
    - OB1: Corked-stopped whiskey measuring 10-3/4" tall; 5-5/8" wide; and 2-1/2" thick. Embossed on back is "Medley Distilling Company Owensboro, Kentucky 4/5 Quart." Color: clear.
    - OB2: Produced in Italy for 8" to 12" liquor bottles. Base embossing with "Patent Nello Gori." Color: clear.
    - OB3: Possible miniature, 4-1/2" tall, cobalt salt and pepper shakers in the image of a banjo. Produced by Maryland Glass Company in the 1930s.

Violin Bottle Pricing:

LV1a1 (United Church Bandstand)
Amethyst $150-250

LV1a2 (Auburn Die Company)
Amethyst $250-350

Large violin bottle (LV1a3),
cobalt blue, $50-100.

LV1a3 (VBCA, 1997)
Cobalt..$50-100

LV1a4 (VBCA, 1999)
Amethyst $50-150

LV1 (Clevenger)
Blue $20-30
Green..$20-30
Amethyst $30-45
Jersey Green $30-45

Large violin bottle (LV1),
amber, $40-50.

Amber...$40-50
Cobalt..$50-100
Amberina..$400-550

LV2 (Dell)
Blue $15-25
Green..$15-25
Amethyst $30-45

Large violin bottle (LV3), amethyst, $30-45.

LV3 (Dell)
Blue $15-25
Green..$15-25
Amethyst $30-45

LV4 (Clevenger)
Green..$50-60
Amethyst $50-60
Amber..$50-60
Cobalt..$80-100

Large violin bottle (LV5), yellow, $100-120.

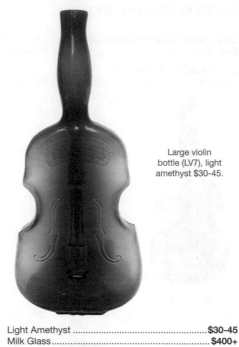

Large violin bottle (LV7), light amethyst $30-45.

LV5 (Dell Glass)
Royal Blue	$50-70
Clear	$50-70
Deep Green	$90-110
Golden Amber	$100-120
Yellow	$100-120
Florescing Green	$250-350

Light Amethyst	$30-45
Milk Glass	$400+

Large violin bottle (LV6), blue $20-30; green $20-30; amber $40-50.

Large violin bottle (LV8), light blue $60-80.

LV6 (Clevenger)
Blue	$20-30
Green	$20-30
Jersey Green	$25-40
Amethyst	$30-45
Amber	$40-50
Clear	$40-50
Cobalt	$50-100
Vaseline	$250-350

LV7 (Dell Glass)
Light Blue	$25-35
Light Green	$25-35

LV8 (Japan)
Light Blue	$60-80
Dark Blue	$60-80
Dark Green	$60-80
Dark Amethyst	$60-80

Small violin bottles (SV1), green $25-35; clear $45-60; cobalt blue $45-60; blue $25-35; amber $45-60.

SV1 (Clevenger)
Blue	$25-35
Green	$25-35
Amethyst	$35-45
Jersey Green	$35-45
Amber	$45-60
Clear	$45-60
Cobalt	$45-60

SV2 (Dell)
Blue	$15-25
Green	$15-25
Amethyst	$20-30

SV3 (Clevenger)
Blue	$25-35
Green	$25-35
Amethyst	$35-45
Amber	$45-60
Cobalt	$45-60

SV3app (Pairpoint Glass)
Ruby Red	$60+

EV's (Maryland Glass Company)
Light Cobalt	$10-20
Dark Cobalt	$10-20
Amber	$10-20
Clear	$10-20

Small violin bottle (SV2), amethyst, $20-30.

Definitive violin bottles (DV1), blue $30-50.

DV1 (Unknown)

Blue $30-50
Green...$30-50

Clear $30-50
Amber..$40-60
Red $80-100

Definitive violin bottles (DV 2 and 3), ruby red, $60-100 (each).

DV2 (Unknown)

Clear $15-25
Blues..$20-30
Greens...$20-30
Ambers $25-40
Red $60-100

DV3 (Unknown)

Clear $15-25
Blues..$20-30
Greens...$20-30
Ambers $25-40
Red $60-100

French violin bottle (FV1-3), blue tint $40-60;
green tint $40-60; light peach $50-75.

FV1-3 (French)
Clear $15-30
Blue Tint $40-60
Green Tint..$40-60
Light Peach $50-75

OV2 (Wheaton)
Clear $5-10
Blue $5-10
Green $5-10

OV 12 (George West)
Amber..$150-250
Cobalt... $500+

OV14 (Stumpy)
Light Blue $40-60
Green...$50-80
Amethyst $50-80

OV16 (Decanter)
Light Blue $150-300
Green..$150-300
Amethyst $150-300
Clear $150-300

Special style violin bottle, amber $150-250.

Banjo Bottle Pricing:

Large banjo
(LB1-9"), green
$75-125.

LB1: 9" - No Base Or Embossing, Mottled Glass, Small Applied Tooled Lip. Unknown Origin.
Green .... $75-$125

LB2: 9-1/2" - Oval Base, No Embossing. Unknown Origin.
Blue .... $40-$70
Amethyst .... $40-$70
Green .... $60-$100

LB3: 9-1/2" - 107 R44 41 Embossed On Base. "Federal Law Forbids Sale Or Reuse Of This Bottle" Embossed On Reverse. Maryland Glass Pre-1966.
Blue .... $60-$100

LB4: 9-1/2" – 107 R44 41 Embossed On Base, Strings And Soundholes. Dell Glass 1940s.
Blue .... $25-$40
Amethyst .... $25-$40
Green .... $25-$40

LB5: 9-1/2" – No Embossing On Base, Strings And Soundholes. Dell Glass 1940s.
Blue .... $25-$40
Amethyst .... $25-$40
Green .... $25-$40

LB6: 9-1/2" – No Embossing On Base, Strings And Soundholes. Clevenger 1940s.
Type E Neck
Blue .... $25-$50
Amethyst .... $25-$50
Green .... $25-$50
Cobalt .... $75-$100
Flared Lip
Blue .... $75-$100
Amethyst .... $50-$75
Green .... $50-$75
Amber .... $150-$200

LB6: 9-1/2" – Embossed Slug Plate Commemoratives. No Embossing On Base, Strings And Sound Holes. Clevenger 1970s.
LB6a: Depiction Of East Bridgewater Church
Amber .... $150-$250

Large banjo (LB4
and LB5 - 9-1/2"),
blue, amethyst,
green $25-40.

Large banjo (LB6b), amber, $100-150.

LB6b: Just The Words "American Handmade, Clevenger Brothers Glass Works, Clayton, NJ"
Amber ....$100-$150

LB6c: Depiction Of Two Glassblowers, Words "Clevenger Brothers Glass Works, American Made Mouth Blown"
Blue ....$75-$100

Amethyst ....$75-$100
Green...$75-$100
Amber..$75-$100

LB6d: Bicentennial "Celebrating 200 Years Of Freedom 1776-1976"
Green...$50-$100

LB6: 9-1/2" – Embossed Slug Plate Commemoratives. No Embossing On Base, Strings And Sound Holes. Pairpoint Glass 2001.

Lb6e: VBCA 2000 Commemorative.
Cobalt..$45-$65

LB6f: VBCA Blank Slug Plate
Cobalt..$45-$65
Lb6g: Chelmsford Historical Society/Ezekial Byam Commemorative
Teal ....$30-$50

SB1: 7"– Embossed Strings And Sound Holes. Old Jersey Glass/Dell 1940's
Blue ....$25-$50
Amethyst ....$25-$50
Green...$75-$100

SB2: 7-7/8" With 4-1/2" Diameter Disc Body, Embossed Strings, No Sound Holes. Origin Unknown
Blue ....$35-$60
Amethyst ....$35-$60
Green...$75-$100

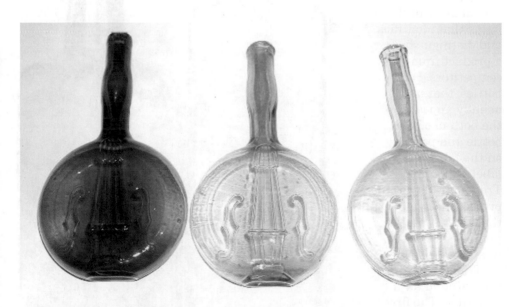

Small banjo (SB1, 7"), blue $25-50; amethyst $25-50; green $75-100.

Trademarks

History

Trademarks are helpful for determining the history, age, and value of bottles. In addition, researching trademarks gives the bottle collector a deeper knowledge of the many glass manufacturers that produced bottles and the bottling companies that provided the contents.

What is a trademark? By definition, a trademark is a word, name, letter, number, symbol, design, phrase, or a combination of these items that identifies and distinguishes a product from its competitors. For bottles, that mark usually appears on the bottom of the bottle and possibly on the label if a label still exists. Trademark laws only protect the symbol that represents the product, not the product itself.

Trademarks have been around for a long time. The first use an identification mark on glassware was the 1st century

glassmaker Ennion of Sidon and two of his students, Jason and Aristeas. They were the first glassmakers to identify their products by placing letters in the sides of their molds. In the 1840s, English glass manufacturers continued this practice using a similar technique.

Identifying marks have been found on antique Chinese porcelain, on pottery from ancient Greece and Rome, and on items from India dating back to 1300 B.C. In addition, stonecutters' marks have been found on many Egyptian structures dating back to 4000 B.C. In medieval times, craft and merchant owners relied on trademarks to distinguish their products from inferior goods and gain buyers' loyalty. They were applied to almost everything, including paper, bread, weapons, gold, silver, and leather goods.

In the late 1600s, bottle manufacturers began to mark their products with a glass seal that was applied while the bottle was still hot. A die with the manufacturer's initials, date, or design, was thus permanently molded on the bottle. This was both efficient and effective because cutting wasn't required, and the mark could be easily seen by the buyer.

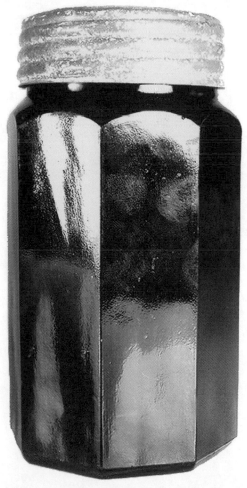

The use of trademarks spread beyond Europe; they were quickly adopted in North America as immigration of Europeans increased, but for many manufacturers of antique bottles, protection for the trademark owner was virtually nonexistent. While the U.S. Constitution provided rights of ownership in copyrights and patents, there was no trademark protection until Congress enacted the first federal trademark law in 1870. Significant revisions and changes were made to the 1870 trademark law in 1881, 1905, 1920, and 1946. Research indicates that registrations of trademarks began in 1860 on glassware, with a major increase in the 1890s by all types of glass manufacturers.

Determining Bottle Makers and Dates

If you are able to determine the producer of a trademark, as well as when it might have been used, you will likely be able to determine the date of a piece. If the mark wasn't used long, it is much easier to pinpoint the bottle's age. If, however, the mark was used over an extended period of time, you will have to rely on additional references. Unfortunately, most numbers appearing with trademarks are not a part of the trademark and, therefore, will not provide any useful information.

There are approximately 1,200 trademarks for bottles and fruit jars, which are comprised of 900 older marks (1830s-1940) and 300 more modern marks (1940s to 1970). Very few manufacturers used identical marks, which is amazing considering how many companies have produced bottles.

Note: Words and letters in bold are the trademarks as they appeared on the bottles. Each trademark is followed by the complete name and location of the company and the approximate time in which the trademark was used.

United States Trademarks

A

A: Adams & Co., Pittsburgh, Pa., 1861-1891.

A: John Agnew & Son, Pittsburgh, Pa., 1854-1866.

A: Arkansas Glass Container Corp., Jonesboro, Ark., 1958 to date (if machine made).

A (in a circle): American Glass Works, Richmond, Va. and Paden City, W.V., 1908-1935.

AB: Adolphus Busch Glass Manufacturing Co, Belleville, Ill., and St. Louis, Mo., 1904-1907.

A.B.C.: Albion Bottle Co., LTD., Oldbury, Worcs., England, 1928-1969.

ABC: Atlantic Bottle Co., New York City and Brackenridge, Pa., 1918-1930.

ABCo.: American Bottle Co., Chicago, Ill., 1905-1916; Toledo, Ohio, 1916-1929.

ABCO (in script): Ahrens Bottling Company, Oakland, Calif., 1903-1908.

A B G M Co.: Adolphus Busch Glass Manufacturing Co, Belleville, Ill., 1886-1907; St. Louis, Mo., 1886-1928.

A & Co.: John Agnew and Co., Pittsburgh, Pa., 1854-1892.

A C M E: Acme Glass Co., Olean, N.Y., 1920-1930.

A & D H C: A. & D.H. Chambers, Pittsburgh, Pa., Union Flasks, 1843-1886.

AGCo : Arsenal Glass Co. (or Works), Pittsburgh, Pa., 1865-1868.

AGEE and Agee (in script): Hazel Atlas Glass Co., Wheeling, W.V., 1919-1925.

AGNEW & CO.: Agnew & Co., Pittsburgh, Pa., 1876-1886.

AGWL, PITTS PA: American Glass Works, Pittsburgh, Pa., 1865-1880, American Glass Works Limited, 1880-1905.

AGW: American Glass Works, Richmond, Va., & Paden City, W.V., 1908-1935.

AMF & Co.: Adelbert M. Foster & Co., Chicago, Ill.; Millgrove, Upland, and Marion, Ind., 1895-1911.

Anchor figure with H in center: Anchor Hocking Glass Corp., Lancaster, Ohio, 1955.

A. R. S.: A.R. Samuels Glass Co., Philadelphia, Pa., 1855-1872.

A S F W W Va.: A.S. Frank Glass Co., Wellsburg, W.V., 1859.

ATLAS: Atlas Glass Co., Washington, Pa., and later Hazel Atlas Glass Co., 1896-1965.

B

B: Buck Glass Co., Baltimore, Md., 1909-1961.

B (in circle): Brockway Machine Bottle Co., Brockway, Pa., 1907-1933.

Ball and Ball (in script): Ball Bros. Glass Manufacturing Co., Muncie, Ind., and later Ball Corp., 1887-1973.

Baker Bros. Balto. MD.: Baker Brothers, Baltimore, Md., 1853-1905.

BAKEWELL: Benjamin P. Bakewell Jr. Glass Co., 1876-1880.

BANNER: Fisher-Bruce Co., Philadelphia, Pa., 1910-1930.

BB Co: Berney-Bond Glass Co., Bradford, Clarion, Hazelhurst, and Smethport, Pa., 1900.

BB & Co: Berney-Bond Glass Co., Bradford, Clarion, Hazelhurst, and Smethport, Pa., 1900.

BB48: Berney-Bond Glass Co., Bradford, Clarion, Hazelhurst, and Smethport, Pa., 1920-1930.

BBCo: Bell Bottle Co, Fairmount, Ind., 1910-1914.

Bennett's: Gillinder & Bennett (Franklin Flint Glass Co.) Philadelphia, Pa., 1863-1867.

Bernardin (in script): W.J. Latchford Glass Co., Los Angeles, Calif., 1932-1938.

The Best: Gillender & Sons, Philadelphia, Pa., 1867-1870.

B F B Co.: Bell Fruit Bottle Co., Fairmount, Ind., 1910.

B. G. Co.: Belleville Glass Co. Ill., 1882.

Bishop's: Bishop & Co., San Diego and Los Angeles, Calif., 1890-1920.

BK: Benedict Kimber, Bridgeport and Brownsville, Pa., 1825-1840.

BLUE RIBBON: Standard Glass Co., Marion, Ind., 1908.

BOLDT: Charles Boldt Glass Manufacturing Co., Cincinnati, Ohio, and Huntington, W.V., 1900-1929.

Boyds (in script): Illinois Glass Co., Alton, Ill., 1900-1930.

BP & B: Bakewell, Page & Bakewell., Pittsburgh, Pa., 1824-1836.

Brelle (in script) Jar: Brelle Fruit Jar Manufacturing Co., San Jose, Calif., 1912-1916.

Brilliante: Jefferis Glass Co., Fairton, N.J. and Rochester, Pa., 1900-1905.

C

C (in circle): Chattanooga Bottle & Glass Co., and later Chattanooga Glass Co., 1927-present.

C (in square): Crystal Glass Co., Los Angeles, Calif., 1921-1929.

C (in star): Star City Glass Co., Star City, W.V., 1949-present.

C (in upside down triangle): Canada Dry Ginger Ale Co., N.Y.C., 1930-1950.

Canton Domestic Fruit Jar: Canton Glass Co., Canton, Ohio, 1890-1904.

C & Co. or C Co: Cunninghams & Co., Pittsburgh, Pa., 1880-1907.

CCCo: Carl Conrad & Co. (Beer), St. Louis, Mo., 1860-1883.

C.V.Co. No. 1 & No 2: Milwaukee, Wis., 1880-1881.

C C Co.: Carl Conrad & Co., St. Louis, Mo., 1876-1883.

C C G Co.: Cream City Glass Co., Milwaukee, Wis., 1888-1894.

C.F.C.A.: California Fruit Canners Association, Sacramento, Calif., 1899-1916.

CFJCo: Consolidated Fruit Jar Co., New Brunswick, N.J., 1867-1882.

C G I: California Glass Insulator Co., Long Beach, Calif., 1912-1919.

C G M Co: Campbell Glass Manufacturing Co., West Berkeley, Calif., 1885.

C G W: Campbell Glass Works, West Berkeley, Calif., 1884-1885.

C & H: Coffin & Hay, Hammonton, N.J., 1836-1838, or Winslow, N.J., 1838-1842.

C L G Co.: Carr-Lowrey Glass Co., Baltimore, Md., 1889-1920.

CLARKE: Clarke Fruit Jar Co., Cleveland, Ohio, 1886-1889.

CLOVER LEAF (in arch with picture of clover leaf): 1890 (marked on ink and mucilage bottles).

Clyde, N.Y.: Clyde Glass Works, Clyde, N.Y., 1870-1882.

The Clyde (in script): Clyde Glass Works, Clyde, N.Y., 1895.

C Milw: Chase Valley Glass Co., Milwaukee, Wis., 1880-1881.

Cohansey: Cohansey Glass Manufacturing Co., Philadelphia, Pa., 1870-1900.

C R: Curling, Robertson & Co., Pittsburgh, Pa., 1834-1857 or Curling, Ringwalt & Co., Pittsburgh, Pa., 1857-1863.

CRYSTO: McPike Drug Co., Kansas City, Mo., 1904.

CS & Co: Cannington, Shaw & Co., St. Helens, England, 1872-1916.

D

D 446: Consolidated Fruit Jar Co., New Brunswick, N.J., 1871-1882.

DB: Du Bois Brewing Co., Pittsburgh, Pa., 1918.

Dexter: Franklin Flint Glass Works, Philadelphia, Pa., 1861-1880.

Diamond: (Plain) Diamond Glass Co. 1924-present.

The Dictator: William McCully & Co., Pittsburgh, Pa., 1855-1869.

Dictator: William McCully & Co., Pittsburgh, Pa., 1869-1885.

D & O: Cumberland Glass Mfg. Co., Bridgeton, N.J., 1890-1900.

D O C: D.O. Cunningham Glass Co., Pittsburgh, Pa., 1883-1937.

DOME: Standard Glass Co., Wellsburg, W.V., 1891-1893.

D S G Co.: De Steiger Glass Co., LaSalle, Ill., 1879-1896.

Duffield: Dr. Samuel Duffield, Detroit, Mich., 1862-1866, and Duffield, Parke & Co., Detroit, Mich., 1866-1875.

Dyottsville: Dyottsville Glass Works, Philadelphia, Pa., 1833-1923.

E

E4: Essex Glass Co., Mt. Vernon, Ohio, 1906-1920.

Economy (in script) TRADE MARK: Kerr Glass Manufacturing Co., Portland, Ore., 1903-1912.

Electric Trade Mark (in script): Gayner Glass Works, Salem, N.J., 1910.

Electric Trade Mark: Gayner Glass Works, Salem, N.J., 1900-1910.

The EMPIRE: Empire Glass Co., Cleveland, N.Y., 1852-1877.

Erd & Co., E R Durkee: E.R. Durkee & Co., New York, N.Y., post-1874.

E R Durkee & Co: E.R. Durkee & Co., New York, NY., 1850-1860.

Eureka (in script): Eurkee Jar Co., Dunbar, W.V., 1900-1910.

Eureka 17: Eurkee Jar Co., Dunbar, W.V., 1864.

Everett and EHE: Edward H. Everett Glass Co. (Star Glass Works) Newark, Ohio, 1893-1904.

Everlasting (in script) JAR: Illinois Pacific Glass Co., San Francisco, Calif., 1904.

Excelsior: Excelsior Glass Co., St. John, Quebec, Canada, 1878-1883.

F

F (inside a jar outline or keystone): C.L. Flaccus Glass Co., Pittsburgh, Pa., 1900-1928.

F WM. Frank & Sons: WM. Frank & Co., Pittsburgh, Pa., 1846-1966, WM. Frank & Sons, Pittsburgh, Pa., 1866-1876.

F & A: Fahnstock & Albree, Pittsburgh, Pa., 1860-1862.

FERG Co: F.E. Reed Glass Co., Rochester, N.Y., 1898-1947.

FF & Co: Fahnstock, Fortune & Co., Pittsburgh, Pa., 1866-1873.

F G: Florida Glass Manufacturing Co., Jacksonville, Fla., 1926-1947.

FL or FL & Co.: Frederick Lorenz & Co., Pittsburgh, Pa., 1819-1841.

FLINT–GREEN: Whitney Glass Works, Glassborough, N.J., 1888.

FOLGER, JAF&Co., Pioneer, Golden Gate: J. A. Folger & Co., San Francisco, Calif., 1850-present.

G

G (in circle, bold lines): Gulfport Glass Co., Gulfport, Miss., 1955-1970.

G E M: Hero Glass Works, Philadelphia, Pa., 1884-1909.

G & H: Gray & Hemingray, Cincinnati, Ohio, 1848-1851; Covington, Ky., 1851-1864.

G & S: Gillinder & Sons, Philadelphia, Pa., 1867-1871 and 1912-1930.

Gillinder: Gillinder Bros., Philadelphia, Pa., 1871-1930.

Gilberds: Gilberds Butter Tub Co., Jamestown, N.Y., 1883-1890.

GLENSHAW (G in box under name): Glenshaw Glass Co., Glenshaw, Pa., 1904.

GLOBE: Hemingray Glass Co., Covington, Ky. (The symbol "Parquet-Lac" was used beginning in 1895), 1886.

Greenfield: Greenfield Fruit Jar & Bottle Co., Greenfield, Ind., 1888-1912.

G W K & Co.: George W. Kearns & Co., Zanesville, Ohio, 1848-1911.

H

H and H (in heart): Hart Glass Manufacturing Co., Dunkirk, Ind., 1918-1938.

H (with varying numerals): Holt Glass Works, West Berkeley, Calif., 1893-1906.

H (in diamond): A.H. Heisey Glass Co., Oakwood Ave., Newark, Ohio, 1893-1958.

H (in triangle): J.T. & A. Hamilton Co., Pittsburgh, Pa., 1900.

Hamilton: Hamilton Glass Works, Hamilton, Ontario, Canada, 1865-1872.

Hazel: Hazel Glass Co., Wellsburg, W.V., 1886-1902.

H.B.Co: Hagerty Bros. & Co., Brooklyn, N.Y., 1880-1900.

F. J. Heinz: H.J. Heinz Co., Pittsburgh, Pa., 1876-1888.

H. J. Heinz: H.J. Heinz Co., Pittsburgh, Pa., 1860-1869.

H. J. Heinz Co.: H.J. Heinz Co., Pittsburgh, Pa., 1888-present.

Heinz & Noble: H.J. Heinz Co., Pittsburgh, Pa., 1869-1872.

Helme: Geo. W. Helme Co., Jersey City, N.J., 1870-1895.

Hemingray: Hemingray Brothers & Co., and later Hemingray Glass Co., Covington, Ky., 1864-1933.

HELME: Geo. W. Helme Co., N.J., 1870-1890.

HERO: Hero Glass Works, Philadelphia, Pa., 1856-1884 and Hero Fruit Jar Co., Philadelphia, Pa., 1884-1909.

HS (in a circle): Twitchell & Schoolcraft, Keene, N.H., 1815-1816.

Hunyadi Janos: Andreas Saxlehner, Buda-Pesth, Austria-Hungary, 1863-1900.

IDEAL: Hod c. Dunfee, Charleston, W.V., 1910.

I

I G Co.: Ihmsen Glass Co., Pittsburgh, Pa., 1855-1896.

I. G. Co: Ihmsen Glass Co., 1895.

I. G. Co.: Monogram, Illinois Glass Co. on fruit jar, 1914.

IPGCO: Illinois Pacific Glass Company, San Francisco, Calif., 1902-1926.

IPGCO: (in diamond), Illinois Pacific Glass Company, San Francisco, 1902-1926.

IG: Illinois Glass, F inside jar outline, C.L. Flaccus, 1/2 glass, 1/2 co., Pittsburgh, Pa., 1900-1928.

Ill. Glass Co.: 1916-1929.

I G: Illinois Glass Co., Alton, Ill., before 1890.

I G Co. (in diamond): Illinois Glass Co., Alton, Ill., 1900-1916.

Improved G E M: Hero Glass Works, Philadelphia, Pa., 1868.

I P G: Illinois Pacific Glass Co. San Francisco, Calif., 1902-1932.

I X L: I X L Glass Bottle Co., Inglewood, Calif., 1921-1923.

J

J (in keystone): Knox Glass Bottle Co., Jackson, Miss., 1932-1953.

J (in square): Jeannette Glass Co., Jeannette, Pa., 1901-1922.

JAF & Co., Pioneer and Folger: J.A. Folger & Co., San Francisco Calif., 1850-present.

J D 26 S: Jogn Ducan & Sons, New York, N.Y., 1880-1900.

J.P.F.: Pitkin Glass Works, Manchester, Conn., 1783-1830.

J R: Stourbridge Flint Glass Works Pittsburgh, Pa., 1823-1828.

JBS monogram: Joseph Schlitz Brewing Co., Milwaukee, Wis., 1900.

JT: Mantua Glass Works, and later Mantua Glass Co., Mantua, Ohi 1824.

JT & Co: Brownsville Glass Works Brownsville, Pa., 1824-1828.

J. SHEPARD: J. Shepard & Co., Zanesville, Ohio, 1823-1838.

Kensington Glass Works: Kensington Glass Works, Philadelphia, Pa., 1822-1932.

K

Kerr (in script): Kerr Glass Manufacturing Co., and later Alexander H. Kerr Glass Co., Portland, Ore.; Sand Spring, Okla.; Chicago, Ill.; Los Angeles, Calif., 1912-present.

K H & G: Kearns, Herdman & Gorsuch, Zanesville, Ohio, 1876-1884.

K & M: Knox & McKee, Wheeling, W.V., 1824-1829.

K & O: Kivlan & Onthank, Boston, Mass., 1919-1925.

K Y G W and KYGW Co: Kentucky Glass Works Co., Louisville, Ky., 1849-1855.

L

L (in keystone): Lincoln Glass Bottle Co., Lincoln, Ill., 1942-1952.

L: W.J. Latchford Glass Co., Los Angeles, Calif., 1925-1938.

Lamb: Lamb Glass Co., Mt. Vernon, Ohio, 1855-1964.

LB (B inside L): Long Beach Glass Co., Long Beach, Calif., 1920-1933.

L & W: Lorenz & Wightman, Pa. 1862-1871.

LGW: Laurens Glass Works, Laurens, S.C., 1911-1970.

L G Co: Louisville Glass Works, Louisville, Ky., 1880.

Lightning: Henry W. Putnam, Bennington, Vt., 1875-1890.

L I P: Lea & Perrins, London, England, 1880-1900.

L K Y G W: Louisville Kentucky Glass Works, Louisville, Ky., 1873-1890.

M

Mascot, "Mason" and M F G Co.: Mason Fruit Jar Co., Philadelphia, Pa., 1885-1890.

Mastadon: Thomas A. Evans Mastadon Works, and later Wm. McCully & Co., Pittsburgh, Pa., 1855-1887.

MB Co: Muncie Glass Co., Muncie, Ind., 1895-1910.

M B & G Co: Massillon Bottle & Glass Co., Massillon, Ohio, 1900-1904.

M B W: Millville Bottle Works, Millville, N.J., 1903-1930.

McL (in circle): McLaughlin Glass Co., Vernon, Calif., 1920-1936, Gardena, Calif., 1951-1956.

MEDALLION: M.S. Burr & Co. (mfgr. of nursing bottles), Boston, Mass., 1874.

MG: Maywood Glass, Maywood, Calif.; straight letters, 1930-1940; slant letters, 1940-1958.

M.G. CO.: Modes Glass Co., Cicero, Ind., 1895-1904.

M.G. W.: Middletown Glass Co., N.Y., 1889.

Moore Bros.: Moore Bros., Clayton, N.J., 1864-1880.

MOUNT VERNON: Cook & Bernheimer Co., New York, N.Y., 1890.

N

N (in keystone): Newborn Glass Co., Royersford, Pa., 1920-1925.

N: H. Northwood Glass Co., Wheeling, W.V., 1902-1925.

N (bold N in bold square): Obear-Nester Glass Co., St. Louis, Mo., and East St. Louis, Ill., 1895.

N B B G Co: North Baltimore Bottle Glass Co., North Baltimore, Ohio, 1885-1930.

N G Co: Northern Glass Co., Milwaukee, Wis., 1894-1896.

N-W: Nivison-Weiskopf Glass Co., Reading, Ohio, 1900-1931.

O

O (in square): Owen Bottle Co., 1911-1929.

O B C: Ohio Bottle Co., Newark, Ohio, 1904-1905.

O-D-1-O & Diamond & I: Owens Illinois Pacific Coast Co., Calif. 1932-1943. Mark of Owen-Illinois Glass Co. merger in 1930.

O G W: Olean Glass Co. (Works), Olean, N.Y., 1887-1915.

P

P (in keystone): Wightman Bottle & Glass Co., Parker Landing, Pa., 1930-1951.

PCGW: Pacific Coast Glass Works, San Francisco, Calif., 1902-1924.

PEERLESS: Peerless Glass Co., Long Island City, N.Y., 1920-1935 (was Bottler's & Manufacturer's Supply Co., 1900-1920.

P G W: Pacific Glass Works, San Francisco, Calif., 1862-1876.

Picture of Young Child (in circle): M.S. Burr & Co. (mfgr. of nursing bottles), Boston, Mass., 1874.

Premium: Premium Glass Co., Coffeyville, Kan., 1908-1914.

P (in square) or pine (in box): Pine Glass Corp., Okmulgee, Okla., 1927-1929.

P S: Puget Sound Glass Co., Anacortes, Wash., 1924-1929.

Putnam Glass Works (in circle): Putnam Flint Glass Works, Putnam, Ohio, 1852-1871.

P & W: Perry & Wood, and later Perry & Wheeler, Keene, N.H., 1822-1830.

Q

Queen (in script) Trade Mark (all in a shield): Smalley, Kivian & Onthank, Boston, Mass., 1906-1919.

R

R: Louit Freres & Co., France, 1870-1890.

Rau's: Fairmount Glass Works, Fairmount, Ind., 1898-1908.

R & C Co: Roth & Co., San Francisco, Calif., 1879-1888.

Red with a key through it: Safe Glass Co., Upland, Ind.,1892-1898.

R G Co.: Renton Glass Co., Renton, Wash., 1911.

Root: Root Glass Co., Terre Haute, Ind., 1901-1932.

S

S (inside a star): Southern Glass Co. L.A., 1920-1929.

SB & G Co- Stretor Bottle & Glass Co., Streator, Ill., 1881-1905.

SF & PGW: San Francisco & Pacific Glass Works, 1876-1900.

S & C: Stebbins & Chamberlain or Coventry Glass Works, Coventry, Conn., 1825-1830.

S F G W: San Francisco Glass Works, San Francisco, Calif., 1869-1876.

S & M: Sykes & Macvey, Castleford, England, 1860-1888.

SIGNET (blown in bottom): Chicago Heights Bottle Co., Chicago Heights, Ill., 1913.

Squibb: E.R. Squibb, M.D., Brooklyn, N.Y., 1858-1895.

Standard (in script, Mason): Standard Coop. Glass Co., and later Standard Glass Co., Marion, Ind., 1894-1932.

Star Glass Co: Star Glass Co., New Albany, Ind., 1867-1900.

Swayzee: Swayzee Glass Co., Swayzee, Ind., 1894-1906.

T

T C W: T.C. Wheaton Co., Millville, N.J., 1888-present.

THE BEST (in an arch): Gotham Co., New York, N.Y., 1891.

TIP TOP: Charles Boldt Glass Co., Cincinnati, Ohio, 1904.

T W & Co.: Thomas Wightman & Co., Pittsburgh, Pa., 1871-1895.

T S: Coventry Glass Works, Coventry, Conn., 1820-1824.

U

U: Upland Flint Bottle Co., Upland Inc., 1890-1909.

U S: United States Glass Co., Pittsburgh, Pa., 1891-1938, Tiffin, Ohio, 1938-1964.

W

WARRANTED (in arch) FLASK: Albert G. Smalley, Boston, Mass., 1892.

W & CO: Thomas Wightman & Co., Pittsburgh, Pa., 1880-1889.

W C G Co: West Coast Glass Co., Los Angeles, Calif., 1908-1930.

WF & S MILW: William Franzen & Son, Milwaukee, Wis., 1900-1929.

W G W: Woodbury Glass Works, Woodbury, N.J., 1882-1900.

WYETH: A drug manufacturer, 1880-1910.

W T & Co: Whitall-Tatum & Co., Millville, N.J., 1857-1935.

W T R Co.: W.T. Rawleigh Manufacturing Co., Freeport, Ill., 1925-1936.

Foreign Trademarks

A

A (in circle): Alembic Glass Industries, Bangalore, India.

Big A (in center of GM): Australian Glass Mfg. Co., Kilkenny, So. Australia.

A.B.C.: Albion Bottle Co. Ltd., Oldbury, Nr. Birmingham, England.

A.G.W.: Alloa Glass Limited, Alloa, Scotland.

A G B Co.: Albion Glass Bottle Co., England (trademark is found under Lea & Perrins), 1880-1900.

B

B & C Co. L: Bagley & Co. Ltd., est. 1832, still operating (England).

AVH: A. Van Hoboken & Co., Rotterdam, the Netherlands, 1800-1898.

Beaver: Beaver Flint Glass Co., Toronto, Ontario, Canada, 1897-1920.

Bottle (in frame): Veb Glasvoerk Drebkau, Drebkau, N. L., Germany.

C

Crown with three dots: Crown Glass, Waterloo, N.S. Wales.

Crown with figure of a crown: Excelsior Glass Co., St. Johns, Quebec, and later Diamond Glass Co., Montreal, Quebec, Canada, 1879-1913.

CS & Co.: Cannington, Shaw & Co., St. Helens, England, 1872-1916.

CSTS (in center of hot air balloon): . Stolzles Sohne Actiengeselischaft fur Glasfabrikation, Vienna, Austria, Hungary,1905.

D

D (in center of diamond): Dominion Glass Co., Montreal, Quebec.

D.B. (in book frame): Dale Brown & Co., Ltd., Mesborough, Yorks., England.

E

Excelsior: Excelsior Glass Co., St. John, Quebec, Canada, 1878-1883.

F

Fish: Veb Glasvoerk Stralau, Berlin.

H

HH: Werk Hermannshutte, Czechoslovakia.

Hamilton: Hamilton Glass Works, Hamilton, Ontario, Canada, 1865-1872.

Hat: Brougba, Bulgaria.

Hunyadi Janos: Andreas Saxlehner, Buda-Pesth, Austria-Hungary, 1863-1900.

I

IYGE (all in circle): The Irish Glass Bottle, Ltd., Dublin.

K

KH: Kastrupog Holmeqaads, Copenhagen.

L

L (on a bell): Lanbert, S.A. Belgium.

LIP: Lea & Perrins, London, England, 1880-1900.

LS (in a circle): Lax & Shaw Ltd., Leeds, York, England.

M

M (in a circle): Cristales Mexicanos, Monterey, Mexico.

N

N (in a diamond): Nippon Glass Co., Ltd. Tokyo, Japan.

NAGC: North American Glass Co., Montreal, Quebec, Canada, 1883-1890.

NP: Imperial Trust for the Encouragement of Scientific and Industrial Research, London, England, 1907.

NS (in middle of bottle shape): Edward Kavalier of Neu Sazawa, Austria-Hungary, 1910.

P

P & J A: P. & J. Arnold, LTD., London, England, 1890-1914.

PRANA: Aerators Limited, London, England, 1905.

PG: Verreries De Puy De Dome, S.A. Paris.

R

R: Louit Freres & Co., France, 1870-1890.

S

S (in a circle): Vetreria Savonese, A. Voglienzone, S.A. Milano, Italy.

S.A.V.A. (all in a circle): Asmara, Ethiopia.

S & M: Sykes & Macvey, Castleford, England, 1860-1888.

T

T (in a circle): Tokyo Seibin Ltd., Tokyo, Japan.

V

vFo: Vidreria Ind., Figuerras, Oliveiras, Brazil.

VT: Ve.Tri S.p.a., Vetrerie Trivemta, Vicenza, Italy.

VX: Usine de Vauxrot, France.

W

WECK (in frame): Weck Glaswerk, G. mb.H, ofigen, Bonn, Germany.

Y

Y (in circle): Etaria Lipasmaton, Athens, Greece.

Bottle Clubs

Bottle clubs are some of the best sources for beginners and offer a great opportunity to meet veteran bottle collectors, learn from them, gather information, and in general have a good time. The bottle clubs listed here reflect the latest information available at the time of publication and are subject to change. The list represents an excellent cross-section across the United States, Europe, and Asia-Pacific. Any active bottle club or organization that requires a change in information, or wishes to be included in the next edition of this book, should send the required information to Michael F. Polak, P.O. Box 30328, Long Beach, CA 90853 or send an e-mail to bottleking@earthlink.net.

Note: Clubs are listed alphabetically by state, country and club name.

United States

Alabama

Alabama Bottle Collectors Society, 2768 Hanover Circle, Birmingham, AL 35205, (205) 933-7902

Azalea City Beamers Bottle & Spec. Club, 100 Bienville Avenue, Mobile, AL 36606, (205) 473-4251

Heart of Dixie Beam Bottle & Spec. Club, 2136 Rexford Road, Montgomery, AL 36116

Mobile Bottle Collectors Club, 8844 Lee Circle, Irvington, AL 36544, (205) 957-6725

Montgomery Bottle & Insulator Club, 2021 Merrily Drive, Montgomery, AL 36111, (205) 288-7937

North Alabama Bottle & Glass Club, P.O. Box 109, Decatur, AL 35602-0109

Tuscaloosa Antique Bottle Club, 1617 11th Street, Tuscaloosa, AL 35401

Vulcan Beamers Bottle & Spec. Club, 5817 Avenue Q, Birmingham, AL 35228, (205) 831-5151

Alaska

Alaska Bottle Club, 8510 E. 10th, Anchorage, AK 99504

Arizona

Avon Collectors Club, P.O. Box 1406, Mesa, AZ 86201

Kachina Ezra Brooks Bottle Club, 3818 W. Cactus Wren Drive, Phoenix, AZ 85021

Phoenix A.B.C. Club, 4712 W. Lavey Road, Glendale, AZ 85306

Pick & Shovel A.B.C. of Arizona, Inc, P.O. Box 7020, Phoenix, AZ 85011

Southern AZ Historical Collector's Association, Ltd., 6211 Piedra Seca, Tucson, AZ 85718

Tri-City Jim Beam Bottle Club, 2701 E. Utopia Road, Sp. #91, Phoenix, AZ 85024, (602) 867-1375

Valley of the Sun Bottle & Specialty Club, 212 E. Minton, Tempe, AZ 85281

White Mountain Antique Bottle Collectors Association, P.O. Box 503, Eager, AZ 85925

Wildcat Country Beam Bottle & Spec. Club, 2601 S. Blackmoon Drive, Tucson, AZ 85730, (602) 298-5943

Arkansas

Fort Smith Area Bottle Collectors Assn., 2201 S. 73rd Street, Ft. Smith, AR 72903

Hempsted County Bottle Club, 710 S. Hervey, Hope AR 71801

Indian Country A.B. & Relic Soc., 3818 Hilltop Dr., Jonesboro, AR 72401

Little Rock Antique Bottle Collectors Club, 16201 Highway 300, Roland, AR 72135

Madison County Bottle Collectors Club, Rt. 2, Box 304, Huntsville, AR 72740

Razorback Jim Beam Bottle & Spec. Club, 2609 S. Taylor, Little Rock, AR 72204, (501) 664-1335

California

American Cut Glass Assoc., P.O. Box 482, Ramona, CA 92065-0482

Amethyst Bottle Club, 3245 Military Avenue, Los Angeles, CA 90034

Antique Bottle Collectors of Orange County, 223 E. Pomona, Santa Ana, CA 92707

Antique Poison Bottle Collectors Association, 3739 Amador Court, Chino, CA 91710

Argonaut Jim Beam Bottle Club, 8253 Citadel Way, Sacramento, CA 95826, (916) 383-0206

Avon Bottle & Specialties Collectors, Southern California Division, 9233 Mills Avenue, Montclair, CA 91763

Bakersfield Bottle & Insulator Collectors, 1023 Baldwin Road, Bakersfield, CA 93304

Bay Area Vagabonds Jim Beam Club, 224 Castleton Way, San Bruno, CA 94066, (415) 355-4356

Bidwell Bottle Club, Box 546, Chico, CA 95926

Bishop Belles & Beaux Bottle Club, P.O. Box 1475, Bishop, CA 93514

Blossom Valley Jim Beam Bottle & Spec. Club, 431 Grey Ghost Avenue, San Jose, CA 95111, (408) 227-2759

California Milk Bottle Collectors, 2592 Mayfair Court, Hanford, CA 93230

California Miniature Bottle Club, 1911 Willow Street, Alameda, CA 94501

California Ski Country Bottle Club, 212 South El Molino Street, Alhambra, CA 91801

Camellia City Jim Beam Bottle Club, 3734 Lynhurst Way, North Highlands, CA 95660

Cherry Valley Beam Bottle & Specialty Club, 6851 Hood Drive, Westminster, CA 92683

Fiesta City Beamers, 329 Mountain Drive, Santa Barbara, CA 93103

First Double Springs Collectors Club, 13311 Illinois Street, Westminster, CA 92683

Five Cities Beamers, 756 Mesa View Drive, Sp. 57, Arroyo Grande, CA 93420

Fostoria Glass Collectors, Inc., P.O. Box 1625, Orange, CA 92668

Fresno Antique Bottle & Collectors Club, 4318 Kenmore Drive South, Fresno, CA 92703

Glass Belles of San Gabriel, 518 W. Neuby Avenue, San Gabriel, CA 91776

Glasshopper Figural Bottle Association, P.O. Box 6642, Torrance, CA 90504

Golden Gate Beam Club, 35113 Clover Street, Union City, CA 94587, (415) 487-4479

Golden Gate Historical Bottle Society, 752 Murdell Lane, Livermore, CA 94550

Highland Toasters Beam Bottle & Spec. Club, 1570 E. Marshall, San Bernardino, CA 92404, (714) 883-2000

Hoffman's Mr. Lucky Bottle Club, 2104 Rhoda Street, Simi Valley, CA 93065

International Perfume Bottle Association, 3519 Wycliffe Drive, Modesto, CA 95355

Jewels of Avon, 2297 Maple Avenue, Oroville, CA 95965

Jim Beam Bottle Club, 139 Arlington, Berkley, CA 94707

Jim Beam Bottle Club of So. Calif., 1114 Coronado Terrace, Los Angeles, CA 90066

Lilliputian Bottle Club, 5626 Corning Avenue, Los Angeles, CA 90056, (213) 294-3231

Livermore Avon Club, 6385 Claremont Avenue, Richmond, CA 94805

Los Angeles Historical Bottle Club, 42243 Brighton St., Lancaster, CA 93536

Miniature Bottle Club of Southern California, 836 Carob, Brea, CA 92621

Mission Bells (Beams), 1114 Coronada Terrace, Los Angeles, CA 90026

Mission Trail Historical Bottle Club, 1075 Hart Street, Seaside, CA 93955

Modesto Beamers, 1429 Glenwood Drive, Modesto, CA 95350, (209) 523-3440

Modesto Old Bottle Club (MOBC), P.O. Box 1791, Modesto, CA 95354

Monterey Bay Beam Bottle & Specialty Club, P.O. Box 258, Freedom, CA 95019

Motherlode Antique Bottle Club, P.O. Box 165, Downieville, CA 95936

Mt. Diablo Bottle Club, 4166 Sandra Circle, Pittsburg, CA 94565

Napa-Solano Bottle Club, 1409 Delwood, Vallejo, CA 94590

National Insulator Assoc., 28390 Saffron Ave., Highland, CA 92346, (909) 862-4312

Northwestern Bottle Collectors Association, P.O. Box 1121, Santa Rosa, CA 95402

Northwestern Bottle Collectors Association, 1 Keeler Street, Petaluma, CA 94952

Ocean Breeze Beamers, 4841 Tacayme Drive, Oceanside, CA 92054, (714) 757-9081

Orange County Jim Beam Bottle & Specialties Club, 546 W. Ash Ave, Fullerton, CA 92632-2702, (714) 875-8241

Original Sippin Cousins Ezra Brooks Specialties Club, 12206 Malone Street, Los Angeles, CA 90066

Pepsi-Cola Collectors Club, P.O. Box 817, Claremont, CA 91711

Painted Soda Bottle Collectors Assn, 9418 Hilmer Dr., La Mesa, CA, 91942, (619) 461-4354

Relic Accumulators, P.O. Box 3513, Eureka, CA 95501

Santa Barbara Beam Bottle Club, 5307 University Drive, Santa Barbara, CA 93111

San Bernardino County Historical Bottle and Collectible Club, P.O. Box 6759, San Bernardino, CA 92412, (619) 244-5863

San Diego Antique Bottle Club, 4214 Tacoma Street, San Diego, CA, 92117, (858) 581-2787

San Joaquin Valley Jim Beam Bottle & Specialties Club, 4085 N. Wilson Avenue, Fresno, CA 93704

San Luis Obispo Bottle Society, 124-21 St., Paso Robles, CA 93446, (805) 238-1848

Sequoia Antique Bottle Society, 1900 4th Avenue, Kingsburg, CA 93631

Sequoia Antique Bottle and Collectors Society, P.O. Box 3695, Visalia, CA 93278

Sierra Gold Ski Country Bottle Club, 5081 Rio Vista Avenue, San Jose, CA 95129

Ski-Country Bottle Club of Southern California, 3148 N. Walnut Grove, Rosemead, CA 91770

Solar Country Beamers, 940 Kelly Drive, Barstow, CA 92311, (714) 256-1485

South Bay Antique Bottle Club, 2589 1/2 Valley Drive, Manhattan Beach, CA 90266

Southern Wyoming Avon Bottle Club, 301 Canyon Highlands Drive, Oroville, CA 95965

Sunnyvale Antique Bottle Collectors Assn, 613 Torrington, Sunnyvale, CA 94087

Superior California Bottle Club, 3220 Stratford Avenue, Redding, CA 96001

The California Miniature Club, 1911 Willow St., Alameda, CA 94501

Tinseltown Beam Club, 4117 E. Gage Avenue, Bell, CA 90201, (213) 699-8787

Violin Bottle Collector's Assoc., Karen Larkin, Newsletter Editor, 1210 Hiller Road, McKinleyville, CA 95519

Wildwind Jim Beam Bottle & Spec. Club, 905 Eaton Way, Sunnyvale, CA 94087, (408) 739-1558

'49er Historical Bottle Assn., P.O. Box 561, Penryn, CA 95663, (916) 663-3681

Colorado

American Breweriana Association, Inc, P.O. Box 11157, Pueblo, CO 81001

Antique Bottle Collectors of Colorado, P.O. Box 1895, Englewood, CO 80150-1895

Colorado Antique Bottle Club, 9545 Oak Tree Ct., Colorado Springs, CO 80925, (719) 390-5621

Colorado Mile-High Ezra Brooks Bottle Club, 7401 Decatur Street, Westminster, CO 80030

Mile-Hi Jim Beam Bottle & Spec. Club, 13196 W. Green Mountain Drive, Lakewood, CO 80228, (303) 986-6828

National Ski Country Bottle
Club, 1224 Washington Avenue,
Golden, CO 80401, (303) 279-
3373

Northern Colorado Antique
Bottle Club, 227 W. Beaver
Avenue, Ft. Morgan, CO 80701

Northern Colorado Beam Bottle
& Spec. Club, 3272 Gunnison
Drive, Ft. Collins, CO 80526,
(303) 226-2301

Ole Foxie Jim Beam Club, 7530
Wilson Court, Westminster, CO
80030, (303) 429-1823 Attn:
Shirley Engel, President

Pikes Peak Antique Bottle &
Collectors Club, 308 Maplewood
Drive, Colorado Springs, CO
80907-4326

Southern Colorado Antique
Bottle Club, 843 Ussie Ave,
Canon City, CO 81212, (719)
275-3719

Western Slope Bottle Club, P.O.
Box 354, Palisade, CO 81526,
(303) 464-7727

Connecticut

The National Assn. of Milk
Bottle Collectors, 18 Pond Place,
Cos Cob, CT 06807

The Somers Antique Bottle
Club, Box 373, Somers, CT
06071

Southern Connecticut Antique
Bottle Collectors Assn, 11
Paquonnock Road, Trumbull CT
06033

Delaware

Blue Hen Jim Beam Bottle &
Spec. Club, 303 Potomac Drive,
Wilmington, DE 19803, (302)
652-6378

Delmarva Antique Bottle
Collectors, 50 Syracuse St.,
Ocean View, DE 19970

Tri-State Bottle Collectors and
Diggers Club, 2510 Cratchett
Road, Wilmington, DE 19808

Florida

Antique Bottle Collectors of Florida, Inc., 2512 Davie Boulevard, Ft. Lauderdale, FL 33312

Antique Bottle Collectors of North Florida, 3867 Winter Berry Road, Jacksonville, FL 32210

Avon Collectors Club, P.O. Box 11004, Ft. Lauderdale, FL 33339

Central Florida Insulator Collectors Club, 707 N.E. 113th St., Miami, FL 33161-7239,

Central Florida Jim Beam Bottle Club, 1060 W. French Avenue, Orange City, FL 32763, (904) 775-7392

Crossarms Collectors Club, 1756 N.W. 58th Avenue, Lauderhill, FL 33313

Emerald Coast Bottle Collectors, P.O. Box 863, DeFuniak Springs, FL 32435, (850) 892-5474

Everglades Antique Bottle Club, 6981 S.W. 19th Street, Pompano, FL 33068

Everglades Antique Bottle & Collectors Club, 400 S. 57 Terrace, Hollywood, FL 33023, (305) 962-3434

International Perfume Bottle Assoc., 3314 Shamrock Rd., Tampa, FL 33629, (813) 837-5845

Mid-State Antique Bottle Collectors, 3400 East Grant Street, Orlando, FL 32806

M.T. Bottle Collectors Assn. Inc., P.O. Box 1581, Deland, FL 32721

Ridge Area Antique Bottle Collectors, 1219 Carlton, Lake Wales, FL 33853

Sanford Antique Bottle Collectors, 2656 Grandview Avenue, Sanford, FL 33853, (305) 322-7181

South Florida Jim Beam Bottle & Spec. Club, 7741 N.W. 35th Street, West Hollywood, FL 33024

Suncoast Antique Bottle Club, 6720 Park St., South Pasadena, FL 33707

Treasure Coast Bottle Collectors, 6301 Lilyan Parkway, Ft. Pierce, FL 34591

Georgia

The Desoto Trail Bottle Collectors Club, 406 Randolph Street, Cuthbert, GA 31740

The Dixie Jewels Insulator Club, 6220 Carriage Court, Cummings, GA 30130, (707) 781-5021

Flint Antique Bottle & Coin Club, C/O Cordele-Crisp Co., Recreation Dept, 204 2nd Street North, Cordele, GA 31015

Georgia Bottle Club, 2996 Pangborn Road, Decatur, GA 30033

Macon Antique Bottle Club, P.O. Box 5395, Macon, GA 31208

The Middle Georgia Antique Bottle Club, 2746 Alden Street, Macon, GA 31206

Peanut State Jim Beam Bottle & Spec. Club, 767 Timberland Street, Smyra, GA 30080, (404) 432-8482

Southeastern Antique Bottle Club, 143 Scatterfoot Drive, Peachtree City, GA 30269

Hawaii

Hauoli Beam Bottle Collectors Club of Hawaii, 45-027 Ka-Hanahou Place, Kaneohe, HI 96744

Hawaii Historic Bottle Collectors Club, P.O. Box 90456, Honolulu, HI 96835

Hilo Bottle Club, 287 Kanoelani Street, Hilo, HI 96720

Idaho

Buhl Antique Bottle Club, 500 12th, N. Buhl, ID 83316

Eagle Rock Beam & Spec. Club, 3665 Upland Avenue, Idaho Falls, ID 83401, (208) 522-7819

Em Tee Bottle Club, P.O. Box 62, Jerome, ID 83338

Idaho Beam & Spec. Club, 2312 Burrell Avenue, Lewiston, ID 83501, (208) 743-5997

Illinois

Alton Area Bottle Club, 2448 Alby Street, Alton, IL (618) 462-4285

Antique Bottle Club of Northern Illinois, 270 Stanley Ave, Waukegan, IL 60085

Blackhawk Jim Beam Bottle & Spec. Club, 2003 Kishwaukee Street, Rockford, IL 61101

Central & Midwestern States Beam & Spec. Club, 44 S. Westmore, Lombard, IL 60148

Chicago Ezra Brooks Bottle & Spec. Club, 3635 W. 82nd Street, Chicago, IL 60652

Dreamers Beamers, 5721 Vial Parkway, LaGrange, IL 60525, (312) 246-4838

1st Chicago Antique Bottle Club, P.O. Box-224, Dolton, IL 60419

Greater Chicago Insulator Club, 11728 Leonardo Dr., St. John, IN 46373

Heart of Illinois Antique Bottle Club, 2010 Bloomington Road, East Peoria, IL 61611

International Assn. of Jim Beam Bottle and Specialties Clubs, P.O. Box 486, Kewanee IL 661443 www.beam-wade.org, 309-853-3370

Land of Lincoln Bottle Club, 2515 Illinois Circle, Decatur, IL 62526

Lewis & Clark Jim Beam Bottle & Spec. Club, P.O. Box 451, Wood River, IL 62095

Metro East Bottle & Jar Assn, 309 Bellevue Drive, Delleville, IL 62223

Pekin Bottle Collectors Assn., 409 E. Forrest Hill Ave, Peoria, IL 61603

Rock River Valley Jim Beam Bottle & Spec. Club, 1107 Avenue A., Rock Falls, IL 61071, (815) 625-7075

The Greater Chicago Insulator Club, 34273 Homestead Rd., Gurnee, IL 60031, (708) 855-9136

Tri-County Jim Beam Bottle Club, 3702 W. Lancer Road, Peoria, IL 61615, (309) 691-8784

Indiana

City of Bridges Jim Beam Bottle & Spec. Club, 1017 N. 6th Street, Logansport, IN 46947, (219) 722-3197

Crossroads of America Jim Beam Bottle Club, 114 S. Green Street, Brownsburg, IN 46112, (317) 852-5168

Hoosier Jim Beam Bottle & Spec. Club, P.O. Box 24234, Indianapolis, IN 46224

Jelly Jammers, 6086 West Boggstown Road, Boggstown, IN 46110

Lafayette Antique Bottle Club, 3664 Redondo Drive, Lafayette, IN 47905

Mid-West Antique Fruit Jar & Bottle Club, P.O. Box 38, Flat Rock, IN 47234

National Greentown Glass Association, P.O. Box 107, Greentown, IN 46936-0107

The Ohio Valley Antique Bottle and Jar Club, 214 John Street, Aurora, IN 47001

Wabash Valley Antique Glass & Pottery Club, P.O. Box 690, Farmersburg, IN 47868

We Found 'Em Bottle & Insulator Club, P.O. Box 578, Bunker Hill, IN 46914

Iowa

Early American Pattern Glass Society, P.O. Box 266, Colesburg, IA 52035

Five Seasons Beam & Spec. Club of Iowa, 609 32nd Street, NE, Cedar Rapids, IA 52402, (319) 365-6089

Gold Dome Jim Beam Bottle & Spec. Club, 2616 Hull, Des Moines, IA 50317, (515) 262-8728

Hawkeye Jim Beam Bottle Club, 658 Kern Street, Waterloo, IA 60703, (319) 233-9168

Iowa Antique Bottlers, 2815 Druid Hill Dr., Des Moines, IA 50315

Iowa Great Lakes Jim Beam Bottle & Spec. Club, Green Acres Mobile Park, Lot 88, Estherville, IA 51334, (712) 362-2759

Larkin Bottle Club, 107 W. Grimes, Red Oak, IA 51566

Quad Cities Jim Beam Bottle & Spec. Club, 2425 W. 46th Street, Davenport, IA 52806

Shot Tower Beam Club, 284 N. Booth Street, Dubuque, IA 52001, (319) 583-6343

Kansas

Air Capital City Jim Beam Bottle & Spec. Club, 3256 Euclid, Wichita, KS 67217, (316) 942-3162

Cherokee Strip Ezra Brooks Bottle & Spec. Club, P.O. Box 631, Arkansas City, KS 67005

Kansas City Bottle Collectors -1050 West Blue Ridge Blvd, Kansas City, MO 64145

National Depression Glass Assoc., P.O. 8264, Wichita, KS 67208

Southeast Kansas Bottle & Relic Club, 612 E. 10th, Chanute, KS

Walnut Valley Jim Beam Bottle & Spec. Club, P.O. Box 631, Arkansas City, KS 67005, (316) 442-0509

Kentucky

Derby City Jim Beam Bottle Club, 4105 Spring Hill Road, Louisville, KY 40207

Gold City Jim Beam Bottle Club, 286 Metts Court, Apt. 4, Elizabethtown, KY 42701, (502) 737-9297

Kentucky Bluegrass Ezra Brooks Bottle Club, 6202 Tabor Drive, Louisville, KY 40218

Kentucky Cardinal Beam Bottle Club, 428 Templin, Bardstown, KY 41104

Louisiana

Bayou Bottle Bugs, 216 Dahlia, New Iberia, LA 70560

"Cajun Country Cousins" Ezra Brooks Bottle & Spec. Club, 1000 Chevis Street, Abbeville, LA 70510

Crescent City Jim Beam Bottle & Spec. Club, 733 Wright Avenue, Gretna, LA 70053, (504) 367-2182

Historical Bottle Assn. of Baton Rouge, 1843 Tudor Drive, Baton Rouge, LA 70815

New Orleans Antique Bottle Club, 2605 Winifed Sreet, Metairie, LA 70003

North East Louisiana Antique Bottle Club, P.O. Box 4192, Monroe, LA 71291, (318) 322-8359

Maine

New England Bottle Club, 45 Bolt Hill Road, Eliot, ME 03903

Pine Tree State Beamers, 15 Woodside Avenue, Saco, ME 04072, (207) 284-8756

Maryland

Baltimore Antique Bottle Club, P.O. Box 36061, Towson, MD 21286-6061

International Chinese Snuff Bottle Society, 2601 North Charles Street, Baltimore, MD 21218

Mid-Atlantic Miniature
Whiskey Bottle Club, 208
Gloucester Drive, Glen Burnie,
MD 21061, (301) 766-842

Paperweight Collectors Assoc.,
P.O. Box 1263, Beltsville, MD
20704-1263

Massachusetts

Berkshire Antique Bottle Assn.,
Box 971, Lenox, MA 01240

Candy Container Collectors
of American, P.O. Box 426,
Reading, MA 01864-0426

Little Rhody Bottle Club, 2739
Elm Street, Dighton, MA 02715

Merrimack Valley Antique
Bottle Club, 3 Forrest St.,
Chelmsford MA 01824-2861,
(978) 256-9561

Scituate Bottle Club, 54
Cedarwood Road, Scituate, MA
02066

Violin Bottle Collectors
Association of America, 24
Sylvan St. Danvers, MA 01923

Yankee Pole Cat Insulator Club,
C/O Jill Meier, 103 Canterbury
Court, Carlisle, MA 01741-1860,
(508) 369-0208

Michigan

Central Michigan Krazy
Korkers Bottle Club, Mid-
Michigan Community College,
Clare Avenue, Harrison, MI
48625

Dickinson County Bottle Club,
717 Henford Avenue, Iron
Mountain, MI 49801

Flint Antique Bottle Collectors
Assn., 450 Leta Avenue, Flint,
MI 48507

Flint Antique Bottle &
Collectors Club, 11353 W. Cook
Rd., Gaines, MI 48436

Flint Eagles Ezra Brooks Club,
1117 W. Remington Avenue,
Flint, MI 48507

Grand Rapids Antique Bottle
Club, 1368 Kinney N.W.,
Walker, MI 49504

Grand Valley Bottle Club, 31
Dickinson S.W., Grand Rapids,
MI 49507

Great Lakes Miniature
Bottle Club, P.O. Box 230460,
Fairhaven, MI 48023

Huron Valley Bottle Club, 12475 Saline-Milan Road, Milan, MI 48160

Huron Valley Bottle & Insulator Club, 4122 Lakeside, Beaverton, MI 84612

Jelly Jammers, 4300 W. Bacon Rd., Hillsdale, MI 49242

Kalamazoo Antique Bottle Club, 607 Crocket Ave, Portage, MI 49024

Lionstone Collectors Bottle & Spec. Club of Michigan, 3089 Grand Blanc Road, Swartz Creek, MI 48473

Manistee Coin & Bottle Club, 207 E. Piney Road, Manistee, MI 49660

Metropolitan Detroit Antique Bottle Club, 26251 Koontz, Roseville, MI 48066

Michigan Bottle Collectors Assn., 144 W. Clark Street, Jackson, MI 49203

Michigan's Vehicle City Beam Bottles & Spec. Club, 907 Root Street, Flint, MI 48503

Mid-Michee Pine Beam Club, 609 Webb Drive, Bay City, MI 48706

Red Run Jim Beam Bottle & Spec. Club, 172 Jones Street, Mt. Clemens, MI 48043, (313) 465-4883

W.M.R.A.C.C., 331 Bellevue S.W., Grand Rapids, MI 49508

World Wide Avon Bottle Collectors Club, 22708 Wick Road, Taylor, MI 48180

Ye Old Corkers, C/O Janet Gallup, Box 7, Gaastra, MI 49927

Minnesota

Hey! Rube Jim Beam Bottle Club, 1506 6th Avenue N.E., Austin, MN 55912, (507) 433-6939

Lake Superior Antique Bottle Club, P.O. Box 67, Knife River, MN 55609

Minnesota 1st Antique Bottle Club, 5001 Queen Ave N., Minneapolis, MN 55430

North-Star Historical Bottle Assn. Inc., 3308-32 Ave. So., Minneapolis, MN 55406

Red Wing Collectors Society Inc. (Red Wing & American Pottery), P.O. Box 50, Red Wing, MN 550660-0050

Society of Inkwell Collectors, 5136 Thomas Ave. S., Minneapolis, MN 55410

Truman, Minnesota Jim Beam Bottle & Spec. Club, Truman, MN 56088, (507) 776-3487

Viking Jim Beam Bottle & Spec. Club, 8224 Oxborough Avenue S., Bloomington, MN 55437, (612) 831-2303

Mississippi

Gum Tree Beam Bottle Club, 104 Ford Circle, Tupelo, MS 38801

Magnolia Beam Bottle & Spec. Club, 1079 Maria Drive, Jackson, MS 39204-5518, (601) 372-4464

Missouri

Arnold, Missouri Jim Beam Bottle & Spec. Club, 1861 Jean Drive, Arnold, MO 63010, (314) 296-0813

Barnhart, Missouri Jim Beam Bottle & Spec. Club, 2150 Cathlin Court, Barnhart, MO 63012

Beer Can Collectors of America, 747 Merus Ct., Fenton, MO 63026-2092, (636) 343-6486

Chesterfield Jim Beam Bottle & Spec. Club, 2066 Honey Ridge, Chesterfield, MO 63017

"Down in the Valley" Jim Beam Bottle Club, 528 St. Louis Avenue, Valley Park, MO 63088

The Federation of Historical Bottle Clubs, 10118 Schuessler, St. Louis, MO 63128, (314) 843-7573

Florissant Valley Jim Beam Bottles & Spec. Club, 25 Cortez, Florissant, MO 63031

Greater Kansas City Jim Beam Bottle & Spec. Club, P.O. Box 6703, Kansas City, MO 64123

Kansas City Antique Bottle Collectors Assn., 1131 E. 77 Street, Kansas City, MO 64131

Maryland Heights Jim Beam Bottle & Spec. Club, 2365 Wesford, Maryland Heights, MO 63043

Midwest Miniature Bottle Collectors, 12455 Parkwood Lane, Blackjack, MO 63033

Missouri Arch Jim Beam Bottle & Spec. Club, 2900 N. Lindbergh, St. Ann, MO 63074, (314) 739-0803

Mound City Jim Beam Decanter Collectors, 42 Webster Acres, Webster Groves, MO 63119

North-East County Jim Beam
Bottle & Spec. Club, 10150
Baron Drive, St. Louis, MO
63136

Rock Hill Jim Beam Bottle &
Spec. Club, 9731 Graystone
Terrace, St. Louis, MO 63119,
(314) 962-8125

Sho Me Jim Beam Bottle &
Spec. Club, Rt. 7, Box 314-D,
Springfield, MO 65802, (417)
831-8093

St. Louis Antique Bottle
Collectors Assn., MO 63039

St. Louis Jim Beam Bottle &
Spec. Club, 2900 Lindbergh, St.
Ann, MO 63074, (314) 291-3256

Troy, Missouri Jim Beam Bottle
& Spec. Club, 121 E. Pershing,
Troy, MO 63379

Vaseline Glass Collectors, P.O.
Box 125, Russellville, MO 65074

Vera Young, Avon Times, P.O.
Box 9868, Kansas City, MO
64134, (816) 537-8223

West County Jim Beam Bottle
& Spec. Club, 11707 Momarte
Lane, St. Louis, MO 63141

Nebraska
Cornhusker Jim Beam Bottle &
Spec. Club, 5204 S. 81st Street,
Ralston, NE 68127, (402) 331-
4646

Nebraska Antique Bottle &
Collectible Club, 407 N. 13th
Street, Ashland, NE 68003

Nebraska Big Red Bottle &
Spec. Club, N Street Drive-in,
200S. 18th Street, Lincoln, NE
68508

Nevada
Las Vegas Antique Bottle &
Collectibles Club, 3901 E.
Stewart #16, Las Vegas, NV
89110, (702) 452-1263

Las Vegas Bottle Club, 2632 E.
Harman, Las Vegas, NV 89121,
(702) 731-5004

Lincoln County Antique Bottle
Club, P.O. Box 191, Calente, NV
89008, (702) 726-3655

Reno/Sparks Antique Bottle
Club, P.O. Box 1061, Verdi, NV
89439

Virginia & Truckee Jim Beam
Bottle & Spec. Club, P.O. Box
1596, Carson City, NV 89701

New Hampshire
Yankee Bottle Club, 382 Court
Street, Keene, NH 03431-2534

New Jersey
Antique Bottle Collectors Club
of Burlington County, 18 Willow
Road, Bordentown, NJ 08505

Artifact Hunters Assn. Inc, C/O 29
Lake Road, Wayne, NJ 07470

Central Jersey Bottle & Collectible Club, 92 North Main Street, New Egypt, NJ 98553

Glass Research Society of New Jersey, Wheaton Village, Millville, NJ 08332

Jersey Jackpot Jim Beam Bottle & Spec. Club, 197 Farley Avenue, Fanwood, NJ 07023, (201) 322-7287

Jersey Shore Bottle Club, P.O. Box 995, Toms River, NJ 08753

North Jersey Antique Bottle Club Assn., 24 Charles St., South River, NJ 08882

South Jersey Heritage Bottle & Glass Club, Inc., 65 N. Main St., Woodstown, NJ 08098

Trenton Jim Beam Bottle Club, Inc., 17 Easy Street, Freehold, NJ 07728

West Essex Bottle Club, 76 Beaufort Avenue, Livingston, NJ 07039

New Mexico

New Mexico Historical Bottle Society, 140 W. Coronado Road, Santa Fe, NM 87501

Roadrunner Bottle Club of New Mexico, 2341 Gay Road S.W., Albuquerque, NM 87105

New York

Ball Metal Container Group, One Adams Road, Saratoga Springs, NY 12866-9036

Capital District Insulator Club, 41 Crestwood Drive, Schenectady, NY 12306

Capital Region Antique Bottle & Insulator Club, 463 Loudon Road, Loudonville, NY 12211

Chautauqua County Bottle Collectors Club, Morse Motel, Main Street, Sherman, NY 14781

Eastern Monroe County Bottle Club, C/O Bethelem Lutheran Church, 1767 Plank Road, Webster, NY 14580

Empire State Bottle Collectors Assn., P.O. Box 3421, Syracuse, NY 13220, (315) 689-6460

Finger Lakes Bottle Collectors Assn., P.O. Box 3894, Ithaca, NY 14852

Genessee Valley Bottle Collectors Assn., P.O. Box 15528., Rochester, NY 14615

Greater Buffalo Bottle Club, 66 Chassin Avenue, Amherst, NY 14226, (716) 834-2249

Hudson River Jim Beam Bottle & Spec. Club, 48 College Road, Monsey, NY 10952

Hudson Valley Bottle Club, 201 Filors Lane, Stony Point, NY 10980

Lions Club of Ballston Spa, 37 Grove Street, Ballston Spa, NY 12020

Long Island Antique Bottle Assn., 10 Holmes Court, Sayville, NY 11782

Mohawk Valley Antique Bottle Club, 8646 Aitken Avenue, Whitesboro, NY 13492

National Bottle Museum, 76 Milton Avenue, Ballston Spa, NY 12020, (518) 885-7589

National Insulator Association, 41 Crestwood Drive, Schenectady, NY 12306

Society of Inkwell Collectors, Jane Betrus, Executive Director, 10 Meadow Drive, Spencerport, N.Y. 14459, (716) 352-4114

The Corning Museum of Glass, One Museum Way, Corning, NY 14830-2253

Tryon Bottle Badgers, P.O. Box 146, Tribes Hill, NY 12177

Western New York Bottle Club Assn., 62 Adams Street, Jamestown, NY 14701, (716) 487-9645, Attn: Tom Karapantso

Western New York Miniature Liquor Club, P.O. Box 182, Cheektowaga, NY 14225

West Valley Bottleique Club, P.O. Box 204, Killbuck, NY 14748, (716) 945-5769

North Carolina

Catawba Valley Jim Beam Bottle & Spec. Club, 265 5th Avenue, N.E. Hickory, NC 28601, (704) 322-5268

Kinston Collectors Club, Inc., 1905 Greenbriar Rd, Kinston, NC 28501-2129, (919) 523-3049

Tar Heel Jim Beam Bottle & Spec. Club, 6615 Wake Forest Road, Fayetteville, NC 20301, (919) 488-4849

The Johnnyhouse Inspector's Bottle Club, 1972 East US 74 Highway, Hamlet, NC 28345

Raleigh Bottle Club, P.O. Box 18083, Raleigh, NC 27619

Southeast Bottle Club, P.O. Box 13736, Durham, NC 27709

The Robeson Antique Bottle Club, 1830 Riverside Blvd, Lumberton, NC 28358

Western North Carolina Antique Bottle Club, P.O. Box 1391, Candler, NC 28715

Wilmington Bottle & Artifact Club,183 Arlington Drive, Wilmington, NC 28401, (919) 763-3701

Yadkin Valley Bottle Club, General Delivery, Gold Hill, NC 28071

Ohio

Buckeye Bottle Club, 229 Oakwood Street, Elyria, OH 44035

Central Ohio Bottle Club, 931 Minerva Avenue, Columbus, OH 43229

Collectors of Findlay Glass, P.O. Box 256, Findlay, OH 45939-0256

Diamond Pin Winners Avon Club, 5281 Fredonia Avenue, Dayton, OH 45431

The Federation of Historical Bottle Clubs, C/O Gary Beatty, Treasurer, 9326 Court Road 3C, Galion, OH 44833

Findlay Antique Bottle Club, P.O. Box 243, Bowling Green, OH 43402

Gem City Beam Bottle Club, 1463 E. Stroop Road, Dayton, OH 45429

Glass Collectors Club of Toledo, 6122 Cross Trails Rd., Sylvania, OH 43560-1714

Greater Cleveland Jim Beam Club, 5398 W. 147th Street, Brook Park, OH 44142, (216) 267-7665

Heart of Ohio Bottle Club, P.O. Box 353, New Washington, OH 44854, (419) 492-2829

Jeep City Beamers, 531A Durango, Toledo, OH 43609, (419) 382-2515

Maple Leaf Beamers, 8200 Yorkshire Road, Mentor, OH 44060, (216) 255-9118

Midwest Minature Bottle Club, 5537 Cleander Dr., Cincinnati, OH 45238

National Fenton Glass Society, P.O. Box 4008, Marietta, OH 45750

Northern Ohio Jim Beam Bottle Club, 43152 Hastings Road, Oberlin, OH 44074, (216) 775-2177

North Eastern Ohio Bottle Club, P.O. Box 57, Madison, OH 44057, (614) 282-8918

Ohio Bottle Club, P.O. Box 585, Barberton, OH 44203, (216) 753-2115

Ohio Ezra Brooks Bottle Club, 8741 Kirtland Chardon Road, Kirtland Hills, OH 44094

Pioneer Beamers, 38912 Butternut Ridge, Elyria, OH 44035, (216) 458-6621

Rubber Capitol Jim Beam Club, 151 Stephens Road, Akron, OH 44312

Southwestern Ohio Antique Bottle & Jar Club, 273 Hilltop Drive, Dayton, OH 45415, (513) 836-3353

St. Bernard Swigin Beamers, 4327 Greenlee Avenue, Cincinnati, OH 45217, (513) 641-3362

Superior Bottle Club, 22000 Shaker Boulevard, Shaker Heights, OH 44122

West Virginia Bottle Club, 39304 Bradbury Road, Middleport, OH 45760

Oklahoma

Bar-Dew Antique Bottle Club, 817 E. 7th Street, Dewey, OK 74029

Frontier Jim Beam Bottle & Spec. Club, P.O. Box 52, Meadowbrook Trailer Village, Lot 101, Ponca City, OK 74601, (405) 765-2174

Midwest Miniature Bottle Collector, 3108 Meadowood Drive, Midwest City, OK 73110-1407

Oklahoma Territory Bottle & Relic Club, 1300 S. Blue Haven Dr., Mustang, OK 73064, (405) 376-1045

Sooner Jim Beam Bottle & Spec. Club, 5913 S.E. 10th, Midwest City, OK 73110, (405) 737-5786

Tri-State Historical Bottle Club, 817 E. 7th Street, Dewey, OK 74029

Oregon

Central Oregon Bottle & Relic Club, 671 N.E. Seward, Bend, OR 97701

Frontier Collectors, 504 N.W. Bailey, Pendleton, OR 97801

Gold Diggers Antique Bottle Club, 1958 S. Stage Road, Medford, OR 97501

Lewis & Clark Historical Bottle & Collectors Soc., 8018 S.E. Hawthorne Boulevard, Portland, OR 97501

Oregon Beamers Beam Bottle & Spec., P.O. Box 7, Sheridan, OR 97378

Oregon Bottle Collectors Assn., 3565 Dee Highway, Hood River, OR 97031

Pioneer Fruit Collectors Assn., P.O. Box 175, Grand Ronde, OR 97347

Promotional Glass Collectors Association, 528 Oakley, Central Point, OR 97502

Siskiyou Antique Bottle Collectors Assn., 2668 Montana Drive, Medford, OR 97504

Pennsylvania

American Collectors of Infant Feeders, 1819 Ebony Drive, York, PA 17402-4706

Beaver Valley Jim Beam Club, 1335 Indiana Avenue, Monaca, PA 15061

Camoset Bottle Club, P.O. Box 252, Johnstown, PA 15901

Coal Crackers Bottle Club, Rod Walck, 168 Sunrise Terrace Ln., Lehighton, PA 18235 (610) 377-1484

Delaware Valley Bottle Club, 12 Belmar Road, Halboro, PA 19040

Del Val Miniature Bottle Club, 57-104 Delaire Landing Road, Philadelphia, PA 19114

East Coast Ezra Brooks Bottle Club, 2815 Fiddler Green, Lancaster, PA 17601

Endless Mountain Antique Bottle Club, P.O. Box 75, Granville Summit, PA 16926

H.C. Fry Glass Society, P.O. Box 41, Beaver, PA 15009

Indiana Bottle Club, 240 Oak Street, Indiana, PA 15701

International Perfume Bottle Association, 295 E. Swedesford Road, PMB 185, Wayne, PA 19087

Jefferson County Antique Bottle Club, 6 Valley View Drive, Washington, PA 15301

Kiski Mini Beam and Spec. Club, C/O John D. Ferchak Jr., 816 Cranberry Drive, Monroeville, PA 15146, (412) 372-0387

Laurel Valley Bottle Club, P.O. Box 201 Hostetter, PA 15638, (412) 238-9046

Middletown Area Bottle Collectors Assn., P.O. Box 1, Middletown, PA 17057, (717) 939-0288

National Milk Glass Collectors Society, 500 Union Cemetery Rd., Greensburg, PA 15601

Pagoda City Beamers, 735 Florida Avenue, Riverview Park, Reading, PA 19605, (215) 929-8924

Penn Beamers' 14th, 15 Gregory Place, Richboro, PA 18954

Pennsylvania Bottle Collectors, 251 Eastland Ave, York, PA 17402 Pennsylvania Dutch Jim Beam Bottle Club, 812 Pointview Avenue, Ephrata, PA 17522

Philadelphia Bottle Club, 8203 Elberon Avenue, Philadelphia, PA 19111

Pittsburgh Antique Bottle Club, 694 Fayette City Road, Fayette City, PA 15438

Pittsburgh Bottle Club, 1528 Railroad Street, Sewickley, PA 15143

Susquehanna Valley Jim Beam Bottle & Spec. Club, 64 E. Park Street, Elizabethtown, PA 17022, (717) 367-4256

The American Collectors of Infant Feeders, 1849 Ebony Drive, York, PA 17402-4706

Valley Forge Jim Beam Bottle Club, 1219 Ridgeview Drive, Phoenixville, PA 19460

Washington County Antique Bottle Club & Insulator Club, 588 E. George Stl, Carmichaels, PA 15320

Rhode Island

Little Rhody Bottle Club, P.O. Box 15142, Riverside, RI 02915-0142, Web:littlerhodybottleclub.org

Seaview Jim Beam Bottle & Spec. Club, 362 Lakepoint Drive, Harrisburg, PA 17111, (717) 561-2517

South Carolina

Anderson Collectors Club, 2318 Hwy. 29, N. Anderson, SC 29621

Horse Creek Antique Bottle Club, P.O. Box 1176, Langley, SC 29834

Palmetto State Beamers, 908 Alton Circle, Florence, SC 29501, (803) 669-6515

South Carolina Bottle Club, 238 Farmdale Drive, Lexington, SC 29073

Tennessee

Cotton Carnival Beam Club, P.O. Box 17951, Memphis, TN 38117

East Tennessee Bottle Society, 220 Carter School Road, Strawberry Plains, TN 37871

Memphis Bottle Collectors Club, 3706 Deerfield Cove, Bartlett, TN 38135

Middle Tennessee Bottle Collectors Club, 1221 Nichol Lane, Nashville, TN 37205

Music City Beam Bottle Club, 2008 June Drive, Nashville, TN 37214, (615) 883-1893

Painted Soda Bottle Collectors Association (PSBCA), 1966 King Springs Road, Johnson City, TN 37601

State of Franklin Antique Bottle & Collectibles Association-230 Rockhouse Rd., Johnson City, TN 27709

Tennessee Valley Traders and Collectors Club, 821 Hiwassee St., Newport, TN 37821 (865) 471-0146

Texas

Cowtown Jim Beam Bottle Club, 2608 Roseland, Ft. Worth, TX 76103, (817) 536-4335

El Paso Insulator Club, Martha Stevens, Chairman, 4556 Bobolink, El Paso, TX 79922

The Exploration Society, 603 9th Street NAS, Corpus Christie, TX 78419, 922-2902

Foursome (Jim Beam), 1208 Azalea Drive, Longview, TX 75601

Gulf Coast Bottle and Jar Club, 907 W. Temple, Houston, TX 77009

Houston Glass Club, 5338 Creekbend Drive, Houston, TX 77096

Republic of Texas Jim Beam Bottle & Spec. Club, 616 Donley Drive, Euless, TX 76039

Sidewinders Jim Beam Club, 522 Reinosa Drive, Garland, TX 75043

Utah

Utah Antique Bottle Collectors Club, P.O. Box 27152 Salt Lake City, UT 84127

Virginia

Antique Poison Bottle Collectors Assoc., 312 Summer Lane, Huddleston, VA 24104, (540) 297-4498

Apple Valley Bottle Collectors Club, P.O. Box 2201, Winchester, VA 22604

Buffalo Beam Bottle Club, P.O. Box 434, Buffalo Junction, VA 24529, (804) 374-2041

Historical Bottle Diggers of Virginia, 2516 Hawksbill Road, McGaheysville, VA 22840

International Perfume Bottle Assoc., Box 529, Vienna, VA 22183

Merrimac Beam Bottle & Spec. Club, 433 Tory Road, Virginia Beach, VA 23462, (804) 497-0969

Metropolitan Antique Bottle Club, 109 Howard Street, Dumfries, VA 22026, (804) 221-8055

Potomac Bottle Collectors- 8411 Porter Lane, Alexandria, VA 22308

Richmond Area Bottle Collectors Assn., 4718 Kyloe Lane, Moseley, VA 23120

Shenandoah Valley Beam Bottle & Spec. Club, 11 Bradford Drive, Front Royal, VA 22630, (703) 743-6316

The Richmond Area Bottle Collectors Association, 4718 Kyloe Lane, Moseley, VA 23120

Washington

Apple Capital Beam Bottle &
Spec. Club, 300 Rock Island
Road, E. Wenatchee, WA 98801,
(509) 884-6895

Inland Empire Bottle &
Collectors Club, 7703 E. Trent
Avenue, Spokane, WA 99206

Mt. Rainer Ezra Brooks Bottle
Club, P.O. Box 1201, Lynwood,
WA 98178

Northwest Treasure Hunter's
Club, E. 107 Astor Drive,
Spokane, WA 99208

Pacific Northwest Avon Bottle
Club, 25425 68th S. Kent, WA
98031

Skagit Bottle & Glass
Collectors, 1314 Virginia, Mt.
Vernon, WA 98273

Violin Bottle Collectors
Association of America, 21815
106th Street East, Buckley, WA
98321

Washington County Antique
Bottle Club, 905 24th Street,
Seattle, WA 92144

West Virginia

Fenton Art Glass Collectors,
P.O. Box 384, Williamstown, WV
26187

Wild Wonderful W. Virginia Jim
Beam Bottle & Spec. Club, 3922
Hanlin Way, Weirton, WV 26062,
(304) 748-2675

Wisconsin

Badger Jim Beam Club of
Madison, P.O. Box 5612,
Madison, WI 53705

Belle City Jim Beam Bottle
Club, 8008 104th Avenue,
Kenosha, WI 53140, (414) 694-
3341

Central Wisconsin Bottle
Collectors, 1608 Main Street,
Stevens Point, WI 54481

Cream Separator Collectors
Association, W20772 State Road
95, Arcadia, WI 54612

Heart of the North Beam Bottle
and Bottle Club, 1323 Eagle
Street, Rhinelander, WI 54501,
(715) 362-6045

Milwaukee Antique Bottle &
Advertising Club, Inc., 4090
Lake Drive, West Bend, WI
53095

Milwaukee Jim Beam Bottle
and Spec. Club, Ltd., N. 95th
Street W. 16548 Richmond Dr.,
Menomonee Falls, WI 53051

Packerland Beam Bottle & Spec.
Club, 1366 Avondale Dr., Green
Bay, WI 54303, (414) 494-4631

Sportsman's Jim Beam Bottle
Club, 6821 Sunset Strip,
Wisconsin Rapids, WI 54494,
(715) 325-5285

Watkins Collectors Club,
W24024 St. Rd. 54/93,
Galesville, WI 54630

Wyoming

Cheyenne Antique Bottle Club,
4417 E. 8th Street, Cheyene,
WY 82001

Foreign

Australia

Miniature Bottle Collectors
of Australia, P.O. Box 59,
Ashburton, Victoria 3147
Australia

Canada

Bytown Bottle Seekers' Club,
564 Courtenay Ave., Ottawa,
Ontario, Canada K2A 3B3

Four Seasons Bottle Collectors
Club, 5 Greystone Walk Drive,
Apt. 1902, Scarborough,
Ontario, Canada M1K 515

Sleeping Giant Bottle Club,
P.O. Box 1351, Thunder Bay,
Ontario, Canada P7C 5W2

Violin Bottle Collectors
Association, 33 East 35th St.,
Hamilton, Ontario, Canada L8V
3R7

China

Hong Kong Miniature Liquor
Club LTD, 180 Nathan Road,
Bowa House, Tsim Sha Tsui,
Kowloon, Hong Kong, (852) 721-
3200

England

The Mini Bottle Club, 47
Burradon Rd., Burradon,
Cramlington, Northumberland,
NE 237NF England

Additional Bottle Clubs in England contact: Ian Whittaker @ www.bolwin1.demon.co.uk/ northc.HTM

Germany

Miniatur Flaschensammler Duetschlands E.V:, Keltenstrasse 1a, 5477 Nickenich, Germany

Ireland

Northern Ireland Antique Bottle Club, David Scott, 52 Ormiston Crescent, Belfast B74 3JQ, Ireland

Italy

Club Delle Mignonnettes, Via Asiago 16, 60124 Ancona, AN, Italy

Japan

Osaka Miniature Bottle Club, 11-2 Hakucho 1-Chome, Habikinoshi, Osaka 583, Japan

Miniature Bottle Club of Kobe, 3-5-41, Morigocho, Nada-ku, Kobe, 657 Japan

New Zealand

Port Nicholson Miniature Bottle Club, 86 Rawhiti Rd., Pukerua Bay, Wellington, New Zealand

Scotland

Cumbria Antique Bottle Club, Steve Davison, 01228-26634, Scotland

Moray Bottle Club, Iain Cosling, 01343-830-512, Scotland

Northumberland & Durham Bottle Club, D. Robertson, 0191-236-4304, Scotland

Bottle Dealers

Note: Dealers are listed alphabetically by state and city.

United States

Alabama

Bert and Margaret Simard, Rt. 1 Box 49D, Ariton, AL 36311, (334) 762-2663 (Ink bottles and Ink Wells)

Matt Lambert, 501 Hall, Bay Minette, AL 36507

Steve Demedicis, 2764 Hanover Circle, Birmingham, AL 35205, (205) 930-9550

Steve Holland, 1740 Serene Dr., Birmingham, AL, 35215, (205) 853-7929

Tom Lines, P.O. Box 382831, Birmingham, AL 35238, (205) 987-0650

Dwain Armentrout, P.O. Box 888, Fayette, AL 35555, (205) 932-8989

Terry Gillis, P.O. Box 680598, Ft. Payne, AL 35968, (205) 845-0410

Frank and Nancy Harrison, 815 Troy Street, Gadsden, AL 35901, (205) 546-9112 (Glassware and Stoneware)

Lee Ivey, P.O. box 21, Henagar, AL 35798

Charles Breland, 3533 Nauvoo Rd., Nauvoo, AL 35578, (205) 924-9773

Ray Turner, 415 Boxwood Dr., Needham, AL 36915

Old Time Bottle House & Museum, 306 Parker Hills Dr., Ozark, AL 36360 (Stone Jugs and Fruit Jars)

Julie Pounders, 150 Old Drive In Rd., Pell City, AL 35125, (205) 338-9346

Bob Broadbooks, 6050 Victoria Lane, Pinson, AL 45126, (205) 680-0999

Elroy Webb, 203 Spanish Main, Spanish Fort, AL 36527, (334) 626-1067 (Bottles, Appraisals)

Bill Thompson, Box 18, Troy, AL 36081, (334) 566-1202

Alaska

Kathryn Hoffer, P.O. Box 111633, Anchorage, AK 99511-1633

Marcy Larson, 5429 Shaune Dr., Juneau, AK, 99801-9540, (907) 780-5866

Arizona

Tom and Jacque Floerchinger, P.O. Box 1622, Arizona City, AZ 85223, (520) 466-9497

Roy and Gwen Erwin, 20432 W. Arlington Rd., Buckeye, AZ 85326, (602) 386-2324

Bottle Barn, Ivan and Lois Dankenbring, 17 S. Silverado, Gilbert, AZ 85296, (480) 497-3869 (Milk Bottles)

Russ and Bonnie Carlson, 2931 E. Millbrae Ln., Gilbert, AZ 85234, (602) 641-9828

Charles and Julie Blake, 4702 W. Lavey Rd., Glendale, AZ 85306, (602) 938-7277 (Cobalt Bottles)

John and Steffany Knirsch, 12335 N. 58th Ave., Glendale, AZ 85304, (602) 334-3527

Bruce Young, Lake Havasu City, AZ, (602) 855-3396 (Insulators)

Brant and Kathy Clinard, 720 N. Stewart St., Mesa, AZ 85021, (602) 962-9182

Tom and Sandra Hallack, 1318 W. Pepper Pl., Mesa, AZ 85201, (602) 962-0249

Shirley Henderson, 117 W. Main St., Mesa, AZ 85201, (602) 655-0968

Fred Liebert, 150 N. 88th Way, Mesa, AZ 85207, (602) 986-5232

Sam Michael, P.O. Box 8025, Mesa, AZ 85214, (480) 962-6523

Michael and Karen Miller, 9214 W. Gary Rd., Peoria, AZ 85345, (602) 486-3123 Arizona Bottles

Chuck and Joice Braden, 4201 N. 20th St. #215, Phoenix, AZ, (602) 955-1166

The Antique Center, 3601 E. Indian School Rd., Phoenix, AZ 85018, (602) 957-3600

Earl and Anne Colton, 1640 W. Hatcher Rd., Phoenix, AZ 85021, (602) 866-9219

Bryan Grapentine, 1939 W. Waltann Lane, Phoenix, AZ 85023, (602) 993-9757 (Bottles and Advertising)

John and Marlene Hallinan, 3102 E. Onyx Avenue, Phoenix, AZ 85028, (602) 482-8237

Don and Sandy Crenshaw, 1503 Eagle Point Dr., Prescott, AZ 86301-5450, (520) 778-7923

Craig and Susie Harris, 7525 E. Highland, Scottsdale, AZ 85251, (602) 946-2285

Russ and Pat Peterson, 814 N. 86th Way, Scottsdale, AZ, (602) 970-3380 (Dr. Pepper Bottles)

The Antique Center, 1290 N. Scottsdale Rd., Tempe, AZ, (602) 966-3350

Gilbert Rodriguez, 332 E. District St., Tucson, AZ 85714, (520) 294-7531

Robert and Dorothy Cross, 10825 Cameo Dr., Sun City, AZ 85351-2648, (602) 977-5379

Keith Curtis, 6871 E. Lurlene Dr., Tucson, AZ 85703, (602) 790-4336

Ed and Arlene Anderson, 13547
E. 49th St., Yuma, AZ 85367,
(606) 839-4773

Clayton and Patty Mullis, 5430
W. 8th St., Yuma, AZ 85364,
(520) 783-3361

Arkansas

Rex Hickox, P.O. Box 584,
Bentonville, AR 72712, (501)
273-5287

Dexter Combs, 835 County Road
844, Green Forest, AR 72638,
(870) 437-2331

Bill Burrows, 2204 Aspen,
Greenwood, AR 72936, (501)
996-7155

Robert Polk, 107 W. Ave C, Hope,
AR 71801

Patrick Schueller, 107 Violet,
Hot Springs, AR 71901, (501)
321-4115

Charles and Mary Garner, 620
Carpenter Dr., Jacksonville, AR
72076, (501) 982-8381

Don and Jackie Leonard, 1118
Green Mt. Dr., Little Rock, AR
72211, (501) 224-5432 (Bottles)

Terry Fields, Route 1, Box 167-
7, McCrory, AR 72101, (501)
697-3132 (Bottles and Indian
Artifacts)

E. Wayne Byrd, 12 Kay Lynn
Dr., Morrilton, AR 72110, (501)
354-4855

Rufus Buie, P.O. Box 226, Rison,
AR 71665, (501) 325-6816

Edwin R. Tardy, 16201 Hwy.
300, Roland, AR 72135, (501)
868-9548 (Coca-Cola Bottles)

M.D. Anglin, P.O. Box 292,
Siloam Springs, AR 72761, (501)
524-5425

California

D & E Collectables & Antiques,
14925 Apple Valley Road, Apple
Valley, CA 92307, (619) 946-
1767 (Bottles)

Mark Accardi, 130 Vistamar Ct.,
Aptos, CA 95003, (831) 688-547

Dan Bell, 323 Kenna Drive,
Auburn, CA 95603, (530) 823-
0950

Gene Bothello, 2381 Andregg
Rd., Auburn, CA 95603, (830)
885-6962

Diane Pingree, 345 Commercial
St., Auburn, CA 95603, (916)
885-5537

Tom Chapman, 390 Ranch Rd.,
Bishop, CA 93514, (760) 872-
2427 (Western Bottles, Nevada
Bottles)

Shirley Morrison, 7640 Sullivan
Pl., Buena Park, CA 90621,
(714) 521-3317

W. Scott Yeargain, 6222 San
Lorenzo Dr., Buena Park, CA
90620, (714) 826-5264 (Bottles)

Fred Hawley, 1311 Montero Ave., Burlingame, CA 94010, (415) 342-7085 (Miniature Bottles)

Wayne Hortman, P.O. Box 183, Butler, CA 31006, (912) 862-3699

Bruce D. Kendall, Erma's Country Store, P.O. Box 1761, Carmel, CA 93921, (408) 394-3257

Robert Porter, P.O. Box 346, Carmichael, CA 95609, (916) 944-1713 (Milk Bottles)

Don Ayers, P.O. Box 1515, Chico, CA 95927, (916) 895-0813 (Coca-Cola Bottles)

Barbara Edmundson, 701 E. Lassen #308, Chico, CA 95973, (916) 343-8460 (Shot Glasses)

Randy Taylor, P.O. Box 1065, Chico, CA 95927, (530) 345-0519 (Fruit Jars)

Don Pelkey, 7508 Pintail Cir., Citrus Heights, CA 95621-1642

John Walker, 281 W. Magill Ave., Clovis, CA 93612, (209) 297-4613 (Bottles)

Stoney and Myrt Stone, 1925 Natoma Dr., Concord, CA 94519, (415) 685-6326

Kitty Yarborough, 4106 Modoc Ct., Concord, CA 94521, (925) 685-0495

Russell Brown, P.O. Box 441, Corona, CA 91720, (714) 737-7164

Gary and Harriet Miller, 5034 Oxford Dr., Cypress, CA 90630, (714) 828-4778

Jim and Monica Baird, P.O. Box 106, Descanso, CA 91916, (619) 445-4771 (Western Americana)

Cal Frederick, 539 South Orange Avenue, El Cajon, CA 92020, (619) 588-2423 (Pot Lids, Poisons, ACL Sodas, Medicines)

Rick Hall, 2265 Needham Road #18, El Cajon, CA 92020, (619) 698-0167 (Western Bottles)

Jay Turner, 5513 Riggs Rd., El Cajon, CA 92019, (619) 445-3039 (Bottles)

Ken Salter, P.O. Box 1549, El Cerrito, CA 94530, (510) 527-5779 (French and U.S. Mustards)

Tim Blair, 418 W. Palm Ave., El Segundo, CA 90245, (310) 640-2089 (Los Angeles Bottles)

Floyd Brown, 532 South "E" Street, Exeter, CA 93221, (209) 592-2525 (Marbles, Games)

Steve Abbot, 8060 Sierra St., Fair Oaks, CA 95628, (919) 961-7171

Noel Baldwin, 13 Rolling View Lane, Fallbrook, CA 92028

James Musser, P.O. Box T, Forest Knolls, CA 94933, (415) 488-9491 (Heroin, Cocaine, and Opium Bottles)

Gary Egorov, 346 E. Cornell, Fresno, CA 93704, (209) 228-1772 (Gems)

Lyle Banks, 12917 Halldale Ave., Gardena, CA 90249, (310) 715-6355

Vincent Madruga, P.O. Box 1261, Gilroy, CA 95021, (408) 847-0639 (Bitters, Whiskeys, Historicals)

Gary and Sheran Johnston, 22853 De Berry, Grand Terrace, CA 92313, (909) 783-4101 Fruit Jars

Scott Grandstaff, Box 154, Happy Camp, CA 96039, (916) 493-2032 (Mason's SGCO—Monogram—Pat. 1858s)

Kitty Roach, Box 409, Happy Camp, CA 96039, (916) 493-2032 (Whittemore Bottles)

Mike and Deanna Delaplain, P.O. Box 787, Hemet, CA 92343, (714) 766-9725

Larry Caddell, 15881 Malm Circle, Huntington Beach, CA 92647, (714) 897-8133

Jim and Sandy Lindholm, 2001 Sierra, Kingsburg, CA 93631, (209) 897-4083 (Western Bottles, Machine and Handmade Marbles, Free Appraisals)

Joss Grandeau, P.O. Box 1508, Laguna Beach, CA 92652, (714) 588-6091 (Milk Bottles)

Rick Sweeney, 9418 Hilmer Dr., La Mesa, CA 91942, (619) 461-4354 (Painted Label Soda Bottles)

Fred Padgett, P.O. Box 1122, Livermore, CA 94551-1122, (510) 443-8841 (Glass Insulators and Bottles)

Lars Houske, 2075 W. Lomita Blvd, Lomita, CA 90717, (310) 325-4425

Susan Anderson, 3604 Via Semi, Lompoc, CA 93436, (805) 733-1435

Mike Polak, P.O. Box 30328, Long Beach, CA 90853, (562) 438-9209, e-mail: bottleking@earthlink.net, web-www.bottlebible@earthlink.com (Nevada Bottles and Associated Items - Tonopah and Goldfield)

Ted Haigh, 1852 Miceltorena, Los Angeles, CA 90026, (213) 666-4408 (Miniature Bottles)

Chiisasi Bin Imports, P.O. Box 90245, Los Angeles, CA 90009 (310) 370-8993 (Miniature Bottles)

Stephen Patra, 10636 Wilshire Blvd, #304, Los Angeles, CA 90024, (310) 446-9621 (Milk Bottle Caps)

Sally Shishmanian, P.O. Box 39463, Los Angeles, CA 90039

Louis and Cindy Pellegrini, 1231 Thurston, Los Alton, CA 94022, (415) 965-9060

Gail Perez, 1261 14th St., Los Osos, CA 93402

John and Estelle Hewitt, 366 Church St., Marietta, CA 30060, (404) 422-5525

Ed Kuskie, 27465 Sereno, Mission Viejo, CA 92691, (949) 597-2165 Southern California Bottles

Steve Viola, 827 Wake Forest Rd., Mountain View, CA 94043, (415) 968-0849 (Glass Insulators)

John Hiscox, 10475 Newtown Rd. P.O. Box 704, Nevada City, CA 95959 (Bottles)

Les Whitman, 1328 Huntoon, Oroville, CA 95965, (916) 532-6377 (Bottles and Beer Cans)

Gary Frederick, 1030 Mission St., Pasadena, CA 91030, (818) 799-1917 (Soda Pop Bottles, Owls, Medicines)

Henry and Cecilia, 5595 Smoketree Ave, 29 Palms, CA 92277, (619) 367-6009 (Bottles)

Pat and Shirley Patocka, P.O. Box 326, Penryn, CA 95663, (916) 663-3681 (Insulators)

Bob's Bottle Shop, Robert Glover, 2500 Hwy. 128, Philco, CA 95466, (707) 895-3259 (Bottles and Fruit Jars)

Mel and Barbara De Mello, P.O. Box 186, Pollock Pines, CA 95726, (916) 644-6133 (Antique Advertising)

Robert Jones, 1866 N. Orange Grove #202, Pomona, CA 91767, (909) 920-0840 (Rexall Drug Bottles and Items)

Ed Lemmon, 13432 Scots Way, Poway, CA 92064

Cecil Munsey, 13541 Willow Run Road, Poway, CA 92064 (All Bottles)

Stan Wilker, P.O. Box 2081, Rancho Palos Verdes, CA, (310) 377-7780 (Gaming and Western Americana)

Dennis Fox, 3600 Data Dr. #227, Rancho Cordova, CA 95670, (916) 638-4378 (All Nevada and Alaska Bottles)

Charlie's Ore House, POB 293, 153 Butte, Randsburg, CA, (760) 374-2238

J. Bart Parker, P.O. Box 356, Randsburg, CA 93554, (760) 374-2382 (Louis Taussig Whiskey Items, Tokens)

Byrl and Grace Rittenhouse, 3055 Birch Way, Redding, CA 96002, (916) 243-0320

Norm Brown, 631 Lakeview Way, Redwood City, CA 94062-3322, (50) 366-7082 Eyecups

Norman Fasig, 1149 N. Heritage Dr., Ridgecrest, CA 93555-5510, (760) 446-4777

Jeff Hargrove, 2002 Midway Road, Ridgecrest, CA 93555, (619) 446-8986 (Insulators)

Richard Aldridge
5047 Olivewood Ave.
Riverside, CA 92506
(951) 276-7184 (Black Glass and Bleach Bottles)

Harold and Virginia Lyle, 11259 Gramercy Pl., Riverside, CA 92505, (714) 689-3662 (Bottles)

James Fennelly, 520 54th St., Sacramento, CA 95819, (916) 457-3695 (Ezra Brooks, Jim Beams, and Ski Country Bottles)

Bill Grolz, 22 Mad River Ct., Sacramento, CA 95831, (916) 424-7283 (Violin Bottles)

Frank Feher, 1624 Maryland Avenue, West Sacramento, CA 95691, (916) 371-7731 - (Glass Insulators)

George and Rose Reidenbach, 2816, "P" St., Sacramento, CA 95816, (916) 451-0063

Grant Salzman, 427 Safflower Place, West Sacramento, CA 95691, (916) 372-7272 (Glass Insulators)

Peck and Audie Markota, 4627 Oakhallow Dr., Sacto, CA 95842, (916) 334-3260

Dwayne Anthony, 1066 Scenic Dr., San Bernardino, CA 92408, (909) 888-6417 (Insulators)

Michael Corvi, 476 Hawthorne, San Bruno, CA 94066

Mike Bryant, 4214 Tacoma St., San Diego, CA 92117, (858) 581-2787 (San Diego Bottles)

Jack E. Coffin, 4429 Ohio St., San Diego, CA 92116, (619) 516-1340 (Jim Beam, Ezra Brooks, Avon)

Frank Console, 4156 Arizona St., San Diego, CA 92104, (619) 295-0696 (Hires Root Beer Bottles/Items)

Clair Cunningham, 8815 Whiteport Lane, San Diego, CA 92119, (619) 466-4705 (Glass Insulators)

Rhudy Fowler, 2622 Bayside Walk, San Diego, CA 92109, (858) 488-5551

Don, Derick and Garet Frace, 7516 Rock Canyon Drive, San Diego, CA 92126, (858) 578-0069 (Early Medicines)

Bob Gilbert, 14490 Rimgate Court, San Diego, CA 92129, (858) 484-8485 (Toys and Soda Marbles)

Clarice Gordon, 3269 N. Mtn. View Dr., San Diego, CA 92116, (619) 282-5101 (Glass Insulators)

Bill Gore, 3098 Rue D'Orleans #315, San Diego, CA 92110, (619) 223-8082 (Stoneware)

Richard Hager, 4712 Redland Drive, San Diego, CA 92115, (619) 287-5499 (Advertising, Brewery Trays)

Richard and Camille Horak, 7841 Melotte Street, San Diego, CA 92119, (619) 469-9629 (Soda and Depression Glass)

Norm and Doris James, San Diego, CA 92115, (619) 466-0652 (Insulators)

Jon, Matt and A.J. Lawson, 6261 Estrella Avenue, San Diego, CA 92120, (619) 287-6338 (Western Botles, Flasks, Whiskeys)

Ed and Carol Lowe, 3027 Wing Street, San Diego, CA 92110, (619) 222-6300 (Insulators, Bottles)

Tim McLeod, 4343 44th Street #4, San Diego, CA 92115 (San Diego Bottles)

Naomi Kent Medlock, 6757 Parkside Avenue, San Diego, CA 92139 Glass, (Old Cooking Items)

Linda and Norman Meeder, 2741 Luna Avenue, San Diego, CA 92117, (858) 274-9857 (R.C. Cola Items)

Roy Nelson, 4132 Vermont Street, San Diego, CA 92103, (619) 691-6296 (Crocks)

Al Sparacino, 743 La Huerta Way, San Diego, CA 92154, (619) 690-3632 (Miniature Bottles)

Jim Walker, 4784 Aberdeen Street, San Diego, CA 92117, (858) 490-9019 (San Diego Items)

Whitney Alexander, 365 S. 19th Street, San Jose, CA 95116, (408) 292-4641

Thierry Stanich, 946 Terra Bella Ave., San Jose, CA 95125, (408) 267-7703 (Miniature Bottles - Cognacs)

Jim Gibson, 8573 Atlas View Dr., Santee, CA 92071 (Bottles)

Randolph M. Haumann, 415 Amherst St., San Francisco, CA 94134, (415) 239-5807 - (Colored Figural Bitters)

Robert Dannebaum, 122 Seabright Ave., Santa Cruz, CA 95062, (831) 423-2224

Valvern and Mary Kille Mcluff, 214 S. Ranch Rd., Santa Maria, CA 93454, (805) 925-7014

Derek Abrams, 129 E. El Camino, Santa Maria, CA 93454, (805) 922-4208 (Whiskeys, Western Bottles)

Fireside Cellars, 1421 Montana Ave., Santa Monica, 90403, (310) 393-2888 (Miniature Bottles)

Lewis Lambert, Santa Rosa, CA,
(707) 823-8845 (Early Western
Bottles)

Richard Siri, P.O. Box 3818,
Santa Rosa, CA 95402,
rtsiri@sonic.net, (Cutters
Whiskeys)

Gene Baker, 39108 Granite
Lane, Shaver Lake, CA 93664

Tim Costello, 3903 Los Padres
Ln., Shingle Springs, CA 95682

James Doty, 2026 Finch
Ct., Simi Valley, CA 93063
(Insulators)

T.R. Schweighart, 1123 Santa
Luisa Dr., Solana Beach, CA
92075

Marilyn Wallace, 13005 Covey
Circle, Sonora, CA 95370

Flask Liquor, Inc., 12194
Ventura Blvd., Studio City,
CA 91604, (818) 761-5373
(Miniature Bottles)

Frank and Judy Brockman, 104
W. Park, Stockton, CA 95202,
(209) 948-0746

Paul Woodward, P.O. Box 325,
811 Thomas Rd., Taft, CA
93268, (661) 765-6563

John R. Swearingen, 3227 N.
Wildhorse Ct., Thousand Oaks,
CA 91360, (805) 492-5036 (Fruit
Jars)

Rich Burnham, P.O. Box 4056,
Torrance, CA 90503, (310) 320-
2552 (Civil War Relics)

David Spaid, 2916 Briarwood
Dr., Torrance, CA 90505, (310)
534-4943 (Miniature Bottles)

Steve and Cris Curtiss, 34641 S. Bernard Dr., Tracy, CA 95376, (209) 836-0903 (Northern and Central Calif. Hutchinsons and Sodas)

Dennis Rogers, 2459 Euclid Crescent East, Upland, CA 91784, (909) 982-3416 (Cathedral Pickle Bottles)

Tom Quinn, P.O. Box 5503, Vallejo, CA 94591, (707) 864-0564 (Western Whiskeys)

Don and Linda Yount, P.O. Box 4459, Ventura, CA 93004, (805) 656 2707 (Bottles)

Tom Eccles, 747 Magnolia, West Covina, CA 91791, (626) 339-9107 (Sarsaparilla Bottles)

David Hall, 1217 McDonald Ave., Wilmington, CA 90744, (310) 834-6368 (Glass Insulators)

Betty and Ernest Zumwalt, 5519 Kay Dr., Windsor, 95492, (707) 545-8670

Mitri Manneh, 11415 Whittier Blvd, Whittier, CA 90601, (310) 692-2928 (Miniature Bottles)

Mike and Lilarae Smith, P.O. Box 2347, Yucca Valley, CA 92286, (760) 228-9640 (Indian Bottles)

Colorado

Ken Schneider, 7156 Jay St. Arvada, CO 80003 (Colorado Bottles)

Fred Shattuck, 12230 Wiagara St., Brighton, CO 80602

Tom Burt, 4711 Starfire Circle, Castle Rock, CO 80104

Bob Dewitt, P.O. Box 25012, Colorado Springs, CO 80936

Rebecca Harris, 9545 Oak Tree Ct., Colorado Springs, CO 80952, (790) 390-5621

Ron Jones, 2204 W. Colorado Ave, Colorado Springs, CO 80904

Michael Bliss, Ft. Collins, CO, (970) 225-0800 (Insulators and Bottles)

Ann Nelson, 30997 Niakwa Rd., Evergreen, CO 80437, (303) 670-4957

Mike and Jodee Holzwarth, 2224 Laporte Ave., Ft. Collins, CO 80521, (970) 224-4464 (Colorado Bottles)

Fort Collins Bottles, Bill Thomas, 2000 Rangeview Dr., Ft. Collins, CO 80524, (303) 493-8177 (Miniature Bottles)

Jim Keilman, 3101 F Road, Grand Junction, CO 81501, (303) 434-3275 (Bottles, Bimal Miniatures)

Karl Knapp, 401 N. Taylor, Gunnison, CO 81230

Marc Sagrillo, 555 Aspen Ridge Drive, Lafayette, CO 80026, (303) 661-9800 (Colorado Bottles)

Larry Volmer, 890 Depew St., Lakewood, CO 80214, (303) 235-0587 (Colorado Bottles)

Craig Collier, 8077 RDMM 3. Lamar, CO 80152, (719) 336-2908

Bruce McCallister, 123 W. 4th Street, Leadville, CO 80461, (719) 486-3934

Bill Frederick, 5118 S. Osceola, Littleton, CO 80123, (303) 347-9771

Jeff Johnson, 5509 S. Iris St., Littleton, CO 80123, (303) 933-4480 (Colorado Bottles)

Marietta LeBlanc, 5592 W. Geddes Place, Littleton, CO 80123, (303) 979-4943 (Miniature Bottles)

David Kratky, 2424 Collyer, Longmont, CO 80501, (303) 772-0558

Dennis Bradley, P.O. Box 1002, New Castle, CO 81647, (970) 984-2625

Jody Grandpre, 7958 Cistera Way, Parker, CO 80134, (720) 851-2720

Joyce Rector, 2037County Rd. 129, Simla, CO 80835, (719) 541-2974 (Fruit Jars)

Jim Bishop, Box 5554, Snowmass Village, CO 81615, (303) 923-2348 (Miniature Liquor)

David Watson, 495 Broken Wagon Road, Woodland Park, CO 80863, (719) 687-7503

Connecticut

Rick Ciralli, 48 Birch Street, Bristol, CT 06010, (860) 585-0713 (Bottles, Flasks, Glass from Connecticut Glasshouses)

Todd James Maynard, P.O. Box 326, Centerbrook, CT 06409 (860) 767-9037 (Saratoga-Type Mineral Water Bottles)

Julian Gottlieb, 18 Pond Pl., Cos Cob, CT 06807, (203) 869-8411

Arthur Morse, 15 Parky Drive, Enfield, CT 06082

Phil Pockoski, 174 Hungary Road, Granby, CT 06035

Ole Severson, 34 Dartmouth Dr., Huntington, CT. 06484, (203) 929-5197

Mary's Old Bottles, White Hollow Rd., Lakeville, CT Lime Rock, CT 06039, (203) 435-2961

Ralph Foster, 180 Exeter Rd., Lebanon, CT 06249-1320

Jerry Jaffe, P.O. Box 287, Madison, CT 06443

Doug MacGillvary, 79 New Bolton Road, Manchester, CT 06040, (203) 649-0477 (Northeast Insulators)

Miriam Giannone, 57 E. Brodway, Milford, CT 06460-6108

Bob's Old Bottles, 656 Noank Rd., Rt. 215, Mystic, CT 06355, (203) 536-8542

Louise Baker, 17 Hyvue Dr., Newtown, CT 06470-1706

Albert Corey, 153 W. Main St., Niantic, CT 06357, (203) 739-7493

Robert Garbauskas, 49 Gertrude Avenue, Waterbury, CT 06708-1738

George E. Johnson, 2339 Litchfield Rd., Watertown, CT 06795, (203) 274-1785

Norman and Elizabeth Heckler, Woodstock, CT 06282, (203) 974-1634

Al and Ginny Way, 68 Cooper Drive, Waterbury, CT 06704, (203) 575-9964 (Insulators)

Delaware

Ferd Meyer, 16 Cove View Dr., Long Neck, DE 19966, (410) 592-3565

August Stenholm, 11 Morris Road, New Castle, DE 19720, (302) 328-7862

Rowland L. Hearn, 10 Wordsworth Drive, Wilmington, DE 19808, (302) 994-2036 (Delaware Books and Bottles)

Florida

Roy and Jean Baither, 1205
40th Street West, Bradenton,
FL 34205, (941) 747-7157

Don Bosket, 1230 N. Kings
Road, Callahan, FL 32011, (904)
845-1987

Russell and Linda Maston, 6700
150th Ave N. #828, Clearwater,
FL 33764

Larry Craft, 403 Woodville
Hwy., Crawfordville, FL 32327,
(904) 421-6907 (Insulators)

Scott Clary, P.O. Box 863,
Defuniak Springs, FL 32435,
(850) 892-5474

Bud Hastin, P.O. Box 11004,
Ft. Lauderdale, Fl 33339, (954)
566-0691

M & S Bottles and Antiques,
421 Wilson St., Fort Meade FL
33841, (941) 285-9421

Pat Besinger, 5719 Casino
Drive, Holiday, FL 34690, (813)
934-3986 (Nursing Bottles)

Arlene Caruso, 1377 Riviera Dr.,
Green Cove Springs, FL 32043,
(904) 284-1499

This-N-That Shop, Albert
B. Coleman, P.O. Box 185,
Hollister, FL 32047, (904) 328-
3658

Hickory Stick Antiques, 400 So. 57 Terr., Hollywood, CA 33023, (904) 962-3434 (Canning Jars, Black Glass, Household Bottles)

Richard King, 1002 San Remo Circle, Homestead, FL 33035, (305) 248-3035

The Browns, 6512 Mitford Rd., Jacksonville, FL 32210, (904) 771-2091 (Sodas, Mineral Waters, Milk, Black Glass)

Wayne Harden, 3867 Winter Berry Rd., Jacksonville, FL 32210, (904) 781-2620, www. waynesbottles.com

Pacer Henry, 5858 Theed Street, Jacksonville, FL 32211, (904) 744-8458 Florida (Pottery Jugs and Crocks)

Dwight Pettit, 33 Sea Side Dr., Key Largo, FL 33037, (305) 852-8338

Carl Sturm, 88 Sweetbriar Branch, Longwood, FL 32750 (407) 332-7689 (Cure Bottles)

Wayne Boynton, Box 1428, Loxahatchee, FL 33470, (561) 793-3530

Bob Adams, 707 N.E. 113th Street, Miami, FL 33161, (305) 895-0843

David Pupo, 563 Raven Way, Naples, FL 34110, (813) 592-0314

Jim Meyer, 3310 St. RD 40, Ormond Beach, FL 32174, (904) 677-0530 (Insulators)

Gary Beatty, 1580 N. Hinton St., Port Charlotte, FL 33952, (941) 255-5812

Alan McCarthy, 2415 W. 15th St., Panama City, FL 32401, (904) 784-3903 Black Glass, (Early Medicines)

Tom and Alice Moulton, 2903 Aston Avenue, Plant City, FL 33567, (813) 754-1396 (Insulators and Fruit Jars)

Gary Drayton, 1531 N.E. 32nd Street, Pompano Beach, FL 33841, (954) 202-0818

Hidden Bottle Shop, 2656 Grandview, Sanford, FL 32771, (813) 322-7181

Juanne and Ed Herrold, P.O. Box 3105, Sarasota, FL, (941) 923-6550 (Bitters, Cathedral Pickles)

Harry O. Thomas, 2721 Parson's Rest, Tallahassee, 32308, (904) 893-3834

Richard Brown, 3130 W. Oaklyn Ave., Tampa, FL 33609, (813) 286-0643

L.L. Linscott, 3557 Nicklaus Dr., Titusville, FL 32780, (305) 267-9170 (Fruit Jars and Porcelain Insulators)

Charles O'Neil, 2235 Talmage Dr., Titusville, FL 32780

Art Besinger, P.O. Box 293,
Zephyr Hills, FL 33593, (813)
934-3986

Georgia

Bob Simmons, 449 Princeton
Way NE, Atlanta, GA 30307,
(770) 455-3065

Allen Vegotsky, 2215 Greencrest
Dr. NE, Atlanta, GA 30345

Bill Babb, 2352 Devere St.,
Augusta, GA 30904, (706) 736-
8097

James McPherson, 3125
Ramsgate Rd., Augusta, GA
30909

Michael D. (Mike) Newman,
3716 Pebble Beach Drive,
Augusta, GA 30907, (706) 868-
8391 (Southern Colored Sodas)

Ken Evans, 7175 Moon Rd.,
Apt 1013, Columbus, GA 31909,
(706) 653-9115

Bob Brown, 274 Riverhill Rd.,
Cornelia, GA 30531 (Saratoga-
Type Bottles)

Keith Roloson, 6220 Carriage
Court, Cumming, GA 30130
(770) 781-5021 (Insulators)

John and Dorothy Wood, P.O.
Box 98, Danielsville, GA 30663,
(706) 795-2745

Marshall Cooper, 1424 Diamond
Head Circle, Decatur, GA 30033,
(678) 417-4006

Carl Barnett, 1211 St. Andrews
Drive, Douglas, GA 31533, (912)
384-0651

James T. Hicks, Rt. 4, Box 265,
Eatonton, GA 31024, (404) 485-
9280

Paul H. Irby, 5862 Meadowview
Lane, Flowery Branch, GA
30542, (770) 967-3946 (Bottles
and Insulators)

Jim Scharnagel, 3601 Laura
Lane, Gainesville, GA 30506,
(770) 536-5690 (Inks and
Female Medicines)

Kim Kerley, P.O. Box 763,
Harlem, GA 30814-0763

Jack Hewitt, 1765 Potomac Ct.,
Lawrenceville, GA 30043, (770)
963-0220

Susan Petard-Acree, 4805
Highway 28, NW #116-190,
Lilbum, GA 30047 (Violin
Bottles)

Butch Alley, P.O. Box 358, Lithia
Springs, GA 30057, (770) 942-
4493 (Bottles)

Jerry Schmitt, 11514 Carriage
Dr., Macon, GA 31210

Schmitt House Bottle Diggers,
5532 Jane Rue Circle, Macon,
GA 31206, (912) 781-6130

Ken Nease, Rt. 1, Box 149,
Manassas, GA 30438, (912) 739-
7355 (Bottles)

Karen Larkin, 1210 Hiller Rd., McKinleyville, GA 95519, (707) 839-0261 (Violin Bottles)

John Joiner, 173 Green Tree Dr., Newman, GA 30265, (770) 502-9565

Steve Schingler, 40 Spring Branch Ct., Newnan, GA 30256, (770) 253-7028

Bob and Barbara Simmons, 152 Greenville St., Newnan, GA 30263, (404) 251-2471

Jimmy Bray, Box 517, Oglethorpe, GA 31068, (912) 472-8442

Thurman Spangler, 391 Hickory Ridge Trail, Ringgold, GA 30736, (706) 965-2925

Ed Nelson, 110 Wickersham Drive, Savannah, GA 31411

David Powell, Savannah, GA, (912) 354-3576 (Bottles and Jars)

George Miller, 502 Wesley Oaks Dr., St. Simons Is, GA 31522, (912) 634-0522

Bill Wrenn, 1060 Calls Creek Drive, Watkinsville, GA 30677 (Mini Jugs)

Jim Hewitt, 214 Parkridge, Woodstock, GA 30189

Hawaii

Matthew Kalalare Sr., P.O. Box 142, Hana, HI 96713

Will Poston, P.O. Box 664, Hana, HI 96713

Alton Chow, 387 Nehe St., Hilo, HI 96720, (808) 935-4107

Francis Markham, 1664 Alu Street, Hilo, HI 96720

James Turner, 115 Paulele Street, Hilo, HI 96720, (808) 959-3664

Steve Goodenow, 625 Iolani Ave., Honolulu, HI 96813, (808) 526-3245 (Hawaiian Bottles)

John Honi, Box 1201, Kailua-Kona, HI 96745, (808) 325-9905

Derek Espirith, 92-1246 Hookeha St., Kapolie, HI 96707, (808) 672-7573 (Sodas)

Peter Underwood, P.O. Box 742, Kealakekua, HI 96750, (808) 323-2239

Celia Rahel, Box 806, Lawai, Kauia, HI 96765, (808) 332-9763

Ruth Newport, 84-6988 Ala Mahiku St. #171A, Waianae, HI 96792, (808) 695-1212

Idaho

Bud Thompson, 2910 S. Cloverdale Rd., Boise, ID 83709, (208) 362-9434 (Insulators)

John Cothern, Rt. 1, Buhl, ID 83316, (208) 543-6713

Rudy Burns, 1238 Eagle Hills Way, Eagle, ID 83616

Larry Banks, RR 1, Box 5B, Kooskia, ID 83539

Betty Zumwalt, Box 1914, Sandpoint, ID 83864, (208) 263-0969

Idaho Hotel, Jordan St., Box 75, Murphy, ID Silver City, ID 86350, (208) 495-2520

Illinois

Sean Mullikin, 5014 Alicia Dr., Alton, IL 62002, (312) 466-7506

Mike Spiiroff, 1229 Alton St., Alton, IL 62002, (618) 462-2283

Joe Bielat, 401 N. Pine, Arlington Heights, IL 60004, (847) 255-7324

Bob Kay, 216 N. Batavia Ave, Batavia, IL 60510 (Miniature Bottles)

Wayne and Jacqueline Brammer, 309 Bellevue Dr., Belleville, IL 62223, (618) 213-8841

Kent Knowles, 910 S. 29th St., Belleville, IL 62226, (618) 235-1412 (Beer Items)

Ernest Brooks, 9023 S. East End, Chicago, IL 60617, (312) 375-9233

1st Chicago Bottle Club, P.O. Box A3382, Chicago, IL 60690

Jerry McCann, 5003 West Berwyn, Chicago, IL 60630, (312) 777-0443 (Fruit Jars)

Carl Malik, 8655 S. Keeler, Chicago, IL 60652, (312) 767-8568

Paul R. Welko, 5727 S. Natoma Ave., Chicago, Il 60638, (312) 229-0424 (Blob Tops and Hutchinson Sodas)

Al and Sue Verley, 486 Longwood Ct., Chicago, IL 60411, (312) 754-4132, (312) 541-5788, (312) 945-5493

Russell and Lynn Sineni, P.O. Box 154, DeKalb, IL (815) 758-3072

Ray's and Betty Antiques, Box 5, Dieterich, IL 62424, (217) 925-5449 (Bitters)

Bob Harms, P.O. Box 142, Dolton, Il 60419 (708) 758-5788 (Hutchinson Sodas)

Keith and Ellen Leeders, 1728 N. 76th Ave, Elmwood, IL 60635, (708) 453-2085

Jeff Cress, 3403 Morkel Dr., Godfrey, IL 62035, (618) 466-3513

Rosemary Brandenburg, P.O. Box 651, Greeup, IL 62428, (217) 923-3245

Kelly Dziak, 5886 Constitution Ave., Gurnee, IL 60031, (847) 263-0417

Jim and Jodi Hall, 5185 Conifer Lane, Gurnee, IL 60031, (708) 541-5788 (Bottles-All Types)

Doug and Eileen Wagner, 9225 S. 88th Ave, Hickory Hills, IL 60457, (312) 598-4570

Jim and Perry Lang, 628 Mechanic, Hillsboro, IL 62049, (217) 532-2915

John Murray, 301 Hillgrove, LaGrange, IL 60525, (312) 352-2199

Lloyd Bindscheattle, P.O. Box 11, Lake Villa, IL 60046

Scott Garrow, 130 S. Stewart Ave., Lombard, IL 60148, (630) 916-7623

Neal and Marianne Vander Zande, 18830 Sara Rd., Mokena, IL 60448, (312) 479-5566

Seve Kehrer, Box 151, New Memphis, IL 62266, (618) 588-7785 (Fruit Jars)

Tom and Ann Feltman, 425 North Oak St., O'Fallon, IL 62269, (618) 632-3327

Vern and Gloria Nitchie, 300 Indiana St., Park Forest, IL 60466, (312) 748-7198

Harry's Bottle Shop, 612 Hillyer St., Pekink, IL 61555, (309) 346-3476 (Pottery, Beer, Sodas, Medicines)

Oertel's Bottle House, Box 682, Pekin, IL 61555, (309) 347-4441 (Peoria Pottery, Embossed Picnic Beer Bottles, Fruit Jars)

Bob Rhinberger, Rt. 7, Quincy, IL 62301, (217) 223-0191

Bob and Barbara Harms, 14521 Atlantic, Riverdale, IL 60627, (312) 841-4068

Ruth Ann Wasson, 6061 Carriage Green Way, Rockford, IL 61108, (815) 397-5677

Ed McDonald, 3002 23rd., Sauk Village, IL 60511, (312) 758-0373

Jon and Char Granada, 631 S. Main, Trenton, IL 62293, (618) 224-7308

Theo Adams, 508 Main St., Venice, IL 62090, (618) 451-5629 (Sodas)

Lenny Veneziano, 27W115 Vale Road, West Chicago, IL 60185, (708) 293-1435

John Watkins, 2456 Bryant Rd., West Frankfort, IL 62896-4045, (818) 932-3618

Lawrence Powers, 4628 Howard, Western Springs, IL 60558, (708) 246-1559

Craig Wright, 4332 Wolf Rd., Western Springs, Il 60558, (708) 246-5240 (ACL Painted Sodas)

Ben Crane, 1700 Thompson Dr., Wheaton, IL 60187, (312) 665-5662

Hall, 940 E. Old Willow Rd., Wheeling, IL 60090, (312) 541-5788 (Sodas, Inks, Medicines)

Steve Miller, 623 Ivy Ct., Wheeling, IL 60090, (312) 398-1445

Michael Davis, 1652 Tappan, Woodstock, IL 66098, (815) 338-5147

Mike Henrich, 402 McHenry Ave., Woodstock, IL 66098, (815) 338-5008

Indiana

Dave Spaulding, 1607 E. Co. Rd. 250N, Connersville, IN 47331, (765) 827-1142

Anthony Augustyn, 5927 Carol Court, Demotte, IN 46310, (219) 987-7306

Anne Szopa, 11199 US 35, Economy, IN 47339

June and Norm Barnett, Box 38, Flat Rock, IN 47234, (812) 587-5560

Annett's Antiques, 6910 Lincoln Hwy. E., Fort Wayne, IN 46803, (219) 749-2745

John Elliott, 4531 W. Jackson St., Frankfort, IN 46041, (219) 654-5602

Neil Wood, P.O. Box 69, Gas City, IN 46933, (765) 674-6450

Chuck Grueb, 17110 Antwerp RD RR3, Harlan, IN 46743-7438, (219) 657-5296

John Brezko, 207 N. Richie, Indianapolis, IN 46234, (317) 271-2524

Charles Davaney, 8888 Classic View Dr., Indianapolis, IN 46217, (317) 888-8401

Lloyd Martin, 1582 Gregory Lane, Jasper, IN 47546, (812) 482-2492

Oren Hammond, 550 North 1885 East, Kokomo, IN 46901, (317) 457-2895

Louis Ebert, 711 W. 6th St., Marion, IN 46953

Sonny Mallory, 3960 Middle Patton Pk. Rd., Martinsville, IN 46151, (765) 342-3357

Ann and Tim Miller, 859 S.
Harriett, Martinsville, IN
46151, (765) 342-1262

Ball State University,
University Libraries, Muncie,
IN 47306

Melvin Aishe, 110 N. Spring St.,
Odon, IN 47562

Owen Glendening, 1200 No.
Minnestrista Parkway, Muncie,
IN 47303, (765) 213-3540

Dean Higginbotham, 208 E.
State St., Princeton, IN 47670,
(812) 386-3040

Greg Spurgeon, 10644 US 41
North, Rosedale, IN 47874,
(812) 466-6521 (Fruit Jars)

Fort Harrod Glass Works, 160
N. Gardner Rd., Scottsburg, IN
47170, (812) 752-5170

Gil Hughes, 61985 31 So., South
Bend, IN 46614, (219) 291-0421

Ned Pennington, 367 S. 22nd
St., Terre Haute, IN 47803,
(812) 234-2214

John Schreiner, 427 Westchester
Lane, Valparaiso, IN 46385,
(219) 465-1190

LeeAnn Hathaway, 7600 W.
Kilgore Avenue, Yorktown, IN
47396-3838, (765) 759-5786

Iowa

Don Faas, 6235 Hwy 69 N,
Ames, IA 50010, (515) 232-9228
(Iowa Sodas)

C. Dean Hoffman, 2668 147 St.,
Aurora, IA 50607

Bill Brown, RR3 Box 322,
Chariton, IA 50049, (515) 862-
4482

Tom Southward, 2815 Druid
Hill Drive, Des Moines, IA
50315, (515) 82-6901

Mark Wiseman, 3505 Sheridan
Ave., Des Moines, IA 50310,
(515) 255-2620

Wyatt Yon, Box 30067, Des
Moines, IA 50310, (515) 255-
8209

The Bottle Shop, 206 Chestnut,
Elkader, IA 52043, (319) 245-
2359 (Sarsaparilla and Bitters)

Mike Burggraaf, 305 E.
Burlington, Fairfield, IA 53556,
(515) 469-6018 (Iowa Bottles)

Dale Schatzberg, 10037 W.
Marquis Rd., Janesville, IA
50647, (319) 987-2120

Reggie Shoeman, 105 E. First,
Madrid, IA 50156

Clyde Jones, 719 e. 4th Street
N., Newton, IA 50208

Stewart Daniels, 2023 West 3rd
St., Waterloo, IA 50701, (319)
235-2443

Matt Schaeffer, P.O. Box 58,
Wellman, IA 52356

Kansas

Mikey Stafford, 507 On The
Mall, Atchison, KS 66002, (913)
367-0056 (Antiques and Books)

Richard Sevart, 1016 S. Rutter
Av. Chanute, KS 66720

Janet Hines, 131 South 2nd St.,
Fredonia, KS 66736

Donald Haury, 208 Main,
Halstead, KS 67056, (316) 283-
5876, (316) 835-2356

Jim Hovious, 6617 N. Kent Rd.,
Butler, KS 67522, (620) 543-
6633,e-mail jimsantqbottles@
earthlink.net

Mel Shootman, 406 Spruce,
Jamestown, KS 66948, (785)
439-6421

Stewart and Sons Old Bottle Shop, 610 E. Kaskaskia, Paola, KS 66071, (913) 294-3434 (Drugstore Bottles, Blob-Top Beers)

David Fath, 1811 Sidney, Kingman, KS 67068, (316) 532-2925 (Bitter Bottles)

Linda Wilbur, P.O. Box 105, Peck, KS 67120, (316) 524-1427

Richard Becker, 901 S. Pine, Pratt, KS 67124, (316) 672-2432

Bob Barbour, 14207 W. 74th Terrace, Shawnee, KS 66216, (913) 248-1478

Joe and Alyce Smith, 4706 West Hills Dr., Topeka, 66606, (913) 272-1892

John Moore, 2818 Milro Circle, Witchita, KS 67204, (316) 838-7161

Kentucky

B.J. Summers, 233 Darnell Rd., Benton, KY 42025, (606) 898-3097

Mike Ritter, 1824 Smallhouse Road, Bowling Green, KY 42104, (502) 781-1825

Roy Brown, RR3 Box 320, Grayson, KY 42243

Paul Van Vactor, 100004 Cardigan Dr., Jeffersontown, KY 40299

Thomas Noel, 1385 Norsworthy Rd., Kirksey, KY 42054, (502) 489-2440 (Stoneware)

Edwin Snyder, P.O. Box 156, Lancaster, KY 40444, (606) 792-4816

Roy and Cordie Willis, Heartland of Kentucky, Lebanon Junction, KY 40150 (502) 833-2827 (Jim Beam, Ski Country)

William Leonard, D.V.M., 1109 Commercial Drive, Lexington, KY 40505, (606) 231-1032 (Patented Vet Bottles)

Freeman Ross, 3560 Lansdowne Drive, Lexington, KY 40571, (606) 273-2640 (Poisons)

Gene Blasi, 5801 River Knolls Dr., Louisville, 40222, (502) 425-6995

Earl and Ruth Cron, 808 N. 25th St., Paducah, KY 42001, (502) 443-5005

Sheldon Baugh, 252 West Valley Dr., Russellville, KY 42276, (502) 726-2712 (Shaker Bottles)

Jerry McKinley, 221 Winding Way, Shelbyville, KY 40065, (502) 633-0105 (Stoneware)

Phillip Smith, 2281 Clarkson Lane, Union, KY 41091, (606) 384-9651

Louisiana

Sidney and Eulalle Genius, 1843 Tudor Dr., Baton Rouge, LA 70815, (504) 925-5774

Joyce Frugia, 122 E. Dazet Ln., Buras, LA 70041, (985) 657-7928

Robert Raynor, 18073 Brandon Dr. E HM, Hammond, LA 70403, (504) 429-2627

Cajun Pop Factory, P.O. Box 1113, Jennings, LA 70546, (318) 824-7078 (Hutchinson, Blob-Tops, Pontil Sodas)

Alvord Fryday, Box 188, Kilbourne, LA 71253, (318) 428-3831

Eddie Cunningham, 4617 Tabony St., Metairie, LA 70006-2341

Bep's Antiques, 3923 Magazine St., New Orleans, LA 70115, (504) 891-3468 (Imports)

Dan Brown, 1021 Burdette Street, New Orleans, LA 70118, (504) 865-1778

Francis Cole, 7442 Dominican St., New Orleans, LA 70119, (504) 866-8596

The Dirty Digger, 1804 Church St., Ruston, LA 71270, (318) 255-6112

Jim Daspit, 244 Marlin Dr., Slidell, LA 70461, (540) 649-6442

Terry Guidroz, Bryson's Antiques, 511 St., Phillips St., Thibodeaus, LA 70301, (985) 447-1800

Maine

John and Althea Hathaway, Bryant Pond, ME 04219

Bitters Bottle Man, P.O. Box 6163, China Village, ME 04926, E-mail danoa@uniets.net

Guy Kelley, RFD 4 Box 6225, Gardiner, ME 04345, (207) 582-7042

John L. Pelletier, 211 Main St., Gorham, ME 04038, (207) 838-4389 (Early American Bottles)

Carol Rose, 355 Sheepscot Rd., Newcastle, ME 04553

Spruce's Antiques, Main St., P.O. Box 295, Milford, ME 04461, (207) 827-4756

Jinny Brodsky, 13 Tide Meadow Lane, York, ME 03909, (207) 3636239

Maryland

Chester Otto, 956 Fish Hatchery Rd., Accident, MD 21520, (301) 746-8148

Jim Bready, 329 Homeland Southway-2A/B, Baltimore, MD 21212, (410) 323-4084

Robert Ford, 5912 Trotter Rd., Clarksville, MD 21029, (410) 531-9459

J. Phillipi, 8815 Jasper, Darksville, MD 21234, (410) 668-8376

Barry Bernas, 4335 O'Kane Court, Ft. Meade, MD 20755, (410) 674-6110

Robert Webber, P.O. Box 96, Linthicom, MD 21090, (410) 833-6849

Dan Walker, P.O. Box 99, Lisbon, MD 21765, (410) 876-8833

Jimmy Breen, 5524 Wicomicao Dr., New Market, MD 21774

Jay Banks, 4399 Wilhan Lane, Preston, MD 21655

Fran and Bill Lafferty, Box 142, Sudlersville, MD 21668

Janet Allen, 15102 Mud College
Rd., Thurmont, MD 21788, (301)
271-7161

Massachusetts

Arthur Channell, 11 Madison
Ave., Beverly, MA 01915, (508)
922-6663

Gregory Bair, 25 Porter Road,
Chelmsford, MA 01824

Robert Parsons, 24 Sylvan
Street, Danvers MA 01923

Paul Tutko, 108 Ash St.,
Danvers, MA 01923, (508) 774-
2061

Gloria Swanson Antiques, 611
Main St., Dennis, MA 02675,
(508) 385-4166

Joe Furgal, 205 Golden Hill
Rd., Lee MA 012238-9598, (413)
243-3320

Metamorphosis, 46 Teewaddle,
RFD 3, Leverett, MA 01002
(Hair Tonics and Medicines)

Phyllis Chamberlin, 11 Crowley
Street, Lowell, MA 01852

Shop in My Home, 211 East St.,
Mansfield, MA 02048, (617) 339-
6086 (Historic Flasks)

Steve Lawrence, 1311 Purchase
St., New Bedford, MA 02740,
(508) 997-3195 (Milk Bottles)

The Applied Lip Place, 26
Linden St., North Easton,
MA 02356, (617) 238-1432
(Medicines, Whiskeys)

Leo Goudreau, 11 Richfield Ave,
Ware, MA 01902, (413) 967-5054

Carlyn Ring, 59 Livermore
Road, Wellesley, MA 02181,
(617) 235-5675

Michigan

John Pastor, 7288 Thorncrest Dr., SE, Ada, MI 49301, (616) 285-7604 (Early Bottles, Flasks)

John Wolfe, 1622 E. Stadium Blvd, Ann Arbor, MI 48104, (313) 665-6106

Pat Keefe, 2290 Hiller Rd. W., Bloomfield, MI 48324, (313) 363-2068 (Miniature Bottles)

Old Chicago, 316 Ross Dr., Buchanan, MI 49107, (616) 695-5896 (Hutchinson Sodas, Blob-Top Beers)

Fred and Shirley Weck, 8274 S. Jackson, Clarklake, MI 49234, (517) 529-9631

Ray and Hillaine Hoste, 366 Main St., Dundee, MI 48131, (313) 529-2193

Ralph Finch, 34007 Hillside Ct., Farmington Hills, MI 48335-2513, (248) 476-4893, rfinch@twmi.rr.com (Target Balls - Publishes "On Target," International Newsletter for Target Ball collectors)

Linda Bobcean, 27051 James Ave., Flat Rock, MI 48134, (734) 782-4143

E & E Antiques, 9441 Grand Blanc Road, Gaines, MI 48436, (517) 271-9063 (Fruit Jars, Beer Bottles, Milks)

Bill Burgess, P.O. Box 381, Grass Lake, MI 49240, (517) 522-8969 (Fruit Jars)

Mark Churchill, 841 Burton St. S.E., Grand Rapids, MI 49507, (616) 248-3808 (Bottle Cleaning Service)

Daniel Moonan, 35 Shoreham, Grosse Pointe Shores, MI 48236

Sarge's, 111 E. Hemlock, Iron River, MI 49935, (906) 265-4223 (Old Mining Town Bottles, Hutchinsons)

Alan Holden, 2132 Chaparral, Kalamazoo, MI 49006, (616) 685-1776

Mark and Marty McNee, 1009 Vassar Dr., Kalamazoo, MI 49001, (616) 343-9393 (Medicine Bottles)

Lew and Leon Wisser, 2837 Parchmount, Kalamazoo, MI 49004, (616) 343-7479

Richard Franks, 6349 W. Silver Lake Rd., Linden, MI 48451, (810) 735-7381 (Fruit Jars, Milk Bottles, Medicine Bottles)

James Priestley, P.O. Box 416, Linden, MI 48451, (810) 266-5710

Don and Glenn Burkett, 3942 West Dunbar Rd., Monroe, MI 48161, (313) 241-6740 (Fruit Jars)

Doug Leybourne, Box 5417, No. Muskegon, MI 48445, (616) 722-1671 (Fruit Jars)

Barbara Sprague, 5546 Washington Ave, Muskegon, MI 49442-1852

Bill Heatlye, P.O. Box 114, Otisville, MI 48463

Ken Eddy, 12115-4 Mile Rd., Palinwell, MI 49080-9001

Dan Louis, 7923 East T.S. Avenue, Scotts, MI 49088, (616) 649-2069 (Cures)

Anvil Antiques, 3439 Hollywood Rd., St. Joseph MI, 49085, (616) 429-5132 (Insulators)

Shaun Kotlarsky, 2475 West Walton Blvd, Waterford, MI 48329, (313) 705-8255 (Insulators)

Earnest Griffin, 1200 South Harris, Ypsilanti, MI 48198, (734) 482-8029

Minnesota

Bradley Durling, 8309 Emerson Ave. So., Bloomington, MN 55420, (612) 881-2031

Ron and Vernie Feldhaus, 5117 W. 92nd St., Bloomington, MN 55437, (612) 545-2698

Austin Fjerestad, 5804 Olson Memorial Hwy., Golden Valley, MN 55422, (763) 595-8733

Pat Stambaugh, 718 S. Lakeshore Drive, Lake City, MN 55041

James Carlson, 4145-27th Ave. S., Minneapolis, MN 55406

Steve Ketcham, P.O. Box 24114, Minneapolis, MN 55424, (612) 920-4205

David Robertus, 5001 Queen Ave. N., Minneapolis, MN 55430

Doug Shilson, 3308-32 Ave So., Minneapolis, MN 55406, (612) 721-4165 (Bitters, Beers, and Sodas)

Neal and Pat Sorensen, 132 Peninsula Rd., Minneapolis, MN 55441, (612) 545-2698

Gerald Dannheim, 416 Summit Ave., New Ulm, MN 56073, (507) 354-1001

Larry Zirbes, Box 516, Richmond, MN 56368

Steve Showers, 25900 130th Ave., Welch, MN 55089, (507) 263-3272

Boyd Beccue, 3773-17th St. N.E., Willmar, MN 56201, (320) 235-5801 (Minnesota Patent Medicine Bottles)

Mississippi

Gordon Logan, P.O. Box 109, Calhoun City, MS 38916, (601) 628-5844

Robert A. Knight, 516 Dale St., Columbia, MS 39429 (601) 736-4249 (Mississippi Bottles and Jugs)

Trisha Schad, 1108 W. Jefferson Ave, Greenwood, MS 38930

Larry Hicks, 1100 Crestwood Drive, Hattiesburg, MS 39402, (601) 261-3228

Wayne Flannigan, P.O. Box 8733, Jackson, MS 39204, (601) 878-6684

Frances Steel, 943 Forest Hill Rd., Jackson, MS 39272-5733

Robert Smith, 623 Pearl River Ave., McComb, MS 39648, (601) 684-1843

John Sharp, P.O. Box 164, Sebastopol, MS 39359, (601) 625-8162 (Mississippi Bottles)

Jerry Drott, 710 Persimmon Dr., P.O. Box 714, Starkville, MS 39759, (601) 323-8796 (Liniments, Drug Store Bottles)

Ronald Lawyer, 2350 Rawhide Rd., Vicksburg, MS 39180

Missouri

Nancy Cummins, 24825 Robin Dr., Center, MO 63436, (573) 267-3639

Dave Hausgen, Rt. 1, Elsberry, MO 63343, (314) 898-2500

Sam and Eloise Taylor, 3002 Woodlands Terrace, Glencoe, MO 63038, (314) 273-6244

Randee and Susan Kaiser, 2400 Country Road 40030, Holts Summit, MO 65043, (573) 896-9052 (ACL Painted Sodas)

Mike and Carol Robinson, 1405 N. River, Independence, MO 64050, (816) 836-2337

Rod McCullough, 2302 S. Prosperity Ave., Joplin, MO 64081, (417) 782-2149

Gary and Vickie Lewis, P.O. Box 922, Liberty, MO 64069 (Soda Pop Bottles)

H. James Maxwell, 1050 W. Blue Ridge Blvd., Kansas City, MO 64145, (816) 942-6300

Robert Stevens, 1131 E. 77th, Kansas City, MO 64131, (816) 333-1398

The Bottle House, Rt. 1, Box 111, Linn Creek, MO 65052, (314) 346-5890

Bruce Mobley, P.O. Box 163, Macon, MO 63552-0163, (660) 385-6256

Ron Christian, 30581 295th, Maryville, MO 64468, (660) 582-8774

Trade Fair Mall, 1690 Se. Hwy 13, Osceola, MO 64776, (417) 646-8085

John Hinkel, 2236 South Hwy N., Pacific, MO 63069, (314) 271-7914

Wayne Lowry, 401 Johnston Ct., Raymore, MO 64083, (816) 318-0161 (Fruit Jars)

Leon Shores, Route 2, Shelbyville, MO 63469, (816) 284-6261 (Fruit Jars)

Patrick Moss, 3020 W. Farm Rd.,164 H-6, Springfield, MO 65807

David Crancer, P.O. Box 29303, St. Louis, MO 63126, (314) 225-2755

Jerry Mueller, 4520 Langtree, St. Louis, MO 63128, (314) 843-8357

Terry and Luann Phillips, 1014 Camelot Gardens, St. Louis, MO 63125, (314) 892-6864

Hal and Vern Wagner, 10118 Schuessler, St. Louis, MO 63128, (314) 843-7573 (Historical Flasks, Colognes, Early Glass)

Barkely Museum, U.S. 61, Taylor, MO, (314) 393-2408

Carol Hilton, 17197 Lawrence 2220, Verona, MO 65769, (417) 678-4523

Tiffany Rank, RT 2 Box 240-A, Warsaw, MO 65355

Randy and Jan Haviland, American Systems Antiques, Westphalia, MO 65085, (314) 455-2525

Tim Dorsey, 19217 Melrose Road, Wildroad, MO 63038, (636) 273-6552

Montana

R.J. Reid, 1102 E. Babcock St., Bozeman, MT 59715, (406) 587-9602 (Montana Sodas, Glass Figurals, Violin Bottles)

Ben Ayers, 393 Charlos Loop, Hamilton, MT 59840

Marc Lutsko, P.O. Box 8655, Kalispell, MT 59904, (406) 756-0224 (Montana Bottles and Items)

Larry and Hazel Munson, Devon Star Rte., Shelby, MT 59474 (Violin Bottles)

Mike Mefford, 6477 Hwy 93 South #352, Whitefish, MT 59937

Nebraska

Herk Karcher, HC85 Box 77, Bridgeport, NE 69336, (308) 262-1539

LaVonne Weber, 2001 E. Railroad Rd., Cozad, NE 69130, (308) 784-2775

Mark Waterbury, 7913 Edgewood Blvd., La Vista, NE 68128, (402) 339-4209

Ward Haessle, 2800 N. 79th St., Lincoln, NE 68507, (402) 325-9740

Terry and Pat Schmitt, 7340 Skyhawk Circle, Lincoln, NE 68506, (402) 489-7418

Brian Schilz, 1205 Westlawn, Ogallala, NE 69153, (308) 284-8297

Born Again Antiques, 1402 Williams St., Omaha, NE 68108, (402) 341-5177

Karl Person, 10210 "W" St., Omaha, NE 68127, (402) 331-2666

Fred Williams, 5712 N. 33rd St., Omaha, NE 68111, (402) 453-4317

Nevada

Lost River Trading Co., Larry Gray, P.O. Box 621, Beatty, NV 89003, (775) 583-9049

Bob Ferraro, 515 Northridge Dr., Boulder City, NV 89005, (702) 293-3114 (Nevada Items, Figural Whiskeys, Bitters)

Tom George, P.O. Box 21195, Carson City, NV 89721, (702) 884-4766 (Nevada Tokens)

Doug Southerland, Box 1345, Carson City, NV 89702

Loren D. Love, P.O. Box 412, Dayton, NV 89403, (702) 246-0142 (Beer Cans, Bottles)

Ed Hoffman, P.O. Box 6039, Elko, NV 89802, (702) 753-2435 (Coins and Paper)

The Gloryhole, Virginia Ridgway, P.O. Box 219, 115 Columbia, Goldfield, NV 89013

Ed and Nell Jennings, P.O. Box 277, Goldfield, NV 89013-0277, (775) 485-3505 (Goldfield), (702) 395-9415 (Las Vegas) (Nevada Tokens, Mining Stocks)

Coleen Garland, HC71 Box 30Q, Goldfield, NV 89013, (775) 485-3729 (Soda Pop and Beer Bottles)

Mike Beales, 4208 Mountain View Dr., Las Vegas, NV 89102, (702) 878-9630 (Fruit Jars)

Jo Bourgeois, 2401 Karli Dr., Las Vegas, NV 89102, (702) 870-0136 (Coca-Cola Bottles and Collectibles)

Terry and Cherly Boyer, 5825 N. Durango Dr., Las Vegas, NV 89149, (702) 645-2951 (Nevada Bottles, Lanterns, Lamps)

June Bramble, 10421 Willamette Pl., Las Vegas, NV 89134, (702) 256-7265 (Heisey Glass)

James Campiglia, 4371 Lucas, Las Vegas, NV 89120, (702) 456-6855 (Casino Collectibles, Postcards, Bottles)

Frank Gafford, 5716 West Balzar, Las Vegas, NV 89108

Tim Gittus, 8233 Abercrombe Way, Las Vegas, NV 89119, (702) 363-0546 (Insulators)

Dennis Larson, 301 Oakford St., Las Vegas, NV 89110, (702) 437-0721 (Beer Bottles and Associated Items)

Joe Martin, 2632 E. Harmon, Las Vegas, NV 89121, (702) 731-5004 (Nevada Trade Tokens)

John Nutting, 1309 Pauline Way, Las Vegas, NV (702) 382-7043

Brad Rodgers, 3385 Rossana St., Las Vegas, NV 89117

Allen Wilson, P.O. Box 29, Montello, NV 89830, (702) 776-2511 (Bottles)

Marty Hall, 15430 Sylvester Rd., Reno, NV 89511, (775) 852-6045 (Western Whiskeys and Nevada Bottles, Glass Repairs), e-mail: rosemulet@charter.net

Fred Holabird, 701 Goldrun Court, Reno, NV 89511, (702) 851-0836 (Nevada Bottles and Paper Items)

Bill Lynch, P.O. Box 13169, Reno, NV 89507, (702) 747-3730 (Whiskey Bottles)

Steve Williams, 2580 Everett Drive, Reno, NV 89503, (702) 747-1166

Willy Young, 80 Promontory Pointe, Reno, NV 89509, (702) 746-0922 (Fire Grenades)

Tom Orzech, 11405 Vicksburg Rd., Reno, NV 89506-8285 (Nevada Mining –Tonopah and Goldfield)

Edwin Upson, 3874 Zoe Lane, Reno, NV 89504

Pegasus Parlon. P.O. Box 33, Silver Peak, NV 89047, (702) 937-2314

Don and Bonnie McLane, 1846 F. St., Sparks, NV 89431, (702) 359-2171

Walt Walker, P.O. Box 21, Verde, NV 89439, (702) 345-0171

Mark Twain's Museum of Memories, Joe Curtis, P.O. Box 449, Virginia City, NV 89440 (702) 847-0454 (Rare Nevada Documents)

Gene and Merleen Wambolt, 493 Ida Ave., Winnemucca, NV 89445, (775) 623-4982

Don Wellman, 5565 Van Diest RD #189-13, Winnemucca, NV 89445, (775) 623-4982

Dan Famas, 320 Kay Way, Yerington, NV 89447

New Hampshire

Dave and Carol Waris, Boston Post Rd., Amherst, NH 03031, (603) 882-4409

Peter Austin, Austin's Antiques,
114 Dover Road, Rte. #4,
Chichester, NH 03234, (603)
798-3116

Karen Gray, 8 Spoiler Dr., Derry,
NH 03038, (603) 434-5215

Lucille Stanley, 9 Oak St.,
Exeter, NH 03833, (603) 772-
2296

Dana Mason, 57 Tyler St. #701,
Nashua, NH 03060

Jim and Joyce Rogers, Harvey
Rd., Rt. 10, Manchester, NH
03103, (603) 623-4101

Dave Bowers, Box 1224,
Wolfeboro, NH 03894

New Jersey

Historic Glass House, John
Brandt and Chris Woods,
Basking Ridge, NJ 07920, (908)
647-6183

Edmund and Ruth DeHaven,
Golden Oak Lane, Beesley's
Point, NJ 08223

Richard and Lesley Harris, Box 400, Branchville, NJ 07826, (201) 948-3935

Marlene Rafferty, 141 Meridian Dr., Brick, NJ 08724

Phil and Flo Alvarez, P.O. Box 107,Califon, NJ 07830, (201) 832-7438

Robert Liebesman, 52 Jerome Ave, Deal, NJ 07723

Glenn Vogel, 201 Knox Ave., Eatontown, NJ 07724, (732) 544-9249

Ed and Carole Clemens, 81 Chester Pl., Apt. D-2, Englewood, NJ 07631, (201) 569-4429

Richard Gibbs, P.O. Box 126, Essex Fells, NJ, 07021, (973) 228-1459

Sally Streeter, 23 Herman St., Glen Ridge, NJ 07028

Michael Mascioli, 118 Empire Ave., Gloucester Township, NJ 08012

Hubert Mertes, 31 Valley Rd., Hillsborough, NJ 08844-4108

Tom and Marion McCandless, 62 Lafayette St., Hopewell, NJ 08525, (609) 466-0619

Bob and Sandy Strickhart, 61 E. Prospect St., Hopewell, NJ 08525, (609) 466-0377 (Bitters and Fruit Jars)

Bruce and Pat Egeland, 3 Rustic Drive Howell, NJ 07731, (201) 363-0556

Dick and Elma Watson, 10 South Wendover Road, Medford, NJ 08055, (856) 983-1364

Sam Fuss, Harmony Rd., Mickleton, NJ 08056, (609) 423-5038

Brian Kutner, 707 Columbia Ave. Box 584, Millville, NJ 08332

Robert Garrett, 311 G. Street, Millville, NJ 08332, (856) 293-0886

Williard Saul and Sons, Millville, NJ 08332, (609) 825-8479 (Milk Products)

Joseph Biringer, 104 Garden Street, Mount Holley, NJ 08060, (609) 261-0159

Bill Herbolsheimer, 211 Suzanne Ave., North Cape May, NJ 08204

Frank Leotta, 342 Whig Cane Rd., Pilesgrove, NJ 08098

Old Bottle Museum, 4 Friendship Dr., Salem, NJ 08079, (609) 935-5631

Vivian Flowers, 9 Letts Court, Sayreville, NJ 08872

Joe Filippi, 561 E. Wheat Rd, Vineland, NJ 08360, (856) 794-2179

Tom Branigan, 117 Emerald Ave., West Cape May, NJ 08204

New Mexico

Irv and Ruth Swalwell, 8826 Fairbanks, Albuquerque, NM 87112, (505) 299-2977

Bill Tanner, 3608 Dakota, NE, Albuquerque, NM 87110-1431, (505) 878-9038

Bill Lockart, 1313-14th St. Apt 21, Almagordo, NM 88310

Greg Hoglin, 209 N. 5th Street, Belen, NM 87002, (505) 864-6634

Mavis Lee, 44 Rd. 5474, Farmington, NM 87401, (505) 325-7084

Zang Wood, P.O. Box 890/#21 Road 3461, Flora Vista, NM 87415, (505) 334-8966 (Seltzers, Hutchinsons)

John Clark, 2190 Kent Road, Las Cruces, NM 88001, (505) 522-9051

Scott Given, Bottle Shop, 200 E. Motel Dr., Lordsburg NM 88045, (505) 542-3402

Tino Romero, 2917 Canada del Humo, Santa Fe, NM 87505, (505) 474-6353 (Poisons, Inks, Dr. Kilmer and New Mexico)

New York

Barbara McEnroe, 5201 RT 22, Amenia, NY 12501

Tom and Alice Moulton, 88 Blue Spruce Lane, RD 5, Ballston Lake, NY 12019

Jim Chamberlain, RD 8, 607 Nowland Rd., Binghamton, NY 13904, (607) 772-1135

Edward Petter, P.O. Box 1, Blodgett Mills, NY 13738, (607) 756-7891 (Inks)

Old Bottle Shop, Horton Rd., P.O. Box 105, Blooming Grove, NY 10914, (914) 496-6841

Nancy Hartwick, 16 Trefoil Lane, Brockport, NY 14420

Al Manuel, 1225 McDonald Ave., Brooklyn, NY 11230, (718) 253-8308 (Miniature Bottles)

The Bottle Shop Antiques, P.O. Box 503, Cranberry Lake, NY, (315) 848-2648

Robert Sapienza, 9945 67th Rd. Apt. 615, Forest Hills, NY 11375

Brian Wade, 39 East 16th Street, Huntington Station, NY 11746, (516) 271-7226 Embossed Crowntop Sodas

William Schwarting, 6046 Sandbank Road, Jordan, NY 13080, (315) 689-6460

Kenneth Cornell, 9232 Warsaw Road, Route 19 South, Le Roy, NY 14482 (Barber Bottles)

Jack Fortmeyer, 83 Palm Street, Lindenhurst, NY 11757, (516) 226-5965 (Fire Grenades)

Robert Latham, 463 Loudon Road, Loudonville, NY 12211, (518) 463-1053

Michael Anderson, 702 Broadway 2nd Fl., Mechanicsville, NY 12118, (518) 664-2847

Manor House Collectibles, Rt. 42, South Forestburg, RD 1, Box 67, Monticello, NY 12701, (914) 794-3967 (Whiskeys, Beers, Sodas)

Chris Davis, 522 Woodhill, Newark, NY 14513, (315) 331-4078 (Bottles and Glass)

Timothy Dupay, 595 Lakeside Road, Newburgh, NY 12550 (914) 564-3053

Schumer's Wine & Liquors, 59 East 54th Street, New York, NY 10022, (Miniature Bottles)

Ken Gore, 646 Pennsylvania Ave, Palenville, NY 12463, (518) 678-2102

Tom Andriach, 1007 N. Madison St., Rome, NY 13440, (315) 339-4338

John Spellman, 1530 High Street, P.O. Box 61, Savannah, NY 13146, (315) 365-3156 (Bottles, Flasks, Jars Produced at Clyde, NY)

Matt Warne, 2924 Brent Dr., Sanborn, NY 14132

Kevin Lawless, 41 Crestwood Drive, Schenectady, NY 12306, (518) 355-5688 (Insulators)

Robert Sheffield, 345 Gillett Road, Spencerport, NY 14559 (716) 352-4604

Thomas Babcock, 115 Marshia Ave., N. Syracuse, NY 13212

William Geduhn, 64 Pelton Ave., Staten Island, NY 10310

James Cookinham, 611 W. Cooper St., Utica, NY 13502, (315) 732-8563

Dick and Evelyn Bowman, 1253 LaBaron Circle, Webster, NY 14580, (716) 872-4015 (Insulators)

Jon Landers, 8646 Aitken Ave., Whiteboro, NY 13492, (315) 768-7091

North Carolina

J. B. Young, 1012 Davis Dr., Apex, NC 27502, (919) 362-6596

Luke Yarbrough, P.O. Box 1023, Blowing Rock, 28605, (704) 963-4961

Howard Kaufman, 17 Tsataga Ct., Brevard, NC 28712

Clement's Bottles, 5234 Willowhaven Dr., Durham, 27712, (919) 383-2493 (Commemorative Soft Drink Bottles)

Gary Allred, P.O. Box 399, Ellerbe, NC 28338, (910) 652-4265

Howard Crowe, P.O. Box 133, Gold Hill, NC 28071, (704) 279-3736 (Figural Bottles)

Vernon Capps, 2216 Rosewood Rd., Goldsboro, NC 27530 (919) 734-8964

John Parks, 1712 Bear Pond Rd., Henderson, NC 27536

Howard McElrath, R #1, Box 179, Horseshoe, NC 28742, (828) 891-7794

Stan Tart, 1408 Applecross Ct., Kernersville, NC 27284, (336) 788-3200

Alice Hatcher, 1905 Greenbriar Rd., Kinston, NC 28501-2129

Scott Berry, 7160 Franklin Rd., Lewisville, NC 27023, (336) 946-2020 (APL Soda Bottles)

Fred Jones, 3556 Mountain View Dr., North Wilkesboro, NC 28659

Doug Williams, 131 Pinelake Circle, S.W., Ocean Isle Beach, NC 28469 (910) 579-9965 (Insulators)

Rex D. McMillan, 4101 Glen Laurel Dr., Raleigh, NC 27612, (919) 787-0007 (North Carolina Blobs, Saloon Bottles, Colored Drugstore Bottles)

C.H. McDonald Jr., 4101 Lower Stone Ch. Rd., Rockwell, NC 28138

J & J Collectibles, 2002 S. Hwy. 301, Wilson, NC 27893, (252) 243-1569

Ohio

Ralph Bowman, 1627 Wooster Ave., Akron, OH 44320, (440) 745-9996

Adam and Phyllis Koch, 763 Jolson Ave., Akron, OH 44319, (330) 633-0274 (Stoneware)

Jim Salzwimmer, 3391 Tisen Rd., Akron, OH 44312, (216) 699-3990

Jerry Tebbano, 63 Carriage Square, Aurora, OH 44202, (216) 562-5329 (Stoneware)

John Miller, 10254 Lawnfield Rd. NW, Beach City, OH 44608

Allan Hodges, 25125 Shaker Blvd., Beachwood, OH 44122, (216) 464-8381

Richard Baldwin, 1931 Thorpe Circle, Brunswick, OH 44212, (330) 225-3576 (Insulators/ Bottles)

Charles Burkart, 27 E. Ridgeway Dr., Centerville, OH 45459

Edna Damon, 811 Dow St., Dayton, OH 45407

Don and Paula Spangler, 2554 Loris Dr., Dayton, OH 45449, (513) 435-7155

John and Mary Wolf, 1186 Latchwood Ave., Dayton, OH 45405, (513) 275-1617 (Cures)

Gilbert Nething, P.O. Box
96, Hannibal, OH 43931
(Hutchinson Sodas)

Sandy Andromeda, P.O. Box
338, Hillard, OH 43026, (614)
527-1957

Robert Black, 1741 Glenmar
Dr., Lancaster, OH 43130, (614)
654-5866

R.J. and Freda Brown, 125 S.
High St., Lancaster, OH 43130,
(614) 687-2899

Pat McNeeley, 1255 Irene Rd.,
Lyndhurst, OH 44124-1315,
(440) 449-6174

A. Waxman, 1928 Camberly Dr.,
Lyndhurst, OH 44124, (216)
449-4765 (Miniature Bottles,
Whiskey, Rye, Scotch)

Dan Deever, 660 Satinwood Cir.,
Mansfield, OH 44903

Alan and Elaine DeMaison,
1605 Clipper Cove, Painesville,
OH 44077, (440) 358-1223,
a.demaison@sbcglobal.net

Kathryn Miller, 17634 Peters
Rd., Middlefield, OH 44062-
8455

Charlie Perry, 39304 Bradbury
Rd., Middleport, OH 45760,
(614) 992-5088 (Miniature
Sodas)

Tim and Cheryl Kearns,
11560 Parkway Road, Munson
Township, OH 44024, (216) 285-
7576 (K.T.K. Whiskey Jugs)

John and Margie Bartley, 160
South Main, North Hampton,
OH 45319, (513) 964-1080

Joseph Franchino, 6034 Bayleaf
Ln., North Royalton, OH 44133

Bob and Dawn Jackson, 107
Pine St., Powhatan Point, OH
43942, (614) 795-5565

Darl Fifer, 5118 New Milford
Rd., Ravenna, OH 44266, (330)
296-3504

Bob and Phyllis Christ, 1218
Creekside Place Reynoldsburg,
OH 43068, (614) 866-2156

Ralph Kovel, 22000 Shaker
Blvd., Shaker Hts. OH 44122,
(440) 752-2252

Ballentine's Bottles, 710 W.
First St., Springfield, OH 45504,
(513) 399-8359

Larry R. Henschen, 3222 Delrey
Rd., Springfield, OH 45504,
(513) 399-1891

Tom Chickery, 70707 Kagg Hill
Rd., St. Clarisville, OH 43950,
(740) 695-2958

Tom and Deena Caniff, 1223
Oak Grove Ave., Steubenville,
OH 43952, (614) 282-8918
(Fruit Jars)

Jerry Pajak, 4457-285th St.,
Toledo, OH 43611, (419) 726-
4325

Bill Orr, 1680 Glenwood Drive, Twinsburg, OH 44087, (216) 425-2365 (Miniature Bottles)

Michael Cetina, 3272 Northwest Blvd. N.W., Warren, OH 44485, (216) 898-1845

Bob and Sue Gilbert, The Bottleworks, 70 N. Main St., P.O. Box 446 Waynesville, OH 45068, (513) 897-3861, (Shaker Medicines)

Charles Spurlock, 1112 Eastwood Ave, Tallmadge, OH 44278 (330) 630-4449

Mary Trenkamp, 215 W. 3rd St., Van Wert, OH 45891-1120

Bill and Wanda Dudley, 393 Franklin Ave., Xenia, OH 45385, (513) 372-8567

Oklahoma

Russell Maddock, 400 N. Santa Fe, Bartlesville, OK 74003, (918) 336-7425

Joann Stinnett, 425 W. 10th St., Chelsea, OK 74016

J. Horton, Rt. 1 Box 119, Cleveland, OK 74020, (918) 243-7892

Ronald and Carol Ashby, 831 E. Pine, Enid, OK 73701 (Rare and Scarce Fruit Jars)

Marvin Johnston, 105 Briarwood Ln., Guthrie, OK 73044, (405) 282-1200

Stephen Skinner, 706 W. Industrial, Guthrie, OK 73044, (405) 282-2031

Bob Barnett, Box 109, Lakeview, OR 97630, (541) 947-2415, (Western Whiskeys)

Timothy Gill, 1111 Birch, Lawton, OK 74507, (580) 248-3852 (Drug Store Items)

Kenneth Long, 2626 North 5th St., McCalester, OK 74501, (918) 423-4277

Rich Carte, 719 S. 11th, Muskogee, OK 74401

Johnnie W. Fletcher, 1300 S. Blue Haven Dr., Mustang, OK 73064, (405) 376-1045 (Kansas and Oklahoma Bottles)

Joe and Hazel Nagy, 3540 NW 23, Oklahoma City, OK 73107, (405) 942-0882

Gary Bracken, 1223 E. Highland, Suite 311, Ponca City, OK 74601, (580) 762-3100

M.S. Yancey, 7326 River Ridge Drive, Ponca City, OK 74604

John Whitney, 6703 E.
Independence St., Tulsa, OK
74115, (918) 835-8823

Oregon

Carl Ott, 1903 26th Ave., Forest
Grove, OR 97116, (503) 357-
2374

Tom and Bonnie Kasner,
380 E. Jersey St., Gladstone,
OR 97027, (503) 655-9127
(Insulators, Marbles, Bottles,
Jars)

Ken Busse, P.O. Box 831,
Gresham, Oregon 97030, (503)
709-6376 (Glass Fishing Net
Floats)

Robert and Marguerite Ornduff,
Rt. 4, Box 236-A, Hillsboro, OR
97123, (503) 538-2359

Bob Woods, 6719 Westridge Ct.
N., Keizer, OR 97303

R.E. Barnett, P.O. Box 109,
Lakeview, OR 97630, (503) 947-
2415 (Western Whiskey Bottles)

Randy Littlefield, 5654 S.E.
King Rd., Milwaukie, OR 97222,
(503) 659-0266

Gerald Burton, 611 Taylor St.,
Myrtle Creek, OR 97457, (503)
863-6670

Alan Amerman, 2311 S.E.
147th, Portland, OR 97233,
(503) 761-1661 (Fruit Jars)

Lena Erickson, 6128 SE
Gladstone St., Portland, OR
97206-3755

The Glass House, 4620 S.E.
104th, Portland, OR 97266,
(503) 760-3346 (Fruit Jars)

Garth Ziegenhagen, 2596 S.W.
Pumice Ave., Redmond, OR
97256, (541) 548-4776

Stuart Kammerman, 3262 W.
Chateau Ave., Roseburg, OR
97470-2411, (541) 440-6754
(Glass Paperweights)

Larry Soper, 1322 Newton
Creek Rd., Roseburg, OR 97470,
(503) 673-5237 (Nevada/Oregon
Tokens)

Terry Talbott, 1589 Mistwood
Dr. N.E., Salem, OR 97303, (503)
393-4822

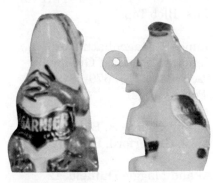

Dennis Young, 677 Lakonen
Loop, Springfield, OR 97478,
(541) 764-4430

Linda White, 26227 Fawver Dr.,
Veneta, OR 97487, (541) 935-
2861

Pennsylvania

R.S. Riovo, 686 Franklin St., Alburtis, PA 18011-9578, (610) 966-2536 (Milk Bottles, Dairy Go-Withs)

Dick and Patti Mansour, 458 Lambert Dr., Bradford, 16701, (814) 368-8820

Claude and Ethel Lee, 643 Bolivar Drive, Bradford, PA 16701, (814) 362-3663 (Jars, Bottles, Pocket Knives)

Ed and Kathy Gray, 1049 Eighth Avenue, Brockway, PA 15824, (814) 268-4503 (Flasks)

Galen Ware, 125 N. 11th Street, Connellsville, PA 15425, (412) 626-1672

The Old Bottle Corner, 508 South Main St., Coudersport, PA 16915, (814) 274-7017 (Fruit Jars, Blob Tops)

James A. Hagenbach, 102 Jefferson St., East Greenville, PA 18041, (215) 679-5849 (Pottery Pigs)

Joseph Colavecci, Box 244 #BT-4310, Graterford, PA 19426

Al and Maggie Duffield, 12 Belmar Rd., Hatboro, PA 19040, (215) 675-5175, (Hutchinsons, Inks)

Carol Ambruster, 15 E. Park Rd., Havertown, PA 19083, (610) 449-7962

Eng Johnson, 650 Hood School Rd., Indiana, PA 15701, (724) 465-8287

Barry and Mary Hogan, 3 Lark Lane, Lancaster, PA 17603

James Ignatz, RR 1 Box 907, Leechburg, PA 15656-9711

Ed Lasky, 43 Nightingale, Levittown, PA 19054, (215) 945-1555

Harold Bauer Antique Bottles, 136 Cherry St, Marienville, PA 16239

Harold Hill, 161 E. Water St., Muncy, PA 17756, (717) 546-3388

Steve Bobb, 610 Northampton Rd., Norristown, PA 19401, (215) 539-6533 (Insulators)

Butch Kim, 103 Mellon Ave., Patton, PA 16668

Bob Averill, 1942 W. Market St., Pottsville, PA 17901, (570) 628-3084

Dave Spurlin, 2315 Elm Ave. RD #1, Quakertown, PA 18951, (215) 538-1716

Rayburn Weimer, 265 W. Branch Fishing Creek Rd., Roulette, PA 16746

Bob Trevorah, 309 N. Elizabeth St., Tamaqua, PA 18252

Jonathan Munn, 120 Center St., Titusville, PA 16354, (814) 827-9685

Scott Elmer, P.O. Box 343, Worcester, PA 19490, (610) 584-0561

Rhode Island

Arthur and Pamela Pawlowski, P.O. Box 314, Hope, RI 02831-0314, (401) 647-3585 (Old Bottles and Early Glass)

Wes and Diane Seemann, Box 49, Kenyon, RI 02836, (203) 599-1626

Stanley Sorrentino, 60 S. of Commons Rd., Little Compton, RI 02837

Normand Provencal, 84 Rowe Ave., Warwick, RI 02889, (401) 739-4148 (Miniature Bottles)

South Carolina

Vern Huffstetler, 109 Hartwell Drive, Aiken, SC 29732, (803) 643-3960

Kenneth Jermac, 215 Westridge Court, Chapin, SC 29036, (803) 345-9780

Linda McLain, 1928 Savannah Hwy, Charleston, SC 29407

John Bray, 1960 Mt. Lebanon Rd., Donalds, SC 29638, (864) 379-3479

Tony Shank, 81 Ocean Green Drive, Georgetown, SC 29440

Mack Cantrell, 3768 Berry Mill Rd., Greer, SC 29651, (864) 895-7015

Eric Warren, 238 Farmdale Dr., Lexington, SC 29703, (803) 951-8860

Tony and Marie Shank, P.O. Box 778, Marion, SC 29571, (803) 423-5803

Ralph Howell, 834 Reservation Road, Rock Hill, SC 29730

D.L. Garrison, 309 Long Reach Dr., Salem, SC 29676, (914) 856-1766

South Dakota

Jim Louks, 1230 North Ave, Spearfish, SD 57783, (605) 642-2699

Tennessee

Gail Ledford, 223 Black Hollow Ln., Alpine, TN 38543, (931) 823-8727

Charles Butler, 295 C/R 103, Athens, TN 37303 (Violin Bottles)

Sally Smith, 13545 Old Hickory Blvd., Antioch, TN 37013

Charlie Barnette, 100 N. Coffey St., Bristol, TN, (615) 968-1437 (Whiskeys, Druggists Patent Medicines)

Claude Bellar, 1750 Keyes Rd., Greenbrier, TN 37073, (615) 643-0290

James Coleman, 1215 Green Acres Rd., Joelton, TN, (615) 746-8217

Ralph VanBrocklin, 1021 W. Oakland Ave. #109, Johnson City, TN 37604 (Western Beers and Whiskeys)

Ronnie Adams, 7005 Charlotte Dr., Knoxville, TN 37914, (615) 524-8958

Sheila Briscoe, 8336 Oak Ridge Highway, Lot J-13, Knoxville, TN 37931, (865) 539-8189

Andy Simon, 122 Indiana Ave, Maryville, TN 37803

Terry Pennington, 415 N. Spring St., McMinnville, TN 37110 (Jack Daniels, Amber Coca-Cola)

William Beck, 3540 Rockwood Ave., Memphis, TN 38122, (901) 459-4510

Bluff City Bottlers, 4630 Crystal Springs Dr., Memphis, TN 38123, (901) 353-0541 (Common American Bottles)

Larry and Nancy McCage, 3772 Hanna Dr., Memphis, TN 38128, (901) 388-9329

Tom Phillips, 2088 Fox Run Cove, Memphis, TN 38138, (901) 754-0097

Aaron Shields, Shields Mercantile & Antiques, 926 Center View Road, Seviereville, TN 37862, (65) 774-8009

T.O. Hailey, P.O. Box 248, Spencer, TN 38585, (931) 946-2090

Texas

Alta Hiler, 925 E. North 13th St., Abeline, TX 79601

Robert Snyder, 4235 W. 13th, Amarillo, TX 79106

Jim Bates Jr., 10604 Londonshire Lane, Austin, TX 78739, (512) 288-2723 (Insulators)

John Foster, 4113 Paint Rock
Drive, Austin, TX 787231-1320,
(512) 346-8253

Elton Gish, P.O. Box 1317,
Buna, TX 77612, (409) 994-5662
(Insulators)

Malcolm Dieckow, 317 CR 5720,
Castroville, TX 78009, (830)
931-2199

Russ Clanton, 201 Hillcrest,
Conroe, TX 77303

Kevin McKinney, 6031 Pineland
No. 112, Dallas, TX 75231, (214)
368-8725

Robert Sanders, 2705 Georgia
Ave, Deer Park, TX 77536, (281)
930-1068

Sterling Allen, P.O. Box 101,
Fort Davis, TX 79734

Bill Bush, 1628 Nast Street,
Garland, TX 75042, (972) 276-
9460

Dee and Connie Mondey, P.O.
Box 272, Haslet, TX 76052,
(817) 439-4807 (Soda Pop)

Marilyn Albers, 14615 Oak
Bend Dr., Houston, TX 77079,
(713) 497-4146 (Insulators)

Don Carroll, 3131 Timmons
#403, Houston, TX 77027, (713)
626-1595

JoAnn Todd, 419 Westmoreland,
Houston, TX 77006

Bill Christy, 6105 County Rd.
90 E, Midland, TX 79706, (915)
685-6016

Steve Thompson, 1101 Silver
Spur, Mt. Pleasant, TX 75455,
(903) 572-1234

Gerald Welch, 4809 Gardenia
Trail, Pasadena, TX 77505,
(713) 487-3057

Jimmy and Peggy Galloway, P.O.
Drawer A, Port Isabel, 78578,
(512) 943-2437

Chuck and Reta Bukin, 1325
Cypress Dr., Richardson, TX
75080, (214) 235-4889

Robert Berry Jr., 1010 Wren Court, Round Rock, TX 78681, (512) 255-2006 (Insulators)

Joe Marek, RT 2 Box 380, Shiner, TX 77984, (361) 594-4258

Utah

Dark Canyon Trading Company, Janice and Gary Parker, W. 200 N., Blanding, UT 84511 (Bottles, Pottery Art)

Syd McNeely, 233 East 2450 South, Bountiful, UT 84010, (801) 295-8508 (Insulators)

John and Deborah Compton, 818 Douglas Drive, Brigham City, UT 84302, (435) 723-7865

Mike Jewell, 60 No. Butch Cassidy Tr., Central, UT, (435) 574-3572 (Fruit Jars, Bitters)

Glen and Reid Groberg, P.O. box 461, Cenerville, UT 84014, (801) 298-3957 (Whiskeys)

Bruce Dugger, 1617 W. 4800 So., Salt Lake City 84123

Dave Emett, 1736 North Star Dr., Salt Lake City, UT84116, (801) 596-2103 (Utah Crocks and Jugs)

Shaunna Murie, 1099 N 1800 W, Salt Lake City, UT 84116

Terry Ann Nielson, 5899 Whitewater Cir., Salt Lake City, UT 84121

Stan Sanders, 2743 Blair Street, Salt Lake City, UT 84115

David Sampson, 3842 Bingham Creek Cr., West Jordan, UT 84088, (801) 280-0825

Tom Hatch, 315 N. 500 East, Vernal, UT 84078 (435) 789-7404

Vermont

Kit Barry, 88 High St., Brattleboro, VT 05301, (802) 254-2195

Jeff and Holly Noordsy, 18 Route 74, Cornwall, VT 05753, (802) 462-2901

Samuel Graham-Sharp, 241 Elm St Apt. #5, Montpelier, VT 05602-2208

William Paltrow, 32 North St., Northfield, VT 05663, (802) 485-8217

Virginia

A. E. Steidel, 6167 Cobbs Rd., Alexandria, VA 22310

John Sullivan, 4300 Ivanhoe Pl., Alexandria, VA 22304, (703) 370-3039

Dick and Margie Stockton, 2331 N. Tuckahoe St Arlington, VA 22205, (703) 534-5619

P.H. Cox, 4343 Bruce Road, Chesapeake, VA 23321

Tom Morgan, 3501 Slate Ct., Chesterfield, VA 23832

Fred Arwood, 229 Hillcrest Drive, Gate City, VA 24251, (540) 386-6582

Joan Cabaniss, 312 Summer Lane, Hyddleston, VA 24104, (540) 297-4498 (Poisons)

John Tutton, 1967 Ridgeway Rd., Front Royal, VA 22630

Dan and Judy Corker, 8406 Knollwood Court, Mechanicsville, VA 23116, (804) 730-2166 (Fruit Jars)

Ed Faulkner, 4718 Kyloe Ln., Moseley, VA 23120, (804) 739-2951

Madelyn Cox, 3511 Clydewood Ave., Richmond, VA 23234, (804) 231-1088

Lloyd and Carrie Hamish, 2936 Woodworth Rd., Richmond, VA 23234, (804) 275-7106

Jim and Connie Mitchell, 5106 Glen Alden Dr., Richmond, VA 23234

Glenn Allen, P.O. Box 746, South Hill, VA 23970 (434) 442-6004

Jeannette Cunningham, 1320 Back Mountain Rd., Winchester, VA 22502

Washington

Kent Beach, 1001 Harding Rd., Aberdeen, WA 98520, (206) 532-8556 (Owl Bottles and Related Items)

Dwaine Engler, 1080 W. 53rd Vista, Bellingham, WA 98226, (360) 384-6044

Ron Flannery, 1821 Jackson Dr. NW., Bremerton, WA 98312, (360) 373-7514 (Bottles)

Doris Christensen, 21815 106th
St. E., Buckley, WA 98321, (253)
862-0255

Pete Hendricks, 3005 So. 302nd
Pl., Federal Way, WA 98023,
(206) 874-6345 (Owl Bottles)

Kin Hurlbut, 313 E. Maberry
Dr., Lynden, WA 98264

Ed and Tami Barber, 45659 SE
129th North Bend, WA 98045,
(206) 888-1179 (Early American
Bottles)

Bert Bergman, 1550 Umatilla
Ave., Port Townsend, WA 98368,
(360) 385-1445

John W. Cooper, 4975 - 120th
Ave. S.E., Bellevue WA 98006,
(206) 644-2669 (Bottles)

Rich and Kimberly Miller,
2736-47th Ave SW, Seattle, WA
98116, (206) 324-8846

Alan Gorsuch, 743 Broadway,
Tacoma, WA 98402, (253) 272-
0334

Washington D.C.

William Porter, P.O. Box 39043,
Washington, D.C. 20016, (202)
363-3297 (Coca-Cola Bottles)

West Virginia

J. C. Blume, Fort Scammon, 111
Ankrom St., Fayetteville, WV
25840-1242

Tim Painter, P. O. Box 22,
Shepherds Town, WV 25443

Wisconsin

Allen Christel, 1719 Sherwood
Forest Dr., Altoona, WI 54720,
(715) 830-0939

Jeff Burkhardt, W65 N717
St. John Ave., Cedarburg, WI
53012, (414) 377-9611 (Figural
Bottles)

Susan Andersen, 516 Dahl
Drive, DeForest, WI 53532,
(608) 846-4037

Robert Hagge, P.O. Box 220,
Hazelhurst, WI 54531

Henry Johnston, N4123 W. Townline Road, Marinete, WI 54134

Bob Markiewicz, 11715 W. Bonniwell Rd., Mequon, WI 53092, (414) 242-3968

George Aldrich, 3211 West Michigan Street, Milwaukee WI 53208 (414) 933-1643 Miniature Bottles

John Brahm, 2355 N. 58th St., Milwaukee, WI 53210

Robert Jaeger, 1380 W. Wisconsin Ave., Apt 232, Oconomowoc, WI 53066, (262) 560-1948

Bill and Kathy Mitchell, 703 Linwood Ave., Stevens Point, WI 55431, (715) 341-1471

Wyoming
Bobbi Tenborg, 5002 W. Villa Circle, Cheyenne, WY 82009 (Violin Bottles)

Henry Puffe, Lander, WY 82520, (307) 332-2021 (Painted Label Soda Bottles)

Wayne Sanchez, P.O. Box 143, Medicine Bow, WY 82329

Foreign

Australia
John Lynch, P.O. Box 78, Charters Towers QLD 4820, Australia

Stephen Trill, 5 Acacia Avenue, Warwick, Australia 4370

Canada
Max Sutton, 2015 Barlow Cres, Burlington Ontario L7P 4N7

Ed Gulka, 5901 - 44th Street, Lloydminster, Alberta T9V 1 V6, (403) 875-6677

Dr. John Kelk, RR2 Elgin, Ontario K0G 1E0, (613) 359-1117

Peter Austin, Off Road Bottles & Collectibles, P.O. 171, Pontypool, Ontario LOA 1KO, (705) 277-3704 (Codd Bottles)

Ron Nykolyshyn, 8820-138 Avenue, Edmonton, Alberta T5E 2A8 Canada (Miniature Vodka Bottles)

China

Hong Kong Miniature Liquor Collection, Shop 107, Astor Plaza, 380 Nathan Road, Kowloon, Hong. Fax (852) 2314-8022 (Miniature Bottles)

Man's Chan, Dragon Empire Trading Co., Bowa House, 180 Nathan Road, Tsimshatsui, Kowloon, Hong Kong. Fax (852) 314-8022, Ph (852) 721-3200

England

Rob Goodacre, 44 Arundel Close, BH 25 SUH, New Milton Hants. Tel: 01425 620794, Over Seas Direct Dial 011-441425-620794 (Bitters, Whiskeys)

Alan Blakeman, A. Balkeman BBR Pubs, Elsecar Heritage Center, NR Barnsley York, England S74 8HJ, 011-44-1226-745156

Robin A. Gollan, 6 Broom Mead, Bexleyheath, Kent. DA6 7NY England, 011-441-1322-524246 (Minature Cognac Bottles)

Norm Lewis, 91 Potters Green Road, Walsgrave, Coventry, Warwickshire, England, 011-024-7661-8541

France

Les Caves De La Reine Antiques Bottle Shop, 6 Rue De La Republique, Chantelle 03140, France, Ken and Reine Salter, Proprietors; Open July 9th-Sept16th, PH/FAX: France 011-334-7056-6779 (June-Nov), USA (510) 527-5779 (Dec-May)

Germany

Norbert Lamping, Siegesstr. 5, D-30175 Hannover, Germany, 049-511-544 31 03

Netherlands

Willy Van den Bossche, Kniplaan 3 NL - 2251 Voorschoten, Nederland

Auction Companies

ABC Absentee Auctions, 139 Pleasant Ave., Dundas Ontario Canada L9H 3T9, PH: (519) 443-4162 or (905) 628-3433, E-Mail: info@auctionsbyabc. com, Web Site: http://www. auctionsbyabc.com.

American Bottle Auctions, 1507 21st Street, Suite #203, Sacramento, CA 95814, PH: (800) 806-7722, FAX: (916) 443-3199, E-Mail: info@americanbottle.com, Web Site: http://www.americanbottle. com.

Armans of Newport, 207 High Point Avenue, Portsmouth, RI 02871.

Robert Arner Auctioneer, Lehighton, PA, (717) 386-4586.

Australian & Collectables Auctions, P.O. Box 245, Deniliquin NSW 2710, Australia, David Wescott, PH: 011-61-35881-2200, FAX: 011-61-35881-4740, E-Mail: dwescott@wescottdavid.com, Web Site: www.westcottdavid. com.

B & B Auctions/Bottles & Bygones, 30 Brabant Road, Cheadle Hulme, Cheadle, Cheshire, England SK8 7AU, E-Mail: bygonz@yahoo.com; Web Site: http://members.tripod. com/~MikeSheridan/index.htm; PH: 011-44-7931-812156.

BBR Auctions, 5 Ironworks Row, Wath Rd., Elsecar, Barnsley, S. Yorkshire, S74 844, England PH: 011-44-1226-745156; FAX: 011-44-1226-361561.

Bothroyd & Detwiler On Line Auctions, 1290 South 8th Ave., Yuma AZ, E-Mail: detwiler@primenet.com, Web Site: http://www.primnet. com/~detwiler/index.html.

Bottles and More Galleria, P.O. Box #6, Lehighton, PA 18235, E-Mail: rodwalck@ptd.net, Web Site: http://www.geocities.com/ bammag2002.

Cerebro, Tobacco Ephemera Auctions, P.O. Box 327, East Prospect, PA 17317, (800) 695-2235, E-Mail: cerebrolab@aol. com, Web Site: http://www. cerebro.com.

CB & SC Auctions, 179D Woodridge Cres, Nepean, ON K2B 712, Canada Rhonda Bennett (613) 828-8266.

Collectors Sales & Services, P.O. Box 4037, Middletown, RI 02842, (401) 849-5012, E-Mail: collectors@antiquechina. com, Web Site: http://www. antiqueglass. com/homepage. htm.

Down-Jersey Auction, 15 Southwest Lakeside Dr., Medford, NJ 08055, PH: (609) 953-1755, FAX: 609-953-5351, E-Mail: dja@skyhigh.com, Web Site: http://www.down-jersey. com.

Gallery at Knotty Pine Auction Service, Route 10, P.O. Box 96, W. Swanzey, NH 03469, PH: (603) 352-2313, FAX (603) 352-5019, E-Mail: kpa@inc-net.com ,Web Site: www. knottypineantiques.com.

Garth's Auctions, 2690 Stratford Rd., Box 369, Delaware, OH 43015, (740) 362-4771, FAX: (740) 363-0164, E-Mail; info@garths.com, Web Site: http://www.garths.com.

GLASSCO Auctions, 102 Abbeyhill Drive, Kanata, Ontario, Canada K2L 1H2, 831-4434, E-Mail: phil@glassco.com.

Glass Works Auctions, Box 187, East Greenville, PA 18041, PH: (215) 679-5849, FAX: (215) 679-3068, E-Mail: glswrk@enter.net, Web Site: http://www.glswrk-auction.com.

Gore Enterprises, P.O. Box 158, Huntington, VT 05462, William D. Emberley (802) 453-3311.

Harmer Rooke Galleries, 32 East 57th Street, New York, NY 10022, (212) 751-1900.

Norman C. Heckler & Co., 79 Bradford Corner Road, Woodstock Valley, CT, PH: (860) 974-1634, FAX: (860) 974-2003, E-Mail: heckler@neca.com www.hecklerauction.com

James E. Hill Auctions, P.O. Box 366, Randolph, VT 05060, PH: (802) 728-5465, E-Mail: jehantqs@sover.net.

Randy Inman Auctions, Inc., P.O. Box 726, Waterville, ME 04903-0726, PH: (207) 872-6900, FAX: (207) 872-6966, E-Mail: Inman@InmanAuctions.com, Web Site: http://www.InmanAuctions.com.

KIWI Auctions, P.O. Box 15025, Christchurch, New Zealand, PH: 64-29-233-6846, FAX: 64-3-389-5841, E-Mail: kiwi.auctions@xtra.co.nz, Web site: http://www.kiwiauctions.co.nz.

Lesie's Antiques & Auctions, The American Pharmacy Auctioneer, 934 Main Street, Newberry, SC 29108, (888) 321-8600, E-Mail: frleslie@interpath.com, Web Site: http://www.antiqueusa.com.

McMurray Antiques & Auctions, P.O. Box 393, Kirkwood, NY 13795, PH/FAX: (607) 775 2321.

Wm. Morford, Rural Route #2, Cazenovia, NY 13035, PH: (315) 662-7625, FAX: (315) 662-3570, E-Mail: morf2bid@aol.com, Web Site: http://morfauction.com.

Morphy Auctions, P.O. Box 8, 2000 N. Reading Road, Denver, PA 17517, PH: (717) 335-3435.

New England Absentee Auctions, 16 Sixth Street, Stamford, CT 06905, PH: (203) 975-9055, FAX: (203) 323-6407, E-Mail: NEAAuction@aol.com.

Nostalgia Publications, Inc., P.O. Box 4175, River Edge, NJ 07661, PH: (201) 488-4536, FAX: (201) 883-0938, E-Mail: nostpub@webtv.net.

NSA Auctions/R. Newton-Smith Antiques, 88 Cedar St., Cambridge, Ontario, Canada N1S IV8, E-mail: info@nsaauctions.com, Web Site: http://www.nsaauctins.com.

Open-Wire Insulator Services, 28390 Ave., Highland, CA 92346, PH: (909) 862-9279, E-Mail: insulators@open-wire.com, Web Site: http://www.open-wire.com.

Don Osborne Auctions, 33 Eagleville Rd., Orange, MA 01354, PH: (978) 544-3696, FAX: (978) 544-8271.

Howard B. Parzow, Drug Store & Apothecary Auctioneer, P.O. Box 3464, Gaithersburg, MD 20885-3464, PH: (301) 977-6741.

Pettigrew Antique & Collector Auctions, Division of R.G. Canning Attractions, P.O. Box 38159, Colorado Springs, CO, PH: (719) 633-7963, FAX: (719) 633-5035.

Phillips International Auctioneers & Valuers, 406 E. 79th St., New York, NY 10021, PH: (212) 570-4830, FAX: (212) 570-2207, Web Site: www.phillips-auctions.com.

Pop Shoppe Auctions, 10556 Combie Road #10652, Auburn, CA 95602, (530) 268-6333, E-Mail: PopShoppe@aol.com.

Carl Pratt Bottle Auctions, P.O. Box 2072, Sandwich, MA 02563, PH: (508) 888-8794.

Shot Glass Exchange, Box 219, Western Springs, IL 60558, PH/FAX: (708) 246-1559.

Skinner Inc., The Heritage on the Garden, 63 Park Plaza, Boston, MA 02116, PH: (617) 350-5400, FAX: (617) 350-5429, E-Mail: info@skinnerinc.com, Web Site: http://www.skinnerinc.com.

Mike Smith's Patent Medicine Auction, Veterinary Collectibles Roundtable, 7431 Covington Hwy., Lithonia, GA 30058, PH: (770) 482-5100, FAX: (770) 484-1304, E-Mail: Petvetmike@aol.com.

Steve Ritter Auctioneering, 34314 W. 120th St., Excelsior Springs, MO 64024, PH: (816) 833-2855.

Stuckey Auction Co., 315 West Broad Street, Richmond, VA 23225, (804) 780-0850.

T.B.R. Bottle Consignments, P.O. Box 1253, Bunnell, FL 32110, (904) 437-2807.

Victorian Images, Box 284, Marlton, NJ 08053, PH: (856) 354-2154, FAX: (856) 354-9699, E-Mail: rmascieri@aol.com, Web Site: www.TradeCards.com/vi.

Bruce & Vicki Waasdorp, Antique Pottery/Stoneware Auctions, P.O. Box 434, Clarence, NY 14031, PH: (716) 759-2361, FAX: (716) 759-2379, E-Mail: waasdorp@antiques-stoneware.com, Web Site: http://www.antiques-stoneware.com.

Museums and Research Resources

Canadian Museum of Civilization, 100 Laurier Street, Hull, Quebec J8X 4H2, PH: (819) 776-7000 or (800) 555-5621; Web sites: www.pennynet.org/glmuseum, www.glass.co.nz, www.antiquebottles.com/clubs.html.

Central Nevada Museum, Logan Field Road, P.O. Box 326, Tonopah, NV 89049, PH: (775) 482-9676

Coca-Cola Company archives, P.O. Drawer 1734, Atlanta, GA 30301, PH: (800) 438-2653, Web site: www.cocacola.com.

Corning Museum of Glass, One Museum Way, Corning, NY, 14830-2253, PH: (607) 974-8271 or (800) 732-6845, Web site: www.corningglasscenter.com, www.pennynet.org/glmuseum.

Dr. Pepper Museum, 300 S. 5th St., Waco, TX 76701, PH: (254) 757-2433

The Glass Museum, 309 S. Franklin, Dunkirk, IN, PH/FAX: (765) 768-6872

Hawaii Bottle Museum, 27 Kalopa Mauka Rd., P.O. Box 1635, Honokaa, HI 96727-1635

Henry Ford Museum & Greenfield Village, 20900 Oakwood Blvd., Dearborn, MI 48121, PH: (313) 271-1620

Historical Glass Museum, 1157 Orange Street, Redlands, CA (909) 798-0868

Mark Twain's Museum and Books, 111 S. C Street, P.O. Box 449, Virginia City, NV 89440-0449

Museum of American Glass at Wheaton Village, 1501 Glasstown Road, Millville, NJ, PH: (856) 825-6800 or (800) 998-4552, Web site: www.wheatonvillage.org.

National Bottle Museum, 76 Milton Ave., Ballston Spa, NY 12020, PH: (515) 885-7589, Web site: www.crisny.org/not-for-profit/nbm.

National Heisey Glass Museum, 169 W. Church St., Newark, OH 43055, PH: (740) 345-2932

Nevada State Museum, 600 N. Carson Street, Carson City, NV 89701, PH: (775) 687-4810

Pepsi-Cola Company Archives, One Pepsi Way, Somers, NY 10589, PH: (914) 767-6000, Web site: www.pepsi.com

Sandwich Glass Museum, P.O. Box 103, 129 Main Street, Sandwich, MA 02563, PH: (508) 888-0251, FAX: (508) 888-4941, E-Mail: sgm@sandwichglassmuseum. org.

Seagram Museum, 57 Erb St. W, Waterloo, ON, Canada N2L 6C2, PH: (519) 885-1857, FAX: (519) 746-1673, Web site: www. seagram-museum.ca

Glossary

ABM (Automatic Bottle Machine): The innovation of Michael Owens in 1903 that allowed an entire bottle to be made in one automatic step.

ACL (Applied Color Label): A colored label produced with pyroglazed or enameled lettering; usually used with soda pop bottles from 1920-1960.

Agate Glass: A glass made from mix incorporating blasting furnace slag. Known in tints of chocolate brown, caramel brown, natural agate, tanned leather, showing striations of milk glass in off-white tints. Made from 1850-1900s.

Amethyst-Colored Glass: A clear glass that when exposed to the sun or bright light for a long period of time turns various shades of purple. Only glass that contains manganese turns purple.

Amber-Colored Glass: Nickel was added in glass production to obtain this common bottle color. It was believed that the dark color prevented sunlight from ruining the contents of the bottle.

Annealing: The gradual cooling of hot glass in a cooling chamber or annealing oven.

Applied Lip/Top: On pre-1880s bottles, the neck was applied after removal from thc blow-pipe. This may be only a ring of glass trailed around the neck.

Aqua-Colored Glass: The natural color of glass, of which the shade depends on the iron oxide contained in the glass production. Produced until the 1930s.

Bail: Wire clamp consisting of a wire placed the top of the lid or lip, and a "locking" wire that is pushed down to cause pressure on the bail and the lid, resulting in an airtight closure.

Barber Bottle: In the 1880s, these colorful bottles decorated the shelves of barbershops and usually were filled with bay rum.

Batch: A mixture of the ingredients necessary in the manufacturing of glass.

Battledore: A wooden paddle used to flatten the bottom or sides of a bottle.

Bitters: An herbal medicine, medicinal and flavoring, that contains a great quantity of alcohol, usually corn whiskey.

Black Glass: This type of glass produced between 1700 and 1875 is actually a dark olive green created by the carbon in the glass production.

Blob Seal: A coin-shaped blob of glass applied to the shoulder of a bottle, into which a seal with the logo or name of the distiller, date, or product name was impressed. The blob seal created a way to identify an unembossed bottle.

Blob Top: A large thick blob of glass placed around the lip of soda or mineral water bottles. A wire held the stopper, which was seated below the blob and anchored the wire when the stopper was closed to prevent carbonation from escaping.

Blown in Mold, Applied Lip (Bimal): The process by which a gather of glass is blown into a mold to take the shape of the mold. The lip was added later and the base often had open pontil scars.

Blowpipe: A hollow iron tube wider and thicker at the gathering end than at the blowing end. It was used by the blower to pick up the molten glass, which was then blown-in-mold or free-blown outside the mold. Blowpipes vary from 2-1/2 feet to 6 feet long.

Blow-Over: A bubble-like extension of glass above a jar or bottle lip created so the blowpipe could be broken free from the jar after blowing. The blow-over was then chipped off and the lip was ground.

Borosilicate: A type of glass originally formulated for making scientific glassware.

Calabash: A type of flask with a rounded bottom. It was known as "Jenny Lind" flask and was common in the 19th century.

Camphor Glass: A white cloudy glass resembling refined gum camphor; made in blown, blown-mold, and pressed forms.

Carboy: A cylindrical bottle with a short neck.

Clapper: A glassmaker's tool used in shaping and forming the footing of an object.

Cobalt-Colored Glass: A dark blue colored glass used with patented medicines and poisons to distinguish them from regular bottles. Excessive amounts of color resulted in the familiar "cobalt blue."

Codd: A bottle enclosure patented in 1873 by Hiram Codd of England. A small glass ball is blown inside of the bottle. The ball forms the seal that protects the contents.

Crown Cap: A metal cap formed from a tin plate pressed tightly over the rolled lip of a bottle. The inside of the cap was filled with a cork disc to create an airtight seal.

Cullet: Cleansed and broken glass added to a batch to bring about rapid fusion to produce new glass.

Date Line: The mold seam or mold line on a bottle. The length and position of the line indicates the approximate age of the bottle.

Decolorizer: A compound that is added to natural aquamarine bottle glass to render the glass clear.

Dip Mold: A one-piece mold open at the top.

Embossed Lettering: Raised or embossed letter denoting the name of the product on the bottle.

Fire Polishing: The reheating of glass to eliminate unwanted blemishes.

Flared Lip: A bottle produced before 1900 with a lip that has been worked out or flared out to reinforce the strength of the opening.

Flint Glass: Glass composed of a silicate of potash and lead. Commonly referred to as "lead crystal" in present terminology.

Freeblown Glass: Items produced with a blowpipe rather than a mold.

Gaffer: A master blower in an early glasshouse.

Gather: A gob of molten glass adhering to the blowpipe.

Glass Pontil: The earliest type of pontil, in which the remaining scar was a sharp glass ring.

Glory Hole: The small furnace used for the frequent reheating necessary during the making of a bottle. The glory hole was also used in fire polishing.

Green Glass: Refers to a composition of glass and not a color. The green color was caused by the iron impurities in the sand, which could not be controlled by the glass makers.

Ground Pontil : When a rough pontil scar has been ground off, the remaining smooth circle is a ground pontil.

Hobbleskirt: The paneled shape of Coca-Cola bottles.

Hobnail: A pattern of pressed glass characterized by an all-over pattern resembling hobnail heads.

Hutchinson : A spring-type internal closure for soda bottles patented in 1879 by Charles Hutchinson.

Imperfections: Flaws, including bubbles (tears) of all sizes and shapes, bent shapes and necks, imperfect seams, and errors in spelling and embossing.

Improved Pontil: A bottle with an improved pontil has reddish or blackish tinges on its base.

ISP (Inserted Slug Plate): A plate inserted into a mold to emboss the names of companies or people on ale, whiskey, wine or other bottles.

Iron Pontil: The solid iron rod heated and affixed to a bottle's base created a black circular depression in the glass, which often turned red upon oxidation.

Kickup: A deep indentation in the bottom of a bottle. It was formed by pressing a wood or metal tool in the base of the mold while the glass was still hot. Kickups are common on wine bottles and calabash flasks.

Laid-On-Ring: A bead of glass trailed around the neck opening of a bottle to reinforce it.

Lady's Leg: A bottle with a long curving neck.

Lightning Closure: A closure that used an intertwined wire bale to hold the lid on fruit jars. This closure was also common on soda bottles.

Lipper: A wood tool used to widen lips and form rims and spouts of pitchers, carafes, and wide-mouthed jars.

Manganese: A substance used as a decolorizer between 1850 and 1910. Over time, exposure to intense sunlight will cause it to turn glass purple.

Melting Pot: A clay container used to melt silicate in the process of making glass.

Metal: Molten glass.

Milk Glass: A white glass primarily used for cosmetic bottles. Tin was added to the glass during production to obtain this color.

Mold, Full-Height , Three-Piece: A mold that allowed an entire bottle to be formed at once. The two seams run the height of the bottle to below the lip on both sides.

Mold, Three-Piece Dip: A mold that made a bottle in three pieces. The bottom of the bottle was molded in one piece, while the top, from the shoulder up, was made in two pieces. Mold seams appear circling the bottle at the shoulder and on each side of the neck.

Opalescence: A frosted or variegated color created when minerals in mud or silt have interacted with glass.

Open Pontil : A raised or depressed circular scar called a moile formed on the bottom of a bottle by a blowpipe rather than a rod.

Painted Label: An abbreviation for an applied color label (ACL), which was baked on the outside of the bottle. Painted labels were commonly used on soda pop and milk bottles.

Panelled: A bottle that isn't circular or oval, but rather is formed from four to twelve flat surfaces, or panels.

Paste Mold: A mold made from two or more pieces of iron coated with paste to prevent scratches on the glass. The paste eliminated seams as the glass was turned in the mold.

Pattern Mold: A mold used to make glass that was patterned before it was completed by blowing.

Pontil, Puntee, or Punty Rod: The iron rod attached to the base of a bottle by a gob of glass to hold the bottle during the finishing.

Pontil Mark: To remove a bottle from a blowpipe, an iron pontil rod with a small amount of molten glass was attached to the bottom of the bottle after the neck and lip were finished. A sharp tap removed the bottle from the pontil rod, leaving a jagged glass scar.

Potstone: Glass resembling white stone, formed by impurities in the glass batch.

Pressed Glass: Glass that has been pressed into a mold to take the shape of the mold or the pattern within the mold.

Pucellas: Called "the tool" by glassmakers. This tool is essential in shaping both the body and opening in blown bottles.

Pumpkinseed: A small round flat flask, generally made of clear glass, often found in the American West. The flask receives its name from its shape, which resembles a pumpkin seed. These bottles are also known as "Mickies," "Saddle Flasks," and "Two-Bit Ponies."

Ribbed: A bottle with vertical or horizontal lines embossed on it.

Round Bottom: A torpedo-shaped heavy glass soda bottle. The long, narrow shape enabled the bottle to lie on its side, keeping the liquid in contact with the cork, which prevented the cork from drying and popping out of the bottle.

Seal: A circular or oval glass slug applied to the shoulder of a bottle with an imprint of the manufacturer's name, initials, or mark.

Sheared Lip: After a bottle was blown, a pair of scissors like shears was used to clip the hot glass from the blowpipe. No top was applied, and sometimes a slight flange was created.

Sick Glass: Glass bearing a superficial decay or deterioration that takes on a grayish tinge caused by erratic firing.

Slug Plate: A metal plate about 2 inches x 4 inches with a firm's name on it was inserted into a mold so that the glass house could use the same mold for many companies.

Smooth Base: The bottom of a bottle without a pontil, or scar.

Snap Case (or Snap Tool): The snap case replaced the pontil as a tool for holding the bottle during finishing. The snap case's curving arms gripped the bottle firmly during finishing of the neck and lip, thus eliminating pontil scars or marks. A bottle made with a snap case may have grip marks on the side, however.

Squat: A bottle used to hold beer, porter, and soda.

Tooled Top: Bottles manufactured after 1885 had tops that were a part of the original bottle mold.

Torpedo: A beer or soda bottle with a rounded base meant to lie on its side to keep the cork wet.

Turn-Mold Bottle: A bottle that was turned while forming in a mold. The continuous turning, with the aid of special solvents, eventually erased all the seam and mold marks and gave a distinct luster to the bottle.

Whittle Marks: Marks found on bottles formed in carved wood molds. Similar marks were also formed on hot glass poured early in the morning in cold molds. The cold molds created "goose pimples" on the surface of the glass. As the mold warmed, the bottles became smoother.

Xanthine Glass: Yellow glass formed by adding silver.

Bibliography

Books

Agee, Bill. *Collecting All Cures*. East Greenville, PA: Antique Bottle & Glass Collector, 1973.

Albers, Marilyn B. *Glass Insulators from Outside North America*. 2nd revision. Houston, TX: Self-Published, 1993.

Apuzzo, Robert. *Bottles of Old New York, A Pictorial Guide to Early New York City Bottles, 1680-1925*. New York: R & L Publishing, 1997.

Ayers, James. *Pepsi-Cola Bottles Collectors Guide*. Mount Airy, N.C.: R. J. Menter Enterprises, 1998.

——*Pepsi-Cola Bottles & More*, Mount Airy, N.C., R. J. Menter Enterprises, 2001.

Arnold, Ken. *Australian Preserving & Storage Jars Pre-1920*. Chicago, IL: McCann Publishing, 1996.

Badders, Veldon, *The Collector's Guide to Inkwells: Identification & Values*. Paducah, KY: Collector Books, 2001.

Barnett, Carl, and Ken Nease. *Georgia Crown Top Bottle Book*. 1211 St. Andrews Drive, Douglas, GA 31533, 2003.

Barnett, Carl, and Ken Nease. *Georgia Soda Bottle Book*. 1211 St. Andrews Drive, Douglas, GA 31533, 2003.

Barnett, R. E. *Western Whiskey Bottles*. 4th ed. Bend, OR: Maverick Publishing, 1997.

Barrett, William J. II. *Zanesville and the Glass Industry, A Lasting Romance*. Zanesville, OH: Self-Published, 1997.

Beck, Doreen. *The Book of Bottle Collecting*. Gig Harbor, WA: Hamlin Publishing Group, Ltd., 1973.

Berguist, Steve. *Antique Bottles of Rhode Island*. Cranston, RI: Self-Published, 1998.

Binder, Frank and Sara Jean. *A Guide to American Nursing Bottles*, revised edition of 1992 edition: Self-Published, 2001. 1819 Ebony Drive, York, PA 17402.

Blake, Charles E. *Cobalt Medicine Bottles*. Glendale, AZ: Self-Published, 2001. (602) 938-7277.

Blakeman, Alan. *A Collectors Guide: Inks*. Elsecar, England: BBR Publishing, 1996.

————A Collectors Guide: Miller's Bottles & Pot Lids. Octopus Publishing Group Ltd., 2002.

Bossche, Willy Van den. Antique Glass Bottles, A Comprehensive Illustrated Guide. Self-Published, Antique Collectors Club, Wappinger Falls, NY 2001.

Bound, Smyth. 19th Century Food in Glass. Sandpoint ID: Midwest Publishers, 1994.

Bowman, Glinda. Miniature Perfume Bottles. Schiffer Publishing, Inc., 2000.

Bredehoft, Tom and Neila. Fifty Years of Collectible Glass 1920-1970, Identification and Price Guide. Vol. I. Dubuque, IA: Antique Trader Books, 1998.

Breton, Anne. Collectible Miniature Perfume Bottles. Flammarion Publications, 2001.

Burnet, Robert G. Canadian Railway Telegraph History. Ontario, Canada: Self-Published, 1996.

Champlin, Nat. Nat Champlin's Antique Bottle Cartoons. Bristol, RI: Self-Published, 1998.

Chapman, Tom. Bottles of Eastern California. Hungry Coyote Publishing, 2003. Tom Chapman, 390 Ranch Rd., Bishop, CA 93514, (760) 872-2427.

Christensen, Don and Doris, Violin Bottles: Guitars & Other Novelty Glass. Privately Published, 1995. 21815 106th St. E. Buckley, WA 98321.

Cleveland, Hugh. Bottle Pricing Guide, 3rd Edition. Paducah, KY: Collector Books, 1996.

Creswick, Alice M. Redbook Number 6: The Collectors Guide to Old Fruit Jars. Privately Published, 1992. 0-8525 Kewowa SW. Grand Rapids, MI 49504

DeGrafft, John. American Sarsaparilla Bottles. East Greenville, PA: Antique Bottle & Glass Collector, 1980.

————Supplement to American Sarsaparilla Bottles. Self-Published, John DeGrafft, 8941 E. Minnesota Ave., Sun Lakes, AZ 85248, 2004.

Diamond, Freda. Story of Glass. New York: Harcourt, Brace and Co., 1953.

Dodsworth, Roger. Glass and Glassmaking. London, England: Shire Publications, 1996.

Dumbrell, Roger. *Understanding Antique Wine Bottles*. Ithaca, NY: Antique Collectors Club, 1983.

Duncan, Ray H. *Dr. Pepper Collectible Bottles, Identification & Values*. Black Creek Publishing, 1606 CR 761, Devine TX 78016, 2004.

Eatwell, John M., and David K. Clint III, *Pike's Peak Gold*. Denver, CO: Self-Published, 2002. 2345 So. Federal Blvd, Suite 100, Denver, CO 80219.

Edmondson, Bill. *The Milk Bottle Book of Michigan*. Privately Published, 1995. 317 Harvest Ln., Lansing, MI 48917.

Edmundson, Barbara. *Historical Shot Glasses*. Chico, CA: Self-Published, 1995.

Eilclberner, George and Serge Agadjanian. *The Complete American Glass Candy Containers Handbook*. Adele Bowden, 1986.

Elliott, Rex R., and Stephen C. Gould. *Hawaiian Bottles of Long Ago*. Honolulu, HI: Hawaiian Service Inc., 1988.

Ferraro, Pat and Bob. *A Bottle Collector's Book*. Sparks, NV: Western Printing & Publishing Co., 1970.

Ferguson, Joel. *A Collectors Guide to New Orleans Soda Bottles*. Slidell, LA: Self-Published, 1999.

Field, Anne E. *On the Trail of Stoddard Glass*. Dublin, NH: William L. Bauhan, 1975.

Fletcher, W. Johnnie. *Kansas Bottle Book*. Mustang, OK: Self-Published, 1994.

———*Oklahoma Bottle Book*. Mustang, OK: Self-Published, 1994.

Gardner, Paul Vickens. *Glass*. NY: Smithsonian Illustrated Library of Antiques, Crown Publishers, 1975.

Graci, David. *American Stoneware Bottles, A History and Study*. South Hadley, MA: Self-Published, 1995.

———*Soda and Beer Bottle Closures, 1850-1910*, 2003. P.O. Box 726, South Hadley, MA 01075.

Ham, Bill. *Bitters Bottles*. Self-Published, 1999. Supplement 2004, P.O. Box 427, Downieville, CA 95936.

———*The Shaving Mug Market*. Downieville, CA: Self-Published, 1997.

Hastin, Bud. *AVON Products & California Perfume Co. Collector's Encyclopedia*. 16th ed. Kansas City, MO: Bud Hastin Publications, 2001.

———*AVON Products & California Perfume Co. Collector's Encyclopedia*. 17th ed. Kansas City, MO: Bud Hastin Publications, 2003.

Haunton, Tom. *Tippecanoe and E.G. Booz Too!*. Tom Haunton, 48 Hancock Ave, Medford, MA 02155, 2003.

Heetderks, Dewey R., M.D. *Merchants of Medicine, Nostram Peddlers-Yesterday & Today*. Dewey Heetderks, 4907 N. Quail Crest Drive, Grand Rapids, MI 49546, 2003.

Higgins, Molly. *Jim Beam Figural Bottles*. Atglen, PA: Schiffer Publishing, 2000.

Holiner, Richard. *Collecting Barber Bottles.* Paducah, KY: Collector Books, 1986.

Hudson, Paul. *Seventeenth Century Glass Wine Bottles and Seals Excavated at Jamestown, Journal of Glass Studies.* Vol. III, Corning, NY: The Corning Museum of Glass, 1961.

Holabird, Fred, and Jack Haddock. *The Nevada Bottle Book.* Reno, NV: R. F. Smith, 1981.

Hopper, Philip. *Anchor Hocking Commemorative Bottles and other Collectibles.* Atglen, PA: Schiffer Publishing, 2000.

Hudgeons, Thomas E. III, *Official Price Guide to Bottles Old & New.* Orlando, FL: House of Collectibles, 1983.

Hunter, Frederick William. *Stiegel Glass.* New York: Dover Publications, 1950.

Hunting, Jean and Franklin. *The Collector's World of Inkwells.* Schiffer Publishing, 2000.

Husfloen, Kyle. *American Pressed Glass & Bottles Price Guide.* 1st ed. Dubuque, IA: Antique Trader Books, 1999.

Husfloen, Kyle. *American Pressed Glass & Bottles Price Guide.* 2nd ed., Dubuque,

IA: Antique Trader Books, 2001.

Innes, Lowell. *Pittsburgh Glass 1797-1891.* Boston, MA: Houghton Mifflin Company, 1976.

Jackson, Barbara and Sonny. *American Pot Lids.* East Greenville, PA: Antique Bottle & Glass Collector, 1992.

Jarves, Deming. *Reminiscences of Glass Making.* New York: Hurd and Houghton, 1865.

Kendrick, Grace. *The Antique Bottle Collector.* Ann Arbor, MI: Edwards Brothers Inc., 1971.

Ketchum, William C. Jr. *A Treasury of American Bottles.* Los Angeles: Rutledge Publishing, 1975.

Klesse, Brigitt, and Hans Mayr. *European Glass from 1500-1800, The Ernesto Wolf Collection.* Germany: Kremayr and Scheriau, 1987.

Knittle, Rhea Mansfield. *Early American Glass.* NY: Garden City Publishing Company, 1948.

Kovel, Terry and Ralph. *Kovels' Bottle Price List,* 11th ed. NY: Crown Publishers, Inc., 1996

Kovill, William E. Jr., *Ink Bottles and Ink Wells.* Taunton, MA: William L. Sullwold, 1971.

Kosler, Rainer. *Flasche, Bottle Und Bouteille.* Ismaning, Germany: WKD-Druck Gmbh Publishing Company, 1998.

Lee, Ruth Webb. *Antique Fakes and Reproductions.* Privately Published, Northborough, MA, 1971.

Lefkowith, Christie Mayer. *Masterpieces of the Perfume Industry.* Editions Stylissimo Publications, 2000.

Leybourne, Doug. *Red Book #8, Fruit Jar Price Guide.* Privately Published, North Muskegon, MI, 1998.

———*Red Book #9, Fruit Jar Price Guide,* Privately Published, North Muskegon, MI, 2001.

Linden, Robert A. *The Classification of Violin Shaped Bottles.* 2nd ed. Privately Published, 1999.

———*Collecting Violin & Banjo Bottles, A Practical Guide.* 3rd ed., Privately Published, 2004.

Maust, Don. *Bottle and Glass Handbook.* Union Town, PA: E. G. Warman Publishing Co., 1956.

Markota, Peck and Audie. *Western Blob Top Soda and Mineral Water Bottles.* 1st ed. Sacramento, CA: Self-Published, 1998.

———*California Hutchinson Type Soda Bottles.* 2nd ed. Sacramento, CA: Self-Published, 2000.

Markowski, Carol. *Tomart's Price Guide To Character & Promotional Glasses.* Dayton, OH: Tomart Publishing, 1993.

Martin, Byron and Vicky. *Here's To Beers, Blob Top Beer Bottles 1880-1910,* 1973, Supplemented 2003, Byron Martin, P.O. Box 838, Angels Camp, CA 95222

McCann, Jerry. *2002 Fruit Jar Annual.* Chicago, IL: J. McCann Publisher, 2002.

McDougal, John and Carol. *1995 Price Guide for Insulators.* St. Charles, IL: Self-Published, 1995.

McKearin, Helen and George S., *American Glass.* New York, NY: Crown Publishers, 1956.

———*Two Hundred Years of American Blown Glass.* New York, NY: Crown Publishers, 1950.

McKearin, Helen, and Kenneth M. Wilson. *American Bottles and Flasks and Their Ancestry.* New York: Crown Publishers, 1978.

Megura, Jim. *Official Price Guide to Bottles.* 12th ed. New York: House of Collectibles, The Ballantine Publishing Group, 1998.

Meinz, David. *So Da Licious, Collecting Applied Color Label Soda Bottles.* Norfolk, VA: Self-Published, 1994.

Metz, Alice Hulett. *Early American Pattern Glass.* Paducah, KY: Collector Books, 2000.

———*Much More Early American Pattern Glass.* Paducah, KY: Collector Books, 2000.

Miller, Mike. *Arizona Bottle Book.* Self-Published. 9214 W. Gary Rd., Peoria, AZ 2000.

Milroy, Wallace. *The Malt Whiskey Almanac.* Glasgow, Scotland: Neil Wilson Publishing Ltd., 1989.

Monsen and Baer. *The Beauty of Perfume, Perfume Bottle Auction VI.* Vienna, VA: Monsen & Baer Publishing, 1998.

———*The Legacies of Perfume, Perfume Bottle Auction VII.* Vienna, VA: Monsen & Baer Publishing, 1998.

Montague, H.F., *Montague's Modern Bottle Identification and Price Guide.* 2nd ed. Overland Park, KS: H.F. Montague Enterprises, Inc., 1980.

Morgan, Roy, and Gordon Litherland. *Sealed Bottles: Their History and Evolution (1630-1930).* Burton-on-Trent, England, Midland Antique Bottle Publishing, 1976.

Munsey, Cecil. *The Illustrated Guide to Collecting Bottles.* New York, NY: Hawthorn Books, Inc., 1970.

———*The Illustrated Guide to The Collectibles of Coca-Cola.* New York, NY: Hawthorn Books, Inc. 1972.

Murschell, Dale L. *American Applied Glass Seal Bottles.* Self-Published, 1996. Dale Murschell, HC 65 Box 2610, Arnold Stickley Rd., Springfield, WV.

Namiat, Robert. *Barber Bottles with Prices.* Radnor, PA: Wallace Homestead Book Company, 1977.

Newman, Harold. *An Illustrated Dictionary of Glass.* London, England: Thames and Hudson Publishing, 1977.

Nielsen, Frederick. *Great American Pontiled Medicines.* Cherry Hill, NJ: The Cortech Corporation, 1978.

North, Jacquelyne. *Perfume, Cologne, and Scent Bottles, Revised 3rd Edition Price Guide.* Atglen, PA: Schiffer Publishing Inc., 1999.

Northend, Mary Harrod. *American Glass.* New York: Tudor Publishing Company, 1940.

Odell, John. *Digger Odell's Official Antique Bottle & Glass Price Guides, I - 11.* Lebanon, OH: Odell Publishing, 1995.

———*Indian Bottles & Brands.* Lebanon, OH: Odell Publishing, 1998.

———*Pontil Medicine Encyclopedia.* Lebanon, OH: Odell Publishing, 2003.

Ojea, Ed and Jack Stecher. *Warner's Reference Book.* Self-Published, 1999. 1192 San Sebastian Ct., Grover Bend, CA 93433.

Ostrander, Diane. *A Guide to American Nursing Bottles.* York, PA: ACIF Publications, 1992.

Padgett, Fred. *Dreams of Glass, The Story of William McLaughlin and His Glass Company.* Livermore, CA: Self-Published, 1997.

Pepper, Adeline. *The Glass Gaffers of New Jersey.* New York: Charles Scribners Sons, 1971.

Peterson, Arthur G., Ph. D., *400 Trademarks on Glass.* L-W Book Sales, P.O. Box 69, Gas City, IN 46933, 2002.

Petretti, Alan. *Petretti's Coca-Cola Collectibles Price Guide.* 11th ed. Dubuque, IA: Antique Trader Books, 1998.

———*Petretti's Soda Pop Collectibles Price Guide.* 1st ed. Dubuque, IA: Antique Trader Books, 2001.

———*Petretti's Soda Pop Collectibles Price Guide.* 3rd ed. Dubuque, IA: Antique Trader Books, 2003.

Pickvet, Mark. *The Encyclopedia of Glass.* Atglen, PA: Schiffer Publishing, 2001.

Polak, Michael. *Antique Trader: Bottles Identification and Price Guide.* 4th ed. Iola, WI: Krause Publications, 2002.

Polak, Michael. *Warman's Bottles Field Guide: Values and Identification.* Iola, WI: Krause Publications, 2005.

———*Official Price Guide to American Patriotic Memorabilia.* 1st ed. New York: House of Collectibles, 2002.

Putnam, H. E. *Bottle Identification.* New York: H.E. Putnam, 1965.

Richardson, Charles G. and Lillian C. *The Pill Rollers, Apothecary Antiques and Drug Store Collectibles.* 3rd ed., 2003. Charles G. Richardson, 1176 S. Dogwood Dr., Harrisonburg, VA 22801-1535.

Ring, Carlyn. *For Bitters Only.* Concord, MA: The Nimrod Press, Inc., 1980.

Ring, Carlyn, and W. C. Ham, *Bitters Bottles.* Downieville, CA, 2000. Self-Published, (530) 289-0809.

Roller, Dick. *Fruit Jar Patents Volume III 1900-1942.* Chicago, IL: McCann Publisher, 1996.

———*Indiana Glass Factories Notes.* Chicago, IL: McCann Publisher, 1994.

Russell, Mike. *Collectors Guide to Civil War Period Bottle and Jars.* 3rd ed. Herndon, VA: Self-Published, 2000.

Schwartz, Marvin D., *"American Glass" Antiques.* Volume 1, 1974, *Blown and Molded,* Princeton, NJ: Pyne Press

Seeliger, Michael. *H.H. Warner, His Company & His Bottles.* East Greenville, PA: Antique Bottle & Glass Collector, 1974.

Sloan, Gene, *Perfume and Scent Bottle Collecting.* Radnor, PA: Wallace Homestead Book Company, 1986.

Snyder, Bob. *Bottles in Miniature.* Amarillo, TX: Snyder Publications, 1969.

———*Bottles in Miniature II.* Amarillo, TX: Snyder Publications, 1970.

————*Bottles in Miniature III.* Amarillo,TX: Snyder Publications, 1972.

Soetens, Johan. *Packaged in Glass: European Bottles, Their History and Production.* Batavlan Lion International, Amsterdam, October 2001.

Spaid, David M. and Harry A. Ford. *101 Rare Whiskey Flasks (Miniature).* Palos Verdes, CA: Brisco Publications, 1989.

Spiegel, Walter Von. *Glas.* Battenberg Verlag, Munchen,1979.

Spillman, Jane Shadel. *Glass Bottles, Lamps and Other Objects.* New York: Alfred A. Knopf, 1983.

Southard, Tom, and Mike Burggraaf. *The Antique Bottles of Iowa.* Des Moines, IA: Self-Published, 1998.

Sweeney, Rick. *Collecting Applied Color Label Soda Bottles.* 2nd ed. La Mesa, CA: Painted Soda Bottles Collectors Assoc., 1995.

————*Collecting Applied Color Label Soda Bottles.* 3rd ed. La Mesa, CA: Painted Soda Bottles Collectors Assoc., 2002.

Thompson, J. H. *Bitters Bottles.* Watkins Glen, NY: Century House, 1947.

Toulouse, Julian Harrison. *Bottle Makers and Their Marks.* Camden, NJ: Thomas Nelson Incorporated, 1971.

Townsend, Brian. *Scotch Missed (The Lost Distilleries of Scotland).* Glasgow, Scotland: Neil Wilson Publishing Ltd., 1994.

Tyson, Scott. *Glass Houses of the 1800s.* East Greenville, PA: Antique Bottle & Glass Collector, 1971.

Tucker, Donald. *Collectors Guide to the Saratoga Type Mineral Water Bottles.* East Greenville, PA.: Antique Bottle & Glass Collector, 1986.

Tutton, John. *Udderly Delightful.* Stephens City, VA: Commercial Press, Inc., 1996.

————*Udderly Splendid,* Stephens City, VA: Commercial Press, Inc., 2003.

Umberger, Joe and Arthur. *Collectible Character Bottles.* Tyler, TX: Corker Book Company, 1969.

Van Wieren, Dale P. *American Breweries II.* North Wales, PA: Eastern Coast Breweriana Association, 1995.

Van Rensselaer, Stephen. *Early American Bottles and Flasks.* Peterborough, NH: Transcript Printing Company, 1926.

————*Early American Bottles and Flasks.* Stratford, CT: J. Edmund Edwards Publisher, 1969.

Watkins, Laura Woodside. *American Glass and Glassmaking.* New York: Chanticleer Press, 1950.

Watson, Richard. *Bitters Bottles.* New York, NY: Thomas Nelson & Sons, 1965.

————*Supplement to Bitters Bottles.* New York, NY: Thomas Nelson & Sons, 1968.

Wichmann, Jeff. *Antique Western Bitters Bottles. 1st ed.* Sacramento, CA: Pacific Glass Books Publishing, 1999.

Wilson, Betty and William. *Spirit Bottles of the Old West.* Wolfe City: Henington Publishing Company, 1968.

Wilson, Kenneth M. *New England Glass and Glass Making.* New York: Thomas Y. Crowell Company, 1972.

Wood, Zang. *New Mexico Bottle Book.* Flora Vista, NM: Self-Published, 1998.

Yates, Don. *Ginger Beer & Root Beer Heritage 1790-1930.* Don Yates, 8300 River Corners Road, Homerville, OH 44235, (330) 625-1025, 2004.

Young, Susan H. *"A Preview of Seventh-Century Glass from the Kourin Basilica, Cyprus."* Journal of Glass Studies, Vol. 35, Corning Museum of Glass, 1993.

Yount, John T. *Bottle Collector's Handbook & Pricing Guide.* Action Printery, 10 No. Main, San Angelo, TX 76901, 1967.

Zumwalt, Betty. *Ketchup, Pickles, Sauces.* Sandpoint, ID: Mark West Publishers, 1980.

Resources

Sanborn Fire Insurance Maps

EDR Sanborn Maps

Environmental Data Resources, Inc.
3530 Post Road
Southport, CT 06890
(800) 352-0050
Web Sites: www.edrnet.com
www.edrnet.com/reports.html

Chadwyck-Healy Inc.

1101 King Street Suite 380
Alexandria, VA 22314
PH: (800) 752-0515 or (703) 683-4890
FAX: (703) 683-7589
Web Site: www.chadwyck.com
E-Mail: sales@chadwyck.com

San Jose Public Library – San Jose California

Web Sites: www.sjpl.lib.ca.us
www.sjlibrary.org

Stanford University – Stanford, California

Web Site: www.sul.stanford.edu
E-Mail: seleniteman@comcast.net

University of California at Berkley – Berkley, California

Web Sites: www.lib.berkeley.edu
www.lib.berkeley.edu/EART/sanborn.html

Vlad Shkurkin, Publisher

6025 Rose Arbor
San Pablo, CA 94806-4147
PH: (510) 232-7742
FAX: (510) 236-7050
E-Mail: Shkurkin@ix.netcom.com

Vista

505 Huntmar Park Drive, Suite 200
Herndon, VA 20170
PH: (800) 989-0402 or (703) 834-0600
FAX: (703) 834-0606

Periodicals

Ale Street News, P.O. Box 1125, Maywood, NJ 07607, E-Mail: JamsOD@aol.com, Web Site: www. AleStreetNews.com

Antique Bottle Collector UK Limited, Llanerch, Carno, Caersws, Powys SY17 5JY Wales

Australian Antique Bottles and Collectibles, AABS, Box 235, Golden Square, 3555 Australia

BAM (*Bottles and More*) Magazine, P.O. Box #6, Lehighton, PA 18235

Bottles & Bygones, 30 Brabant Rd, Cheadle Hulme, Cheadlek, Cheshire, SKA 7AU England

Bottles & Extra Magazine, 1966 King Springs Road, Johnson City, TN 37601

British Bottle Review (BBR), Elsecar Heritage Centre, Barnsley, S.York, S74 8HJ England

Canadian Bottle & Stoneware Collector Magazine, 102 Abbeyhill Drive, Kanata, ON K2L 1H2 Canada, Web-Site: www.cbandsc. com

Crown Jewels of the Wire, P.O. Box 1003, St. Charles, IL 60174-1003

Fruit Jar Newsletter, FJN Publishers, 364 Gregory Avenue, West Orange, NH 07052-3743

Antique Bottle & Glass Collector, Jim Hagenbuch, 102 Jefferson Street, P.O. Box 187, East Greenville, PA 18041

Root Beer Float, P.O. Box 571, Lake Geneva, WI 53147

The Miniature Bottle Collector, P.O. Box 2161, Palos Verdes Peninsula, CA 92074, Brisco Publications

The Soda Spectrum, A Publication by Soda Pop Dreams, P.O Box 23037, Krug Postal Outlet, Kitchener, Ontario Canada N2B 3V1

Treasure Hunter's Gazette (*Collector's Newsletter*), 14 Vernon St., Keene, N.H., 03431, George Streeter, Publisher and Editor